Ethical Issues

Ethical Issues

Perspectives for Canadians

edited by Eldon Soifer

broadview press

Cataloguing in Publication Data

Soifer, Eldon, 1960–
    Ethical issues

ISBN   0-921149-71-9

1. Social Ethics. 2. Ethics. 3. Social problems. I. Title.

BJ1012.S6 1992   170   C92-093422-6

broadview press   OR   broadview press
P.O. Box 1243   269 Portage Rd.
Peterborough, Ontario   Lewiston, NY
K9J 7H5   Canada   14092   USA

printed in Canada

CONTENTS

Introduction

This book contains discussions of a number of moral issues which are currently being debated in a variety of places: in government and other policy-making bodies, in the courts, in the press, within professional organizations, and in ordinary everyday conversations. What makes them "issues" is that reasonable people disagree about how to act in regard to these subjects, yet agree that it is important to decide how to act. (There would be little point to discussing whether torturing innocent people is wrong, or whether one should tie one's left shoe before one's right). No doubt most readers have already discussed many of these issues with friends, family, and others. The purpose of this book is to provide thought-provoking ideas and systematic presentations of various positions which will help sort out each individual's views on these issues. There are new aspects one has never thought of before, and even points one *has* considered may be put in ways which make them seem much more difficult to ignore or reject. Ultimately, however, each individual must decide his or her own views on these matters. It is no part of the purpose of this book to try to sway people from any particular stance. Rather, the purpose is to provide readings which will entertain the reader, promote further discussion of the issues, and stimulate thought.

There are many different ways of thinking about these issues. This book is first and foremost "philosophical" in its orientation. I do not mean this word in the off-hand sense it often has in everyday speech of being resigned, as in "she took her friend's anger philosophically," but it has proven notoriously difficult to provide an exact account of what *is* meant by this term. The word derives from the ancient Greek, meaning "love of wisdom," and originally applied to virtually every area of human search for knowledge (hence today's "Doctor of Philosophy" degree in every subject from English literature to atomic physics). The readings in this book are "philosophical" in the sense that they attempt to proceed (in connection with their respective issues) by a certain method involving reasoning, argument, criticism, and insight. The fact that the authors included here take a calm, reasoned approach to their subjects should not be taken to mean that they do not feel passionately about the issues they discuss. It is possible to have strong opinions, and yet be able to discuss them (and the reasons for holding them) in a cool and rational manner. It is assumed here that there is a communal interest in discussing these issues and progressing in some way toward truth, or consensus, or at least an appreciation of the basis of disagreement.

This book is also Canadian in its orientation. The issues it deals with apply to people everywhere, and most of the points raised here could be applied very broadly, but there are places where specific aspects of the issues may be viewed from a distinctly Canadian perspective. This book tries to reflect that perspective by including references to Canadian law and policy, and by including many selections written by Canadians.

The book contains readings which are organized into seven categories, dealing with seven different issues. Needless to say, these are not the only moral issues of interest to people today. The issues here have been chosen largely because they seem to be of particular interest to a large number of people, and because they provide an indication of the broad range of concerns being discussed in the philosophical community today. It is important to note, however, that there is something a bit artificial about dividing contemporary moral concerns into distinct areas. People who discuss one issue usually find they need to say something about some other matter as well. To give just one example of such an interlocking chain, writers on employment equity in Canada frequently make reference to Aboriginal rights, since Aboriginal peoples have been identified as potential beneficiaries of employment equity programs. It is difficult to discuss Aboriginal rights, however, without making some reference to different conceptions of how human beings are related to their cultures and to the environment and the resources it contains. Discussion of the environment is likely to involve discussion of the status of animals: are they merely "resources," or do they have standing in their own right? And so it goes. This spilling over of one issue into another is characteristic of philosophy. It is nevertheless useful to consider different aspects of these questions separately (one has to start somewhere!), and thus the division into different issues helps make the debates manageable. It should also be noted that it is not necessary to read the sections of this book in order—each of the "issues" can be considered on its own, at least up to a point.

There is another way in which the different issues are linked as well. This is that they are all *moral* issues. (Note: many people distinguish between "moral" and "ethical," and the distinction is drawn in a variety of different ways. For the purposes of this book, however, I see no need to draw such a distinction, and so these words will be used interchangeably.) "Moral" is another word notoriously difficult to define. I will take it that calling an issue a "moral" issue implies that it has something to do with how people *should* act; with what is right or wrong, or what states of affairs are good or bad. In this broad sense, it seems everyone has *some* moral beliefs—people who say they "don't believe in morality" usually mean that they do not accept the particular moral "rules" dominant in their societies at the time, not that they have no beliefs whatsoever about what sorts of things people should or should not do.

It is not necessary, of course, for individuals to have a fully worked out moral system, or firmly established set of moral rules. People can function perfectly well with only a vague set of moral beliefs or intuitions. Nevertheless, philosophers have often tried to provide some sort of systematic account of morality. There is considerable debate within philosophy about whether it is even possible to develop such a "moral theory," and I do not want to pre-judge that issue here. Nevertheless, I believe it to be useful for any reader interested in these issues to have some sort of background understanding of how the issues might be described in terms of various moral theories. (For one thing, writers on these issues often refer to these theories, assuming a background knowledge. For example, writers on scarcity of medical resources often refer to a "utilitarian" method of deciding who should get scarce medical resources, without explaining the moral theory this word describes.) Accordingly, this book begins with an introduction to some of the most influential strands of moral theory. I leave it to the reader to decide how these might apply to the issues at hand.

Utilitarianism

Perhaps the single most influential moral theory over the past couple of centuries has been one called "utilitarianism." One of its best-known advocates, John Stuart Mill, described utilitarians in the 1860s as people who believe that "actions are right in proportion as they tend to promote happiness; wrong as they tend to produce the reverse of happiness."[1] The basic intuition here seems to be that, if anything matters, happiness does, and it makes sense to try to get as much as possible of what matters. There are other theories tell us to aim at the maximum possible amount of some other thing held to have value, such as beauty, knowledge, etc. Any such theories are commonly called "consequentialist," because they claim that the rightness of an act depends on its having the right sort of *consequences*. Utilitarianism, then, is a particular form of consequentialist theory, which states that the value to be maximized is happiness (or "utility"). Therefore, the way to decide which action to pursue is to add up the increase in happiness for each individual affected by the action (subtracting all unhappiness, if there is any), and do whichever action will produce the most happiness for the most people.

Before getting into more detail about utilitarianism, it is worth mentioning another theory which is also concerned with bringing about happiness and which is commonly called "ethical egoism." According to this view, the right thing for individuals to do is to aim at their own happiness, whether or not that coincides with the happiness of others. Some people would deny that ethical egoism is a "moral" theory at all, maintaining that morality requires people to be self-sacrificing, at least sometimes, but insofar as egoism tries to provide a guide for how people should live, it deserves some mention when discussing morality.

One argument often put forward for ethical egoism is that, if people pursue their own interests, everyone will be better off. This could be because each person knows his or her own interests best, and so will be in the best position to achieve them, or because such an approach would avoid the ill effects of people's "butting in" and generally interfering with others' business. It has also been suggested along these lines that charity is always demeaning to the recipient, and that only ethical egoism can avoid some such element of charity.

Of course, all of these are empirical claims, which might turn out to be false. For example, there could be cases where people are *not* the best judges of what is in their best interests, or it may be that such an egoist approach might turn out to be in the interests of some at the expense of others, rather than being better for everyone. But the main thing to note here is that these arguments are not really arguments for egoism at all, so much as arguments for a particular view of utilitarianism. The expressed goal here is "everyone's happiness," or "maximum happiness," not just one's own good. It is simply that having each pursue his or her own good is held to be the best means for bringing about the utilitarian goal. There may be other arguments which really are for ethical egoism directly, but for now I will return to utilitarianism.

There is an obvious appeal to a theory that tells us to aim at maximum happiness, but there are problems as well. This is not the place to recite all of the arguments for and against this theory, but I will touch on some of the most important aspects of the on-going debate.

The first point to be noted is that, in order to use this theory, we have to have a pretty good idea of what sorts of things contribute to a person's happiness. Although everyone has at least some rough idea about this, there are certainly cases where people might disagree; for instance, whether a particular action has made a given individual "better off" or not. Utilitarians generally try to explain what is meant by "happiness" either in terms of some pleasant mental state, or in terms of having one's desires satisfied. (Note that there may be cases in which these accounts have to separate, such as times when satisfaction of one's desires does not produce the mental state one expected.) Some people, however, might claim that people can be better off in one condition than another, whether they realize it or not. For example, someone might think a person is better off doing something active with one's leisure time, rather than sitting around watching television. Calling this sort of being better off a state of "happiness" might involve stretching the term a bit, but nevertheless there have been "utilitarians" who have claimed that happiness along these lines is what is to be maximized.

Another problem utilitarianism faces is in deciding how to compare one person's happiness with another's. To take a simple case: if two children each want the last candy, how can one decide which one to give it to? Utilitarianism seems to say that we should give it to the one who will enjoy it more, but it may be very hard to tell which one that is. When it comes to making decisions for large numbers of people, the problem is even greater. If a town has to decide whether to build a theatre or a gymnasium, each of which would be used by different people, how can we compare the amounts of happiness involved in either decision? These problems are compounded by the fact that we cannot foresee *all* the consequences of our actions, and so can't even tell exactly how many people will be affected in the long run.

These are certainly problems utilitarians should consider, but they may not be strong enough to destroy the theory. Perhaps utilitarians can claim that all we need for guiding our decisions are rough estimates. After all, nobody claims that human beings will always succeed in doing the right moral thing all the time. Perhaps *trying* to bring about the most happiness is all we can demand. And it seems clear that people often do use such considerations in trying to make decisions. For example, if several people want to go out to dinner together and are trying to decide where to go, it seems likely they will use elements of utilitarian reasoning—if some people like Chinese food and others prefer Italian, for example. Often the decision will be made by some sort of estimate of which choice will maximize the overall happiness.

Even if utilitarianism is able to deal with these problems, however, it is still not off the hook. One of the most persistent criticisms of the theory has been that it fails to give the required prominence to considerations of justice. Utilitarianism says that utility is to be maximized overall, but what if the way to achieve that is to sacrifice some individual (or group of individuals) so that others may enjoy greater benefits? Is it all right to do so, or do the individuals involved have rights that they not be treated in certain ways?

A classic example of the sort of question at issue here goes as follows: suppose you are a law officer, and you are holding a person in custody. There is a mob outside threatening to riot unless you turn this person over to them, in which case the person will be abused and ultimately killed. You know that this person has done no wrong, and the mob would therefore be killing an innocent person. On the other hand, you know that if you do not turn the person over, there will be no way to prevent the mob from rioting (assume it is too late for any rational persuasion). If they do riot, there is a very good chance not only of a great deal of damage to property in the neighbourhood, but also that more innocent people (say, local residents) will be killed in the chaos. Assuming that each person's life would contain equal happiness, it seems that the way to maximize utility would be by turning over this individual, thereby stopping the riot and saving the lives of some innocent residents. Yet many people believe that the person in custody has a right not to be treated in this way, and that one is not allowed to sacrifice this one person for the overall good. What should you do in such a case?

Some people claim that in these and similar cases the only way to maximize happiness overall would be by doing something which we are not morally allowed to do. If that is right, then it cannot be the case that maximizing happiness is what we are morally required to do—there must at least be some additional guidelines. Theories which maintain that there are some moral considerations which do not depend on the consequences of our actions are sometimes called "deontological" theories.

Deontological Theories

Deontological theories do not have to say consequences are *always* unimportant, but they do have to say that the rightness of actions at least sometimes depends on qualities of the action itself, rather than its consequences. A deontologist might claim, for example, that it is always wrong to tell a lie, even if that lie will not harm anyone. Deontological theories often begin with either rights or duties. In recent political debate, it has become popular to try to draw support for one's cause by describing it in terms of rights. Thus, people make claims ranging from "a right to treatment as an equal" and a "right to life," through "animal rights" and "rights to national self-determination," to "rights to a university education" and "rights to holidays with pay." Often, people on each side of an issue claim rights which seem to conflict with those claimed by the other side.

In philosophy, some care must be taken in introducing a rights claim. It may be that some moral claims cannot properly be put in terms of rights. What sorts of entities can have rights? Must rights-holders be individuals, or can there be collective rights? What is the relationship between interests and rights? Must rights be the sort of things one can choose whether or not to exercise, such as the right to free expression? Can there be "special" rights which belong to some people and not others (for example, rights police officers must have, but others should not)? And what happens when rights claims conflict?

It has been suggested that rights claims should be understood in terms of several elements. One way to do this is in terms of a formula such as the following: "X has a right to Y against Z in virtue of V." In these terms, if people make rights claims, it is permissible to press them to explain exactly what is to be substituted for each of the letters in the formula. Who has the right (X)? How did they qualify for it (V)? What is it a right to (Y)? And what does its existence imply by way of duties for others (Z)? With regard to the last of these questions, it is also possible to ask whether others have a "positive" duty to provide something for the right-holder, or merely a "negative" duty not to interfere. Raising these questions will often make rights claims less obvious than they may have seemed at first.

The other common forms of deontological theories take "duties" as the central notion of morality. Certainly much of our common moral discourse can be described in terms of duties. For example, one might assert we have a duty to refrain from murdering, or a duty not to make promises we do not intend to keep. It is possible, though, that some aspects of morality are more difficult to describe in this way. For example, if we see someone trapped in a burning building, do we have a duty to try to rescue him or her, even at the risk of our own lives, or is that something which it would be nice to do, but which is "beyond the call of duty"?

Even if there is a way to describe all of our moral beliefs in terms of duties, however, there is still a problem. How do we come to know which duties we have? Where do they come from? This problem becomes more acute when we discover that different duties conflict with each other, and that people (both in different cultures and within a single one) disagree about which duties they have. For example, if I have promised to keep a secret, but it turns out someone I care about will be harmed if I do, I may be unsure about what to do. It may seem that in these sorts of cases I have two conflicting duties, and I need some way of knowing which one should give way. Similarly, at the inter-personal level, people might disagree about whether there is a duty to abstain from pre-marital sex, for example. How are we to decide which is right in such cases?

A) Intuitionism

Some deontological theorists have claimed that we have a faculty called "intuition" which informs us about our duties. This faculty is often seen as being similar to our senses. Just as sight can perceive colour and hearing can perceive sound, so intuition might be said to perceive moral facts.

One problem many people have with this view is that there may not be any moral "facts" out there waiting to be perceived. The most common objection, however, is that talk of this faculty does not really explain how different people can have such different moral beliefs, nor indeed how it can come to be that whole cultures can agree within themselves, but disagree with other cultures.

The intuitionist can reply that some people are simply better than others at using this faculty, just as some people may have better vision or hearing than others. Perhaps also the faculty needs to be "trained" by proper upbringing. Such a reply raises questions, however, about how we can tell which people are using the faculty "correctly" and which are not. In any case, many people do not find this intuitionist approach satisfactory.

B) Kantian Ethics

How else might we learn which duties we have? Perhaps the most influential deontological theorist of all has been eighteenth-century philosopher Immanuel Kant who believed that we could discover our moral duties through the use of reason alone. He suggested that any time we are contemplating an action we should apply a rational test to it, and if it fails the test, it is an action we are not allowed to perform. This test, known as the "categorical imperative," has a few different formulations. The best known of these are, first, that we should act as if the principle we are acting on is a universal law,[2] and, second, that we must "treat humanity...always at the same time as an end and never simply as a means."[3] There has been a great deal of debate about how these principles are to be interpreted. One way to understand the first one might be by considering the question often raised when someone does a thing of which we do not approve, which is "what if everyone did that?" (or, perhaps, "how would you like it if people did that to you?"). The second one might be understood as a requirement that we treat people with respect and concern for their integrity as people.

Few would deny that these are good general guidelines for action, but many would question whether they give a full account of morality, or whether they are indeed given by reason alone. For example, one might ask what it means to treat a person as an end and not simply as a means. Does that mean we should consider each person's well-being before we act? But that is exactly what a utilitarian would say, and Kant's deontological approach was supposed to solve some of the problems utilitarianism runs into. And as for the "universalizing" version of the test, does it matter how we describe the circumstances? If we describe a given action as an act of lying, then it would seem we could not want that universalized. But if we describe it as an act of lying to a would-be murderer so as to save the life of a friend, we might come to a very different conclusion.

It is not clear whether a rational test such as the categorical imperative can provide us with all the moral guidance we might want. Kant's principles have unquestionably inspired many moral philosophers, but there is still no consensus as to how successfully he addressed pressing ethical questions. It is also not clear whether there is another way to discover which duties apply, such as through a faculty of intuition. These deontological approaches raise some promising ideas, but cannot be said to have provided unquestionable solutions to the problems of moral philosophy.

Virtue Ethics

As we have seen, utilitarianism and deontology each has its appeal, but each has problems as well. Many philosophers continue to believe that one of these approaches is the best one to take, and the debate rages on. Others, however, have decided that some alternative must be found.

One such alternative which has been around for centuries but which has become increasingly popular in recent years is what is often known as "virtue ethics."

This approach focuses on the state of character of a morally good person, rather than on a state of affairs (as utilitarianism seems to do) or on particular actions (as deontology seems to do). According to this view, the primary usage of moral terminology should be to evaluate individuals' characters as "good" or "bad," where a "good" person is one who chooses actions because they are of the right moral kind. Such a person acts out of a disposition to do what is morally right, rather than by weighing the alternatives of what one could do, and deciding between them.

The most common objection to virtue ethics is that it is too vague to be of much use in moral decision-making. One could agree that we do evaluate people in terms of having or not having various good characteristics, but insist that we do so only because those people generally do the right sort of actions, or bring about the right sort of consequences. The fact that we do make evaluations of these various types does not by itself establish anything about which of them is most fundamental. Both utilitarians and deontologists would claim that we can decide which character traits to encourage as "virtues" only because we already know what sorts of actions we believe to be right, and then can decide which personal characteristics are most likely to lead one to perform the right actions.

Ethical Relativism

When faced with the various difficulties which confront the leading moral theories, some philosophers have suggested that there are no universal moral truths at all—that what is "right" in a given society is whatever people in that society *believe* is right. This view is often called "relativism," or, to distinguish it from other theories which sometimes go by this name, it could be called "cultural ethical relativism."

In order to assess this relativist claim, it may be useful to distinguish several different issues. First of all, it should be noted that relativists say more than that there are different beliefs in different cultures. They also make the claim that what each of these cultures believes to be right *is* right. One could believe the first without believing the second, however—one might think that one culture has it right while another has it wrong. It may be very difficult to *prove* that one is right and the other wrong, but that does not necessarily mean that it is not true to say it. For example, people might have different theories about why the dinosaurs died out, only one of which could be true, even if it were never possible to prove which one is correct.

On the other hand, even if one is convinced that a particular culture has a mistaken moral belief, that does not automatically tell us anything about what we are allowed to do to try to change the situation. Certainly much harm has been done over the years by people who felt certain about their own moral beliefs and tried to impose these beliefs on others. Mistakes of that sort have no doubt helped convince many people that a relativist approach is the only one we can adopt, practically speaking. However, one might think that tolerance of others' difference is a very important moral value all by itself, and therefore one might disapprove of such impositions of moral belief, even while believing that one particular set of beliefs is morally best in some objective sense. Indeed, many people's common-sense moral beliefs seem to reflect such a value, but also place a limitation upon it. If, for example, the dominant view in another culture is that women should not be treated as equals or that slavery or torture are acceptable, many people might think we have an obligation to try to convince that culture of the error of its ways. We may or may not be entitled to use force to bring about the change, but many would say we should do more than simply say "Well, that's their business" and stay out of the picture.

So far I have suggested that some of the reasons people have put forward for accepting cultural ethical relativism fail to establish the truth of that approach. However, I have not tried to argue that the approach must be false. So far, all we know is that some arguments for it do not seem to work, but it is still possible that there are other arguments which would work. To that extent, relativism is still a live issue.

One problem which cultural ethical relativists must face is in explaining how to identify a culture, or what a culture believes. Many countries, including Canada, are made up of several different cultural groups. Whether one refers to them as "cultures" or "sub-cultures" or by some other name, the problem remains that it is difficult to make any strong claims about what the present culture of Canada believes. Some issues relating to this observation are among those discussed in the chapter on "Cultural, Linguistic, and Aboriginal Rights." Nevertheless, issues such as those raised in this book must be approached from within some sort of cultural framework, and some of the questions (such as what laws, if any, there should be governing such things as abortion, treatment of the environment, and distribution of pornography) seem to require answers which can be applied to all Canadians. Perhaps it is enough to try to discover answers which apply here first, and postpone the question of whether these answers can be universally applicable. Nevertheless, the issue of relativism does raise interesting questions about the very nature of moral reasoning.

Contractarianism

There is one other approach to the subject of morality which deserves some mention here, and that is "contractarianism." The main idea of this approach is that moral rules are justified by an agreement (or "social contract") between the members of a society. Sometimes this "contract" is viewed as an actual historical event, but more commonly it is used as a hypothetical device—we should feel obliged to stick to rules which we *would have* agreed to in the contracting situation. People describe this original contracting situation differently (and often get different outcomes as a result), but there are some common elements. The basic view is that individuals are primarily interested in their own well-being, and realize that they will be better off joining forces with other people to form one society. However, the advantages of society can only be gained if everyone follows certain rules, which become the essence of morality.

This approach to ethics has been criticized in a number of ways. Some people argue that it is too individualistic—that it depends too heavily on the unwarranted assumption that people are necessarily most interested in their own well-being. Other people might argue that contractarianism excludes from the scope of morality all beings which lack the mental capacity to be parties to a contract. Finally, people have objected that this approach is incomplete in that it still requires us to give a fairly full description of the situation in which the contract is made. By the time one has done that, the argument goes, one has already done most of the controversial work about which moral principles should be adopted. In other words, this objection states that one gets out of a contractarian approach only what one has already put into it. Nevertheless, contractarianism continues to have supporters throughout the philosophical community.

Application

As we have seen, there is a great deal of question about which moral theory is the best, or even about whether we should aim for moral theories at all. Much interesting work is being done in this area, and it is well worth investigating further, but this is not the place to do so. Instead, I will now turn to the question of how moral theories might apply to specific moral issues.

The classic view has been that one should work out the best moral theory, and then apply it to specific issues (hence the common term "applied ethics" for discussion of such contemporary moral issues). According to this view, one might decide, for example, that utilitarianism is the best view available, and then simply resolve the issues by trying to determine which action or policy would maximize happiness. Alternatively, one might test various policies to see if they conform to the categorical imperative, and so on.

Not everyone accepts this approach, however. Some argue that we can be much more certain of our beliefs about these concrete cases than we can about rather abstract moral theories. Others point out that in the heat of the moment, we often do not have time to calculate what our chosen moral theory dictates, and so must simply apply, as well as we can, general common-sense rules which we have adopted earlier.

I do not propose to settle these issues here. One could write a whole book on whether moral issues are best dealt with by applying moral theories—but that would be a different book. The information in this introduction is meant to familiarize the reader with some of the terms which may be referred to in the pieces which follow, and to provide some introductory background information about the nature of moral philosophy. What you make of that information, and of the arguments and ideas which follow, is up to you.

Notes

1 J.S. Mill, *Utilitarianism*, originally published 1861; as printed by Hackett Publishing Company, Inc., 1979, p.7.

2 I. Kant, *Grounding for the Metaphysic of Morals*, (J.W. Ellington, trans.), (Hackett: Indianapolis, 1981), p.30, or p.421 in the standard pagination.

3 *Ibid.*, p.36, or p.429 in the standard pagination.

PART 1

distribution of scarce resources

It has been suggested that there would be no need for morality at all if there were enough material goods around for all people to have whatever they wanted. Whether this is correct or not, it is certainly the case that one of the problems of today's world concerns the distribution and use of limited resources. This problem arises at several different levels. There is the global dilemma of how relatively wealthy nations should act toward poorer nations, and (what may be a different issue) how individual citizens of wealthy nations should respond to widespread poverty in many parts of the world. There is also the problem of how the goods within society should be distributed among members of that society—for example the extent to which some sort of social welfare system is required by considerations of justice. A related question concerns decisions about which of several competing groups should receive government support.

One of the most visible areas in which the problem of distribution of scarce resources within a society has arisen is in relation to medical resources. Obviously health has a tremendous influence on how well people live; indeed, sometimes medical assistance is needed if people are to go on living at all. Modern medical technology has made it possible to extend the lives of a great many people. However, much of this technology is very expensive, and providing everyone with all treatments which could be expected to benefit them may not be feasible. Of course, that might be a reason to advocate a large-scale reorganization of society's priorities, a reorganization that might well have other consequences which would outweigh its benefits. In any case, in society as it stands, there is a very real question about the best way to distribute medical care.

This issue is often divided into two major sub-categories: "macro-allocation" and "micro-allocation," although in practice the distinction may not be completely clear-cut. Macro-allocation has to do with the broad questions about how nations should go about providing health care for their citizens. Should the government provide all necessary health care, or leave medical care to market forces? Assuming society takes some responsibility for medical care, what proportion of its resources should be devoted to such care? Macro-allocation is also concerned with providing rough guidelines for how allocated resources are to be divided. For example, one might ask how much should be spent on treatment of the unhealthy, how much on education and preventative measures, and how much on research to improve our ability to do each of the first two things in the future. For another example, one might wonder how much should go to treatment of life-threatening conditions (such as heart disease), and how much to conditions which are not life-threatening but seriously impair the sufferers' quality of life (such as arthritis).

Micro-allocation, on the other hand, is concerned with the specific distribution of resources at an individual level. For example, if a hospital can only afford to provide dialysis for ten patients, and there are twenty who could benefit from such treatment, how are the fortunate ten to be selected? Should they be evaluated on the basis of likely contribution to the community at large? Past contributions? Likelihood of responding well to treatment? First-come first-served? The questions multiply.

As mentioned above, the distribution of medical resources is only one question about how resources should be used within a community, albeit an important and much-discussed one. A similar quandary concerns the notion of a welfare state. To what extent do needy people have a legitimate claim against those better off within their society? How did those who control more of society's resources come to be in such a position? Are people entitled to whatever they are able to "earn" under existing systems, or should government intervene to redistribute wealth?

Finally, there are questions about how much responsibility members of societies should take for those of other societies who are less well off. It might be the case that one could always do more good by sending money for food for a starving child rather than spending it on a movie or new clothes. Are we morally required to keep giving rather than spending on ourselves so long as the recipient of the money can use it for greater benefit than we can? Or would giving to poor countries in that way be counter-productive, or foolhardy?

There are many facets to the question of how scarce resources should be distributed. The writings which follow cannot possibly cover all of them adequately, but do serve to introduce some of the important issues, and suggest ways of approaching them.

A Definition of Health

From Preamble to the Constitution of the World Health Organization

World Health Organization

One reason often put forward for being concerned about the distribution of scarce resources is that people have a right to a fair chance at a healthy life. Whether there is such a right or not, it is

clear that health is a very important moral value. However, it is not easy to define exactly what is meant by "health." The World Health Organization has offered the following broad definition.

*   *   *

The States Parties to this Constitution declare, in conformity with the Charter of the United Nations, that the following principles are basic to the happiness, harmonious relations and security of all peoples:

Health is a state of complete physical, mental and social well-being and not merely the absence of disease or infirmity.

The enjoyment of the highest attainable standard of health is one of the fundamental rights of every human being without distinction of race, religion, political belief, economic or social condition.

The health of all peoples is fundamental to the attainment of peace and security and is dependent upon the fullest co-operation of individuals and States.

The achievement of any State in the promotion and protection of health care is of value to all.

Unequal development in different countries in the promotion of health and control of disease, especially communicable disease, is a common danger.

Healthy development of the child is of basic importance; the ability to live harmoniously in a changing total environment is essential to such development.

The extension to all peoples of the benefits of medical, psychological and related knowl-edge is essential to the fullest attainment of health.

Informed opinion and active co-operation on the part of the public are of the utmost importance in the improvement of the health of the people.

Governments have a responsibility for the health of their peoples which can be fulfilled only by the provision of adequate health and social measures.

Accepting these principles, and for the purpose of co-operation among themselves and with others to promote and protect the health of all peoples, the Contracting Parties agree to the present Constitution and hereby establish the World Health Organization as a specialized agency within the terms of Article 57 of the Charter of the United Nations.

Questions for Discussion

1   Does the WHO definition go too far in equating health with "complete physical, mental and social well-being"? If this broad definition is accepted, is it still plausible to claim that people have a "right to health care"?

2   To what extent would the full promotion of health require a restructuring of the existing economic order? Is this desirable?

Allocating Scarce Medical Resources

Case Presentation: Selection Committee for Dialysis

Ronald Munson

One of the central cases where issues arise with respect to how to distribute scarce resources is the case in which there is not enough medical care available for the number of people who need it. How is one to decide which people will receive the needed care, and which will have to do without? In the following somewhat speculative account of such a decision procedure, Ronald Munson raises some of the factors which might be considered relevant.

* * *

In 1966 Brattle, Texas, proper had a population of about ten thousand people. In Brattle County there were twenty thousand more people who lived on isolated farms deep within the pine forests, or in crossroads towns with a filling station, a feed store, one or two white, frame churches, and maybe twenty or twenty-five houses.

Brattle was the marketing town and county seat, the place all the farmers, their wives, and children went to on Saturday afternoon. It was also the medical center because it had the only hospitals in the county. One of them, Conklin Clinic, was hardly more than a group of doctors' offices. But Crane Memorial Hospital was quite a different sort of place. Occupying a relatively new three-story brick building in downtown Brattle, the hospital offered new equipment, a well-trained staff, and high quality medical care.

This was mostly due to the efforts of Dr. J.B. Crane, Jr. The hospital was dedicated to the memory of his father, a man who practiced medicine in Brattle County for almost fifty years. Before Crane became a memorial hospital, it was Crane Clinic.

But J.B. Crane, Jr., after returning from the Johns Hopkins Medical School, was determined to expand the clinic and transform it into a modern hospital. The need was there, and private investors were easy to find. Only a year after his father's death, Dr. Crane was able to offer Brattle County a genuine hospital.

It was only natural that when the County Commissioner decided that Brattle County should have a dialysis machine, he would turn to Dr. Crane's hospital. The machine was bought with county funds, but Crane Memorial Hospital would operate it under a contract agreement. The hospital was guaranteed against loss by the county, but the hospital was also not permitted to make a profit on dialysis. Furthermore, although access to the machine was not restricted to county residents, residents were to be given priority.

Dr. Crane was not pleased with this stipulation. "I don't like to have medical decisions influenced by political considerations," he told the Commissioner. "If a guy comes in and needs dialysis, I don't want to tell him that he can't have it because somebody else who doesn't need it as much is on the machine and that person is a county resident."

"I don't know what to tell you," the Commissioner said. "It was county tax money that paid for the machine, and the County Council decided that the people who supplied the money ought to get top priority."

"What about the kind of case that I mentioned?" Dr. Crane asked. "What about somebody who could wait for dialysis who is a resident as opposed to somebody who needs it immediately who's not a resident?"

"We'll just leave that sort of case to your discretion," the Commissioner said. "People around here have confidence in you and your doctors. If you say they can wait, then they can wait. I know you won't let them down. Of course if somebody died while some outsider was on the machine.... Well, that would be embarrassing for all of us, I guess."

Dr. Crane was pleased to have the dialysis machine in his hospital. Not only was it the only one in Brattle County, but none of the neighboring counties had even one. Only the big hospitals in places like Dallas, Houston, and San Antonio had the machines. It put Crane Memorial up in the top rank.

Dr. Crane was totally unprepared for the problem when it came. He hadn't known there were so many people with chronic renal disease in Brattle County. But when news spread that there was a kidney machine available at Crane Memorial Hospital, twenty-three people applied for the dialysis program. Some were Dr. Crane's own patients or patients of his associates on the hospital staff. But a number of them were ones referred to the hospital by other physicians in Brattle and surrounding

towns. Two of them were from neighboring Lopez County.

Working at a maximum, the machine could accommodate fourteen patients. But the staff decided that maximum operation would be likely to lead to dangerous equipment malfunctions and breakdowns. They settled on ten as the number of patients that should be admitted to the program.

Dr. Crane and his staff interviewed each of the program's applicants, reviewed their medical history, and got a thorough medical workup on each. They persuaded two of the patients to continue to commute to Houston, where they were already in dialysis. In four cases, renal disease had already progressed to the point that the staff decided that the patients could not benefit sufficiently from the program to make them good medical risks. In one other case, a patient suffering intestinal cancer and in generally poor health was rejected as a candidate. Two people were not in genuine need of dialysis but could be best treated by a program of medication.

That left fourteen candidates for the ten positions. Thirteen were from Brattle County and one from Lopez County.

"This is not a medical problem," Dr. Crane told the Commissioner. "And I'm not going to take the responsibility of deciding which people to condemn to death and which to give an extra chance at life."

"What do you want me to do?" the Commissioner asked. "I wouldn't object if you made the decision. I mean, you wouldn't have to tell everybody about it. You could just decide."

"That's something I won't do," Dr. Crane said. "All of this has to be open and aboveboard. It's got to be fair. If I decide, then everybody will think I am just favoring my own patients or just taking the people who can pay the most money."

"I see what you mean. If I appoint a selection committee, will you serve on it?"

"I will. So long as my vote is the same as everybody else's."

"That's what I'll do then," the Commissioner said.

The Brattle County Renal Dialysis Selection Committee was appointed and operating within the week. In addition to Dr. Crane, it was made up of three people chosen by the Commissioner. Amy Langford, a Brattle housewife in her middle fifties whose husband owned the largest automobile and truck agency in Brattle County, was one member. Reverend David Johnson was another member. He was the only black on the committee and the pastor of the largest predominantly black church in Brattle. The last member was Jacob Sims, owner of a hardware store in the nearby town of Silsbee. He was the only member of the committee not from the town of Brattle.

"Now I'm inclined to favor this fellow," said Mr. Sims at the Selection Committee's first meeting. "He's twenty-four years old, he's married and has a child two years old."

"You're talking about James Nelson?" Mrs. Langford asked. "I had some trouble with him. I've heard that he used to drink a lot before he got sick, and from the looks of his record he's had a hard time keeping a job."

"That's hard to say," said Reverend Johnson. "He works as a pulp-wood hauler, and people who do that change jobs a lot. You just have to go where the work is."

"That's right," said Mr. Sims. "One thing, though. I can't find any indication of his church membership. He says he's a

Methodist, but I don't see where he's told us what his church is."

"I don't either," said Mrs. Langford. "And he's not a member of the Masons or the Lions Club or any other sort of civic group. I wouldn't say he's made much of a contribution to this community."

"That's right," said Reverend Johnson. "But let's don't forget that he's got a wife and baby depending on him. That child is going to need a father."

"I think he is a good psychological candidate," said Dr. Crane. "That is, I think if he starts the program he'll stick to it. I've talked with his wife, and I know she'll encourage him."

"We should notice that he's a high school dropout," Mrs. Langford said. "I don't think we can ever expect him to make much of a contribution to this town or to the county."

"Do you want to vote on this case?" asked Mr. Sims, the chairman of the committee.

"Let's talk about all of them, then go back and vote," Reverend Johnson suggested.

Everyone around the table nodded in agreement. The files were arranged by date of application, and Mr. Sims picked up the next one from the stack in front of him.

"Alva Algers," he said. "He's a fifty-three-year-old lawyer with three grown children. His wife is still alive, and he's still married to her. He's Secretary of the Layman's Board of the Brattle Episcopal Church, a member of the Rotary Club and the Elks. He used to be a scoutmaster."

"From the practical point of view," said Dr. Crane, "he would be a good candidate. He's intelligent and educated and understands what's involved in dialysis."

"I think he's definitely the sort of person we want to help," said Mrs. Langford. "He's the kind of a person who makes this a better town. I'm definitely in favor of him."

"I am too," said Reverend Johnson. "Even if he does go to the wrong church."

"I'm not so sure," said Mr. Sims. "I don't think fifty-three is old—I'd better not, because I'm fifty-two myself. Still, his children are grown, he's led a good life. I'm not sure I wouldn't give the edge to some younger fellow."

"How can you say that," Mrs. Langford said. "He's got a lot of good years left. He's a person of good character who might still do a lot for other people. He's not like that Nelson, who's not going to do any good for anybody except himself."

"I guess I'm not convinced that lawyers and members of the Rotary Club do a lot more good for the community than drivers of pulp-wood trucks," Mr. Sims said.

"Perhaps we ought to go on to the next candidate," Reverend Johnson said.

"We have Mrs. Holly Holton, a forty-three-year-old housewife from Mineral Springs," Mr. Sims said.

"That's in Lopez County, isn't it?" Mrs. Langford asked. "I think we can just reject her right off. She didn't pay the taxes that bought the machine, and our county doesn't have any responsibility for her."

"That's right," said Reverend Johnson.

Mr. Sims agreed and Dr. Crane raised no objection.

"Now," said Mr. Sims, "here's Alton Conway. I believe he's our only black candidate."

"I know him well," said Reverend Johnson. "He owns a dry cleaning business, and people in the black community think very highly of him."

"I'm in favor of him," Mrs. Langford said. "He's a married man and seems quite settled and respectable."

"I wouldn't want us to take him just because he's black," Reverend Johnson said. "But I think he's got a lot in his favor."

"Well," said Mr. Sims, "unless Dr. Crane wants to add anything, let's go on to Nora Bainridge. She's a thirty-year-old divorced woman whose eight-year-old boy lives with his father over in Louisiana. She's a waitress at the Pep Cafe."

"She is a very vital woman," said Dr. Crane. "She's had a lot of trouble in her life, but I think she's a real fighter."

"I don't think she's much of a church-goer," said Reverend Johnson. "At least she doesn't give us a pastor's name."

"That's right," said Mrs. Langford. "And I just wonder what kind of morals a woman like her has. I mean, being divorced and working as a waitress and all."

"I don't believe we are trying to award sainthood here," said Mr. Sims.

"But surely moral character is relevant," said Mrs. Langford.

"I don't know anything about her moral character," said Mr. Sims. "Do you?"

"I'm only guessing," said Mrs. Langford. "But I wouldn't say that a woman of her background and apparent character is somebody we ought to give top priority to."

"I don't want to be the one to cast the first stone," said Reverend Johnson. "But I wouldn't put her at the top of our list either."

"I think we had better be careful not to discriminate against people who are poor and uneducated," said Dr. Crane.

"I agree," said Mrs. Langford. "But surely we have to take account of a person's worth."

"Can you tell us how we can measure a person's worth?" asked Mr. Sims.

"I believe I can," Mrs. Langford said. "Does the person have a steady job? Is he or she somebody we would be proud to know? Is he a churchgoer? Does he or she do things for other people? We can see what kind of education the person has had, and consider whether he is somebody we would like to have around."

"I guess that's some of it all right," said Mr. Sims. "But I don't like to rely on things like education, money, and public service. A lot of people just haven't had a decent chance in this world. Maybe they were born poor or have had a lot of bad luck. I'm beginning to think that we ought to make our choices just by drawing lots."

"I can't approve of that," said Reverend Johnson. "That seems like a form of gambling to me. We ought to choose the good over the wicked, reward those who have led a virtuous life."

"I agree," Mrs. Langford said. "Choosing by drawing straws or something like that would mean we are just too cowardly to make decisions. We would be shirking our responsibility. Clearly, some people are more deserving than others, and we ought to have the courage to say so."

"All right," said Mr. Sims. "I guess we'd better get on with it then. Simon Gootz is a forty-eight-year-old baker. He's got a wife and four children. Owns his own bakery—probably all of us have been there. He's Jewish."

"I'm not sure he's the sort of person who can stick to the required diet and go through with the dialysis program," Dr. Crane said.

"I'll bet his wife and children would be a good incentive," said Mrs. Langford.

"There's not a Jewish church in town," said Reverend Johnson. "So of course we can't expect him to be a regular churchgoer."

"He's an immigrant," said Mr. Sims. "I don't believe he has any education to speak of, but he did start that bakery and build it up from nothing. I think that says a lot about his character."

"I think we can agree he's a good candidate," said Mrs. Langford.

"Let's just take one more before we break for dinner," Mr. Sims said. "Rebecca Scarborough. She's a sixty-three-year-old widow. Her children are all grown and living somewhere else."

"She's my patient," Dr. Crane said. "She's a tough and resourceful old woman. I believe she can follow orders and stand up to the rigors of the program, and her health in general is good."

Reverend Johnson said, "I just wonder if we shouldn't put a lady like her pretty far down on our list. She's lived a long life already, and she hasn't got anybody depending on her."

"I'm against that," Mrs. Langford said. "Everybody knows Mrs. Scarborough. Her family has been in this town for ages. She's one of our most substantial citizens. People would be scandalized if we didn't select her."

"Of course I'm not from Brattle," said Mr. Sims. "And maybe that's an advantage here, because I don't see that she's got much in her favor except being from an old family."

"I think that's worth something," said Mrs. Langford.

"I'm not sure if it's enough, though," said Reverend Johnson.

After dinner at the Crane Memorial Hospital cafeteria, the Selection Committee met again to discuss the seven remaining candidates. It was past ten o'clock before their final decisions were made. James Nelson, the pulp-wood truck driver, Holly Holton, the housewife from Mineral Springs, and Nora Bainridge, the waitress, were all rejected as candidates. Mrs. Scarborough was rejected also. The lawyer, Alva Algers, the dry cleaner, Alton Conway, and the baker, Simon Gootz, were selected to participate in the dialysis program. Others selected were a retired secondary school teacher, an assembly-line worker at the Rigid Box Company, a Brattle County Sheriff's Department patrolman, and a twenty-seven-year-old woman file clerk in the office of the Texas Western Insurance Company.

Dr. Crane was glad that the choices were made so that the program could begin operation. But he was not pleased with the selection method and resolved to talk to his own staff and with the County Commissioner about devising some other kind of selection procedure.

Without giving any reasons, Mr. Sims sent a letter to the County Commissioner resigning from the Renal Dialysis Selection Committee.

Mrs. Langford and Reverend Johnson also sent letters to the Commissioner. They thanked him for appointing them to the Committee and indicated their willingness to continue to serve.

Questions for Discussion

1 Among the factors considered relevant by various members of the committee were: number of dependants, civic participation, expected future contribution to the community, conformity to accepted moral standards, likelihood of sticking with the treatment, and age. Are all of these factors worth taking into account? How should they be ranked in order of importance?

2 Should the likelihood of a person's sticking to treatment be considered, even if there is a practical tendency for it to work against already disadvantaged groups?

3 Is it true that making selections on the basis of a random process such as drawing straws is "cowardly" and amounts to shirking the responsibility of deciding which people are most deserving?

Quality of Life and Resource Allocation

Michael Lockwood

One proposal which has been made for allocating scarce medical resources involves measuring "quality adjusted life years," or "QALYs." The idea here is that a year of life in one condition might be worth two years in some other condition, and so on, and it is possible to measure particular types of care in terms of both expected lengthening of life and expected improvement in quality of life. In the following article, Lockwood examines the strengths and weaknesses of such a proposal.

*   *   *

A new word has recently entered the British medical vocabulary. What it stands for is neither a disease nor a cure. At least, it is not a cure for a disease in the medical sense. But it could, perhaps, be thought of as an intended cure for a medicosociological disease: namely that of haphazard or otherwise ethically inappropriate allocation of scarce medical resources. What I have in mind is the term 'QALY,' which is an acronym standing for *quality adjusted life year.* Just what this means and what it is intended to do I shall explain in due course. Let me first, however, set the scene.

I

Problems of resource allocation within medicine arise at a number of different levels. First, one might ask how much of a society's resources should be devoted to health care at all, as opposed to housing, say, or defence. (For what it may be worth, the United States is usually said to devote 10 per cent of its gross national product to health care—though some authors claim that the true figure is substantially higher. By contrast, most Western European countries devote about 7 or 8 per cent, whereas Britain devotes only 5.6 per cent. It is widely held, however, that Britain's relatively low figure is largely compensated for by substantially greater cost efficiency, as compared with other countries. Perhaps; certainly this argument is regularly paraded by the British Government whenever it is suggested that the National Health Service is underfunded!) Given some overall allocation of resources to health care in general, one can then ask how these resources should be distributed amongst various different sorts of health care expenditure: for example, primary versus hospital care, or

preventive medicine versus care of the already ill. Then, within such broader categories, one can ask how one should distribute between different specializations: cardiac versus obstetric units, say, in the case of hospital medicine. And both within and across specializations, one can ask what should be the relative funds allocated for different forms of treatment: kidney transplants versus renal dialysis, hip replacement operations versus coronary bypass surgery, cervical smears versus primary geriatric nursing care.

It is customary to lump together questions of all these different sorts as problems of *macroallocation. Micro*allocation questions, by contrast, arise when decisions have already been made about matters of the kinds just instanced. One has, let us suppose, more patients who stand to benefit by a certain form of treatment than it is possible, given limited resources, to give the treatment to. And the question is: who then gets it? What sorts of criteria should one then appeal to? What selection procedures should one adopt? This problem assumes a special poignancy, of course, when the treatment in question is one without which patients will die. The dramatic potential of such decisions has been widely exploited in fiction, from Bernard Shaw's *The Doctor's Dilemma* (1911)[1] to James Balfour's (1969) short story 'The Junior Physician and the Court of Final Appeal'[2] and a 1966 *Dr Kildare* series, in which a lay panel is established by Dr Gillespie to decide which of a number of clinically eligible patients should be chosen for a limited number of places on a newly installed artificial kidney machine. (The model for Dr Gillespie's committee appears to have been the so-called 'God Committee' of the Seattle Artificial Kidney Center, which from

1961 to 1967 sat in judgement over patients suffering from end-stage renal failure).[3]

Now a natural response to allocation problems, both at macro and micro levels, is to say simply: one should put one's resources where they will do the most good. Well, yes, perhaps one should. But that then raises the further question: what does one mean by 'the most good'? One kind of good, arguably the most important kind of good, that health care may achieve is the saving of lives, or more precisely (if less optimistically) postponing death. So one measure—albeit a very crude and one-sided measure—of the good that health care does would be the overall extension of live [sic] expectancy that it generates: years of life gained. Some writers have argued that we should give a very high priority to this aim of maximizing aggregate years of life gained; and that, moreover, this aim morally requires an allocation of resources, both within and outside medicine, that is radically at odds with the present allocation pattern in developed countries. So argued Dr Donald Gould in 1975:

> In the name of justice, as well as efficiency, we have got to adopt new methods of medical accounting. One such assesses the relative importance of threats to health in terms of the loss of life-years they cause. Calculations are based upon the assumption that all who survive their first perilous year ought then to live on to the age of 70 (any extra years are a bonus). In Denmark, for example, there are 50,000 deaths a year, but only 20,000 among citizens in the 1-70 bracket. These are the ones that count. The annual number of life-years lost in this group totals 264,000. Of these, 80,000 are lost because of accidents and suicides, 40,000 because of coronary heart disease, and 20,000 are due to lung disease. On the basis of these figures, a large proportion of the 'health' budget ought to be spent on pre-

venting accidents and suicides and a lesser but still substantial amount on attempting to prevent and cure heart and lung disease. Much less would be spent on cancer, which is predominantly a disease of the latter half of life, and which therefore contributes relatively little to the total sum of life-years lost. Little would go towards providing kidney machines, and even less toward treating haemophiliacs. No money at all would be available for trying to prolong the life of a sick old man of 82.[4]

There are several things that might be said in response to this passage. First, it is unclear why Gould thinks that *justice*, as well as efficiency, calls for these methods of medical accounting. What is involved in being just, in such contexts, is a question to which we shall return in due course. Secondly, Gould is here concentrating on quantity of life lived to the exclusion of its quality. Most of what is done in the name of health care is directed towards the alleviation of pain, discomfort and disability, rather than the extension of life, but is surely no less valuable on that account. Moreover, things which rank equal in terms of the threat to life that they pose, may well rank unequal in terms of their effect on the quality of life, or in terms of the typical quality of the lives that they threaten to cut short; both sorts of consideration are surely relevant to the question of the relative priority to be given to their prevention or cure.

Thus, judgements about which of several forms of health care expenditure does the most good calls, in general, for one to balance against each other the life-enhancing and the life-extending aspects of health care: quality and quantity of life have somehow to be rendered mutually commensurable. This is where QALYs come in. I quote from Alan Williams, of the University of York, who has done most to develop this approach:

> The essence of a QALY is that it takes a year of healthy life expectancy to be worth 1, but regards a year of unhealthy life expectancy as worth less than 1. Its precise value is lower the worse the quality of life of the unhealthy person (which is what the 'quality adjusted' bit is all about). If being dead is worth zero, it is, in principle, possible for a QALY to be negative, i.e. for the quality of someone's life to be judged worse than being dead.

> The general idea is that a beneficial health care activity is one that generates a positive amount of QALYs, and that an efficient health care activity is one where the cost per QALY is as low as it can be. A high priority health care activity is one where the cost-per-QALY is low, and a low priority activity is one where cost-per-QALY is high.[5]

The assumption here is that there is some rational way of trading off length of life against quality of life, so that one could say, for example, that three years of life with some specified degree of discomfort, loss of mobility or whatever was worth two years of normal life. Such tradeoffs are, of course, often inescapable in medical practice. Take, for example, a patient suffering from laryngial carcinoma, where the choice of treatments is between laryngectomy, which is incompatible with normal speech, but has a 60 per cent five-year survival rate, and radiotherapy, which preserves normal speech, but has only a 30-40 per cent five-year survival rate. Here, presumably, the ethically appropriate thing for the doctor to do is put the choice to the patient—both on the grounds of autonomy and on the grounds that the patient is probably better able to judge, in terms of his own values and way of life, what sort of impact on the quality of his own life the inability

to speak normally is likely to have. (For what it is worth, nearly all patients faced with this particular choice, in fact opt for surgery.) But the resource of passing the decision back to the individual patient is unavailable in microallocation cases, where different patients are competing for the same resource, and would both choose to be treated, or in macroallocation cases, where again we are dealing with different patients, this time mainly future patients, and with questions of overall funding.

What economists who favour the QALY approach do, in a macroallocation context, is take a checklist of health factors that are likely to affect the perceived quality of life of normal people, and assign weightings to them. (Most work done in Britain has been based on the *Rosser distress and disability index*, which health economists would be the first to admit provides only rather a crude measure of quality, but one which they would hope to improve upon in time.[6]) There is, of course, an inescapable element of arbitrariness here, both in the choice of factors to be taken into account and in the relative weightings that are attached to them, which, as already pointed out, would differ markedly from patient to patient. (Immobility, for example, is likely to prove far more irksome to the athlete than to the philosopher.) But the factors and their associated weightings are mostly so chosen as to reflect the feelings and considered judgements which the average or representative patient is likely to evince in practice, when faced with various forms of disability or discomfort, either in prospect or, better, having actually experienced them. On this basis, a given form of treatment is assigned a QALY value, corresponding to the number of QALYs such a patient can look forward to with the treatment minus the number of

QALYs the patient can look forward to if untreated. One then calculates what each QALY gained by these means actually costs.

Whatever philosophical reservations one might have about such an exercise (and I will turn to these in due course), it has yielded some interesting, indeed surprising, results. In Britain there is (or certainly was in the recent past) a widespread feeling that heart transplants represent a wasteful use of medical resources, that the benefits yielded are simply not sufficiently great to justify the cost. But on the other hand, people who say this will usually argue that not enough funds are, in Britain, allocated to long-term renal dialysis. It is widely regarded as a scandal that a treatment that is so effective in extending life should not be made universally available. Williams, evaluating these and other forms of treatment using the notion of a QALY, has come to a very different conclusion. Williams assigns to heart transplantation a QALY value of 4.5 (the point, neglected by most critics of heart transplants, being that their effect, when successful, on the quality of life is dramatic), whereas home and hospital dialysis receive QALY values of 6 and 5 respectively (the neglected point here being that, for most people, long-term dialysis represents a considerable ordeal).[7] Nevertheless, dialysis, so far, comes out somewhat ahead of heart transplants. But now the cost per patient of long-term dialysis is considerably greater than that of a heart transplant. So the cost per QALY is only £5,000 in the case of heart transplants, as compared to £11,000 and £14,000 respectively, in the case of home and hospital dialysis.[8]

Actually, all three figures turned out to be very high as compared with, say, hip replacement or heart valve replacement and pacemaker implantation, whereas Williams

assesses the costs per QALY gained as, respectively, £750, £900 and £700;[9] in these latter operations one gets far more QALYs for one's money. In most parts of Britain there are waiting lists for all these operations; in the case of hip replacement operations the average waiting list under the National Health Service is three years (and in some areas is as high as five years)—it is not in the least unusual for people to die before they reach the head of the queue! Someone who believed that macroallocation in health care should be determined wholly on the basis of directing funds to where they can generate the maximum number of QALYs might well conclude from these figures that given a fixed health care budget, it would be rationally appropriate actually to transfer funds from such relatively high cost-per-QALY, albeit life-saving, forms of treatment as renal dialysis, to such things as hip-replacement operations, right up to the point at which the waiting lists had been eliminated—even if this meant providing no long-term dialysis at all! A pretty startling conclusion, hardly less radical than Gould's.

II

Appealing to QALYs in a macroallocation context, despite the fact that, as we have just seen, it is likely to result in recommendations wildly at odds with present practice, tends to raise fewer hackles than its application to problems of microallocation. Indeed, the advocates of this approach tend to talk less about microallocation than macroallocation. But the approach has clear implications for microallocation too. It implies, for example, that life-saving treatment should, other things being equal, go to those who, with the treatment, will have a longer life expectancy; thus, generally speaking, it will favour younger over older patients. This is in line with actual policy within the British National Health Service with regard to renal dialysis: most centres operate an effective 65-year cut-off. It also implies that, if there appeared, on other grounds, to be nothing to choose between two rival candidates for some life-saving treatment, but one was suffering from a condition, whether or not related to whatever it was that threatened his life, that detracted from its quality, then one should prefer to treat the other candidate. These two sorts of consideration were run together in an example that became a bone of contention at the British Medical Association Annual Scientific Meeting at Oxford in April 1986.

> [S]ay two people needed lifesaving treatment and there were the resources to treat only one, say one who was young and fit and the other was older with arthritis, who should get the treatment? If QALYs were used the younger patient would inevitably and always get the treatment but was that fair?[10]

The economist, Professor Alan Maynard, a champion of the QALY approach, defended such a policy; the philosopher John Harris attacked it, arguing that it was indefensibly discriminatory, and advocated instead the use of a lottery in such cases.

These health-care economists have, it appears, rediscovered utilitarianism. Indeed the QALY approach has a pleasantly nostalgic air, for those familiar with Jeremy Bentham's 'felicific calculus.'[11] Most of the philosophical doubts one might have had about the QALY approach would be particular instances of familiar charges that have been laid against utilitarianism. It should be emphasized, however, that the use of QALYs does not commit one to *classical* or *eudaimonic* utilitarianism: that is to say, there is no suggestion that the good is to be equated with happiness. If we adopt a terminology recently advocated by Amartya Sen,[12] the QALY approach to allocation is, strictly speaking, *welfarist* rather than utilitarian—welfarism being the doctrine that we should so act as to maximize aggregate benefit. Classical utilitarianism is thus a particular form of welfarism, characterized by its equation of benefit with happiness. The concept of a QALY is, of course, committed to no such equation. Indeed, it is in one sense only a framework, requiring to be fleshed out by some substantive conception of what contributes to or detracts from the intrinsic value or worthwhileness of a life, and to what degree—a conception, that is, of what it is about a life that determines of how much benefit it is to the person whose life it is. To this extent, the concept is highly permissive: one can, as it were, plug in whatever conception of value one personally favours. The quality of life indices that are used in practice, as I indicated earlier, seem to be grounded in people's actual expressed values, preferences and attitudes. Is this because people are supposed, by and large, to be their own best judges of the degree to which various things do or would contribute to or detract from the value of their lives? Or is it because, whether they are the best judges or not, it is thought democratically proper that resource allocation reflect, as far as possible, people's actual preferences—a kind of oblique appeal to personal autonomy? It is unclear, though it perhaps does not much matter for practical purposes. My own view is that there are actually three ways in which people's preferences are of moral relevance here. First, what people here and now want is something that ought to be given weight (though not necessarily decisive weight) in the name of a principle of collective or individual self-determination. Secondly, it is, other things being equal, in people's interests that their preferences are satisfied; to that extent the degree to which people's actual circumstances are consonant with their preferences is one of the things, but by no means the only thing, that should be taken into account in making an overall assessment of the quality of someone's life. And finally, people have what philosophers call 'privileged access' to their own lives; they know, better than anyone else can, just what it is like to be them. To that extent, their own judgements about conditions they have actually experienced, whilst far from infallible (especially where what it is that detracts from the quality of their lives is itself something that may affect their judgement, or, where relevant, memory), nevertheless have great authority.

Supposing that one were clear about *what* it was that one was trying to measure, there would still, of course, be room for considerable scepticism about the extent to which it was possible to measure it. From a certain point of view, the idea of putting a yardstick up against a life, whether real or hypothetical, and reading off some numerical value representing its quality or degree of worthwhileness, may seem simply preposterous. On the other hand, one might reasonably doubt whether the moral universe was so constituted that there was a fact of the matter as to just how many years of life under circumstances A were equivalent in value to one year of life under circumstances B, whether one were comparing within or across lives. And even assuming that there were uniquely correct answers to such questions, one might reasonably doubt whether there was any reliable method of

divining them. (Interpersonal comparisons have, historically, been the subject of particular scepticism here, on both these grounds).

But one must be careful here. It would be a mistake to suppose that the validity or usefulness of the QALY approach hinged either on there being, or on one's being able to determine, a *precise* answer to the question of how many QALYs a given span of life added up to. Faced with the sort of comparisons that the QALY approach requires, most people, I imagine, would say this sort of thing: 'Well, a year of normal life would certainly, for me, be worth at least eighteen months of life paralysed from the waist down, but it wouldn't be worth three years under those conditions.' In other words, most people would feel able to set numerical *limits* with some confidence—limits that would generally be narrower if they were judging for themselves than if they were judging for others. Now the point of the QALY approach is to help determine how resources should be allocated, especially as a matter of general policy. And for that purpose, it may be important to know *whether* renal dialysis, say, represents a better use of National Health Service funds than coronary bypass surgery; but it is probably not nearly so important, if important at all, to know just *how much* better. Suppose, then, one were to make the experiment of varying the numerical values one put into the equation, within the limits of what would strike one as intuitively reasonable. In many cases one would find that that made no difference to the *ordinal* conclusions that one ended up with, that is to say conclusions as to what was better than what. Such conclusions would then have the feature that economists sometimes describe as *robustness*—invariance with respect to adjustments of the input values, within the range of one's uncertainty. Thus, only a very radical scepticism, according to which one could not even, with any confidence, set numerical limits in such comparisons, would have the effect of rendering the QALY approach wholly useless. And such wholesale scepticism would, I should have thought, be very difficult convincingly to sustain.

III

Any sane moral theory is bound, it seems to me, to incorporate a welfarist element: other things being equal, it should be regarded as morally preferable to confer greater aggregate benefit than less. To this extent, it seems to me that QALY calculations, or something equivalent to them, should certainly be regarded as highly germane to the resolution of allocation problems within medicine. And, as I have just indicated, the fact that any assignment of precise QALY values is bound, in practice, to involve a degree of arbitrariness need not invalidate the qualitative conclusions that emerge, to the extent that the latter prove robust. But of course, it is one thing to say that welfarist considerations deserve to be given weight (great weight, even) in decisions regarding allocation, quite another to say that they should invariably be regarded as decisive.

The intuition from which we started was that medical resources should be allocated in such a way that they do the most good. But it is far from clear that 'the most good,' here, should simply be equated with 'the greatest aggregate benefit.' And even if one thought it should, it is far from clear that allocation according to QALYs is what would best promote aggregate benefit,

given that there are many things relevant to aggregate benefit that QALY calculations leave totally out of account. If one reflects on what actually goes to determine the overall quality of one's life, one will find that this is dependent on many things that are likely to be overlooked in the rather crude quality of life indices used by the health care economists. This will include one's material and social circumstances: where one lives, what sort of job one has, if any, whether one lives alone or has a family—to what extent, in particular, one possesses those things that Rawls refers to as the 'social and material bases of self-respect.' But it will also include a host of less tangible things, some of them closely bound up with the latter. These will include, for example, one's temperament and psychological make-up in general, the character of one's relationships with others, the extent to which one has a sense of security and of consonance between what one feels oneself to be and what one finds oneself doing, and also a sense of being in command of one's life and of being free to pursue one's chosen projects, but neither effortlessly nor with too much fruitless struggle, and quite generally, the degree of stress, boredom and frustration, or satisfaction and fulfilment that is involved in day-to-day living.

Then there is *social worth*: a calculation confined to QALYs leaves out of account the effects that deciding to treat this person rather than that might have on the lives of others—something that greatly exercises the doctors, Sir Patrick Cullen and Sir Colenso Ridgeon, in Shaw's play.

The situation is that Ridgeon has found a cure for tuberculosis, but only has the time, staff and laboratory facilities to take on one more patient. Two patients then present themselves. The one, Louis

Dubedat, is an artist of genius but morally totally unscrupulous: he borrows money under false pretences which he never returns, and worse, turns out to be a bigamist. The other, Blenkinsop, is an impoverished doctor, hardworking and morally upright, but possessing no great skill or experience. The following conversation ensues:

SIR PATRICK: Well, Mr. Saviour of Lives: which is it to be? that honest decent man Blenkinsop, or that rotten blackguard of an artist, eh?

RIDGEON: It's not an easy case to judge, is it? Blenkinsop's an honest decent man; but is he any use? Dubedat's a rotten blackguard; but he's a genuine source of pretty and pleasant and good things.

SIR PATRICK: What will he be a source of for that poor innocent wife of his, when she finds him out?

RIDGEON: That's true. Her life will be a hell.

SIR PATRICK: And tell me this. Suppose you had this choice put before you: either to go through life and find all the pictures bad but all the men and women good, or to go through life and find all the pictures good and all the men and women rotten. Which would you choose?... To me it's a plain choice between man and a lot of pictures.

RIDGEON: It's easier to replace a dead man than a good picture.[13]

Social worth will be highly sensitive to such considerations as whether one has dependants and, if so, how one's death would affect the quality of their lives, how important is the job one does, and how easy it would be to find someone else to do it comparably well.

There are economic considerations too. Some health care economists have advocated taking into account prospective earnings, on the grounds that if taxpayers' money is being used to pay for a given treatment its *real* cost (or real cost per QALY) will be less in the case of those patients treatment of whom will make the greatest positive impact on their net future contribution to government funds, and thus on the government's capacity to fund health care and welfare programs generally. The economic cost, to the state, of someone's death or continued incapacitation also enters under this heading. I have seen it argued on the basis that, given a cardiac patient with dependants, incapacitated to the point of being unable to work, it may, all things being considered, actually be less costly for the state to pay for him to have a heart transplant (assuming this to be the only suitable treatment) than to allow him to die or to continue living in a severely incapacitated state. (The point here is that if the transplant enables someone to return to work and support his family, then both he and they will cease to be a charge upon the state.) Such considerations may cast doubt on Alan Williams' conclusion, based on QALY calculations, that 'Heart transplantation does not seem to be a serious contender [for National Health Service funds]'.[14]

Save, perhaps, for the most intangible, all the broader types of welfarist consideration just surveyed have entered (in one centre or another) into decisions as to whom to select for some scarce life-saving procedure. So also have a number of other considerations having to do rather with some notion of *desert* (which will be sensitive to what one has done for society in the past, rather than what one is likely to do in the future). The Seattle 'God Committee' (officially, the Admissions and Policies

Committee of the Seattle Artificial Kidney Center) is a case in point:

> In selecting those to receive treatment, the Committee...considered...age, sex, marital status, and number of dependants, income, net worth, psychological stability, and past performance and future potential.[15]

Even from a welfarist perspective, however, it is far from clear that it is, all things considered, desirable that decisions about who should receive, e.g. renal dialysis, be made on this kind of basis. Consistent application of the broader sorts of criteria, especially the economic ones, is likely, in practice, to generate a heavy bias in favour of the white middle class, in a way that is potentially socially divisive.

(Actually, one finds just such a bias in the majority of British renal dialysis units. It is, for example, a fact in Britain, and a disturbing fact, that very few blacks receive renal dialysis, even though it is unlikely that racial discrimination, as such, has much to do with it—simply that the criteria employed tend *de facto* to exclude blacks. It seems unlikely, in fact, that this class/race/income bias has much to do even with doctors applying the kind of generalized quality of life considerations we have been surveying. What seems to be happening is that doctors prefer to give dialysis to those that their past experience suggests are most likely to do well on it. And statistically, educated middle class professionals are likely to do better than, say, unskilled labourers. They are, for example, likely to adhere more closely to the doctor's dietary and other instructions, and they tend to cope better with the psychological stress of being attached to a machine for a period of several hours two or three days a week.)

To the extent that such criteria are employed in a discretionary way at a microallocation level, a different kind of worry arises: is it really desirable that doctors should be allowed to sit in judgement on people's lives in the way that application of such a broad range of criteria implies? Do we want them to have that kind of power? Do we, in fact, want anyone to have that kind of power, even (or perhaps especially) the sort of predominantly lay panel set up in Seattle?[16] This sort of doubt may well be extended to QALY considerations too, if it is a matter of deciding, at a microallocation level, which of two rival contenders for some treatment is to get it. But the fact that QALYs are estimated mainly on the basis of quality of life as it is affected by a patient's overall health at any rate makes it something relatively objective, and something regarding which the doctor may at least claim some professional expertise—albeit that that expertise hardly extends to questions of the evaluative implications of these various health factors (the negative impact of which on the quality of people's lives there is evidence that doctors tend systematically to overestimate).[17]

IV

But I mention all these other sorts of welfarist consideration mainly to put them to one side. For what I really want to focus on here is the philosophically more fundamental objection that can be levelled against the QALY approach: namely that, precisely *because* it is uncompromisingly welfarist, it is in principle liable to result in forms of allocation that are *unjust* or *unfair*.

I shall not attempt here to define justice or unfairness. (All of the well-known philosophical theories of justice seem to me to be subject to decisive objections; and yet I have no alternative theory to offer.) Intuitively, however, justice has something to do with equality, and something also to do with giving appropriate weight to certain sorts of moral *claim*. From a commonsense point of view, the fact that A could confer some benefit, X, on B does not, as such, give B any claim upon A. Only if it is a particular kind of benefit, and A has a particular kind of responsibility for B, does it follow that A is even *prima facie* morally obliged to confer X upon B, or, consequently, that his refusal to do so constitutes any kind of injustice towards B. Now, continuing in this rather abstract vein, the claim that any patient would plausibly be thought to have on the health services (or on the state, in so far as it in turn is responsible for the health of its citizens) is a function not so much of the amount of *benefit* that the health services are in a position to confer, as of the person's health *needs* in relation to the services' capacity effectively to meet those needs.

One reason, then, why the QALY approach can strike one as intuitively unjust is that the principle 'To each according to what will generate the most QALYs' is potentially in conflict with the principle 'To each according to his need.' A patient suffering from end-stage renal failure may be said to *need* dialysis or a kidney transplant, just as a patient with an arthritic hip *needs* a hip replacement. But the first patient's need is clearly the greater. Following David Wiggins,[18] one can think of the degree to which a person, P, needs something, X, as a function of the degree to which his lack of X compromises P's capacity to flourish as a human being ('flourishing' now being, in British philosophical circles, the most favoured translation of Aristotle's *eudaimonia*.) Someone, then, who will die without some particular

treatment needs it in the strongest possible sense; for one cannot flourish at all if one is dead. Other things being equal, one would think, the greater the need the weightier the claim on available resources. But the QALY arithmetic is inherently insensitive to differences in degree of need, except in so far as they happen to correlate with the degree of benefit per unit cost that treatment can confer. It attaches just as much value to the QALYs generated by treating those in a state of lesser need as it does to those generated by treating those in a state of greater need.

Indeed, it is arguable that some forms of medical treatment, whilst they confer a genuine benefit, do not minister to any *need*, as such, at all. I have in mind, for example, cosmetic surgery designed to remove normal wrinkles from the faces of middle-aged ladies. A model or an actress might, to be sure, need such an operation if she was to flourish, if the wrinkles compromised her ability to find employment (and so might a woman who was neurotically obsessed with her looks, if the operation could remove the obsession). But for the rest, the wrinkles do not compromise their capacity to flourish; it is merely that, with the operation, they may be enabled to flourish at a higher level. Such operations are, in short, a luxury. Suppose, then, as seems to me entirely possible, that some health care economist were able to show that face-lifts, say, generated even more QALYs per unit cost than do hip-replacement operations. Would anyone really think that was sufficient reason for switching resources from hip replacements towards such cosmetic surgery?

Surely not. And if not, then by the same token it is far from clear that the QALY calculations cited by Williams constitute a sufficient reason for transferring resources from renal dialysis to hip replacements. One could plausibly argue that someone who will die, if he or she doesn't receive a certain form of treatment, has an intrinsically much stronger claim on available resources than someone whose life is not at stake, even if there is a sense in which greater aggregate benefit could be achieved by neglecting those whose life was threatened in favour of those suffering from reduced mobility or discomfort. And if so, then the greater moral weight that attaches to the claim could be held to outweigh the greater cost of the life-saving treatment per unit QALY generated.

Another respect in which allocation according to QALYs can result in modes of allocation which would intuitively seem unjust is that it will tend, in certain circumstances, to favour those who are (from a health point of view) already relatively fortunate over those who are less fortunate. This, indeed, was the force of the example cited earlier, where it was pointed out that the logic of QALYs would work to the disadvantage of elderly arthritic patients. But I want, for the moment, to set aside the age factor, since it raises important points of principle in its own right which are better dealt with separately. Let us simply suppose that there are two candidates for renal dialysis, and that the only relevant difference between them is that one is suffering from arthritis and the other is not. Assume that the quality of life of the arthritic patient is significantly impaired by his arthritis, but that there is no reason to suppose that it will in any way affect the chances of the dialysis proving successful. Assume, further, that both patients have an equally intense wish to go on living. Under these circumstances, the QALY approach says:

give the dialysis to the patient who does not have arthritis. For every extra year of life we give him will correspond to a higher QALY value than a year given to the other.

There is a clear sense in which this is inequitable, for what it amounts to is taking the fact that someone is already unfortunate, in one respect, as a reason for visiting further misfortunes upon him (or at least denying him benefits). One might reasonably ask whether it was consistent with natural justice to allocate life-saving resources on the basis: 'From him who hath not shall be taken away even that which he hath,' namely his life.

In cases such as this, I find myself in agreement with John Harris's assertion that allocation by QALYs 'amounts to unjust discrimination between individuals.' On the other hand, if doctors are faced with a choice of treating either of two patients, who are in an equivalent state of need, it does not seem to me unjust to choose to treat the patient for whom the treatment is more likely to prove successful. Nor does it seem to me unjust to prefer to treat the patient who can be treated at less cost, whether at the level of microallocation or macroallocation. Harris, by contrast, finds this an objectionable feature of the QALY approach:

If a 'high priority health care activity is one where the cost-per-QALY is low and a low priority is one where cost-per-QALY is high' then people who just happen to have conditions which are relatively cheap to treat are always to be given priority over those who happen to have conditions which are relatively expensive to treat. This will inevitably involve not only a systematic pattern of disadvantage to particular groups of patients, or to people afflicted with particular diseases or conditions, but perhaps also a systematic preference for the survival of some kinds of patients at the expense of others. We usually think that justice requires that we do not allow certain sections of the community or certain types of individual to become the victims of systematic disadvantage....[19]

This line of reasoning seems to me fallacious. The principal basis of just dealing in a health care context is, surely, that people are thought of as having a claim on available health care resources that is proportional to their degree of need. (In the absence, that is, of other considerations bearing upon what is just or fair.) From this point of view, if two patients (whether suffering from the same or different diseases) are equally in need of treatment, then they have the same claim on available resources. In the context of finite resources, this implies that if the resources required to treat them effectively are the same, neither has a better claim to being treated than the other (again, in the absence of other considerations). But if the resources required to treat the one are greater than those required to treat the other, it is perfectly compatible with recognizing that they have an equal claim on resources to say that the patient whose treatment requires a lesser expenditure of resources should be treated to the exclusion of the other.

Putting it schematically, suppose that the two patients, Andrew and Brian, in virtue of their health needs, were both thought to have a claim on medical resources of weight W, and that effective treatment of Andrew would call for an expenditure of resources X, whereas effective treatment of Brian would call for an expenditure of resources Y, where Y is less than X. (Any claim on resources is, after all, clearly going to be contingent on their effectiveness in ministering to the need that grounds the claim.) It is then entirely consistent with

recognizing that they both have a prior claim of weight W to say that Brian should be treated in preference to Andrew. For what that implies is that, in the circumstances, a claim of weight W carries with it an entitlement to an expenditure of resources Y (conditional upon its being effective), but not to the larger expenditure of resources X. And that is surely perfectly reasonable. Indeed, to devote a disproportionate amount of one's health care resources to the treatment of people in a given state of need, when a lesser expenditure would enable one effectively to treat more people in an equivalent or greater sense of need, would itself, from this point of view, be a violation of the principle that the claim on resources is proportional to need.

I do not, incidentally, think it is true, *absolutely in general*, that 'justice requires that we do not allow certain sections of the community to become the victims of systematic disadvantage.' If it were true, then justice would require, absurdly, that we not allow, say, more able people to get better jobs. What justice actually requires is that we do not discriminate between people on the basis of unjust criteria—race and sex being obvious cases in point. Thus if someone claims, as Harris does, that it is unjust to allocate health care on the basis of how great an expenditure of resources is required to minister effectively to a given need, the burden is on him to show that this *particular* criterion is unjust. But this he does not attempt to do; and the argument I have just presented seems to lead to quite the opposite conclusion, that it is perfectly just. This is not to deny, of course, that it is thoroughly bad luck if someone finds himself suffering from a condition the treatment for which is just too expensive to constitute a justifiable use of limited health care resources. But bad luck is not, *ipso facto*, injustice.

I alluded, in passing, to 'other considerations' that might be thought relevant to justice. Given two people who are equally in need of a given form of treatment, some would think it morally appropriate to take into account the fact that one of them has, through irresponsible behaviour, brought his condition upon himself. An example which featured in a recent television program on the allocation of renal dialysis[20] was that of a patient suffering from renal failure consequent upon drug abuse (though it should have been pointed out, on this program, that a history of drug abuse may, for purely medical reasons, cause difficulties when it comes to dialysis). For my own part, I am somewhat sceptical about the claim that *justice* requires that one should be sensitive to this kind of consideration. And this is because I am sceptical about free will. I am personally inclined to think that, in an important sense, we are all of us victims of our genetic inheritance, upbringing and so forth, and that it is not true that people who bring certain kinds of health care need on themselves—e.g. by driving dangerously, overeating, smoking or abusing drugs or alcohol—really *could*, in the final analysis, have acted any differently. (That said, I have heard it argued that there might be good welfarist reasons for according the claims of such people on health care resources a relatively low priority, if the fact were to be widely publicized and could act as an effective deterrent to such irresponsible behaviour. But I doubt whether it would. Someone who is undeterred by the prospect of seriously damaging his health is hardly likely, in my opinion, to be deterred

by the prospect of less than ideal health care thereafter. An alternative and more promising proposal might be to give people some kind of tax incentive towards healthy living—say, in a British context, by making National Insurance payments depend in some degree on doctor's reports, so that someone who was overweight or who smoked, for example, would find himself paying more. But such a scheme might prove, in practice, very difficult to administer satisfactorily.)

A second point on which I find myself in disagreement with Harris concerns the relevance of *age* to allocation questions. Harris[21] maintains that it is *ageist* to take the fact that one of two rival contenders for renal dialysis, say, is younger as a reason for preferring to treat him, ageism, here, meaning wilful discrimination on the basis of age, parallel to racism, sexism and, most recently, speciesism (taking the fact that an animal does not belong to the human species as a reason for saying that its suffering, say, matters less than equivalent suffering in the case of a human being). Now it goes without saying that some ways of taking someone's age into account, whether in a health care context or elsewhere, would be unjust. But I do not think it is unjust to allocate life-extending treatment on the basis that the younger one is, the weightier, other things being equal, is one's claim upon available resources.

The reason I say this is that I am impressed, as Harris is not, by what is commonly referred to as the 'fair innings argument.' The thought here, which seems to me absolutely correct, is that an older person seeking dialysis, for example, has already by definition lived for longer than a younger person. To treat the older person, letting the younger person die, would thus be inherently inequitable in terms of years of life lived: the younger person would get no more years than the relatively few he has already had, whereas the older person, who has already had more than the younger person, will get several years more.

Of course, this argument only works if one takes seriously the identity of persons over time. If one does not, then one can mount a counter-argument parallel to that which led us to the conclusion that it is inequitable to take the fact that someone has arthritis, for example, as a contraindication, in a situation of scarcity, to providing him with life-extending treatment. 'It is bad enough being old,' someone might argue. 'To cite that as a reason for denying life-saving measures is to take the fact that one is already unfortunate in one respect as a reason for imposing yet a further misfortune, namely death. How can that be fair?' Well, quite easily; it is fair, inasmuch as the person referred to has already had a reasonably long life, longer, anyway, than that of rival contenders for the treatment. Fairness must be assessed on the basis of someone's life as a whole, unless one thinks of each 'time-slice' of a person as an independent contender for available resources, which would seem to me perverse. (But then I am not a sceptic about personal identity. Someone who took a more sceptical position than I, such as that defended by Derek Parfit in his influential *Reasons and Persons*,[22] might well be disposed to find great merit in the counter-argument to the fair innings argument that I have just cited.)

I mentioned earlier the fact that, from a welfarist perspective, it would be appropriate to take into consideration whether a patient had dependants, and if so how many and of what age—something that is not taken into account in a QALY calculation.

How does this criterion look from the standpoint of justice? Well it depends, it seems to me, on the precise grounds on which the interests of dependants are included in the equation. The central principle of justice that is operative here, I have been suggesting, is that one's claim on resources is proportional to one's need (in the absence of other factors). Now such a principle not only permits but actually requires one to take dependants into account, to the extent that these dependants themselves have a stake in the life or health of the patient *that in itself amounts to a need*, in the strongest sense of that term. What one must ask, then, is whether the death or continued ill-health of the patient compromises the capacity of these dependants to flourish as human beings. If it does, then the health care needs of the patient are, in an extended sense, their health care needs too, and should be taken into account as such. Under such circumstances one may favour a mother with young children over a single person in an equivalent state of need, not because she herself has a greater claim on health care resources than does the single person, but because her children have, in virtue of their own need of the mother, claims in their own right—claims which can only be satisfied (or at least which can best be satisfied) through treating her.

Both here and as regards whether one should take age into account, it therefore seems to me that welfarist considerations, on the one hand, and considerations having to do with justice, on the other, will tend to converge on the same conclusion. (QALY calculations, as we have seen, tend statistically to favour the young for life-extending treatment, on grounds of life expectancy, quality of life, as gauged in terms of distress and disability, and also, in the case of renal dialysis, on the basis of the prospects for an eventual transplant.) Here the conclusions may be 'robust' in a new, wider sense: they may be invariant with respect to variations in one's moral assumptions, whether uncompromisingly welfarist or highly sensitive to considerations of justice.

But I see no particular reason to suppose that in general one will find any such convergence between justice and welfare (though there are many philosophers who argue that our intuitions about what is just are likely in practice to converge with what welfarism would enjoin, when we take sufficiently many factors into account in our welfarist calculations, or, like Richard Hare, that our intuitions about what is just are intuitions that it is, by and large, best from a welfarist point of view for people to have and act upon).[23] What then, since I have argued that any sane moral theory must include a welfarist element, should happen when justice and welfare come into conflict with each other, as I have argued that they do, in many QALY calculations? To give a wholly general answer to this question is as difficult as giving a theory of justice in the first place. But, at the level of moral phenomenology, it would seem that, over a considerable middle range of cases, where the cost in welfarist terms of giving priority to considerations of justice is not that enormous, we think it morally appropriate to favour justice. Indeed, one could view justice as *constraining* one's pursuit of welfarist aims: it is morally legitimate, indeed laudable, to aim for greater aggregate benefit, *provided* one acts justly in the pursuit of that aim.

One logical mechanism whereby justice can thus constrain welfarism may be via Joseph Raz's interesting concept of *exclusionary reasons*. An exclusionary reason is a

reason for *not* taking something else as a reason. For example, justice gives the judge in a court of law a reason for not taking as a reason for giving a lenient sentence the fact that the accused is an old friend. Indeed, the image of justice as standing blindfold is a perfect symbolic embodiment of this notion of exclusionary reasons. Now in the context of the allocation of scarce lifesaving therapy, our earlier arguments might suggest that justice should be blind, for example, to the patient's quality of life, in respects that have nothing to do with the likely effectiveness of the treatment or the patient's wish to go on living.

This notion of justice as constraining welfarism constitutes the element of truth in John Rawls' claim that justice should be given what he calls *lexical priority* over other values, such as efficiency,[24] by which he means that the demands of justice have to be met before one starts discriminating amongst different policies or courses of action on other grounds: any policy or course of action which violates justice is excluded at the outset. But that, whilst it may be the right way to look at matters in a middle range of cases, becomes grossly implausible if insisted upon right across the board. It is moral fanaticism to say, with William Watson, 'Fiat justitia et ruant coeli' (Let justice be done though the heavens fall) or with the Emperor Ferdinand I, 'Fiat justitia, et pereat mundi' (Let justice be done, though the world perish). Whilst differences in quality of life should perhaps, in the name of justice, be ignored over a large middle range of cases, when allocating scarce resources, there comes a point where differences in prospective distress and disability are so great that it would be morally irresponsible not to take them into account, on welfarist grounds. And of course one ought, by the logic of what I have been saying, to take such factors into account when choosing amongst policies or courses of action which are none of them unjust. What I have been proposing is a pluralistic scheme of values in which welfare is one amongst a number of elements, which will also include justice, autonomy, and no doubt other things too. We should not let enthusiasm for QALYs blind us to these other values, nor let the fact that unconstrained maximization of QALYs may be a recipe for injustice blind us to the crucial importance of the welfarist considerations that QALY calculations embody. The allocation of scarce medical resources is an area where rationality is sorely called for, where we urgently need to examine our priorities in the light of argument and evidence of their relative efficacy. As a contribution to this task—but only as a contribution, not the last word on allocation matters—QALYs are greatly to be welcomed.

Postscript 1987[25]

Since writing this article, I have come to think (partly as a result of some very stimulating conversations with John Broome) that what I say in response to John Harris's claims needs to be amended. Harris, as we have seen, argues that a policy of thoroughgoing QALY maximization is ageist, and to that extent unjust. My response in the text was to argue that this is not unjust, and that, from the standpoint of justice, we ought, other things being equal, to favour younger patients in the allocation of scarce life-saving resources. What I should now argue is that Harris is mistaken in thinking that the QALY approach is ageist. For it is not true that QALY maximization involves discriminating against older patients as

such; what it discriminates against are those with relatively low life expectancy, given that they receive the treatment. The situation is parallel to that of selecting amongst applicants for a job that calls for a high degree of physical strength. In such circumstances, men would be most likely to be chosen in preference to women; but that would not be sexist, provided that weaker men were not chosen in preference to demonstratively stronger women. Clearly, the QALY approach is not committed to selecting younger people in preference to older people that demonstrably have a higher post-treatment life expectancy. But that very fact now seems to me to be an objection to unconstrained QALY maximization. For if, as I have been arguing, the fair innings argument is sound, then one ought, in the name of fairness, to prefer a younger over an older patient, for life-saving treatment, even if the post-treatment life-expectancy of the younger patient is no greater than that of the older patient. As I now see it, what is objectionable, here, about unconstrained QALY maximization, is not that it involves discriminating on the basis of age, but, on the contrary, that it fails to take age into account in circumstances where, in fairness, it ought to do so. It fails to be ageist when it should be, rather than being ageist when it should not.

The second point involves Harris's claim that it is unfair, when faced with limited resources, to favour patients that can be treated at less cost. In the article I argued that this was not unfair to the patients who needed relatively costly treatment; but merely a case of bad luck. Now, however, I am inclined to think that this is, after all, unfair, but that to treat a smaller number of people at greater cost, at the expense of failing to treat a larger number of equally needy patients, would be more unfair still. Suppose Tom, Dick and Harriet are in a state of equal need, and that for each of their conditions there exists a unique corresponding treatment that will be wholly effective. However, Tom's treatment costs £6,000, whereas Dick's and Harriet's both cost £3,000. Suppose, further, that nothing useful can be done for these patients for any amounts less than these, and that there is only £6,000 in the kitty. Given that they are all equally needy, Tom, Dick, and Harriet each have, *a priori*, an equal claim on available resources. But we cannot just split the money three ways, since £2,000 will not, for any of them, buy effective treatment. By treating Dick and Harriet, at the expense of Tom, we are, it seems to me, being unfair to Tom, since his need is the same as that of Dick and Harriet, and yet he gets nothing. But in treating Tom, at the expense of Dick and Harriet, we would be being even more unfair, since then two of them would get nothing; and the numerical disparity between the actual allocation of resources and the unattainable ideal of £2,000 worth of effective treatment apiece, would be twice as great, in this case. The fairest thing we could do, in this situation, would be to have a weighted lottery, in which Tom was given a one-third chance of getting treated, at a cost of £6,000, while Dick and Harriet were given a two-thirds chance of being treated, at a cost of £3,000 apiece. For then the *expected* resource allocation, that is to say the probability of getting treated multiplied by the cost, would be the same for all of them, namely £2,000, thus matching their equal need. But even that is not perfectly fair, since it ameliorates but does not eliminate the inevitable inequality of the final outcome.

Two final points. First, I quite deliberately say 'unfair' here, rather than 'unjust.' We are sometimes it seems to me, faced with situations in which whatever we do will result in an outcome that is, to some extent, unfair. But it strikes me a bit odd to describe it as unjust. We might perhaps say that an outcome is perfectly just when it reduces unfairness to the absolute minimum that the situation allows. But anyway, a pattern of distribution of scarce medical resources that, other things being equal, will favour those who can be treated at less cost, is not perfectly just if, as I now believe, a weighted lorry would be fairer. Nevertheless, I should not advocate such a lottery. First, it would be an administrative nightmare. But secondly, it would be significantly less efficient at generating QALYs. Given that, in any case, considerations of justice have, to some extent, to be weighed against welfarist considerations, I would judge that favouring those who can be treated at less cost gives about the right weight to both.

Notes

1   Bernard Shaw, *The Doctor's Dilemma: A Tragedy* (first published in 1911), A.C. Ward (ed.) (London: Longman's Green, 1960).

2   'The Junior Physician and the Court of Last Appeal,' in James Balfour, *Court Short* (London: Hutchison, 1969), 171-189.

3   Guido Calebresi and Philip Bobbit, *Tragic Choices* (New York: W.W. Norton, 1978), 187-188, 209 n., 232-233 n.

4   Donald Gould, 'Some Lives Cost Too Dear,' *New Statesman* November (1975), quoted in Jonathan Glover, *Causing Death and Saving Lives* (Harmondsworth: Penguin Books, 1977), 220-221.

5   Alan Williams, 'The Value of QALYs,' *Health and Social Service Journal* July (1985), 3.

6   P. Kind, R. Rosser, and A. Williams, 'Valuation of quality of life: Some Psychometric Evidence,'

in M.W. Jones-Lee, *The Value of Life and Safety* (Amsterdam: Elsevier/North-Holland, 1982).

7   Alan Williams, 'Economics of Coronary Bypass Grafting,' *British Medical Journal* **291** (3 August 1985), 328.

8   *Ibid.*

9   *Ibid.*

10 Tessa Richards and Linda Beecham, 'The BMA in Oxford,' *British Medical Journal* **292** (26 April 1986), 1119-1120.

11 Jeremy Bentham, *The Principles of Morals and Legislation* (1789), Chs. 1-5.

12 See Amartya Sen, 'Utilitarianism and Welfarism,' *Journal of Philosophy* **76** (September 1979).

13 *The Doctor's Dilemma*, op. cit., 84-85.

14 Alan Williams, op. cit., 328.

15 Calebresi and Bobbit, op. cit., 233 n.

16 The Committee's membership 'consisted of a lawyer, a minister, a housewife, a banker, a state government official, a labor leader, and a surgeon' assisted by 'a medical advisory panel made up of personnel associated with the kidney treatment program' (Calebresi and Bobbit, op. cit., 209 n.).

17 Alan Williams, op. cit., 327.

18 David Wiggins, 'Claims of Need,' in Ted Honderich (ed.), *Morality and Objectivity* (London: Routledge & Kegan Paul, 1984), 149-202.

19 John Harris, 'Rationing Life: Quality or Justice' (unpublished), paper presented to the British Medical Association Annual Scientific Meeting, Oxford, 10-12 April 1986, p. 9.

20 In the *Doctor's Dilemma* series, Granada Television, 1984.

21 Harris, op. cit., 8. This line of thought is developed at greater length in his *The Value of Life: An Introduction to Medical Ethics* (London: Routledge & Kegan Paul, 1985), Ch. 5.

22 Derek Parfit, *Reasons and Persons* (Oxford University Press, 1984), Part III.

23 Hare's theory was originally put forward in R.M. Hare, 'Ethical Theory and Utilitarianism,' in H.D. Lewis (ed.), *Contemporary Moral Philosophy 4* (London: Allen and Unwin, 1976); it is developed in greater detail in his *Moral Thinking* (Oxford University Press, 1981).

24 John Rawls, *A Theory of Justice* (Oxford University Press, 1973), para. 8.

25 The preceding text appears originally in French in the *Revue de Métaphysique et de Morale*, No.3/1987, 307-328. The postscript which follows has been added for this volume.

Questions for Discussion

1   Can QALYs be measured well enough for use in decision-making?

2   Does use of QALYs interfere with considerations of justice? Are there any other factors which need to be taken into consideration?

Excerpts from Anarchy, State, and Utopia

Robert Nozick

One issue concerning distribution of scarce resources involves the question of how people come to "own" particular resources at all. The classical view has been that natural resources are originally unowned, but people may then stake a claim to the unowned property. One of the most famous accounts of how this might take place was offered by John Locke in the seventeenth century. Locke claimed people acquire previously unowned objects by mixing their labour with them. Contemporary philosopher Robert Nozick follows in this tradition, maintaining that we can determine whether people have a just claim to their holdings simply by seeing if they have acquired them justly ("justice in acquisition," if converted directly from an unowned state, or "justice in transfer" if originally appropriated by someone else but then transferred to the current owner). In the following selection

*from his influential book, Nozick offers a critical discussion of Locke's account of property acqui-
sition, including an attempt at understanding Locke's "proviso" that others not be made worse off
by one's acquisition. Nozick believes that a free market system, with a minimal social safety net,
will satisfy the requirements of justice, viewed in this way.*

*   *   *

Locke's Theory of Acquisition

Locke views property rights in an unowned object as originating through someone's mixing his labor with it. This gives rise to many questions. What are the boundaries of what labor is mixed with? If a private astronaut clears a place on Mars, has he mixed his labor with (so that he comes to own) the whole planet, the whole uninhabited universe, or just a particular plot? Which plot does an act bring under ownership? The minimal (possibly disconnected) area such that an act decreases entropy in that area, and not elsewhere? Can virgin land (for the purposes of ecological investigation by high-flying aiplane) come under ownership by a Lockean process? Building a fence around a territory presumably would make one the owner of only the fence (and the land immediately underneath it).

Why does mixing one's labor with something make one the owner of it? Perhaps because one owns one's labor, and so one comes to own a previously unowned thing that becomes permeated with what one owns. Ownership seeps over into the rest. But why isn't mixing what I own with what I don't own a way of losing what I own rather than that a way of gaining what I don't? If I own a can of tomato juice and spill it in the sea so that its molecules (made radioactive, so I can check this) mingle evenly throughout the sea, do I thereby come to own the sea, or have I foolishly dissipated my tomato juice? Perhaps the idea, instead, is that laboring on something improves it and makes it more valuable; and anyone is entitled to own a thing whose value he has created. (Reinforcing this, perhaps, is the view that laboring is unpleasant. If some people made things effortlessly, as the cartoon characters in *The Yellow Submarine* trail flowers in their wake, would they have lesser claim to their own products whose making didn't *cost* them anything?) Ignore the fact that laboring on something may make it less valuable (spraying pink enamel paint on a piece of driftwood that you have found). Why should one's entitlement extend to the whole object rather than just to the *added value* one's labor has produced? (Such reference to value might also serve to delimit the extent of ownership; for example, substitute "increases the value of" for "decreases entropy in" in the above entropy criterion.) No workable or coherent value-added property scheme has yet been devised, and any such scheme presumably would fall to objections (similar to those) that fell the theory of Henry George.

It will be implausible to view improving an object as giving full ownership to it, if the stock of unowned objects that might be improved is limited. For an object's coming under one person's ownership changes the situation of all others. Whereas previously they were at liberty (in Hohfeld's sense) to use the object, they now no longer are. This change in the situation of others (by removing their liberty to act on a previously unowned object) need not worsen their situation. If I appropriate a grain of sand from Coney Island, no one else may now do as they will with *that* grain of sand. But there are plenty of other grains left for them to do the same with. Or if not grains of sand, then other things. Alternatively, the things I do with the grains of sand I appropriate might improve the position of others, counterbalancing their loss of the liberty to use that grain. The crucial point is whether appropriation of an unowned object worsens the situation of others.

Locke's proviso that there be "enough and as good left in common for others" (sect. 27) is meant to ensure that the situation of others is not worsened. (If this proviso is met is there any motivation for his further condition of nonwaste?) It is often said that this proviso once held but now no longer does. But there appears to be an argument for the conclusion that if the proviso no longer holds, then it cannot ever have held so as to yield permanent and inheritable property rights. Consider the first person Z for whom there is not enough and as good left to appropriate. The last person Y to appropriate left Z without his previous liberty to act on an object, and so worsened Z's situation. So Y's appropriation is not allowed under Locke's proviso. Therefore the next to last person X to appropriate left Y in a worse position, for X's act ended permissible appropriation. Therefore X's appropriation wasn't permissible. But then the appropriator two from last, W, ended permissible appropriation, and so, since it worsened X's position, W's appropriation wasn't permissible. And so on back to the first person A to appropriate a permanent property right.

This argument, however, proceeds too quickly. Someone may be made worse off by another's appropriation in two ways: first, by losing the opportunity to improve his situation by a particular appropriation or any one; and second, by no longer being able to use freely (without appropriation) what he previously could. A *stringent* requirement that another not be made worse off by an appropriation would exclude the first way if nothing else counterbalances the diminution in opportunity, as well as the second. A *weaker* requirement would exclude the second way, though not the first. With the weaker requirement, we cannot zip back so quickly from Z to A, as in the above argument; for though person Z can no longer *appropriate*, there may remain some for him to *use* as before. In this case Y's appropriation would not violate the weaker Lockean condition. (With less remaining that people are at liberty to use, users might face more inconvenience, crowding, and so on; in that way the situation of others might be worsened, unless appropriation stopped far short of such a point.) It is arguable that no one legitimately can complain if the weaker provision is satisfied. However, since this is less clear than in the case of the more stringent proviso, Locke may have intended this stringent proviso by "enough and as good" remaining, and perhaps he meant the nonwaste condition to delay the end point from which the argument zips back.

Is the situation of persons who are unable to appropriate (there being no more accessible and useful unowned objects) worsened by a system allowing appropriation and permanent property? Here enter the various familiar social considerations favoring private property: it increases the social product by putting means of production in the hands of those who can use them most efficiently (profitably); experimentation is encouraged, because with separate persons controlling resources, there is no one person or small group whom someone with a new idea must convince to try it out; private property enables people to decide on the pattern and types of risks they wish to bear, leading to specialized types of risk bearing; private property protects future persons by leading some to hold back resources from current consumption for future markets; it provides alternate sources of employment for unpopular persons who don't have to convince any one person or small group to hire them, and so on. These considerations enter a Lockean theory to support the claim that appropriation of private property satisfies the intent behind the "enough and as good left over" proviso, *not* as a utilitarian justification of property. They enter to rebut the claim that because the proviso is violated no natural right to private property can arise by a Lockean process. The difficulty in working such an argument to show that the proviso is satisfied is in fixing the appropriate base line for comparison. Lockean appropriation makes people no worse off than they would be *how?*[1] This question of fixing the baseline needs more detailed investigation than we are able to give it here. It would be desirable to have an estimate of the general economic importance of original appropriation in order to see how much leeway there is for differing theories of appropriation and of the location of the baseline. Perhaps this importance can be measured by the percentage of all income that is based upon un-

transformed raw materials and given resources (rather than upon human actions), mainly rental income representing the unimproved value of land, and the price of raw material *in situ*, and by the percentage of current wealth which represents such income in the past.[†]

We should note that it is not only persons favoring *private* property who need a theory of how property rights legitimately originate. Those believing in collective property, for example those believing that a group of persons living in an area jointly own the territory, or its mineral resources, also must provide a theory of how such property rights arise; they must show why the persons living there have rights to determine what is done with the land and resources there that persons living elsewhere don't have (with regard to the same land and resources).

The Proviso

Whether or not Locke's particular theory of appropriation can be spelled out so as to handle various difficulties, I assume that any adequate theory of justice in acquisition will contain a proviso similar to the weaker of the ones we have attributed to Locke. A process normally giving rise to a permanent bequeathable property right in a previously unowned thing will not do so if the position of others no longer at liberty to use the thing is thereby worsened. It is important to specify *this* particular mode of worsening the situation of others, for the

---

[†] I have not seen a precise estimate. David Friedman, *The Machinery of Freedom* (N.Y.: Harper & Row, 1973), pp. xiv, xv, discusses this issue and suggests 5 percent of US national income as an upper limit for the first two factors mentioned. However he does not attempt to estimate the percentage of current wealth which is based upon such income in the past. (The vague notion of "based upon" merely indicates a topic needing investigation.)

Ethical Issues

proviso does not encompass other modes. It does not include the worsening due to more limited opportunities to appropriate (the first way above, corresponding to the more stringent condition), and it does not include how I "worsen" a seller's position if I appropriate materials to make some of what he is selling, and then enter into competition with him. Someone whose appropriation otherwise would violate the proviso still may appropriate provided he compensates the others so that their situation is not thereby worsened; unless he does compensate these others, his appropriation will violate the proviso of the principle of justice in acquisition and will be an illegitimate one.[†] A theory of appropriation incorporating this Lockean proviso will handle correctly the cases (objections to the theory lacking the proviso) where someone appropriates the total supply of something necessary for life.[*]

A theory which includes this proviso in its principle of justice in acquisition must also contain a more complex principle of justice in transfer. Some reflection of the proviso about appropriation constrains later actions. If my appropriating all of a certain substance violates the Lockean proviso, then so does my appropriating some and purchasing all the rest from others who obtained it without otherwise violating the Lockean proviso. If the proviso excludes someone's appropriating all the drinkable water in the world, it also excludes his purchasing it all. (More weakly, and messily, it may exclude his charging certain prices for some of his supply.) This proviso (almost?) never will come into effect; the more someone acquires of a scarce substance which others want, the higher the price of the rest will go, and the more difficult it will become for him to acquire it all. But still, we can imagine, at least, that something like this occurs: someone makes simultaneous secret bids to the separate owners of a substance, each of whom sells assuming he can easily purchase more from the other owners; or some natural catastrophe destroys all of the supply of something

---

[†] Fourier held that since the process of civilization had deprived the members of society of certain liberties (to gather, pasture, engage in the chase), a socially guaranteed minimum provision for persons was justified as compensation for the loss (Alexander Gray, *The Socialist Tradition* (New York: Harper & Row, 1968), p. 188). But this puts the point too strongly. This compensation would be due those persons, if any, for whom the process of civilization was a *net loss*, for whom the benefits of civilization did not counterbalance being deprived of these particular liberties.

[*] For example, Rashdall's case of someone who comes upon the only water in the desert several miles ahead of others who will also come to it and appropriates it all. Hastings Rashdall, "The Philosophical Theory of Property," in *Property, its Duties and Rights* (London: MacMillan, 1915). We should note Ayn Rand's theory of property rights—"Man's Rights" in *The Virtue of Selfishness* (New York: New American Library, 1964), p. 94—wherein these follow from the right to life, since people need physical things to live. But a right to life is not a right to whatever one needs to live; other people may have rights over these other things (see Chapter 3 of [Nozick's] book). At most, a right to life would be a right to have or strive for whatever one needs to live, provided that having it does not violate anyone else's rights. With regard to material things, the question is whether having it does violate any right of others. (Would appropriation of all unowned things do so? Would appropriating the water hole in Rashdall's example?) Since special considerations (such as the Lockean proviso) may enter with regard to material property, one *first* needs a theory of property rights before one can apply any supposed right to life (as amended above). Therefore the right to life cannot provide the foundation for a theory of property rights.

except that in one person's possession. The total supply could not be permissibly appropriated by one person at the beginning. His later acquisition of it all does not show that the original appropriation violated the proviso (even by a reverse argument similar to the one above that tried to zip back from Z to A). Rather, it is the combination of the original appropriation *plus* all the later transfers and actions that violates the Lockean proviso.

Each owner's title to his holding includes the historical shadow of the Lockean proviso on appropriation. This excludes his transferring it into an agglomeration that does violate the Lockean proviso and excludes his using it in a way, in coordination with others or independently of them, so as to violate the proviso by making the situation of others worse than their baseline situation. Once it is known that someone's ownership runs afoul of the Lockean proviso, there are stringent limits on what he may do with (what it is difficult any longer unreservedly to call) "his property." Thus a person may not appropriate the only water hole in a desert and charge what he will. Nor may he charge what he will if he possesses one, and unfortunately it happens that all the water holes in the desert dry up, except for his. This unfortunate circumstance, admittedly no fault of his, brings into operation the Lockean proviso and limits his property rights.[†] Similarly, an owner's property right in the only island in an area does not allow him to order a castaway from a shipwreck off his island as a trespasser, for this would violate the Lockean proviso.

Notice that the theory does not say that owners do have these rights, but that the rights are overridden to avoid some catastrophe. (Overridden rights do not disappear; they leave a trace of a sort absent in the cases under discussion.)[2] There is no such external (and *ad hoc?*) overriding. Considerations internal to the theory of property itself, to its theory of acquisition and appropriation, provide the means for handling such cases. The results, however, may be coextensive with some condition about catastrophe, since the baseline for comparison is so low as compared to the productiveness of a society with private appropriation that the question of the Lockean proviso being violated arises only in the case of catastrophe (or a desert-island situation).

The fact that someone owns the total supply of something necessary for others to stay alive does *not* entail that his (or anyone's) appropriation of anything left some people (immediately or later) in a situation worse than the baseline one. A medical researcher who synthesizes a new substance that effectively treats a certain disease and who refuses to sell except on his terms does not worsen the situation of others by depriving them of whatever he has appropriated. The others easily can possess the same materials he appropriated; the researcher's appropriation or purchase of chemicals didn't make those chemicals scarce in a way so as to violate the Lockean proviso. Nor would someone else's pur-

† The situation would be different if his water hole didn't dry up, due to special precautions he took to prevent this. Compare our discussion of the case in the text with Hayek, *The Constitution of Liberty*, p. 136; and also with Ronald Hamowy, "Hayek's Concept of Freedom; A Critique," *New Individualist Review*, April 1961, pp. 28-31.

chasing the total supply of the synthesized substance from the medical researcher. The fact that the medical researcher uses easily available chemicals to synthesize the drug no more violates the Lockean proviso than does the fact that the only surgeon able to perform a particular operation eats easily obtainable food in order to stay alive and to have the energy to work. This shows that the Lockean proviso is not an "end-state principle"; it focuses on a particular way that appropriative actions affect others, and not on the structure of the situation that results.[3]

Intermediate between someone who takes all of the public supply and someone who makes the total supply out of easily obtainable substances is someone who appropriates the total supply of something in a way that does not deprive the others of it. For example, someone finds a new substance in an out-of-the-way place. He discovers that it effectively treats a certain disease and appropriates the total supply. He does not worsen the situation of others; if he did not stumble upon the substance no one else would have, and the others would remain without it. However, as time passes, the likelihood increases that others would have come across the substance; upon this fact might be based a limit to his property right in the substance so that others are not below his baseline position; for example, its bequest might be limited. The theme of someone worsening another's situation by depriving him of something he otherwise would possess may also illuminate the example of patents. An inventor's patent does not deprive others of an object which would not exist if not for the inventor. Yet patents would have this effect on others who independently invent the object. Therefore, these independent inventors, upon whom the burden of proving independent discovery may rest, should not be excluded from utilizing their own invention as they wish (including selling it to others). Furthermore, a known inventor drastically lessens the chances of actual independent invention. For persons who know of an invention usually will not try to reinvent it, and the notion of independent discovery here would be murky at best. Yet we may assume that in the absence of the original invention, sometime later someone else would have come up with it. This suggests placing a time limit on patents, as a rough rule of thumb to approximate how long it would have taken, in the absence of knowledge of the invention, for independent discovery.

I believe that the free operation of a market system will not actually run afoul of the Lockean proviso.

Notes

1   Compare this with Robert Paul Wolff's "A Refutation of Rawls' Theorem on Justice," *Journal of Philosophy*, March 31, 1966, sect. 2. Wolff's criticism does not apply to Rawls' conception under which the baseline is fixed by the difference principle.

2   I discuss overriding and its moral traces in "Moral Complications and Moral Structures," *Natural Law Forum*, 1968, pp. 1-50.

3   Does the principle of compensation (Chapter 4) introduce patterning considerations? Though it requires compensation for the disadvantages imposed by those seeking security from risks, it is not a patterned principle. For it seeks to remove only those disadvantages which prohibitions inflict on those who might present risks to others, not all disadvantages. It specifies an obligation on those who impose the prohibition, which stems from their own particular acts, to remove a particular complaint those prohibited may make against them.

Questions for Discussion

1 Should natural resources be viewed as "unowned" but there for the taking?

2 Is "mixing one's labour" with something a good enough explanation of how we can come to acquire unowned things?

3 What should the relevant comparison be for saying that a person has been made worse off by a series of acquisitions and transfers? Can a resulting inequality provide a justification for requiring people to surrender some of their possessions to those worse off?

The Right to Eat and the Duty to Work

Trudy Govier

In the following selection, first published in 1975, Govier surveys different views people might have about the welfare state, which she calls the "Individualist," "Permissive," and "Puritan" views. She argues that the view of the individualists (such as Nozick) is least convincing, while the permissive view is her preferred choice.

*　　*　　*

Although the topic of welfare is not one with which philosophers have often concerned themselves, it is a topic which gives rise to many complex and fascinating questions—some in the area of political philosophy, some in the area of ethics, and some of a more practical kind. The variety of issues related to the subject of welfare makes it particularly necessary to be clear just which issue one is examining in a discussion of welfare. In a recent book on the subject, Nicholas Rescher asks:

In what respects and to what extent is society, working through the instrumentality of the state, responsible for the welfare of its members? What demands for the promotion of his welfare can an individual reasonably make upon his society? These are questions to which no answer can be given in terms of some *a priori* approach with reference to universal ultimates. Whatever answer can

appropriately be given will depend, in the final analysis, on what the society decides it should be.[1]

Rescher raises this question only to avoid it. His response to his own question is that a society has all and only those responsibilities for its members that it thinks it has. Although this claim is trivially true as regards legal responsibilities, it is inadequate from a moral perspective. If one imagines the case of an affluent society which leaves the blind, the disabled, and the needy to die of starvation, the incompleteness of Rescher's account becomes obvious. In this imagined case one is naturally led to raise the question as to whether those in power ought to supply those in need with the necessities of life. Though the needy have no legal right to welfare benefits of any kind, one might very well say that they ought to have such a right. It is this claim which I propose to discuss here.[2]

I shall approach this issue by examining three positions which may be adopted in response to it. These are:

1. The Individualist Position: Even in an affluent society, one ought not to have any legal right to state-supplied welfare benefits.

2. The Permissive Position: In a society with sufficient resources, one ought to have an unconditional legal right to receive state-supplied welfare benefits. (That is, one's right to receive such benefits ought not to depend on one's behaviour; it should be guaranteed).

3. The Puritan Position: In a society with sufficient resources one ought to have a legal right to state-supplied welfare benefits; this right ought to be conditional, however, on one's willingness to work.

But before we examine these positions, some preliminary clarification must be attempted....

Welfare systems are state-supported systems which supply benefits, usually in the form of cash income, to those who are in need. Welfare systems thus exist in the sort of social context where there is some private ownership of property. If no one owned anything individually (except possibly his own body), and all goods were considered to be the joint property of everyone, then this type of welfare system could not exist. A state might take on the responsibility for the welfare of its citizens, but it could not meet this responsibility by distributing a level of cash income which such citizens would spend to purchase the goods essential for life. The welfare systems which exist in the western world do exist against the background of extensive private ownership of property. It is in this

context that I propose to discuss moral questions about having a right to welfare benefits. By setting out my questions in this way, I do not intend to endorse the institution of private property, but only to discuss questions which many people find real and difficult in the context of the social organization which they actually do experience. The present analysis of welfare is intended to apply to societies which (*a*) have the institution of private property, if not for means of production, at least for some basic good; and (*b*) possess sufficient resources so that it is at least possible for every member of the society to be supplied with the necessities of life.

The Individualist View

It might be maintained that a person in need has no legitimate moral claim on those around him and that the hypothetical inattentive society which left its blind citizens to beg or starve cannot rightly be censured for doing so. This view, which is dramatically at odds with most of contemporary social thinking, lives on in the writings of Ayn Rand and her followers.[3] The Individualist sets a high value on uncoerced personal choice. He sees each person as a responsible agent who is able to make his own decisions and to plan his own life. He insists that with the freedom to make decisions goes responsibility for the consequences of those decisions. A person has every right, for example, to spend ten years of his life studying Sanskrit—but if, as a result of this choice, he is unemployable, he ought not to expect others to labour on his behalf. No one has a proper claim on the labour of another, or on the income ensuing from that labour, unless he can repay the labourer in a way acceptable to that labourer himself. Government welfare schemes provide benefits from funds gained largely by taxing earned income. One cannot "opt out" of such schemes. To the Individualist, this means that a person is forced to work part of his time for others.

Suppose that a man works forty hours and earns two hundred dollars. Under modern-day taxation, it may well be that he can spend only two-thirds of that money as he chooses. The rest is taken by government and goes to support programs which the working individual may not himself endorse. The beneficiaries of such programs—those beneficiaries who do not work themselves—are as though they have slaves working for them. Backed by the force which government authorities can command, they are able to exist on the earnings of others. Those who support them do not do so voluntarily, out of charity; they do so on government command.

> Someone across the street is unemployed. Should you be taxed extra to pay for his expenses? Not at all. You have not injured him, you are not responsible for the fact that he is unemployed (unless you are a senator or bureaucrat who agitated for further curtailing of business which legislation passed, with the result that your neighbour was laid off by the curtailed business). You may voluntarily wish to help him out, or better still, try to get him a job to put him on his feet again; but since you have initiated no aggressive act against him, and neither purposefully nor accidentally injured him in any way, you should not be legally penalized for the fact of his unemployment.[4]

The Individualist need not lack concern for those in need. He may give generously to charity; he might give more generously still, if his whole income were his to use, as he would like it to be. He may also believe that, as a matter of empirical fact, existing government programs do not actually help the poor. They support a cumbersome bureaucracy and they use financial resources which, if untaxed, might be used by those with initiative to pursue job-creating endeavours. The thrust of the Individualist's position is that each person owns his own body and his own labour; thus each person is taken to have a virtually unconditional right to the income which that labour can earn him in a free market place.[5] For anyone to pre-empt part of a worker's earnings without that worker's voluntary consent is tantamount to robbery. And the fact that the government is the intermediary through which this deed is committed does not change its moral status one iota.

On an Individualist's view, those in need should be cared for by charities or through other schemes to which contributions are voluntary. Many people may wish to insure themselves against unforeseen calamities and they should be free to do so. But there is no justification for non-optional government schemes financed by taxpayers' money....

The Permissive View

Directly contrary to the Individualist view of welfare is what I have termed the Permissive view. According to this view, in a society which has sufficient resources so that everyone could be supplied with the necessities of life, every individual ought to be given the legal right to social security, and this right ought not to be conditional in any way upon an individual's behavior. *Ex hypothesi* the society which we are discussing has sufficient goods to provide everyone with food, clothing, shelter and other necessities. Someone who does without these basic goods is scarcely living at all, and a society which takes no steps to change this state of affairs implies by its inaction that the life of such a person is without value. It does not execute him; but it may allow him to die. It does not put him in prison; but it may leave him with a life of lower quality than that of some prison inmates. A society which can rectify these circumstances and does not can justly be accused of imposing upon the needy either death or lifelong deprivation. And those characteristics which make a person needy—whether they be illness, old age, insanity, feeblemindedness, inability to find work, or even poor moral character—are insufficient to make him deserve the fate to which an inactive society would in effect condemn him. One would not be executed for inability or failure to find work; neither should one be allowed to die for this misfortune or failing.

A person who cannot or does not find his own means of social security does not thereby forfeit his status as a human being. If other human beings, with physical, mental and moral qualities different from his, are regarded as having the right to life and to the means of life, then so too should he be regarded. A society which does not accept the responsibilities for supplying such a person with the basic necessities of life is, in effect, endorsing a difference between its members which is without moral justification....

The adoption of a Permissive view of welfare would have significant practical implications. If there were a legal right, unconditional upon behaviour, to a specified level of state-supplied benefits, then state investigation of the prospective welfare recipient could be kept to a minimum. Why he is in need, whether he can work, whether he is willing to work, and what he does while receiving welfare benefits are on this view quite irrelevant to his right to receive those benefits. A welfare recipient is a person who claims from his society that to which he is legally entitled under a morally based welfare scheme. The fact that he makes this claim licenses no special state or societal interference with his behaviour. If the Permissive view of welfare were widely believed, then there would be no social stigma attached to being on welfare. There is such a stigma, and many long-term welfare recipients are considerably demoralized by their dependent status.[6] These facts suggest that the Permissive view of welfare is not widely held in our society.

The Puritan View

This view of welfare rather naturally emerges when we consider that no one can have a right to something without someone else's, or some group of other persons', having responsibilities correlative to this right. In the case in which the right in question is a legal right to social security, the correlative responsibilities may be rather extensive. They have been deemed responsibilities of "the state." The state will require resources and funds to meet these responsibilities, and these do not emerge from the sky miraculously, or zip into existence as a consequence of virtually effortless acts of will. They are taken by the state from its citizens, often in the form of taxation on earned income. The funds given to the welfare recipient and many of the goods which he purchases with these funds are produced by other members of society, many of whom give a considerable portion of their time and their energy to this end. If a state has the moral responsibility to ensure the social security of its citizens then all the citizens of that state have the responsibility to provide state agencies with the means to carry out their duties. This responsibility, in our present contingent circumstances, seems to generate an obligation to *work*.

A person who works helps to produce the goods which all use in daily living and, when paid, contributes through taxation to government endeavours. The person who does not work, even though able to work, does not make his contribution to social efforts towards obtaining the means of life. He is not entitled to a share of the goods produced by others if he chooses not to take part in their labours. Unless he can show that there is a moral justification for his not making the sacrifice of time and energy which others make, he has no legitimate claim to welfare benefits. If he is disabled or unable to obtain work, he cannot work; hence he has no need to justify his failure to work. But if does choose not to work, he would have to justify his choice by saying "others should sacrifice their time and energy for me; I have no need to sacrifice time and energy for them." This principle, a version of what Rawls refers to as a **freerider's principle**, simply will not stand up to criticism.[7] To deliberately avoid working and benefit from the labours of others is morally indefensible.

Within a welfare system erected on these principles, the right to welfare is conditional upon one's satisfactorily accounting for his failure to obtain the necessities of life by his own efforts. Someone who is severely disabled mentally or physically, or who for some other reason cannot work, is morally entitled to receive welfare benefits. Someone who chooses not to work is not. The Puritan view of welfare is a kind of compromise between the Individualist view and the Permissive view....

The Puritan view of welfare, based as it is on the inter-relation between welfare and work, provides a rationale for two connected principles which those establishing welfare schemes in Canada and in the United States seem to endorse. First of all, those on welfare should never receive a higher income than the working poor. Secondly, a welfare scheme should, in some way or other, incorporate incentives to work. These principles, which presuppose that it is better to work than not to work, emerge rather naturally from the contingency which is at the basis of the Puritan view: the goods essential for social security are products of the labour of some members of society. If we wish to have a continued supply of such goods, we must encourage those who work to produce them....

Appraisal of Policies: Social Consequences and Social Justice

In approaching the appraisal of prospective welfare policies under these two aspects I am, of course, making some assumptions about the moral appraisal of suggested social policies. Although these cannot possibly be justified here, it may be helpful to articulate them, at least in a rough way.

Appraisal of social policies is in part teleological. To the extent that a policy, P, increases the total human welfare more than does an alternative policy, P', P is a better social policy than P'. Or, if P leaves the total human welfare as it is, while P' diminishes it, then to that extent, P is a better social policy than P'. Even this skeletal formulation of the teleological aspect of appraisal cannot be entirely teleological. We consider total consequences—effects upon the total of "human well-being" in a society. But this total is a summation of consequences on different individuals. It includes no judgements as to how far we allow one individual's well-being to decrease while another's increases, under the same policy. Judgements relating to the latter problems are judgements about social justice.

In appraising social policies we have to weigh up considerations of total well-being against considerations of justice. Just how this is to be done, precisely, I would not pretend to know. However, the absence of precise methods does not mean that we should relinquish attempts at appraisal: some problems are already with us, and thought which is necessarily tentative and imprecise is still preferable to no thought at all.

Consequences of Welfare Schemes

First, let us consider the consequences of the non-scheme advocated by the Individualist. He would have us abolish all non-optional government programs which have as their goal the improvement of anyone's personal welfare. This rejection extends to health schemes, pension plans and education, as well as to welfare and unemployment insurance. So following the Individualist would lead to very sweeping changes.

The Individualist will claim (as do Hospers and Ayn Rand) that on the whole his non-scheme will bring beneficial consequences. He will admit, as he must, that there are people who would suffer tremendously if welfare and other social security programs were simply terminated. Some would even die as a result. We cannot assume that spontaneously developing charities would cover every case of dire need. Nevertheless the Individualist wants to

point to benefits which would accrue to businessmen and to working people and their families if taxation were drastically cut. It is his claim that consumption would rise, hence production would rise, job opportunities would be extended, and there would be an economic boom, if people could only spend all their earned income as they wished. This boom would benefit both rich and poor.

There are significant omissions which are necessary in order to render the Individualist's optimism plausible. Either workers and businessmen would have insurance of various kinds, or they would be insecure in their prosperity. If they did have insurance to cover health problems, old age and possible job loss, then they would not be spending their whole earned income on consumer goods. Those who run the insurance schemes could, of course, put this money back into the economy—but government schemes already do this. The economic boom under Individualism would not be loud as originally expected. Furthermore the goal of increased productivity must be questioned from an ecological viewpoint: many necessary materials are only available in limited quantities.

Finally, a word about charity. It is not to be expected that those who are at the mercy of charities will benefit from this state, either materially or psychologically. Those who prosper will be able to choose between giving a great deal to charity and suffering from the very real insecurity and guilt which would accompany the existence of starvation and grim poverty outside their padlocked doors. It is to be hoped that they would opt for the first alternative. But, if they did, this might be every bit as expensive for them as government-supported benefit schemes are now. If they did not give generously to charity, violence might result. However one looked at it, the consequences of Individualism are unlikely to be good.

Welfare schemes operating in Canada today are almost without exception based upon the principles of the Puritan view. To see the consequences of that type of welfare scheme we have only to look at the results of our own welfare programs. Taxation to support such schemes is high, but not so intolerably so as to have led to widescale resentment among taxpayers. Canadian welfare programs are attended by complicated and often cumbersome bureaucracy, some of which results from the interlocking of municipal, provincial and federal governments in the administration and financing of welfare programs. The cost of the programs is no doubt increased by this bureaucracy; not all the tax money directed to welfare programs goes to those in need. Puritan welfare schemes do not result in social catastrophe or in significant business stagnation—this much we know, because we already live with such schemes. Their adverse consequences, if any, are felt primarily not by society generally, nor by businessmen and the working segment of the public, but rather by recipients of welfare.

Both the Special Senate Committee Report on Poverty and the Real Poverty Report criticize our present system of welfare for its demoralization of recipients, who often must deal with several levels of government and are vulnerable to arbitrary interference on the part of administering officials. Welfare officials have the power to check on welfare recipients and to cut off or limit their benefits under a large number of circumstances. The dangers to welfare recipients in terms of anxiety, threats to privacy and loss of dignity are obvious. According to the Senate Report, the single aspect shared by all Canada's welfare systems is "a record of failure and insufficiency, of bureaucratic rigidities that often result in the degradation, humiliation and alienation of recipients."[8] The writers of this report cite many instances of humiliation, leaving the impression that these are too easily found to be "incidental aberrations."[9] Concern that a welfare recipient either be unable to work or be willing to work (if unemployed) can easily turn into concern about how he spends the income supplied him, what his plans for the future are, where he lives, how many children he has. And the rationale underlying the Puritan scheme makes the degradation of welfare recipients a natural consequence of welfare institutions. Work is valued and only he who works is thought to contribute to society. Welfare recipients are regarded as parasites and spongers—so when they are treated as such, this is only what we should have expected. Being on welfare in a society which thinks and acts in this fashion can be psychologically debilitating. Welfare recipients who are demoralized by their downgraded status and relative lack of personal freedom can be expected to be made less capable of self-sufficiency. To the extent that this is so, welfare systems erected on Puritan principles may defeat their own purposes.

In fairness, it must be noted here that bureaucratic checks and controls are not a feature only of Puritan welfare systems. To a limited extent, Permissive systems would have to incorporate them too. Within those systems, welfare benefits would be given only to those whose income was inadequate to meet basic needs. However, there would be no checks on "willingness to work," and there would be no need for welfare workers to evaluate the merits of the daily activities of recipients. If a Permissive guaranteed income system were administered through income tax returns, everyone receiving the basic income and those not needing it paying it back in taxes, then the special status of welfare recipients would fade. They would no longer be singled out as a special group within the population. It is to be expected that living solely on government-supplied benefits would be psychologically easier in that type of situation.

Thus it can be argued that for the recipients of welfare, a Permissive scheme has more advantages than a Puritan one. This is not a very surprising conclusion. The Puritan scheme is relatively disadvantageous to recipients, and Puritans would acknowledge this point; they will argue that the overall consequences of Permissive schemes are negative in that these schemes benefit some at too great a cost to others. (Remember, we are not yet concerned with the *justice* of welfare policies, but solely with their consequences as regards *total* human well-being within the society in question.) The concern which most people have regarding the Permissive scheme relates to its costs and its dangers to the "work ethic." It is commonly thought that people work only because they have to work to survive in a tolerable style. If a guaranteed income scheme were adopted by the government, this incentive to work would disappear. No one would be faced with the choice between a nasty and boring job and starvation. Who would do the nasty and boring jobs then? Many of them are not eliminable and they have to be done somehow, by someone. Puritans fear that a great many people—even some with relatively pleasant jobs—might simply cease to work if they

could receive non-stigmatized government money to live on. If this were to happen, the permissive society would simply grind to a halt.

In addressing these anxieties about the consequences of Permissive welfare schemes, we must recall that welfare benefits are set to ensure only that those who do not work have a bearable existence, with an income sufficient for basic needs, and that they have this income regardless of why they fail to work. Welfare benefits will not finance luxury living for a family of five! If jobs are adequately paid so that workers receive more than the minimum welfare income in an earned salary, then there will still be a financial incentive to take jobs. What guaranteed income schemes will do is to raise the salary floor. This change will benefit the many non-unionized workers in service and clerical occupations.

Furthermore it is unlikely that people work solely due to (i) the desire for money and the things it can buy and (ii) belief in the Puritan work ethic. There are many other reasons for working, some of which would persist in a society which had adopted a Permissive welfare system. Most people are happier when their time is structured in some way, when they are active outside their own homes, when they feel themselves part of an endeavour whose purposes transcend their particular egoistic ones. Women often choose to work outside the home for these reasons as much as for financial ones. With these and other factors operating I cannot see that the adoption of a Permissive welfare scheme would be followed by a level of slothfulness which would jeopardize human well-being.

Another worry about the Permissive scheme concerns cost. It is difficult to comment on this in a general way, since it would vary so much from case to case. Of Canada at the present it has been said that a guaranteed income scheme administered through income tax would cost even less than social security payments administered through the present bureaucracies. It is thought that this saving would result from a drastic cut in administrative costs. The matter of the work ethic is also relevant to the question of costs. Within a Puritan framework it is very important to have a high level of employment and there is a tendency to resist any reorganization which results in there being fewer jobs available. Some of these proposed reorganizations would save money; strictly speaking we should count the cost of keeping jobs which are objectively unnecessary as part of the cost of Puritanism regarding welfare.

In summary, we can appraise Individualism, Puritanism and Permissivism with respect to their anticipated consequences, as follows: Individualism is unacceptable; Puritanism is tolerable, but has some undesirable consequences for welfare recipients; Permissivism appears to be the winner. Worries about bad effects which Permissive welfare schemes might have due to high costs and (alleged) reduced work-incentives appear to be without solid basis.

Social Justice Under Proposed Welfare Schemes

We must now try to consider the merits of Individualism, Puritanism and Permissivism with regard to their impact on the distribution of the goods necessary for well-being. [Robert] Nozick has argued against the whole conception of a distributive justice on the grounds that it presupposes that goods are like manna from heaven: we simply get them and then have a problem—to whom to give them. According to Nozick

we know where things come from and we do not have the problem of to whom to give them. There is not really a problem of distributive justice, for there is no central distributor giving out manna from heaven! It is necessary to counter Nozick on this point since his reaction to the (purported) problems of distributive justice would undercut much of what follows.[10]

There is a level at which Nozick's point is obviously valid. If A discovers a cure for cancer, then it is A and not B or C who is responsible for this discovery. On Nozick's view this is taken to imply that A should reap any monetary profits which are forthcoming; other people will benefit from the cure itself. Now although it cannot be doubted that A is a bright and hardworking person, neither can it be denied that A and his circumstances are the product of many co-operative endeavours: schools and laboratories, for instance. Because this is so, I find Nozick's claim that "we know where things come from" unconvincing at a deeper level. Since achievements like A's presuppose extensive social co-operation, it is morally permissible to regard even the monetary profits accruing from them as shareable by the "owner" and society at large.

Laws support existing income levels in many ways. Governments specify taxation so as to further determine net income. Property ownership is a legal matter. In all these ways people's incomes and possibilities for obtaining income are affected by deliberate state action. It is always possible to raise questions about the moral desirability of actual conventional arrangements. Should university professors earn less than lawyers? More than waitresses? Why? Why not? Anyone who gives an account of distributive justice is trying to specify principles which will make it possible to answer questions such as these, and nothing in Nozick's argument suffices to show that the questions are meaningless or unimportant.

Any human distribution of anything is unjust insofar as differences exist for no good reason. If goods did come like manna from heaven and the Central Distributor gave A ten times more goods than B, we should want to know why. The skewed distribution might be deemed a just one if A's needs were objectively ten times greater than B's, or if B refused to accept more than his small portion of goods. But if no reason at all could be given for it, or if only an irrelevant reason could be given (e.g., A is blue-eyed and B is not), then it is an unjust distribution. All the views we have expounded concerning welfare permit differences in income level. Some philosophers would say that such differences are never just, although they may be necessary, for historical or utilitarian reasons. Whether or not this is so, it is admittedly very difficult to say just what would constitute a good reason for giving A a higher income than B. Level of need, degree of responsibility, amount of training, unpleasantness of work—all these have been proposed and all have some plausibility. We do not need to tackle all this larger problem in order to consider justice under proposed welfare systems. For we can deal here solely with the question of whether everyone should receive a floor level of income; decisions on this matter are independent of decisions on overall equality or principles of variation among incomes above the floor. The Permissivist contends that all should receive at least the floor income; the Individualist and the Puritan deny this. All would claim justice for their side.

The Individualist attempts to justify extreme variations in income, with some people below the level where they can fulfill their basic needs, with reference to the fact of people's actual accomplishments. This approach to the question is open to the same objections as those which have already been raised against Nozick's non-manna-from-heaven argument, and I shall not repeat them here. Let us move on to the Puritan account. It is because goods emerge from human efforts that the Puritan advances his view of welfare. He stresses the unfairness of a system which would permit some people to take advantage of others. A Permissive welfare system would do this, as it makes no attempt to distinguish between those who choose not to work and those who cannot work. No one should be able to take advantage of another under the auspices of a government institution. The Puritan scheme seeks to eliminate this possibility, and for that reason, Puritans would allege, it is a more just scheme than the Permissive one.

Permissivists can best reply to this contention by acknowledging that any instance of free-riding would be an instance where those working were done an injustice, but by showing that any justice which the Puritan preserves by eliminating free-riding is outweighed by *injustice* perpetrated elsewhere. Consider the children of the Puritan's free-riders. They will suffer greatly for the "sins" of their parents. Within the institution of the family, the Puritan cannot suitably hurt the guilty without cruelly depriving the innocent. There is a sense, too, in which Puritanism does injustice to the many people on welfare who are not free-riders. It perpetuates the opinion that they are non-contributors to society and this doctrine, which is over-simplified if not downright false, has a harmful effect upon welfare recipients.

Social justice is not simply a matter of the distribution of goods, or the income with which goods are to be purchased. It is also a matter of the protection of rights. Western societies claim to give their citizens equal rights in political and legal contexts; they also claim to endorse the larger conception of a right to life. Now it is possible to interpret these rights in a limited and formalistic way, so that the duties correlative to them are minimal. On the limited, or negative, interpretation, to say that A has a right to life is simply to say that others have a duty not to interfere with A's attempts to keep himself alive. This interpretation of the right to life is compatible with Individualism as well as with Puritanism. But it is an inadequate interpretation of the right to life and of other rights. A right to vote is meaningless if one is starving and unable to get to the polls; a right to equality before the law is meaningless if one cannot afford to hire a lawyer. And so on.

Even a Permissive welfare scheme will go only a very small way towards protecting people's rights. It will amount to a meaningful acknowledgement of a right to life, by ensuring income adequate to purchase food, clothing and shelter—at the very least. These minimum necessities are presupposed by all other rights a society may endorse in that their possession is a precondition of being able to exercise these other rights. Because it protects the rights of all within a society better than do Puritanism and Individualism, the Permissive view can rightly claim superiority over the others with regard to justice.

Notes

1 Nichols Rescher, *Welfare: Social Issues in Philosophical Perspective*, p. 114.

2 One might wish to discuss moral questions concerning welfare in the context of **natural rights** doctrines. Indeed, Article 22 of the United Nations Declaration of Human Rights states, "Everyone, as a member of society, has the right to social security and is entitled, through national effort and international cooperation and in accordance with the organization and resources of each State, to the economic, social and cultural rights indispensable for his dignity and the free development of his personality." I make no attempt to defend the right to welfare as a **natural right**. Granting that rights imply responsibilities or duties and that "ought" implies "can," it would only be intelligible to regard the right to social security as a natural right if all states were able to ensure the minimum well-being of their citizens. This is not the case. And a natural right is one which is by definition supposed to belong to all human beings. The analysis given here in the permissive view is compatible with the claim that all human beings have a *prima facie* natural right to social security. It is not, however, compatible with the claim that all human beings have a natural right to social security if this right is regarded as one which is so absolute as to be inviolable under any and all conditions.

3 See, for example, Ayn Rand's *Atlas Shrugged, The Virtue of Selfishness*, and *Capitalism: The Unknown Ideal*.

4 John Hospers, *Libertarianism: A Political Philosophy for Tomorrow*, p. 67.

5 I say virtually unconditional, because an Individualist such as John Hospers sees a legitimate moral role for government in preventing the use of force by some citizens against others. Since this is the case, I presume that he would also regard as legitimate such taxation as was necessary to support this function. Presumably that taxation would be seen as consented to by all, on the grounds that all "really want" government protection.

6 Ian Adams, William Cameron, Brian Hill, and Peter Penz, *The Real Poverty Report*, pp. 167-187.

7 See *A Theory of Justice*, pp. 124, 136. Rawls defines the free-rider as one who relies on the principle "everyone is to act justly except for myself, if I choose not to," and says that his position is a version of egoism which is eliminated as a

morally acceptable principle by formal constraints. This conclusion regarding the tenability of egoism is one which I accept and which is taken for granted in the present context.

8   *Senate Report on Poverty*, p. 73.

9   The Hamilton Public Welfare Department takes automobile licence plates from recipients, making them available again only to those whose needs meet with the Department's approval. (*Real Poverty Report*, p. 186.) The *Globe and Mail* for 12 January 1974 reported that welfare recipients in the city of Toronto are to be subjected to computerized budgeting. In the summer of 1973, the two young daughters of an Alabama man on welfare were sterilized against their own wishes and without their parents' informed consent. (See *Time*, 23 July, 1973.)

10 Robert Nozick, "Distributive Justice," *Philosophy and Public Affairs*, Fall 1973.

Questions for Discussion

1   Govier argues that the permissive approach would actually cost less in financial terms, and that there would still be sufficient incentive to cause people to work rather than live on welfare. Is she right?

2   Do the injustices suffered by some under the permissive view (imposed by people "free-riding" on the backs of others) outweigh the injustices suffered by others (e.g. innocent children born into families below the minimum welfare line, or welfare recipients who are not free-riders) if the permissive view is not adopted?

Living on a Lifeboat

Garrett Hardin

Looking at distribution of resources on a global scale, Hardin argues against the common view that wealthy nations have some obligation to help the starving of the world. Using the image of a lifeboat in a sea full of drowning people, Hardin argues that the eventual result of giving large amounts of humanitarian aid and loosening immigration laws would not be a raising of the disadvantaged to the level of the well-off, but rather a lowering of the wealthy to the level of the poor. This paper was first published in the mid-1970s, but remains one of the classic statements of warning against large-scale humanitarian aid.

*   *   *

Susanne Langer (1942) has shown that it is probably impossible to approach an unsolved problem save through the door of metaphor. Later, attempting to meet the demands of rigor, we may achieve some success in cleansing theory of metaphor, though our success is limited if we are unable to avoid using common language, which is shot through and through with fossil metaphors. (I count no less than five in the preceding two sentences.)

Since metaphorical thinking is inescapable it is pointless merely to weep about our human limitations. We must learn to live with them, to understand them, and to control them. "All of us," said George Eliot in *Middlemarch*, "get our thoughts entangled in metaphors, and act fatally on the strength of them." To avoid unconscious suicide we are well advised to pit one metaphor against another. From the interplay of competitive metaphors, thoroughly developed, we may come closer to metaphor-free solutions to our problems.

No generation has viewed the problem of the survival of the human species as seriously as we have. Inevitably, we have entered this world of concern through the door of metaphor. Environmentalists have emphasized the image of the earth as a spaceship—Spaceship Earth. Kenneth Boulding (1966) is the principal architect of this metaphor. It is time, he says, that we replace the wasteful "cowboy economy" of the past with the frugal "spaceship economy" required for continued survival in the limited world we now see ours to be. The metaphor is notably useful in justifying pollution-control measures.

Unfortunately, the image of a spaceship is also used to promote measures that are suicidal. One of these is a generous immigration policy, which is only a particular instance of a class of policies that are in error because they lead to the tragedy of the commons (Hardin 1968). These suicidal policies are attractive because they mesh with what we unthinkingly take to be the ideals of "the best people." What is missing in the idealistic view is an insistence that rights and responsibilities must go together. The "generous" attitude of all too many people results in asserting inalienable rights while ignoring or denying matching responsibilities.

For the metaphor of a spaceship to be correct the aggregate of people on board would have to be under unitary sovereign control (Ophuls 1974). A true ship always has a captain. It is conceivable that a ship could be run by a committee. But it could not possibly survive if its course were determined by bickering tribes that claimed rights without responsibilities.

What about Spaceship Earth? It certainly has no captain, and no executive committee. The United Nations is a toothless tiger, because the signatories of its charter wanted it that way. The spaceship metaphor is used only to justify spaceship demands on common resources without acknowledging corresponding spaceship responsibilities.

An understandable fear of decisive action leads people to embrace "incrementalism"—moving toward reform by tiny stages. As we shall see, this strategy is counterproductive in the area discussed here if it means accepting rights before responsibilities. Where human survival is at stake, the acceptance of responsibilities is a precondition to the acceptance of rights, if the two cannot be introduced simultaneously.

Lifeboat Ethics

Before taking up certain substantive issues let us look at an alternative metaphor, that of a lifeboat. In developing some relevant examples the following numerical values are assumed. Approximately two-thirds of the world is desperately poor, and only one-third is comparatively rich. The people in poor countries have an average per capita GNP (Gross National Product) of about $200 per year; the rich, of about $3,000. (For the United States it is nearly $5,000 per year.) Metaphorically, each rich nation amounts to a lifeboat full of comparatively rich people. The poor of the world are in other, much more crowded lifeboats. Continuously, so to speak, the poor fall out of their lifeboats and swim for a while in the water outside, hoping to be admitted to a rich lifeboat, or in some other way to benefit from the "goodies" on board. What should the passengers on a rich lifeboat do? This is the central problem of "the ethics of a lifeboat."

First we must acknowledge that each lifeboat is effectively limited in capacity. The land of every nation has a limited carrying capacity. The exact limit is a matter for argument, but the energy crunch is convincing more people every day that we have already exceeded the carrying capacity of the land. We have been living on "capital"—stored petroleum and coal—and soon we must live on income alone.

Let us look at only one lifeboat—ours. The ethical problem is the same for all, and is as follows. Here we sit, say fifty people in a lifeboat. To be generous, let us assume our boat has a capacity of ten more, making sixty. (This, however, is to violate the engineering principle of the "safety factor." A new plant disease or a bad change in the weather may decimate our population if we don't preserve some excess capacity as a safety factor.)

The fifty of us in the lifeboat see 100 others swimming in the water outside, asking for admission to the boat, or for handouts. How shall we respond to their calls? There are several possibilities.

One. We may be tempted to try to live by the Christian ideal of being "our brother's keeper," or by the Marxian ideal (Marx 1875) of "from each according to his abilities, to each according to his needs." Since the needs of all are the same, we take all the needy into our boat, making a total of 150 in a boat with a capacity of sixty. The boat is swamped, and everyone drowns. Complete justice, complete catastrophe.

Two. Since the boat has an unused excess capacity of ten, we admit just ten more to it. This has the disadvantage of getting

rid of the safety factor, for which action we will sooner or later pay dearly. Moreover, *which* ten do we let in? "First come, first served?" The best ten? The neediest ten? How do we *discriminate*? And what do we say to the ninety who are excluded?

Three. Admit no more to the boat and preserve the small safety factor. Survival of the people in the lifeboat is then possible (though we shall have to be on our guard against boarding parties).

The last solution is abhorrent to many people. It is unjust, they say. Let us grant that it is.

"I feel guilty about my good luck," say some. The reply to this is simple: *Get out and yield your place to others*. Such a selfless action might satisfy the conscience of those who are addicted to guilt but it would not change the ethics of the lifeboat. The needy person to whom a guilt-addict yields his place will not himself feel guilty about his sudden good luck. (If he did he would not climb aboard.) The net result of conscience-stricken people relinquishing their unjustly held positions is the elimination of their kind of conscience from the lifeboat. The lifeboat, as it were, purifies itself of guilt. The ethics of the lifeboat persist, unchanged by such momentary aberrations.

This then is the basic metaphor within which we must work out our solutions. Let us enrich the image step by step with substantive additions from the real world.

Reproduction

The harsh characteristics of lifeboat ethics are heightened by reproduction, particularly by reproductive differences. The people inside the lifeboats of the wealthy nations are doubling in numbers every eighty-seven years; those outside are doubling every thirty-five years, on the average. And the relative difference in prosperity is becoming greater.

Let us, for a while, think primarily of the US lifeboat. As of 1973 the United States had a population of 210 million people, who were increasing by 0.8% per year, that is, doubling in number every eighty-seven years.

Although the citizens of rich nations are outnumbered two to one by the poor, let us imagine an equal number of poor people outside our lifeboat—a mere 210 million poor people reproducing at a quite different rate. If we imagine these to be the combined populations of Colombia, Venezuela, Ecuador, Morocco, Thailand, Pakistan, and the Philippines, the average rate of increase of the people "outside" is 3.3% per year. The doubling time of this population is twenty-one years.

Suppose that all these countries, and the United States, agreed to live by the Marxian ideal, "to each according to his needs," the ideal of most Christians as well. Needs, of course, are determined by population size, which is affected by reproduction. Every nation regards its rate of reproduction as a sovereign right. If our lifeboat were big enough in the beginning it might be possible to live *for a while* by Christian-Marxian ideals. *Might*.

Initially, in the model given, the ratio of non-Americans to Americans would be one to one. But consider what the ratio would be eighty-seven years later. By this time Americans would have doubled to a population of 420 million. The other group (doubling every twenty-one years) would now have swollen to 3,540 million. Each American would have more than eight people to share with. How could the lifeboat possibly keep afloat?

All this involves extrapolation of current trends into the future, and is consequently suspect. Trends may change. Granted: but the change will not necessarily be favorable. If—as seems likely—the rate of population increases falls faster in the ethnic group presently inside the lifeboat than it does among those now outside, the future will turn out to be even worse than mathematics predicts, and sharing will be even more suicidal.

Ruin in the Commons

The fundamental error of the sharing ethics is that it leads to the tragedy of the commons. Under a system of private property the man (or group of men) who own property recognize their responsibility to care for it, for if they don't they will eventually suffer. A farmer, for instance, if he is intelligent, will allow no more cattle in a pasture than its carrying capacity justifies. If he overloads the pasture, weeds take over, erosion sets in, and the owner loses in the long run.

But if a pasture is run as a commons open to all, the right of each to use it is not matched by an operational responsibility to take care of it. It is no use asking independent herdsmen in a commons not to act responsibly, for they dare not. The considerate herdsman who refrains from overloading the commons suffers more than a selfish one who says his needs are greater. (As Leo Durocher says, "Nice guys finish last.") Christian-Marxian idealism is counterproductive. That it *sounds* nice is no excuse. With distribution systems, as with individual morality, good intentions are no substitute for good performance.

A social system is stable only if it is insensitive to errors. To the Christian-Marxian idealist a selfish person is a sort of "error." Prosperity in the system of the commons cannot survive errors. If *everyone* would only restrain himself, all would be well; but it takes *only one less than everyone* to ruin a system of voluntary restraint. In a crowded world of less than perfect human beings—and we will never know any other—mutual ruin is inevitable in the commons. This is the core of the tragedy of the commons.

One of the major tasks of education today is to create such an awareness of the dangers of the commons that people will be able to recognize its many varieties, however disguised. There is pollution of the air and water because these media are treated as commons. Further growth of population and growth in the per capita conversion of natural resources into pollutants require that the system of the commons be modified or abandoned in the disposal of "externalities."

The fish populations of the oceans are exploited as commons, and ruin lies ahead. No technological invention can prevent this fate; in fact, all improvements in the art of fishing merely hasten the day of complete ruin. Only the replacement of the system of the commons with a responsible system can save oceanic fisheries.

The management of western range lands, though nominally rational, is in fact (under the steady pressure of cattle ranchers) often merely a government-sanctioned system of the commons, drifting toward ultimate ruin for both the rangelands and the residual enterprisers.

World Food Banks

In the international arena we have recently heard a proposal to create a new commons, namely an international depository of food reserves to which nations will contribute according to their abilities, and from which nations may draw according to their needs. Nobel laureate Norman Borlaug has lent the prestige of his name to this proposal.

A world food bank appeals powerfully to our humanitarian impulses. We remember John Donne's celebrated line, "Any man's death diminishes me." But before we rush out to see for whom the bell tolls let us recognize where the greatest political push for international granaries comes from, lest we be disillusioned later. Our experience with Public Law 480 clearly reveals the answer. This was the law that moved billions of dollars worth of US grain to food-short, population-long countries during the past two decades. When P.L. 480 first came into being, a headline in the business magazine *Forbes* (Paddock and Paddock 1970) revealed the power behind it: "Feeding the World's Hungry Millions: How it will mean billions for US business."

And indeed it did. In the years 1960 to 1970 a total of $7.9 billion was spent on the "Food for Peace" program, as P.L. 480 was called. During the years 1948 to 1970 an additional $49.9 billion were extracted from American taxpayers to pay for other economic aid programs, some of which went for food and food-producing machinery. (This figure does *not* include military aid.) That P.L. 480 was a giveaway program was concealed. Recipient countries went through the motions of paying for P.L. 480 food—with IOUs. In December 1973 the charade was brought to an end as far as India was concerned when the United

States "forgave" India's $3.2 billion debt (Anonymous 1974). Public announcement of the cancellation of the debt was delayed for two months; one wonders why.

"Famine—1974!" (Paddock and Paddock 1970) is one of the few publications that points out the commercial roots of this humanitarian attempt. Though all US taxpayers lost by P.L. 480, special interest groups gained handsomely. Farmers benefited because they were not asked to contribute the grain—it was bought from them by the taxpayers. Besides the direct benefit there was the indirect effect of increasing demand and thus raising prices of farm products generally. The manufacturers of farm machinery, fertilizers, and pesticides benefited by the farmers' extra efforts to grow more food. Grain elevators profited from storing the grain for varying lengths of time. Railroads made money hauling it to port, and shipping lines by carrying it overseas. Moreover, once the machinery for P.L. 480 was established an immense bureaucracy had a vested interest in its continuance regardless of its merits.

Very little was ever heard of these selfish interests when P.L. 480 was defended in public. The emphasis was always on its humanitarian effects. The combination of multiple and relatively silent selfish interests with highly vocal humanitarian apologists constitutes a powerful lobby for extracting money from taxpayers. Foreign aid has become a habit that can apparently survive in the absence of any known justification. A news commentator in a weekly magazine (Lansner 1974), after exhaustively going over all the conventional arguments for foreign aid—self-interest, social justice, political advantage, and charity—and concluding that none of the known arguments really held water, concluded: "So

the search continues for some logically compelling reasons for giving aid...." In other words, *Act now, justify later*—if ever. (Apparently a quarter of a century is too short a time to find the justification for expending several billion dollars yearly).

The search for a rational justification can be short-circuited by interjecting the word "emergency." Borlaug uses this word. We need to look sharply at it. What is an "emergency?" It is surely something like an accident, which is correctly defined as *an event that is certain to happen, though with a low frequency* (Hardin, 1972a). A well-run organization prepares for everything that is certain, including accidents and emergencies. It budgets for them. It saves for them. It expects them—and mature decision-makers do not waste time complaining about accidents when they occur.

What happens if some organizations budget for emergencies and others do not? If each organization is solely responsible for its own well-being, poorly managed ones will suffer. But they should be able to learn from experience. They have a chance to mend their ways and learn to budget for infrequent but certain emergencies. The weather, for instance, always varies and periodic crop failures are certain. A wise and competent government saves out of the production of the good years in anticipation of bad years that are sure to come. This is not a new idea. The Bible tells us that Joseph taught this policy to Pharoah in Egypt more than 2,000 years ago. Yet it is literally true that the vast majority of the governments of the world today have no such policy. They lack either the wisdom or the competence, or both. Far more difficult than the transfer of wealth from one country to another is the transfer of wisdom between sovereign powers or between generations.

"But it isn't their fault! How can we blame the poor people who are caught in an emergency? Why must we punish them?" The concepts of blame and punishment are irrelevant. The question is, what are the operational consequences of establishing a world food bank? If it is open to every country every time a need develops, slovenly rulers will not be motivated to take Joseph's advice. Why should they? Others will bail them out whenever they are in trouble.

Some countries will make deposits in the world food bank and others will withdraw from it; there will be almost no overlap. Calling such a depository-transfer unit a "bank" is stretching the metaphor of *bank* beyond its elastic limits. The proposers, of course, never call attention to the metaphorical nature of the word they use.

The Ratchet Effect

An "international food bank" is really, then, not a true bank but a disguised one-way transfer device for moving wealth from rich countries to poor. In the absence of such a bank, in a world inhabited by individually responsible sovereign nations, the population of each nation would repeatedly go through a cycle of the sort shown in Exhibit A. P_2 is greater than P_1, either in absolute numbers or because a deterioration of the food supply has removed the safety factor and produced a dangerously low ratio of resources to population. P_2 may be said to represent a state of over-population, which becomes obvious upon the appearance of an "accident," e.g., a crop failure. If the "emergency" is not met by outside help, the population drops back

to the "normal" level—the "carrying capacity" of the environment—or even below. In the absence of population control by a sovereign, sooner or later the population grows to P_2 again and the cycle repeats. The long-term population curve (Hardin 1966) is an irregularly fluctuating one, equilibrating more or less about the carrying capacity.

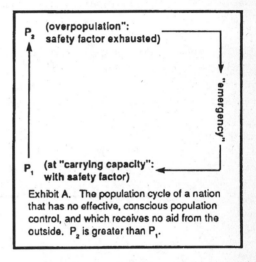

Exhibit A. The population cycle of a nation that has no effective, conscious population control, and which receives no aid from the outside. P_2 is greater than P_1.

A demographic cycle of this sort obviously involves great suffering in the restrictive phase, but such a cycle is normal to any independent country with inadequate population control. The third century theologian Tertullian (Hardin, 1969a) expressed what must have been the recognition of many wise men when he wrote: "The scourges of pestilence, famine, wars, and earthquakes have come to be regarded as a blessing to overcrowded nations, since they serve to prune away the luxuriant growth of the human race."

Only under a strong and farsighted sovereign—which theoretically could be the people themselves, democratically organized—can a population equilibrate at some set point below the carrying capacity, thus avoiding the pains normally caused by periodic and unavoidable disasters. For this happy state to be achieved it is necessary that those in power be able to contemplate with equanimity the "waste" of surplus food in times of bountiful harvests. It is essential that those in power resist the temptation to convert extra food into extra babies. On the public relations level it is necessary that the phrase "surplus food" be replaced by "safety factor."

But wise sovereigns seem not to exist in the poor world today. The most anguishing problems are created by poor countries that are governed by rulers insufficiently wise and powerful. If such countries can draw on a world food bank in times of "emergency," the population *cycle* of Exhibit A will be replaced by the population *escalator*

of Exhibit B. The input of food from a food bank acts as the pawl of a ratchet, preventing the population from retracting its steps to a lower level. Reproduction pushes the population upward, inputs from the world bank prevent its moving downward. Population size escalates, as does the absolute magnitude of "accidents" and "emergencies." The process is brought to an end only by the total collapse of the whole system, producing a catastrophe of scarcely imaginable proportions.

Such are the implications of the well-meant sharing of food in a world of irresponsible reproduction.

I think we need a new word for systems like this. The adjective "melioristic" is applied to systems that produce continual improvement; the English word is derived from the Latin *meliorare*, to become or

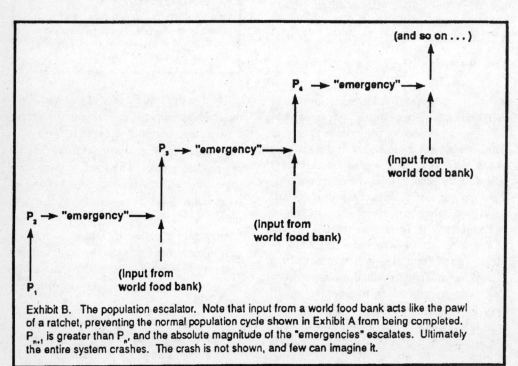

Exhibit B. The population escalator. Note that input from a world food bank acts like the pawl of a ratchet, preventing the normal population cycle shown in Exhibit A from being completed. P_{n+1} is greater than P_n, and the absolute magnitude of the "emergencies" escalates. Ultimately the entire system crashes. The crash is not shown, and few can imagine it.

make better. Parallel with this it would be useful to bring in the word *pejoristic* (from the Latin *pejorare*, to become or to make worse). This word can be applied to those systems that by their very nature, can be relied upon to make matters worse. A world food bank coupled with sovereign state irresponsibly in reproduction is an example of a pejoristic system.

This pejoristic system creates an unacknowledged commons. People have more motivation to draw from than to add to the common store. The license to make such withdrawals diminishes whatever motivation poor countries might otherwise have to control their populations. Under the guidance of this ratchet, wealth can be steadily moved in one direction only, from the slowly-breeding rich to the rapidly-breeding poor, the process finally coming to a halt only when all countries are equally and miserably poor.

All this is terribly obvious once we are acutely aware of the pervasiveness and danger of the commons. But many people still lack this awareness and the euphoria of the "benign demographic transition" (Hardin 1973) interferes with the realistic appraisal of pejoristic mechanisms. As concerns public policy, the deductions drawn from the benign demographic transition are these:

1. If the per capita GNP rises the birth rate will fall; hence, the rate of population increase will fall, ultimately producing ZPG (Zero Population Growth).

2. The long-term trend all over the world (including the poor countries) is of a rising per capita GNP (for which no limit is seen).

3. Therefore, all political interference in population matters is unnecessary; all we need to do is foster economic "development"—*note the metaphor*—and population problems will solve themselves.

Those who believe in the benign demographic transition dismiss the pejoristic mechanism of Exhibit B in the belief that each input of food from the world outside fosters development within a poor country thus resulting in a drop in the rate of population increase. Foreign aid has proceeded on this assumption for more than two decades. Unfortunately it has produced no indubitable instance of the asserted effect. It has, however, produced a library of excuses. The air is filled with plaintive calls for more massive foreign aid appropriations so that the hypothetical melioristic process can get started.

The doctrine of demographic laissez-faire implicit in the hypothesis of the benign demographic transition is immensely attractive. Unfortunately there is more evidence against the melioristic system than there is for it (Davis 1963). On the historical side there are many counter-examples. The rise in per capita GNP in France and Ireland during the past century has been accompanied by a rise in population growth. In the twenty-five years following the Second World War the same positive correlation was noted almost everywhere in the world. Never in world history before 1950 did the worldwide population growth reach one percent per annum. Now the average population growth is over two percent and shows no signs of slackening.

On the theoretical side, the denial of the pejoristic scheme of Exhibit B probably springs from the hidden acceptance of the "cowboy economy" that Boulding castigated. Those who recognize the limitations of a spaceship, if they are unable to achieve population control at a safe and comfortable level, accept the necessity of the corrective feedback of the population cycle shown in Exhibit A. No one who knew in his bones that he was living on a true spaceship would countenance political support of the population escalator shown in Exhibit B.

Eco-destruction via the Green Revolution

The demoralizing effect of charity on the recipient has long been known. "Give a man a fish and he will eat for a day; teach him how to fish and he will eat for the rest of his days." So runs an ancient Chinese proverb. Acting on this advice the Rockefeller and Ford Foundations have financed a multipronged program for improving agriculture in the hungry nations. The result, known as the "Green Revolution," has been quite remarkable. "Miracle wheat" and "miracle rice" are splendid technological achievements in the realm of plant genetics.

Whether or not the Green Revolution can increase food production is doubtful (Harris 1972, Paddock 1970, Wilkes 1972), but in any event not particularly important. What is missing in this great and well-meaning humanitarian effort is a firm grasp of fundamentals. Considering the importance of the Rockefeller Foundation in this effort it is ironic that the late Alan Gregg, a much-respected vice-president of the Foundation, strongly expressed his doubts of the wisdom of all attempts to increase food production some two decades ago. (This was before Borlaug's work—supported by Rockefeller—had resulted in the development of "miracle wheat.") Gregg (1955) likened the growth and spreading of humanity over the surface of the earth to the metastasis of cancer in the human body, wryly remarking that "Cancerous growths demand food; but, as far as I know, they have never been cured by getting it."

"Man does not live by bread alone"— the scriptural statement has a rich meaning even in the material realm. Every human being born constitutes a draft on all aspects of the environment—food, air, water, unspoiled scenery, occasional and optional solitude, beaches, contact with wild animals, fishing, hunting—the list is long and incompletely known. Food can, perhaps, be significantly increased, but what about clean beaches, unspoiled forests, and solitudes? If we satisfy the need for food in a growing population we necessarily decrease the supply of other goods, and thereby increase the difficulty of equitably allocating scarce goods (Hardin 1969b, 1972b).

The present population of India is 600 million, and it is increasing by fifteen million per year. The environmental load of this population is already great. The forests of India are only a small fraction of what they were three centuries ago. Soil erosion, floods, and the psychological costs of crowding are serious. Every one of the net fifteen million lives added each year stresses the Indian environment more severely. *Every life saved this year in a poor country diminishes the quality of life for subsequent generations.*

Observant critics have shown how much harm we wealthy nations have already done to poor nations through our well-intentioned but misguided attempts to help them (Paddock and Paddock 1973). Particularly reprehensible is our failure to carry out post-audits of these attempts (Farvar and Milton 1972). Thus have we shielded our tender consciences from knowledge of the harm we have done. Must we Americans continue to fail to monitor the consequences of our external "do-gooding?" If, for instance, we thoughtlessly make it possible for the present 600 million Indians to swell to 1,200 million by the year 2001—as their present growth rate promises—will posterity in India thank *us* for facilitating an even greater destruction of *their* environment? Are good intentions ever a sufficient excuse for bad consequences?

Immigration Creates a Commons

I come now to the final example of a commons in action, one for which the public is least prepared for rational discussion. The topic is at present enveloped by a great silence that reminds me of a comment made by Sherlock Holmes in A. Conan Doyle's story, "Silver Blaze." Inspector Gregory had asked, "Is there any point to which you wish to draw my attention?" To this Holmes responded:

> "To the curious incident of the dog in the night-time."
> "The dog did nothing in the night-time," said the Inspector.
> "That was the curious incident," remarked Sherlock Holmes.

By asking himself what would repress the normal barking instinct of a watch dog Holmes realized that it must be the dog's recognition of his master as the criminal trespasser. In a similar way we should ask ourselves what repression keeps us from discussing something as important as immigration?

It cannot be that immigration is numerically of no consequence. Our government acknowledges a *net* inflow of 400,000 a year. Hard data are understandably lacking on the extent of illegal entries, but a not implausible figure is 600,000 per year. (Buchanan 1973). The natural increase of the resident population is now about 1.7 million per year. This means that the yearly gain from immigration is at least nineteen

percent and may be thirty-seven percent, of the total increase. It is quite conceivable that educational campaigns like that of Zero Population Growth, Inc., coupled with adverse social and economic factors—inflation, housing shortage, depression, and loss of confidence in national leaders—may lower the fertility of American women to a point at which all of the yearly increase in population would be accounted for by immigration. Should we not at least ask if that is what we want? How curious it is that we so seldom discuss immigration these days!

Curious, but understandable—as one finds out the moment he publicly questions the wisdom of the status quo in immigration. He who does so is promptly charged with *isolationism, bigotry, prejudice, ethnocentrism, chauvinism*, and *selfishness*. These are hard accusations to bear. It is pleasanter to talk about other matters, leaving immigration policy to wallow in the crosscurrents of special interests that take no account of the good of the whole—*or of the interests of posterity*.

We Americans have a bad conscience because of things we said in the past about immigrants. Two generations ago the popular press was rife with references to *Dagos, Wops, Pollacks, Japs, Chinks*, and *Krauts*—all pejorative terms that failed to acknowledge our indebtedness to Goya, Leonardo, Copernicus, Hiroshige, Confucius, and Bach. Because the implied inferiority of foreigners was *then* the justification for keeping them out, it is *now* thoughtlessly assumed that restrictive policies can only be based on the assumption of immigrant inferiority. *This is not so.*

Existing immigration laws exclude idiots and known criminals; future laws will almost certainly continue this policy. But should we also consider the quality of the average immigrant, as compared with the quality of the average resident? Perhaps we should, perhaps we shouldn't. (What is "quality" anyway?) But the quality issue is not our concern here.

From this point on, *it will be assumed that immigrants and native-born citizens are of exactly equal quality*, however quality may be defined. The focus is only on quantity. The conclusions reached depend on nothing else, so all charges of ethnocentrism are irrelevant.

World food banks move food to the people, thus facilitating the exhaustion of the environment of the poor. By contrast, unrestricted immigration moves people to the food, thus speeding up the destruction of the environment in rich countries. Why poor people should want to make this transfer is no mystery, but why should rich hosts encourage it? This transfer, like the reverse one, is supported by both selfish interests and humanitarian impulses.

The principal selfish interest in unimpeded immigration is easy to identify: it is the interest of the employers of cheap labor, particularly that needed for degrading jobs. We have been deceived about the forces of history by the lines of Emma Lazarus inscribed on the Statue of Liberty:

Give me your tired, your poor,
Your huddled masses yearning to breathe free,
The wretched refuse of your teeming shore,
Send these, the homeless, tempest-tossed to me:
I lift my lamp beside the golden door.

The image is one of an infinitely generous earth-mother, passively opening her arms to hordes of immigrants who come here on their own initiative. Such an image may have been adequate for the early days of colonization, but by the time these lines were written (1886) the force for immigration was largely manufactured inside our own borders by factory and mine owners who sought cheap labor not to be found among laborers already here. One group of foreigners after another was thus enticed into the United States to work at wretched jobs for wretched wages.

At present, it is largely the Mexicans who are being so exploited. It is particularly to the advantage of certain employers that there be many illegal immigrants. Illegal immigrant workers dare not complain about their working conditions for fear of being repatriated. Their presence reduces the bargaining power of all Mexican-American laborers. Cesar Chavez has repeatedly pleaded with congressional committees to close the doors to more Mexicans so that those here can negotiate effectively for higher wages and decent working conditions. Chavez understands the ethics of a lifeboat.

The interests of the employers of cheap labor are well served by the silence of the intelligentsia of the country. WASPs—White Anglo-Saxon Protestants—are particularly reluctant to call for a closing of the doors to immigration for fear of being called ethnocentric bigots. It was, therefore, an occasion of pure delight for this particular WASP to be present at a meeting when the points he would like to have made were made better by a non-WASP speaking to other non-WASPs. It was in Hawaii, and most of the people in the room were second-level Hawaiian officials of Japanese ancestry. All Hawaiians are keenly aware of the limits of their environment, and the speaker had asked how it might be practically and constitutionally possible to close the doors to more immigrants to the islands. (To Hawaiians, immigrants from the other forty-nine states are as much of a threat as those from other nations. There is only so much room in the islands, and the islanders know it. Sophistical arguments that imply otherwise do not impress them.)

Yet the Japanese-Americans of Hawaii have active ties with the land of their origin. This point was raised by a Japanese-American member of the audience who asked the Japanese-American speaker: "But how can we shut the doors now? We have many friends and relations in Japan that we'd like to bring to Hawaii some day so that they can enjoy this beautiful land."

The speaker smiled sympathetically and responded slowly, "Yes, but we have children now and someday we'll have grandchildren. We can bring more people here from Japan only by giving away some of the land that we hope to pass on to our grandchildren some day. What right do we have to do that?"

To be generous with one's own possessions is one thing; to be generous with posterity's is quite another. This, I think, is the point that must be gotten across to those who would, from a commendable love of **distributive justice**, institute a ruinous system of the commons, either in the form of a world food bank or that of unrestricted immigration. Since every speaker is a member of some ethnic group it is always possible to charge him with ethnocentrism. But even after purging an argument of ethnocentrism the rejection of the commons is still valid and necessary if we are to save at least some parts of the world from environmental ruin. Is it not desirable that at least some of the grandchildren of people now living should have a decent place in which to live?

The Asymmetry of Door-Shutting

We must now answer this telling point: "How can you justify slamming the door once you're inside? You say that immigrants should be kept out. But aren't we all immigrants, or the descendants of immigrants? Since we refuse to leave, must we not, as a matter of justice and symmetry, admit all others?"

It is literally true that we Americans of non-Indian ancestry are the descendants of thieves. Should we not, then, "give back" the land to the Indians, that is, give it to the now-living Americans of Indian ancestry? As an exercise in pure logic I see no way to reject this proposal. Yet I am unwilling to live by it, and I know no one who is. Our reluctance to embrace pure justice may spring from pure selfishness. On the other hand, it may arise from an unspoken recognition of consequences that have not yet been clearly spelled out.

Suppose, becoming intoxicated with pure justice, we "Anglos" should decide to turn our land over to the Indians. Since all our other wealth has also been derived from the land, we would have to give that to the Indians, too. Then what would we non-Indians do? Where would we go? There is no open land in the world on which men without capital can make their own living (and not much unoccupied land on which men with capital can either). Where would 209 million putatively justice-loving, non-Indian Americans go? Most of them—in the persons of their ancestors—came from Europe, but they wouldn't be welcomed back there. Anyway, Europeans have no better title to their land than we to ours. They also would have to give up their homes. (But to whom? And where would *they* go?)

Clearly, the concept of pure justice produces an **infinite regress**. The law long ago invented statutes of limitations to justify the rejection of pure justice, in the interest of preventing massive disorder. The law zealously defends property rights—but only *recent* property rights. It is as though the physical principle of exponential decay applies to property rights. Drawing a line in time may be unjust, but any other action is practically worse.

We are all the descendants of thieves, and the world's resources are inequitably distributed, but we must begin the journey to tomorrow from the point where we are today. We cannot remake the past. We cannot, without violent disorder and suffering, give land and resources back to the "original" owners—who are dead anyway.

We cannot safely divide the wealth equitably among all present peoples, so long as people reproduce at different rates, because to do so would guarantee that our grandchildren—everyone's grandchildren—would have only a ruined world to inhabit.

Must Exclusion be Absolute?

To show the logical structure of the immigration problem I have ignored many factors that would enter into real decisions made in a real world. No matter how convincing the logic may be, it is probable that we would want, from time to time, to admit a few people from the outside to our lifeboat. Political refugees in particular are likely to cause us to make exceptions: We remember the Jewish refugees from Germany after 1933, and the Hungarian refugees after 1956. Moreover, the interests of national defense, broadly conceived, could justify admitting many men and women of unusual talents, whether refugees or not.

(This raises the quality issue, which is not the subject of this essay.)

Such exceptions threaten to create runaway population growth inside the lifeboat, i.e., the receiving country. However, the threat can be neutralized by a population policy that includes immigration. An effective policy is one of flexible control.

Suppose, for example, that the nation has achieved a stable condition of ZPG, which (say) permits 1.5 million births yearly. We must suppose that an acceptable system of allocating birth-rights to potential parents is in effect. Now suppose that an inhumane regime in some other part of the world creates a horde of refugees, and that there is a widespread desire to admit some to our country. At the same time, we do not want to sabotage our population control system. Clearly, the rational path to pursue is the following. If we decide to admit 100,000 refugees this year we should compensate for this by reducing the allocation of birth-rights in the following year by a similar amount, that is, downward to a total of 1.4 million. In that way we could achieve both humanitarian and population control goals. (And the refugees would have to accept the population controls of the society that admits them. It is not inconceivable that they might be given proportionately fewer rights than the native population.)

In a democracy, the admission of immigrants should properly be voted on. But by whom? It is not obvious. The usual rule of a democracy is votes for all. But it can be questioned whether a universal franchise is the most just one in a case of this sort. Whatever benefits there are in the admission of immigrants presumably accrue to everyone. But the costs would be seen as falling most heavily on potential parents, some of whom would have to postpone or forego having their (next) child because of the influx of immigrants. The double question *Who benefits? Who pays?* suggests that a restriction of the usual democratic franchise would be appropriate and just in this case. Would our particular quasi-democratic form of government be flexible enough to institute such a novelty? If not, the majority might, out of humanitarian motives, impose an unacceptable burden (the foregoing of parenthood) on a minority, thus producing political instability.

Plainly many new problems will arise when we consciously face the immigration question and seek rational answers. No workable answers can be found if we ignore population problems. And—if the argument of this essay is correct—so long as there is no true world government to control reproduction everywhere it is impossible to survive in dignity if we are to be guided by spaceship ethics. Without a world government that is sovereign in reproductive matters mankind lives, in fact, on a number of sovereign lifeboats. For the foreseeable future survival demands that we govern our actions by the ethics of a lifeboat. Posterity will be ill served if we do not.

References

Anonymous. 1974. *Wall Street Journal* 19 Feb.

Borlaug, N. 1973. Civilization's future: a call for international granaries. *Bulletin of Atomic Science* 29: 7-15.

Boulding, K. 1966. The economics of the coming Spaceship Earth. *In* H. Jarrett, ed. *Environmental Quality in a Growing Economy*. Baltimore: John Hopkins Press.

Buchanan, W. 1973. Immigration statistics. *Equilibrium* 1(3): 16-19.

Davis, K. 1963. Population. *Scientific American* 209(3): 62-71.

Farvar, M.T., and J.P. Milton. 1972. *The Careless Technology*. Garden City, NY: Natural History Press.

Gregg, A. 1955. A medical aspect of the population problem. *Science* 121:681-682.

Hardin, G. 1966. Chap. 9 in *Biology: Its Principles and Implications*, 2nd ed. San Francisco: Freeman.

___. 1968. The tragedy of the commons. *Science* 162: 1243-1248.

___. 1969a Page 18 in *Population, Evolution, and Birth Control*, 2nd ed. San Francisco: Freeman.

___. 1969b. The economics of wilderness. *Nat.Hist.* 78(6): 20-27.

___. 1972a. Pages 81-82 in *Exploring New Ethics for Survival: The Voyage of the Spaceship* Beagle. New York: Viking.

___. 1972b. Preserving quality on Spaceship Earth. *In* J.B. Trefethen, ed. *Transactions of the Thirty-Seventh North American Wildlife and Natural Resources Conference*. Wildlife Management Institute, Washington, D.C.

___. 1973. Chap. 23 in *Stalking the Wild Taboo*. Los Altos, CA: Kaufmann.

Harris, M. 1972. How green the revolution. *Nat.Hist.* 81(3): 28-30.

Langer, S.K. 1942. *Philosophy in a New Key*. Cambridge, MA: Harvard University Press.

Lansner, K. 1974. Should foreign aid begin at home? *Newsweek*, 11 Feb., p. 32.

Marx, K. 1875. Critique of the Gotha program. Page 388 in R.C. Tucker, ed. *The Marx-Engels Reader*. New York: Norton, 1972.

Ophuls, W. 1974. The scarcity society. *Harpers* 248(1487): 47-52.

Paddock, W.C. 1970. How green is the green revolution? *BioScience* 20: 897-902.

Paddock, W., and E. Paddock. 1973. *We Don't Know How*. Ames, IA: Iowa State University Press.

Paddock, W., and P. Paddock. 1967. *Famine—1975!* Boston: Little, Brown.

Wilkes, H.G. 1972. The green revolution. *Environment* 14(8): 32-39.

Questions for Discussion

1 Is it fair to say that nations should take responsibility for managing their own resources? Does it

matter if some nations have exploited others in the past?

2   Hardin states that "Every life saved this year in a poor country diminishes the quality of life for subsequent generations." Is he right? If so, how powerful an argument is this against trying to save lives in poor countries?

Rich and Poor

Peter Singer

In the following article, Singer argues that citizens of affluent nations are morally obliged to give assistance to those who are starving up to the point at which such assistance would involve sacrificing something of equal moral worth. Since starvation is a much more serious evil than being deprived of some new clothing, or entertainment, etc., this would mean there is a positive obligation to give much more than what is commonly considered a virtuous amount.

*   *   *

Some facts

...Consider these facts: by the most cautious estimates, 400 million people lack the calories, protein, vitamins and minerals needed for a normally healthy life. Millions are constantly hungry; others suffer from deficiency diseases and from infections they would be able to resist on a better diet. Children are worst affected. According to one estimate, 15 million children under five die every year from the combined effect of malnutrition and infection. In some areas, half the children born can be expected to die before their fifth birthday.

Nor is lack of food the only hardship of the poor. To give a broader picture, Robert McNamara, President of the World Bank, has suggested the term 'absolute poverty.' The poverty we are familiar with in industrialized nations is relative poverty—meaning that some citizens are poor, relative to the wealth enjoyed by their neighbours. People living in relative poverty in Australia might be quite comfortably off by comparison with old-age pensioners in Britain, and British old-age pensioners are not poor in comparison with the poverty that exists in Mali or Ethiopia. Absolute poverty, on the other hand, is poverty by any standard. In McNamara's words:

> Poverty at the absolute level...is life at the very margin of existence.
>
> The absolute poor are severely deprived human beings struggling to survive in a set of squalid and degraded circumstances almost beyond the power of our sophisticated imaginations and privileged circumstances to conceive.
>
> Compared to those fortunate enough to live in developed countries, individuals in the poorest countries have:
>
> An infant mortality rate eight times higher
>
> A life expectancy one-third lower
>
> An adult literacy rate 60% less
>
> A nutritional level, for one out of every two in the population, below acceptable

standards; and for millions of infants, less protein than is sufficient to permit optimum development of the brain.

And McNamara has summed up absolute poverty as:

> a condition of life so characterized by malnutrition, illiteracy, disease, squalid surroundings, high infant mortality, and low life expectancy as to be beneath any reasonable definition of human decency.

Absolute poverty is, McNamara has said, responsible for the loss of countless lives, especially among infants and young children. When absolute poverty does not cause death it still causes misery of a kind not often seen in the affluent nations. Malnutrition in young children stunts both physical and mental development. It has been estimated that the health, growth, and learning capacity of nearly half the young children in developing countries are affected by malnutrition. Millions of people on poor diets suffer from deficiency diseases, like goitre, or blindness caused by a lack of vitamin A. The food value of what the poor eat is further reduced by parasites such as hookworm and ringworm, which are endemic in conditions of poor sanitation and health education.

Death and disease apart, absolute poverty remains a miserable condition of life, with inadequate food, shelter, clothing, sanitation, health services and education. According to World Bank estimates which define absolute poverty in terms of income levels insufficient to provide adequate nutrition, something like 800 million people—almost 40% of the people of developing countries—live in absolute poverty. Absolute poverty is probably the principal cause of human misery today.

This is the background situation, the situation that prevails on our planet all the time. It does not make headlines. People died from malnutrition and related diseases yesterday, and more will die tomorrow. The occasional droughts, cyclones, earthquakes and floods that take the lives of tens of thousands in one place and at one time are more newsworthy. They add greatly to the total amount of human suffering; but it is wrong to assume that when there are no major calamities reported, all is well.

The problem is not that the world cannot produce enough to feed and shelter its people. People in the poor countries consume, on average, 400 lbs of grain a year, while North Americans average more than 2000 lbs. The difference is caused by the fact that in the rich countries we feed most of our grain to animals, converting it into meat, milk and eggs. Because this is an inefficient process, wasting up to 95% of the food value of the animal feed, people in rich countries are responsible for the consumption of far more food than those in poor countries who eat few animal products. If we stopped feeding animals on grains, soybeans and fishmeal the amount of food saved would—if distributed to those who need it—be more than enough to end hunger throughout the world.

These facts about animal food do not mean that we can easily solve the world food problem by cutting down on animal products, but they show that the problem is essentially one of distribution rather than production. The world does produce enough food. Moreover the poorer nations themselves could produce far more if they made more use of improved agricultural techniques.

So why are people hungry? Poor people cannot afford to buy grain grown by American farmers. Poor farmers cannot afford to buy improved seeds, or fertilizers, or the machinery needed for drilling wells and pumping water. Only by transferring some of the wealth of the developed nations to the poor of the undeveloped nations can the situation be changed.

That this wealth exists is clear. Against the picture of absolute poverty that McNamara has painted, one might pose a picture of 'absolute affluence.' Those who are absolutely affluent are not necessarily affluent by comparison with their neighbours, but they are affluent by any reasonable definition of human needs. This means that they have more income than they need to provide themselves adequately with all the basic necessities of life. After buying food, shelter, clothing, necessary health services and education, the absolutely affluent are still able to spend money on luxuries. The absolutely affluent choose their food for the pleasures of the palate, not to stop hunger; they buy new clothes to look fashionable, not to keep warm; they move house to be in a better neighbourhood or have a play room for the children, not to keep out the rain; and after all this there is still money to spend on books and records, colour television, and overseas holidays.

At this stage I am making no ethical judgements about absolute affluence, merely pointing out that it exists. Its defining characteristic is a significant amount of income above the level necessary to provide for the basic human needs of oneself and one's dependents. By this standard Western Europe, North America, Japan, Australia, New Zealand and the oil-rich Middle Eastern states are all absolutely affluent, and so are many, if not all, of their citizens. The USSR and Eastern Europe might

also be included on this list. To quote McNamara once more:

> The average citizen of a developed country enjoys wealth beyond the wildest dreams of the one billion people in countries with per capita incomes under $200....

These, therefore, are the countries—and individuals—who have wealth which they could, without threatening their own basic welfare, transfer to the absolutely poor.

At present, very little is being transferred. Members of the Organization of Petroleum Exporting Countries lead the way, giving an average of 2.1% of their Gross National Product. Apart from them, only Sweden, The Netherlands and Norway have reached the modest UN target of 0.7% of GNP. Britain gives 0.38% of its GNP in official development assistance and a small additional amount in unofficial aid from voluntary organizations. The total comes to less than £1 per month per person, and compares with 5.5% of GNP spent on alcohol, and 3% on tobacco. Other, even wealthier nations, give still less: Germany gives 0.27%, the United States 0.22% and Japan 0.21%.

The moral equivalent of murder?

If these are the facts, we cannot avoid concluding that by not giving more than we do, people in rich countries are allowing those in poor countries to suffer from absolute poverty, with consequent malnutrition, ill health and death. This is not a conclusion which applies only to governments. It applies to each absolutely affluent individual, for each of us has the opportunity to do something about the situation; for instance, to give our time or money to voluntary organizations like Oxfam, War on Want, Freedom From Hunger, and so on. If then, allowing someone to die is not intrinsically different from killing someone, it would seem that we are all murderers.

Is this verdict too harsh? Many will reject it as self-evidently absurd. They would sooner take it as showing that allowing to die cannot be equivalent to killing than as showing that living in an affluent style without contributing to Oxfam is ethically equivalent to going over to India and shooting a few peasants. And no doubt, put as bluntly as that, the verdict *is* too harsh.

There are several significant differences between spending money on luxuries instead of using it to save lives, and deliberately shooting people.

First, the motivation will normally be different. Those who deliberately shoot others go out of their way to kill; they presumably want their victims dead, from malice, sadism, or some equally unpleasant motive. A person who buys a colour television set presumably wants to watch television in colour—not in itself a terrible thing. At worst, spending money on luxuries instead of giving it away indicates selfishness and indifference to the sufferings of others, characteristics which may be undesirable but are not compatible with actual malice or similar motives.

Second, it is not difficult for most of us to act in accordance with a rule against killing people: it is, on the other hand, very difficult to obey a rule which commands us to save all the lives we can. To live a comfortable, or even luxurious life it is not necessary to kill anyone; but it is necessary to allow some to die whom we might have saved, for the money that we need to live comfortably could have been given away. Thus the duty to avoid killing is much easier to discharge completely than the duty to save. Saving every life we could would mean cutting our standard of living down to the bare essentials needed to keep us alive. (Strictly, we would need to cut down to the minimum level compatible with earning the income which, after providing for our needs, left us most to give away. Thus if my present position earns me, say, £10,000 a year, but requires me to spend £1,000 a year on dressing respectably and maintaining a car, I cannot save more people by giving away the car and clothes if that will mean taking a job which, although it does not involve me in these expenses, earns me only £5,000.) To discharge this duty completely would require a degree of moral heroism utterly different from what is required by mere avoidance of killing.

A third difference is the greater certainty of the outcome of shooting when compared with not giving aid. If I point a loaded gun at someone and pull the trigger, it is virtually certain that the person will be injured, if not killed; whereas the money that I could give might be spent on a project that turns out to be unsuccessful and helps no one.

Fourth, when people are shot there are identifiable individuals who have been harmed. We can point to them and to their grieving families. When I buy my colour television, I cannot know who my money would have saved if I had given it away. In a time of famine I may see dead bodies and grieving families on my new television, and I might not doubt that my money would have saved some of them; even then it is impossible to point to a body and say that had I not bought the set, that person would have survived.

Fifth, it might be said that the plight of the hungry is not my doing, and so I cannot be held responsible for it. The starving would have been starving if I had never existed. If I kill, however, I am responsible for my victims' deaths, for those people would not have died if I had not killed them.

These differences need not shake our previous conclusion that there is no intrinsic difference between killing and allowing to die. They are extrinsic differences, that is, differences normally but not necessarily associated with the distinction between killing and allowing to die. We can imagine cases in which someone allows another to die for malicious or sadistic reasons; we can imagine a world in which there are so few people needing assistance, and they are so easy to assist, that our duty not to allow people to die is as easily discharged as our duty not to kill; we can imagine situations in which the outcome of not helping is as sure as shooting; we can imagine cases in which we can identify the person we allow to die. We can even imagine a case of allowing to die in which, if I had not existed, the person would not have died—for instance, a case in which if I had not been in a position to help (though I don't help) someone else would have been in my position and would have helped.

[A] discussion of euthanasia illustrates the extrinsic nature of these differences, for they do not provide a basis for distinguishing active from passive euthanasia. If a doctor decides, in consultation with the parents, not to operate on—and thus to allow to die—a mongoloid infant with an intestinal blockage, his motivation will be similar to that of a doctor who gives a lethal injection rather than allow the infant to die. No extraordinary sacrifice or moral heroism will be required in either case. Not operating will just as certainly end in death as administering the injection. Allowing to die

does have an identifiable victim. Finally, it may well be that the doctor is personally responsible for the death of the infant he decides not to operate upon, since he may know that if he had not taken this case, other doctors in the hospital would have operated.

Nevertheless, euthanasia is a special case, and very different from allowing people to starve to death. (The major difference being that when euthanasia is justifiable, death is a good thing.) The extrinsic differences which *normally* mark off killing and allowing to die do explain why we *normally* regard killing as much worse than allowing to die.

To explain our conventional ethical attitudes is not to justify them. Do the five differences not only explain, but also justify, our attitudes? Let us consider them one by one:

(1) Take the lack of an identifiable victim first. Suppose that I am a travelling salesman, selling tinned food, and I learn that a batch of tins contains a contaminant, the known effect of which when consumed is to double the risk that the consumer will die from stomach cancer. Suppose I continue to sell the tins. My decision may have no identifiable victims. Some of those who eat the food will die from cancer. The proportion of consumers dying in this way will be twice that of the community at large, but which among the consumers died because they ate what I sold, and which would have contracted the disease anyway? It is impossible to tell; but surely this impossibility makes my decision no less reprehensible than it would have been had the contaminant had more readily detectable, though equally fatal, effects.

(2) The lack of certainty that by giving money I could save a life does reduce the

wrongness of not giving, by comparison with deliberate killing; but it is insufficient to show that not giving is acceptable conduct. The motorist who speeds through pedestrian crossings, heedless of anyone who might be on them, is not a murderer. She may never actually hit a pedestrian; yet what she does is very wrong indeed.

(3) The notion of responsibility for acts rather than omissions is more puzzling. On the one hand we feel ourselves to be under a greater obligation to help those whose misfortunes we have caused. (It is for this reason that advocates of overseas aid often argue that Western nations have created the poverty of Third World nations, through forms of economic exploitation which go back to the colonial system.) On the other hand any consequentialist would insist that we are responsible for all the consequences of our actions, and if a consequence of my spending money on a luxury item is that someone dies, I am responsible for that death. It is true that the person would have died even if I had never existed, but what is the relevance of that? The fact is that I do exist, and the consequentialist will say that our responsibilities derive from the world as it is, not as it might have been.

One way of making sense of the non-consequentialist view of responsibility is by basing it on a theory of rights of the kind proposed by John Locke or, more recently, Robert Nozick. If everyone has a right to life, and this right is a right *against* others who might threaten my life, but not a right *to* assistance from others when my life is in danger, then we can understand the feeling that we are responsible for acting to kill but not for omitting to save. The former violates the rights of others, the latter does not.

Should we accept such a theory of rights? If we build up our theory of rights by imagining, as Locke and Nozick do, individuals living independently from each other in a 'state of nature,' it may seem natural to adopt a conception of rights in which as long as each leaves the other alone, no rights are violated. I might, on this view, quite properly have maintained my independent existence if I had wished to do so. So if I do not make you any worse off than you would have been if I had had nothing at all to do with you, how can I have violated your rights? But why start from such an unhistorical, abstract and ultimately inexplicable idea as an independent individual? We now know that our ancestors were social beings long before they were human beings, and could not have developed the abilities and capacities of human beings if they had not been social beings first. In any case we are not, now, isolated individuals. If we consider people living together in a community, it is less easy to assume that rights must be restricted to rights against interference. We might, instead, adopt the view that taking rights to life seriously is incompatible with standing by and watching people die when one could easily save them.

(4) What of the difference in motivation? That a person does not positively wish for the death of another lessens the severity of the blame she deserves; but not by as much as our present attitudes to giving aid suggest. The behaviour of the speeding motorist is again comparable, for such motorists usually have no desire to kill anyone. They merely enjoy speeding and are indifferent to the consequences. Despite their lack of malice, those who kill with cars deserve not only blame but also severe punishment.

(5) Finally, the fact that to avoid killing people is normally not difficult, whereas to save all one could possibly save is heroic, must make an important difference to our attitude to failure to do what the respective principles demand. Not to kill is a minimum standard of acceptable conduct we can require of everyone; to save all one possibly could is not something that can realistically be required, especially not in societies accustomed to giving as little as ours do. Given the generally accepted standards, people who give, say, £100 a year to Oxfam are more aptly praised for above average generosity than blamed for giving less than they might. The appropriateness of praise and blame is, however, a separate issue from the rightness or wrongness of actions. The former evaluates the agent: the latter evaluates the action. Perhaps people who give £100 really ought to give at least £1,000, but to blame them for not giving more could be counterproductive. It might make them feel that what is required is too demanding, and if one is going to be blamed anyway, one might as well not give anything at all.

(That an ethic which put saving all one possibly can on the same footing as not killing would be an ethic for saints or heroes should not lead us to assume that the alternative must be an ethic which makes it obligatory not to kill, but puts us under no obligation to save anyone. There are positions in between these extremes, as we shall soon see.)

To summarize our discussion of the five differences which normally exist between killing and allowing to die, in the context of absolute poverty and overseas aid. The lack of an identifiable victim is of no moral significance, though it may play an important role in explaining our attitudes. The idea that we are directly responsible for those we kill, but not for those we do not help, depends on a questionable notion of responsibility, and may need to be based on a controversial theory of rights. Differences in certainty and motivation are ethically significant, and show that not aiding the poor is not to be condemned as murdering them; it could, however, be on a par with killing someone as a result of reckless driving, which is serious enough. Finally the difficulty of completely discharging the duty of saving all one possibly can makes it inappropriate to blame those who fall short of this target as we blame those who kill; but this does not show that the act itself is less serious. Nor does it indicate anything about those who, far from saving all they possibly can, make no effort to save anyone.

These conclusions suggest a new approach. Instead of attempting to deal with the contrast between affluence and poverty by comparing not saving with deliberate killing, let us consider afresh whether we have an obligation to assist those whose lives are in danger, and if so, how this obligation applies to the present world situation.

The obligation to assist

The argument for an obligation to assist

The path from the library at my university to the Humanities lecture theatre passes a shallow ornamental pond. Suppose that on my way to give a lecture I notice that a small child has fallen in and is in danger of drowning. Would anyone deny that I ought to wade in and pull the child out? This will mean getting my clothes muddy, and either cancelling the lecture or delaying it until I can find something dry to change into; but compared with the avoidable death of a child this is insignificant.

A plausible principle that would support the judgement that I ought to pull the child out is this: if it is in our power to prevent something very bad happening, without thereby sacrificing anything of comparable moral significance, we ought to do it. This principle seems quite uncontroversial. It will obviously win the assent of consequentialists; but non-consequentialists should accept it too, because the injunction to prevent what is bad applies only when nothing comparably significant is at stake. Thus the principle cannot lead to the kinds of actions of which non-consequentialists strongly disapprove—serious violations of individual rights, injustice, broken promises, and so on. If a non-consequentialist regards any of these as comparable in moral significance to the bad thing that is to be prevented, he will automatically regard the principle as not applying in those cases in which the bad thing can only be prevented by violating rights, doing injustice, breaking promises, or whatever else is at stake. Most non-consequentialists hold that we ought to prevent what is bad and promote what is good. Their dispute with consequentialists lies in their insistence that this is not the sole ultimate ethical principle: that it is *an* ethical principle is not denied by any plausible ethical theory.

Nevertheless the uncontroversial appearance of the principle that we ought to prevent what is bad when we can do so without sacrificing anything of comparable moral significance is deceptive. If it were to be taken seriously and acted upon, our lives and our world would be fundamentally changed. For the principle applies, not just to rare situations in which one can save a child from a pond, but to the everyday situation in which we can assist those living in absolute poverty. In saying this I assume that absolute poverty, with its hunger and malnutrition, lack of shelter, illiteracy, disease, high infant mortality and low life expectancy, is a bad thing. And I assume that it is within the power of the affluent to reduce absolute poverty, without sacrificing anything of comparable moral significance. If these two assumptions and the principle we have been discussing are correct, we have an obligation to help those in absolute poverty which is no less strong than our obligation to rescue a drowning child from a pond. Not to help would be wrong, whether or not it is intrinsically equivalent to killing. Helping is not, as conventionally thought, a charitable act which it is praiseworthy to do, but not wrong to omit; it is something that everyone ought to do.

This is the argument for an obligation to assist. Set out more formally, it would look like this.

FIRST PREMISE: If we can prevent something bad without sacrificing anything of comparable significance, we ought to do it.

SECOND PREMISE: Absolute poverty is bad.

THIRD PREMISE: There is some absolute poverty we can prevent without sacrificing anything of comparable moral significance.

CONCLUSION: We ought to prevent some absolute poverty.

The first premise is the substantive moral premise on which the argument rests, and I have tried to show that it can be accepted by people who hold a variety of ethical positions.

The second premise is unlikely to be challenged. Absolute poverty is, as McNamara puts it, 'beneath any reasonable definition of human decency' and it would be hard to find a plausible ethical view which did not regard it as a bad thing.

The third premise is more controversial, even though it is cautiously framed. It claims only that some absolute poverty can be prevented without the sacrifice of anything of comparable moral significance. It thus avoids the objection that any aid I can give is just 'drops in the ocean' for the point is not whether my personal contribution will make any noticeable impression on world poverty as a whole (of course it won't) but whether it will prevent some poverty. This is all the argument needs to sustain its conclusion, since the second premise says that any absolute poverty is bad, and not merely the total amount of absolute poverty. If without sacrificing anything of comparable moral significance we can provide just one family with the means to raise itself out of absolute poverty, the third premise is vindicated.

I have left the notion of moral significance unexamined in order to show that the argument does not depend on any specific values or ethical principles. I think the third premise is true for most people living in industrialized nations, on any defensible view of what is morally significant. Our affluence means that we have income we can dispose of without giving up the basic necessities of life, and we can use this income to reduce absolute poverty. Just how much we will think ourselves obliged to give up will depend on what we consider to be of comparable moral significance to the poverty we could prevent: colour television, stylish clothes, expensive dinners, a sophisticated stereo system, overseas holidays, a (second?) car, a larger house, private schools for our children.... For a utilitarian, none of these is likely to be of comparable significance to the reduction of absolute poverty; and those who are not utilitarians surely must, if they subscribe to the principle of universalizability, accept that at least *some* of these things are of far less moral significance than the absolute poverty that could be prevented by the money they cost. So the third premise seems to be true on any plausible ethical view—although the precise amount of absolute poverty that can be prevented before anything of moral significance is sacrificed will vary according to the ethical view one accepts.

Objections to the argument

Taking care of our own Anyone who has worked to increase overseas aid will have come across the argument that we should look after those near us, our families and then the poor in our own country, before we think about poverty in distant places.

No doubt we do instinctively prefer to help those who are close to us. Few could stand by and watch a child drown; many can ignore a famine in Africa. But the question is not what we usually do, but what we ought to do, and it is difficult to see any sound moral justification for the view that distance, or community membership, makes a crucial difference to our obligation.

Consider, for instance, racial affinities. Should whites help poor whites before helping poor blacks? Most of us would reject such a suggestion out of hand: ...people's need for food has nothing to do with their race, and if blacks need food more than whites, it would be a violation of the principle of equal consideration to give preference to whites.

The same point applies to citizenship or nationhood. Every affluent nation has some relatively poor citizens, but absolute poverty is limited largely to the poor nations. Those living on the streets of Calcutta, or in a drought-stricken region of the Sahel, are experiencing poverty unknown in the West. Under these circumstances it would be wrong to decide that only those fortunate enough to be citizens of our own community will share our abundance.

We feel obligations of kinship more strongly than those of citizenship. Which parents could give away their last bowl of rice if their own children were starving? To do so would seem unnatural, contrary to our nature as biologically evolved beings—although whether it would be wrong is another question altogether. In any case, we are not faced with that situation, but with one in which our own children are well-fed, well-clothed, well-educated, and would now like new bikes, a stereo set, or their own car. In these circumstances any special obligations we might have to our children have been fulfilled, and the needs of strangers make a stronger claim upon us.

The element of truth in the view that we should first take care of our own, lies in the advantage of a recognized system of responsibilities. When families and local communities look after their own poorer members, ties of affection and personal relationships achieve ends that would otherwise require a large, impersonal bureaucracy. Hence it would be absurd to propose that from now on we all regard ourselves as equally responsible for the welfare of everyone in the world; but the argument for an obligation to assist does not propose that. It applies only when some are in absolute poverty, and others can help without sacrificing anything of comparable moral significance. To allow one's own kin to sink into absolute poverty would be to sacrifice something of comparable signifi-

cance; and before that point had been reached, the breakdown of the system of family and community responsibility would be a factor to weigh the balance in favour of a small degree of preference for family and community. This small degree of preference is, however, decisively outweighed by existing discrepancies in wealth and property.

Property rights Do people have a right to private property, a right which contradicts the view that they are under an obligation to give some of their wealth away to those in absolute poverty? According to some theories of rights (for instance, Robert Nozick's) provided one has acquired one's property without the use of unjust means like force and fraud, one may be entitled to enormous wealth while others starve. This individualistic conception of rights is in contrast to other views, like the early Christian doctrine to be found in the works of Thomas Aquinas, which holds that since property exists for the satisfaction of human needs, 'whatever a man has in superabundance is owed, of natural right, to the poor for their sustenance.' A socialist would also, of course, see wealth as belonging to the community rather than the individual, while utilitarians, whether socialist or not, would be prepared to override property rights to prevent great evils.

Does the argument for an obligation to assist others therefore presuppose one of these other theories of property rights, and not an individualistic theory like Nozick's? Not necessarily. A theory of property rights can insist on our *right* to retain wealth without pronouncing on whether the rich *ought* to give to the poor. Nozick, for example, rejects the use of compulsory means like taxation to redistribute income, but suggests that we can achieve the ends we deem morally desirable by voluntary means. So Nozick would reject the claim that rich people have an 'obligation' to give aid to the poor, in so far as this implies that the poor have a right to our aid, but might accept that giving is something we ought to do and failing to give, though within one's rights, is wrong—for rights is not all there is to ethics.

The argument for an obligation to assist can survive, with only minor modifications, even if we accept an individualistic theory of property rights. In any case, however, I do not think we should accept such a theory. It leaves too much to chance to be an acceptable ethical view. For instance, those whose forefathers happened to inhabit some sandy wastes around the Persian Gulf are now fabulously wealthy, because oil lay under those sands; while those whose forefathers settled on better land south of the Sahara live in absolute poverty, because of drought and bad harvests. Can this distribution be acceptable from an impartial point of view? If we imagine ourselves about to begin life as a citizen of either Kuwait or Chad—but we do not know which—would we accept the principle that citizens of Kuwait are under no obligation to assist people living in Chad?

Population and the ethics of triage Perhaps the most serious objection to the argument that we have an obligation to assist is that since the major cause of absolute poverty is overpopulation, helping those now in poverty will only ensure that yet more people are born to live in poverty in the future.

In its most extreme form, this objection is taken to show that we should adopt a policy of 'triage.' The term comes from medical policies adopted in wartime. With too few doctors to cope with all the casualties, the wounded were divided into three cate-gories: those who would probably survive without medical assistance, those who might survive if they received assistance, but otherwise probably would not, and those who even with medical assistance probably would not survive. Only those in the middle category were given medical assistance. The idea, of course, was to use limited medical resources as effectively as possible. For those in the first category, medical treatment was not strictly necessary; for those in the third category, it was likely to be useless. It has been suggested that we should apply the same policies to countries, according to their prospects of becoming self-sustaining. We would not aid countries which even without our help will soon be able to feed their populations. We would not aid countries which, even with our help, will not be able to limit their population to a level they can feed. We would aid those countries where our help might make the difference between success and failure in bringing food and population into balance.

Advocates of this theory are understandably reluctant to give a complete list of the countries they would place in the 'hopeless' category; but Bangladesh is often cited as an example. Adopting the policy of triage would, then, mean cutting off assistance to Bangladesh and allowing famine, disease and natural disasters to reduce the population of that country (now around 80 million) to the level at which it can provide adequately for all.

In support of this view Garrett Hardin has offered a metaphor: we in the rich nations are like the occupants of a crowded lifeboat adrift in a sea full of drowning people. If we try to save the drowning by bringing them aboard our boat will be overloaded and we shall all drown. Since it is better that some survive than none, we should leave the others to drown. In the world today, according to Hardin, 'lifeboat ethics' apply. The rich should leave the poor to starve, for otherwise the poor will drag the rich down with them.

Against this view, some writers have argued that overpopulation is a myth. The world produces ample food to feed its population, and could, according to some estimates, feed ten times as many. People are hungry not because there are too many but because of inequitable land distribution, the manipulation of Third World economies by the developed nations, wastage of food in the West, and so on.

Putting aside the controversial issue of the extent to which food production might one day be increased, it is true, as we have already seen, that the world now produces enough to feed its inhabitants—the amount lost by being fed to animals itself being enough to meet existing grain shortages. Nevertheless population growth cannot be ignored. Bangladesh could, with land reform and using better techniques, feed its present population of 80 million; but by the year 2000, according to World Bank estimates, its population will be 146 million. The enormous effort that will have to go into feeding an extra 66 million people, all added to the population within a quarter of a century, means that Bangladesh must develop at full speed to stay where she is. Other low income countries are in similar situations. By the end of the century, Ethiopia's population is expected to rise from 29 to 54 million; Somalia's from 3 to 7 million, India's from 620 to 958 million, Zaire's from 25 to 47 million. What will happen then? Population cannot grow indefinitely. It will be checked by a decline in birth rates or a rise in death rates. Those

who advocate triage are proposing that we allow the population growth of some countries to be checked by a rise in death rates—that is, by increased malnutrition, and related diseases; by widespread famines; by increased infant mortality; and by epidemics of infectious diseases.

The consequences of triage on this scale are so horrible that we are inclined to reject it without further argument. How could we sit by our television sets, watching millions starve while we do nothing? Would not that...be the end of all notions of human equality and respect for human life? Don't people have a right to our assistance, irrespective of the consequences?

Anyone whose initial reaction to triage was not one of repugnance would be an unpleasant sort of person. Yet initial reactions based on strong feelings are not always reliable guides. Advocates of triage are rightly concerned with the long-term consequences of our actions. They say that helping the poor and starving now merely ensures more poor and starving in the future. When our capacity to help is finally unable to cope—as one day it must be—the suffering will be greater than it would be if we stopped helping them now. If this is correct, there is nothing we can do to prevent absolute starvation and poverty, in the long run, and so we have no obligation to assist. Nor does it seem reasonable to hold that under these circumstances people have a right to our assistance. If we do accept such a right, irrespective of the consequences, we are saying that, in Hardin's metaphor, we would continue to haul the drowning into our lifeboat until the boat sank and we all drowned.

If triage is to be rejected it must be tackled on its own ground, within the framework of consequentialist ethics. Here it is vulnerable. Any consequentialist ethics must take probability of outcome into account. A course of action that will certainly produce some benefit is to be preferred to an alternative course that may lead to a slightly larger benefit, but is equally likely to result in no benefit at all. Only if the greater magnitude of the uncertain benefit outweighs its uncertainty should we choose it. Better one certain unit of benefit than a 10% chance of 5 units; but better a 50% chance of 3 units than a single certain unit. The same principle applies when we are trying to avoid evils.

The policy of triage involves a certain, very great evil: population control by famine and disease. Tens of millions would die slowly. Hundreds of millions would continue to live in absolute poverty, at the very margin of existence. Against this prospect, advocates of the policy place a possible evil which is greater still: the same process of famine and disease, taking place in, say, fifty years time, when the world's population may be three times its present level, and the number who will die from famine, or struggle on in absolute poverty, will be that much greater. The question is: how probable is this forecast that continued assistance now will lead to greater disasters in the future?

Forecasts of population growth are notoriously fallible, and theories about the factors which affect it remain speculative. One theory, at least as plausible as any other, is that countries pass through a 'demographic transition' as their standard of living rises. When people are very poor and have no access to modern medicine their fertility is high, but population is kept in check by high death rates. The introduction of sanitation, modern medical techniques and other improvements reduces the death

rate, but initially has little effect on the birth rate. Then population grows rapidly. Most poor countries are now in this phase. If standards of living continue to rise, however, couples begin to realize that to have the same number of children surviving to maturity as in the past, they do not need to give birth to as many children as their parents did. The need for children to provide economic support in old age diminishes. Improved education and the emancipation and employment of women also reduce the birthrate, and so population growth begins to level off. Most rich nations have reached this stage, and their populations are growing only very slowly.

If this theory is right, there is an alternative to the disasters accepted as inevitable by supporters of triage. We can assist poor countries to raise the living standards of the poorest members of their population. We can encourage the governments of these countries to enact land reform measures, improve education, and liberate women from a purely child-bearing role. We can also help other countries to make contraception and sterilization widely available. There is a fair chance that these measures will hasten the onset of the demographic transition and bring population growth down to a manageable level. Success cannot be guaranteed; but the evidence that improved economic security and education reduce population growth is strong enough to make triage ethically unacceptable. We cannot allow millions to die from starvation and disease when there is a reasonable probability that population can be brought under control without such horrors.

Population growth is therefore not a reason against giving overseas aid, although it should make us think about the kind of aid to give. Instead of food handouts, it may be better to give aid that hastens the demographic transition. This may mean agricultural assistance for the rural poor, or assistance with education, or the provision of contraceptive services. Whatever kind of aid proves most effective in specific circumstances, the obligation to assist is not reduced.

One awkward question remains. What should we do about a poor and already overpopulated country which, for religious or nationalistic reasons, restricts the use of contraceptives and refuses to slow its population growth? Should we nevertheless offer development assistance? Or should we make our offer conditional on effective steps being taken to reduce the birthrate? To the latter course, some would object that putting conditions on aid is an attempt to impose our own ideas on independent sovereign nations. So it is—but is this imposition unjustifiable? If the argument for an obligation to assist is sound, we have an obligation to reduce absolute poverty; but we have no obligation to make sacrifices that, to the best of our knowledge, have no prospect of reducing poverty in the long run. Hence we have no obligation to assist countries whose governments have policies which will make our aid ineffective. This could be very harsh on poor citizens of these countries—for they may have no say in the government's policies—but we will help more people in the long run by using our resources where they are most effective. (The same principles may apply, incidentally, to countries that refuse to take other steps that could make assistance effective—like refusing to reform systems of land holding that impose intolerable burdens on poor tenant farmers.)

Leaving it to the government We often hear that overseas aid should be a government

responsibility, not left to privately-run charities. Giving privately, it is said, allows the government to escape its responsibilities.

Since increasing government aid is the surest way of making a significant increase to the total amount of aid given, I would agree that the governments of affluent nations should give much more genuine, no strings attached, aid than they give now. One quarter of one percent of GNP is a scandalously small amount for a nation as wealthy as the United States to give. Even the official UN target of 0.7% seems much less than affluent nations can and should give—though it is a target few have reached. But is this a reason against each of us giving what we can privately, through voluntary agencies? To believe that it is seems to assume that the more people there are who give through voluntary agencies, the less likely it is that the government will do its part. Is this plausible? The opposite view—that if no one gives voluntarily the government will assume that its citizens are not in favour of overseas aid, and will cut its program accordingly—is more reasonable. In any case, unless there is a definite probability that by refusing to give we would be helping to bring about an increase in government assistance, refusing to give privately is wrong for the same reason that triage is wrong: it is a refusal to prevent a definite evil for the sake of a very uncertain gain. The onus of showing how a refusal to give privately will make the government give more is on those who refuse to give.

This is not to say that giving privately is enough. Certainly we should campaign for entirely new standards for both public and private overseas aid. We should also work for fairer trading arrangements between rich and poor countries, and less domination of the economies of poor countries by multinational corporations more concerned to produce profits for shareholders back home than food for the local poor. Perhaps it is more important to be politically active in the interests of the poor than to give to them oneself—but why not do both? Unfortunately many use the view that overseas aid is the government's responsibility as a reason against giving, but not as a reason for being politically active.

Too high a standard? The final objection to the argument for an obligation to assist is that it sets a standard so high that none but a saint could attain it. How many people can we really expect to give away everything not comparable in moral significance to the poverty their donation could relieve? For most of us, with commonsense views about what is of moral significance, this would mean a life of real austerity. Might it not be counterproductive to demand so much? Might not people say: 'As I can't do what is morally required anyway, I won't bother to give at all.' If, however, we were to set a more realistic standard, people might make a genuine effort to reach it. Thus setting a lower standard might actually result in more aid being given.

It is important to get the status of this objection clear. Its accuracy as a prediction of human behaviour is quite compatible with the argument that we are obliged to give to the point at which by giving more we sacrifice something of comparable moral significance. What would follow from the objection is that public advocacy of this standard of giving is undesirable. It would mean that in order to do the maximum to reduce absolute poverty, we should advocate a standard lower than the amount we think people really ought to give. Of course we ourselves—those of us who accept the original argument, with its higher standard—would know that we ought to do more than we publicly propose people ought to do, and we might actually give more than we urge others to give. There is no inconsistency here, since in both our private and our public behaviour we are trying to do what will most reduce absolute poverty.

For a consequentialist, this apparent conflict between public and private morality is always a possibility, and not in itself an indication that the underlying principle is wrong. The consequences of a principle are one thing, the consequences of publicly advocating it another.

Is it true that the standard set by our argument is so high as to be counterproductive? There is not much evidence to go by, but discussions of the argument, with students and others, have led me to think it might be. On the other hand the conventionally accepted standard—a few coins in a collection tin when one is waved under your nose—is obviously far too low. What level should we advocate? Any figure will be arbitrary, but there may be something to be said for a round percentage of one's income like, say, 10%—more than a token donation, yet not so high as to be beyond all but saints. (This figure has the additional advantage of being reminiscent of the ancient tithe, or tenth, which was traditionally given to the church, whose responsibilities included care of the poor in one's local community. Perhaps the idea can be revived and applied to the global community.) Some families, of course, will find 10% a considerable strain on their finances. Others may be able to give more without difficulty. No figure should be advocated as a rigid minimum or maximum; but it seems safe to advocate that those earning average or above average incomes in affluent societies, unless they have an unusually large number of dependents or other special needs, ought to give a tenth of their income to reducing absolute poverty. By any reasonable ethical standards this is the minimum we ought to do, and we do wrong if we do less.

Questions for Discussion

1   Is Singer right that failing to provide assistance to those who are dying is virtually equivalent to killing people?

2   Is there any relevant moral difference between Singer's example of saving a child from drowning in a fountain on one's way to a lecture, and providing humanitarian aid to the many starving people in the world?

3   Does Singer provide an adequate response to the sort of argument raised by Hardin?

PART 2

the beginning and end of life

Life itself is one of the central values of common-sense morality, and in most cases very little doubt arises about this. However, there are some cases in which it is not quite so obvious how valuable a given life is, or even sometimes whether a being counts as a living person at all. These questions arise most obviously at the margins of life—the beginning and the end—and become more pronounced as we become capable of more and more technological manipulations of nature. At the beginning-of-life stage are the issues of abortion, and the usage of new reproductive technologies such as in vitro fertilization, and surrogate motherhood. At the end-of-life stage are issues concerning euthanasia and the definition of death, which are again much complicated by our capacity to keep the body "alive" under a variety of circumstances which once would have been fatal. In all of these issues, ethical thought is hard-pressed to keep up with the new possibilities and dangers technology offers.

Abortion is the issue which is probably the most frequently and hotly debated of the issues within this general area. Often the debate is put in terms of a conflict between the rights of an unborn fetus (I use that term loosely here, to cover all stages of development from fertilization of an egg to birth) and the rights of the woman in whose uterus the fetus exists. Traditionally, this debate has been largely between two views, commonly known as the "conservative" (or "pro-life") and the "liberal" (or "pro-choice") view. The conservative view asserts that a fetus is a human being, and that all human beings have an inviolable right to life. Procuring an abortion is equivalent to murder—the taking of an innocent human life—and is never permissible (except perhaps to save another innocent life, such as the mother's). The liberal view, on the other hand, usually maintains that a fetus is not a full human being with rights, and that a woman's right to do as she chooses with her own body extends to choosing to have an abortion.

Much of the discussion, then, has revolved around the question of when a fetus can be said to become a person, with the idea that only a person can properly be said to have "rights" such as the right to life. Does "personhood" occur at the moment of live birth, but not before? Is it at some set stage of fetal development, specifiable in terms of number of weeks? Is it at the moment of conception?

Some of this discussion, in turn, involves the question of what characteristics a being must have to be a "person." Is it a question of having a soul? Can we be sure that anyone has a soul, and if so, how do we know at what point we acquire it? Is it a question of the capacity to reason, or use language? If so, it should be noted that these capacities are not acquired until some time after birth, suggesting that infants (and perhaps some handicapped adults) are not "persons." Should we treat "potential" persons as actual persons? But then how remote can the potential be? Is an unfertilized egg or a sperm cell a potential person in the requisite sense? Is personhood a question of viability—of when one is able to survive without external support? If so, would that mean that rational adults who require an iron lung or some such technological intervention to survive do not count as persons?

It is not easy to identify the characteristics which are required for a being to count as a person. However, this issue does not come up only in connection with abortion. A very similar debate is involved when one tries to decide how non-human animals should be treated. Much of the discussion of that aspect of the abortion issue will be covered in this book under the heading of the "Status of Non-Human Animals."

Even people who agree that a fetus has rights may disagree about what that implies for the abortion debate. It is possible to maintain that the fetus has a right to life, but that that right is not absolute. There are decisions that societies make for the overall good which may predictably result in the deaths of some people—even decisions as trivial as raising the speed limit on highways—so there is at least some precedent for claiming that the right to life is not absolute. One might also argue that there is a limit to how much one person can be required to sacrifice to preserve the life of another, in which case a woman may not be required to carry a fetus to term, even if it has a right to life. (Judith Jarvis Thomson presents a classic argument along these lines in her article, "A Defense of Abortion." The question of what lengths a person is required to go to to save the life of another also comes up in connection with the obligations of the rich to help the poor, discussed in the chapter on "Distribution of Scarce Resources.") It may also become possible, as technology is developed, that a fetus may be removed from a woman's uterus without killing it, which might change the nature of the abortion issue. It is clear that there will still be room for debate even once the question of the moral status of the fetus is settled.

One other issue which should be mentioned along these lines is what is known as the "doctrine of double effect." According to this doctrine (originally employed by the Roman Catholic Church), it may be allowable under particular conditions to perform an action which will have results that would usually be unacceptable. Specifically, the main requirement for the employment of this doctrine is that the "evil" must be a foreseen but unintended consequence of some other action which is itself good enough to outweigh the evil consequence. It is also considered important that the evil effect be another consequence of the same action, and not a means to the desired end. For example, bombing innocent civilians in a just war so as to demoralize the enemy and bring about victory is not justified, since one is not allowed to kill civilians. However, deciding to attack a military target situated in a populated area and knowing the attack is likely to lead to civilian casualties, may be permissible.

The doctrine of double effect is often applied to abortion in cases where an operation is needed to save a pregnant woman's life, and it is foreseen that performing this operation is likely to kill the fetus. If one believes that killing a fetus is generally impermissible, one might apply the doctrine of double effect to allow the operation in such a case.

In addition to cases where the mother's health is endangered by the pregnancy, many people who are generally opposed to abortions believe they can be justified in cases where the pregnancy is the result of rape. If the reason for being opposed to abortion is related to a claim that the fetus has rights, this is a puzzling attitude. How could the details of how a fetus came into existence affect the rights it has once it is in existence? More likely, such a view reveals a belief that a woman can be expected to endure a pregnancy rather than abort because she is considered responsible for her condition, and people should bear the consequences of their own actions. Such a belief could explain why a pregnant woman would be freed of the responsibility in a case of rape. This raises questions about whether people who have actively tried to avoid pregnancy (e.g. by contraception) should be considered responsible if their preventive measures fail. There is also a question of whether it is fair for women to bear such consequences of their actions, when the father is equally responsible.

The current Canadian legal situation concerning issues about unborn humans is extremely unsettled. The Supreme Court of Canada struck down the previously existing abortion legislation in 1988 on the grounds that it violated a woman's right to fair treatment (section 7 of the Charter of Rights). The decision left it unclear, however, whether the problem was that the particular law in question was too restrictive, or whether *any* law restricting abortions would be unconstitutional. There is not even agreement on whether Canada needs a law governing abortion at all. The courts' decisions have been similarly inconclusive in a number of related areas, although the arguments the judges consider often reveal much of the current thought on these issues. Accordingly, this chapter includes an account of the way in which many of these issues have appeared in Canadian law-making and in court.

Many of the issues concerning the status of unborn humans are rendered even more complex by the availability of new reproductive technologies. To explain one such new option, it is now possible for couples who cannot conceive naturally to fertilize several eggs outside the womb (in vitro fertilization). These fertilized eggs ("pre-embryos") may then be allowed to develop to the eight- or sixteen-cell stage, at which point some of them may be implanted in a mother's uterus, while the rest are frozen and preserved. If the pregnancy resulting from the implant does not succeed, it may be possible to try again with one of the remaining pre-embryos.

There are a number of issues raised by in vitro fertilization. Some of these again involve the status of the unborn human being. Suppose, for example, that the procedure outlined above is followed, and that the first attempted implant does succeed. What is to be done with the remaining pre-embryos? Is there an obligation to try to develop them into full-grown human beings? If so, who has that obligation? Should they be viewed as the "property" of those who arranged for their existence, to be disposed of as they see fit? Again, it is important to decide when a living being becomes a person.

New reproductive technologies raise other issues as well. One might question how large a portion of society's resources should be dedicated to such procedures. One might also wonder how the severing of the link between biological parenthood and birth, made possible by the technology, might affect societal assumptions and behaviours. Indeed, one might fear that such capacities have a tendency to encourage undesirable social attitudes on a large scale. For example, people might be encouraged to think of human beings as commodities to be bought and sold, or to become intolerant of "imperfections" in human beings. All of these issues bear scrutiny, as does the question of how we as a society should make decisions about these issues.

Similar questions are raised in issues concerning the end of life, issues complicated by the question of what makes life valuable. If we could know what it is that makes life valuable, then it would be easier to decide what lengths one is required to go to in order to sustain it, or indeed whether it is permissible to take deliberate steps to end a person's life in some circumstances.

The most prominent issue in this area concerns "euthanasia," sometimes known loosely as "mercy-killing." The word euthanasia comes from the ancient Greek for "good death," and still carries some shades of meaning from that origin, although this meaning has changed somewhat in the context of the modern debate. Indeed, one of its most controversial aspects is finding an adequate characterization of what euthanasia means. It is generally understood to refer to the inducement of a gentle, easy death so as to avoid an unreasonable amount of suffering, or loss of dignity.

The main reasons offered to justify hastening death or refusing to prolong life have to do with the best interests of a person, or the desire to treat people with dignity and respect. A person who is in great pain may be considered "better off dead," although of course we do not really know what it is like to be dead. Can a life ever be "not worth living"? Alternatively, the decision may be based on a belief that certain conditions threaten the dignity of people, either because they reduce them to states in which they are not capable of doing what they previously could, or simply because they are too physically intrusive. Finally, one important case involving dignity concerns the belief that human beings should have "autonomy" (the ability to govern themselves). That could mean that they should be allowed to decide for themselves what is to happen in their lives. In this case, it may be morally required that we accept people's decisions if they decide they want to end their own lives. (One problematic possibility this raises is that a person may decide to die so as to avoid becoming a burden on friends and family.)

There are several distinctions which have traditionally been raised in connection with euthanasia. Perhaps the most basic of these is a distinction between killing a person, and letting a person die (sometimes described as "active" vs. "passive" euthanasia). Many people believe that it is sometimes permissible to refrain from taking steps which would prolong a life, but that it is never permissible to take active steps to hasten the end of a life. (Indeed, some people use the word euthanasia only for those cases in which active steps are taken, and not for "letting die.") It might be claimed that actively killing a person amounts to "playing

God," and allowing such killings might lead people (including health care professionals, who are presumed to be dedicated to preserving life and health) to lower the value they place on human life in other contexts (the "slippery slope" argument). Simply letting someone die, when there doesn't seem to be much for that person to live for, is not considered to have the same dire consequences.

On the other side of this issue, one might argue that refraining from life-sustaining treatment and waiting for natural death may sometimes be less humane than bringing about a quick and painless end. If the reason for refusing to prolong life is that the person is suffering greatly, it might seem kinder to put such a person "out of his or her misery." People on this side of the issue deny that there is any relevant difference between passive and active euthanasia. Both sides can agree that there could be cases in which both passive and active euthanasia would be wrong.

Another important distinction is that between "voluntary" and "non-voluntary" euthanasia. A voluntary decision about death is one in which the decision-maker is considered competent to make decisions regarding his or her own life. In such cases, many people would say that we have to respect the autonomy of that person, and accept her or his decision (although of course this obligation might not reach so far as to require us to take positive steps to bring it about, if the person is not able to bring it about without our help). Some writers have suggested that in cases of competent individuals, the right to life should be understood to extend to the "right to death."

The more complicated cases here involve people who are not able to make decisions for themselves. Such people cannot act voluntarily, and so a decision to perform euthanasia would have to be non-voluntary. (It might also be possible to perform euthanasia on a person against that person's own stated desires, which might be called "involuntary euthanasia." Most people would find this generally unacceptable, however, and it is not discussed much in the literature.)

There are a variety of reasons why people may be unable to express a view regarding their own fate. One extreme circumstance would be one in which the person is unconscious. People may also be considered incompetent to make such a decision if, for example, they are too young, or suffer from some mental impairment which leaves them unable to understand their situation.

How are we to go about deciding whether euthanasia can be performed on a person not competent to speak for him or herself? There are two standards which have been applied to such cases. The first, called the "best interests" standard, requires the decision-makers to decide what they believe to be in the best interests of the incompetent person and act accordingly. Of course different decision-makers might have different ideas about what makes for a good life, and so this standard may yield different results depending on who is using it. There is, however, some precedent for the state's assuming a duty to look after the best interests of those who cannot look after themselves, for example by protecting children from abusive parents.

The "substituted judgement" standard maintains that the decision properly belongs to the individual involved, because of that person's rights to autonomy and privacy. However, since that person is unable to decide, the task of the decision-maker should be to figure out what the individual *would* decide if he or she were competent to do so. This may or may not correspond to the decision-maker's own opinion about what would be best for that person.

There may be cases in which the calculation of what a person would decide is made easier by an opinion expressed by that person before becoming incompetent. Although it is true that people sometimes change their minds, there is at least some reason to think that a request such as "If I am ever in condition x, please let me die" should be heeded if the person does indeed end up in condition x. The acceptability of this sort of statement has been tested in many places by the making of a so-called "living will."

In many cases, however, the individual concerned was never competent, or did not express a clear preference. It might be very difficult to apply the substituted judgement standard in such cases. Indeed, asking people to decide what they would do if they were not who they are, or were in very different circumstances, is always going to be difficult, although it might still be the best approach available.

One final issue which needs to be raised about non-voluntary euthanasia is that of who is to make the decision. Should it be the family of the individual affected? The attending physicians? A hospital ethics committee? The courts? Each may have some advantages over the others. Of course, if all agree, there may be no problem, but conflicts are inevitable.

The selections which follow discuss several of these issues concerning ethics at the beginning and end of life.

Abortion and the Criminal Code

As things stand in Canada today, there is no federal law governing abortion. There was a part of the criminal code prohibiting abortions, except under specified conditions, until 1988. In that year, the Supreme Court of Canada, in the case of R. v. Morgentaler, Smoling and Scott, found that the law violated section 7 of the Charter of Rights, and was therefore unconstitutional. The following two articles contain the text of the original law, and some of the text of the Supreme Court decision which struck it down. Note that different justices on the Supreme Court who reached the same conclusion seem to have disagreed about which reasons for that conclusion were the most appealing.

* * *

Abortion in the Criminal Code (S.287)

PROCURING MISCARRIAGE / Woman procuring her own miscarriage / Definition of "means" / Exceptions / Information requirement / Definitions / "accredited hospital" / "approved hospital" / "board" / "Minister of Health" / "qualified medical practitioner" / "therapeutic abortion committee" / Requirement of consent not affected.

287. (1) Every one who, with intent to procure the miscarriage of a female person, whether or not she is pregnant, uses any means for the purpose of carrying out his intention is guilty of an indictable offence and liable to imprisonment for life.

(2) Every female person who, being pregnant, with intent to procure her own miscarriage, uses any means or permits any means to be used for the purpose of carrying out her intention is guilty of an indictable offence and liable to imprisonment for a term not exceeding two years.

(3) In this section, "means" includes

(a) the administration of a drug or other noxious thing;

(b) the use of an instrument; and

(c) manipulation of any kind.

(4) Subsections (1) and (2) do not apply to

(a) a qualified medical practitioner, other than a member of a therapeutic abortion committee for any hospital, who in good faith uses in an accredited or approved hospital any means for the purpose of carrying out his intention to procure the miscarriage of a female person, or

(b) a female person who, being pregnant, permits a qualified medical practitioner to use in an accredited or approved hospital any means for the purpose of carrying out her intention to procure her own miscarriage, if, before the use of those means, the therapeutic abortion committee for that accredited or approved hospital, by a majority of the members of the committee and at a meeting of the committee at which the case of the female person has been reviewed,

(c) has by certificate in writing stated that in its opinion the continuation of the pregnancy of the female person would or would be likely to endanger her life or health, and

(d) has caused a copy of such certificate to be given to the qualified medical practitioner.

(5) The Minister of Health of a province may by order

(a) require a therapeutic abortion committee for any hospital in that province, or any member thereof, to furnish him with a copy of any certificate described in paragraph (4)(c) issued by that committee, together with such other information relating to the circumstances surrounding the issue of that certificate as he may require, or

(b) require a medical practitioner who, in that province, has procured the miscarriage of any female person named in a certificate described in paragraph (4)(c), to furnish him with a copy of that certificate, together with such other information relating to the procuring of the miscarriage as he may require.

(6) For the purposes of subsections (4) and (5) and this subsection,

"accredited hospital" means a hospital accredited by the Canadian Council on Hospital Accreditation in which diagnostic services and medical, surgical and obstetrical treatment are provided;

"approved hospital" means a hospital in a province approved for the purposes of this section by the Minister of Health of that province;

"board" means the board of governors, management or directors, or the trustees, commission or other group of persons having the control and management of an accredited or approved hospital;

"Minister of Health" means

(a) in the Provinces of Ontario, Quebec, New Brunswick, Prince Edward Island, Manitoba and Newfoundland, the Minister of Health,

(b) in the Provinces of Nova Scotia and Saskatchewan, the Minister of Public Health, and

(c) in the Province of British Columbia, the Minister of Health Services and Hospital Insurance,

(d) in the Province of Alberta, the Minister of Hospitals and Medical Care,

(e) in the Yukon Territory and the Northwest Territories, the Minister of National Health and Welfare;

"qualified medical practitioner" means a person entitled to engage in the practice of medicine under the laws of the province in which the hospital referred to in subsection (4) is situated;

"therapeutic abortion committee" for any

hospital means a committee, comprised of not less than three members each of whom is a qualified medical practitioner, appointed by the board of that hospital for the purpose of considering and determining questions relating to terminations of pregnancy within that hospital.

(7) Nothing in subsection (4) shall be construed as making unnecessary the obtaining of any authorization or consent that is or may be required, otherwise than under this Act, before any means are used for the purpose of carrying out an intention to procure the miscarriage of a female person. R.S., c. C-34, s. 251; 1974-75-76, c.93, s.22.1.

* * *

Morgentaler, Smoling and Scott v. The Queen

Supreme Court of Canada (1988) 44 D.L.R. (4th) 385

Chief Justice Dickson:

Although the "principles of fundamental justice" referred to in s. 7 have both a substantive and a procedural component,....it is not necessary in this appeal to evaluate the substantive content of s. 251 of the *Criminal Code*. My discussion will therefore be limited to various aspects of the administrative structure and procedure set down in s. 251 for access to therapeutic abortions.

In outline, s. 251 operates in the following manner. Subsection (1) creates an indictable offence for any person to use any means with the intent "to procure the miscarriage of a female person." Subsection

(2) establishes a parallel indictable offence for any pregnant woman to use or to permit any means to be used with the intent "to procure her own miscarriage".... The crucial provision for the purposes of the present appeal is s.-s. (4) which states that the offences created in s.-ss. (1) and (2) "do not apply" in certain circumstances....

The procedure surrounding the defence is rather complex. A pregnant woman who desires to have an abortion must apply to the "therapeutic abortion committee" of an "accredited or approved hospital." Such a committee is empowered to issue a certificate in writing stating that in the opinion of a majority of the committee, the continuation of the pregnancy would be likely to endanger the woman's life or health. Once a copy of the certificate is given to a qualified medical practitioner who is not a member of the therapeutic abortion committee, he or she is permitted to perform an abortion on the pregnant woman and both the doctor and the woman are freed from any criminal liability....

As is so often the case in matters of interpretation, however, the straightforward reading of this statutory scheme is not fully revealing. In order to understand the true nature and scope of s. 251, it is necessary to investigate the practical operations of the provisions. The court has been provided with a myriad of factual submissions in this area. One of the most useful sources of information is the Badgley report [the final report of the Committee on the Operation of the Abortion Law issued in 1978]....

The Badgley report contains a wealth of detailed information which demonstrates...that many of the most serious problems with the functioning of s. 251 are created by the procedural and administrative requirements established in the law.... [For example,] the seemingly neutral requirement of s. 251(4) that at least four physicians be available to authorize and to perform an abortion meant in practice that abortions would be absolutely unavailable in almost one quarter of all hospitals in Canada.

Other administrative and procedural requirements of s. 251(4) reduce the availability of therapeutic abortions even further. For the purposes of s. 251, therapeutic abortions can only be performed in "accredited" or "approved" hospitals.... [A]n "approved" hospital is one which a provincial minister of health has designated as such for the purposes of performing therapeutic abortions. The minister is under no obligation to grant any such approval. Furthermore, an "accredited" hospital must not only be accredited by the Canadian Council on Hospital Accreditation, it must also pro-

vide specific services. Many Canadian hospitals do not provide all of the required services, thereby being automatically disqualified from undertaking therapeutic abortions.... Moreover, even if a hospital is eligible to create a therapeutic abortion committee, there is no requirement in s. 251 that the hospital need do so....

...The requirement that therapeutic abortions be performed only in "accredited" or "approved" hospitals effectively means that the practical availability of the exculpatory provisions of s.-s. (4) may be heavily restricted, even denied, through provincial regulation....

A further flaw in the administrative system established in s. 251 is the failure to provide an adequate standard for therapeutic abortion committees which must determine when a therapeutic abortion should, as a matter of law, be granted. Subsection (4) states simply that a therapeutic abortion committee may grant a certificate when it determines that a continuation of a pregnancy would be likely to endanger the "life or health" of the pregnant woman. It was noted above that "health" is not defined for the purposes of the section....

...Various expert doctors testified at trial that therapeutic abortion committees apply widely differing definitions of health. For some committees, psychological health is a justification for therapeutic abortion; for others it is not. Some committees routinely refuse abortions to married women unless they are in physical danger, while for other committees it is possible for a married woman to show that she would suffer psychological harm if she continued with a pregnancy, thereby justifying an abortion. It is not typically possible for women to know in advance what standard of health will be applied by any given committee....

The combined effect of all of these problems with the procedure stipulated in s. 251 for access to therapeutic abortions is a failure to comply with the principles of fundamental justice.... One of the basic tenets of our system of criminal justice is that when Parliament creates a defence to a criminal charge, the defence should not be illusory or so difficult to attain as to be practically illusory. The criminal law is a very special form of governmental regulation, for it seeks to express our society's selective disapprobation of certain acts and omissions. When a defence is provided, especially a specifically-tailored defence to a particular charge, it is because the legislator has determined that the disapprobation of society is not warranted when the conditions of the defence are met.

Consider then the case of a pregnant married woman who wishes to apply for a therapeutic abortion certificate because she fears that her psychological health would be impaired seriously if she carried the fetus to term. The uncontroverted evidence appears that there are many areas in Canada where such a woman could simply not have access to a therapeutic abortion. She may be in an area where no hospital has four doctors; no therapeutic abortion committee can be created. Equally, she may live in a place where the treatment functions of the nearby hospitals do not satisfy the definition of "accredited hospital" in s. 251(6). Or she may be in a province where the provincial government has posed such stringent requirements on hospitals seeking to activate therapeutic abortion committees that no hospital can qualify. Alternatively, our hypothetical woman may confront a therapeutic abortion committee in her local hospital

which defines "health" in purely physical terms or which refuses to countenance abortions for married women. In each of these cases, it is the administrative structures and procedures established by s. 251 itself that would in practice prevent the woman from gaining the benefit of the defence held out to her in s.251(4).

The facts indicate that many women do indeed confront these problems....

I conclude that the procedures created in s. 251 of the *Criminal Code* for obtaining a therapeutic abortion do not comport with the principles of fundamental justice. It is not necessary to determine whether s. 7 also contains a substantive content leading to the conclusion that, in some circumstances at least, the deprivation of a pregnant woman's right to security of the person can never comport with fundamental justice. Simply put, assuming Parliament can act, it must do so properly. For the reasons given earlier, the deprivation of security of the person caused by s. 251 as a whole is not in accordance with the second clause of s. 7.

Madam Justice Wilson:

At the heart of this appeal is the question whether a pregnant woman can, as a constitutional matter, be compelled by law to carry the fetus to term. The legislature has proceeded on the basis that she can be so compelled and, indeed, has made it a criminal offence punishable by imprisonment under s. 251 of the *Criminal Code*...for her or her physician to terminate the pregnancy unless the procedural requirements of the section are complied with.

My colleagues...have attacked those requirements in reasons which I have had the privilege of reading. They have found that the requirements do not comport with the principles of fundamental justice in the procedural sense and have concluded that, since they cannot be severed from the provisions creating the substantive offence, the whole of s. 251 must fall.

With all due respect, I think that the court must tackle the primary issue first. A consideration as to whether or not the procedural requirements for obtaining or performing an abortion comport with fundamental justice is purely academic if such requirements cannot as a constitutional matter be imposed at all. If a pregnant woman cannot, as a constitutional matter, be compelled by law to carry the fetus to term against her will, a review of the procedural requirements by which she may be compelled to do so seems pointless. Moreover, it would, in my opinion, be an exercise in futility for the legislature to expend its time and energy in attempting to remedy the defects in the procedural requirements unless it has some assurance that this process will, at the end of the day, result in the creation of a valid criminal offence. I turn, therefore, to what I believe is the central issue that must be addressed....

In order to ascertain the content of the right to liberty we must...commence with an analysis of the purpose of that right.... We are invited, therefore, to consider the purpose of the Charter in general and of the right to liberty in particular.

The Charter is predicated on a particular conception of the place of the individual in society. An individual is not a totally independent entity disconnected from the society in which he or she lives. Neither, however, is the individual a mere cog in an impersonal machine in which his or her values, goals and aspirations are subordinated to those of the collectivity. The individual is a bit of both. The Charter reflects this

reality by leaving a wide range of activities and decisions open to legitimate government control while at the same time placing limits on the proper scope of that control. Thus, the rights guaranteed in the Charter erect around each individual, metaphorically speaking, an invisible fence over which the state will not be allowed to trespass. The role of the courts is to map out, piece by piece, the parameters of the fence.

The Charter and the right to individual liberty guaranteed under it are inextricably tied to the concept of human dignity. Professor Neil MacCormick, *Legal Right and Social Democracy: Essays in Legal and Political Philosophy,* speaks of liberty as "a condition of human self-respect and of that contentment which resides in the ability to pursue one's own conception of a full and rewarding life." He says...:

> To be able to decide what to do and how to do it, to carry out one's own decisions and accept their consequences, seems to me essential to one's self-respect as a human being, and essential to the possibility of that contentment. Such self-respect and contentment are in my judgement fundamental goods for human beings, the worth of life itself being on condition of having or striving for them. If a person were deliberately denied the opportunity of self-respect and that contentment, he would suffer deprivation of his essential humanity....

The idea of human dignity finds expression in almost every right and freedom guaranteed in the Charter. Individuals are afforded the right to choose their own religion and their own philosophy of life, the right to choose with whom they will associate and how they will express themselves, the right to choose where they will live and what occupation they will pursue. These are all examples of the basic theory underlying the Charter, namely, that the state will respect choices made by individuals and, to the greatest extent possible, will avoid subordinating these choices to any one conception of the good life.

Thus, an aspect of the respect for human dignity on which the Charter is founded is the right to make fundamental personal decisions without interference from the state. This right is a crucial component of the right to liberty. Liberty...is a phrase capable of a broad range of meaning. In my view, this right, properly construed, grants the individual a degree of autonomy in making decisions of fundamental personal importance.

This view is consistent with the position I took in the case of *Jones v. The Queen* (1986).... One issue raised in that case was whether the right to liberty in s. 7 of the Charter included a parent's right to bring up his children in accordance with his conscientious beliefs. In concluding that it did I stated...:

> I believe that the framers of the Constitution in guaranteeing "liberty" as a fundamental value in a free and democratic society had in mind the freedom of the individual to develop and realize his potential to the full, to plan his own life to suit his own character, to make his own choices for good or ill, to be non-conformist, idiosyncratic and even eccentric—to be, in today's parlance, "his own person" and accountable as such. John Stuart Mill described it as "pursuing our own good in our own way." This, he believed, we should be free to do "so long as we do not attempt to deprive others of theirs or impede their efforts to obtain it." He added:

> > "Each is the guardian of his own health, whether bodily *or* mental or spiritual. Mankind are greater gainers by suffering each other to live as seems good to themselves than by compelling each to live as seems good to the rest."

Liberty in a free and democratic society does not require the state to approve the personal decisions made by its citizens; it does, however, require the state to respect them....

...I would conclude, therefore, that the right to liberty contained in s. 7 guarantees to every individual a degree of personal autonomy over important decisions intimately affecting their private lives.

The question then becomes whether the decision of a woman to terminate her pregnancy falls within this class of protected decisions. I have no doubt that it does. This decision is one that will have profound psychological, economic and social consequences for the pregnant woman. The circumstances giving rise to it can be complex and varied and there may be, and usually are, powerful considerations militating in opposite directions. It is a decision that deeply reflects the way the woman thinks about herself and her relationship to others and to society at large. It is not just a medical decision; it is a profound social and ethical one as well. Her response to it will be the response of the whole person.

It is probably impossible for a man to respond, even imaginatively, to such a dilemma not just because it is outside the realm of his personal experience (although this is, of course, the case) but because he can relate to it only by objectifying it, thereby eliminating the subjective elements of the female psyche which are at the heart of the dilemma....

Given then that the right to liberty guaranteed by s. 7 of the Charter gives a woman the right to decide for herself whether or not to terminate her pregnancy, does s. 251 of the *Criminal Code* violate this right? Clearly it does. The purpose of the section is to take the decision away from the woman and give it to a committee. Furthermore, as the Chief Justice correctly points out, the committee bases its decision on "criteria entirely unrelated to [the pregnant woman's] priorities and aspirations." The fact that the decision whether a woman will be allowed to terminate her pregnancy is in the hands of a committee is just as great a violation of the woman's right to personal autonomy in decisions of an intimate and private nature as it would be if a committee were established to decide whether a woman should be allowed to continue her pregnancy. Both these arrangements violate the woman's right to liberty by deciding for her something that she has the right to decide for herself...

...[A]s the Chief Justice and Beetz J. point out, the present legislative scheme for the obtaining of an abortion clearly subjects pregnant women to considerable emotional stress as well as to unnecessary physical risk. I believe, however, that the flaw in the present legislative scheme goes much deeper than that. In essence, what it does is assert that the woman's capacity to reproduce is not to be subject to her own control. It is to be subject to the control of the state. She may not choose whether to exercise her existing capacity or not to exercise it. This is not, in my view, just a matter of interfering with her right to liberty in the sense (already discussed) of her right to personal autonomy in decision-making, it is a direct interference with her physical "person" as well. She is truly being treated as a means—a means to an end which she does not desire but over which she has no control. She is the passive recipient of a decision made by others as to whether her body is to be used to nurture a new life. Can there be anything that comports less with human dignity and self-respect? How can a woman in this position have any sense of security with respect to her person? I believe that s. 251 of the *Criminal Code* deprives the pregnant woman of her right to security of the person as well as her right to liberty.

Questions for Discussion

1   Justice Wilson argues that preventing a woman from controlling her own reproductive capacity (e.g. by requiring her to carry a pregnancy to term) treats her as merely a means to an end, and a "passive recipient of a decision made by others." Is she right, and if so, does that imply that it is morally forbidden to act in such a manner?

2   Justice Wilson states that "It is probably impossible for a man to respond, even imaginatively, to such a dilemma." Are men in a different situation from women who have never been pregnant, in this respect? Is abortion an issue which should be decided by women exclusively?

3   To what extent should the law take account of the fact that the same legal requirements may have a different impact on different people?

Bill C-43   *An Act respecting abortion*

After the old abortion law was struck down, the government introduced a new bill concerning abortion. This new bill tried to take account of the Supreme Court's objections to the old law by, for example, dispensing with the requirement of approval by a hospital committee, which had in practice made abortions very difficult for many women to obtain. This bill was attacked by many pro-choice advocates for leaving ultimate control of women's reproduction in the hands of the medical profession, and by many pro-life advocates for making it too easy to meet the requirements for an abortion (especially by allowing mental and psychological health to be considered).

* * *

1. Sections 287 and 288 of the *Criminal Code* are repealed and the following substituted therefor:

"**287.** (1) Every *person who induces an abortion on a female person* is guilty of an indictable offence and liable to imprisonment for *a term not exceeding two* years, unless the abortion is induced by or under the direction of a medical practitioner who is of the opinion that, if the abortion were not induced, the health or life of the female person would be likely to be threatened.

(2) For the purposes of this section,

"health" includes, for greater certainty, physical, mental and psychological health;

"medical practitioner," in respect of an abortion induced in a province, means a person who is entitled to practise medicine under the laws of that province;

"opinion" means an opinion formed using generally accepted standards of the medical profession.

(3) For the purposes of this section and section 288, inducing an abortion does not include using a drug, device or other means on a female person that is likely to prevent implantation of a fertilized ovum.

Question for discussion

1 Does there need to be a law concerning abortion?

Abortion Injunction Vacated:

Daigle v. Tremblay

A. Anne McLellan

One important legal case concerning Canadian abortion law arose in the period after the Morgentaler decision and before the new law was proposed: This was the case of Daigle v. Tremblay. In this case, a pregnant woman decided to have an abortion, and the biological father of the fetus (whose romantic relationship with the woman had ended) tried to get an injunction to prevent the abortion. In this article concerning the Supreme Court's decision in that case, McLellan surveys the prevailing Canadian legal thinking about the status of the fetus and the authority of the father concerning it.

* * *

On July 8, 1989 Chantal Daigle left her home in Chibougamau, Québec, with her brother, to drive to Sherbrooke, where she had made an appointment to have an abortion. As she began this trip, the purpose of which was intensely private, she had no idea that she soon would become, for both the pro- and anti-choice movements in Canada, symbolic of all that they believe to be wrong with the present state of the law regarding abortion. In a very few weeks, Chantal Daigle would go from being an unknown 21-year-old to "newsmaker of the year."[1]

The "story" of Chantal Daigle is well known to everyone; her pregnancy, her failed relationship with Jean-Guy Tremblay, her decision to terminate her pregnancy, Tremblay's attempts to stop the abortion, the Québec courts' granting Tremblay's request for an injunction,[2] her decision to have an abortion, in defiance of the order of the Québec Court of Appeal[3] and, finally, vindication from the Supreme Court of Canada when it allowed her appeal.[4]

This comment will focus primarily upon the decision of the Supreme Court of Canada, the result of which was rendered on August 8, but the reasons for which were released only on November 16, 1989. I will consider what, if anything, this decision adds to our knowledge and understanding of a woman's right to choose to terminate her pregnancy, the rights of the fetus and the rights of fathers.

It should be pointed out that this case does not deal, strictly speaking, with "constitutional" issues.[5] The decision of the Supreme Court of Canada is an exercise in statutory interpretation, in particular, the interpretation of the Québec *Charter of Rights and Freedoms*. The task of the Court was to determine if the phrase "human being," as used in the Québec *Charter of Rights and Freedoms*, included a fetus. In answering this question, the Supreme Court of Canada relied primarily upon a consider-

ation of the status of the fetus under the Civil Code of Québec.

The Supreme Court of Canada enumerated three arguments which were made by counsel for the Respondent, Jean-Guy Tremblay, to support the injunction: (1) that the fetus had a right to life under the Québec *Charter of Rights and Freedoms*; (2) that the Appellant, Chantal Daigle, would violate this right by having an abortion; (3) that an injunction was an appropriate remedy by which to protect this right.

Ultimately, the Supreme Court of Canada concluded that it needed to address only the first of these issues, since if there were no substantive rights of the fetus upon which to base an injunction, it would be vacated. Therefore, two of the issues raised by the Appellant, in response to the Respondent's arguments, were never addressed by the Court; the appropriateness of the remedy of injunction, if the fetus were found to have rights of some sort, and the federalism argument, that an injunction would have the effect of prohibiting abortion, a matter within exclusive federal jurisdiction. The Court, exercising its characteristic judicial restraint,[6] simply declared that it would answer no more questions than required to determine the appeal. Based on its decision that there were no substantive rights to justify the issuing of an injunction in the first place, the Court needed to go no further in its deliberations.

The Respondent argued that the substantive rights upon which an injunction could be based were: (1) that the fetus had a right to life, under the Québec *Charter of Rights and Freedoms*; (2) that the fetus had a right to life under the *Canadian Charter of Rights and Freedoms*; and (3) that the Respondent, as "potential father,"[7] had a right to be heard in respect of decisions regarding his potential child.

It is the first of these three arguments to which the Supreme Court of Canada devotes most of its judgement. The Québec *Charter* guarantees that, "Every human being has a right to life...he also possesses juridical personality."[8] It should be pointed out that there is no reference in the Québec *Charter* to the fetus or foetal rights. In addition, the Court found no cases dealing with foetal rights under the Québec *Charter*.

Counsel for the Respondent made much of the linguistic interpretation of the phrase "human being," seemingly based on something akin to the plain meaning rule. The Respondent argued that "human" was in reference to the human race and that "being" related to the state of being in "existence," and that the fetus was included within both notions.

If this argument seems somewhat mechanistic and one-dimensional, do not be alarmed; the Court viewed it in much the same way. The Court makes it plain that the question which it was asked to resolve is a "legal" one, not a philosophical, theological, scientific or linguistic one,[9] although all might provide some assistance or background in resolving the "legal" issue. Indeed, the asserted linguistic approach would make strangely simple the most contentious of issues, that of the definition of human being. Questions of when life begins, and when a "life form" becomes a human being, are deeply divisive and morally difficult issues which cannot be resolved by reference to a dictionary.

Much was made of the differing uses of the words "human being" and "person" in the Québec *Charter*. It is only to human beings that the right of life is guaranteed. Persons are guaranteed other, and arguably, lesser rights, such as respect for their private life and peaceful enjoyment of their property. Although the Court makes no final decision on this issue, it appears likely that the choice of words was dictated by a desire on the part of the Québec National Assembly to make clear that only natural persons or human beings possess the right to life, while artificial persons, such as corporate entities, might assert and enjoy the other rights guaranteed.

The Supreme Court of Canada quite reasonably concluded that the Québec *Charter* displayed no clear intent on the issue of who was to be included within the term "human being." Indeed, as the Court pointed out, one would expect that on such a controversial issue, if the National Assembly had intended to include protection for the fetus within this term, they would have explicitly said so.

Since the language of the Québec *Charter* displayed no clear intent on the meaning of the phrase "human being," the Court turned to the Civil Code to see if the provisions of the Code, or its interpretation, offered an answer to this definitional problem. The Court involved itself in a lengthy analysis of various provisions of the Code[10] and ultimately concluded that the Code "does not generally accord a fetus legal personality."[11] Indeed, the Court suggested that a fetus is treated as a person under the Civil Code only where it is necessary to do so, in order to protect its interests after it is born.

The Court found further confirmation for its interpretation of the Civil Code in Anglo-Canadian common law, in which it has been recognized generally that, to enjoy rights, a fetus must be born alive and have a separate existence from its mother.[12] It is interesting that in its survey of Canadian law, the Court refers to three recent cases involving foetal protection under provincial child welfare legislation. In two of these cases,[13] the Courts found that the fetus was a "child" in need of protection. In the third case, that of Baby R,[14] the BC Supreme Court concluded that a fetus was not a child, for the purposes of such legislation. This latter case is in line with English authority, which has reached the same conclusion under similar legislation.[15] While the Supreme Court offers no opinion on the merits of these conflicting authorities, it is not unreasonable to suggest that the Court feels some discomfort, and likely disagreement, with the above-noted cases, which interpreted "child" as including the fetus.

After this fairly lengthy exercise in statutory interpretation, the Supreme Court of Canada concluded that for the purposes of the Québec *Charter of Rights and Freedoms*, the term "human being" did not include a fetus.

The Court quickly dealt with the remaining two substantive rights arguments of the Respondent. The first of these was that the *Canadian Charter of Rights and Freedoms* provided the fetus with an independent right to life, under s.7. Yet again, the Supreme Court of Canada avoided answering this question.[16] The Supreme Court invoked its decision in *Dolphin Delivery*,[17] in which it concluded that the *Charter* did not apply to private disputes. It should be remembered that the facts of this case involve Jean Tremblay seeking an injunction against Chantal Daigle, a matter which the Court describes as a private civil dispute. There was no law to which Tremblay could point, nor any government action, which created the asserted violation of s.7. However, there may be an argument involving government "inaction," which the respondent could have invoked. The argument would be that, by not legislating to protect the rights of the fetus, either the Québec National Assembly or the federal Parliament was violating the right to life of the fetus. This raises an issue of major significance in the interpretation of the *Charter*, that of whether the *Charter* can be construed as imposing positive obligations upon government to act, in certain circumstances.[18]

The s.7 *Charter* argument raised by the Respondent was preemptively discarded by the Supreme Court of Canada, on the basis that none of the counsel present chose to offer arguments challenging the correctness of *Dolphin Delivery*. Hence, the Supreme Court saw it as a "full answer" to the *Charter* argument. It is interesting to speculate as to whether the Supreme Court is indicating that it would be receptive to arguments, questioning the broad proposition stated in *Dolphin Delivery* that the *Charter* does not apply to so-called private disputes.

The Supreme Court of Canada concluded in its assessment of the substantive rights arguments by briefly addressing the father's rights issue. The Respondent argued that, since he had played an equal part in the conception of the potential child, he should have an equal say in that which happened to it. The Supreme Court found no case law to support this proposition, the practical effect of which would be to provide a "potential father" with a veto over a woman's decision in relation to the fetus she was carrying.

The Supreme Court of Canada declined to answer many of the interesting *Charter* questions raised in this appeal. Some of them are: (1) the rights of the fetus, if any, under s.7 of the *Canadian Charter of*

Rights and Freedoms, an issue which the Court has successfully avoided in both this case and *Borowski*; (2) the balance that must be struck between a woman's right to liberty and security and the rights or interest of the fetus; (3) the rights, if any, of potential fathers; (4) the possibility that the *Charter* may give rise to positive obligations upon government to act, at least in certain circumstances, to protect guaranteed rights and; (5) the possibility that the Supreme Court will reconsider its decision in *Dolphin Delivery*, in relation to the application of the *Charter* to private disputes.

In some ways, this was an easy case for the Supreme Court of Canada. Undoubtedly, it was correct that the Québec National Assembly did not intend to extend protection to a fetus when it used the expression "human being" in s.1 of the Québec *Charter*. Therefore, if there is no right to life recognized for a fetus, in either Québec human rights legislation or the Civil Code, then the only alternative would appear to be the *Canadian Charter of Rights and Freedoms*. The Court was able to deny the *Charter's* application to these facts in three short paragraphs. Further, the right of the "potential father" to assert a claim over his unborn progeny, notwithstanding the objections of the mother, is a claim that has virtually no support in English, Canadian, and American law and hence could be dismissed with even greater speed and certainty.

What do we know at the end of that which the Supreme Court of Canada referred to as the "ordeal" of Chantal Daigle? Simply, that neither the civil law of Québec nor the common law of the other nine provinces, recognizes the right to life of a fetus. In the absence of either provincial or federal law recognizing such a right, a woman's right to seek an abortion seems clear. Fathers' rights, in this context, are viewed as nonexistent. Therefore, we can conclude that, until the federal Parliament, or a provincial legislature, attempts to place new restrictions upon a woman's right to control her body, there will be no further "ordeals," such as that endured by Chantal Daigle.[19]

Notes

1   As described in Chatelaine, January, 1990.

2   An interlocutory injunction was granted against Daigle by Mr. Justice Viens of the Québec Superior Court, on July 17, 1989. An appeal from this decision was heard by the Québec Court of Appeal on July 20, 1989. It rendered its judgement on July 26, and in a 3-2 decision, denied the request of the Appellant to vacate the injunction.

3   In fact, the Québec Court of Appeal upheld the interlocutory injunction issued by Mr. Justice Viens. It stated, in part:

   ...the Court grants the request for an interlocutory injunction, orders the Respondent to refrain, under threat of legal penalty, from having an abortion or taking recourse voluntarily to any method which directly or indirectly would lead to the death of the fetus which she is presently carrying.

4   During the summer recess, due to the urgency of the matter, five Justices of the Supreme Court of Canada heard the Appellant's application for leave to appeal, on August 1. Leave was granted the same day and the appeal was heard on August 8, before the entire Court.

5   There is a brief reference in the judgement to the inapplicability of the *Canadian Charter of Rights and Freedoms*. I suppose that if one views provincial human rights legislation as being of a "quasi constitutional" status, then, any interpretation thereof might be described as raising a "constitutional" question.

6   See Morgentaler (No. 2), [1988] 1 S.C.R. 30; *Borowski* v. *Canada* [1989] 1 S.C.R. 342.

7   The language of "potential father" is that used by the Supreme Court.

8   Section 1 of the Québec *Charter of Rights and Freedoms*, R.S.Q., c.C-12. In addition, Section 2

of the Québec *Charter* states: "Every human being whose life is in peril has a right to assistance."

9 The question the Supreme Court had to answer was whether the Québec legislature had accorded the fetus personhood. I think the Court rightly suggests that classifying the fetus for the purpose of a particular law or for scientific or philosophical purposes may be fundamentally different tasks. The Court describes the ascribing of personhood to the fetus, in law, as a fundamentally normative task.

10 In particular, *Civil Code of Lower Canada*, arts. 18, 338, 345, 608, 771, 838, 945, 2543.

11 Unreported decision of the Supreme Court of Canada, File no. 21553, Nov. 16, 1989, at 23.

12 This view can be contrasted with that of Bernier, J.C.A., of the Québec Court of Appeal, where he states:

"He (the fetus) is not an inanimate object nor anyone's property but a living human being distinct from that of the mother who bears him,...and who from the outset has the right to life and to the protection of those who conceived him."

13 *Re Children's Aid Society of City of Belleville and T* (1987), 590 O.R. (2d) 204 (Ont. Prov. Ct.); *Re Children's Aid Society for the District of*

Kenora and J.L. (1981), 134 D.L.R. (3d) 249 (Ont. Prov. Ct).

14 *Re Baby R* (1988), 15 R.F.L. (3d) 225 (B.C.S.C.)

15 *In Re F*, [1988] 2 W.L.R. 128 (C.A.).

16 As it did in *Borowski, supra*, fn.6.

17 *R.W.D.S.U.* v. *Dolphin Delivery Ltd.*, [1986] 2 S.C.R. 573.

18 See generally, Slattery, Brian, "A Theory of the *Charter*," (1987) 2 Osgoode H.L.J. 701.

19 Indeed, the reason offered by the Court for continuing the hearing, after Daigle's counsel announced that she had obtained an abortion in defiance of the terms of the interlocutory injunction, was "so that the situation of women in the position in which Ms. Daigle found herself could be clarified." Technically, the issues raised in this appeal became moot upon Daigle obtaining an abortion.

Questions for Discussion

1 How much say should a "potential father" have concerning what is to become of a fetus?

2 Should a fetus be considered a "human being"? How much of a role should the courts play in making this decision?

Making Distinctions About Abortion

Christine Overall

In the following article, Overall discusses the distinction, made possible by modern technology, between removing a fetus from a woman's uterus, and killing the fetus. She argues that there may be some hope for the abortion debate in this distinction, but warns us to consider the entire social atmosphere, including education about options, attitudes toward parenting, and various kinds of support for women.

*　　　*　　　*

(Excerpts from Chapter 4: Abortion)

Until recently it seems fair—and obvious—to say, the main objection to abortion by those who find it morally wrong has depended primarily upon the indubitable empirical fact that abortion results in the death of the embryo/fetus.[1] (Some objections to abortion may also be founded upon overt or covert misogyny: a desire to punish women for "illicit" sexual behaviour or to control women through the denial of reproductive choice.[2] In later chapters I shall examine both the patriarchally enforced connections and disconnections between sexuality and reproduction, and the use of reproductive technology to control women. For now, however, I shall assume that the central and arguably most defensible objection to abortion is that it kills the embryo/fetus.)

But with the arrival of new developments in reproductive technology and neonatal care, what was once an indubitable empirical fact is changing. It is becoming clear that abortion really consists of two potentially distinct aspects: (1) the (premature) emptying of the uterus (that is, the expulsion of the embryo/fetus), and (2) causing the death of the embryo/fetus.[3] In the past (1) has virtually always resulted in (2); the embryo/fetus dies either during or immediately after the process of prematurely removing it from the uterus. So closely linked have these two events been that some philosophers have even denied abortion as consisting essentially of (2).[4] However, that (1) and (2) are distinct, though causally related, has been recognized at least implicitly by other philosophers—for example, within the context of discussion of the Roman Catholic doctrine of double effect.[5]

It is because abortion consists of these two events that two alleged rights are commonly discussed in connection with the abortion issue. These are (a) the alleged right of the pregnant woman to control her own body, and (b) the alleged right of the embryo/fetus to life. The two are in conflict, and this is because until now the exercise of one alleged right has precluded the exercise of the other. If the woman exercises her alleged right to control her body by having her uterus emptied, the embryo/fetus dies; if the embryo/fetus exercises, or better, is permitted to exercise, its alleged right to life, this severely reduces (if not eliminates) the woman's control over her body.

Furthermore, the fact that abortion consists of these two events and that therefore the two alleged rights are in apparent conflict has led to the generation of two staunchly opposed positions about the morality of abortion, commonly called the "liberal" position and the "conservative" position. The liberal position, putting its emphasis on event (1) of the abortion process and alleged right (a), avows that abortion is not (at least in most cases) morally wrong. The conservative position, putting its emphasis on event (2) of the abortion process and alleged right (b), avows that abortion is (at least in most cases) morally wrong.[6] The liberal position has ordinarily been associated with feminism, whereas the conservative position appears to be nonfeminist or antifeminist in character.

However, the very nature of abortion and of the related moral issues is changing and will change further because of recent developments in reproductive technology. These developments will mean that the two hitherto causally linked events, (1) the emptying of the uterus and (2) the death of the embryo/fetus, can be severed. The expulsion of the embryo/fetus will no longer mean its death.

This possibility is suggested by the production of embryos through in vitro fertilization.[7] Ordinarily, if fertilization and embryo development proceed normally, the embryo is either implanted in its donor mother or a surrogate or is stored in a frozen state for possible future use. So far embryos are usually developed in vitro only to the sixteen-cell stage before being implanted. However, the development of frozen embryo banks suggest that the actual length of time of the embryo's independence of the uterus can be considerably extended beyond a few days.[8] Moreover, perhaps even more important, a type of "embryo adoption" can be effected by removing an embryo through uterine lavage from the uterus of one woman and implanting it directly in that of another.[9]

What these processes suggest is that there is a time, near the beginning of its development, albeit so far a very limited time, when the embryo/fetus need not be so dependent for its existence upon the occupancy of a uterus, or at least, of any particular uterus—for example, that of its biological mother. And of course at the other end of prenatal existence the age of viability—the point at which a relatively developed fetus is able to survive ex utero with the help of sophisticated support systems—is gradually declining. Therefore although it remains true that the embryo/fetus in utero is fully dependent upon the woman who sustains it, in such a way that its well-being is not usually separable from hers, it can be anticipated that in the future, expulsion from the uterus will ordinarily not result in the death of the embryo/fetus. This potential development provides the opportunity for a reexamination of the issue of the morality of abortion. It permits us to keep quite separate the two alleged rights mentioned earlier, of the woman to control her body and of the embryo/fetus to its life.

In this chapter I shall recast the issues surrounding abortion in a way that may satisfy both the liberal and the conservative. It preserves the woman-oriented insights of the liberal position without being forced to sacrifice all of the conservative's concern for the embryo/fetus. This new approach emerges by focusing upon what seems to be rather wide consensus about some aspects of abortion. The consensus may not have been very apparent until now because of the fact that the emptying of the uterus resulted in the death of the embryo/fetus. But if, instead, we examine our responses—our "intuitions," as some have called them— about each of these events separately, a surprising degree of agreement appears. This agreement may help to reduce the confusion discussed in chapter 3 [of *Ethics and Human Reproduction*] in attitudes toward and treatment of the embryo/fetus. (However, it does not by any means solve all the problems associated with abortion. Rather, it would be fair to say that it displaces them.)

Abortion and the Embryo/Fetus

Like many others, I propose to discuss abortion in terms of rights. To say that a person has a right to have or to do something is to imply that it would be wrong to interfere with her having it or doing it.[10] I do not assume that any rights are necessarily absolute—that is, that they hold whatever else may be the case. However, rights must be regarded as special claims or entitlements that can be set aside or interfered with, if at all, only on the basis of other compelling moral grounds.

R.M. Hare points out that rights are "the stamping grounds of institutionists,"[11] and as I have indicated, I shall argue on the basis of our responses to, or "intuitions" about, some specific moral situations. However, the intuitions advanced here are not in support of claims about the possession of rights. Instead, they are used to support claims about the *absence* of rights.

Let us begin with the heart of the conservative position: claim (b), that the embryo/fetus has a right to life. Does it indeed have such a right? If so, when is the right acquired—at the time of conception, motility, viability? If not, why not? What distinguishes it from beings that do in fact possess this right? These questions are apparently endlessly debatable. In this discussion I assume no views about the embryo/fetus' alleged right to life; I am agnostic as to the answers to the questions listed above.

Instead I offer a different statement about rights and the embryo/fetus—or rather, about the absences of rights: (c) The pregnant woman (or anyone else, e.g., a physician) has no right to kill the embryo/fetus.

The claim is not without precedents, and indeed seems to match the intuitions of many who have written about abortion. Judith Jarvis Thomson, for example, who espouses a liberal view about the morality of abortion, has this to say:

> I am not arguing for the right to secure the death of the unborn child. It is easy to confuse these two things in that up to a certain point in the life of the fetus it is not able to survive outside the mother's body; hence removing it from her body guarantees its death. But they are importantly different.... A woman may be utterly devastated by the thought of a child, a bit of herself, put out for adoption and never seen or heard of

> again. She may therefore want not merely that the child be detached from her, but more, that it die.... [But] the desire for the child's death is not one which anybody may gratify, should it turn out to be possible to detach the child alive.[12]

Other philosophers have expressed agreement with this view;[13] for example, Mary Anne Warren remarks, "if abortion could be performed without killing the fetus, she [the mother] would never possess the *right* to have the fetus destroyed, for the same reasons that she has no right to have an infant destroyed."[14] Margaret A. Somerville argues that it is both unethical and illegal (within the context of Canadian law) for a physician intentionally and unnecessarily to kill the fetus, because even when an abortion is legally performed neither the mother nor the physician has the moral or legal right to kill it unnecessarily.[15]

What exactly does (c) mean? In general, if X has a right to life, then Y has no right to kill X. Conversely, if Y has a right to kill X, then X has no (or a very minimal) right to life. However, even if X (in this case, the embryo/fetus) has itself no right to life (i.e., no right not to be killed) or even if we do not know whether it has a right to life, this does not imply that another being, Y, has the right to kill X. Nor does this imply that it is morally right to kill X. There is no prima facie obligation on any other being, Z, to permit Y to kill X; and indeed, under some circumstances, Z may even have an obligation to prevent Y from killing X. That is, even if X has no right to life, it may nevertheless be wrong to kill X;[16] therefore Y does not have a right to kill X.

Claim (c) may appear to threaten the heart of the liberal position and to be inconsistent with a feminist approach to abortion.

But notice that in both Thomson's and Warren's formulation in (c), explicit reference is made to the important distinction between events (1) expelling the embryo/fetus from the uterus, and (2) causing the death of the embryo/fetus. It is this distinction that helps to make the claim plausible. Reflection upon several actual and possible cases will illustrate and lend support to (c).

Consider first that occasionally, after a late abortion involving the injection of a saline solution into the woman's uterus, the fetus is born alive. An attempt is ordinarily made to resuscitate the baby, damaged though it may be by the abortion process. No one would suppose that the mother of such a baby has a right to strangle it, slit its throat, suffocate it, or otherwise kill it. Nor has anyone else, including the physician who performed the abortion and subsequent delivery, any such right on behalf of the mother.

Similarly, imagine that a baby is born very prematurely to a woman who had wanted an abortion but failed to obtain one (whether because of legal barriers, lack of access to abortion facilities, or whatever). Babies born as early as twenty-six weeks' gestational age, and sometimes less, may survive.[17] Suppose, then, that this unwanted baby is delivered spontaneously at twenty-six weeks. Once again, no one would be inclined to say that the mother or anyone else (whether acting independently or on the mother's behalf) has a right to kill it.

Third (and this is the most difficult example), consider the case of a typical "test-tube baby": that is, a one- to sixteen-cell embryo existing outside its biological mother's uterus in a culture medium. Tiny and undeveloped as it is, its parents (and anyone else) do not have a *right* to destroy it or have it destroyed. Here I disagree with arguments put forward by Helga Kuhse and Peter Singer. The former states, "there is no moral difference between discarding surplus human embryos and deliberately not creating them in the first place."[18] In another paper, Kuhse and Singer together appear to maintain that a couple who have donated sperm and eggs for in vitro fertilization have a right to refuse to permit excess embryos resulting therefrom either to be implanted (in the woman herself or in a surrogate) or to be frozen; in other words, they have a right to have the embryos "tipped down the sink" and thus destroyed.[19]

This, however, is mistaken. The parents do not have this right, mainly because they do not own the embryo. An individual does, in a limited sense at least, own his or her genetic material: a woman can be said to be the owner of her ova; a man of his sperm.[20] Women may soon donate or sell their eggs to egg banks, just as men now sell or donate their sperm to sperm banks. While objections deserve to be raised about the selling of genetic materials—in other words, about *what* can be done with them and the *ways* in which they are disposed of—there can be no doubt that one's gametes are one's own to dispose of, at least in the sense that they do not belong to anyone else. The individual from whom they are obtained has the clearest entitlement to determine their disposal, including their destruction—although there may be good consequentialist reasons to limit that entitlement (for example, to limit the person's ability to determine which individuals may be the recipients of the gametes). To the extent that an individual may be said to be the owner of her or his body parts, that individual also owns her or his own gametes and has some rights as to their preservation and destruction. There are, of course, problems in regarding parts of the body as one's property,[21] and there are important limitations on what one can do with parts of one's body. But there is at least an important sense in which my arm *is* mine (and no one else's), and in that sense my gametes are also mine.[22] Thus the couple in Kuhse and Singer's example does have the right to have these materials "tipped down the sink" (destroyed)—if, for example, one of them should change his or her mind about participation in the in vitro fertilization process.

By contrast, the sense of "mine" that pertains to one's body parts or one's gametes does not extend to embryos, even to embryos produced by means of one's own gametes. No one owns the embryo or fetus: for as an entity that may become a person, it is not something that can be owned. Joel Feinberg shows this very clearly by means of two arguments:[23] First,

> if fetuses were property, we would find nothing odd in the notion that they can be bought or sold, rented out, leased, used as collateral on loans, and so on. But no one has ever seriously entertained such suggestions.

Of course, as human reproduction becomes increasingly commodified, these suggestions may be entertained more seriously, but their conceptual and moral inappropriateness remains. According to Feinberg's second argument,

> one would think that the father would have equal or near-equal rights of disposal if the fetus were "property." It is not in his body, to be sure, but he contributed as much genetically to its existence as did the mother and might therefore make just as strong (or just as weak) a claim to ownership over it.

But neither claim would make very good conceptual sense.

Once again, the claim fails to make sense because the embryo/fetus is not the sort of thing that can be owned. Unlike an individual egg or sperm cell, an embryo may become a person, and it is therefore different from mere body parts.

Some might be tempted to argue that an individual ovum or sperm may become a person also. For example, Peter Singer and Deane Wells state that since it is not wrong to destroy one's gametes, it is also not wrong to destroy an embryo, an embryo being simply a fortuitous coming together of egg and sperm.[24] But that that claim is misleading at best is shown by the fact that it is an embryo, not an egg or sperm cell, which is transferred to a woman's uterus after external fertilization. The embryo, but not the ovum or sperm alone, may become a person.

Thus because no one—not even its parents—owns the embryo/fetus, no one has the *right* to destroy it, even at a very early developmental stage, and the couple in Kuhse and Singer's example are not entitled to tip the embryo down the sink. This is not to deny that the genetic parents are ordinarily authorized to make some decisions about the fate of the embryo/fetus[25]. The point here is simply that to destroy an embryo is not an automatic entitlement held by anyone, including its genetic parents.

If the three cases cited so far are persuasive with regard to the claim that the mother (and everyone else) has no right to kill the embryo/fetus, it might be thought that this absence of a right is due to the location of the embryo/fetus. In the first two examples the fetus is born; it is now a baby outside the mother's body. In the third case the embryo exists independently in a petri dish.

However, it is not because of some change in location, or because of development in a location independent of the mother's body, that there exists no right to kill it. To suppose that merely location determines this absence of right is to confuse claim (c) with some aspect of another claim, to be called (d), which will be discussed later. From the perspective of a woman experiencing pregnancy, the location of the embryo/fetus is naturally of the utmost importance, and that fact must be taken account of. But the point being made here is just that the location itself of the embryo/fetus can neither endow a right upon it nor deny a right to it.

At this point it should be noted that although the mother (and everyone else) has no right to kill the embryo/fetus, it may nevertheless in some cases not be wrong for her—or, more likely, a physician deputized by her—to kill the embryo/fetus or to permit it to die. For to say that a person has no right to do something does not preclude her doing it, on occasion, and being morally right in doing so. An obvious example in this context is a case in which the embryo is threatening the mother's health—for example, when growing in the fallopian tube. Other possible examples include cases of severe fetal deformity or illness. Thus the general possibility must be recognized that at times it might be right for someone in some circumstances to kill the embryo/fetus or to allow it to die, and this might be so regardless of its location—whether in its mother's uterus or growing in a petri dish, and regardless of the fact that she (and everyone else) has no general right to kill it.

Abortion and the Pregnant Woman

Now consider the heart of the liberal position: claim (a), that the mother has the right to control her own body. Like (b), about fetal rights, (a) has been endlessly debated. Thomson states, "if a human being has any just, prior claim to anything at all, he [sic] has a just, prior claim to his own body," and she suggests that "everyone would grant that."[26] But as she indicates, much of the dispute has concerned the possible limitations on that alleged right and the degree to which it can be overcome by other rights, such as alleged rights of the embryo/fetus. In this discussion, although I assume that the parts of a woman's body are hers and no one else's, I make no general assumptions about women's alleged right to control their bodies; I am agnostic as to the solutions to the problems just cited.

Instead, I offer a different statement about rights and women, or rather, once again, about the absence of rights: (d) The embryo/fetus has no right to occupancy of its mother's (or anyone else's) uterus.[27]

This claim is a specific instance of the more general principle that no one has the right to the use of anyone's body: that is, presumably, part of what makes rape and slavery wrong. Maintaining our bodily integrity and autonomy is essential to our identity and sense of ourselves as persons; this is true no less in the case of pregnancy than in other cases.... [T]he relationship of a pregant woman to her reproductive organs and capacities cannot be likened to the relationship of landlord to rental property. It is precisely because her body in no way resembles a building awaiting occupancy that it is impossible for anything—including the embryo/fetus—to have a right to the use of it.

Claim (d) is very clearly illustrated by Thomson's famous violinist example. Suppose that a famous violinist is ill and will survive only by being hooked up to some specific individual's kidneys. "[N]obody has any right to use your kidneys unless you give him such a right; and nobody has the right against you that you shall give him this right—if you do allow him to go on using your kidneys, this is a kindness on your part, and not something he can claim against you."[28]

Claim (d) appears to undermine the conservative position on abortion. But once again, the distinction between emptying the uterus and causing the death of the embryo/fetus must be maintained, and a brief consideration of some possible cases will lend support to (d).

Imagine, first, that an egg is withdrawn from a woman and is fertilized in vitro with her partner's sperm. However, during the time in which the embryo is growing to a multicellular stage, the woman unfortunately is killed in a car accident. No one could plausibly say that another woman must be made the host(ess?) of the "orphan" embryo. For the embryo has no right to the occupancy of another woman's body. The fact that it is dependent—first on the culture medium in which it divides and then upon a uterus, should one be available—does not give it the right to inhabit a woman's body.

Now suppose that in the same type of case, several eggs are withdrawn and fertilized. One is reimplanted, develops, and becomes a healthy baby successfully delivered nine months later. The other embryos are frozen for possible later use. But then several years go by and the woman enters her forties: she feels too old to have another baby. Or imagine that in the meantime she develops diabetes, a condition that may make pregnancy perilous for her and the embryo/fetus. The frozen embryos then have no right—against the interests of her health and her life situation—to be implanted. For they too have no right to the occupancy of their biological mother's uterus. Those who may be inclined to say that these embryos do have such a right are confusing that claim either with the more usual but unproved conservative claim that the embryo/fetus has a right to life, or with claim (c), that no one has the right to kill the embryo/fetus.

However, it should also be noted that claim (d), that the embryo/fetus has no right to occupancy of any woman's uterus, does not imply that it will never be wrong for a woman to terminate its occupancy—that is, to abort it. Circumstances may be such that it would be wrong for her to end the pregnancy, in that she has incurred some degree of responsibility for the embryo/fetus. For example, it might be wrong for a mother to abort her embryo/fetus when its conception was planned, it is well advanced in development, and her only reason is that she is tired of her pregnancy;[29] the abortion might also be wrong when its only justification is that the embryo/fetus has been discovered to be of the "wrong" sex. Thus the general possibility should be recognized that it might sometimes be wrong for a woman in some circumstances to end the embryo/fetus' occupancy of her uterus, and this might be so regardless of the fact that it has no general right to such occupancy.

Some Implications

If it were not for developing reproductive technology, the two claims, (c) and (d), put forward here would continue to generate an insoluble conflict, in practice if not in theory. To say that no one has a right to kill the embryo/fetus seems to say that abortion is wrong; but to say that the embryo/fetus has no right to occupancy of its mother's (or anyone else's) uterus seems to say that abortion is not wrong.

If, however, it is becoming more and more possible for an embryo/fetus to survive outside its mother's body, or to be transferred successfully to the uterus of another woman who wants a child, abortion need no longer entail so much moral conflict. It could then be said that a woman may have an abortion, in the sense of expelling the embryo/fetus from her body, and the embryo/fetus may live. The solution could satisfy both the liberal, whose desire is to provide abortions for women who want them, and the conservative, whose aim is the preservation of fetal life. The feminist concern for women's reproductive control is not necessarily incompatible with a concern for the embryo/fetus.

Thus the position on abortion outlined here has both theoretical and practical advantages over the old battle lines. That is, it both helps to make sense of moral beliefs about the topic and it suggests actual positive consequences for behavior. I turn now to a consideration of these potential advantages.

When a spontaneous miscarriage occurs, people mourn—and perhaps not only for the woman whose pregnancy has ended but for the loss of a being they regard as valuable. In fact, great efforts have been made and are being made to preserve and enhance the life of the embryo/fetus in utero. While some treatments (such as fetal surgery) have the potential to oppress both the pregnant woman and her fetus, other forms of care (such as a nutritious diet and adequate prenatal care) are ususally beneficial to both and willingly assumed by pregnant women.

Yet these practices are rather difficult to reconcile with the usual liberal view on abortion, which tends to see the embryo/fetus as merely a disposable part of the mother's body. From an extreme liberal point of view, care for the embryo/fetus can be understood only by reference to the woman's care for herself, or by her desire to have a healthy child at the end of her pregnancy, or perhaps by the need to avoid unnecessary medical costs of providing for disabled children. And the liberal view is not improved by arguing that no body part is a *mere* part; or that a part takes its meaning from the whole, and that a person may value or despise parts of her body. For a woman may freely and legitimately choose to undergo cosmetic surgery, to donate a kidney, or to have her uterus removed: while such choices may be foolish or wise, hasty or well thought out, informed or ignorant, no one would argue that she should consider her moral responsibilities to her face, her kidney, or her uterus.

But the view defended here—that there is no general right to kill the embryo/fetus—raises the possibility that individuals also have responsibilities to the embryo/fetus itself. They lead us to suspect that perhaps no one has a *right* to injure, mutilate, or cause pain to it—that is, that there is at least a prima facie responsibility of nonmaleficence to it. The embryo/fetus therefore appears to have a different moral status than that which is possessed by a body part.

In saying this I wish to emphasize not just the responsibility of the pregnant woman, as do most advocates of prenatal care, but the social responsibility toward the embryo/fetus on the part of entities such as the state, corporations, and the medical care system. Furthermore, these responsibilities should not be permitted to override the consideration of the pregnant woman's health; that is, performance of the least mutilating type of abortion procedure for the fetus should not impose serious health risks upon the woman.

> If abortion is justified, then it should be performed in a way that gives the child a chance of survival, if there is any chance at all. The effort to save the aborted child and to find ways of saving all who are justifiably aborted would be a token of sincerity that the death of the child really was not in the scope of the intention.[30]

What exactly is the intention of a woman seeking an abortion is, surely, an empirical question. Often she may not have thought beyond the immediate goal of no longer being pregnant. In addition, she may feel that she does not want and/or is not able to care for an infant, or the child that it will become. Most people do not regard a desperate woman who attempts to abort herself as a potential killer. It is recognized, implicitly, that what she is trying to do is to end her pregnancy, to remove the embryo/fetus from her body. Moreover, most people probably feel particularly sympathetic to women who seek abortions when pregnancy results from rape or incest, or when it seriously threatens their life or health. Once again, the woman seems to be saying that she does not want, and will not permit, the embryo/fetus to occupy her uterus. Her goal is clearly to end her pregnancy, but not necessarily to kill the embryo/fetus. And to say that the former may not be wrong, although the latter may be, is preferable to the more peculiar view of

those who seem inclined to believe that an embryo/fetus has a right to life—except when it is the product of rape.

Is it the case that some women seeking abortions specifically desire the death of the embryo/fetus? Steven L. Ross argues that, indeed, some women "cannot be satisfied *unless* the fetus is killed; nothing else will do."[31] This desire, he says, is derived from the unique relationship of the parent to the embryo/fetus: that it is genetically related to her, and that she (as well as the father) has the most legitimate claim to raise the child. Thus for some, the feeling that "she and not any one else ought to raise whatever children she brings into the world" is a "deeply felt personal preference";[32] failure to raise one's own child can be avoided only by killing the embryo/fetus.

This kind of feeling, however, if and when it occurs (and the existence of surrogate mothers proves that it is not universal), does not justify killing the embryo/fetus. Although the relationship to the embryo/fetus is unique (and Ross does not fully understand it, for he says, "We cannot...love the fetus even if we wanted to, as we cannot be said to love anything we have not interacted with"[33]—there are certainly some women who would claim that they have both interacted with and loved their fetus), the mother does not own it and therefore is not entitled to have it killed. (Moreover, as I [argue elsewhere], it is important not to overestimate the moral significance of the link with one's own genetically related offspring.)

Hence writers like H. Tristram Engelhardt, Jr., are mistaken when they claim that the use of abortifacient devices that guarantee the death of the embryo/fetus is justified by "a woman's interests in not being a mother," and that "one would wish as well to forbid attempts, against the will of the mother, to sustain the life of an abortus prior to the established [legal] upper limit for abortions."[34] The policy at many North American hospitals that perform abortions is to attempt to resuscitate aborted fetuses that show signs of life. And surely, if abortion is seen primarily as the emptying of the uterus and no one has the right to kill the embryo/fetus, then some of the irony attendant upon "requiring a lifesaving medical team to be prepared to rush into the operating clinic in the event that the abortion team fails to achieve the fetus's death"[35] is reduced. There is, perhaps, an important moral distinction between killing and letting die. But once the mother's personal autonomy is respected by honoring her request to end her pregnancy (because the embryo/fetus has no right to occupy her uterus), there seems to be little reason for assuming that there is never anything morally wrong with letting the aborted fetus die. There may be cases in which this would be right—for example, if the embryo/fetus is irretrievably deformed or damaged by the abortion process—but this will not be true in all cases, and, as I suggested earlier, the abortion procedure itself should ideally be designed to minimize damage to the embryo/fetus. That is, the mother (and everyone else) is entitled to demand neither that the embryo/fetus be killed after abortion nor that it not be resuscitated.

This position permits the reexamination of some morally peculiar views about viability. Many have been inclined to agree with American abortion policy, which treats viability as the cutoff point for most permissible abortions. This view suggests that it is all right to expel the embryo/fetus from the uterus until the point in its devel-opment when it is able to survive outside the uterus—at which time it becomes impermissible to expel it. The anomaly is made even worse by the fact that while the age of fetal viability is declining, the age at which abortions can be performed safely (for the woman) is moving up. But neither sheer length of gestation nor capacity for survival outside the uterus confers on the embryo/fetus a right to occupancy of the uterus. Engelhardt points out that if reproductive technology develops to the point that an embryo/fetus could be brought to term in vitro, then "all conceptuses would be viable in the sense of being at a stage at which there are known survivors."[36] He then asks whether this should result in the prohibition of all abortions. But if we agree that the embryo/fetus has no right to occupancy of the uterus, we can see that such a general prohibition would not be justified in these circumstances. Achievement of viability does not confer rights on the embryo/fetus.

Having detailed some advantages of this approach to the abortion issue, it must be conceded that it also raises a good many problems. If fetal survival outside the uterus becomes more and more frequent, and the two claims (c) and (d) are accepted, then the moral quandaries will merely shift from the actual process of abortion to the events that follow the abortion. These problems include, but are not confined to, the following.

First, if fetal survival becomes commonplace, would there be an obligation to preserve all aborted fetuses? As Somerville points out, "arguing that the lives of viable to-be-aborted fetuses should be preserved even though they may be aborted is artificially to create a group of new-borns at much higher risk of being defective than babies born at term." These babies "are at a high risk of being mentally or physically handicapped by their premature expulsion into the world and...therefore require specialized and expensive treatment."[37]

Second, what limitations, if any, should be placed on the availability of abortion, understood as the emptying of the uterus? Those who advocate "embryo adoption"—the transfer of an embryo from an unwilling woman to a willing adoptive mother—argue that a woman "should be free to surrender her fetus for adoption at any time during pregnancy."[38] Since the embryo/fetus has no right to occupancy of its mother's uterus, this appears justifiable. But "embryo adoption" at all points during pregnancy is not yet technically possible, and in any case it raises its own moral problems: Should all aborted embryo/fetuses be candidates for adoption? What about those with defects? What women should be able to become their adoptive mothers? How should the decision be made?

Finally, the present reality is that there is still a period, perhaps about twenty-three weeks in length, in which an embryo/fetus is totally dependent upon the body of a woman for its continued existence. So it is necessary to consider the general policy implications of the position adumbrated here for this period of time in prenatal life. I suggest that claim (d) is most relevant to the early months of embryonic development. The fact that the embryo/fetus has no right to occupancy of its mother's (or any other woman's) uterus would sanction very early abortions on request, despite the fact that the embryos aborted will not now survive. Claim (c), on the other hand, is most relevant to later months of fetal development. The fact that the mother (or anyone else) has no right to kill the embryo/fetus

requires the performance of abortions in a way that, without compromising the pregnant woman's medical care, causes least mutilation and maximizes the fetus' chances of survival.[39]

It should now be clear that the development of new reproductive technologies both permits and requires the reevaluation of existing views about abortion. When fetal survival becomes routinely possible, it will be necessary to confront some very difficult practical questions about the treatment of the embryo/fetus. But these developments also enable us to make the crucial distinction between emptying the uterus and killing the embryo/fetus, and to see that while the embryo/fetus has no right to occupancy of its mother's (or anyone's) uterus, she (along with everyone else) has no right to kill the embryo/fetus.

Notes

An earlier version of part of this chapter, entitled "New Reproductive Technology: Some Implications for the Abortion Issue," appeared in *The Journal of Value Inquiry* 19 (1985): 279-292. The material is used here with the permission of the journal's editor.

1   Once again, "embryo/fetus" will be used here generally to refer to the developing zygote/embryo/fetus throughout its nine-month gestation, except when referring specifically to very early stages of gestation, when the term "embryo" will be used.

2   Cf. Janet Radcliffe Richards, *The Sceptical Feminist: A Philosophical Inquiry* (Harmondsworth, England: Penguin Books, 1980), pp. 263-290.

3   Mary B. Mahowald makes a similar distinction between different concepts of abortion. Abortion, she says, is either the "premature termination of pregnancy" or the "termination of fetal life." See "Concepts of Abortion and Their Relevance to the Abortion Debate," *Southern Journal of Philosophy* 20 (Summer 1982): 195. Compare Sissela Bok, Bernard N. Nathanson, and LeRoy Walters, "Commentary: The Unwanted Child: Caring for

the Fetus Born Alive after an Abortion," *Cases in Bioethics*, rev. ed. ed. Carol Levine and Robert M. Veatch (Hastings-on-Hudson: The Hastings Center, 1984), pp. 3, 5.

4   For example, see Joel Feinberg, "Abortion," in *Matters of Life and Death: New Introductory Essays in Moral Philosophy*, ed. Tom Regan (New York: Random House, 1981), p. 183.

5   See Susan T. Nicholson, "The Roman Catholic Doctrine of Therapeutic Abortion," in *Feminism and Philosophy*, ed. Mary Vetterling-Braggin, Frederick A. Elliston, and Jane English (Totowa, N.J.: Littlefield, Adams, 1978), p. 392. The distinction is also employed by John Morreall in "Of Marsupials and Men: A Thought Experiment on Abortion," *Dialogos* 37 (1981): 16; by Steven L. Ross in "Abortion and the Death of the Fetus," *Philosophy and Public Affairs* 11 (1982): 232; by Daniel I. Wikler in "Ought We to Save Aborted Fetuses?" *Ethics* 90 (1978): 64; and by Raymond M. Herbenick in "Remarks on Abortion, Abandonment, and Adoption Opportunities," in *Philosophy and Publics Affairs* 5 (1975): 98.

6   A "moderate" position on abortion, not discussed here, has also been defended. See L.W. Sumner, "Toward a Credible View of Abortion," *Canadian Journal of Philosophy* 4 (1974): 163-181.

7   An informative discussion of in vitro fertilization is given by John F. Leeton, Alan O. Trounson, and Carl Wood, in "IVF and ET: What It Is and How It Works," in *Test-Tube Babies: A Guide to Moral Questions, Present Techniques and Future Possibilities*, ed. William A.W. Walters and Peter Singer (Melbourne, Australia: Oxford University Press, 1982), pp. 2-10.

8   Ectogenesis, the growth of the fetus outside the human uterus, is discussed by William A.W. Walters in "Cloning, Ectogenesis, and Hybrids: Things to Come?" in *Test-Tube Babies*, pp. 115-117.

9   See Robert A. Freitas, Jr., "Fetal Adoption: A Technological Solution to the Problem of Abortion Ethics," *The Humanist* (May/June 1980): 22-23.

10 Cf. Ronald Dworkin, *Taking Rights Seriously* (Cambridge, Mass.: Harvard University Press, 1977), p. 188.

11 R.M. Hare, "Abortion and the Golden Rule," in *Philosophy and Sex*, ed. Robert Baker and Frederick Elliston (Buffalo: Prometheus Books, 1975), p. 357.

12 Judith Jarvis Thomson, "A Defense of Abortion,"

in *Moral Problems*, 2d ed., ed. James Rachels (New York: Harper & Row, 1975), p. 106.

13 Jane English, "Abortion: Introduction," in Vetterling-Braggin et al., *Feminism and Philosophy*, p. 422; Frances Myrna, "The Right to Abortion," in *Ethics for Modern Life*, ed. Raziel Abelson and Marie-Louise Friquegnon (New York: St. Martin's Press, 1982), pp. 114-115; David S. Levin, "Abortion, Personhood and Vagueness," *Journal of Value Inquiry* 19 (1985): 202-203.

14 Mary Anne Warren, " On the Moral and Legal Status of Abortion," in *Today's Moral Problems*, ed. Richard Wasserstrom (New York: Macmillan, 1975), p. 136, my emphasis.

15 Margaret A. Somerville, "Reflections on Canadian Abortion Law: Evacuation and Destruction—Two Separate Issues," *University of Toronto Law Journal* 31, no. 1 (1981), p. 12.

16 Cf. Charles B. Daniels, "Abortion and Potential," *Dialogue* 18 (1979): 223, 1 n.

17 Ernie W.D. Young, "Caring for Disabled Infants," *Hastings Center Report* 13 (August 1983): 16.

18 Helga Kuhse, "An Ethical Approach to IVF and ET: What Ethics is All About," in Walters and Singer, *Test-Tube Babies*, p. 34.

19 Helga Kuhse and Peter Singer, "The Moral Status of the Embryo," in Walters and Singer, *Test-Tube Babies*, pp. 57 ff.

20 See Robert P.S. Jansen, "Sperm and Ova as Property," *Journal of Medical Ethics* 11 (September 1985): 123-126.

21 See, for example, Warren, "On the Moral and Legal Status of Abortion," p. 121; Feinberg, "Abortion," p. 204; Sara Ann Ketchum, "The Moral Status of the Bodies of Persons," *Social Theory and Practice* 10 (Spring 1984): 25-27; and Leon R. Kass, "Thinking about the Body," *Hastings Center Report* 15 (February 1985): 23.

22 See Lori B. Andrews, "My Body, My Property," *Hastings Center Report* 16 (October 1986): 28-38. However, Andrews regards embryos as well as gametes as personal property and enthusiastically endorses financial compensation for body parts. For a dissenting view, that gametes "are, strictly speaking, not our private property, in the sense of individual interest, control and possession," see Joseph Fletcher, *Humanhood: Essays in Biomedical Ethics* (Buffalo: Prometheus Books, 1979), p. 118.

23 Feinberg, "Abortion," p. 204.

24 Peter Singer and Deane Wells, *The Reproduction*

Revolution: New Ways of Making Babies (Oxford: Oxford University Press, 1984), pp. 87-89. For criticisms of this view, see B.F. Scarlett, "The Moral Status of Embryos," *Journal of Medical Ethics* 2 (1984): 79-81. See also the response to Scarlett's arguments by Peter Singer and Helga Kuhse, *Journal of Medical Ethics* 2 (1984): 80-81.

25 The position taken here is very like that taken in *A Question of Life: The Warnock Report on Human Fertilisation and Embryology*, by Mary Warnock (Oxford: Basil Blackwell, 1985), p. 56.

26 Thomson, "A Defense of Abortion," pp. 95, 90.

27 Cf. Ellen Frankel Paul and Jeffrey Paul, "Self-Ownership, Abortion and Infanticide," *Journal of Medical Ethics* 5 (1979): 134.

28 Thomson, "A Defense of Abortion," p. 96.

29 Thomson gives a similar example, p. 105. Cf. Morreall, "Of Marsupials and Men," p. 11.

30 Germain Grisez, "Abortion: Ethical Arguments," in Wasserstrom, *Today's Moral Problems,* p. 102.

31 Ross, "Abortion and the Death of the Fetus," p. 238, his emphasis.

32 *Ibid.,* p. 240.

33 *Ibid.,* p. 243.

34 H. Tristram Engelhardt, Jr., "Viability and the Use of the Fetus," in *Ethics and Public Policy*, ed. Tom L. Beauchamp and Terry P. Pinkard (Englewood Cliffs, N.J.: Prentice-Hall, 1980), pp. 307-308.

35 Wikler, "Ought we to Save Aborted Fetuses?" p. 60. Cf. Paul and Paul, "Self-Ownership," p. 133; and Thomas P. Carney, *Instant Evolution: We'd Better Get Good at It* (Notre Dame, Ind.: University of Notre Dame Press, 1980), p. 16.

36 Engelhardt, "Viability and the Use of the Fetus," p. 307.

37 Somerville, "Birth Technology," pp. 23, 22.

38 Freitas, "Fetal Adoption," p. 23.

39 Cf. Sissela Bok, Bernard N. Nathanson, and LeRoy Walters, "Commentary: The Unwanted Child," pp. 2, 3, and 6.

Questions for Discussion

1 If a woman does have a right to an abortion, does that extend to having a right to have the fetus killed?

2 Should the decision about whether to save the life of an aborted fetus (where possible) depend in part on whether it is irretrievably deformed or damaged by the abortion process?

3 Is there anything wrong with the view that it is permissible to have an abortion before the fetus is viable, but then not permissible to have an abortion from the time when the fetus could survive outside the mother's uterus?

Comparative Judicial Embryology: Judges' Approaches to Unborn Human Life

Bernard M. Dickens

In this article, Dickens considers some recent legal cases which have stretched our ordinary thinking about the status of unborn humans. In these cases, judges have had to consider the point at which a fetus becomes a human being, the notion of "best interests" and its relation to rights, and the idea of "ownership" of undifferentiated pre-embryos.

*   *   *

In Canada, the United States, England and Australia judges have recently had occasion to address the law's approach to unborn human life, and to resolve how the law should treat claims or threats made to pre-embryos and to embryonic and fetal life. The outcome has been generally unremarkable in that the long-standing common jurisprudence has been maintained that the pre-condition to full legal protection of human life is live birth. Some trial judges and even appellate judges have departed from this jurisprudence, however, and thereby demonstrated the role that idiosyncrasy and ideology can play in adjudication. This itself is not novel either, particularly where the issue of abortion furnishes the backdrop against which parties act out the drama of litigation. The abortion issue has already led to troubling distortions of justice,[1] and the recent cases show that when judges face or allow themselves to be drawn into social controversy about abortion, they are at some risk of losing sight of the transcending jurisprudence. The exceptions to the general law in Canada, demonstrated in the case of *Tremblay v. Daigle* in the summer of 1989 in the Quebec superior court[2] and the Quebec Court of Appeal,[3] which respectively granted and upheld an injunction to restrain an abortion, were corrected in the Supreme Court of Canada.[4] Transcending Canadian law which denies embryonic and fetal rights had been followed earlier in the Saskatchewan Court of Appeal[5] and the British Columbia Court of Appeal,[6] but the *Daigle* case was argued in a civil law context under the Quebec Charter of Human Rights and Freedoms.[7] The US exception, the frozen pre-embryo case of *Davis v. Davis* in the Tennessee Circuit Court,[8] stands in sharp contrast to the slightly earlier decision of the federal US

District Court for the Eastern District of Virginia in *York v. Jones*,[9] which followed the general law in not personifying a pre-embryo, and perhaps for that reason attracted relatively little news media attention. The English Court of Appeal decision in *R. v. Tait*[10] and the Federal Family Court of Australia decision in *In the Marriage of F*[11] were similarly consistent with the pre-existing understanding of the law, the latter case being almost identical with the material facts and final outcome of the *Daigle* case.[12]

The *Daigle* case merits analysis in its own right not only in terms of the law[13] but also in terms of sociology, psychology and legal hermeneutics. The techniques by which the trial judge and majority judges of the Quebec Court of Appeal brought themselves to an interpretation of the law that was so inconsistent with the prevailing jurisprudence is of somewhat less interest, however, than are their incentives to grant and uphold the injunction. In its instant, unanimous decision to quash the injunction (the more emphatic because of its unnecessary promptness in light of the Court having been informed that the abortion enjoined had already been performed) the Supreme Court of Canada held that "the foundation of substantive rights on which the injunction could possibly be founded is lacking."[14] This suggests that the attempt by the lower judges to create such a foundation was inspired by an anti-abortion commitment not simply to interpret the law, but rather, to use the words of a poet-philosopher, to "shatter it to bits—and then remould it nearer to the heart's desire."[15]

The Tennessee *Davis* case will primarily be reviewed here, not simply because it shows how a judge, contrary to the background jurisprudence, can make the law do his bidding,[16] subject to the response of a court of appeal or of higher appeal, but also because it shows how a judge who does not honestly review his own motivations can create a law with implications that contradict the philosophy he embraces; or in more colloquial language, how a judge who fires without looking about can shoot himself in the foot. Before the anomalous *Davis* case is considered, however, it may be useful to review the general law disclosed in a different but relevant way in the English criminal case of *R. v. Tait.*[17]

The circumstances of the case were so unusual that it is easy to sympathize with the incentive of the trial jury to convict the defendant, after the judge ruled as a matter of law that the relevant charge in the indictment disclosed an indictable offence on the facts of the case. The facts were that the defendant with others broke into a house, intending to frighten the owner. He was not there, but his daughter was. The defendant committed a burglary, and before the intruders left they warned the daughter, who was five months pregnant, that if she told the police, the intruder would come back for her and kill her baby. The defendant was charged, *inter alia*, with committing an offence against section 16 of the Offences against the Person Act 1861, as amended,[18] which provides that: "A person who...makes to another a threat...to kill that other or a third person shall be guilty of an offence...."

The trial judge rejected a preliminary defence submission that the count be quashed on the ground that, since any threat to kill was directed at a fetus, there was no threat to kill a "person." There was discussion at trial about whether the threat might have been to return four or so

months later after the fetus had been born, but the judge directed the jury that:

> "Parliament, in its wisdom, has not put any restriction on the definition of a third person. It has left it to the good sense of juries to decide. Was there a threat to kill? Would you call the baby a third person, notwithstanding that it had not been born?"[19]

The Court of Appeal quashed the consequent conviction on grounds of the trial judge having materially misdirected the jury, since under the 1861 Act, "the fetus in utero was not, in the ordinary sense, 'another person,' distinct from its mother."[20] The Court found no available alternative offence of which the defendant could be convicted on that count, and that there could be no question of applying the proviso[21] by which conviction may be upheld if the error in direction of the jury resulted in no substantial wrong or miscarriage of justice.

The lack of an alternative verdict in *Tait* may be contrasted with the British Columbia case of *R. v. Sullivan,*[22] in which midwives who attended the delivery of a fetus that failed to survive birth were charged with the offence against the present section 220 of the Criminal Code of committing criminal negligence causing death "to another person," and an offence against section 221 of similarly causing bodily harm. A conviction on the basis of section 220 was set aside by the British Columbia Court of Appeal on the ground that a fetus that was not living on complete removal from its mother's body was not a "person," but the Court substituted a verdict of guilty of criminal negligence causing bodily harm to another person, namely the pregnant woman, contrary to section 221. The fetus in the birth canal was found to be part of the mother, so that injury to the fetus constituted injury to her. The conviction is being appealed to the Supreme Court of Canada on the ground, *inter alia*, that a fetus is not a part of the mother's body, and that no bodily harm was found to have been caused to the woman herself. This ground does not necessarily claim, of course, that the fetus has rights or personhood on its own behalf, which was denied in the English High Court Case of *Paton* v. *British Pregnancy Advisory Service*.[23] This was the case followed by the Family Court of Australia in *In the Marriage of F*,[24] which was decided consistently with the *Daigle* case and indicates a cohesive Commonwealth jurisprudence on the point.[25]

The very language in which the Tennessee *Davis* case was argued and decided relates to the pro-choice and pro-life sides[26] of the dichotomy of preferences on the legal status of induced abortion.[27] Several expert witnesses described the subject-matter of the case as "pre-embryos", a word in increasingly common use among embryologists, biologists, obstetricians and gynecologists and other reproductive health scientists to describe apparently largely undifferentiated cells that are the product of conception before their attachment to the uterine wall. At the point of completed implantation in the uterine wall, which occurs at about 11 to 14 days of development, the cells form an embryo. Many modern means described as contraception obstruct development of the pre-embryo,[28] which description tends to be favoured by pro-choice adherents. In constrast, pro-life adherents favour the opinion that protected human life begins at conception and recognize no differentiation between the immediate products of conception, embryos that have implanted themselves in the uterine wall or pre-viable or viable fetuses.

Dr. Jerome Lejeune, an expert witness who had appeared with other public advocates of the pro-life cause on behalf of Joseph Borowski in his 1983 trial before the Saskatchewan Court of Queen's Bench,[29] consistently testified that there is no such word as pre-embryo, and that there is no need for a subclass of embryo.[30] The trial judge observed that he had decided the case "on legal principles alone" and that he "must not manage morality or temper theology,"[31] but adopted the major tenets of the pro-life conviction and echoed Dr. Lejeune, a highly distinguished geneticist but not an embryologist, in finding "there is no such term as pre-embryo."[32] In contrast, the US District Court in the Virginia case of *York v. Jones*,[33] which considered identical subject-matter to that in issue in *Davis*, used the analogous description "pre-zygote" throughout. Judgement in that case was given on July 10, 1989. Testimony in the *Davis* case commenced on August 7, 1989. In his September 21, 1989 judgement the trial judge described the case as one of first impression,[34] which it was in Tennessee, but made no reference to the earlier judgement, or indeed to any of the guiding jurisprudence.

The *Davis* case arose when Mr. and Mrs. Davis's marriage failed after they had tried to overcome their inability to have a child by turning to in vitro fertilization. The technique employed induced superovulation, recovery of multiple ova from Mrs. Davis, and their exposure to Mr. Davis's sperm in vitro. Nine pre-embryos resulted, two of which were placed in Mrs. Davis without success, and seven remained in freezing (cryopreservation). Following the couple's separation, Mrs. Davis sought a court order that these seven pre-embryos be available to her for implantation. Having had her fallopian tubes tied on health grounds, she was incapable of natural conception, and considered the pre-embryos to represent her only opportunity to have her own genetic child.

Mr. Davis objected to this proposal, since he did not want control of whether he would become a father, with its attendant moral and financial responsibilities, to be in the hands solely of another person, such as his separated, and in time to be divorced, wife. He accordingly opposed the grant of an order that would permit her to use the pre-embryos in attempts to have a child, and similarly opposed their anonymous donation to another woman for the same purpose. The trial judge found, however, that Mr. Davis was too late to object to the pre-embryos being used for the creation of children, because "Mr. and Mrs. Davis have accomplished their original intent to produce a human being to be known as their child."[35] Finding as a matter of law that human life begins at conception, the judge concluded that legal provisions governing "a human being existing as an embryo, in vitro"[36] to be those of child custody law, dominated by the obligation to seek, protect and advance the best interests of the child. These were found to be served by implantation in Mrs. Davis rather than in non-implantation, evidence indicating that after two years in cryopreservation they would be incapable of gestation *in utero*. Mrs. Davis was granted the order she sought.

The reasoning of the judgement is flawed in many ways. As opposed to laypeople who equate "human" with "human being," for instance, lawyers in the common law tradition usually know that the expression "human being" is a contraction of the historic legal description of a human who is "in being," meaning born alive.[37]

The Criminal Code embodies many centuries of consistent understanding of both criminal and civil law[38] in providing in section 223(1) that:

A child becomes a human being...when it has completely proceeded, in a living state, from the body of its mother whether or not
(a) it has breathed,
(b) it has an independent circulation, or
(c) the navel string is severed.

Section 238 compatibly governs the offence of deliberately causing "the death, in the act of birth, of any child that has not become a human being," which is concerned with a human child that is not legally "in being." The trial judge's reference to a "human being existing as an embryo"[39] reflects fundamentalist pro-life ideology rather than legal learning when applied to a pre-embryo that has not only not "proceeded...from the body of its mother" but has not yet entered her body.

Defective though the reasoning in the case was regarding both historic law and, as will be discussed, prospective law, the decision itself may be upheld on appeal, because it may be consistent with the outcome of more orthodox reasoning. In *York v. Jones*[40] the court interpreted the property-based language of the cryopreservation agreement to afford the gamete donors control of a resultant pre-embryo and the right to order it transferred to a different facility from the one that created it *in vitro*, in order for implantation to be undertaken. In *Davis* the disagreement was not between the freezing facility and the gamete donors but between the gamete donors themselves, but an inference of their genetic contribution to creation of their child might have been that Mr. Davis surrendered his control of the pre-embryo once it came into existence *in vitro*, because he had then done all that he could towards paternity, and the choice and timing of further use of the pre-embryo depended on his wife. The analogy would be with natural insemination, where following intercourse a man has no further control of whether the woman allows, terminates or continues pregnancy.

Mrs. Davis's claim might have been favoured in addition on the related contractual or consensual ground that, while her husband could not compel the introduction of the pre-embryo into her uterus involuntarily, her continuation of their formerly joint intervention of implantation was not dependent on any bodily invasion of him or action by him, and that her initiative to employ the pre-embryos consistently with their intentions in combining gametes to create pre-embryos should be favoured over his subsequently formed unilateral preference that they be wasted. The *Davis* decision could satisfactorily have been based on the comparable outcome reached by a French court, in the *Parpalaix* case.[41] The court awarded a widow control of frozen semen that had been provided to a gamete preservation bank before death by her husband, which she wanted for purposes of insemination. The court respected and gave effect to the parties' original intentions notwithstanding a change in circumstances.

Contractual and proprietary grounds are available in law to result in such an outcome. Although traditionally courts were disposed to find that purely domestic arrangements were not intended by the parties to be contractually binding,[42] both legislatures and courts in recent years have come to recognize that legally binding agreements have a place in marital relations, particularly where control of property is concerned. A court might accordingly find that when partners have acted consensually to undertake *in vitro* fertilization, the man cannot frustrate the woman's pursuit of the agreement by a unilateral act of disallowing implantation in her. The woman can frustrate his intention of implantation because her bodily integrity to refuse unwanted implantation prevails over the agreement, in the same way as preservation of his bodily integrity would allow him to refuse to contribute his sperm.

The *York v. Jones* judgement[43] discussed the property aspects of cryopreservation in detail, with no suggestion of the relevance of custody laws. The court looked to the property agreement between the couple and the clinic, interpreted in terms and gave effect to their agreement. Reinforcing its findings on the clinic's breach of contract regarding disposition of the pre-embryo, the court concluded that there was an agreement for bailment of goods, found that "plaintiffs have properly alleged a cause of action in detinue,"[44] and discussed liability for conversion. The agreement by which the Yorks placed their pre-embryos (called pre-zygotes) in the clinic included the term:

> Our frozen pre-zygotes will not be released from storage for the purpose of intrauterine transfer without the written consents of us both. In the event of divorce, we understand legal ownership of any stored pre-zygotes must be determined in a property settlement and will be released as directed by order of a court of competent jurisdiction.[45]

Such a provision in the Davis's circumstances would have prevented Mrs. Davis from succeeding unless a court applied custody law or, for instance, found that actual or judicial separation was intended to be analogous to divorce, and control of the pre-embryos was to be determined by settlement or according to a judicial ruling.

The *Davis* case may be an anachronism in that the couple entered into no express agreement regarding storage and disposition of cryopreserved pre-embryos. The *York v. Jones* arrangement, although perhaps not comprehensive, is more typical of modern practice in which participants in in vitro fertilization specify what is to happen to stored materials in a number of possible eventualities. The *York* case offers the prospect that these arrangements would be judicially respected *per se*, but the *Davis* case indicates that they would not be respected but, like custody agreements, apply only if courts find them consistent with, or not inconsistent with, a pre-embryo's "best interests."

The absurdity of the *Davis* approach to regulation of pre-embryos through custody law is evident in several regards. The judge found the best interests of the pre-embryos in implantation in Mrs. Davis, but paid no attention to the fact that, once Mrs. Davis had commenced gestation, she could arbitrarily choose abortion with no legal duty to consider the best interests of any embryo or fetus she bore. Even if constitutional US abortion legislation becomes less accommodating of free choice, following the Missouri *Webster* decision of the US Supreme Court,[46] it is doubtful that prohibition of abortion from the moment after conception will be constitutional, the US Supreme Court finding it unnecessary to interpret Missouri's fundamentalist anti-abortion legislation's preamble that observed that human life begins at conception. Further, even anti-abortion laws may permit abortion on grounds not only of danger to the woman's life or permanent health but also of rape or incest, or perhaps gross fetal handicap. These latter grounds may be invoked without reference to the embryo's or fetus's best interests. Equally significantly, intrauterine devices may operate to cause the discharge of more advanced pre-embryos than were involved in the *Davis* case, but these are widely accepted and in *Webster* the US Solicitor General and others defending the Missouri statute denied that it affected or limited the practice of contraception, which most recognize intrauterine devices to offer.

Artificial contraception and induced abortion are secondary to the high rate of spontaneous wastage of pre-embryos and embryos that occurs in nature. The rates of natural failure of a pre-embryo to become implanted in the uterine wall, and of implanted embryos to continue their natural gestation have not been precisely determined, but estimates run to the extent of claiming that "total embryonic loss is very high, 62% of all detected pregnancies terminating prior to 12 weeks."[47] When embryo loss in undetected pregnancies and pre-embryonic failure to implant and so produce pregnancy are considered as well, there are evidently vast numbers of embryos and pre-embryos wasted in natural reproduction of the human species, outnumbering by far the number of children born alive. For a court to require that the "best interests" of each of these be protected in accordance with the principles of child custody law, and that modern means of contraception be prohibited because they may prejudice the best interests of unimplanted pre-embryos, is eccentric and unrealistic. The trial judge in *Davis* missed the importance of the biological distinction between unimplanted pre-embryos as separate from embryos.

Although the pro-life movement takes no official position on artificial contraception, many of its leaders, particularly those who adhere to the position of the Roman Catholic Church on contraception, condemn intra-uterine devices in so far as they operate after conception but before completion of implantation of a pre-embryo in the uterine wall, and describe them as abortifacients. This explains their modern emphasis of the philosophy that human life begins at conception reflecting historic religious conflicts about the moment of ensoulment, which the judge in *Davis*, and the lower courts' judges in *Tremblay v. Daigle*, tried to introduce into the law.[48] This philosophy opposes many techniques of assisted or artificial reproduction, and has been particularly vehement in its condemnation of surrogate motherhood.[49] The trial judge in *Davis* made several approving references to the New Jersey Supreme Court decision in the *Baby M* case,[50] in which agreements for surrogate motherhood were comprehensively condemned. Paradoxically, however, the *Davis* judgement would compel legal recognition and strict enforcement of even the most oppressive and exploitive surrogate motherhood agreement. Inadvertently, the *Davis* decision opened a trap-door beneath the ideological basis on which it stands.

The trial judge applies custody law in order to protect the pre-embryos' best interests, which on the facts of the case were served by granting the application made by Mrs. Davis. Had Mrs. Davis requested non-implantation and wastage, however, and Mr. Davis sought implantation in another woman such as one he had hired as a surrogate mother, the trial judge would have favoured the claim of Mr. Davis, because "it is to the manifest best interest of the children, in vitro, that they be made available for implantation to assure their opportunity for live birth."[51] Had the surrogate mother then threatened to deviate from the terms of an agreement, such as by not obtaining pre-natal monitoring and care, or had she proposed, for instance, to consume alcohol, the judge would presumably have subjected her to the same constraints courts use in custody cases to serve children's best interests, such as prohibitive or mandatory injunctions enforceable by citation and punishment for contempt of court.

Further, had a surrogate mother retained by Mr. Davis been unaffected by a source of potential congenital damage to embryos and fetuses from which Mrs. Davis might have suffered, such as diabetes, the judge appears disposed to favour the surrogate's gestation of the pre-embryos on a request by Mr. Davis even over Mrs. Davis's wish to gestate her own genetic child. He stated that the law "turns its full focus on the best interests of the child; its concern is not for those who claim 'rights' to the child, nor for those who claim custody of the child, nor for those who may suffer perceived or real inequities resulting from scrupiously (*sic*) guarding the child's best interests."[52]

There are no doubt limits to how far a court will go and permit itself to be pressed in serving the best interests of children, born or unborn. The activist pro-life movement has not distinguished itself through efforts in courts or legislatures to compel governments to provide, for instance, pre-natal health services or nutritional supplements to pregnant women who are unable to serve the best interests of their unborn children due to poverty. Similarly, the pro-life movement has not litigated against the unnecessarily high rate of pre-embryonic loss due to human causes of infertility, and has opposed embryo research intended to reduce the rate of spontaneous wastage that results in infertility. As against this, however, its members might tolerate surrogate motherhood to gestate embryos when the biological mother has a history of chronic spontaneous abortion due to a uterine dysfunction.

More problematic would be surrogate motherhood when a genetic mother has such a condition as phenylketonuria (PKU) or uncontrolled diabetes, which threatens to cause severe neurological damage to the embryo or fetus *in utero*. Similarly, a woman with AIDS or HIV infection presents a risk of vertical transmission of infection *in utero* which the embryo or fetus may be spared by lavage removal from her uterus and transfer to that of a suitably prepared surrogate or adoptive mother. Whether this is acceptable to pro-life adherents and to the *Davis* judge's commitment to the best interests of pre-embryos is a measure of their dedication to their convictions.

A further paradox of the *Davis* trial decision is more apparent in the US than in modern Canada, but it has implications here too. The judicial approach in *Davis* responds to pro-life advocacy that is frequently called, and indeed calls itself, "conservative." If pre-embryos were to be given the legal status of persons or human beings, however, a radical revolution in our public, constitutional and private law would be achieved with repercussions extending far beyond the areas of abortion and management of reproductive choice. From private inheritance and succession law to public revenue law affecting allowances for dependent children,[53] from provincial law on the protection of children by parents and by officers of child welfare agencies to federal law on Criminal Code liability for manslaughter and police investigational duties where manslaughter is suspected, pro-

visions and effects of laws would have to be fundamentally reassessed. Women's privacy would be devastated by tests mandated to determine if they were abusing unborn children, whom they might not realise they had yet conceived, and innumerable strangers would acquire legal powers and perhaps duties to ask women, married and unmarried, from post-puberty to their post-menopausal age, if they might be pregnant, and perhaps to insist on testing such women to guard against deception and mistake in negative answers. This radical change in law, wrought in the name of "conservative" values, has been spared Canada through Supreme Court of Canada decisions such as *Morgentaler*[54] and *Tremblay v. Daigle*.[55]

Perhaps the most corrosive effect on our values threatened by the *Davis* reasoning, however, concerns the impact on public attitudes of its finding of law that pre-embryos are human beings. Natural reproduction results in the spontaneous wastage of uncountable millions of pre-embryos in our society, and routine contraception many millions more. In contrast, the volume of induced abortions is trivial, although the pro-life movement targets these for its attention and disregards the volume of avoidable spontaneous abortions, including those that couples and medical scientists are desperately striving to prevent. By equating spontaneous and induced wastage of pre-embryos with the deaths of human beings, the *Davis* decision diminishes death, and dilutes its impact on us. The true vice of the *Davis* reasoning is that it not only reduces human choice, but also cheapens human death.

Postscript: Mrs. Davis subsequently remarried and decided not to have a child but to make the pre-embryos available to others. The Tennessee Court of Appeal subsequently reversed the trial decision and awarded joint custody to both genetic parents.

Notes

1 See B.M. Dickens, "Abortion and Distortion of Justice in the Law" (1989) *17 Law, Medicine and Health Care* 395.

2 [1989] R.J.Q. 1980.

3 (1989), 59 D.L.R. (4th) 609.

4 (1989), 62 D.L.R. (4th) 634.

5 *Borowski v. Canada (Attorney General)* (1987), 39 D.L.R. (4th) 731.

6 *R. v. Sullivan* (1988), 43 C.C.C. (3d) 65, leave to appeal to the Supreme Court of Canada granted.

7 R.S.Q. 1977, c. C-12.

8 (1989), 15 FLR 2097.

9 717 F. Supp. 421 (E.D. Va. 1989).

10 [1989] 3 W.L.R. 891.

11 (1989), 13 Fam LR 189.

12 For comparative European law, see R.J. Cook, "International Dimensions of the Department of Justice Arguments in the *Webster* case" (1989) *17 Law, Medicine and Health Care* 384.

13 Academic discussion will focus on the *Quebec civil code* and the *Quebec Charter of Human Rights and Freedoms*; the *Canadian Charter of Rights and Freedoms* was not implicated in the case.

14 *Daigle, supra,* note 4 at 665.

15 *Rubaiyat of Omar Khayyam*, trans. E. Fitzgerald, verse LXXIII.

16 The male gender is used here not generically, but because the judge in the *Davis* case was male.

17 *Supra,* note 10.

18 24 & 25 Vict., c. 100, s. 16 (as substituted by Criminal Law Act 1977 (U.K.), c.45, s.65, sch. 1).

19 *Tait, supra,* note 10 at 895.

20 *Ibid.* at 899.

21 Compare the Canadian *Criminal Code*, R.S.C. 1985, c. C-46, s. 686(1)(b)(iii).

22 *Supra,* note 6.

23 [1979] 1 Q.B.276, upheld by the European Commission of Human Rights in *Paton v. United Kingdom* (1980), 3 E.H.R.R. 408.

24 *Supra,* note 11.

25 See also, e.g., *Wall v. Livingston*, [1982] 1 N.Z.L.R. 734 (N.Z.C.A.); *Att.-Gen. for Queensland*; *Ex. rel. Kerr v. T.* (1983), 46 A.L.R. 275 (Aust. High Ct.).

26 The practice is adopted here of giving each side the name it usually gives itself.

27 Positions appear polarized or separated by a dichotomy rather than linked by a continuum, although some scholars are seeking a middle ground; see e.g. R. Colker, "Abortion and Dialogue" (1989) *63 Tulane Law Review* 1363.

28 See R.J. Cook, "Antiprogestin Drugs: Medical Legal Issues" (1989) *21 Family Planning Perspectives* 267.

29 *Borowski v. Canada (Attorney General)* [1984] 1 W.W.R. 15. For the Saskatchewan Court of Appeal affirmation, see *Supra,* note 5. The Supreme Court of Canada, following its decision in *R. v. Morgentaler*, [1988] 1 S.C.R. 30, found the issue moot; see *Borowski v. Canada (Attorney General)* [1989] 1 S.C.R. 342.

30 *Supra,* Note 8 at 2100.

31 *Ibid.* at 2106 (judgement Appendix A), quoting *In Re: Baby M*, 525 A. 2d 128 (N.J. 1987) at 1138.

32 *Ibid.* at 2101.

33 *Supra,* note 9.

34 *Supra,* note 8 at 2097.

35 *Ibid.* at 2103.

36 *Ibid.*

37 Glanville Williams, *Textbook of Criminal Law*, 2nd ed. (London: Stevens & Sons, 1983), 245, 289.

38 As discussed in *Daigle, supra,* note 4 at 661-665.

39 *Supra,* note 36.

40 *Supra,* note 9.

41 See D. Jones, "Artificial Procreation, Societal Reconceptions: Legal Insight from France" (1988) *36 American Journal of Comparative Law* 525.

42 *Balfour v. Balfour* [1919] 2 K.B. 571 C.A.

43 *Supra,* note 9.

44 *Ibid.* at 427.

45 *Ibid.* at 424.

46 *Webster v. Reproductive Health Services*, 109 S. Ct.3040 (1989).

47 D.K. Edwards, "Early Embryonic Mortality in Women" (1982) *38 Fertility and Sterility* 447.

48 *Supra,* note 3 at 613.

49 See Congregation for the Doctrine of the Faith,

Instruction on Respect for Human Life in its Origin and on the Dignity of Procreation (Vatican City, 1987).

50 *Supra*, note 31.

51 *Supra*, note 8 at 2104.

52 *Ibid.*

53 See e.g. D. Westfall, "Beyond Abortion: The Potential Reach of a Human Life Amendment" in M.W. Shaw and A.E. Doudera, *Defining Human Life: Medical, Legal and Ethical Implications* (Ann Arbor: AUPHA Press, 1983).

54 [1988] 1 S.C.R. 30.

55 *Supra*, note 4.

Questions for Discussion

1 Who should have "custody" of undifferentiated pre-embryos?

2 Is it reasonable to claim that harm done to a fetus is bodily harm to the woman carrying the fetus?

The Ethics of In Vitro Fertilization

Arthur L. Caplan, Ph.D.

Modern technology has had a serious impact on many aspects of human life, and often ethical thinking has had trouble keeping up with the new possibilities. One area in which this is clearly true is with respect to new reproductive technologies. In this article, Caplan discusses some of the new problems which result from our expanding abilities to manipulate nature in this area.

*   *   *

Assisted Reproduction—A Cornucopia of Moral Muddles

There has been an explosion in recent years in the demand for and resources devoted to the treatment of infertility in the United States. Many parents have benefitted from the availability of new techniques such as artificial insemination, microsurgery, fertility drugs, and the various forms of what is generically known as "in vitro fertilization." At the same time, increases in the demand for and allocation of resources to the medical treatment of infertility raise profoundly disturbing and complex moral issues.

The scientific status of the current generation of infertility interventions remains unclear. Some commentators assert that it is obvious that artificial reproduction is still in its infancy. Others, usually more directly involved in providing the technology to patients, avow that the level of success is so high that many forms of artificial reproduction can be viewed only as therapies. The issue of whether medicine is capable of treating infertility is important not only for scientific reasons but also because basic moral issues concerning informed consent, liability for untoward results, and public policies concerning reimbursement pivot around the answer. Where should artificial reproduction be placed on the experiment/therapy continuum?

Little consensus exists either within the medical profession or among the general public as to the moral status of the entities that are the objects of a great deal of medical manipulation in any attempt to treat infertility: ova, sperm, and embryos. The ethics of manipulating, storing, or destroying reproductive materials raise basic questions about the moral status of possible and potential human beings.

It is not even clear whether infertility is or ought to be viewed as a disease requiring or meriting medical intervention. Many of the causes of infertility and many of the possible remedies are as much a function of social, cultural, and economic factors as they are physiologic or biologic abnormalities. Attitudes about conception, child rearing, and the nature of the family are greatly influenced by social and ethical beliefs concerning individual rights, the duties of marriage, and the desirability of passing on a particular set of genetic information into the next generation.

The treatment of infertility also raises basic questions concerning equity and justice. These fall roughly into two broad categories: questions of social justice and questions of individual justice.

Questions of Social Justice

At the social level, increasing amounts of scarce medical resources are being invested in the provision of services for those suffering from impaired fertility. It is estimated conservatively that the United States is now spending more than 200 million dollars annually on medical interventions intended to correct infertility. In the years from 1981 to 1983, more than 2 million visits were made to physicians in private practice by those seeking assistance regarding procreation.

Not only are many persons seeking help, but also an increasing proportion of medical resources are being devoted to this problem. The number of programs offering in vitro fertilization doubled in 1984 alone from 60 to 120. Private clinics whose sole interest is the provision of services to treat infertility have opened in many areas of the country.[1]

Increases in both the supply and demand for medical services to treat infertility can be expected to continue. The number of persons seeking medical assistance is still far below the number of persons in the general population estimated to have serious impairments for fertility.

The expenditure of scarce funds for health resources is not the only social issue raised by technologic progress with respect to reproduction. It is not uncommon for fertility services to be located in the same building, if not on the same floor, as services devoted to the termination of pregnancies. If this situation were not ironic enough in itself, it is surely odd to contemplate increases in the resources devoted to the alleviation of infertility at a time when millions of children in the United States and around the world lack parents as well as the basic necessities of life.

In the United States itself, there are still thousands of children who cannot be placed with either foster families or adoptive parents. This situation raises obvious issues of social justice and individual rights, particularly when many of the children requiring adoption have special physical, cognitive, and emotional needs.

Issues regarding the priority that should be given to the development of fertility-enhancing services are made all the more pressing at a time when both federal and state governments have been moving rapidly to institute cost-containment measures such as prospective payment and reimbursement by diagnosis related groups (DRGs). These efforts are likely to curtail sharply access to proven therapeutic services for the elderly, the disabled, and the poor, who depend on public expenditures for their care.

Questions of Individual Justice

At an individual or familial level, access to infertility services frequently is limited to those who can pay for them, either out of pocket or, in some cases, through private insurance. Access to services also is constrained by patient awareness of the existence of medical options, geography, and the ability to bear the often onerous financial, psychosocial, and time commitments associated with many of the available forms of assisted reproduction.

The proper role of the law and of the state in influencing or controlling individual decisions concerning reproduction is also a matter of much disagreement and dispute. Traditionally, American courts have been loathe to countenance any interference with matters pertaining to the family and individual decisions concerning procreation. As one philosopher has observed, parental decisions concerning children have been seen as "a right against all the rest of society to be indulged within wide limits,...immune from the scrutiny of and direction of others."[2]

However, in recent years, federal and state law has begun to acknowledge a powerful state interest in the welfare of children, particularly newborns. Child abuse statutes in many states have recently been revised and strengthened. The federal government has expressed its wish that children born with handicaps or congenital defects receive access to the same opportunities for medical assistance as would be available to other children. The traditional assumption in American law and morality that privacy provides an inviolate shield against intervention by other parties or the state has weakened somewhat in the face of increasing concern about protecting the interests of especially vulnerable human beings such as newborns and children and assuring that no one is subject to invidious discrimination on the basis of handicap, race, sex, or ethnic origin.[3]

The Growing Demand for Medical Assistance in Procreation

Infertility is a major problem in the United States. Almost one in six couples who have tried to conceive a child for 1 year fail to do so. Although the overall incidence of infertility appears to be relatively stable, the demand for infertility services is increasing rapidly.

The increase in demand for medical assistance in conceiving children is due to a variety of factors. Many couples have chosen to delay conception, thereby exposing themselves to the increased risks of infertility associated with aging. There appears to be some increase in the number of women encountering Iatrogenic fertility problems as a result of difficulties associated with various forms of birth control, such as intra-uterine devices (IUDs). Many women have entered the work force and, as a result, have been exposed to reproductive hazards and pollutants that may adversely affect fertility. Increases in the incidence of sexually transmitted diseases, especially pelvic inflammatory disease, have also produced a higher incidence of infertility among some subgroups within the general population.

The causes of increased demand for fertility services are not confined to physiologic factors. Couples who might have considered adoption in earlier decades are now turning in increasing numbers to the medical profession for assistance with respect to conception. Moreover, there has been a dramatic increase in the availability of infertility services in the United States. Advances in diagnostic techniques such as laparoscopy and hormonal and genetic analysis also allow health care professionals to identify with increasing reliability those suffering from impairments in fertility.[4]

Attitudes toward human variability, the desirability of marriage and family, and the importance of biologic kinship between parent and child also play a powerful role in influencing the demand for medical assistance with respect to infertility. There is some evidence that parental expectations concerning pregnancy and reproduction have changed drastically during the past decade.

Lawsuits against and malpractice rates among those engaged in obstetrics have increased dramatically in recent years. Our society has come, whether wisely or not, to expect physicians to facilitate the conception of optimally healthy children at the conclusion of every pregnancy.

The power of medical intervention to influence procreation and reproduction challenges social norms concerning human differences and variability that are, at best, poorly understood by social scientists and moral philosophers. A growing emphasis on perfection in procreation and child rearing contributes to a situation in which those who are disabled, dysfunctional, or merely different from the norm may encounter increasing difficulties in securing social acceptance and material security. The availability of technologic methods for facilitating procreation in those for whom this would not have been an option in earlier times means that personal autonomy and individual choice are enhanced. However, it may also mean that such gains are purchased at the cost of lowering public tolerance for differences and diversity among individual human beings and about decisions concerning child-bearing, child rearing, childlessness, and disability.[5]

In Vitro Fertilization: A Case Study

Perhaps the most controversial and provocative of all the new forms of medically assisted reproduction available today is in vitro fertilization. Although it has been common practice for decades in the United States as well as in other nations to utilize sperm donated by either spouses or strangers for the purpose of facilitating procreation, it is only in the past 10 years that efforts have been made to utilize donated ova by various means in order to facilitate reproduction.

It is not merely the novelty of in vitro fertilization that makes it worthy of special comment and ethical reflection. The fact that in vitro fertilization is a technology that severs the traditional link between gestation and maternal identity raises serious and novel issues for both the law and morality. The prevailing ideology of equality, at least with respect to opportunity, in the United States makes it easy to overlook the fact that one of our society's most basic and fundamental beliefs about reproduction and the family is that the mothers of children are undeniably that, the mothers. Although it is true that artificial insemination by donor (AID) raises questions about paternal identity, the fact is that paternal identity, whether men like to admit it or not, has always been subject to a certain degree of uncertainty—with or without artificial insemination by donor.

Prior to the appearance of in vitro fertilization, there has never been any doubt, much less any empiric reason for doubting, that the woman who bore a child bore a direct familial relationship to that child. It is difficult to know exactly what the social reverberations of a technology capable of severing the tie between genetic relationship and gestation will be. However, the fact that this new technology can change a previously basic and undeniable reality of the human condition makes this particular technology worthy of serious and special moral consideration.

Standard In Vitro Fertilization

In vitro fertilization actually refers to a family of procedures that all involve the fertilization of an ovum outside of the human body. In the most commonly utilized technique, which might be termed "standard in vitro fertilization," one or more eggs are removed from the ovaries using a syringe known as a laparoscope. Egg cells are exceedingly small, so that the process of retrieval requires considerable skill and experience.

In many but not in all centers in which standard in vitro fertilization is practiced, the ovaries are stimulated artificially by hormones administered to the donor to produce more than one egg in the menstrual cycle. The eggs that are removed are subjected to microscopic inspection to determine which appears to be structurally most sound. One or more of the eggs is then fertilized in vitro using the husband's or a donor's sperm. The egg or eggs are then observed until they have grown to the eight-cell stage in an artificial medium. A decision is then made as to which of the developing embryos will be reimplanted into the prospective mother's womb.[6]

Reimplantation or, as it is often termed, "embryo transfer," also requires careful monitoring of the prospective mother in order to ascertain the optimal time for reimplanting the egg back into the uterus. Timing is critical to the success of reimplantation.

In some centers, some of the embryos that are produced are frozen for later use should the initial attempt at reimplantation fail. Techniques for freezing fertilized eggs at very low temperatures are well developed. The decision to freeze a fertilized egg allows for further efforts at reimplantation, but it also raises questions about the disposition of unused embryos.

The first successful use of standard in vitro fertilization took place in Britain in 1978. Since that time, nearly 1000 infants have been born utilizing this technique in the United States, Australia, the Netherlands, and a number of other countries. The procedure generally costs between $3000 and $5000 per attempt. Several attempts are often required in order to achieve pregnancy. One recent report stated that out of 24,037 oocytes collected, 7722 resulted in fertilized embryos that were reimplanted in the mother's uterus. From this group, 590 children were born, among which were 56 twins, 7 triplets, and 1 set of quadruplets. These multiple births were a result of the simultaneous reimplantation of more than one embryo in order to increase the likelihood of a successful implantation and birth.[7]

These data indicate that the pregnancy rate achieved is about 25 per cent, although the number of pregnancies resulting in a liveborn child is less than 10 per cent. These figures are low, but it should be noted that they do not differ all that much from the rates of pregnancy and birth associated with sexual intercourse between fertile parents.[8]

Nonstandard In Vitro Fertilization

The techniques utilized in standard in vitro fertilization allow for a startling number of permutations and combinations with respect to the donors of sperm and eggs, the choice of a recipient to receive the embryos that result, and the choice of individuals to parent the children who are born as a result of these techniques. Donors of sperm or eggs may or may not be persons who are married. Women who cannot produce viable eggs or who for some reason are unwilling or unable to undergo the procedures necessary to perform laparoscopy may ask another woman to supply eggs for in vitro fertilization.

It is also possible to utilize women other than the biologic donor to serve as the "gestational mother" for a fertilized egg. These women may carry an embryo to term and then either keep the resulting child or turn it over to another party—either the biologic donor or yet another person or persons. Because it is possible to freeze embryos, it is also possible to utilize in vitro fertilization techniques to produce a child after the death of the biologic donors or without the knowledge and consent of the biologic donors.

Nonstandard in vitro fertilization techniques allow for a division of the roles of mother and parent that was, quite simply, impossible before the appearance of these techniques. It is now possible to produce a child who has one set of biologic parents who may be either alive or dead and who provide eggs and sperm, another person or persons who are involved in pregnancy and gestation, and still a third person or persons who serve as the actual or social parent(s) of the child![9]

The fact that it is now possible to separate the biologic, gestational, and social aspects of mothering and parenting introduces a range of further novel possibilities concerning fertilization, reproduction, and birth. For example, frozen embryos not utilized for in vitro fertilization are available for research directly related to in vitro fertilization techniques or other medical purposes involving therapies not related to procreation (for example, the development of embryos in order to produce and harvest useful organic materials). Nonstandard in vitro fertilization techniques raise the possibility of remuneration of women for their services as either egg donors or gestational mothers, or, as the role is often termed, surrogates. The availability of standard and nonstandard in vitro fertilization techniques may facilitate the application of genetic engineering either for therapeutic purposes, aesthetic reasons, or even eugenic goals.

Major Policy Issues Raised by In Vitro Fertilization

The development of in vitro fertilization techniques of various types poses a direct and pressing challenge to public policy. At present, in vitro fertilization is still a relatively new medical modality, and as such, there are many aspects of the techniques utilized, including hormonal induction of ovulation, the freezing and storage of embryos, and the development of optimal media for embryo growth, in which further research is necessary. Little is known about the long-term psychosocial impacts of in vitro fertilization on children born by these methods or on the families who raise children produced by either standard or nonstandard in vitro fertilization techniques.[10]

Little formal supervision and regulation has been exercised to date by local, state, and federal authorities in the United States over the provision of in vitro fertilization as a therapy. At present, the only form of control over those who provide in vitro fertilization exists in the form of peer regulation through professional societies and individual collegial review. Few courts have ruled on matters pertaining to in vitro fertilization, and there are few legislative statutes that govern either research or therapy in this area....[11]

Major Ethical Issues Raised by In Vitro Fertilization

There is a tendency in the existing literature on in vitro fertilization to move directly to arguments about the moral implications of the nonstandard forms of the technique.[12] In many ways, this is understandable, because as noted earlier, the permutations and combinations of nonstandard in vitro fertilization techniques do allow for the separation of biologic, gestational, and parental functions, especially with respect to women, that pose enormous challenges to the legal system.

However, although issues pertaining to the moral acceptability of surrogacy, the desirability or undesirability of commercial relationships in nonstandard and standard forms of in vitro fertilization, and the policies that should be followed with regard to matters such as inheritance where in vitro fertilization embryos and children are concerned raise obvious moral and legal conundrums, it is not clear that these issues are actually the pivotal ones raised by advances in in vitro fertilization techniques. I suspect that moral matters regarding in vitro fertilization in terms of both research and therapy will actually hinge on the answers that are given to the following questions:

1. Is infertility a disease?

2. What counts as fair and equitable access to in vitro fertilization?

3. What is the moral status of a human embryo?

Is Infertility a Disease?

One common definition of disease often found in medical literature is that disease represents any deviation from the existing norms that prevail for human functioning.[13] Certainly, infertility, although not uncommon, is uncommon enough to qualify as abnormal or deviant relative to the average capacities and abilities of the human population.

Nonetheless, defining disease as abnormality has its own significant problems, not the least of which is that such a definition makes any physical or mental state at the tail ends of normal distributions diseases by definition. Thus, the state of being very tall, very smart, very dark-skinned, or very strong all qualify as diseases according to the abnormality criterion.

One way of avoiding including too much in the disease category is to restrict the definition of disease to those states that represent biologic dysfunction. According to this view, infertility would qualify as a disease because the relevant organ systems are not functioning as they presumably were designed to do.

However, again, a strictly biologic definition of disease flounders on empiric grounds. Not all dysfunctional bodily states constitute sources of symptoms or even problems for those who possess them. One can be afflicted with any number of dysfunctional states and attributes over the course of a normal life span without either knowing or caring very much about them one way or another. It seems odd to argue that a person who does not want children and who also has a low sperm count should be labeled as diseased.

Perhaps the most satisfying way to handle the problem of defining disease is to attempt a definition that captures both physiologic and patient perspectives. Disease would appear to refer to those dysfunctional states that a person recognizes or, if left untreated, will eventually come to recognize as dysfunctional either due to impairments in abilities or capacities as a result of noxious symptoms.[14]

Using a definition that recognizes both the biologic and psychosocial aspects of disease, it would appear defensible to argue that infertility is a disease that falls reasonably within medicine's purview. Although not all persons afflicted with fertility problems find this state distressing or limiting, many certainly do. Furthermore, although it is true that fertility and the ability to have children is a desire that is strongly mediated by social and cultural values, it is also true that this desire comes as close as can be to constituting a universal desire that can be found among every human society.

Indeed, it is the pervasiveness of the importance assigned to the ability to have offspring that provides one of the empiric warrants not only for labeling infertility as a disease but also for assigning its care and treatment a relatively high priority with respect to other disease states. If it is reasonable to include the capacity to bear children among those abilities and skills that constitute basic human goods, such as cognition, locomotion, and perception, infertility not only is a disease but also is one that should receive special attention and concern from physicians and those concerned with health policy.

What Counts As Fair and Equitable Access to In Vitro Fertilization?

If it is true that infertility is a disease that adversely affects a basic and important human capacity, it would seem important to assure access to efficacious and safe diagnostic, therapeutic, and palliative health care services that may contribute to the enhancement of this capacity. Indeed, infertility would appear to constitute so severe an impairment of a basic human capacity that, other things being equal, access to such services should not be contingent upon the individual patient's or family's ability to pay.

However, the major issue requiring resolution with respect to justice and equity in the allocation of resources for the diagnosis and treatment of infertility is not how much to spend or who should foot the bill, but rather whether the diagnostic and therapeutic techniques now in existence are safe and efficacious. Until the requisite empiric information for analyzing this issue has been obtained, it would be unethical to divert resources from other medical interventions already known to be safe and efficacious.

Moreover, although high priority should be accorded to the treatment of infertility, it should not be assumed that in vitro fertilization and other techniques are the only techniques that can be utilized to cope with the dysfunctional consequences of infertility or that the demonstration of a need for services thereby entails that any and all health care practitioners who wish to engage in treatment are thereby entitled to do so. Equity and fairness demand that those afflicted with the disease of infertility be aware of all options available to them, including adoption and foster parenting, and that public policy facilitate the utilization of those options. Equity and fairness also require that the resources devoted to in vitro fertilization and other techniques be used in the most efficient manner possible. This may require that diagnostic and therapeutic services be regionalized and that funding be restricted to those centers that can demonstrate a high level of safety and efficacy with regard to in vitro fertilization techniques.[15]

What Is the Moral Status of a Human Embryo?

One of the most perplexing issues raised by the evolution of in vitro fertilization is the need to examine the moral standing that should be accorded to an embryo. Arguments about research on embryos and about the storage and disposition of embryos will ultimately pivot upon the moral status that should be accorded to these entities.

In general, the scientific and medical communities have tried to shy away from the suggestion that science has anything much to say about the questions of when life begins or what counts as a human being. Recent Congressional hearings on the question of the definition of life produced a barrage of disclaimers, dodges, and apologies from those scientists called upon to testify.

The unwillingness of many members of the scientific and medical communities to address squarely the issue of when life begins and what counts as a human being is perhaps not surprising. After all, the definition of human life raises theologic and psychologic issues that are difficult and disturbing to contemplate.

However, it is important to note that members of the scientific and medical communities have not been reticent about an analogous issue—when does human life end. The existence of brain death statutes in most states is evidence of the fact that the biomedical community has been willing to offer its expert opinion as to both the definition of death and the criteria that should be followed to assess whether a particular person meets this definition.[16]

The issues of when life begins and what entities count as human beings demand similar degrees of courage and attention from the biomedical community. Although biomedical scientists may not be able to formulate definitions of life and personhood among themselves that can command societal assent, they surely have a role to play in participating in the formulation of definitions and criteria that society will have to establish in order to cope with the existence of in vitro fertilization.

Two lessons should be learned from other attempts to define life and personhood in such arenas as the debates about abortion and animal experimentation. First, no single property is likely to serve as a distinct boundary for establishing the existence of personhood or even life. The criteria used in a definition are more likely to constitute a family or cluster of concepts.

Second, the definition of life and the criteria used to assess its presence do not end moral matters. Knowing when life begins and when personhood or humanity can be attributed to a particular entity provides only the starting point for arguments about what to do with embryos. It is still necessary to consider the rights, duties, and obligations of donors, prospective parents, and health care professionals in deciding what is to be done with and to embryos. However, it will not do for the biomedical community to continue to adopt an ostrich-like posture and proclaim that it has nothing whatsoever to contribute in the way of empiric information that might facilitate the formulation of an answer to the question of what moral status should be accorded to human embryos.

Conclusion

The evolution of medicine's capacity to assist those afflicted with impairments of fertility is an exciting and commendable prospect. However, enthusiasm for the techniques and for the benefit they can bring to those afflicted with a disease that impairs a fundamental and universally valued human capacity should not blind us to the fact that these techniques are still new, relatively poorly understood, and surrounded with uncertainty as to their efficacy and safety.

In vitro fertilization is not only a scientific and financial challenge to society but also a moral challenge. The possibility of separating the functions of biologic, gestational, and social parenting raises dilemmas of policy, law and regulation that have never before faced humankind. However, insufficient attention has been given to some of the basic moral issues that underlie much of the current fascination with, and fear of, in vitro fertilization. Given the implications of this technique for basic social

institutions such as the family, kinship, and parenting, it is imperative that our regulatory, legal, and legislative responses to it be wise. We as a society must look much more carefully before we take a leap in any particular regulatory or legal direction.

Notes

1   Henahan, J. Fertilization: Embryo transfer procedures raise many questions. *J.A.M.A.*, 252:877-882, 1984.

2   Schoeman, F. Rights of children, rights of parents and the moral basis of the family. *Ethics*, 91:6-19, 1980.

3   Murray, T., and Caplan, A. (eds.). *Which Babies Shall Live?* Clifton, New Jersey: Humana, 1985.

4   Grobstein, C., Flower, M. and Mendeloff, J. External human fertilization: An evaluation of policy. *Science*, 222:127-133, 1983.

5   Murray and Caplan (eds.). *Which Babies Shall Live?*

6   Blank, R. Making babies: The state of the art. *The Futurist, 19*:1-17, 1985; Warnock, M. *Report of the Committee of Inquiry into Human Fertilization and Embryology*, London: HMSO, 1984.

7   Hodgen, G. *The Need for Infertility Treatment. Testimony in Hearings on Human Embryo Transfer, Subcommittee on Investigations and Oversight, Committee on Science and Technology*, US House of Representatives, August 8, 1984.

8   Sattaur, O. New conception threatened by old morality. *New Scientist, 103*:12-17, 1984.

9   Working Party, Council for Science and Society. *Human Procreation: Ethical Aspects of the New Techniques*, Oxford: Oxford University Press, 1984.

10 Warnock, M. *Report of the Committee of Inquiry into Human Fertilization and Embryology*, London: HMSO, 1984.

11 Annas, G. and Elias, S.. In vitro fertilization and embryo transfer: Medicolegal aspects of a new technique to create a family. *Family Law Quarterly, 17*:199-223, 1983.

12 Robertson, J.A. Procreative liberty and the control of conception, pregnancy and childbirth. *Virginia Law Review, 69*:20-80, 1983; Wadlington, W. Artificial conception: The challenge for family law. *Virginia Law Review, 69*:126-174, 1983.

13 Caplan, A., and Engelhardt, II, T. (eds.). *Con-*

cepts of Health and Disease, Reading, Massachusetts: Addison-Wesley, 1981.

14 Caplan, A. Is aging a disease? *In* Spicker, S., and Ingman, S. (eds.), *Vitalizing Long-Term Care*, New York: Springer-Verlag, 1984, pp. 14-28.

15 Institute of Medicine. *Assessing Medical Technologies*, Washington, D.C.: National Academy Press, 1985.

16 Culver, C., and Gert, B. *Philosophy in Medicine*. New York, Oxford University Press, 1982.

Questions for Discussion

1 Is infertility a disease?

2 Is it ethical to invest considerable resources in producing new children when there are many children already living who need homes? Is it possible or desirable to change the common opinion that it is more desirable to raise one's own biological offspring?

3 What role should scientists play in deciding when life begins?

4 Is there reason to worry that increasing pressure to produce "optimal pregnancies" will lead to a lower tolerance of disability or difference in society?

President's Commission for the Study of Ethical Problems in Medicine and Biomedical and Behavioral Research

Why "Update" Death?

Just as the question of when a human life can be said to have begun is of moral and social policy interest, so is the question of when life ends. In 1981, a President's Commission in the United States published a report which included some technical discussion of the definition of death. The report also discusses how the ability of modern medical technology to keep the heart going and oxygen flowing after various parts of the brain have ceased to function complicates the definition of death.

*   *   *

For most of the past several centuries, the medical determination of death was very close to the popular one. If a person fell unconscious or was found so, someone (often but not always a physician) would feel for the pulse, listen for breathing, hold a mirror before the nose to test for condensation, and look to see if the pupils were fixed. Although these criteria have been used to determine death since antiquity, they have not always been universally accepted.

Developing Confidence in the Heart-Lung Criteria

In the eighteenth century, macabre tales of "corpses" reviving during funerals and exhumed skeletons found to have clawed at coffin lids led to widespread fear of premature burial. Coffins were developed with elaborate escape mechanisms and speaking tubes to the world above (Figure 1), mortuaries employed guards to monitor the newly dead for signs of life, and legislatures passed laws requiring a delay before burial.[1]

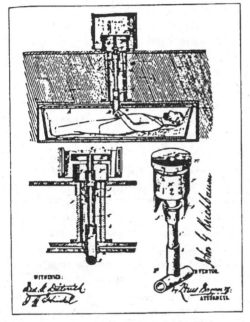

Figure 1. Kirchbaum's device for indicating life in buried persons, Patent sketch, 1882.

The medical press also paid a great deal of attention to the matter. In *The Uncertainty of the Signs of Death and the Danger of Precipitate Interments* in 1740, Jean-Jacques Winslow advanced the thesis that putrefaction was the only sure sign of death. In the years following, many physicians published articles agreeing with him. This position had, however, notable logistic and public health disadvantages. It also dis-

paraged, sometimes with unfair vigor, the skills of physicians as diagnosticians of death. In reply, the French surgeon Louis published in 1752 his influential *Letters on the Certainty of the Signs of Death.* The debate dissipated in the seventeenth century because of the gradual improvement in the competence of physicians and a concomitant increase in the public's confidence in them.

Physicians actively sought to develop this competence. They even held contests encouraging the search for a cluster of signs—rather than a single infallible sign—for the diagnosis of death.[2] One sign did, however, achieve prominence. The invention of the stethoscope in the mid-nineteenth century enabled physicians to detect heartbeat with heightened sensitivity. The use of this instrument by a well-trained physician, together with other clinical measures, laid to rest public fears of premature burial. The twentieth century brought even more sophisticated technological means to determine death, particularly the electrocardiograph (EKG), which is more sensitive than the stethoscope in detecting cardiac functioning.

The Interrelationships of Brain, Heart and Lung Functions

The brain has three general anatomic divisions: the cerebrum, with its outer shell called the cortex; the cerebellum; and the brainstem, composed of the mid-brain, the pons, and the medulla oblongata. Traditionally, the cerebrum has been referred to as the "higher brain" because it has primary control of consciousness, thought, memory and feeling. The brainstem has been called the "lower brain," since it controls spontaneous, vegetative functions such as swallowing, yawning, and sleep-wake cycles. It is important to note that these generalizations are not entirely accurate. Neuroscientists generally agree that such "higher brain" functions as cognition or consciousness probably are not mediated strictly by the cerebral cortex; rather, they probably result from complex interrelations between brainstem and cortex.

Respiration is controlled in the brainstem, particularly the medulla. Neural impulses originating in the respiratory centers of the medulla stimulate the diaphragm and intercostal (ed. note: between the ribs) muscles, which cause the lungs to fill with air. Ordinarily, these respiratory centers adjust the rate of breathing to maintain the correct levels of carbon dioxide and oxygen. In certain circumstances, such as heavy exercise, sighing, coughing or sneezing, other areas of the brain modulate the activities of the respiratory centers, or even briefly take direct control of respiration.

Destruction of the brain's respiratory center stops respiration, which in turn deprives the heart of needed oxygen, causing it too to cease functioning. The traditional signs of life—respiration and heartbeat—disappear: the person is dead. The "vital signs" traditionally used in diagnosing death thus reflect the direct interdependence of respiration, circulation and the brain.

The artificial respirator and concomitant life-support systems have changed this simple picture. Normally, respiration ceases when the functions of the diaphragm and intercostal muscles are impaired. This results from direct injury to the muscles or (more commonly) because the neural impulses between the brain and these muscles are interrupted. However, an artificial respirator (also called a ventilator) can be used to compensate for the inability of the tho-racic muscles to fill the lungs with air. Some of these machines use negative pressure to expand the chest wall (in which case they are called "iron lungs"); others use positive pressure to push air into the lungs. The respirators are equipped with devices to regulate the rate and depth of "breathing," which are normally controlled by the respiratory centres in the medulla. The machines cannot compensate entirely for the defective neural connections since they cannot regulate blood gas levels precisely. But, provided that the lungs themselves have not been extensively damaged, gas exchange can continue and appropriate levels of oxygen and carbon dioxide can be maintained in the circulating blood.

Unlike the respiratory system, which depends on the neural impulses from the brain, the heart can pump blood without external control. Impulses from brain centers modulate the inherent rate and force of the heartbeat but are not required for the heart to contract at a level of function that is ordinarily adequate. Thus, when artificial respiration provides adequate oxygenation and associated medical treatments regulate essential plasma components and blood pressure, an intact heart will continue to beat, despite loss of brain functions. At present, however, no machine can take over the functions of the heart except for a very limited time and in limited circumstances (e.g., a heart-lung machine used during surgery). Therefore, when a severe injury to the heart or major blood vessels prevents the circulation of the crucial blood supply to the brain, the loss of brain functioning is inevitable because no oxygen reaches the brain.

Loss of Various Brain Functions

The most frequent causes of irreversible loss of functions of the whole brain are: (1) direct trauma to the head, such as from a motor vehicle accident or a gunshot wound, (2) massive spontaneous hemorrhage into the brain as a result of ruptured aneurysm or complications of high blood pressure, and (3) anoxic (ed. note: severely depleted in its oxygen supply) damage from cardiac or respiratory arrest or severely reduced blood pressure.[3]

Many of these severe injuries to the brain cause an accumulation of fluid and swelling in the brain tissue, a condition called cerebral edema. In severe cases of edema, the pressure within the closed cavity increases until it exceeds the systolic blood pressure, resulting in a total loss of blood flow to both the upper and lower portions of the brain. If deprived of blood flow for at least 10-15 minutes, the brain, including the brainstem, will completely cease functioning.[4] Other pathophysiologic mechanisms also result in a progressive and, ultimately, complete cessation of intracranial circulation.

Once deprived of adequate supplies of oxygen and glucose, brain neurons will irreversibly lose all activity and ability to function. In adults, oxygen and/or glucose deprivation for more than a few minutes causes some neuron loss.[5] Thus, even in the absence of direct trauma and edema, brain functions can be lost if circulation to the brain is impaired. If blood flow is cut off, brain tissues completely self-digest (autolyze) over the ensuing days.

When the brain lacks all function, consciousness is, of course, lost. While some spinal reflexes often persist in such bodies (since circulation to the spine is separate from that of the brain), all reflexes controlled by the brainstem as well as cognitive, affective and integrating functions are absent. Respiration and circulation in these bodies may be generated by a ventilator together with intensive medical management. In adults who have experienced irreversible cessation of the functions of the entire brain, this mechanically generated functioning can continue only a limited time because the heart usually stops beating within two to ten days. (An infant or small child who has lost all brain functions will typically suffer cardiac arrest within several weeks, although respiration and heartbeat can sometimes be maintained even longer.[6])

Less severe injury to the brain can cause mild to profound damage to the cortex, lower cerebral structures, cerebellum, brainstem, or some combination thereof. The cerebrum, especially the cerebral cortex, is more easily injured by loss of blood flow or oxygen than is the brainstem. A 4-6 minute loss of blood flow—caused by, for example, cardiac arrest—typically damages the cerebral cortex permanently, while the relatively more resistant brainstem may continue to function.[7]

When brainstem functions remain, but the major components of the cerebrum are irreversibly destroyed, the patient is in what is usually called a "persistent vegetative state" or "persistent noncognitive state."[8] Such persons may exhibit spontaneous, involuntary movements such as yawns or facial grimaces, their eyes may be open and they may be capable of breathing without assistance. Without higher brain functions, however, any apparent wakefulness does not represent awareness of self or environment (thus, the condition is often described as "awake but unaware"). The case of Karen Ann Quinlan has made this condition familiar to the general public. With necessary medical and nursing care—including feeding through intravenous or nasogastric tubes, and antibiotics for recurrent pulmonary infections—such patients can survive months or years, often without a respirator. (The longest survival exceeded 37 years.[9])

Conclusion: The Need for Reliable Policy

Medical interventions can often provide great benefit in avoiding *irreversible* harm to a patient's injured heart, lungs, or brain by carrying a patient through a period of acute need. These techniques have, however, thrown new light on the interrelationship of these crucial organ systems. This has created complex issues for public policy as well.

For medical and legal purposes, partial brain impairment must be distinguished from complete and irreversible loss of brain functions or "whole brain death." The President's Commission...regards the cessation of the vital functions of the entire brain—and not merely portions thereof, such as those responsible for cognitive functions—as the only proper neurologic basis for declaring death. This conclusion accords with the overwhelming consensus of medical and legal experts and the public.

Present attention to the "definition" of death is part of a process of development in social attitudes and legal rules stimulated by the unfolding of biomedical knowledge. In the nineteenth century increasing knowledge and practical skill made the public confident that death could be diagnosed reliably using cardiopulmonary criteria. The question now is whether, when medical intervention may be responsible for a patient's respiration and circulation, there are other equally reliable ways to diagnose death.

The Commission recognizes that it is often difficult to determine the severity of a patient's injuries, especially in the first few days of intensive care following a cardiac arrest, head trauma, or other similar event. Responsible public policy in this area requires that physicians be able to distinguish reliably those patients who have died from those whose injuries are less severe or are reversible....

Notes

1   Marc Alexander, "The Rigid Embrace of the Narrow House: Premature Burial and the Signs of Death," 10 *Hastings Ctr. Rpt.* 25 (1980); John D. Arnold, Thomas F. Zimmerman and Daniel C. Martin, "Public Attitudes and the Diagnosis of Death," 206 *J.A.M.A.* 1949 (1968).

2   Alexander, *op. cit.* at 30, citing, Orifila, *A Popular Treatise on the Remedies to be Employed in Case of Poisoning and Apparent Death; Including Means of Detecting Poisons, of Distinguishing Real From Apparent Death, and of Ascertaining the Adulteration of Wines,* trans. from French, Philadelphia (1818) at 154; G. Tourdes, "Mort (Medicine legate)," *Dictionnaire Encyclopedique des Sciences Medicales,* Ser. II, X (1875) at 579-708, 603.

3   Ronald E. Cranford and Harmon L. Smith, "Some Critical Distinctions Between Brain Death and Persistent Vegetative State" 6 *Ethics in Sci. and Med.* 199, 201 (1979).

4   H.A.H. van Till-d'Aulnis de Bourouill, "Diagnosis of Death in Comatose Patients under Resuscitation Treatment: A Critical Review of the Harvard Report," 2 *Am. J.L. & Med.* 1, 21-22 (1976).

5   One exception to this general picture requires brief mention. Certain drugs or low body temperature (hypothermia) can place the neurons in "suspended animation." Under these conditions, the neurons may receive virtually no oxygen or glucose for a significant period of time without sustaining irreversible damage. This effect is being used to try to limit brain injury in patients by giving them barbiturates or reducing temperature; the use of such techniques will, of course, make

neurological diagnoses slower or more complicated.

6 Julius Korein, "Brain Death," in J. Cottrell and H. Turndorf (eds.), *Anesthesia and Neurosurgery*, C.V. Mosby & Co., St. Louis (1980) at 282, 284, 292-293.

7 Cranford and Smith, *op. cit.* at 203.

8 Bryan Jennett and Fred Plum, "The Persistent Vegetative State: A Syndrome in Search of a Name," 1 *Lancet* 734(1972); Fred Plum and Jerome B. Posner, *The Diagnosis of Stupor and Coma*, F.A. David Co., Philadelphia (1980 3rd ed.) at 6-7.

9 See Norris McWhirter (ed.), *The Guinness Book of World Records*, Bantam Books, New York (1981) at 42, citing the case of Elaine Esposito who lapsed into coma following surgery on August 6, 1941, and died on November 25, 1978, 37 years and 111 days later.

Question for Discussion

1 Fill in the blank: A person can be said to have died when his or her _____ has ceased functioning. Give reasons for your answer.

The Wrongfulness of Euthanasia

J. Gay-Williams

The ability to use technology to keep people alive has raised a number of moral problems. The problems are enhanced when one asks whether it is permissible to take active steps to end a person's life under some circumstances. In this article, Gay-Williams raises several arguments against the moral acceptability of taking the life of a presumably hopeless person, under any circumstances. Removal of life-preserving treatment after it has ceased to be of benefit is not considered to be a form of killing, however.

* * *

My impression is that euthanasia—the idea, if not the practice—is slowly gaining acceptance within our society. Cynics might attribute this to an increasing tendency to devalue human life, but I do not believe this is the major factor. The acceptance is much more likely to be the result of unthinking sympathy and benevolence. Well-publicized, tragic stories like that of Karen Quinlan elicit from us deep feelings of compassion. We think to ourselves, "She and her family would be better off if she were dead." It is an easy step from this very human response to the view that if someone (and others) would be better off dead, then it must be all right to kill that person.[1] Although I respect the compassion that leads to this conclusion, I believe the conclusion is wrong. I want to show that euthanasia is wrong. It is inherently wrong, but it is also wrong judged from the standpoints of self-interest and of practical effects.

Before presenting my arguments to support this claim, it would be well to define "euthanasia." An essential aspect of euthanasia is that it involves taking a human life, either one's own or that of another. Also, the person whose life is taken must be someone who is believed to be suffering from some disease or injury from which recovery cannot reasonably be expected. Finally, the action must be deliberate and intentional. Thus, euthanasia is intentionally taking the life of a presumably hopeless person. Whether the life is one's own or that of another, the taking of it is still euthanasia.

It is important to be clear about the deliberate and intentional aspect of the killing. If a hopeless person is given an injection of the wrong drug by mistake and this causes his death, this is wrongful killing but not euthanasia. The killing cannot be the result of accident. Furthermore, if the person is given an injection of a drug that is believed to be necessary to treat his disease or better his condition and the person dies as a result, then this is neither wrongful killing nor euthanasia. The intention was to make the patient well, not kill him. Similarly, when a patient's condition is such that it is not reasonable to hope that any medical procedures or treatments will save his life, a failure to implement the procedures or treatments is not euthanasia. If the person dies, this will be as a result of his injuries or disease and not because of his failure to receive treatment.

The failure to continue treatment after it has been realized that the patient has little chance of benefitting from it has been characterized by some as "passive euthanasia." This phrase is misleading and mistaken.[2] In such cases, the person involved is not killed (the first essential aspect of euthanasia). The aim may be to spare the person additional and unjustifiable pain, to save him from the indignities of hopeless manipula-

tions, and to avoid increasing the financial and emotional burden on his family. When I buy a pencil it is so that I can use it to write, not to contribute to an increase in the gross national product. This may be the unintended consequence of my action, but it is not the aim of my action. So it is with failing to continue the treatment of a dying person. I intend his death no more than I intend to reduce the GNP by not using medical supplies. His is an unintended dying, and so-called "passive euthanasia" is not euthanasia at all.

The Argument from Nature

Every human being has a natural inclination to continue living. Our reflexes and responses fit us to fight attackers, flee wild animals, and dodge out of the way of trucks. In our daily lives we exercise the caution and care necessary to protect ourselves. Our bodies are similarly structured for survival right down to the molecular level. When we are cut, our capillaries seal shut, our blood clots, and fibrogen is produced to start the process of healing the wound. When we are invaded by bacteria, antibodies are produced to fight against the alien organisms, and their remains are swept out of the body by special cells designed for clean-up work.

Euthanasia does violence to this natural goal of survival. It is literally acting against nature because all the processes of nature are bent towards the end of bodily survival. Euthanasia defeats these subtle mechanisms in a way that, in a particular case, disease and injury might not.

It is possible, but not necessary, to make an appeal to revealed religion in this connection.[3] Man as trustee of his body acts against God, its rightful possessor, when he takes his own life. He also violates the commandment to hold life sacred and never to take it without just and compelling cause. But since this appeal will persuade only those who are prepared to accept that religion has access to revealed truths, I shall not employ this line of argument.

It is enough, I believe, to recognize that the organization of the human body and our patterns of behavioural responses make the continuation of life a natural goal. By reason alone, then, we can recognize that euthanasia sets us against our own nature.[4] Furthermore, in doing so, euthanasia does violence to our dignity. Our dignity comes from seeking our ends. When one of our goals is survival, and actions are taken that eliminate that goal, then our natural dignity suffers. Unlike animals, we are conscious through reason of our nature and our ends. Euthanasia involves acting as if this dual nature—inclination towards survival and awareness of this as an end—did not exist. Thus, euthanasia denies our basic human character and requires that we regard ourselves or others as something less than fully human.

The Argument from Self-Interest

The above arguments are, I believe, sufficient to show that euthanasia is inherently wrong. But there are reasons for considering it wrong when judged by standards other than reason. Because death is final and irreversible, euthanasia contains within it the possibility that we will work against our own interest if we practice it or allow it to be practiced on us.

Contemporary medicine has high standards of excellence and a proven record of accomplishment, but it does not possess perfect and complete knowledge. A mis-

taken diagnosis is possible, and so is a mistaken prognosis. Consequently, we may believe that we are dying of a disease when, as a matter of fact, we may not be. We may think that we have no hope of recovery when, as a matter of fact, our chances are quite good. In such circumstances, if euthanasia were permitted, we would die needlessly. Death is final and the chance of error too great to approve the practice of euthanasia.

Also, there is always the possibility that an experimental procedure or a hitherto untried technique will pull us through. We should at least keep this option open, but euthanasia closes it off. Furthermore, spontaneous remission does occur in many cases. For no apparent reason, a patient simply recovers when those all around him, including his physicians, expected him to die. Euthanasia would just guarantee their expectations and leave no room for the "miraculous" recoveries that frequently occur.

Finally, knowing that we can take our life at any time (or ask another to take it) might well incline us to give up too easily. The will to live is strong in all of us, but it can be weakened by pain and suffering and feelings of hopelessness. If during a bad time we allow ourselves to be killed, we never have a chance to reconsider. Recovery from a serious illness requires that we fight for it and anything that weakens our determination by suggesting that there is an easy way out is ultimately against our own interest. Also, we may be inclined towards euthanasia because of our concern for others. If we see our sickness and suffering as an emotional and financial burden on our family, we may feel that to leave our life is to make their lives easier.[5] The very presence of the possibility of euthanasia may keep us from surviving when we might.

The Argument from Practical Effects

Doctors and nurses are, for the most part, totally committed to saving lives. A life lost is, for them, almost a personal failure, an insult to their skills and knowledge. Euthanasia as a practice might well alter this. It could have a corrupting influence so that in any case that is severe doctors and nurses might not try hard enough to save the patient. They might decide that the patient would simply be "better off dead" and take the steps necessary to make that come about. This attitude could then carry over to their dealings with patients less seriously ill. The result would be an overall decline in the quality of medical care.

Finally, euthanasia as a policy is a slippery slope. A person apparently hopelessly ill may be allowed to take his own life. Then he may be permitted to deputize others to do it for him should he no longer be able to act. The judgement of others then becomes the ruling factor. Already at this point euthanasia is not personal and voluntary, for others are acting "on behalf of" the patient as they see fit. This may well incline them to act on behalf of other patients who have not authorized them to exercise their judgement. It is only a short step, then, from voluntary euthanasia (self-inflicted or authorized), to directed euthanasia administered to a patient who has given no authorization, to involuntary euthanasia conducted as part of a social policy.[6] Recently many psychiatrists and sociologists have argued that we define as "mental illness" those forms of behavior that we disapprove of.[7] This gives us li-

cense then to lock up those who display the behavior. The category of the "hopelessly ill" provides the possibility of even worse abuse. Embedded in a social policy, it would give society or its representatives the authority to eliminate all those who might be considered too "ill" to function normally any longer. The dangers of euthanasia are too great to all to run the risk of approving it in any form. The first slippery step may well lead to a serious and harmful fall.

I hope that I have succeeded in showing why the benevolence that inclines us to give approval of euthanasia is misplaced. Euthanasia is inherently wrong because it violates the nature and dignity of human beings. But even those who are not convinced by this must be persuaded that the potential personal and social dangers inherent in euthanasia are sufficient to forbid our approving it either as a personal practice or as a public policy.

Suffering is surely a terrible thing, and we have a clear duty to comfort those in need and to ease their suffering when we can. But suffering is also a natural part of life with values for the individual and for others that we should not overlook. We may legitimately seek for others and for ourselves an easeful death, as Arthur Dyck has pointed out.[8] Euthanasia, however, is not just an easeful death. It is a wrongful death. Euthanasia is not just dying. It is killing.

Notes

1   For a sophisticated defense of this position see Philippa Foot, "Euthanasia," *Philosophy and Public Affairs*, vol. 6 (1977), pp. 85-112. Foot does not endorse the radical conclusion that euthanasia, voluntary and involuntary, is always right.

2   James Rachels rejects the distinction between active and passive euthanasia as morally irrelevant in his "Active and Passive Euthanasia," *New En-*

gland Journal of Medicine, vol. 292, pp. 78-80. But see the criticism by Foot, pp. 100-103.

3   For a defense of this view see J.V. Sullivan, "The Immorality of Euthanasia," in *Beneficent Euthanasia*, ed. Marvin Kohl (Buffalo, New York: Prometheus Books, 1975), pp. 34-44.

4   This point is made by Ray V. McIntyre in "Voluntary Euthanasia: The Ultimate Perversion," *Medical Counterpoint*, vol. 2, pp. 26-29.

5   See McIntyre, p. 28.

6   See Sullivan, "Immorality of Euthanasia," pp. 34-44, for a fuller argument in support of this view.

7   See, for example, Thomas S. Szasz, *The Myth of Mental Illness*, rev. ed. (New York: Harper & Row, 1974).

8   Arthur Dyck, "Beneficent Euthanasia and Benemortasia," Kohl, op. cit., pp. 117-129.

Questions for Discussion

1   Is Gay-Williams right to assert that the aim of health care professionals is saving lives? Would allowing them to bring about death in some cases have a negative effect on their dealings with all patients?

2   Is it possible to stop the "slippery slope" from allowing euthanasia to allowing killings of selected individuals in the interests of social policy?

A Moral Principle About Killing

Richard Brandt

In this paper, Brandt argues that death is wrong if it is also an injury of someone, but that there may be cases in which killing does not injure.

*   *   *

One of the Ten Commandments states: "Thou shalt not kill." The commandment does not supply an object for the verb, but the traditional Catholic view has been that the proper object for the verb is "innocent human beings" (except in cases of extreme necessity), where "innocent" is taken to exclude persons convicted of a capital crime or engaged in an unjust assault aimed at killing, such as members of the armed forces of a country prosecuting an unjust war. Thus construed, the prohibition is taken to extend to suicide and abortion. (There is a qualification: that we are not to count cases in which the death is not wanted for itself or intended as a *means* to a goal that is wanted for itself, provided that in either case the aim of the act is the avoidance of some evil greater than the death of the person.) Can this view that all killing of innocent human beings is morally wrong be defended, and if not, what alternative principle can be?

This question is one the ground rules for answering which are far from a matter of agreement. I should myself be content if a principle were identified that could be shown to be one that would be included in any moral system that rational and benevolent persons would support for a society in which they expected to live. Apparently others would not be so content; so in what follows I shall simply aim to make some observations that I hope will identify a principle with which the consciences of intelligent people will be comfortable. I believe the rough principle I will suggest is also one that would belong to the moral system rational and benevolent people would want for their society.

Let us begin by reflecting on what it is to kill. The first thing to notice is that *kill* is a biological term. For example, a weed may be killed by being sprayed with a chemical. The verb *kill* involves essentially the broad notion of death—the change from the state of being biologically alive to the state of being dead. It is beyond my powers to give any general characterization of this transition, and it may be impossible to give one. If there is one, it is one that human beings, flies, and ferns all share; and to kill is in some sense to bring that transition about. The next thing to notice is that at least human beings do not live forever, and hence killing a human being at a given time must be construed as *advancing the date* of its death, or as *shortening its life*. Thus it may be brought about that the termination of the life of a person occurs at the time t instead of at the time $t+k$. Killing is thus shortening the span of organic life of something.

There is a third thing to notice about *kill*. It is a term of causal agency and has roots in the legal tradition. As such, it involves complications. For instance, suppose I push a boulder down a mountainside, aiming it a person X and it indeed strikes X, and he is dead after impact and not before (and not from a coincidental heart attack); in that case we would say that I killed X. On the other hand, suppose I tell Y that X is in bed with Y's wife, and Y hurries to the scene, discovers them, and shoots X to death; in that case, although the unfolding of events from my action may be as much a matter of causal law as the path of the boulder, we should *not* say that I killed X. Fortunately, for the purposes of principles of the morally right, we can sidestep such complications. For suppose I am choosing whether to do A or B (where one or the other of these "acts" may be construed as essentially *in*action—for example, *not* doing what I know is the one thing that will *prevent* someone's death); then it is enough if I know, or have reason to think it highly probable, that were I to do A, a state of the world including the death of some person or persons would ensue, whereas were I to do B, a state of the world of some specified different sort would ensue. If a moral principle will tell me in this case whether I am to do A or B, that is all I need. It could be that a moral principle would tell me that I am absolutely never to perform any action A, such that were I to do it the death of some innocent human being would ensue, provided there is some alternative action I might perform, such that were I to do it no such death would ensue.

It is helpful, I think, to reformulate the traditional Catholic view in a way that preserves the spirit and intent of that view (although some philosophers would disagree with this assessment) and at the same time avoids some misconceptions that are both vague and more appropriate to a principle about when a person is morally blameworthy for doing something than to a principle about what a person ought morally to do. The terminology I use goes back, in philosophical literature, to a phrase introduced by W.D. Ross, but the conception is quite familiar. The alternative proposal is that there is a *strong prima facie obligation* not to kill any human being except in justifiable self-defense; in the sense (of prima facie) that it is morally *wrong* to kill any human being except in justifiable self-defense *unless* there is an even stronger prima facie moral obligation to do something that cannot be done without killing. (The term *innocent* can now be omitted, since if a person is not innocent, there may be a stronger moral obligation that can only be discharged by killing him; and this change is to the good since it is not obvious that we have no prima facie obligation to avoid killing people even if they are not innocent.) This formulation has the result that sometimes, to decide what is morally right, we have to compare the stringencies of conflicting moral obligations—and that is an elusive business; but the other formulation either conceals the same problem by putting it in another place, or else leads to objectionable implications. (Consider one implication of the traditional formulation, for a party of spelunkers in a cave by the oceanside. It is found that a rising tide is bringing water into the cave and all will be drowned unless they escape at once. Unfortunately, the first man to try to squeeze though the exit is fat and gets wedged inextricably in the opening, with his head inside the cave. Somebody in the party has a stick of dynamite. Either they blast the fat man out, killing him, or all of them, including him, will drown. The traditional formulation leads to the conclusion that all must drown.)

Let us then consider the principle: "There is a strong prima facie moral obligation not to kill any human being except in justifiable self-defense." I do not believe we want to accept this principle without further qualification; indeed, its status

seems not to be that of a basic principle at all, but derivative from some more-basic principles. W.D. Ross listed what he thought were the main prima facie moral obligations; it is noteworthy that he listed a prima facie duty not to cause *injury*, but he did not include an obligation not to kill. Presumably this was no oversight. He might have thought that killing a human being is always an injury, so that the additional listing of an obligation not to kill would be redundant; but he might also have thought that killing is sometimes *not* an injury and that it is prima facie obligatory not to kill only when, and because, so doing would injure a sentient being.

What might be a noninjurious killing? If I come upon a cat that has been mangled but not quite killed by several dogs and is writhing in pain, and I pull myself together and put it out of its misery, I have killed the cat but surely not *injured* it. I do not injure something by relieving its pain. If someone is being tortured and roasted to death and I know he wishes nothing more than a merciful termination of life, I have not injured him if I shoot him; I have done him a favor. In general, it seems I have not injured a person if I treat him in a way in which he would want me to treat him if he were fully rational, or in a way to which he would be indifferent if he were fully rational. (I do not think that terminating the life of a human fetus in the third month is an injury; I admit this view requires discussion.[1])

Consider another type of killing that is not an injury. Consider the case of a human being who has become unconscious and will not, it is known, regain consciousness. He is in a hospital and is being kept alive only through excessive supportive measures. Is there a strong prima facie moral obligation not to withdraw these measures and not to take positive steps to terminate his life? It seems obvious that if he is on the only kidney machine and its use could *save* the life of another person, who could lead a normal life after temporary use, it would be wrong not to take him off. Is there an obligation to continue, or not to terminate, if there is no countering obligation? I would think not, with an exception to be mentioned; and this coincides with the fact that he is *beyond* injury. There is also not an obligation *not* to preserve his life, say, in order to have his organs available for use when they are needed.

There seems, however, to be another morally relevant consideration in such a case—knowledge of the patient's own wishes when he was conscious and in possession of his faculties. Suppose he had feared such an eventuality and prepared a sworn statement requesting his doctor to terminate his life at once in such circumstances. Now, if it is morally obligatory to some degree to carry out a person's wishes for disposal of his body and possessions after his death, it would seem to be equally morally obligatory to respect his wishes in case he becomes a "vegetable." In the event of the existence of such a document, I would think that if he can no longer be injured we are free to withdraw life-sustaining measures and also to take positive steps to terminate life—and are even morally bound, prima facie, to do so. (If, however, the patient had prepared a document directing that his body be preserved alive as long as possible in such circumstances, then there would be a prima facie obligation *not* to cease life-sustaining measures and not to terminate. It would seem obvious, however, that such an obligation would fall far short of giving the patient the right to con-

tinued use of a kidney machine when its use by another could save that person's life.) Some persons would not hesitate to discontinue life-sustaining procedures in such a situation, but would balk at more positive measures. But the hesitation to use more positive procedures, which veterinarians employ frequently with animals, is surely nothing but squeamishness; if a person is in the state described, there can be no injury to him in positive termination more than or less than that in allowing him to wither by withdrawing life-supportive procedures.

If I am right in my analysis of this case, we must phrase our basic principle about killing in such a way as to take into account (1) whether the killing would be an injury and (2) the person's own wishes and directives. And perhaps, more important, any moral principle about killing must be viewed simply as an implicate of more basic principles about these matters.

Let us look for corroboration of this proposal to how we feel about another type of case, one in which termination would be of positive benefit to the agent. Let us suppose that a patient has a terminal illness and is in severe pain, subject only to brief remissions, with no prospect of any event that could make his life good, either in the short or long term. It might seem that here, with the patient in severe pain, at least life-supportive measures should be discontinued, or positive termination adopted. But I do not think we would accept this inference, for in this situation the patient, let us suppose, has his preferences and is able to express them. The patient may have strong religious convictions and prefer to go on living despite the pain; if so, surely there is a prima facie moral obligation not positively to terminate his life. Even if, as seemingly in this case, the situation is one in which it would be *rational* for the agent, from the point of view of his own welfare, to direct the termination of his life,[2] it seems that if he (irrationally) does the opposite, there is a prima facie moral obligation not to terminate and some prima facie moral obligation to sustain it. (I believe, however, that we think a person's expressed wishes have *less* moral force when we think the wishes are irrational.)

What is the effect, in this case, if the patient himself expresses a preference for termination and would, if he were given the means, terminate his own existence? Is there a prima facie moral obligation to sustain his life—and pain—against his will? Surely not. Or is there an obligation *not* to take positive measures to terminate his life immediately, thereby saving the patient much discomfort? Again, surely not. What possible reason could be offered to justify the claim that the answer is affirmative, beyond theological ones about God's will and our being bound to stay alive at His pleasure? The only argument I can think of is that there is some consideration of public policy, to the effect that a recognition of such moral permission might lead to abuses or to some other detriment to society in the long run. Such an argument does seem weak.

It might be questioned whether a patient's request should be honored, if made at a time when he is in pain, on the grounds that it is not rational. (The physician may be in a position to see, however, that the patient is quite right about his prospects and that his personal welfare would be maximized by termination.) It might also be questioned whether a patient's formal declaration, written earlier, requesting termination if he were ever in his present circumstances, should be honored, on the grounds that at the earlier time he did not know what it would be like to be in his present situation. It would seem odd, however, if *no* circumstances are identifiable in which a patient's request for termination is deemed to have moral force, when his request *not* to terminate is thought morally weighty in the same circumstances, even when this request is clearly irrational. I think we may ignore such arguments and hold that, in a situation in which it is rational for a person to choose termination of his life, his expressed wish is morally definitive and removes both the obligation to sustain life and the obligation not to terminate.

Indeed, there is a question whether or not in these circumstances a physician has not a moral obligation at least to withdraw life-supporting measures, and perhaps positively to terminate life. At least there seems to be a general moral obligation to render assistance when a person is in need, when it can be given at small cost to oneself, and when it is requested. The obligation is the stronger when one happens to be the only person in a position to receive such a request or to know about the situation. Furthermore, the physician has acquired a special obligation if there has been a long-standing personal relationship with the patient—just as a friend or relative has special obligations. But since we are discussing not the possible obligation to terminate but the obligation *not* to terminate, I shall not pursue this issue.

The patient's own expression of preference or consent, then, seems to be weighty. But suppose he is unable to express his preference; suppose that his terminal disease not only causes him great pain but has attacked his brain in such a way that he is incapable of thought and of rational speech.

May the physician, then, after consultation, take matters into his own hands? We often think we know what is best for another, but we think one person should not make decisions for another. Just as we must respect the decision of a person who has decided after careful reflection that he wishes to commit suicide, so we must not take the liberty of deciding to bring another's life to a close contrary to his wishes. So what may be done? Must a person suffer simply because he cannot express consent? There is evidence that can be gathered about what conclusions a person would draw if he were in a state to draw and express them. The patient's friends will have some recollection of things he has said in the past, of his values and general ethical views. Just as we can have good reason to think, for example, that he would vote Democratic if voting for president in a certain year, so we can have good reason to think he would take a certain stand about the termination of his own life in various circumstances. We can know of some persons who because of their religious views would want to go on living until natural processes bring their lives to a close. About others we can know that they decidedly would not take this view. We can also know what would be the *rational* choice for them to make, and our knowledge of this can be *evidence* about what they would request if they were able. There are, of course, practical complications in the mechanics of a review board of some kind making a determination of this sort, but they are hardly insurmountable.

I wish to consider one other type of case, that of a person who, say, has had a stroke and is leading, and for some time can continue to lead, a life that is comfortable but one on a very low level, *and* who has antecedently requested that his life be terminated if he comes, incurably, into such a situation. May he then be terminated? In this case, unlike the others, there are probably ongoing pleasant experiences, perhaps on the level of some animals, that seem to be a good thing. One can hardly say that *injury* is being done such a person by keeping him alive; and one might say that some slight injury is being done him by terminating his existence. There is a real problem here. Can the (slight) goodness of these experiences stand against the weight of an earlier firm declaration requesting that life be terminated in a situation of hopeless senility? There is no *injury* in keeping the person alive despite his request, but there seems something *indecent* about keeping a mind alive after a severe stroke, when we know quite well that, could he have anticipated it, his own action would have been to terminate his life. I think that the person's own request should be honored; it should be if a person's expressed preferences have as much moral weight as I think they should have.

What general conclusions are warranted by the preceding discussion? I shall emphasize two. First, there is a prima facie obligation *not* to terminate a person's existence when this would injure him (except in cases of self-defense or of senility of a person whose known wish is to be terminated in such a condition) *or* if he wishes not to be terminated. Second, there is *not* a prima facie obligation not to terminate when there would be *no* injury, or when there would be a positive benefit (release from pain) in so doing, provided the patient has not declared himself otherwise or there is evidence that his wishes are to that effect. Obviously there are two things that are decisive for the morality of terminating a person's life: whether so doing would be an *injury* and whether it conforms to what is known of his *preferences*.

I remarked at the outset that I would be content with some moral principles if it could be made out that rational persons would want those principles incorporated in the consciences of a group among whom they were to live. It is obvious why rational persons would want these principles. They would want injury avoided both because they would not wish others to injure them and because, if they are benevolent, they would not wish others injured. Moreover, they would want weight given to a person's own known preferences. Rational people do want the decision about the termination of their lives, where that is possible; for they would be uncomfortable if they thought it possible that others would be free to terminate their lives without their consent. The threat of serious illness is bad enough without that prospect. On the other hand, this discomfort would be removed if they knew that termination would not be undertaken on their behalf without their explicit consent, except after a careful inquiry had been made, both into whether termination would constitute an injury and whether they would request termination under the circumstance if they were in a position to do so.

If I am right in all this, then it appears that killing a person is not something that is just prima facie wrong *in itself*; it is wrong roughly only if and because it is an *injury* of someone, or if and because it is contrary to the *known preferences* of someone. It would seem that a principle about the prima facie wrongness of killing is *derivative* from principles about when we are prima facie obligated not to injure and when we are prima facie obligated to respect a person's wishes, at least about what happens to his own body. I do not, however, have any suggestions for a general statement of principles of this latter sort.

Notes

1 See my "The Morality of Abortion" in *The Monist*, 56 (1972), pp. 503-26; and in revised form, in a forthcoming volume edited by R.L. Perkins.

2 See my "The Morality and Rationality of Suicide," in James Rachels, ed., *Moral Problems* (in press); and, in revised form, in E.S. Shneidman, ed., *Suicidology: Current Developments* (forthcoming).

Questions for Discussion

1 Brandt suggests that if an animal such as a cat is in pain, killing it to "put it out of its misery" does not injure it. Is he right about this, and can the example be extended to human beings?

2 Brandt claims that people who allow the discontinuation of life-sustaining procedures but not active measures to end life are exhibiting "nothing but squeamishness." Is that true, or is there a relevant difference?

3 If people express different preferences at different times (for example, once before a debilitating condition sets in, and then later in a condition of extreme pain after the onslaught of such a condition), how should we decide which view expresses the person's "real" preference?

When Merely Staying Alive is Morally Intolerable

Editorial, The Globe and Mail, January 7, 1992

Jim Lavery

In Canada, public policy on euthanasia has not been fully worked out, but the recent case of Nancy B. may have wide-ranging repercussions. In this editorial, Lavery argues that the court made the right decision in allowing Nancy B. to have her treatment discontinued, even knowing that was likely to result in her death.

*   *   *

It is unfortunate that the request by Nancy B., the 25-year-old Quebec City woman who wants authorities to turn off the mechanical ventilator keeping her alive, has turned into such a legal and media event. But it would have been even more unfortunate had Quebec Superior Court Judge Jacques Dufour not agreed yesterday to grant her wish.

Ms. B.'s condition—a nerve disorder called Guillain-Barré syndrome—has left her paralyzed from the neck down and unable to breathe without the aid of a machine. With no prospect of recovering, she made a clear and competent decision to forgo further treatment. The Quebec Civil Code states that "no person may be made to undergo care of any nature...except with his (her) consent."

Ms. B. withdrew that consent and, thus, is being treated against her will. But lawyers for the Quebec government fought her, arguing that "consent(ing) to have death inflicted" upon oneself is an offence under Section 14 of the Criminal Code of Canada.

There is no question that allowing a lucid young woman to die is emotionally and psychologically distressing. Such an act appears to fly in the face of the medical and societal interest in preserving and protecting life. But there is a difference between halting a medical treatment and actually wanting to die.

Ms. B. seems to regard her death as a foreseeable and tragic consequence of her illness, not the morally evil objective described by the government. What is morally intolerable for her is her mechanical captivity. She feels the irreversible and forced reliance on a ventilator causes her greater harm than her untimely death. She doesn't actually *want* to die; she just wants to free herself from intolerable technological constraints.

Some consider this case important because it establishes a legal precedent with respect to euthanasia in Canada. This way of framing the issue relies on presumptions concerning the nature of death and the intentions of those involved.

Just as it is not clear that Ms. B. wishes to be killed, neither is it clear that the intention of caregiver or family member in turning off her respirator is to "euthanize" her. Ms. B.'s death would simply be a dramatic and unavoidable consequence of a reasonable decision to end a treatment that holds no promise of improving her condition or well-being.

Rather than euthanasia, this case illustrates the practical difficulty in determining which treatments are medically appropriate and which are not. Ms. B.'s ventilator, as a treatment for her condition, is futile. However, as a means simply of keeping her alive, it is highly effective.

So the onus must be on the caregiver, and the court, not to justify continued treatment simply to preserve a life, especially at the cost of violating the right of patients to determine the nature of their own care. If the state really intends to "care" for people such as Nancy B., it will appreciate their dilemma and respect their ability to determine what is appropriate medical care.

This case should be seen as an opportunity to gain some insight into the tormenting and often hopeless medical options available to dying patients, and to reaffirm the principle of patient self-determination that is fundamental to responsible and ethical care. No one can take Ms. B.'s death lightly, but we all must respect her decision and defend her right to make it.

PART 3

the moral status of non-human animals

Ordinarily, our moral beliefs are geared toward other human beings. However, we share this universe with many other sorts of beings: rocks, pinball machines, computers, fetuses, biospheres, non-human animals, or works of art, for example. Some of these may lack the characteristics which "normal" adult human beings have. Can moral statements be extended so as to apply to some or all of these other beings?

One way this question is often approached is by asking what sorts of beings "matter" (or "count") morally. It is common to assert that normal adult human beings matter morally, but that rocks (for example) do not. A person who hits a rock has probably not done anything wrong, but a person who hits another adult human being probably has. What makes the difference here? Is there some relevant characteristic which the human has, but the rock does not?

Several possible criteria have been suggested for the moral status of a being. If it is true that all normal adult human beings count, then the criterion will have to be something which is common to all such beings. Suggestions for what this characteristic might be have included: the capacity to feel pain, the capacity to use language, or to think abstractly or rationally; the sense of oneself as continuing through time; or the property of having a soul.

Of course there is also disagreement about which particular beings *have* these characteristics. Is there such a thing as a soul at all, and if so, do non-human animals have them? (From now on, for convenience, I will use the word "animals" to refer to non-human animals.) Can fish feel pain? Can insects, or plants? Are non-human primates capable of abstract thought? Do whales use language? The questions are endless.

One way of describing this line of questioning is in terms of an attempt to discover which beings should be considered "persons." One might claim that "persons" count morally, and then leave open the question of which beings might qualify as persons. Of course, in ordinary usage "person" is virtually synonymous with "human being," and indeed many people might claim that human beings count morally, and other beings do not. It is fair to ask, however, what is so special about human beings.

Clearly we are predisposed to favour members of our own group over "outsiders," and it is much easier to identify with other human beings than with rocks or biospheres or even other animals. However, much of what is commonly considered political progress over the past century or two can be usefully understood in terms of an expansion of the circle of beings people have been willing to consider members of their own group. For example, favouring people whose skin colour is the same as one's own has been commonly denounced as "racism," denial of rights to people on the basis of gender has been commonly denounced as "sexism," and so on. Some people would claim that this broadening process should continue, and that failure to include animals in one's own group should be denouned as "speciesism."

It should be noted that saying that certain beings count morally does not necessarily imply that they have to be counted as equals. One might think that the suffering of dogs counts for something, and should be avoided if possible, but that if one has to choose between allowing a dog to suffer and allowing a human being to suffer, one should not be indifferent about the choices. But what if the choice was between one human being and a hundred dogs? Is there any amount of dog suffering which can outweigh the suffering of a human being? If so, how much? If not, why not?

This question of how to compare human well-being with animal well-being is important for the broader issue of how we should treat animals. What if many people enjoy eating meat, but could survive on a strictly vegetarian diet? Is it morally acceptable to sacrifice an animal's life in order to provide the increased pleasure of a tasty meal? How about for a bit of leather, or fur, or ivory?

Many people believe that it is acceptable to use animals for human purposes if the purpose is important enough, but not for "trivial" things such as improved cosmetics. Explaining how this distinction between important and unimportant purposes works may be a difficult task, especially since human beings obviously get different amounts of pleasure from different things. Is eating meat somehow more important than wearing fur, for example? But even in cases where the goal is clearly important, such as medical experimentation which could potentially save many lives, it is not clear what principle is at stake here. Again, the question is how we compare human well-being with that of animals.

Some people, at the extreme "animal rights" end of the scale, argue that it is never permissible to use animals in a way it would not be permissible to use human beings. They point out that many human beings do not have all the capacities of "normal" adult humans. Human infants and severely mentally handicapped people, not to mention people in comas and perhaps fetuses, seem incapable of abstract thought, use of language, etc. Indeed, some animals may seem more advanced in these regards than the human beings in question. Yet most people would claim that it would be wrong to use infants or severely mentally handicapped people for experiments, or to kill them for food. The animal rights advocate might claim that treating animals but not these humans in these ways reveals an unreasonable double standard, and that using animals in such ways should be seen as abhorrent.

Others claim that causing the death of animals is not wrong, but causing their suffering is. In this case, if, for example, it is true that the present-day meat industry causes animals to live miserable lives, then that would be a reason to stop eating meat. If, however, it were possible to kill animals humanely after comfortable lives, perhaps eating meat would not be wrong.

Another view which provides only limited protection for animals maintains that animals do not have any standing in their own right, but that there are good reasons for people to treat them well in any case. One such reason is that people often grow emotionally attached to animals (pets, etc.), and that hurting those animals would indirectly hurt the people who care about them, which is morally impermissible. This is analogous to an argument which might be raised for showing consideration toward works of art, which other people might appreciate. Another such indirect reason for being kind to animals might be that people should foster dispositions of kindness and consideration, for the well-being of human society, and that cruelty toward animals tends to disrupt those dispositions.

Other human-based arguments in favour of some sort of consideration for animals have to do with wastefulness and distribution of resources. It has been claimed that a great deal of plant protein is wasted in the process of nourishing an animal for consumption, so that fewer people can be fed successfully on animal meat than on the grain the animal itself is fed on. It has also been claimed that great quantities of water are similarly used inefficiently in meat-production. It is important to note, however, that these arguments do not depend on the animals' counting morally at all—the claim is simply that human beings will be better off if we adopt certain attitudes toward the use of animals.

The selections in this chapter consider some of the alternative views on the moral status of non-human animals, and try to provide answers to the question of how we should view our relationship to them.

Cruelty to Animals

Section 446,
Canadian Criminal Code

In current Canadian law, non-human animals do not have standing in their own right, but there are limitations on the ways in which people can treat them. The following is the existing law against cruelty to animals.

*　　*　　*

CAUSING UNNECESSARY SUFFERING / Punishment / Failure to exercise reasonable care as evidence / Presence at baiting as evidence / Order of prohibition / Breach of order.

446. (1) Every one commits an offence who

(a) wilfully causes or, being the owner, wilfully permits to be caused unnecessary pain, suffering or injury to an animal or a bird;

(b) by wilful neglect causes damage or injury to animals or birds while they are being driven or conveyed;

(c) being the owner or the person having the custody or control of a domestic animal or a bird or an animal or a bird wild by nature that is in captivity, abandons it in distress or wilfully neglects or fails to provide suitable and adequate food, water, shelter and care for it;

(d) in any manner encourages, aids or assists at the fighting or baiting of animals or birds;

(e) wilfully, without reasonable excuse, administers a poisonous or an injurious drug or substance to a domestic animal or bird or an animal or a bird wild by nature that is kept in captivity or, being the owner of such an animal or a bird, wilfully permits a poisonous or an injurious drug or substance to be administered;

(f) promotes, arranges, conducts, assists in, receives money for or takes part in any meeting, competition, exhibition, pastime, practice, display or event at or in the course of which captive birds are liberated by hand, trap, contrivance or any other means for the purpose of being shot when they are liberated; or

(g) being the owner, occupier, or person in charge of any premises, permits the premises or any part thereof to be used for a purpose mentioned in paragraph (f).

(2) Every one who commits an offence under subsection (1) is guilty of an offence punishable on summary conviction.

(3) For the purposes of proceedings under paragraph (1)(a) or (b), evidence that a person failed to exercise reasonable care or supervision of an animal or a bird thereby causing it pain, suffering, damage or injury is, in the absence of any evidence to the contrary, proof that the pain, suffering, damage or injury was caused or was permitted to be caused wilfully or was caused by wilful neglect, as the case may be.

(4) For the purpose of proceedings under paragraph (1)(d), evidence that an accused was present at the fighting or baiting of animals or birds is, in the absence of any evidence to the contrary, proof that he encouraged, aided or assisted at the fighting or baiting.

(5) Where an accused is convicted of an offence under subsection (1), the court may, in addition to any other sentence that may be imposed for the offence, make an order prohibiting the accused from owning or having the custody or control of an animal or a bird during any period not exceeding two years.

(6) Every one who owns or has the custody or control of an animal or a bird while he is prohibited from doing so by reason of an order made under subsection (5) is guilty of an offence punishable on summary conviction. R.S., c.C-34, s. 402; 1974-75-76, c. 93, s. 35.

The Rights of Animals and Unborn Generations

Joel Feinberg

In this selection, Feinberg tries to determine what characteristics a being must have in order to have rights. His announced intention is to see if future generations of humans can have rights against us, but in the process of exploring that, he considers the claim of non-human animals, vegetables, whole species, dead persons, human vegetables, and fetuses. He claims that, in order to have rights, a being must have interests, and tries to separate authentic uses of that description from metaphorical or mistaken uses.

*   *   *

Every philosophical paper must begin with an unproved assumption. Mine is the assumption that there will still be a world five hundred years from now, and that it will contain human beings who are very much like us. We have it within our power now, clearly, to affect the lives of these creatures for better or worse by contributing to the conservation or corruption of the environment in which they must live. I shall assume furthermore that it is psychologically possible for us to care about our remote descendants, that many of us in fact do care, and indeed that we ought to care. My main concern then will be to show that it makes sense to speak of the rights of unborn generations against us, and that given the moral judgement that we ought to conserve our environmental inheritance for them, and its grounds, we might well say that future generations *do* have rights correlative to our present duties toward them. Protecting our environment now is also a matter of elementary prudence, and insofar as we do it for the next generation already here in the persons of our children, it is a matter of love. But from the perspective of our remote descendants it is basically a matter of justice, of respect for their rights. My main concern here will be to examine the concept of a right to better understand how that can be.

The Problem

To have a right is to have a claim[1] *to* something and *against* someone, the recognition of which is called for by legal rules or, in the case of moral rights, by the principles of an enlightened conscience. In the familiar cases of rights, the claimant is a competent adult human being, and the claimee is an officeholder in an institution or else a private individual, in either case, another competent adult human being. Normal adult human beings, then, are obviously the sorts of beings of whom rights can meaningfully be predicated. Everyone would agree to that, even extreme misanthropes who deny that anyone in fact has rights. On the other hand, it is absurd to say that rocks can have rights, not because rocks are morally inferior things unworthy of rights (that statement makes no sense either), but because rocks belong to a category of entities of whom rights cannot be meaningfully predicated. That is not to say that there are no circumstances in which we ought to treat rocks carefully, but only that the rocks themselves cannot validly claim good treatment from us. In between the clear cases of rocks and normal human beings, however, is a spectrum of less obvious cases, including some bewildering borderline ones. Is it meaningful or conceptually possible to ascribe rights to our dead ancestors? to individual animals? to whole species of animals? to plants? to idiots and madmen? to fetuses? to generations yet unborn? Until we know how to settle these puzzling cases, we cannot claim fully to grasp the concept of a right, or to know the shape of its logical boundaries.

One way to approach these riddles is to turn one's attention first to the most familiar and unproblematic instances of rights, note their most salient characteristics, and then compare the borderline cases with them, measuring as closely as possible the points of similarity and difference. In the end, the way we classify the borderline cases may depend on whether we are more impressed with the similarities or the differences between them and the cases in which we have the most confidence.

It will be useful to consider the problem of individual animals first because their case is the one that has already been debated with the most thoroughness by philosophers so that the dialectic of claim and rejoinder has now unfolded to the point where disputants can get to the end game quickly and isolate the crucial point at issue. When we understand precisely what is at issue in the debate over animal rights, I think we will have the key to the solution of all the other riddles about rights.

Individual Animals

Almost all modern writers agree that we ought to be kind to animals, but that is quite another thing from holding that animals can claim kind treatment from us as their due. Statutes making cruelty to animals a crime are now very common, and these, of course, impose legal duties on people not to mistreat animals; but that still leaves open the question whether the animals, as beneficiaries of those duties, possess rights correlative to them. We may very well have duties *regarding* animals that are not at the same time duties *to* animals, just as we may have duties regarding rocks, or buildings, or lawns, that are not duties *to* the rocks, buildings, or lawns. Some legal writers have taken the still more extreme position that animals themselves are not even the directly intended beneficiaries of statutes prohibiting cruelty to animals. During the nineteenth century, for example, it was commonly said that such statutes were designed to protect human beings by preventing the growth of cruel habits that could later threaten human beings with harm too. Prof. Louis B. Schwartz finds the rationale of the cruelty-to-animals prohibition in its protection of animal lovers from affronts to their sensibilities. "It is not the mistreated dog who is the ultimate object of concern," he writes. "Our concern is for the feelings of other human beings, a large proportion of whom, although accustomed to the slaughter of animals for food, readily identify themselves with a tortured dog or horse and respond with great sensitivity to its sufferings."[2] This seems to me to be factitious. How much more natural is it to say with John Chipman Gray that the true purpose of cruelty-to-animals statutes is "to preserve the dumb brutes from suffering."[3] The very people whose sensibilities are invoked in the alternative explanation, a group that no doubt now includes most of us, are precisely those who would insist that the protection belongs primarily to the animals themselves, not merely to their own tender feelings. Indeed, it would be difficult even to account for the existence of such feelings in the absence of a belief that the animals deserve the protection in their own right and for their own sakes.

Even if we allow, as I think we must, that animals are the intended direct beneficiaries of legislation forbidding cruelty to animals, it does not follow directly that animals have legal rights, and Gray himself, for one,[4] refused to draw this further inference. Animals cannot have rights, he thought, for the same reason they cannot have duties, namely, that they are not genuine "moral agents." Now, it is relatively easy to see why animals cannot have duties, and this matter is largely beyond controversy. Animals cannot be "reasoned with" or instructed in their responsibilities; they are inflexible and unadaptable to future contingencies; they are subject to fits of instinctive passion which they are incapable of repressing or controlling, postponing or sublimating. Hence, they cannot enter into contractual agreements, or make promises; they cannot be trusted; and they cannot (except within very narrow limits and for the purposes of conditioning) be blamed for what would be called "moral failures" in a human being. They are therefore incapable of being moral subjects, of acting rightly or wrongly in the moral sense, of having, discharging, or breeching duties and obligations.

But what is there about the intellectual incompetence of animals (which admittedly disqualifies them for duties) that makes them logically unsuitable for rights? The most common reply to this question is that animals are incapable of *claiming* rights on their own. They cannot make motion, on their own, to courts to have their claims recognized or enforced; they cannot initiate, on their own, any kind of legal proceedings; nor are they capable of even understanding when their rights are being violated, of distinguishing harm from wrongful injury, and responding with indignation and an outraged sense of justice instead of mere anger or fear.

No one can deny any of these allegations, but to the claim that they are grounds for disqualification of rights of animals, philosophers on the other side of this controversy have made convincing rejoinders. It is simply not true, says W.D. Lamont,[5] that the ability to understand what a right is and the ability to set legal machinery in motion by one's own initiative are necessary for the possession of rights. If that were the case, then neither human idiots nor wee babies would have any legal rights at all. Yet it is manifest that both of these classes of intellectual incompetents have legal rights recognized and easily enforced by the courts. Children and idiots start legal proceedings, not on their own direct initiative, but rather through the actions of proxies or attorneys who are empowered to speak in their names. If there is no conceptual absurdity in this situation, why should there be in the case where a proxy makes a claim on behalf of an animal? People commonly enough make wills leaving money to trustees for the care of animals. Is it not natural to speak of the animal's right to his inheritance in cases of this kind? If a trustee embezzles money from the animal's account,[6] and a proxy speaking in the dumb brute's behalf presses the animal's claim, can he not be described as asserting the animal's *rights*? More exactly, the animal itself claims its rights through the vicarious actions of a human proxy speaking in its name and on its behalf. There appears to be no reason why we should require the animal to understand what is going on (so the argument concludes) as a condition for regarding it as a possessor of rights.

Some writers protest at this point that the legal relation between a principal and an agent cannot hold between animals and human beings. Between humans, the relation of agency can take two very different forms, depending upon the degree of discretion granted to the agent, and there is a continuum of combinations between the extremes. On the other hand, there is the agent who is the mere "mouthpiece" of his principal. He is a "tool" in much the same sense as is a typewriter or telephone; he simply transmits the instructions of his principal. Human beings could hardly be the agents or representatives of animals in this sense, since the dumb brutes could no more use human "tools" than mechanical ones. On the other hand, an agent may be some sort of expert hired to exercise his professional judgement on behalf of, and in the name of, the principal. He may be given, within some limited area of expertise, complete independence to act as he deems best, binding his principal to all the beneficial or detrimental consequences. This is the role played by trustees, lawyers, and ghost-writers. This type of representation requires that the agent have great skill, but makes little or no demand upon the principal, who may leave everything to the judgement of his agent. Hence, there appears, at first, to be no reason why an animal cannot be a

totally passive principal in this second kind of agency relationship.

There are still some important dissimilarities, however. In the typical instance of representation by an agent, even of the second, highly discretionary kind, the agent is hired by a principal who enters into an agreement or contract with him; the principal tells his agent that within certain carefully specified boundaries "You may speak for me," subject always to the principal's approval, his right to give new directions, or to cancel the whole arrangement. No dog or cat could possibly do any of those things. Moreover, if it is the assigned task of the agent to defend the principal's rights, the principal may often decide to release his claimee, or to waive his own rights, and instruct his agent accordingly. Again, no mute cow or horse can do that. But although the possibility of hiring, agreeing, contracting, approving, directing, canceling, releasing, waiving, and instructing is present in the typical (all-human) case of agency representation, there appears to be no reason of a logical or conceptual kind why that *must* be so, and indeed there are some special examples involving human principals where it is not in fact so. I have in mind legal rules, for example, that require that a defendant be represented at his trial by an attorney, and impose a state-appointed attorney upon reluctant defendants, or upon those tried *in absentia*, whether they like it or not. Moreover, small children and mentally deficient and deranged adults are commonly represented by trustees and attorneys, even though they are incapable of granting their own consent to the representation, or of entering into contracts, of giving directions, or waiving their rights. It may be that it is unwise to permit agents to represent principals without the latters' knowledge or consent. If so, then no one should ever be permitted to speak for an animal, at least in a legally binding way. But that is quite another thing than saying that such representation is logically incoherent or conceptually incongruous—the contention that is at issue.

H. J. McCloskey,[7] I believe, accepts the argument up to this point, but he presents a new and different reason for denying that animals can have legal rights. The ability to make claims, whether directly or through a representative, he implies, is essential to the possession of rights. Animals obviously cannot press their claims on their own, and so if they have rights, these rights must be assertable by agents. Animals, however, cannot be represented, McCloskey contends, and not for any of the reasons already discussed, but rather because representation, in the requisite sense, is always of interests, and animals (he says) are incapable of having interests.

Now, there is a very important insight expressed in the requirement that a being have interests if he is to be a logically proper subject of rights. This can be appreciated if we consider just why it is that mere things cannot have rights. Consider a very precious "mere thing"—a beautiful natural wilderness, or a complex and ornamental artifact, like the Taj Mahal. Such things ought to be cared for, because they would sink into decay if neglected, depriving some human beings, or perhaps even all human beings, of something of great value. Certain persons may even have as their own special job the care and protection of these valuable objects. But we are not tempted in these cases to speak of "thing-rights" correlative to custodial duties, because, try as we might, we cannot think of

mere things as possessing interests of their own. Some people may have a duty to preserve, maintain, or improve the Taj Mahal, but they can hardly have a duty to help or hurt it, benefit or aid it, succor or relieve it. Custodians may protect it for the sake of a nation's pride and art lovers' fancy; but they don't keep it in good repair for "its own sake," and for "its own true welfare," or "well-being." A mere thing, however valuable to others, has no good of its own. The explanation of that fact, I suspect, consists in the fact that mere things have no conative life: no conscious wishes, desires, and hopes; or urges and impulses; or unconscious drives, aims, and goals; or latent tendencies, direction of growth, and natural fulfillments. Interests must be compounded somehow out of conations; hence mere things have no interests. *A fortiori*, they have no interests to be protected by legal or moral rules. Without interests a creature can have no "good" of its own, the achievement of which can be its due. Mere things are not loci of value in their own right, but rather their value consists entirely in their being objects of other beings' interests.

So far McCloskey is on solid ground, but one can quarrel with his denial that any animals but humans have interests. I should think that the trustee of funds willed to a dog or cat is more than a mere custodian of the animal he protects. Rather his job is to look out for the interests of the animal and make sure no one denies it its due. The animal itself is the beneficiary of his dutiful services. Many of the higher animals at least have appetites, conative urges, and rudimentary purposes, the integrated satisfaction of which constitutes their welfare or good. We can, of course, with consistency treat animals as mere pests and deny that they have any rights; for most animals, especially those of the lower orders, we have no choice but to do so. But it seems to me, nevertheless, that in general, animals *are* among the sorts of beings of whom rights can meaningfully be predicated and denied.

Now, if a person agrees with the conclusion of the argument thus far, that animals are the sorts of beings that *can* have rights, and further, if he accepts the moral judgement that we ought to be kind to animals, only one further premise is needed to yield the conclusion that some animals do in fact have rights. We must now ask ourselves for whose sake ought we to treat (some) animals with consideration and humaneness? If we conceive our duty to be one of obedience to authority, or to one's own conscience merely, or one of consideration for tender human sensibilities only, then we might still deny that animals have rights, even though we admit that they are the kinds of beings that *can* have rights. But if we hold not only that we ought to treat animals humanely but also that we should do so for the animals' own sake, that such treatment is something we owe animals as their due, something that can be claimed for them, something the withholding of which would be an injustice and a wrong, and not merely a harm, then it follows that we do ascribe rights to animals. I suspect that the moral judgements most of us make about animals do pass these phenomenological tests, so that most of us do believe that animals have rights, but are reluctant to say so because of the conceptual confusions about the notion of a right that I have attempted to dispel above.

Now we can extract from our discussion of animal rights a crucial principle for tentative use in the resolution of the other riddles about the applicability of the concept

of a right, namely, that the sorts of beings who *can* have rights are precisely those who have (or can have) interests. I have come to this tentative conclusion for two reasons: (1) because a right holder must be capable of being represented and it is impossible to represent a being that has no interests, and (2) because a right holder must be capable of being a beneficiary in his own person, and a being without interests is a being that is incapable of being harmed or benefitted, having no good or "sake" of its own. Thus, a being without interests has no "behalf" to act in, and no "sake" to act for. My strategy now will be to apply the "interest principle," as we can call it, to the other puzzles about rights, while being prepared to modify it where necessary (but as little as possible), in the hope of separating in a consistent and intuitively satisfactory fashion the beings who can have rights from those which cannot.

Vegetables

It is clear that we ought not to mistreat certain plants, and indeed there are rules and regulations imposing duties on persons not to misbehave in respect to certain members of the vegetable kingdom. It is forbidden, for example, to pick wildflowers in the mountainous tundra areas of national parks, or to endanger trees by starting fires in dry forest areas. Members of Congress introduce bills designed, as they say, to "protect" rare redwood trees from commercial pillage. Given this background, it is surprising that no one[8] speaks of plants as having rights. Plants, after all, are not "mere things"; they are vital objects with inherited biological propensities determining their natural growth. Moreover, we do say that certain conditions are "good" or "bad" for plants, thereby suggesting that plants, unlike rocks, are capable of having a "good." (This is a case, however, where "what we say" should not be taken seriously: we also say that certain kinds of paint are good or bad for the internal walls of a house, and this does not commit us to a conception of walls as being possessed of a good or welfare of their own.) Finally, we are capable of feeling a kind of affection for particular plants, though we rarely personalize them, as we do in the case of animals by giving them proper names.

Still, all are agreed that plants are not the kinds of beings that can have rights. Plants are never plausibly understood to be the direct intended beneficiaries of rules designed to "protect" them. We wish to keep redwood groves in existence for the sake of human beings who can enjoy their serene beauty, and for the sake of generations of human beings yet unborn. Trees are not the sorts of beings who have their "own sakes," despite the fact that they have biological propensities. Having no conscious wants or goals of their own, trees cannot know satisfaction or frustration, pleasure or pain. Hence, there is no possibility of kind or cruel treatment of trees. In these morally crucial respects, trees differ from the higher species of animals.

Yet trees are not mere things like rocks. They grow and develop according to the laws of their own nature. Aristotle and Aquinas both took trees to have their own "natural ends." Why then do I deny them the status of beings with interests of their own? The reason is that an interest, however the concept is finally to be analyzed, presupposes at least rudimentary cognitive equipment. Interests are compounded out of *desires* and *aims*, both of which presuppose something like *belief*, or cognitive awareness. A desiring creature may want X because he seeks anything that is $\emptyset$, and X appears to be $\emptyset$ to him; or he may be seeking Y, and he believes, or expects, or hopes that X will be a means to Y. If he desires X in order to get Y, this implies that he believes that X will bring Y about, or at least that he has some sort of brute expectation that is a primitive correlate of belief. But what of the desire for $\emptyset$ (or for Y) itself? Perhaps a creature has such a "desire" as an ultimate set, as if he had come into existence all "wound up" to pursue $\emptyset$-ness or Y-ness, and his not to reason why. Such a propensity, I think, would not qualify as a desire. Mere brute longings unmediated by beliefs—longings for one knows not what— might perhaps be a primitive form of consciousness (I don't want to beg that question) but they are altogether different from the sort of thing we mean by "desire," especially when we speak of human beings.

If some such account as the above is correct, we can never have any grounds for attributing a desire or a want to a creature known to be incapable even of rudimentary beliefs; and if desires or wants are the materials interests are made of, mindless creatures have no interests of their own. The law, therefore, cannot have as its intention the protection of their interests, so that "protective legislation" has to be understood as legislation protecting the interests human beings may have in them.

Plant life might nevertheless be thought at first to constitute a hard case for the interest principle for two reasons. In the first place, plants no less than animals are said to have needs of their own. To be sure, we can speak even of mere things as having needs too, but such talk misleads one into thinking of the need as belonging, in the final analysis, to the "mere thing" itself. If we were so deceived we would not be thinking of the mere thing as a "mere thing" after all. We say, for example, that John Doe's walls need painting, or that Richard Roe's car needs a washing, but we direct our attitudes of sympathy or reproach (as the case may be) to John and Richard, not to their possessions. It would be otherwise, if we observed that some child is in need of a good meal. Our sympathy and concern in that case would be directed at the child himself as the true possessor of the need in question.

The needs of plants might well seem closer to the needs of animals than to the pseudoneeds of mere things. An owner may need a plant (say, for its commercial value or as a potential meal), but the plant itself, it might appear, needs nutrition or cultivation. Our confusion about this matter may stem from language. It is a commonplace that the word *need* is ambiguous. To say that A needs X may be to say either: (1) X is necessary to the achievement of A's goals, or to the performance of one of its functions, or (2) X is good for A; its lack would harm A or be injurious or detrimental to him (or it). The first sort of need-statement is value-neutral, implying no comment on the value of the goal or function in question; whereas the second kind of statement about needs commits its maker to a value judgement about what is good or bad for A in the long run, that is, about what is in A's interests. A being must have interests, therefore, to have needs in the second sense, but any kind of thing, vegetable or mineral, could have needs in the first sense. An automobile needs gas and oil to function, but it is no tragedy for it if it runs out—an empty gas tank does not hinder or retard its interests. Similarly, to say

that a tree needs sunshine and water is to say that without them it cannot grow and survive; but unless the growth and survival of trees are matters of human concern, affecting human interests, practical or aesthetic, the needs of trees alone will not be the basis of any claim of what is "due" them in their own right. Plants may need things in order to discharge their functions, but their functions are assigned by human interests, not their own.

The second source of confusion derives from the fact that we commonly speak of plants as thriving and flourishing, or withering and languishing. One might be tempted to think of these states either as themselves consequences of the possession of interests so that even creatures without wants or beliefs can be said to have interests, or else as grounds independent of the possession of interests for the making of intelligible claims of rights. In either case, plants would be thought of as conceivable possessors of rights after all.

Consider what it means to speak of something as "flourishing." The verb *to flourish* apparently was applied originally and literally to plants only, and in its original sense it meant simply "to bear flowers: BLOSSOM"; but then by analogical extension of sense it came also to mean "to grow luxuriantly: increase, and enlarge," and then to "THRIVE" (generally) and finally, when extended to human beings, "to be prosperous," or to "increase in wealth, honor, comfort, happiness, or whatever is desirable."[9] Applied to human beings the term is, of course, a fixed metaphor. When a person flourishes, something happens to his interests analogous to what happens to a plant when it flowers, grows, and spreads. A person flourishes when his interests (whatever they may be) are progressing severally and collectively toward their harmonious fulfillment and spawning new interests along the way whose prospects are also good. To flourish is to glory in the advancement of one's interests, in short, to be happy.

Nothing is gained by twisting the botanical metaphor back from humans to plants. To speak of thriving human interests as if they were flowers is to speak naturally and well, and to mislead no one. But then to think of the flowers or plants as if they were interests (or the signs of interests) is to bring the metaphor back full circle for no good reason and in the teeth of our actual beliefs. Some of our talk about flourishing plants reveals quite clearly that the interests that thrive when plants flourish are human not "plant interests." For example, we sometimes make a flowering bush flourish by "frustrating" its own primary propensities. We pinch off dead flowers before seeds have formed, thus "encouraging" the plant to make new flowers in an effort to produce more seeds. It is not the plant's own natural propensity (to produce seeds) that is advanced, but rather the gardener's interest in the production of new flowers and the spectator's pleasure in aesthetic form, color, or scent. What we mean in such cases by saying that the plant flourishes is that our interest in the plant, not its own, is thriving. It is not always so clear that that is what we mean, for on other occasions there is a correspondence between our interests and the plant's natural propensities, a coinciding of what we want from nature and nature's own "intention." But the exceptions to this correspondence provide the clue to our real sense in speaking of a plant's good or welfare.[10] And even when there exists such a correspondence, it is often because we have actually remade the plant's nature so that our own interests in it will flourish more "naturally" and effectively.

Whole Species

The topic of whole species, whether of plants or animals, can be treated in much the same way as that of individual plants. A whole collection, as such, cannot have beliefs, expectations, wants, or desires, and can flourish or languish only in the human interest related sense in which individual plants thrive and decay. Individual elephants can have interests, but the species elephant cannot. Even where individual elephants are not granted rights, human beings may have an interest—economic, scientific, or sentimental—in keeping the species from dying out, and *that* interest may be protected in various ways by law. But that is quite another matter from recognizing a right to survival belonging to the species itself. Still, the preservation of a whole species may quite properly seem to be a morally more important matter than the preservation of an individual animal. Individual animals can have rights but it is implausible to ascribe to them a right to life on the human model. Nor do we normally have duties to keep individual animals alive or even to abstain from killing them provided we do it humanely and non-wantonly in the promotion of legitimate human interests. On the other hand, we do have duties to protect threatened species, not duties to the species themselves as such, but rather duties to future human beings, duties derived from our housekeeping role as temporary inhabitants of this planet.

We commonly and very naturally speak of corporate entities, such as institutions, churches and national states having rights and duties, and an adequate analysis of the conditions for ownership of rights should account for that fact. A corporate entity, of course, is more than a mere collection of things that have some important traits in common. Unlike a biological species, an institution has a charter, or constitution, or bylaws, with rules defining offices and procedures, and it has human beings whose function it is to administer the rules and apply the procedures. When the institution has a duty to an outsider, there is always some determinant human being whose duty it is to do something for the outsider, and when the state, for example, has a right to collect taxes, there are always certain definite flesh and blood persons who have rights to demand tax money from other citizens. We have no reluctance to use the language of corporate rights and duties because we know that in the last analysis these are rights and duties of individual persons, acting in their "official capacities." And when individuals act in their official roles in accordance with valid empowering rules, their acts are imputable to the organization itself and become "acts of state." Thus, there is no need to posit any individual superperson named by the expression "the State" (or for that matter, "the company," "the club," or "the church.") Nor is there any reason to take the rights of corporate entities to be exceptions to the interest principle. The United States is not a superperson with wants and beliefs of its own, but it is a corporate entity with corporate interests that are, in turn, analyzable into the interests of its numerous flesh and blood members.

Dead Persons

So far we have refined the interest principle but we have not had occasion to modify it. Applied to dead persons, however, it will have to be stretched to near the breaking point if it is to explain how our duty to honor commitments to the dead can be thought to be linked to the rights of the dead against us. The case against ascribing rights to dead men can be made very simply: a dead man is a mere corpse, a piece of decaying organic matter. Mere inanimate things can have no interests, and what is incapable of having interests is incapable of having rights. If, nevertheless, we grant dead men rights against us, we would seem to be treating the interests they had while alive as somehow surviving their deaths. There is the sound of paradox in this way of talking, but it may be the least paradoxical way of describing our moral relations to our predecessors. And if the idea of an interest's surviving its possessor's death is a kind of fiction, it is a fiction that most living men have a real interest in preserving.

Most persons while still alive have certain desires about what is to happen to their bodies, their property, or their reputations after they are dead. For that reason, our legal system has developed procedures to enable persons while still alive to determine whether their bodies will be used for purposes of medical research or organic transplantation, and to whom their wealth (after taxes) is to be transferred. Living men also take out life insurance policies guaranteeing that the accumulated benefits be conferred upon beneficiaries of their own choice. They also make private agreements, both contractual and informal, in which they receive promises that certain things will be done after their deaths in exchange for some present service or consideration. In all these cases promises are made to living persons that their wishes will be honored after they are dead. Like all other valid promises, they impose duties on the promisor and confer correlative rights on the promisee.

How does the situation change after the promisee has died? Surely the duties of the promisor do not suddenly become null and void. If that were the case, and known to be the case, there could be no confidence in promises regarding posthumous arrangements; no one would bother with wills or life insurance policies. Indeed the duties of courts and trustees to honor testamentary directions, and the duties of life insurance companies to pay benefits to survivors, are, in a sense, only conditional duties before a man dies. They come into existence as categorical demands for immediate action only upon the promisee's death. So the view that death renders them null and void has the truth exactly upside down.

The survival of the promisor's duty after the promisee's death does not prove that the promisee retains a right even after death, for we might prefer to conclude that there is one class of cases where duties to keep promises are not logically correlated with a promisee's right, namely, cases where the promisee has died. Still, a morally sensitive promisor is likely to think of his promised performance not only as a duty (i.e., a morally required action) but also as something owed to the deceased promisee as his due. Honoring such promises is a way of keeping faith with the dead. To be sure, the promisor will not think of his duty as something to be done for the promisee's "good," since the promisee, being dead, has no "good" of his own. We can think of certain of the deceased's interests, however, (including especially those enshrined in wills and protected by contracts and promises) as surviving their owner's death, and constituting claims against us that persist beyond the life of the claimant. Such claims can be represented by proxies just like the claims of animals. This way of speaking, I believe, reflects more accurately than any other an important fact about the human condition: we have an interest while alive that other interests of ours will continue to be recognized and served after we are dead. The whole practice of honoring wills and testaments, and the like, is thus for the sake of the living, just as a particular instance of it may be thought to be for the sake of one who is dead.

Conceptual sense, then, can be made of talk about dead men's rights; but it is still a wide open moral question whether dead men in fact have rights, and if so, what those rights are. In particular, commentators have disagreed over whether a man's interest in his reputation deserves to be protected from defamation even after his death. With only a few prominent exceptions, legal systems punish a libel on a dead man "only when its publication is in truth an attack upon the interests of living persons."[11] A widow or a son may be wounded, or embarrassed, or even injured economically, by a defamatory attack on the memory of their dead husband or father. In Utah defamation of the dead is a misdemeanor, and in Sweden a cause of action in tort. The law rarely presumes, however, that a dead man himself has any interests, representable by proxy, that can be injured by defamation, apparently because of the maxim that what a dead man doesn't know can't hurt him.

This presupposes, however, that the whole point of guarding the reputations even of living men, is to protect them from hurt feelings, or to protect some other interests, for example, economic ones, that do not survive death. A moment's thought, I think, will show that our interests are more complicated than that. If someone spreads a libelous description of me, without my knowledge, among hundreds of people in a remote part of the country, so that I am, still without my knowledge, an object of general scorn and mockery in that group, I have been injured, even though I never learn what has happened. That is because I have an interest, so I believe, in having a good reputation *simpliciter*, in addition to my interest in avoiding hurt feelings, embarrassment, and economic injury. In the example, I do not know what is being said and believed about me, so my feelings are not hurt; but clearly if I did know, I would be enormously distressed. The distress would be the natural consequence of my belief that an interest other than my interest in avoiding distress had been damaged. How else can I account for the distress? If I had no interest in a good reputation as such, I would respond to news of harm to my reputation with indifference.

While it is true that a dead man cannot have his feelings hurt, it does not follow, therefore, that his claim to be thought of no worse than he deserves cannot survive his death. Almost every living person, I should think, would wish to have this interest protected after his death, at least during the lifetimes of those persons who were his contemporaries. We can hardly expect the law to protect Julius Caesar from defamation in the history books. This might hamper historical research and restrict socially valuable forms of expression. Even inter-

ests that survive their owner's death are not immortal. Anyone should be permitted to say anything he wishes about George Washington or Abraham Lincoln, although perhaps not everything is morally permissible. Everyone ought to refrain from malicious lies about Nero or King Tut, though not so much for those ancients' own sakes as for the sake of those who would now know the truth about the past. We owe it to the brothers Kennedy, however, as their due, not to tell damaging lies about them to those who were once their contemporaries. If the reader would deny that judgement, I can only urge him to ask himself whether he now wishes his own interest in reputation to be respected, along with his interest in determining the distribution of his wealth, after his death.

Human Vegetables

Mentally deficient and deranged human beings are hardly ever so handicapped intellectually that they do not compare favorably with even the highest of the lower animals, though they are commonly so incompetent that they cannot be assigned duties or be held responsible for what they do. Since animals can have rights, then, it follows that human idiots and madmen can too. It would make good sense, for example, to ascribe to them a right to be cured whenever effective therapy is available at reasonable cost, and even those incurables who have been consigned to a sanatorium for permanent "warehousing" can claim (through a proxy) their right to decent treatment.

Human beings suffering extreme cases of mental illness, however, may be so utterly disoriented or insensitive as to compare quite unfavorably with the brightest cats and dogs. Those suffering from catatonic schizophrenia may be barely distinguishable in respect to those traits presupposed by the possession of interests from the lowliest vegetables. So long as we regard these patients as potentially curable, we may think of them as human beings with interests in their own restoration and treat them as possessors of rights. We may think of the patient as a genuine human person inside the vegetable casing struggling to get out, just as in the old fairy tales a pumpkin could be thought of as a beautiful maiden under a magic spell waiting only the proper words to be restored to her true self. Perhaps it is reasonable never to lose hope that a patient can be cured, and therefore to regard him always as a person "under a spell" with a permanent interest in his own recovery that is entitled to recognition and protection.

What if, nevertheless, we think of the catatonic schizophrenic and the vegetating patient with irreversible brain damage as absolutely incurable? Can we think of them at the same time as possessed of interests and rights too, or is this combination of traits a conceptual impossibility? Shocking as it may at first seem, I am driven unavoidably to the latter view. If redwood trees and rosebushes cannot have rights, neither can incorrigible human vegetables.[12] The trustees who are designated to administer funds for the care of these unfortunates are better understood as mere custodians than as representatives of their interests since these patients no longer have interests. It does not follow that they should not be kept alive as long as possible: that is an open moral question not foreclosed by conceptual analysis. Even if we have duties to keep human vegetables alive, however, they cannot be duties *to* them. We may be

obliged to keep them alive to protect the sensibilities of others, or to foster humanitarian tendencies in ourselves, but we cannot keep them alive for their own good, for they are no longer capable of having a "good" of their own. Without awareness, expectation, belief, desire, aim, and purpose, a being can have no interests; without interests, he cannot be benefited; without the capacity to be a beneficiary, he can have no rights. But there may nevertheless be a dozen other reasons to treat him as if he did.

Fetuses

If the interest principle is to permit us to ascribe rights to infants, fetuses, and generations yet unborn, it can only be on the grounds that interests can exert a claim upon us even before their possessors actually come into being, just the reverse of the situation respecting dead men whose interests are respected even after their possessors have ceased to be. Newly born infants are surely noisier than mere vegetables, but they are just barely brighter. They come into existence, as Aristotle said, with the capacity to acquire concepts and dispositions, but in the beginning we suppose that their consciousness of the world is a "blooming, buzzing confusion." They do have a capacity, no doubt from the very beginning, to feel pain, and this alone may be sufficient ground for ascribing both an interest and a right to them. Apart from that, however, during the first few hours of their lives, at least, they may well lack even the rudimentary intellectual equipment necessary to the possession of interests. Of course, this induces no moral reservations whatever in adults. Children grow and mature almost visibly in the first few months so that those future interests that are so rapidly emerging from the unformed chaos of their earliest days seem unquestionably to be the basis of their present rights. Thus, we say of a newborn infant that he has a right now to live and grow into his adulthood, even though he lacks the conceptual equipment at this very moment to have this or any other desire. A new infant, in short, lacks the traits necessary for the possession of interests, but he has the capacity to acquire those traits, and his inherited potentialities are moving quickly toward actualization even as we watch him. Those proxies who make claims in behalf of infants, then, are more than mere custodians: they are (or can be) genuine representatives of the child's emerging interests, which may need protection even now if they are to be allowed to come into existence at all.

The same principle may be extended to "unborn persons." After all, the situation of fetuses one day before birth is not strikingly different from that a few hours after birth. The rights that our law confers on the unborn child, both proprietary and personal, are for the most part, placeholders or reservations for the rights he shall inherit when he becomes a full-fledged interested being. The law protects a potential interest in these cases before it has even grown into actuality, as a garden fence protects newly seeded flower beds long before blooming flowers have emerged from them. The unborn child's present right to property, for example, is a legal protection offered now to his future interest, contingent upon his birth, and instantly voidable if he dies before birth. As Coke put it: "The law in many cases hath consideration of him in respect of the apparent expectation of his birth";[13] but this is quite another thing than recognizing a right actually to be born. Assum-

ing that the child will be born, the law seems to say, various interests that he will come to have after birth must be protected from damage that they can incur even before birth. Thus prenatal injuries of a negligently inflicted kind can give the newly born child a right to sue for damages which he can exercise through a proxy-attorney and in his own name any time *after* he is born.

There are numerous other places, however, where our law seems to imply an unconditional right to be born, and surprisingly no one seems ever to have found that idea conceptually absurd. One interesting example comes from an article given the following headline by the *New York Times*: "Unborn Child's Right Upheld Over Religion."[14] A hospital patient in her eighth month of pregnancy refused to take a blood transfusion even though warned by her physician that "she might die at any minute and take the life of her child as well." The ground of her refusal was that blood transfusions are repugnant to the principles of her religion (Jehovah's Witnesses). The Supreme Court of New Jersey expressed uncertainty over the constitutional question of whether a non-pregnant adult might refuse on religious grounds a blood transfusion pronounced necessary to her own survival, but the court nevertheless ordered the patient in the present case to receive the transfusion on the grounds that "the unborn child is entitled to the law's protection."

It is important to reemphasize here that the questions of whether fetuses do or ought to have rights are substantive questions of law and morals open to argument and decision. The prior question of whether fetuses are the kind of beings that can have rights, however, is a conceptual, not a moral, question, amenable only to what is called "logical analysis," and irrelevant to moral judgement. The correct answer to the conceptual question, I believe, is that unborn children are among the sorts of beings of whom possession of rights can meaningfully be predicated, even though they are (temporarily) incapable of having interests, because their future interests can be protected now, and it does make sense to protect a potential interest even before it has grown into actuality. The interest principle, however, makes perplexing, at best, talk of a noncontingent fetal right to be born; for fetuses, lacking actual wants and beliefs, have no actual interest in being born, and it is difficult to think of any other reason for ascribing any rights to them other than on the assumption that they will in fact be born.[15]

Future Generations

We have it in our power now to make the world a much less pleasant place for our descendants than the world we inherited from our ancestors. We can continue to proliferate in ever greater numbers, using up fertile soil at an even greater rate, dumping our wastes into rivers, lakes, oceans, cutting down our forests, and polluting the atmosphere with noxious gases. All thoughtful people agree that we ought not to do these things. Most would say that we have a duty not to do these things, meaning not merely that conservation is morally required (as opposed to merely desirable) but also that it is something due our descendants, something to be done for their sakes. Surely we owe it to future generations to pass on a world that is not a used up garbage heap. Our remote descendants are not yet present to claim a livable

world as their right, but there are plenty of proxies to speak now in their behalf. These spokesmen, far from being mere custodians, are genuine representatives of future interests.

Why then deny that the human beings of the future have rights which can be claimed against us now in their behalf? Some are inclined to deny them present rights out of a fear of falling into obscure metaphysics, by granting rights to remote and unidentifiable beings who are not yet even in existence. Our unborn great-great-grandchildren are in some sense "potential" persons, but they are far more remotely potential, it may seem, than fetuses. This, however, is not the real difficulty. Unborn generations are more remotely potential than fetuses in one sense, but not in another. A much greater period of time with a far greater number of causally necessary and important events must pass before their potentiality can be actualized, it is true; but our collective posterity is just as certain to come into existence "in the normal course of events" as is any given fetus now in its mother's womb. In that sense the existence of the distant human future is no more remotely potential than that of a particular child already on its way.

The real difficulty is not that we doubt whether our descendants will ever be actual, but rather that we don't know who they will be. It is not their temporal remoteness that troubles us so much as their indeterminacy—their present facelessness and namelessness. Five centuries from now men and women will be living where we live now. Any given one of them will have an interest in living space, fertile soil, fresh air, and the like, but that arbitrarily selected one has no other qualities we can presently envision very clearly. We don't even know who his parents, grandparents, or great-grandparents are, or even whether he is related to us. Still, whoever these human beings may turn out to be, and whatever they might reasonably be expected to be like, they will have interests that we can affect, for better or worse, right now. That much we can and do know about them. The identity of the owners of these interests is now necessarily obscure, but the fact of their interest-ownership is crystal clear, and that is all that is necessary to certify the coherence of present talk about their rights. We can tell, sometimes, that shadowy forms in the spatial distance belong to human beings, though we know not who or how many they are; and this imposes a duty on us not to throw bombs, for example, in their direction. In like manner, the vagueness of the human future does not weaken its claim on us in light of the nearly certain knowledge that it will, after all, be human.

Doubts about the existence of a right to be born transfer neatly to the question of a similar right to come into existence ascribed to future generations. The rights that future generations certainly have against us are contingent rights: the interests they are sure to have when they come into being (assuming of course that they will come into being) cry out for protection from invasions that can take place now. Yet there are no actual interests, presently existent, that future generations, presently nonexistent, have now. Hence, there is no actual interest that they have in simply coming into being, and I am at a loss to think of any other reason for claiming that they have a right to come into existence (though there may well be such a reason). Suppose then that all human beings at a given time voluntarily form a compact never again to produce children, thus leading within a few decades to the end of our species. This of course is a wildly improbable hypothetical example but a rather crucial one for the position I have been tentatively considering. And we can imagine, say, that the whole world is converted to a strange ascetic religion which absolutely requires sexual abstinence for everyone. Would this arrangement violate the rights of anyone? No one can complain on behalf of presently nonexistent future generations that their future interests which give them a contingent right of protection have been violated since they will never come into existence to be wronged. My inclination then is to conclude that the suicide of our species would be deplorable, lamentable, and a deeply moving tragedy, but that it would violate no one's rights. Indeed if, contrary to fact, all human beings could ever agree to such a thing, that very agreement would be a symptom of our species' biological unsuitability for survival anyway.

Conclusion

For several centuries now human beings have run roughshod over the lands of our planet, just as if the animals who do live there and the generations of humans who will live there had no claims on them whatever. Philosophers have not helped matters by arguing that animals and future generations are not the kinds of beings who can have rights now, that they don't presently qualify for membership, even "auxiliary membership," in our moral community. I have tried in this essay to dispel the conceptual confusions that make such conclusions possible. To acknowledge their rights is the very least we can do for members of endangered species (including our own). But that is something.

Appendix

The Paradoxes of Potentiality

Having conceded that rights can belong to beings in virtue of their merely potential interests, we find ourselves on a slippery slope; for it may seem at first sight that anything at all can have potential interests, or much more generally, that anything at all can be potentially almost anything else at all! Dehydrated orange powder is potentially orange juice, since if we add water to it, it will be orange juice. More remotely, however, it is also potentially lemonade, since it will become lemonade if we add a large quantity of lemon juice, sugar, and water. It is also a potentially poisonous brew (add water and arsenic), a potential orange cake (add flour, etc., and bake), a potential orange-colored building block (add cement and harden), and so on, *ad infinitum*. Similarly a two-celled embryo, too small to be seen by the unaided eye, is a potential human being; and so is an unfertilized ovum; and so is even an "uncapacitated" spermatozoan. Add the proper nutrition to an implanted embryo (under certain other necessary conditions) and it becomes a fetus and then a child. Looked at another way, however, the implanted embryo has been combined (under the same conditions) with the nutritive elements, which themselves are converted into a growing fetus and child. Is it then just as proper to say that food is a "potential child" as that an embryo is a potential child? If so, then what isn't a "potential child?" (Organic elements in the air and soil are "potentially food," and hence potentially people!)

Clearly, some sort of line will have to be drawn between direct and proximate potentialities and indirect or remote ones; and however we draw this line, there will be borderline cases whose classification will seem uncertain or even arbitrary. Even though any X can become a Y provided only that it is combined with the necessary additional elements, a, b, c, d, and so forth, we cannot say of any given X that it is a "potential Y" unless certain further—rather strict—conditions are met. (Otherwise the concept of potentiality, being universally and promiscuously applicable, will have no utility.) A number of possible criteria of proximate potentiality suggest themselves. The first is the criterion of causal importance. Orange powder is not properly called a potential building block because of those elements needed to transform it into a building block, the cement (as opposed to any of the qualities of the orange powder) is the causally crucial one. Similarly, any pauper might (misleadingly) be called a "potential millionaire" in the sense that all that need be added to any man to transform him into a millionaire is a great amount of money. The absolutely crucial element in the change, of course, is no quality of the man himself but rather the million dollars "added" to him.

What is causally "important" depends upon our purposes and interests and is therefore to some degree a relativistic matter. If we seek a standard, in turn, of "importance," we may posit such a criterion, for example, as that of the ease or difficulty (to some persons or other) of providing those missing elements which, when combined with the thing at hand, convert it into something else. It does seem quite natural, for example, to say that the orange powder is potentially orange juice, and that is because the missing element is merely common tap water, a substance conveniently near at hand to everyone; whereas it is less plausible to characterize the powder as potential cake since a variety of further elements, and not just one, are required, and some of these are not conveniently near at hand to many. Moreover, the process of combining the missing elements into a cake is rather more complicated than mere "addition." It is less plausible still to call orange powder a potential curbstone for the same kind of reason. The criterion of ease or difficulty of the acquisition and combination of additional elements explains all these variations.

Still another criterion of proximate potentiality closely related to the others is that of degree of deviation required from "the normal course of events." Given the intentions of its producers, distributors, sellers, and consumers, dehydrated orange juice will, in the normal course of events, become orange juice. Similarly, a human embryo securely imbedded in the wall of its mother's uterus will in the normal course of events become a human child. That is to say that if no one deliberately intervenes to prevent it happening, it will, in the vast majority of cases, happen. On the other hand, an unfertilized ovum will not become an embryo unless someone intervenes deliberately to make it happen. Without such intervention in the "normal" course of events, an ovum is a mere bit of protoplasm of a very brief life expectancy. If we lived in a world in which virtually every biologically capable human female became pregnant once a year throughout her entire fertile period of life, then we would regard fertilization as something that happens to every ovum in "the natural course of events." Perhaps we would regard every unfertilized ovum, in such a world, as a potential person even possessed of rights corresponding to its future interests. It would perhaps make conceptual if not moral sense in such a world to regard deliberate nonfertilization as a kind of homicide.

It is important to notice, in summary, that words like *important, easy,* and *normal* have sense only in relation to human experiences, purposes, and techniques. As the latter change, so will our notions of what is important, difficult and usual, and so will the concept of potentiality, or our application of it. If our purposes, understanding, and techniques continue to change in indicated directions, we may even one day come to think of inanimate things as possessed of "potential interests." In any case, we can expect the concept of a right to shift its logical boundaries with changes in our practical experience.

Notes

1 I shall leave the concept of a claim unanalyzed here, but for a detailed discussion, see my "The Nature and Value of Rights," *Journal of Value Inquiry* 4 (Winter 1971): 263-277.

2 Louis B. Schwartz, "Morals, Offenses and the Model Penal Code," *Columbia Law Review* 63 (1963): 673.

3 John Chipman Gray, *The Nature and Sources of the Law,* 2d ed. (Boston: Beacon Press, 1963), p. 43.

4 And W.D. Ross for another. See *The Right and the Good* (Oxford: Clarendon Press, 1930), app. 1, pp. 48-56.

5 W.D. Lamont, *Principles of Moral Judgment* (Oxford: Clarendon Press, 1946), pp. 83-85.

6 Cf. H.J. McCloskey, "Rights," *Philosophical Quarterly* 15 (1965): 121, 124.

7 *Ibid.*

8 Outside of Samuel Butler's *Erewhon.*

9 *Webster's Third New International Dictionary.*

10 Sometimes, of course, the correspondence fails because what accords with the plant's natural propensities is not in our interests, rather than the other way round. I must concede that in cases of this kind we speak even of weeds flourishing, but I doubt that we mean to imply that a weed is a thing with a good of its own. Rather, this way of talking is a plain piece of irony, or else an animistic metaphor (thinking of the weeds in the way we think of prospering businessmen). In any case, when weeds thrive, usually no interests, human or otherwise, flourish.

11 William Salmond, *Jurisprudence*, 12th ed., ed. P.J. Fitzgerald (London: Sweet and Maxwell, 1966), p. 304.

12 Unless, of course, the person in question, before he became a "vegetable," left testamentary directions about what was to be done with his body just in case he should ever become an incurable vegetable. He may have directed either that he be preserved alive as long as possible, or else that he be destroyed, whichever he preferred. There may, of course, be sound reasons of public policy why we should not honor such directions, but if we did promise to give legal effect to such wishes, we would have an example of a man's earlier interest in what is to happen to his body surviving his very competence as a person, in quite the same manner as that in which the express interest of a man now dead may continue to exert a claim on us.

13 As quoted by Salmond, *Jurisprudence*, p. 303. Simply as a matter of policy the potentiality of some future interests may be so remote as to make them seem unworthy of present support. A testator may leave property to his unborn child, for example, but not to his unborn grandchildren. To say of the potential person presently in his mother's womb that he owns property now is to say that certain property must be held for him until he is "real" or "mature" enough to possess it. "Yet the law is careful lest property should be too long withdrawn in this way from the uses of living men in favor of generations yet to come; and various restrictive rules have been established to this end. No testator could now direct his fortune to be accumulated for a hundred years and then distributed among his descendants"— Salmond, *ibid*.

14 *New York Times*, 17 June 1966, p. 1.

15 In an essay entitled "Is There a Right to be Born?" I defend a negative answer to the question posed, but I allow that under certain very special conditions, there can be a "right *not* to be born." See *Abortion*, ed. J. Feinberg (Belmont, Calif.: Wadsworth, 1973).

Questions for Discussion

1 What is the relationship between legal rights and moral rights? Does having one qualify one for the other?

2 Is it possible to make sense of the claim that people should not be cruel to animals without attributing moral weight to the animals themselves?

3 Is Feinberg correct in saying that the kinds of appetites and purposes which animals have should count as the sort of interests needed to have rights?

4 How important is it that a right-holder be able to claim rights on its own behalf? Should we accept such a requirement, even if it means some human beings (e.g. babies and severely mentally handicapped persons) do not qualify as right-holders?

Rights, Interests, Desires, and Beliefs

R.G. Frey

Frey agreyes with Feinberg that a being must have interests in order to have rights, but denies that animals can have interests in the requisite sense. He claims that it makes as much sense to say tractors have rights as to say that non-human animals do.

* * *

I

The question of whether non-human animals possess moral rights is once again being widely argued. Doubtless the rise of ethology is partly responsible for this: as we learn more about the behavior of animals, it seems inevitable that we shall be led to focus upon the similarities between them and us, with the result that the extension of moral rights from human beings to non-human animals can appear, as a result of these similarities, to have a firm basis in nature. (Of course, this way of putting the matter assumes that human beings have moral rights, and on another occasion I should perhaps wish to challenge this assumption.) But the major impetus to renewed interest in the subject of animal rights almost certainly stems from a heightened and more critical awareness, among philosophers and non-philosophers alike, of the arguments for and against eating animals and using them in scientific research. For if animals *do* have moral rights, such as a right to live and to live free from unnecessary suffering, and if our present practices systematically tread upon these rights, then the case for eating and experi-

menting upon animals, especially when other alternatives are for the most part readily available, is going to have to be a powerful one indeed.

It is important, however, not to misconstrue the question: the question is not about *which* rights animals may or may not be thought to possess or about *whether* their alleged rights in a particular regard are on a par with the alleged rights of humans in this same regard but rather about the more fundamental issue of whether animals—or, in any event, the "higher" animals—are a kind of being which can be the logical subject of rights. It is this issue, and a particular position with respect to it, that I want critically to address here.

II

The position I have in mind is the widely influential one which links the possession of rights to the possession of interests. In his *System of Ethics*, Leonard Nelson is among the first, if not the first, to propound the view that all and only beings which have interests can have rights,[1] a view which has attracted an increasingly wide following ever since. For example, in his paper "Rights," H.J. McCloskey embraces this view but goes on to deny that animals have interests;[2] whereas Joel Feinberg, in his seminal paper "The Rights of Animals and Unborn Generations," likewise embraces the view but goes on to affirm that animals do have interests.[3] Nelson himself is emphatic that animals as well as human beings are, as he puts it, "carriers of interests,"[4] and he concludes, accordingly, that animals possess rights, rights which both deserve and warrant our respect. For Nelson, then, it is because animals have interests that they can be the logical subject of rights, and his claim that animals *do have* interests forms the minor premise, therefore, in an argument for the moral rights of animals:

> All and only beings which (can) have interests (can) have moral rights; Animals as well as humans (can) have interests; Therefore, animals (can) have moral rights.

Both McCloskey and Feinberg accept the major premise of this argument, which I shall dub the interest thesis, but disagree over the truth of the minor premise; and it is apparent that the minor premise is indeed the key to the whole matter. For given the truth of the major premise, given, that is, that the possession of interests *is* a criterion for the possession of rights, it is nevertheless only the truth of the minor premise that would result in the inclusion of creatures other than human beings within the class of right-holders. This premise is doubtful, however, and the case against it is a powerful one, or so I want to suggest.

This case is not that developed by McCloskey, whose position is not free of a rather obvious difficulty. He makes the issue of whether animals have interests turn upon their failure and/or inability to grasp and so behave in accordance with the pre-

scriptive overtone which he takes talk of "*X* is in *A*'s interests" to have, when it is not obvious that expressions like "*X* is in *A*'s interests" do have a prescriptive overtone and certainly not obvious that a prescriptive overtone is part of the meaning of such expressions. I have elsewhere tried to show how a McCloskey-like position on interests might be sustained;[5] but I do not think his way of tackling the claim that animals have interests a particularly fruitful one, and I neither adopt nor rely upon it in what follows.

III

To say that "Good health is in John's interests" is not at all the same thing as to say that "John has an interest in good health." The former is intimately bound up with having a good or well-being to which good health is conducive, so that we could just as easily have said "Good health is conducive to John's good or well-being," whereas the latter—"John has an interest in good health"—is intimately bound up with wanting, with John's wanting good health. That these two notions of "interest" are logically distinct is readily apparent: good health may well be in John's interests, in the sense of being conducive to his good or well-being, even if John does not want good health, indeed, even if he wants to continue taking hard drugs, with the result that his health is irreparably damaged; and John may have an interest in taking drugs, in the sense of wanting to take them, even if it is apparent to him that it is not conducive to his good or well-being to continue to do so. In other words, something can be *in* John's interests without John's *having* an interest in it, and John can *have* an interest in something without its being *in* his interests.

If this is right, and there are these two logically distinct senses of "interest," we can go on to ask whether animals can have interests in either of these senses; and if they do, then perhaps the minor premise of Nelson's argument for the moral rights of animals can be sustained.

IV

Do animals, therefore, have interests in the first sense, in the sense of having a good or well-being which can be harmed or benefited? The answer, I think, is that they certainly do have interests in this sense; after all, it is plainly not good for a dog to be fed certain types of food or to be deprived of a certain amount of exercise. This answer, however, is of little use to the Nelsonian cause; for it yields the counter-intuitive result that manmade/manufactured objects and even things have interests, and, therefore, on the interest thesis, have or at least are candidates for having moral rights. For example, just as it is not good for a dog to be deprived of a certain amount of exercise, so it is not good for prehistoric cave drawings to be exposed to excessive amounts of carbon dioxide or for Rembrandt paintings to be exposed to excessive amounts of sunlight.

If, nevertheless, one is inclined to doubt that the notion of "not being good for" in the above examples shows that the object or thing in question "has a good," consider the case of tractors: anything, including tractors, can have a good, a well-being, I submit, if it is the sort of thing that can be good of its kind; and there are obviously good and bad tractors. A tractor which cannot perform certain tasks is not a good trac-

tor, is not good of its kind; it falls short of those standards tractors must meet in order to be good ones. Thus, to say that it is in a tractor's interests to be well-oiled means only that it is conducive to the tractor's being a good one, good of its kind, if it is well-oiled. Just as John is good of his kind (i.e., human being) only if he is in health, so tractors are good of their kind only if they are well-oiled. Of course, farmers *have an interest* in their tractors being well-oiled; but this does not show that being well-oiled is not in a tractor's interest, in the sense of contributing to its being good of its kind. It *may* show that what makes good tractors good depends upon the purposes for which *we* make them; but the fact that we make them for certain purposes in no way shows that, once they are made, they cannot have a good of their own. Their good is being good of their kind, and being well-oiled is conducive to their being good of their kind and so, in this sense, in their interests. If this is right, if tractors do have interests, then on the interest thesis they have or can have moral rights, and this is a counter-intuitive result.

It is tempting to object, I suppose, that tractors cannot be harmed and benefited and, therefore, cannot have interests. My earlier examples, however, suffice to meet this objection. Prehistoric cave drawings are (not benefited but) positively harmed by excessive amounts of carbon dioxide, and Rembrandt paintings are likewise certainly harmed through exposure to excessive amounts of sunlight. It must be emphasized that it is these objects themselves that are harmed, and that their owners are harmed only in so far as and to the extent that the objects themselves undergo harm. Accordingly, on the present objection, interests are present, and the interest thesis once again gives the result that objects or things have or can have moral rights. To accomodate those, should there be any, who just might feel that objects or things can have moral rights, when these objects or things are, e.g., significant works of art, the examples can be suitably altered, so that what is harmed is, e.g., a quite ordinary rug. But if drawings, paintings, and rugs can be harmed, why not tractors? Surely a tractor is harmed by prolonged exposure to rain? And surely the harm the tractor's owner suffers comes through and is a function of the harm to the tractor itself?

In short, it cannot be in this first sense of "interest" that the case for animals and for the truth of Nelson's minor premise is to be made; for though animals do have interests in this sense, so too, do tractors, with awkward results.

V

Do animals, therefore, have interests in the second sense, in the sense of having wants which can be satisfied or left unsatisfied? In this sense, of course, it appears that tractors do not have interests; for though being well-oiled may be conducive to tractors being good of their kind, tractors do not *have an interest* in being well-oiled since they cannot *want* to be well-oiled, cannot, in fact, have any wants whatever. But farmers can have wants, and they certainly have an interest in their tractors being well-oiled.

What, then, about animals? Can they have wants? By "wants," I understand a term that encompasses both needs and desires, and it is these that I shall consider.[6]

If to ask whether animals can have wants is to ask whether they can have needs, then certainly animals have wants. A dog can need water. But *this* cannot be the sense of "want" on which having interests will depend, since it does not exclude things from the class of want-holders. Just as dogs need water in order to function normally, so tractors need oil in order to function normally; and just as dogs will die unless their need for water is satisfied, so trees and grass and a wide variety of plants and shrubs will die unless their need for water is satisfied. Though we should not give the fact undue weight, someone who in ordinary discourse says "The tractor wants oiling" certainly means the tractor needs oiling, if it is not to fall away from those standards which make tractors good of their kind. Dogs, too, need water, if they are not to fall away from the standards which make them good of their kind. It is perhaps worth emphasizing, moreover, as the cases of the tractor, trees, grass, etc., show, that needs do not require the presence either of consciousness or of knowledge of the lack which makes up the need. If, in sum, we are to agree that tractors, trees, grass, etc., do not have wants, and therefore, interests, it cannot be the case that wants are to be construed as needs.

This, then, leaves desires, and the question of whether animals can have wants as desires. I may as well say at once that I do not think that animals can have desires. My reasons for thinking this turn largely upon my doubts that animals can have beliefs, and my doubts in this regard turn partially,[7] though in large part, upon the view that having beliefs is not compatible with the absence of language and linguistic ability. I realize that the claim that animals cannot have desires is a controversial one; but I think the case to be made in support of it, complex though it is, is persuasive. This case, I should stress, consists in an analysis of desire and belief and of what it is to have and to entertain beliefs, and *not* in the adoption of anything like Chomsky's account of language as something radically unlike and completely discontinuous with animal behavior

VI

Suppose I am a collector of rare books and desire to own a Gutenburg Bible; my desire to own this volume is *to be traced* to my belief that I do not now own such a work and that my rare book collection is deficient in this regard. By "to be traced" here, what I mean is this: if someone were to ask *how* my belief that my book collection lacks a Gutenberg Bible is connected with my desire to own such a Bible, what better or more direct reply could be given than that, without this belief, I would not have this desire? For if I believed that my rare book collection *did* contain a Gutenberg Bible and so was complete in this sense, then I would not desire a Gutenberg Bible in order to make up what I now believe to be a notable deficiency in my collection. (Of course, I might desire to own more than one such Bible, but this contingency is not what is at issue here.)

Now what is it that I believe? I believe that my collection lacks a Gutenberg Bible; that is, I believe that the sentence "My collection lacks a Gutenberg Bible" is true. In constructions of the form "I believe that...," what follows upon the "that" is a declarative sentence; and *what* I believe is that that sentence is true. The same is the case with constructions of the form "He believes that...": what follows upon the "that" is a declarative sentence, and what the "he" in question believes is that that sentence is true. The difficulty in the case of animals should be apparent: if someone

were to say, e.g., "The cat believes that the door is locked," then that person is holding, as I see it, that the cat holds the declarative sentence "The door is locked" to be true; and I can see no reason whatever for crediting the cat or any other creature which lacks language, including human infants, with entertaining declarative sentences and holding certain declarative sentences to be true.

Importantly, nothing whatever in this account is affected by changing the example, in order to rid it of sophisticated concepts like "door" and "locked," which in any event may be thought beyond cats, and to put in their place more rudimentary concepts. For the essence of this account is not about the relative sophistication of this or that concept but rather about the relationship between believing something and entertaining and regarding as true certain declarative sentences. If what is believed is that a certain declarative sentence is true, then no creature which lacks language can have beliefs; and without beliefs, a creature cannot have desires. And this is the case with animals, or so I suggest; and if I am right, not even in the sense, then, of wants as desires do animals have interests, which, to recall, is the minor premise in the Nelsonian argument for the moral rights of animals.

But is what is believed that a certain declarative sentence is true? I think there are three arguments of sorts that shore up the claim that this *is* what is believed.

First, I do not see how a creature could have the concept of belief without being able to distinguish between true and false beliefs. When I believe that my collection of rare books lacks a Gutenberg Bible, I believe that it is true that my collection lacks a Gutenberg Bible; put another way, I believe that it is false that my collection contains a Gutenberg Bible. I can distinguish, and do distinguish, between the sentences "My collection lacks a Gutenberg Bible" and "My collection contains a Gutenberg Bible," and it is only the former I hold to be true. According to my view, what I believe in this case is that this sentence is true; and sentences are the sorts of things we regard as or hold to be true. As for the cat, and leaving aside now all questions about the relative sophistication of concepts, I do not see how it could have the belief that the door is locked unless it could distinguish this true belief from the false belief that the door is unlocked. But what is true or false are not states of affairs which correspond to or reflect or pertain to these beliefs; states of affairs are not true or false but either are or are not the case, either do or do not obtain. If, then, one is going to credit cats with beliefs, and cats must be able to distinguish true from false beliefs, and states of affairs are not true or false, then what exactly is it that cats are being credited with distinguishing as true or false? Reflection on this question, I think, forces one to credit cats with language, in order for there to be something that can be true or false in belief; and it is precisely because they lack language that we cannot make this move.

Second, if in order to have the concept of belief a creature must be possessed of the difference between true and false belief, then in order for a creature to be able to distinguish true from false beliefs that creature must—simply must, as I see it—have some awareness of, to put the matter in the most general terms, how language connects with, links up with the world; and I see no reason to credit cats with such an awareness. My belief that my collection lacks a

Gutenberg Bible is true if and only if my collection lacks a Gutenberg Bible; that is, the *truth* of this belief cannot be entertained by me without it being the case that I am aware that the truth of the sentence "My collection lacks a Gutenberg Bible" is *at the very least* partially a function of how the world is. However difficult to capture, it is this relationship between language and the world a grasp of which is necessary if a creature is to grasp the difference between true and false belief, a distinction which it must grasp, if it is to possess the concept of belief at all.

Third, I do not see how a creature could have an awareness or grasp of how language connects with, links up with the world, to leave the matter at its most general, unless that creature was itself possessed of language; and cats are not possessed of language. If it were to be suggested, for example, that the sounds that cats make do amount to a language, I should deny it. This matter is far too large and complex to be tackled here; but the general line of argument I should use to support my denial can be sketched in a very few words. Can cats lie? If they cannot, then they cannot assert anything; and if they lack assertion, I do not see how they could possess a language. And I should be strict: I do not suggest that, lacking assertion, cats possess a language in some attenuated or secondary sense; rather, I suggest that, lacking assertion, they do not possess a language *at all*.

VII

It may be suggested, of course, that there might possibly be a class of desires—let us call them simple desires—which do not involve the intervention of belief, in order to have them, and which do not require that we credit animals with language. Such simple desires, for example, might be for some object or other, and we as language-users might try to capture these simple desires in the case of a dog by describing its behavior in such terms as "The dog simply desires the bone." (This position may have to be complicated, as the result of questions about whether the dog possesses the concept "bone" or even more general concepts such as "material object," "thing" and "thing in my visual field"; but these questions I shall leave aside here.) If all the dog's desires are simple desires, and this is the point, then my arguments to show that dogs lack beliefs may well be beside the point.

A subsidiary argument is required, therefore, in order to cover this possibility. Suppose, then, the dog simply desires the bone: is the dog aware that it has this simple desire or not? If it is alleged to have this desire but to be unaware that it has it, to want but to be unaware that it wants, then a problem arises. In the case of human beings, unconscious desire can be made sense of, but only because we first make sense of conscious desire; but where no desires are conscious ones, where the creature in question is alleged to have only unconscious desires, what cash value can the use of the term "desire" have in such a case? This question must be appreciated against the backdrop of what appears to ensue as a result of the present claim. On the strength of the dog's behavior, it is claimed that the dog simply desires the bone; the desire we claim for it is one which, if we concede that it has it, it is unaware that it has; and no distinction between conscious and unconscious desire is to be drawn in the dog's case. Consider, then, a rubber plant which

shuns the dark and through a series of movements, seeks the light: by parity of reasoning with the dog's case, we can endow the plant with an unconscious desire for the light, and claim as we do so that it, too, is a type of creature for whom no distinction between conscious and unconscious desire is possible. In other words, without an awareness-condition of some sort, it would seem that the world can be populated with an enormous number of unconscious desires in this way, and it no longer remains clear what, if anything, the cash value of the term "desire" is in such cases. If, however, the dog is alleged to have a simple desire for the bone and to be aware that it simply desires the bone; it is, in other words, self-conscious. Now my objection to regarding the dog as self-conscious is not merely founded upon the view that self-consciousness presupposes the possession of language, which is too large a subject to go into here; it is also founded upon the fact that there is nothing the dog can do which can express the difference between desiring the bone and being aware of desiring the bone. Yet, the dog would have to be capable of expressing this difference in its behavior, if one is going to hold, *on the basis of that behavior*, that the dog is aware that it has a simple desire for the bone, aware that it simply desires the bone.

Even, then, if we concede for the sake of argument that there are simple desires, desires which do not involve the intervention of belief in order to have them, the suggestion that we can credit animals with these desires, without also having to credit them with language, is at best problematic.

VIII

I want, finally, to comment upon a contention that is not exactly an objection to my earlier remarks so much as a thesis which might be thought to serve as a possible rallying point for opponents.

In *Belief, Truth and Knowledge*, D.M. Armstrong proposes a way of interpreting "that"-clauses used of animals, such that the attribution of beliefs to animals in sentences of the form "The dog believes that..." remains intelligible but does not commit us to characterizing the exact content of animal beliefs.[8] Briefly, Armstrong suggests that "that"-clauses used of animals be treated as referentially transparent (as opposed to opaque) constructions, so that, "in saying that the dog believes that his master is at the door we are, or should be, attributing to the dog a belief whose exact content we do not know but which can be obtained by substituting *salva veritate* in the proposition 'that his master is at the door.'"[9] There are problems here, as Armstrong says, with the use of human concepts to describe the actual content of animal beliefs, and further problems, which Armstrong does not go into, about the actual categories of things which animals recognize; and these two clusters of problems together, I suspect, prove highly damaging to Armstrong's analysis. But at least his way of proceeding, he claims, "shows that we need not give up our natural inclination to attribute beliefs to animals just because the descriptions we give of the beliefs almost certainly do not fit the beliefs' actual content."[10]

My problem with Armstrong's position is this: on the strength of the dog's behavior, we say "The dog believes that his master is at the door"; but our attributing this belief to the dog is not the same thing as showing that it actually has this belief. What we require, if we are to move from our saying "The dog believes that *p*" to holding that the dog actually has the belief *that p*, is some account of the connection, not between behavior and our attribution of belief, but between behavior and belief. Now if, as Armstrong, one allows belief to have any propositional content whatever, even propositional content that is to be regarded and treated as referentially transparent; and if, as Armstrong, one is prepared to concede that dogs do not possess language; then it must be the case, if one is going to claim that dogs actually do have beliefs, both that they have some grasp (a term which the reader is to interpret as liberally as he desires) of this propositional content and that non-linguistic behavior alone can suffice to show that they have such a grasp. I have two difficulties here. First, I do not understand how non-linguistic behavior can *show* that a dog possesses the belief *that p* unless it is the case that that non-linguistic behavior is connected with the belief *that p* in such a way that that same piece of non-linguistic behavior is not compatible with the belief *that q* or *that r* or *that s*. For if the dog's non-linguistic behavior is compatible both with the belief *that p* and with these other beliefs, then I do not understand how it can be concluded on the basis of that behavior that it has the belief *that p* or that it has a grasp of the propositional content of the belief *that p*. For example, yesterday, my dog wagged its tail when its master was at the door, but it also wagged its tail when its lunch was about to be prepared and when the sun was being eclipsed by the moon. On all three occasions, it barked and jumped about. So far as I could see, its non-linguistic behavior was the same on the last two occasions as it was on the first, and I am not clear how on the basis of that behavior it can possibly be concluded that the dog *had* the belief that his master was at the door or that the dog *had* a grasp of the propositional content of the belief that its master was at the door. Second, I do not understand how a piece of non-linguistic behavior could be connected with the belief *that p* in such a way that we could conclude on the basis of the presence of that piece of behavior that the dog actually had the belief *that p* or had actually grasped the propositional content of the belief *that p* unless it were the case that there were some intrinsic connection between that piece of non-linguistic behavior and the proposition *that p* itself. The dog allegedly believes *that p*: according to Armstrong, *that p* is, even if in a referentially transparent fashion, what is believed, and *that p* is a proposition. In order to show that the dog grasps the proposition *that p*, its behavior must suffice; but if its behavior is in fact to show that it grasps just this particular proposition, just this proposition *that p*, then surely there must be some intrinsic connection between the dog's wagging its tail and its barking and jumping about and the proposition "Its master is at the door," since that behavior is compatible with the widely different propositions "Lunch is about to be served" and "The sun is being eclipsed by the moon." We can describe the dog's behavior in propositional terms, describe it as believing *that p* or as having a grasp of the propositional content of the belief *that p*; but the fact that the dog wags its tail, barks and jumps about does not show that the dog has grasped the proposition *that p* and *could not* show this, I think, unless wagging its tail, barking and jumping about were intrinsi-

cally connected with just that proposition, which they are not, any more than they are so connected with any other proposition.

Put succinctly, then, my complaint against Armstrong is that, even if his analysis of the use of "that"-clauses in respect of animals is correct, it still has not been shown *either* that the dog has a grasp of the proposition *that p* or the propositional content of the belief *that p* or that non-linguistic behavior alone can suffice to establish such a grasp. But it is precisely these things which must be shown, if we are to pass from merely attributing beliefs to animals on the strength of their behavior to concluding on the strength of their behavior that they actually have some beliefs.[11]

IX

I conclude, then, that the Nelsonian position on the moral rights of animals is not a sound one: the truth of the minor premise in his argument—that animals have interests—is doubtful at best, and animals must have interests if, in accordance with the interest thesis, they are to be a logical subject of such rights. For animals either have interests in a sense which allows objects and things to have interests, and so, on the interest thesis, to have or to be candidates for having moral rights or they do not have interests at all, and so, on the interest thesis, do not have and are not candidates for having moral rights. I have reached this conclusion, moreover, without querying the correctness of the interest thesis itself, without querying that is, whether the possession of interests *really* is a criterion for the possession of moral rights.[12]

Notes

1   Leonard Nelson, *System of Ethics* , tr. by Norbert Guterman (New Haven, 1956), Part I, Section 2, Chapter 7, pp. 136-144.

2   H.J. McCloskey, "Rights," *Philosophical Quarterly*, vol. 15 (1965), pp. 115-127.

3   Joel Feinberg, "The Rights of Animals and Unborn Generations," in W.T. Blackstone, (ed.), *Philosophy and Environmental Crisis* (Athens, Georgia, 1974), pp. 43-68.

4   Nelson, *op. cit.*, p. 138.

5   See my paper "Interests and Animal Rights," *Philosophical Quarterly*, vol. 27 (1977), pp. 254-259.

6   See also my paper "Russell and the Essence of Desire," *Philosophy*, forthcoming.

7   I express my doubts of a different kind elsewhere; see note 6.

8   D.M. Armstrong, *Belief, Truth and Knowledge* (Cambridge, 1973), pp. 24-37.

9   *Ibid.*, p. 26.

10   *Ibid.*, p. 27. In this section, because I am addressing Armstrong and others who analyze belief propositionally or at least allow it to have propositional content, I shall allow myself to speak to the belief *that p*, where *that p* is a proposition. I remind the reader, however, that my own account of belief in Section VII is in terms of sentences. What I say here is consistent with what I say there, since in each instance where belief is analyzed propositionally here, I should resort to Quine's method for eliminating propositions in belief contexts in favor of sentences.

11   One may, of course, try to get around my argument by analyzing belief non-propositionally (e.g., by trying to develop a reductionism of belief to behavior in the case of animals), but this is not Armstrong's tack in his discussion of animals. Nor, as it will be apparent from my arguments in this paper, is it one that I think capable of showing that animals actually have the concept of belief, since a reductionism would appear to leave no room for a distinction between true and false belief, a grasp of which is necessary, in my view, if a creature is to have the concept of belief at all.

12   An earlier version of this paper was read to a discussion group in Oxford and to a conference on the philosophy of Leonard Nelson in the University of Göttingen. I am indebted to the participants in each for helpful comments and suggestions.

Questions for Discussions

1   Is Frey correct that only beings capable of using language and forming beliefs can be possessors of rights?

2   How convincing is Frey's claim that cave drawings, paintings, and tractors are just as plausible candidates for rights as non-human animals?

Animal Liberation[1]

Peter Singer

Peter Singer has been one of the leaders in the movement to change common attitudes toward treatment of animals for many years now. The following landmark article first appeared in 1973, and has been extremely influential. Singer argues that all suffering counts equally, no matter whose it is, and that non-human animals are capable of suffering.

*   *   *

I

We are familiar with Black Liberation, Gay Liberation, and a variety of other movements. With Women's Liberation some thought we had come to the end of the road. Discrimination on the basis of sex, it has been said, is the last form of discrimination that is universally accepted and practiced without pretense, even in those liberal circles which have long prided themselves on their freedom from racial discrimination. But one should always be wary of talking of "the last remaining form of discrimination." If we have learned anything from the liberation movements, we should have learned how difficult it is to be aware of the ways in which we discriminate until they are forcefully pointed out to us. A liberation movement demands an expansion of our moral horizons, so that practices that were previously regarded as natural and inevitable are now seen as intolerable.

Animals, Men and Morals is a manifesto for an Animal Liberation movement. The contributers to the book may not all see the issue this way. They are a varied group. Philosophers, ranging from professors to graduate students, make up the largest contingent. There are five of them, including the three editors, and there is also an extract from the unjustly neglected German philosopher with an English name, Leonard Nelson, who died in 1927. There are essays by two novelist/critics, Brigid Brophy and Maureen Duffy, and another by Muriel the Lady Dowding, widow of Dowding of Battle of Britain fame and the founder of "Beauty without Cruelty," a movement that campaigns against the use of animals for furs and cosmetics. The other pieces are by a psychologist, a botanist, a sociologist, and Ruth Harrison, who is probably best

described as a professional campaigner for animal welfare.

Whether or not these people, as individuals, would agree that they are launching a liberation movement for animals, the book as a whole amounts to no less. It is a demand for a complete change in our attitudes to nonhumans. It is a demand that we cease to regard the exploitation of other species as natural and inevitable, and that, instead, we see it as a continuing moral outrage. Patrick Corbett, Professor of Philosophy at Sussex University, captures the spirit of the book in his closing words:

> ...we require now to extend the great principles of liberty, equality and fraternity over the lives of animals. Let animal slavery join human slavery in the graveyard of the past.

The reader is likely to be skeptical. "Animal Liberation" sounds more like a parody of liberation movements than a serious objective. The reader may think: We support the claims of blacks and women for equality because blacks and women really are equal to whites and males—equal in intelligence and in abilities, capacity for leadership, rationality, and so on. Humans and nonhumans obviously are not equal in these respects. Since justice demands only that we treat equals equally, unequal treatment of humans and nonhumans cannot be an injustice.

This is a tempting reply, but a dangerous one. It commits the non-racist and non-sexist to a dogmatic belief that blacks and women really are just as intelligent, able, etc., as whites and males—and no more. Quite possibly this happens to be the case. Certainly attempts to prove that racial or sexual differences in these respects have a genetic origin have not been conclusive. But do we really want to stake our demand for equality on the assumption that there are no genetic differences of this kind between the different races or sexes? Surely the appropriate response to those who claim to have found evidence for such genetic differences is not to stick to the belief that there are no differences, whatever the evidence to the contrary; rather one should be clear that the claim to equality does not depend on IQ. Moral equality is distinct from factual equality. Otherwise it would be nonsense to talk of the equality of human beings, since humans, as individuals, obviously differ in intelligence and almost any ability one cares to name. If possessing greater intelligence does not entitle one human to exploit another, why should it entitle humans to exploit nonhumans?

Jeremy Bentham expressed the essential basis of equality in his famous formula: "Each to count for one and none for more than one." In other words, the interests of every being that has interests are to be taken into account and treated equally with the like interests of any other being. Other moral philosophers, before and after Bentham, have made the same point in different ways. Our concern for others must not depend on whether they possess certain characteristics, though just what that concern involves may, of course, vary according to such characteristics.

Bentham, incidentally, was well aware that the logic of the demand for racial equality did not stop at the equality of humans. He wrote:

The day *may* come when the rest of the animal creation may acquire those rights which never could have been withholden from them but by the hand of tyranny. The French have already discovered that the blackness of the skin is no reason why a human being should be abandoned without redress to the caprice of a tormentor. It may one day come to be recognized that the number of the legs, the villiosity of the skin, or the termination of the *os sacrum*, are reasons equally insufficient for abandoning a sensitive being to the same fate. What else is it that should trace the insuperable line? Is it the faculty of reason, or perhaps the faculty of discourse? But a full-grown horse or dog is beyond comparison a more rational, as well as a more conversable animal, than an infant of a day, or a week, or even a month old. But suppose they were otherwise, what would it avail? The question is not, Can they *reason?* nor Can they *talk?* but, Can they *suffer?*[2]

Surely Bentham was right. If a being suffers, there can be no moral justification for refusing to take that suffering into consideration, and, indeed, to count it equally with the like suffering (if rough comparisons can be made) of any other being.

So the only question is: do animals other than man suffer? Most people agree unhesitatingly that animals like cats and dogs can and do suffer, and this seems also to be assumed by those laws that prohibit wanton cruelty to such animals. Personally, I have no doubt at all about this and find it hard to take seriously the doubts that a few people apparently do have. The editors and contributors of *Animals, Men and Morals* seem to feel the same way, for although the question is raised more than once, doubts are quickly dismissed each time. Nevertheless, because this is such a fundamental point, it is worth asking what grounds we have for attributing suffering to other animals.

It is best to begin by asking what grounds any individual human has for supposing that other humans feel pain. Since pain is a state of consciousness, a "mental event," it can never be directly observed. No observations, whether behavioral signs such as writhing or screaming or physiological or neurological recordings, are observations of pain itself. Pain is something one feels, and one can only infer that others are feeling it from various external indications. The fact that only philosophers are ever skeptical about whether other humans feel pain shows that we regard such inference as justifiable in the case of humans.

Is there any reason why the same inference should be unjustifiable for other animals? Nearly all the external signs which lead us to infer pain in other humans can be seen in other species, especially "higher" animals such as mammals and birds. Behavioral signs—writhing, yelping, or other forms of calling, attempts to avoid the source of pain, and many others, are present. We know, too, that these animals are biologically similar in the relevant respects, having nervous systems like ours which can be observed to function as ours do.

So the grounds for inferring that these animals can feel pain are nearly as good as the grounds for inferring other humans do. Only nearly, for there is one behavioral sign that humans have but nonhumans, with the exception of one or two specially raised chimpanzees, do not have. This, of course, is a developed language. As the quotation from Bentham indicates, this has long been regarded as an important distinction between man and other animals. Other animals may communicate with each other, but not in the way we do. Following Chomsky, many people now mark this distinction by saying that only humans communicate in a form that is governed by rules of syntax. (For the purposes of this argument, linguists allow those chimpanzees who have learned a syntactic sign language to rank as honorary humans.) Nevertheless, as Bentham pointed out, this distinction is not relevant to the question of

how animals ought to be treated, unless it can be linked to the issue of whether animals suffer.

This link may be attempted in two ways. First, there is a hazy line of philosophical thought, stemming perhaps from some doctrines associated with Wittgenstein, which maintains that we cannot meaningfully attribute states of consciousness to beings without language. I have not seen this argument made explicit in print, though I have come across it in conversation. This position seems to me very implausible, and I doubt that it would be held at all if it were not thought to be a consequence of a broader view of the significance of language. It may be that the use of a public, rule-governed language is a precondition of conceptual thought. It may even be, although personally I doubt it, that we cannot meaningfully speak of a creature having an intention unless that creature can use a language. But states like pain, surely, are more primitive than either of these, and seem to have nothing to do with language.

Indeed, as Jane Goodall points out in her study of chimpanzees, when it comes to the expression of feelings and emotions, humans tend to fall back on nonlinguistic modes of communication which are often found among apes, such as a cheering pat on the back, an exuberant embrace, a clasp of hands, and so on.[3] Michael Peters makes a similar point in his contribution to *Animals, Men and Morals* when he notes that the basic signals we use to convey pain, fear, sexual arousal, and so on are not specific to our species. So there seems to be no reason at all to believe that a creature without language cannot suffer.

The second, and more easily appreciated way of linking language and the existence of pain is to say that the best evidence that we can have that another creature is in pain is when he tells us that he is. This is a distinct line of argument, for it is not being denied that a non-language-user conceivably could suffer, but only that we could know that he is suffering. Still, this line of argument seems to me to fail, and for reasons similar to those just given. "I am in pain" is not the best possible evidence that the speaker is in pain (he might be lying) and it is certainly not the only possible evidence. Behavioral signs and knowledge of the animals' biological similarity to ourselves together provide adequate evidence that animals do suffer. After all, we would not accept linguistic evidence if it contradicted the rest of the evidence. If a man was severely burned, and behaved as if he were in pain, writhing, groaning, being very careful not to let his burned skin touch anything, and so on, but later said he had not been in pain at all, we would be more likely to conclude that he was lying or suffering from amnesia than that he had not been in pain.

Even if there were stronger grounds for refusing to attribute pain to those who do not have a language, the consequences of this refusal might lead us to examine these grounds unusually critically. Human infants, as well as some adults, are unable to use language. Are we to deny that a year-old infant can suffer? If not, how can language be crucial? Of course, most parents can understand the responses of even very young infants better than they understand the responses of other animals, and sometimes infant responses can be understood in the light of later development.

This, however, is just a fact about the relative knowledge we have of our own species and other species, and most of this knowledge is simply derived from closer contact. Those who have studied the behavior of other animals soon learn to understand their responses at least as well as we understand those of an infant. (I am not just referring to Jane Goodall's and other well-known studies of apes. Consider, for example, the degree of understanding achieved by Tinbergen from watching herring gulls.)[4] Just as we can understand infant human behavior, so we can understand the behavior of other species in the light of our own behavior (and sometimes we can understand our own behavior better in the light of the behavior of other species).

The grounds we have for believing that other mammals and birds suffer are, then, closely analogous to the grounds we have for believing that other humans suffer. It remains to consider how far down the evolutionary scale this analogy holds. Obviously it becomes poorer when we get further away from man. To be more precise would require a detailed examination of all that we know about other forms of life. With fish, reptiles, and other vertebrates the analogy still seems strong, with molluscs like oysters it is much weaker. Insects are more difficult, and it may be that in our present state of knowledge we must be agnostic about whether they are capable of suffering.

If there is no moral justification for ignoring suffering when it occurs, and it does occur in other species, what are we to say of our attitudes toward these other species? Richard Ryder, one of the contributors to *Animals, Men and Morals*, uses the term "speciesism" to describe the belief that we are entitled to treat members of other species in a way in which it would be wrong to treat members of our own species. The term is not euphonious, but it neatly makes the analogy with racism. The non-racist would do well to bear the analogy in mind when he is inclined to defend human behavior toward nonhumans. "Shouldn't we worry about improving the lot of our own species before we concern ourselves with other species?" he may ask. If we substitute "race" for "species" we shall see that the question is better not asked. "Is a vegetarian diet nutritionally adequate?" resembles the slave-owner's claim that he and the whole economy of the South would be ruined without slave labor. There is even a parallel with skeptical doubts about whether animals suffer, for some defenders of slavery professed to doubt whether blacks really suffer in the way that whites do.

I do not want to give the impression, however, that the case for Animal Liberation is based on the analogy with racism and no more. On the contrary, *Animals, Men and Morals* describes the various ways in which humans exploit nonhumans, and several contributors consider the defenses that have been offered, including the defense of meat-eating mentioned in the last paragraph. Sometimes the rebuttals are scornfully dismissive, rather than carefully designed to convince the detached critic. This may be a fault, but it is a fault that is inevitable, given the kind of book this is. The issue is not one of which one can remain detached. As the editors state in their Introduction:

> Once the full force of moral assessment has been made explicit there can be no rational excuse left for killing animals, be they killed for food, science, or sheer personal indulgence. We have not assembled this book to provide the reader with yet another manual on how to make brutalities less brutal. Compromise, in the traditional sense of the term, is simple unthinking weakness when one considers the actual reasons for our crude relationships with the other animals.

The point is that on this issue there are few critics who are genuinely detached. People who eat pieces of slaughtered nonhumans every day find it hard to believe that they are doing wrong; and they also find it hard to imagine what else they could eat. So for those who do not place nonhumans beyond the pale of morality, there comes a stage when further argument seems pointless, a stage at which one can only accuse one's opponent of hypocrisy and reach for the sort of sociological account of our practices and the way we defend them that is attempted by David Wood in his contribution to this book. On the other hand, to those unconvinced by the arguments, and unable to accept that they are rationalizing their dietary preferences and their fear of being thought peculiar, such sociological explanations can only seem insultingly arrogant.

II

The logic of speciesism is most apparent in the practice of experimenting on nonhumans in order to benefit humans. This is because the issue is rarely obscured by allegations that nonhumans are so different from humans that we cannot know anything about whether they suffer. The defender of vivisection cannot use this argument because he needs to stress the similarities between man and other animals in order to justify the usefulness to the former of experiments on the latter. The researcher who makes rats choose between starvation and electric shocks to see if they develop ulcers (they do) does so because he knows that the rat has a nervous system very similar to man's, and presumably feels an electric shock in a similar way.

Richard Ryder's restrained account of experiments on animals made me angrier with my fellow men than anything else in this book. Ryder, a clinical psychologist by profession, himself experimented on animals before he came to hold the view he puts forward in his essay. Experimenting on animals is now a large industry, both academic and commercial. In 1969, more than 5 million experiments were performed in Britain, the vast majority without anesthetic (though how many of these involved pain is not known). There are no accurate US figures, since there is no federal law on the subject, and in many cases no state law either. Estimates vary from 20 million to 200 million. Ryder suggests that 80 million may be the best guess. We tend to think that this is all for vital medical research, but of course it is not. Huge numbers of animals are used in university departments from Forestry to Psychology, and even more are used for commercial purposes, to test whether cosmetics can cause skin damage, or shampoos eye damage, or to test food additives or laxatives or sleeping pills or anything else.

A standard test for foodstuffs is the "LD50." The object of this test is to find the dosage level at which 50 percent of the test animals will die. This means that nearly all of them will become very sick before finally succumbing or surviving. When the substance is a harmless one, it may be necessary to force huge doses down the animals, until in some cases sheer volume or concentration causes death.

Ryder gives a selection of experiments, taken from recent scientific journals. I will quote two, not for the sake of indulging in gory details, but in order to give an idea of what normal researchers think they may legitimately do to other species. The point is not that the individual researchers are cruel men, but that they are behaving in a way that is allowed by our speciesist attitude. As Ryder points out, even if only 1 percent of the experiments involve severe pain, that is 50,000 experiments in Britain each year, or nearly 150 every day (and about fifteen times as many in the United States, if Ryder's guess is right). Here then are two experiments:

O.S. Ray and R.J. Barrett of Pittsburgh gave electric shocks to the feet of 1,042 mice. They then caused convulsions by giving more intense shocks through cup-shaped electrodes applied to the animals' eyes or through pressure spring clips attached to their ears. Unfortunately some of the mice who "successfully completed Day One training were found sick or dead prior to testing on Day Two." [*Journal of Comparative and Physiological Psychology,* 1969, Vol. 67, pp. 110-116]

At the National Institute for Medical Research, Mill Hill, London, W. Feldberg and S.L. Sherwood injected chemicals into the brains of cats—"with a number of widely different substances, recurrent patterns of reaction were obtained. Retching, vomiting, defaecation, increased salivation and greatly accelerated respiration leading to panting were common features,"...

The injection into the brain of a large dose of Tubocuraine caused the cat to jump "from the table to the floor and then straight into its cage, where it started calling more and more noisily whilst moving about restlessly and jerkily...finally the cat fell with legs and neck flexed, jerking in rapid clonic movements, the condition being that of a major [epileptic] convulsion...within a few seconds the cat got up, ran for a few yards at high speed and fell in another fit. The whole process was repeated several times within the next ten minutes, during which the cat lost faeces and foamed at the mouth."

This animal finally died thirty-five minutes after the brain injection. [*Journal of Physiology,* 1954, Vol. 123, pp. 148-167]

There is nothing secret about these experiments. One has only to open any recent volume of a learned journal, such as the *Journal of Comparative and Physiological Psychology*, to find full descriptions of experiments of this sort, together with the results obtained—results that are frequently trivial and obvious. The experiments are often supported by public funds.

It is a significant indication of the level of acceptability of these practices that, although these experiments are taking place at this moment on university campuses throughout the country, there has, so far as I know, not been the slightest protest from the student movement. Students have been rightly concerned that their universities should not discriminate on grounds of race or sex, and that they should not serve the purposes of the military or big business. Speciesism continues undisturbed, and many students participate in it. There may be a few qualms at first, but since everyone regards it as normal, and it may even be a required part of a course, the student soon becomes hardened and, dismissing his earlier feelings as "mere sentiment," comes to regard animals as statistics rather than sentient beings with interests that warrant consideration.

Argument about vivisection has often missed the point because it has been put in absolutist terms: would the abolitionist be prepared to let thousands die if they could be saved by experimenting on a single animal? The way to reply to this purely hypothetical question is to pose another: Would the experimenter be prepared to experiment on a human orphan under six months old, if it were the only way to save many lives? (I say "orphan" to avoid the complication of parental feelings, although in doing so I am being overfair to the experimenter, since

the nonhuman subjects of experiments are not orphans.) A negative answer to this question indicates that the experimenter's readiness to use nonhumans is simple discrimination, for adult apes, cats, mice, and other mammals are more conscious of what is happening to them, more self-directing, and, so far as we can tell, just as sensitive to pain as a human infant. There is no characteristic that human infants possess that higher mammals do not have to the same or a higher degree.

(It might be possible to hold that what makes it wrong to experiment on a human infant is that the infant will in time develop into more than the nonhuman, but one would then, to be consistent, have to oppose abortion, and perhaps contraception, too, for the fetus and the egg and sperm have the same potential as the infant. Moreover, one would still have no reason for experimenting on a nonhuman rather than a human with brain damage severe enough to make it impossible for him to rise above infant level.)

The experimenter, then, shows a bias for his own species whenever he carries out an experiment on a nonhuman for a purpose that he would not think justified him in using a human being at an equal or lower level of sentience, awareness, ability to be self-directing, etc. No one familiar with the kind of results yielded by these experiments can have the slightest doubt that if this bias were eliminated the number of experiments performed would be zero or very close to it.

III

If it is vivisection that shows the logic of speciesism most clearly, it is the use of other species for food that is at the heart of our attitudes toward them. Most of *Animals, Men and Morals* is an attack on meat-eating—an attack which is based solely on concern for nonhumans, without reference to arguments derived from considerations of ecology, macrobiotics, health, or religion.

The idea that nonhumans are utilities, means to our ends, pervades our thought. Even conservationists who are concerned about the slaughter of wild fowl but not about the vastly greater slaughter of chickens for our tables are thinking in this way—they are worried about what we would lose if there were less wildlife. Stanley Godlovitch, pursuing the Marxist idea that our thinking is formed by the activities we undertake in satisfying our needs, suggests that man's first classification of his environment was into Edibles and Inedibles. Most animals came into the first category, and there they have remained.

Man may always have killed other species for food, but he has never exploited them so ruthlessly as he does today. Farming has succumbed to business methods, the objective being to get the highest possible ratio of output (meat, eggs, milk) to input (fodder, labor costs, etc.). Ruth Harrison's essay "On Factory Farming" gives an account of some aspects of modern methods, and of the unsuccessful British campaign for effective controls, a campaign which was sparked off by her *Animal Machines* (Stuart: London, 1964).

Her article is in no way a substitute for her earlier book. This is a pity since, as she says, "Farm produce is still associated with mental pictures of animals browsing in the fields...of hens having a last forage before going to roost...." Yet neither in her article nor elsewhere in *Animals, Men and Morals* is this false image replaced by a clear idea of the nature and extent of factory farming. We learn of this only indirectly, when we hear of the code of reform proposed by an advisory committee set up by the British government.

Among the proposals, which the government refused to implement on the grounds that they were too idealistic, were: *"Any animal should at least have room to turn around freely."*

Factory farm animals need liberation in the most literal sense. Veal calves are kept in stalls five feet by two feet. They are usually slaughtered when about four months old, and have been too big to turn in their stalls for at least a month. Intensive beef herds, kept in stalls only proportionately larger for much longer periods, account for a growing percentage of beef production. Sows are often similarly confined when pregnant, which, because of artificial methods of increasing fertility, can be most of the time. Animals confined in this way do not waste food by exercising, nor do they develop unpalatable muscle.

"A dry bedded area should be provided for all stock." Intensively kept animals usually have to stand and sleep on slatted floors without straw, because this makes cleaning easier.

"Palatable roughage must be readily available to all calves after one week of age." In order to produce the pale veal housewives are said to prefer, calves are fed on an all-liquid diet until slaughter, even though they are long past the age at which they would normally eat grass. They develop a craving for roughage, evidenced by attempts to gnaw wood from their stalls. (For the same reason, their diet is deficient in iron.)

"Battery cages for poultry should be large enough for a bird to be able to stretch

one wing at a time." Under current British practice, a cage for four or five laying hens has a floor area of twenty inches by eighteen inches, scarcely larger than a double page of the *New York Review of Books*. In this space, on a sloping wire floor (sloping so the eggs roll down, wire so the dung drops through) the birds live for a year or eighteen months while artificial lighting and temperature conditions combine with drugs in their food to squeeze the maximum number of eggs out of them. Table birds are also sometimes kept in cages. More often they are reared in sheds, no less crowded. Under these conditions all the birds' natural activities are frustrated, and they develop "vices" such as pecking each other to death. To prevent this, beaks are often cut off, and the sheds kept dark.

How many of those who support factory farming by buying its produce know anything about the way it is produced? How many have heard something about it, but are reluctant to check up for fear that it will make them uncomfortable? To nonspeciesists, the typical consumer's mixture of ignorance, reluctance to find out the truth, and vague belief that nothing really bad could be allowed seems analogous to the attitudes of "decent Germans" to the death camps.

There are, of course, some defenders of factory farming. Their arguments are considered, though again rather sketchily, by John Harris. Among the most common: "Since they have never known anything else, they don't suffer." This argument will not be put by anyone who knows anything about animal behavior, since he will know that not all behavior has to be learned. Chickens attempt to stretch wings, walk around, scratch, and even dustbathe or build a nest, even though they have never

lived under conditions that allowed these activities. Calves can suffer from maternal deprivation no matter at what age they were taken from their mothers. "We need these intensive methods to provide protein for a growing population." As ecologists and famine relief organizations know, we can produce far more protein per acre if we grow the right vegetable crop, soy beans for instance, than if we use the land to grow crops to be converted into protein by animals who use nearly 90 percent of the protein themselves, even when unable to exercise.

There will be many readers of this book who will agree that factory farming involves an unjustifiable degree of exploitation of sentient creatures, and yet will want to say that there is nothing wrong with rearing animals for food, provided it is done "humanely." These people are saying, in effect, that although we should not cause animals to suffer, there is nothing wrong with killing them.

There are two possible replies to this view. One is to attempt to show that this combination of attitudes is absurd. Roslind Godlovitch takes this course in her essay, which is an examination of some common attitudes to animals. She argues that from the combination of "animal suffering is to be avoided" and "there is nothing wrong with killing animals" it follows that all animal life ought to be exterminated (since all sentient creatures will suffer to some degree at some point in their lives). Euthanasia is a contentious issue only because we place some value on living. If we did not, the least amount of suffering would justify it. Accordingly, if we deny that we have a duty to exterminate all animal life, we must concede that we are placing some value on animal life.

This argument seems to me valid, although one could still reply that the value of animal life is to be derived from the pleasures that life can have for them, so that, provided their lives have a balance of pleasure over pain, we are justified in rearing them. But this would imply that we ought to produce animals and let them live as pleasantly as possible, without suffering.

At this point, one can make the second of the two possible replies to the view that rearing and killing animals for food is all right so long as it is done humanely. This second reply is that so long as we think that a nonhuman may be killed simply so that a human can satisfy his taste for meat, we are still thinking of nonhumans as means rather than as ends in themselves. The factory farm is nothing more than the application of technology to this concept. Even traditional methods involve castration, the separation of mothers and their young, the breaking up of herds, branding or ear-punching, and of course transportation to the abattoirs and the final moments when the animal smells blood and senses danger. If we were to try rearing animals so that they lived and died without suffering, we should find that to do so on anything like the scale of today's meat industry would be a sheer impossibility. Meat would become the prerogative of the rich.

I have been able to discuss only some of the contributions to this book, saying nothing about, for instance, the essays on killing for furs and for sport. Nor have I considered all the detailed questions that need to be asked once we start thinking about other species in the radically different way presented by this book. What, for instance, are we to do about genuine conflicts of interests like rats biting slum children? I am not sure of the answer, but the essential

point is just that we *do* see this as a conflict of interests, that we recognize that rats have interests too. Then we may begin to think about other ways of resolving the conflict—perhaps by leaving out rat baits that sterilize the rats instead of killing them.

I have not discussed such problems because they are side issues compared with the exploitation of other species for food and for experimental purposes. On these central matters, I hope that I have said enough to show that this book, despite its flaws, is a challenge to every human to recognize his attitudes to nonhumans as a form of prejudice no less objectionable than racism or sexism. It is a challenge that demands not just a change of attitudes, but a change in our way of life, for it requires us to become vegetarians.

Can a purely moral demand of this kind succeed? The odds are certainly against it. The book holds out no inducements. It does not tell us that we will become healthier, or enjoy life more, if we cease exploiting animals. Animal Liberation will require greater altruism on the part of mankind than any other liberation movement, since animals are incapable of demanding it for themselves, or of protesting against their exploitation by votes, demonstrations, or bombs. Is man capable of such genuine altruism? Who knows? If this book does have a significant effect, however, it will be a vindication of all those who have believed that man has within himself the potential for more than cruelty and selfishness.

Notes

1   This article originally appeared as a book review of *Animals, Men and Morals*, edited by Stanley and Roslind Godlovitch and John Harris.

2   *The Principles of Morals and Legislation*, Ch. XVII, Sec. 1, footnote to paragraph 4. (Italics in original.)

3   Jane van Lawick-Goodall, *In the Shadow of Man* (Houghton Mifflin, 1971), p. 225.

4   N. Tinbergen, *The Herring Gull's World* (Basic Books, 1961).

Questions for Discussion

1   Is it "speciesist" to believe that human suffering counts more than that of non-human animals? Is this term conceptually analogous to "racist" and "sexist"?

2   Is there any good reason to allow experiments on non-humans which one would not allow on, say, a human orphan under six months old?

3   If there is a part of a city in which rats are biting children, how would we go about weighing the interests of the rats against those of the children?

Utilitarianism and Vegetarianism

Roger Crisp

In this selection, Roger Crisp argues that people who believe that the pleasures and sufferings of animals count may be not only permitted but morally required to eat meat. He claims this will be true so long as the animals live pleasant lives (which is not the case in factory farms), because the meat industry may be responsible for the very existence of the animals, who are better off living and then being killed than never living at all. In the process, Crisp critiques several of the common arguments against eating meat.

*   *   *

The condition of non-human animals—especially those consumed as food by human beings—has been a major concern of many thinkers in the utilitarian tradition. Two main lines of thought have been taken on the ethics of eating meat. It is claimed either that utilitarianism requires Vegetarianism (V)[1], or that it does not, but permits one to eat meat.[2] In this paper, I shall develop a third line: that utilitarianism does not permit V, requiring a form of non-V. This view I shall call the Compromise Requirement view (CR). I shall claim that one is morally required both to abstain from the flesh of intensively reared animals and to eat the flesh of certain non-intensively-reared animals.

The paper will proceed primarily in a negative way, through consideration and refutation of the main utilitarian arguments for V. But a positive case for CR will emerge, particularly in the discussion of the Argument from Suffering.

Before proceeding to the first argument, it might be helpful to outline the utilitarian positions under consideration:

Vegetarianism (V): One is morally required to abstain from meat.

The Compromise Permission View (CP): One is morally required to abstain from the flesh of intensively reared animals, but permitted to eat the flesh of certain non-intensively-reared animals.

The Compromise Requirement View (CR): One is morally required both to abstain from the flesh of intensively reared animals and to eat the flesh of certain non-intensively-reared animals.

The Raymond Frey View (RF): One is morally permitted to eat all kinds of meat, but required to campaign against intensive farming, by means such as political lobbying.

The Full Meat-eating Requirement View (FR): One is morally required to eat all kinds of meat.

1 The Argument from Killing

1. The widespread practice of Meat-eating requires killing sentient beings.
2. Killing sentient beings is wrong.
3. Therefore, the widespread practice of Meat-eating is wrong.

The first premise of this argument is undeniable. Therefore, it can only be vulnerable as regards its second premise. The premise can be supported, in turn, by three subsidiary utilitarian arguments intended to demonstrate the wrongness of killing. Replies to each will show that these arguments do not apply to the case of killing animals for food, and thus that the Argument from Killing fails.

1(a) The Argument from Direct Diminution of Utility

1. Killing a sentient being for food directly reduces the amount of utility in the world by removing that being from the world.
2. Reducing the amount of utility is wrong.

3. Therefore, killing a sentient being for food is wrong.

The second premise here is correct by definition in utilitarian terms. Thus, we must focus on the first. It is not clear that this is correct.

The reason for this is that utilitarianism is committed to replaceability. The replacing of one being by another at a similar level of utility is, other things being equal, morally neutral.

It may be objected that if the utility levels of both the animal to be killed and that intended as a surrogate are above zero, then it would be better that both live. There are two replies to this. The first is that we are concerned with Meat-eating as a widespread practice. And an inherent feature of this practice is that over time some animals will be killed for food, and others will take their places. If animals were not killed, the practice could not exist. The second is that the objection is not anyway to the point. All that needs to be shown is that killing an animal need not be wrong, not that failing to increase the overall level of utility is not wrong. Replaceability makes morally neutral killing a possibility.[3]

In what does an animal's utility consist? Primarily it must be sheer pleasurable experience, and the fulfillment of desires for those experiences.[4] And the pleasures of even the more intelligent domestic animals, such as pigs, will tend to be of the 'low' variety.[5] Indeed, one would not have to be a Socrates dissatisfied to have a life preferable to that of a contented pig. Not all the desires of animals are for pleasurable experiences, however. For example, they also have desires connected with their relations with other animals. If a cow sees her calf being mistreated, she will show signs of acute distress, and perhaps attempt to protect her offspring. It would be more plausible to explain her actions by ascribing to her the desire that her offspring not suffer, than the desire that she not experience the sight of her offspring suffering. No cow is so stupid as not to realize that a more effective way of fulfilling the latter desire would be to turn tail and head for the other end of the field.

The Vegetarian may use the notion of the sophistication of animal desires in the following way. She may accept that merely replacing one pleasurable experience with another is morally neutral. But, she may continue, desires are not like this. An animal may have desires for the future. The frustration of these desires is not counter-balanced by the bringing into existence of a new animal.

The fulfillment of future-related desires, however, does not differ from mental states, as far as replaceability is concerned.[6] Utilitarian theories are neutral as to when or where utility is located. Thus, the surrogate animal will also have future-related desires, and if these desires are fulfilled, replaceability once again ensures the moral neutrality of the killing.[7]

In the context of a widespread practice of Meat-eating, of course, the surrogate animal is highly unlikely to go on living for very long. It too will be killed and eaten. It might be thought that to ensure the moral neutrality of the process one has only to stipulate that the *final* animal in the process will be allowed to survive. Given that the process of rearing animals for food is nowhere near its end, this is a worry that need not afflict us at present.

But this claim misses the same point as the original Vegetarian argument based on desires. Desire-fulfillment, and hence frustration, like pleasure and pain is cumulative. As the process continues, more and more future-related desires will be frustrated, and these are not counter-balanced by the fulfillment of one such set of desires at the end of the process.

To solve the problem, one has to be aware of another mistaken assumption underlying the original Vegetarian argument. This is the view that there is something special about these *particular* future-related desires. The utilitarian must accept that the value of their fulfillment can be outweighed by the value of the fulfillment of other desires (and, depending on the type of utilitarianism in question, other values, such as pleasure or aesthetic appreciation).

Thus, the frustration of the future-related desires of the animal killed is counter-balanced by: i) the utility of the life of the surrogate animal; ii) the utility of the desire-satisfaction, pleasure, or aesthetic appreciation in eating the animal; and (which surely tips the balance in favour of Meat-eating here) iii) the utility of the life of the animal killed, given that, in the context of a widespread practice of Meat-eating, it would not have existed had it not been intended for slaughter. (It is important to bear in mind that i) and iii) will not apply in the case of intensively reared animals, who live at levels of negative utility. But these animals are better off not existing, so killing them is not wrong.)

1(b) The Argument from Indirect Diminution of Utility

1. Killing a sentient being causes grief, anxiety, and thereby suffering in other sentient beings.
2. Thus, killing a sentient being indirectly reduces the amount of utility in the world.
3. Reducing the amount of utility is wrong.
4. Therefore, killing a sentient being is wrong.

Ethical Issues

Premise 3 is correct by definition, and premise 2 is true if premise 1 is true. Thus, we must attend to premise 1.

Now it cannot be denied that killing *certain* sentient beings, in particular humans and other higher primates, almost always causes grief and anxiety among other such beings. But this does not seem to be the case with domestic animals. We are not unduly perturbed at the killing of animals, especially if we do not see it happen. And those who kill them are similarly unaffected.

It may be said that animals become distressed when members of their group are killed in their presence. In the case of domestic animals, this could only occur at the slaughter-house. But there is no argument for not killing, if it is possible to alter the circumstances of the death. And surely it is possible to do this, by changing the methods of slaughtering. Animals could be killed in separate pens, for example.

Animals can also be distressed at the death of a mate. Pair-bonding, however, is not found among the animals we eat. And finally there is the problem of distress caused by the death of a parent or offspring. This again is not an argument for not killing. The problem can be dealt with *either* by slaughtering both parent and offspring at the same time *or* by slaughtering neither parent nor offspring at times when the offspring is young enough to experience distress at the loss or to cause the parent distress at the loss of the offspring.

1(c) The Argument from Autonomy

1. Killing a sentient being, other things being equal, violates its autonomy and deprives it of liberty.
2. Autonomy and liberty are productive of utility.

3. Thus, killing a sentient being reduces the amount of utility in the world.
4. Reducing the amount of utility is wrong.
5. Therefore, killing a sentient being is wrong.

Some utilitarians have appealed to respect for autonomy as a moral principle.[8] And a Vegetarian might think that an ideal utilitarian theory, which included the claim that autonomy is itself *part of utility*, would also support her case.

She will be disappointed, however. For animals do not possess autonomy.[9] They do have desires, and they do make choices. But their choices are not about how their lives should go. They are about immediate things, such as whether to walk in this or that direction, to lie in the shade or under the sun, to flee or stay. Autonomy requires at least some degree of a global conception of one's life, and this it seems clear animals do not have.[10]

Animals can, however, be free. Indeed, the basis of the ethical criticism of our treatment of animals for many people is that we deprive them of liberty. But by killing an animal we do not deprive it of liberty alone. We deprive it of everything. And, if my critique of the Argument from Direct Diminution of Utility is correct, depriving a being of everything including liberty can be justified by replaceability. Thus, even if animals possess liberty, it is not always wrong to deprive them of it.

2 The Argument from Suffering

1. The widespread practice of Meat-eating causes suffering.
2. The causing of suffering is wrong.
3. Therefore, Meat-eating is wrong.

The second premise of this argument requires attention. Utilitarians do, of course, claim that suffering is bad, and that causing suffering is *in itself* a bad thing to do. But causing suffering *can* be a good thing to do when it is not considered in itself. It may lead to better consequences occurring than if suffering had not been caused (*e.g.* the action of a dentist filling a cavity), or it may be part of a series of actions which, taken overall, are productive of utility (*e.g.* the punishing of a child). Thus, as I noted in the discussion of replaceability, doing something that causes a drop in the level of utility can be counter-balanced by doing something else that causes an increase.

In the case of rearing animals for food, it may well be that the suffering they will inevitably endure is analogous to that experienced by a child who is punished in the normal run of things.[11] Most non-intensively-reared animals lead worthwhile lives[12], and we enjoy eating them. The worthwhileness of their lives, and the pleasure we gain from eating them, justify the practice of rearing them, although it inevitably involves causing suffering. And if we were not to eat them, both of these sources of utility would disappear. Thus, there is here the beginning of a case for CR.

Intensively-reared animals, however, fall into a different category. Their lives are frustrating, painful, stunted, and devoid of anything but the slightest pleasure.[13] It would have been better for such animals if they had not been born. The only consideration counter-balancing the severe suffering endured by intensively reared animals is our pleasure in eating them. When we consider the fact that alternative meals are available, it seems patently clear that this consideration will not justify factory-farming.

Thus far, I have ruled out V as an option, and suggested that there is a requirement on us to eat non-intensively-reared meat. This gives *prima facie* support to CR, RF, and FR. I have also suggested that intensively rearing animals cannot be justified in utilitarian terms. This narrows the field to CR and RF.

RF is still in play for the reason that from the claim that the *practice* of intensively rearing animals is wrong, in that it causes more suffering than pleasure overall, one cannot conclude that an *individual* is therefore required to desist from eating the products of factory-farms. For it may be that an individual's actions will have no effect on the practice.

This problem is similar to the Problem of Collective Action in Marxism[14]: *just as* it is not in the interest of individual workers to struggle for socialism, even if they see socialism as a desirable goal, since what an ordinary individual does makes no difference to what others do, and so whether socialism comes about or not does not depend on the actions of that individual; *so* whether or not I abstain from intensively reared meat, given the vast scale of modern meat-production, will be irrelevant as to whether any good effects arise from a widespread practice of abstaining from intensively reared meat.

One response to this problem might be that it is unfair to take advantage of others. If we assume that intensive rearing will decrease in scale if a certain number of people give up eating meat reared in that way, and that no one accepts that this is a good thing, then when others are boycotting such meat, it is unfair not to join them.

This claim, however, is counter to the consequentialism at the heart of utilitarianism. If the consequences alone determine the moral standing of an act, and the only consequences relevant to this determination are benefits and harms, then to claim that an act is wrong, although it does no harm and indeed produces a benefit (the pleasure of eating meat), seems not only churlish, but also contradictory.[15]

A more promising response might be to claim that characterizing the problem in this way makes what Parfit calls the 'fifth mistake in moral mathematics.'[16] One makes this mistake if one thinks that:

> If some act has effects on other people that are imperceptible, this act cannot be morally wrong *because* it has these effects. An act cannot be wrong because of its effects on other people if none of these people could ever notice any difference. Similarly, if some act would have imperceptible effects on other people, these effects cannot make this act what someone ought to do.

Developing Parfit's analysis, one might claim that in order to avoid the paradox that, if imperceptible acts are never wrong, many people who increase the suffering of a person until it is severe, each by an imperceptible amount, are doing no wrong, we should attend to the consequences of what *we together* do.

This response also fails, however, in that it still provides no reason for the *individual* to join the boycott. The group will go on doing the good whether or not any one individual partakes in the boycott.

The following response to the Problem of Collective Action is more successful. There are three possible effects of an individual boycotting intensively reared meat. It will either have no effect, being below the threshold required to make a difference; or a great effect, 'tipping the balance' over a threshold; or a small effect, if thresholds do not exist and the effect on intensive farming is direct.

If thresholds do exist, the action will have one or other of the first two effects. It might be thought that this gives the individual a reason not to join the boycott, in the same way that the fact that there is a very small probability of having an effect in a general election might be thought to supply a good reason for any one individual not to vote. This, however, is to make Parfit's third mistake, that of ignoring small chances.[17] According to utilitarianism, we should act so as to maximize *expected* utility. Thus, a small chance of bringing about a great good does give me a reason to act.

It is also possible that boycotting intensively reared meat will have an effect on intensive farming, regardless of the effects of the acts on others. In fact, it seems likely that this will sometimes be the case. Imagine that I am a Meat-eating individual, who, like most people, enjoys the taste of chicken. In a year, I might buy, say, five chickens. Now information-transfer in a corporate market economy is not perfect. If I chose to boycott Bernard Matthews' chickens, he would not be able to find out that *I* had done so. But neither is it entirely inefficient. If I buy my chickens from the same store, and then stop buying them, the figures for chicken sales for the next year will be less by five than if I had not joined the boycott. The store may order fewer chickens over the next year, and the farmer produce fewer chickens. For farmers surely will supply fewer chickens if demand drops. If this scenario appears unlikely, however, the argument based around thresholds still suffices to solve the Collective Action Problem.

It is also the case that an individual's boycott can be a symbolic gesture, and thus have indirect effects on intensive farming through influencing others to reflect upon the reasons for the boycott and to join it.

On the basis of the discussion so far, then, CR emerges as the most plausible utilitarian view on Meat-eating.

3 The Argument from Callousness

1. The practice of rearing animals and killing them for food engenders a callous attitude in human beings towards other human beings.
2. This attitude will be expressed in callous actions towards other human beings, which cause suffering.
3. Causing suffering is wrong.
4. Therefore, the practice is wrong.

One way to criticize this old argument would be to point out that, once again, only the *bad* consequences are being taken into account. The number of people actually involved in the practice is small, relative to the number of people who benefit from it (the Meat-eaters). Thus, even if animal-farmers and employees of slaughter-houses do cause more suffering to other human beings than they might otherwise have done if employed in a different area, it is still possible that the benefits gained by those who enjoy their products will more than suffice to counter-balance that suffering.

But it seems questionable whether the first premise is anyway correct. If those involved in the practice are made aware of the justifications for it, there need be no presumption that they will become callous in their attitude towards other animals or humans. And even if not only are they not aware of the justifications, but also (as is often claimed) they must think of animals as in some sense inanimate if they are to do their job, there is no reason to think that this is the first step on a slippery slope leading to callous actions towards human beings. For this attitude to animals would be based on the notion that they are even more unlike humans than they in fact are.

The truth of the matter is that there is a place for compassion in the rearing of animals for food, and that even where callousness takes the place of compassion, there is no reason to think that this will spill over into callousness towards human beings.

4 The Argument from Paternalism

1. There is strong evidence that Meat-eating is not conducive to the health of a population.
2. It is the utilitarian duty of a government to minimize harm.
3. Therefore, Meat-eating ought to be forbidden.

The first premise is loosely worded. There is strong evidence that the eating of red meat—and fatty foods in general—in large quantities is linked with conditions such as heart-disease. But there is little, if any, evidence that eating meat, in particular white meat or fish, in moderation is harmful.

The proponent of the argument may then attempt to weaken the conclusion to the claim that eating *red* meat ought to be forbidden. But this ignores the direct and indirect harms of paternalism. Paternalism, by definition, violates a person's autonomy, and infringes upon his or her liberty. And banning red meat would also have obvious bad side-effects, similar to those which occurred during the era of Prohibition of alcohol in the United States. Indeed, it is likely that any such measure would have to be repealed. The conclusion, then, must be weakened still further. The argument can only require a government to disseminate information concerning the dangers to the individual of consuming large amounts of food with a high fat content.

5 The Argument from Starvation

1. The widespread practice of Meat-eating requires the feeding of large amounts of protein to animals.
2. This protein could be used to feed those human beings who are starving.
3. By eating meat, we are causing the deaths of these human beings.
4. Causing the death of human beings is wrong.
5. Therefore, we ought to cease to eat meat.

Utilitarians cannot accept that there is a moral distinction between acts and omissions. Thus, the obvious common-sense reply to the argument, that we are not killing those who starve to death, but merely allowing them to die, is not open to me in a dispute with a utilitarian.

Could I claim that we have property-rights over this protein, in that it is purchased on the open market from its legal owners, either at home, or in other countries, where people may or may not be starving? It is true that utilitarianism does offer a strong rationale for the institution of property.[18] But, given that goods diminish marginally in value, any utilitarian theory of property which would permit the present inequality of wealth, and hence control over resources, between northern and southern hemispheres must be entirely unconvincing.[19]

The problem with this argument is the simplistic conception of economics on which its main assumption rests. This is that the practices of Meat-eating use protein which would otherwise have been available for the starving. But famines are not usually *caused* by shortages of food, but rather more complex issues such as sudden changes in entitlement relations.[20] What those who are starving need is wealth, to buy food and long-term productive capacity, not our ceasing to eat meat. This would be likely to disturb the world grain-market to such an extent that very bad consequences could occur. For example, countries relying on grain-export would become poorer, with adverse effects on their population. And a further likely consequence would be that there would be *less* grain available to those who are starving. This was suggested by a number of economists, reacting to the statement in the nineteen-seventies by the American senator Earl Butt that each American citizen ought to eat one less hamburger a week, with a view to easing starvation in the Third World.[21] Third World grain supplies fluctuate according to surpluses in the First World. Supply in the First World in turn fluctuates according to demand. And the greater the demand, the greater the likely surplus. Thus, as it turned out, Butt should have urged Americans to eat one *more* hamburger a week!

If the proponent of the argument then claims to be aware of these problems, and to be offering a purely tactical or protreptic thesis, designed to bring about a change in people's diets, there is a requirement that V be shown to be justified on grounds *other* than those allegedly supplied by the Argument from Starvation.[22] And those grounds we have yet to find. The Argument from Starvation is valid and true if re-interpreted as a demand that an individual give money to a charity concerned with aid to the Third World. But becoming a Vegetarian will not aid those who are starving.

6 The Argument from Future Generations

1. Extra sentient beings in the world would raise the level of utility.

2. Human beings are the most efficient producers of utility.
3. Therefore, it is wrong to rear animals for food, since the protein consumed by these animals would produce more utility if used to feed extra human beings, until an optimum population is reached.

This argument relies on Total, as opposed to Average, utilitarianism.[23] According to the Total view, we are required to maximize the level of total utility over time, not, say, average utility (total utility divided by the number of beings living).

One important objection to the argument is of course that people do not believe in the Total view, including most members of most governments. Thus, even if more protein becomes available, it is unlikely to support programs of population-growth. It is not only the economics, but also the politics of this argument which are simplistic.

A more trenchant point, however, is that the Total view does not support increasing population in our world. Unless there is some disaster, it will be many millions of years before life on this planet dies out through the sun's being extinguished. Thus, our conception of 'the future' ought to be far broader than that implied by the Argument from Future Generations.

Human beings at present are heavy users of finite resources, such as fossil-fuels and metals. These resources are being used very inefficiently. Imagine future generations classified into three groups: the short-term, the medium-term, and the long-term. And consider the effects of two policies: Depletion of resources, through increasing the population; and Conservation, through maintaining present levels of population. Depletion will benefit the short-term generations, but at the expense of the medium-term. Conservation will benefit the medium-term, but at the expense of the short term. There are two relevant considerations, here. Keeping the population steady will (i) give us more time to develop substitutes for these resources, and (ii) enable us to contrive more efficient ways of using resources that remain. If we fail to develop substitutes, there could be a global disaster. Conservation gives us more time for research, and thus is less likely to result in disaster for medium- *and* long-term generations. And any amount of resources used in the medium-term will almost certainly provide more utility, because of increased efficiency.

Meanwhile, renewable resources, such as protein, should be put to their most efficient use. And the most efficient use of protein will involve feeding both human beings and domestic animals.

I conclude, then, that none of the main utilitarian arguments for V succeeds. The suffering endured by intensively reared animals rules out eating them. Thus RF, FP, and FR are incorrect. The practice of rearing animals non-intensively is productive of utility. Thus, CP is incorrect, and CR is the most plausible utilitarian view on Meat-eating.[24]

Acknowledgement

I am indebted to Raymond Frey, James Griffin, Richard Hare, Michael Lockwood, Peter Singer, and Eldon Soifer for their comments on previous drafts of this paper.

Notes

1   See *e.g.* P. Singer, *Animal Liberation,* London: Jonathan Cape, 1976; *Practical Ethics,* Cambridge: Cambridge University Press, 1979. In 'Killing animals and killing humans,' *Inquiry* 22, 1979, and 'Utilitarianism and vegetarianism,' *Philosophy and Public Affairs* 7, 1979-80, Singer's

position becomes more sympathetic to what I call the Compromise Permission view (CP). Singer does, however, appear to qualify his adherence to CP: i) it may only be suited to a society of 'sophisticated philosophers'; ii) it may be the first step onto a slippery slope leading us back to Full Meat-eating in a factory-farming society. Singer's arguments will be discussed further below.

2 See *e.g.* R. Frey, *Rights, Killing, and Suffering*, Oxford: Basil Blackwell, 1983. Frey does not advocate the Full Meat-eating Permission view (FP) (according to which one can eat all kinds of meat without qualms), but is sympathetic to the motivation behind the Compromise views. One is morally permitted to eat any kind of animal flesh, but also morally required to campaign for the end of intensive farming, by means such as political lobbying. I shall call this the R. Frey view (RF).

3 This incidentally is why one should take care in interpreting Singer's claim about replaceability:

> ...that even if it is valid when the animals in question have a pleasant life, it would not justify eating the flesh of animals reared in modern 'factory farms,' where the animals are so crowded together and restricted in their movements that their lives seem to be more of a burden than a benefit to them. [*Practical Ethics*, p. 100]

4 It has been argued in Frey, *Interests and Rights*, Oxford: Clarendon Press, 1980 and elsewhere that animals cannot have desires. Common sense suggests that this is false, and is supported by *e.g.* T. Regan, *The Case for Animal Rights*, London, Routledge & Kegan Paul, chap. 2.

5 J.S. Mill, *Utilitarianism*, repr. in (ed.) M. Warnock, *Utilitarianism*, London: Fontana, 1962, chap. 2.

6 See M. Lockwood, 'Singer on killing and the preference for life,' *Inquiry* 22, 1979, p. 61.

7 Singer appears to believe that a Desire theory can supply special reasons for not killing 'self-conscious' beings (those with the desire to go on living). See *Practical Ethics*, 80f.; ch. 5; 'Killing humans and killing animals.' He says:

> The replaceability principle applies, regardless of species, to beings who have never had the capacity to desire continued life. ['Killing humans and killing animals,' 154f.]

He also seems to believe that domestic animals lack self-consciousness, and do not therefore have the desire to go on living. The latter claim seems to me false, and I suspect that the former is either

false or confused. But as the main text shows the point is not relevant here, and so does not deserve further discussion.

8 *E.g.*, Singer, *Practical Ethics*, 83ff.; J. Glover, *Causing Death and Saving Lives*, Harmondsworth: Penguin, 1977, chap. 5; J. Griffin, *Well-Being*, Oxford: Clarendon Press, 1986, p. 67.

9 For the opposing view, see Regan, *The Case for Animal Rights*, ch. 3.

10 Again, I am concerned with *domestic* animals here. If someone were to claim that certain chimpanzees or gorillas are autonomous to some degree, I should be less inclined to dismiss her.

11 Singer sometimes seems to pass by this point. For example:

> ...the important question is not whether animal flesh *could* be produced without suffering, but whether the flesh that we are considering buying *was* produced without suffering. Unless we can be confident that it was, the principle of equal consideration of interests implies that it was wrong to sacrifice important interests of the animal to satisfy less important interests of our own; consequently we should boycott the end result of this process. [*Practical Ethics*, p. 56f.]

12 Although they do of course often experience severe suffering. See Singer, *Animal Liberation*, *152ff.*

13 See Singer, *Animal Liberation*, Chap. 3; and J. Mason and Singer, *Animal Factories*, New York: Crown Publishers, 1980.

14 See M. Olson, *The Logic of Collective Action*, Cambridge, Mass: Harvard University Press, 1965.

15 For a different view, see Griffin, 'Some problems of fairness,' *Ethics 96*, 1985.

16 D. Parfit, *Reasons and Persons*, Oxford: Clarendon Press, 1984, pp. 28-9.

17 *Reasons and Persons*, p. 27. See also Singer, 'Utilitarianism and vegetarianism,' p. 336.

18 See A. Ryan, *Property and Political Theory*, Oxford: Basil Blackwell, 1984, Chap. 4.

19 See Singer, 'Famine, affluence and morality,' *Philosophy and Public Affairs* 1, 1972.

20 See A. Sen, *Poverty and Famines*, Oxford: Clarendon Press, 1981.

21 Butt's claim was brought to my attention by Lockwood.

22 I discuss another tactical argument concerning animals in 'The argument from marginal cases,'

Journal of Applied Philosophy 2, 1985. If the utilitarian offers this as an argument for V—on the ground that we would think it wrong to eat mentally defective people—it will fail on grounds similar to those on which the Argument from Indirect Diminution of Utility (1b) failed. The side-effects in each case are markedly different.

23 See H. Sidgwick, *The Methods of Ethics*, London: Macmillan, 1907, p. 415f.

24 It should be noted that CR requires only the consumption of artificially-reared meat. Wild animals, including fish, will not be replaced, and so should not be eaten.

Questions for Discussion

1 Can the pleasures and satisfactions of one animal simply be "replaced" by those of another?

2 What is the relationship between the ethics of eating meat at the individual level, and the ethics of the institution of meat-production?

Trapped

J. Barber

In the following article, Barber argues that the anti-fur movement may be doing more damage than good, both to the environment, and to human beings. He offers a critical examination of some of the claims of the anti-fur movement and discusses the plight of the trappers who depend on the fur trade for their livelihood.

*   *   *

As a wildlife biologist employed by the state of Louisiana, Greg Linscombe fields a lot of calls from journalists on the enormous problems facing his state's magnificent coastal marshes. At four million acres, they form one of the most productive wildlife habitats on the continent. Dozens of species of Canadian waterfowl, among innumerable other animals, depend on them for survival. And they are eroding so fast that they could soon disappear.

When reporters ask him what people can do to help save the marshes, Linscombe always repeats the same message. "If you're really concerned about the wetlands," he says, "buy a fur coat."

Linscombe explains that the marshes face a host of manmade problems. But one of the biggest threats today comes from the otherwise innocuous nutria. A kind of outsize muskrat native to South America, the nutria was accidentally let loose in the bayou country more than 50 years ago. As long as nutria pelts were in demand, trappers combined with alligators to keep them in check. Now that the price of fur of all kinds has collapsed like a penny stock, trappers don't bother much with nutria and the marsh-eating interlopers are multiplying crazily. "They're eating the marshes right down to the mud," says Linscombe.

The solution doesn't exactly jibe with the preconceptions of his callers, most of whom accept uncritically the fashionable view that fur coats are the ultimate symbol of environmental insensitivity. So, like a fourth-grade teacher, Linscombe repeats himself a lot. "Buy a nutria coat and help save the marsh. Wear it with pride."

Linscombe is a biologist, not a moralist, so he doesn't dwell on the obvious irony of the situation: the fact that certain animal lovers who are intent on destroying the fur trade—and would be delighted to claim full responsibility for the worldwide crash in fur prices—are in the process helping to destroy one of the richest wildlife habitats in North America. But it is worth noting, because the nutria explosion is just one of the unintended consequences of their campaign.

The logic and the morality are so simple: You shouldn't kill animals for the sake of luxury and vanity. The images of terrified animals struggling in steel leg-hold traps are so persuasive. The suffering seems inarguable. The targets, the furriers and their wealthy clientele, are so easy. Never mind that virtually every Native group in Canada thinks of the anti-fur campaign as nothing less than the white man's attempt at cultural genocide. Or that biologists from Siberia to the Yukon predict that its victory will result in outright environmental disaster. That the movement, in the words of Valerius Geist, a professor of environmental science at the University of Calgary, "stands ultimately for brutalized landscapes and wildlife depleted and squeezed into tiny enclaves." That view, like Linscombe's, is irritatingly complex. It has no validity amid the cozy simplicities of the anti-fur protest. Never mind that it's right.

There is no hint of the anti-fur protest at Montreal's huge and bustling Canadian International Fur Fair, not a single sidewalk placard. Inside the Place Bonaventure there are literally miles of coat racks groaning with the weight of fur. There are buyers and sellers from around the world, rural Louisianians mingling with Milanese couturiers—all the brisk chaos of a long-established, nuts-and-bolts trade fair. Even the army of models, dressed identically in their uniform of black, have an air more businesslike than glamorous as they don coat after coat for stony-faced buyers sitting behind order books and pocket calculators.

Yet there is a pervasive unease in Montreal this year. Nothing reflects that better than the variety of excuses being offered for the second straight year of rock-bottom prices. Retailers and manufacturers talk about the overall decline in the fashion industry. European overproduction of ranch mink—anything but the effects of the fur protest. But those effects are undeniable: Fur coat sales have almost disappeared in many European countries, where the campaign is most active and where simply appearing on the streets in fur invites attack from paint-throwing zealots. British department stores, most famously Harrods, have abandoned the fur business altogether, while specialty furriers, who are stuck with it, learn to live with constant vandalism and death threats. In magazines and on television, the issue is presented as a "debate" that pits the hollow legal rights of furriers to engage in a distasteful business against the shocking cruelty and barbarism of the trappers. Guess which side is winning. A recent survey found that almost 80 per cent of Americans think it is wrong to kill an animal for a fur coat.

Nothing, it would seem, provokes easier outrage in 1990 than wearing fur. "They come at me with such incredible fanatical energy and such hatred on their faces, I'm afraid they're going to attack me physically," says one Toronto woman who persists in wearing a fur coat. Men leading small children shout obscenities; others stalk her along the street, sometimes for blocks at a time.

Respectable and sincere anti-fur activists understandably distance themselves from the lunatics and terrorists. Nevertheless, the movement seems infested with people who are addicted to the pleasure of moral disapproval and, as all the old orthodoxies crumble away, turn to fur for their fix. As *The Wall Street Journal* pointed out last February, "These are not your typical pet lovers. Their actions show less a love for furry rodents than a certain hatred for their own species."

At Montreal this year, the fur trade is countering with its own propaganda. Exhibitors wear buttons that say "FUR, naturally yours," part of a campaign to promote fur as a "green" product. It is questionable whether anyone will be persuaded to buy a fur coat by the fact that it is biodegradable, but not all of the fur trade's efforts are so feeble. It learned important lessons from the destruction of the seal hunt earlier this decade. One is that if it's going to survive, the fur trade needs to become as slick as its media-savvy opposition. For this year's fair they have assembled a crack team of pro-fur activists to send the message out. The keynote speaker is Pierre Berton.

Berton is impressively thunderous. A seasoned campaigner against animal rights extremism, mainly in support of scientific research, he calls the anti-fur movement "a tragedy and a scandal, and whenever I get a chance to say it I do. Nothing short of an all-out campaign will prevent these people from ruining the country." Anti-fur activists "are at best misinformed and at worst fanatics, and whether misinformed or fanatics, they are certainly dangerous." The story of what happened to the Inuit of the eastern Arctic as a result of the European ban on imports of sealskin is depressingly familiar. "Their lives have been ruined and the result has been suicide, drugs, alcohol and murder. That's what's going on in the high Arctic. The suicide rate is due entirely to the animal rights movement.

"We've got to ask ourselves when cruelty to animals stops and cruelty to humans begins."

Berton's speech is the emotional equivalent of an anti-fur film, the kind that shows foxes struggling desperately to free themselves from the steel jaws of a leg-hold trap. (Berton argues that most such films are fakes, like the notorious footage obtained by activists who paid a hunter to skin a seal pup alive; on the other hand, less passionate observers hesitate to attribute all Inuit suicides to the destruction of the seal hunt.) But the problem with more rational appeals is that they invariably run into an impassable emotional roadblock. How do you justify death?

Alcide Giroux has come up against that question many times, and has never been able to provide a soothing answer. The Ontario trapper has come to Montreal to do business and speak up for his cause and he doesn't go in for euphemisms like "harvest." He talks about killing animals, plain talk that sets him apart from the PR apparatus as clearly as his Rotarian suit, white socks and bent nose. "It's a fact of life that people who don't even know where milk comes from cannot accept that you can kill an animal," says Giroux.

He can't fight people who oppose swatting mosquitoes and eating fish. He doesn't even try to argue against animal-rights activists. What he can and does fight are the misconceptions they foster about trappers. "When people say that trapping's cruel and inhumane, they don't have a clue what trapping is and what a trapper does," says Giroux.

Giroux was one of the first trappers in Canada to urge his colleagues to get serious about animal welfare, and he takes personal pride in the wave of new humane trapping regulations quickly advancing across the country. The anti-fur campaign continues to focus dogmatically on the steel-jawed leg-hold trap, a device that can lead to a lingering and painful death. But as Giroux points out, the propaganda bears no relationship to the trap's role in the fur trade today. About three-quarters of all animals trapped in Canada every year die in quick-kill traps. And in the vast majority of cases in which the leg-hold trap is still used, it is set so the animal drowns within a few minutes. Giroux says that 98 per cent of all fur-bearers trapped in Canada die either instantly or within a few minutes of being caught. Federal officials, more cautious, would lower that figure—many trappers continue to resist the new methods. Even so, says Giroux, "It's the law of the land. We made it the law of the land and a trapper must abide by it or lose his licence."

Currently Giroux is helping government researchers field-test a new padded trap that could eliminate the use of conventional leg-holds on wolves, coyotes, foxes, bobcats and lynx. Although it is uncommon even for standard traps to injure these animals, padded traps promise to cause no pain and minimal stress to the animals held in them, even over a period of several hours.

Such innovations are the result of campaigns initiated decades ago by old-fashioned animal-welfare groups. Modern anti-fur campaigners flatly dismiss them, saying that humane trapping is a contradiction in terms. But, as Giroux points out, trapping will continue even if wearing fur

becomes a capital offence in every country on earth. Northerners will trap for food and people all over the world will trap nuisance animals like rats and moles. Dutch trappers kill 200,000 muskrats per year to prevent the country's dikes from washing away into the North Sea—and now, with knowledge gained from Canadian research, they can do it humanely. "No matter what people say, animals will still be killed," says Giroux. "So what responsibility do we have? It's to use the most humane and effective trapping programs possible." In response, anti-fur campaigners distribute pictures of wolves with stakes shoved down their throats, saying, "This is how a trapper kills an animal caught in a trap"; they capture animals out of season in illegal traps and shove cameras in their faces, filming as the animal struggles desperately to get away; they produce videos showing corrupt paparazzi at a fashion show being showered with blood. Blood is a favorite tool. Giroux recalls the disappointment of a CBC film crew that spent a week on his trap line. "They kept asking me, 'Where's the blood?'" he says. He couldn't show them blood, because there wasn't any. All the animals in his traps were dead.

As well as characterizing trappers as bloodthirsty brutes, many anti-fur campaigners take it as a matter of faith that they are also wiping out whole populations of animals. Faith is necessary in this case, because no fur-bearing species in Canada is endangered or even threatened by trapping. Charles Dauphine, the biologist who advises the Canadian government on the application of the Convention on International Trade in Endangered Species, keeps a close watch on the rarest fur-bearers—especially when prices for their pelts are high—and has consistently concluded that trapping does not threaten their numbers. The only animal about which he has doubts is the prairie long-tailed weasel. "I have told this to the anti-trapping groups and they just go, 'Ho hum,'" says Dauphine. "They just want more exciting animals."

As evidence for their charge that wildlife is being wiped out indiscriminately, anti-fur campaigners say there is insufficient data to prove that it is not being wiped out. It is a conveniently endless argument. But the truly astonishing thing about fur-bearing animals in Canada is that there are so many of them, especially large predators such as wolves, bears and coyotes. Wild wolves in Europe are all but extinct; meanwhile there are as many wolves in Alcide Giroux's backyard—Ontario cottage country—as anywhere else on earth.

Gazing down from the moral high ground, anti-fur campaigners care little for the complexities of conservation policy or humane trapping. Some of them say it is wrong to kill animals, period; they would like to see an end to commercial fisheries as well as the fur trade. Others, more realistic, say merely that it is wrong to kill for frivolous reasons, adding that nothing could be more frivolous than "luxury furs." It seems like a reasonable argument, except when one considers that trappers are among the poorest-paid people in the country; to them, fur is hardly a luxury. But more important, it ignores the vital role they play in environmental protection.

For Bob Stevenson, the imposing, long-haired Métis who heads the Aboriginal Trappers Federation of Canada, that role is as real as the bearclaw necklace around his neck. Stevenson has set up his fur-draped teepee right at the entrance to the Montreal show, where he functions as a kind of moral doorman and an irresistible magnet for the long-legged models killing time between shows. "The trapper is the true environmentalist," he says simply. "He will always be the first to complain about pollution or oil spills or clear-cutting. You can't take him away from the land. Once you do, these people come bulldozing in, they destroy the land and create all kinds of problems for the animals."

Trappers and hunters have a vested interest in maintaining an unspoiled environment. The wildlife they rely on cannot survive on land polluted by mine tailings or flooded by hydro megaprojects. And anyone who has paid the slightest attention to northern development in Canada, especially since the historic Berger Inquiry quashed the Mackenzie Valley pipeline, knows the vital role played by trappers and hunters who live on the land. Their role as guardians is real, not theoretical.

Canadian hunters and trappers are the exact equivalent of the Brazilian rubber-tree trappers whose heroic defence of the rain forest against slash-and-burn cattle ranchers transformed them into international heroes. The lessons of that struggle have led environmentalists to search frantically for other renewable resources that could be extracted from the rain forest without harming it, creating sustainable economic activity to forestall destructive practices like ranching and logging. In other words, making the rain forest more valuable intact than in ashes. A luxury trade, which by definition is characterized by high prices and an eager market, would be perfect. The Canadian fur trade provides the ideal model. If there was anything like it in the tropics, the future of the rain forest would not be nearly so grim.

The argument that fur is a luxury, ergo bad, has an impregnable simplicity that complicated facts can't breach. What knocks it all to hell is strictly human: the tens of thousands of Native families who rely on trapping as one of their last links with an embattled way of life. They saw what happened to the Inuit of the eastern Arctic in the wake of the European ban on sealskin—the widespread social breakdown is well documented by academics and by the federal government's royal commission on the seal hunt—and they know that the anti-fur campaign threatens more than their livelihood. It threatens a way of life that, despite intense persecution, has persisted for thousands of years. Stephen Kakfwi, former president of the Dene Nation, notes that the anti-fur campaign is "potentially far more dangerous than the threat to our lands posed by resource developers and far more oppressing than colonial governments." In the eyes of Bob Stevenson, its goal—perhaps unintended but no less real for that—is simply "cultural genocide." On that subject, of course, Natives are expert.

European anti-fur activists generally dismiss the Native right to continue trapping with straightforward utilitarian arguments. "If you look at the figures it turns out that one-tenth of one per cent of fur coming onto the international market comes from those northern communities," says Mark Glover of the British animal-rights group Lynx. "For me that's not a good enough reason for us to stop the campaign." The Europeans are far enough away from the 50,000 human victims of their campaign that they can afford to treat them like statistics. Many Canadians, however, confronted with real people demanding they take responsibility for their actions, respond with evasion, sanctimonious lectures and outright contempt.

The attitude was typified by an exchange that took place at a forum on the fur trade held at McGill University in 1987. Thomas Coon, a James Bay Cree and executive of the Native pro-fur lobby, Indigenous Survival International, was talking to Cynthia Drummond, coordinating director of the Canadian Society for the Prevention of Cruelty to Animals. Coon said, "Those people who killed the seal market will eventually kill the fur trade and the fur market. But the people who are truly suffering, people who are facing hardships, my people, want an answer to this question: What are the alternatives?"

Drummond refused to answer, "because our position with the SPCA is to speak about what's happening to the animals."

"What is happening to the human beings?" asked Coon. "Us, people that are suffering? What about us? Do animal rights supersede human rights? What about us? What about me? What am I going to feed my little ones with?"

There was no answer.

When there is an answer, however, it tends to be offensive. Anti-fur people often suggest that Natives who argue against them—and that includes virtually every Native in the country—are simply being "manipulated" by the fur industry. The assumption is that Natives haven't the wit to recognize their real self-interest and that if they did, they would oppose the fur trade. They are merely, in the words of Stephen Best, the Toronto-based vice-president of the International Wildlife Coalition, "a public relations tool."

Best is famous for his anti-Native arguments. He has made a close study of the poverty and desperation that exists on many Canadian reserves, and in a speech he has given more than once he describes it in astonishing detail—long lists of all the most depressing statistics. "This is what the heritage of the fur fashion industry has wrought," he declares. Past exploitation by the fur trade is something no Native denies, even though the historical fur trade allowed Natives an important measure of independence and figures strongly in much of their nostalgia for the good old days. But Best's audacious claim that all contemporary Native problems are exclusively due to the fur trade—"There does not appear to be anything else in particular that caused it," he says—is palpably absurd.

What then, is the point of describing Native despair in such loving detail? One suspects that Best merely enjoys rubbing their noses in it. Here are his views on Native culture: "I own the Native culture. I bought it with my taxes.... There would be no Indian culture today if it wasn't for the fact that southern Canadians pay for it. Native people have got to develop a culture that is sufficiently apart from southern interests, and they have to do it on their own terms. When they do, they will be able to call all their own shots." Until then, of course, they will remain "public relations tools" mired in desperate poverty, with no ability—and presumably no right—to run their own lives.

The depressing thing about such arguments is that they are so familiar. They were invented by missionaries and educators who used them to justify their deliberate attempt to eradicate a stubbornly persistent Native culture. As Justice Berger noted in his famous report, long before anyone had heard of Stephen Best, the exact same arguments were adopted holus-bolus by the powerful industrial interests urging him to approve a pipeline down the Mackenzie Valley. The argument that Native culture is "a pathetic and diminishing remnant of what existed in the past," wrote

Berger, "arises as much from our attitudes toward Native people as from any process of reasoning.... We simply do not see Native culture as defensible. Many of us do not even see it as a culture at all."

Among the nonracist arguments brought against Native people, the most serious one claims that they are no longer engaged in subsistence hunting and trapping, that using snowmobiles and accepting cash disqualifies them from the right to trap. Such simplistic assertions ignore the reality of life in the north. For the Native people, the food value of the animals they hunt and trap far outweighs the price they receive for the pelts: The replacement value of food obtained from fur-bearing animals in the Northwest Territories alone amounts to $50 million a year. But the cash they do earn can be vital in sustaining their independence—keeping them off welfare and on the land. That is why they hold on to trapping so seriously.

Life in the high Arctic presents a classic study in the nature of true subsistence, which has little to do with the artifacts of technology. The Inuit readily adopt high technology, but they do it to improve their life: For them, satellite TV is a means to preserve and promote their language and culture, not a cheap way to get *Mork and Mindy* reruns. So it is with hunting and trapping. George Wenzel, a professor of geography at McGill University who has spent 20 years studying the Inuit of Baffin Island, points out that subsistence is a matter of cooperation, of perpetuating the system of social relations that is centred on the hunt. Those relations haven't changed with modern technology or with the cash needed to buy gas and bullets. But without the hunt, they disappear. Without the hunt, says Wenzel, Inuit lose their economic in-

dependence and the basic organizing principle of their culture. "The anti-fur movement is an ideology, just like capitalism,
and it takes no account of the Native perspective at all. It's basically saying, 'We're
right and you're wrong.' That's what white
men have always done."

The consequences of imposing rigid
definitions of subsistence on Native hunters—in effect forcing them into unworkable
museum cultures—were revealed tragically
in the Pribilof Islands of Alaska, where in
1983 animal-rights campaigners succeeded
in halting a centuries-old seal hunt conducted by local Aleuts. The ban ostensibly
permitted subsistence hunting. But John
Grandy, vice-president of the Humane Society of the United States, explains that
when the Aleuts tried to sell the pelts of
seals killed for food, "we frankly said, 'No
way, José. You can't do that. That's not
what we mean by subsistence.'" The absurd
result, duplicated in the Canadian arctic, is
that the Aleuts are now forced to bury those
pelts—a criminal waste that offends every
principle of traditional culture and true subsistence.

Another result, not incidental, was that
a formerly self-sufficient society was
plunged into desperate poverty. Domestic
violence and alcohol abuse reached crisis
proportions among the 700 Aleuts of the
Pribilofs, and over a single year there were
four suicides, 100 documented suicide attempts and three murders. Meanwhile, US
animal-rights activists stepped up their campaign, demanding an end to the "subsistence" hunt.

Clearly, the only endangered animals in
the fur trade are human beings. Not just
any humans, but the last of the hunter-gath-
erers, the stubborn survivors of the greatest
epic of human evolution.

Two years after Greenpeace succeeded in
destroying the seal hunt, a British representative of the group visited Greenland for the
first time to see the conditions prevailing in
the seal-hunting communities along the
west coast. He said, "We didn't really
know what it was like in a community like
this…. Maybe if we had known about these
things earlier, it [the anti-sealing campaign]
wouldn't have happened like that." The admission gave little solace to the Inuit people, who might well have asked why
Greenpeace didn't research the facts before
it launched its long and vigorous campaign.
But as a result, the group has dropped out
of the wider anti-fur campaign. The fur
trade "is just not a priority for us," says a
spokesperson.

It seems incredible that so many other
groups, despite clear evidence of the human
suffering they threaten to cause, remain im-
placably determined to wipe out the entire
fur trade. The reason probably lies in the
philosophical gulf that separates the two
sides. That gulf is so wide that the Native
people have virtually become invisible to
their oppressors; they are seen only as statistics, or distant criminals.

"The further you are from the wilderness," says Pierre Berton, "the more
chance you have of becoming an animal
rights advocate." The statement is not
merely funny; it is a fact. For people raised
in cities and garden-like countrysides,
where nature is strictly controlled if not
downright suppressed, nature becomes a
marvellous park. For people who buy their
meat in cellophane packages and are raised
on stories in which hedgehogs wear aprons
and muskrats smoke pipes, it becomes impossible not to see all wild animals as pets.
Who would not protect their pet against a
killer?

People who live close to nature can never afford such a cozy view. If an Inuk's dog faltered in its traces, it was cut loose and left to freeze to death on the tundra. People who live close to nature know that there is no such thing as old age in the animal world, that every wild animal meets a horrible, often violent death. They know that for man to live, he must kill. The same Mother Nature that succors and supports them is also fundamentally and utterly hostile. As the myths of every aboriginal culture prove, intimacy with nature breeds attitudes and beliefs that are so complex they are incomprehensible to civilized people. When they are trying to explain their "side" in the fur debate, Native people invariably attempt to describe their relationship with nature. It's a lost cause; they might as well lecture on Martian ballet.

The most pragmatic behave like Dave Monture, secretary-treasurer of Indigenous Survival International. Monture wears a three-piece suit, speaks in well-crafted sound bites and is a veteran of the bureaucratic corridors in cities such as Brussels and Strasbourg. His latest campaign was to stop the European Community from moving up the deadline on its proposed ban on fur imports, currently scheduled to take effect January 1, 1995. To that end he organized a tour, wittily titled "A Few Acres of Snow," that took five key members of the European Parliament to northern Manitoba in the dead of winter. They gained a "first-time glimpse of reality," says Monture. "They saw what the price of hamburger was at the 59th parallel, and at minus-30 Centigrade they didn't notice any banana plantations."

The diplomacy, actively supported by the federal government, is having some effect. The European ban will be enforced if by 1995 there are no international standards for humane trapping. Canada recently put a proposal to that effect before the International Organization for Standardization and appears to have secured the agreement of the European Community to help in its development.

But such successes, as anti-fur activists are quick to point out, mean little. The fact is, they are winning the hearts and minds of virtually all well-intentioned people who like animals. As Stephen Best said, testifying before a parliamentary committee four years ago, "I may be completely morally bankrupt in dealing with this, and all the people I deal with and all the people who support us, who are in the millions, may all be wrong; but they exist.... It is a practical fact you have to deal with, whether it is right or wrong...."

Never mind all the tedious arguments—the fur trade is dying. Thomas Coon knows it. "We are the weak, we are the poor, we will lose," he says simply. A hard fact of life. "Taking life is definitely a cruelty," says Coon. "No matter how we die as human beings, no matter how we take life, it is cruelty. Killing a culture, killing a society and killing a way of life is definitely a cruelty. My culture will die in agony."

Question for Discussion

1 How convincing are Barber's arguments that people should stop objecting to the fur trade?

PART 4

ethics and the environment

The twentieth century has witnessed an unprecedented increase both in the number of human beings, and in our technological capability. As a result, we now create larger changes in the world around us than ever before. With this increased impact, there has been a growth in concern about those changes. What will be the long-term costs of our actions? Are we doing irreparable harm to our environment? How much change in ordinary attitudes is required to reflect this concern?

It is clear that people have often acted without knowing the full consequences of their actions, often with tragic results. For example, when the United States was conducting experiments with nuclear weapons after the Second World War, it warned visitors to cover their eyes to protect themselves from the radiation. Now we know that such "protection" was woefully inadequate and that many people were needlessly harmed. The same can be said about unseen hazards such as underground toxic wastes and asbestos fibres. Even visible pollution, such as industrial smoke, was once believed to dissipate harmlessly; now it is thought to be responsible for (among other things) acid rain and the corresponding deaths of many kinds of fish and wildlife.

There are many different views about what follows from these sorts of observations. The most straightforward approach—people should take greater care to discover the consequences of their actions—agrees with the traditional view that nature is there for our use, but emphasizes that we must take care to make *good* use of it. This approach has led to the imposition of "environmental impact assessments" of many major projects. Before people do anything which might have a serious impact on the environment, they should conduct a study to determine exactly what consequences can be expected, and perhaps to investigate alternatives with their accompanying costs in both financial and environmental terms. After the assessment is completed, it is then possible to decide whether the benefits of the project are important enough to warrant the foreseen risks to the environment.

Practical objections to this approach point out that, the way the system stands, environmental assessments tend to weigh economic considerations too heavily, and environmental concerns correspondingly lightly. For example, it has been claimed that the people proposing the projects in question are likely to be fairly wealthy, organized groups, who have a vested interest in the project's success. Those who are likely to suffer the consequences, on the other hand, are often isolated individuals, in many cases already socially disadvantaged, who are less able to mount an organized opposition. Indeed, some potential victims may not even be aware of proposed changes. Furthermore, there is sometimes a question about who is allowed to have standing to make a presentation before the body conducting the assessment. Some viewpoints may be shut out of the process, simply because the process is not public enough.

Another objection to environmental impact assessments is that they tend to view things in exclusively economic terms, and systematically undervalue some societal "goods." For example, it is very difficult to place a monetary value on the benefit of a pleasing natural landscape, and so such values may fail to be taken into account when considering the "costs" of a proposed project.

Extremists opposed to environmental impact assessments as commonly practiced claim that no interference with natural environments should be tolerated. This could be maintinaed on the ground that we know too little about the interconnectedness of different aspects of the environment, and simply cannot estimate the full consequences of our actions.

Making a claim as strong as saying we should freeze all interference with the environment might require one to explain what counts as an "interference." Any human activity, even one as basic as breathing, has *some* impact on the environment; certainly activities such as building shelters and consuming food can have negative effects on the non-human world. Nevertheless, it is clear that some human activities have more broad-ranging and intrusive effects than others, and one could argue that no activities of the larger sort should be undertaken. Whether one believes we should put a "hold" on all projects with significant environmental ramifications will depend in part on how serious one believes the long-term harm is likely to be. Of course nobody knows for certain, but perhaps people should simply make their best estimate of what will have the best consequences, and act accordingly.

One objection to freezing our activities at the status quo is that this would be unfair to people who have not yet been able to benefit from the advantages of technology. For example, it might be claimed that the "developed" nations have benefitted from exploiting the "third world" nations, and that it is only fair now to give those nations a chance to catch up, even if this means further destruction of the environment. It may be that North Americans, for example, could live reasonably well without any further major development of the environment, but that some nations which face tremendous poverty have no choice but to exploit their resources to avoid a tremendous human cost. Furthermore, it might be argued that it is technological advance which makes it possible to keep more people alive, by making more efficient use of existing resources. If humankind suddenly stopped employing its technology, the results might be even greater infringement of the environment, or a great extension of human poverty and suffering. This then seems to become an empirical question, about whether technology tends to do more harm or good.

Many people would argue that the threats to the environment cannot be overcome without serious changes in common attitudes toward material goods. The "consumerism" of people in wealthy nations seems to be responsible for much of the rampant depletion of resources in the poverty-stricken third world. Meanwhile, the industries, transportation, and conveniences of the developed nations require increasing amounts of energy. Using traditional sources of energy such as coal, oil, and gas not only depletes the world's irreplaceable resources, but also leaves a polluting residue, and generates heat which may affect the climate of the planet. What is more, it has been argued that our economic system is based on a notion of continuous exponential growth which simply cannot be maintained. To what extent must we change our assumptions, attitudes, and behaviour in order to preserve our planet?

One question this gives rise to concerns the goal of preserving the planet itself. Should we be concerned only with the long-term interests of human beings (and perhaps other sentient beings), or should we be concerned about the interests of entities such as trees, prairies, or wetlands? The dominant tradition in Canada has been for people to see themselves as somehow separate from nature, having either been given, or simply legitimately taking, dominion over it. However, it is possible to view ourselves as *part* of the environment—as one more feature which should try to fit in to the whole. One way to put this view would be to say that we should stop viewing ourselves as the only things which have value in the universe, and come to recognize the intrinsic value of such things as forests, species, and perhaps even rock formations. We might also want to assert that the whole earth (or at least everything living on it) has value, and that people should view their relationship to it as one of stewardship rather than ownership. People who advocate attributing intrinsic moral value to things independently of their impact on human lives are sometimes known as "deep ecologists."

It is very difficult to tell what properties something must have in order to have value in its own right. (For more on this issue, see the chapter on "The Moral Status of Non-Human Animals.") Can the "biosphere" as a whole have rights? Can individual plants? How about species? This issue about whether our environmental concern should be based, ultimately, on human good, or on some broader good, is one of the central issues of environmental ethics.

Some people argue that, although of course most people do feel some sorrow at the prospect of a species dying out, or of a beautiful forest that has existed for centuries being felled to make room for a shopping mall or equivalent, this feeling can be associated with the sense of loss we feel when we hear someone has destroyed a priceless painting. Perhaps our appreciation of such objects is aesthetic, rather than moral, and perhaps it does not reveal a belief that the species, or tree, has any moral status in its own right, any more than works of art do. If this is the case, then it is still an open question how such value should be balanced against other values, such as the well-being of human beings.

Another objection often raised against deep ecologists has to do with the question of whether concern for non-human entities does necessarily lead (as deep ecologists commonly suggest) to non-interference on our part. If diversity of species is itself a good, should we feel an obligation to use our technology to produce new species? If forests (for example) have interests, should we go out and water them in times of drought, or trim the trees so that they can reach their full potential?

A similar objection to deep ecology grows from the claim that we should view ourselves as simply one part of nature. If that is true, it would seem that any intervention we make in the world around us could be viewed as a "natural" development. To call ourselves "stewards" with an obligation to protect the natural world (of a sort plants, habitats, and species presumably do not have) does seem to involve setting ourselves apart from the rest of the world in some way.

This chapter explores some of the alternatives for how we might view the relationship between human beings and the non-human environment. Virtually everyone would agree that we must change some of our behaviours and attitudes in light of a new appreciation of the interconnectedness of things in the natural order, and the long-term consequences of our activities. However, the degree of change required is still very much open to debate.

Crimes Against the Environment

Law Reform Commission of Canada

Traditionally, the legal remedy for excessive pollution has been the imposition of fines on the polluters. Some people have objected that this amounts to the same thing as establishing a licensing fee for polluting—would-be polluters can simply calculate whether it will cost them more to change their behaviour so as to avoid the fine, or pay it and continue polluting. In 1985, the Law Reform Commission of Canada published a working paper which considered the idea that damaging the environment might be considered a criminal offense. In the process, the Commission considered several aspects of environmental ethics, including the question of which rights (if any) are violated by harm to the environment, and whether the environment should be protected for its own sake, apart from any relevance it may have for human beings.

*   *   *

The present *Criminal Code* in effect prohibits offences against persons and property. It does not, in any explicit or direct manner, prohibit offences against the natural environment itself. In this Working Paper, the Commission makes and supports the proposition that the natural environment should now become an interest explicitly protectable in some cases in the *Criminal Code*. Some acts or omissions seriously harmful or endangering to the environment should, if they meet the various tests of a real crime, be characterized and prohibited for what they really are in the first instance, crimes against the environment....

In terms of harm done, risks caused, degree of intent and values threatened, environmental pollution spans a continuum from minor to catastrophic; from what is harmless, to what is tolerable if controlled in view of various social benefits thereby achieved, to what is intolerable and deserving of social abhorrence and denunciation; from what is only accidental, careless or negligent, to what is grossly negligent, reckless or intentional....

That wide range regarding harm, values threatened and degree of intent calls for a similar range of legal controls and responses. In this Working Paper, the focus is on those pollution activities at the most serious end of the scale, those which in the view of this Commission, merit the most severe societal deterrence, repudiation and sanction available, namely, that provided by their clear and explicit prohibition in the *Criminal Code*. The problems addressed are those of: determining at what point on the pollution continuum these offences should be considered real crimes; deciding what the essential elements of environmental crimes should be; and demonstrating that their prohibition fulfils an urgent need which cannot otherwise be met.

It must be emphasized at this point that no claim will be made that the explicit prohibition by the *Criminal Code* of some pollution activity will provide in one stroke the solution to all pollution problems. In fact it is almost certain that from a practical and long-range point of view, a number of other existing and evolving legal and administrative approaches, controls and incentives, especially those focused on prevention and compliance, will do much more to limit and lessen pollution than will recourse to the *Criminal Code*. It should be acknowledged that what will count far more towards environmental protection than *any* law reform, criminal or otherwise, is an increasingly informed and environmentally sensitive public combined with an evolution in economic and political priorities.

It is the view of this Commission that a fundamental and widely shared value is indeed seriously contravened by some environmental pollution, a value which we will refer to as the *right to a safe environment*.

To some extent, this right and value appears to be new and emerging, but in part because it is an extension of existing and very traditional rights and values already protected by criminal law, its presence and shape even now are largely discernible. Among the new strands of this fundamental value are, it may be argued, those such as *quality of life*, and *stewardship* of the natural environment. At the same time, traditional values as well have simply expanded and evolved to include the environment now as an area and interest of direct and primary concern. Among these values fundamental to the purposes and protections of criminal law are the *sanctity of life*, the *inviolability and integrity of persons*, and the *protection of human life and health*. It is increasingly understood that certain forms and degrees of environmental pollution can directly or indirectly, sooner or later, seriously harm or endanger human life and human health.

"Environmental Rights": The Options

An indisputable task in exploring and justifying our proposal to add environmental crimes to the *Criminal Code* is that of determining, with as much precision as possible, the particular value and interest legitimately within the scope of criminal law protection. There can, in other words, be a number of reasons why one might wish to make serious harm or danger to the environment a crime. But it does not follow that each reason has the same weight, or that each of the interests in mind equally merit the involvement of criminal law. The principle of restraint in the use of criminal law obliges us not to extend its already wide scope, except to include identifiable and deserving targets.

Expressed very broadly and in terms of environmental rights, there are potentially five related but different levels of "environmental rights" one might wish to enshrine in law, and corresponding activities one may wish the law to prohibit:

(1) *A right not to have one's life or health harmed or endangered as a result of environmental pollution, the health effects of which are known, predictable, serious, and relatively immediate.*

In effect this category can be thought of as an extension and application of the more general right and interest already the primary focus of the *Criminal Code*—that of physical integrity and security.

(2) *A right to a reasonable level of environmental quality, even when a specific pollutant or pollution source cannot now be identified with certainty as the cause of specific health damage or risk, on the grounds that sooner or later serious pollution of the environment will threaten human life and health as well.*

Although the right in this case would be to environmental quality, the ultimate concern and basis, as in the first category, is human health. Unlike the first category, however, its scope would extend beyond just those instances of pollution with known, predictable and serious dangers to human life and health, to include all instances of serious environmental pollution. Proponents of this view would and do argue

that, in the long run, to badly damage particular aspects of the natural environment, especially in an irreversible manner, may do serious harm to human health—if not to those now living, then to those in a future generation; in other words that, from an ecological perspective, there is no discontinuity between serious environmental harm and harm to the health of humans in general. Because of that risk, the law should directly prohibit all pollution which seriously harms or endangers environmental quality. This level and category of right does not assume or promote victimless crimes. Rather, it assumes that there will be specific and identifiable victims; it is simply that we do not yet know their identity or the particular form of their victimization.

(3) *A right to a reasonable level of environmental quality, but one which is violated by pollution instances which deprive people of the use and enjoyment of the environment, even when there are no health effects or dangers.*

This right and category differs from the previous two in that the interest underlying the right is not the protection of human life and health, but a wide range of uses of the natural environment and natural resources which can be seriously interfered with by pollution ranging from noise to toxic contamination. These amenity considerations could range from a dirty (but not unhealthy) river, to the ability to exploit a particular natural resource for commercial purposes because of pollution damage. The fundamental question which must be faced in this regard is whether the scope of criminal law should be extended into the environmental arena to protect amenity rights alone, when there are no significant human health implications. Important rights can, of course, be infringed in both cases, and various branches of law other than criminal already are involved in protecting, for various purposes, the use and enjoyment of the environment; but the case for involving the *criminal* law would appear to be much stronger when claims to the use and enjoyment of the environment also involve direct or indirect health risks. In other words, the emission of very large quantities of highly carcinogenic or mutagenic compounds into city air would appear to constitute a much more serious and hence potentially criminal infringement of environmental rights than the emission of pollutants making a river objectionable to swim in, but not unhealthy.

(4) A right of the environment to be protected from serious pollution for its own sake, even if pollution incidents should result in no direct or indirect risk or harm to human health or limitation upon the use and enjoyment of nature.

The previous three categories permit the focus upon, and protection of, the environment *itself*, although ultimately for the sake of human life, human health, and the use and enjoyment of the environment by humans. However, this last right would protect the environment *for its own sake*, quite apart from health or amenity considerations. From this perspective, it is the environment which should have various rights, not people who should have environmental rights. The implications of environmental pollution for humans would be quite incidental to this right. The extension of criminal law protection to encompass the first three rights could be considered *evolutionary* (although not necessarily justifiable in each case). However, for the criminal law, or law generally for that matter, to acknowledge this fourth category and right in the strict and literal sense would be truly *revolutionary*. It would be, in effect, to as-

sign rights to nonhuman entities, and it has always been thought that only humans can have rights. Interesting and tempting though it may be to do so, efforts to argue that case have so far not been met with anything approaching general support, whether in philosophical or legal thinking. Some very real conceptual problems stand in the way of such efforts.[1] In our view, there are more than adequate grounds for more rigorous environmental protection right now, whether or not nonhuman entities are granted legal rights at some future date.

(5) A right to have one's private property protected from damage by pollution caused by others.

It is doubtful in our view that this new environmental crime should include within its scope pollution which only damages or endangers the private property of others. The implications of some pollution for private property can be very serious; but when there are no serious dangers to human health or the environment itself as well, what is at issue is not environmental rights, but (private) property rights. To include property considerations as a direct and exclusive object of this new crime against the environment would be to blunt its focus and diffuse its effect. It is in part at least to focus clearly on the environment itself as opposed to (private) property that this new environmental crime is being proposed. When only private property is harmed or endangered by pollution, the more direct and effective legal routes would seem to be the civil route for prosecutions for crimes against property....

The Public Trust Doctrine, Environmental Quality and Bills of Environmental Rights

Another strand of an environmental ethic given increased attention in our times is the notion of "public trust" applied to environmental rights and duties. That notion is contributing to an evolution in our concept of private ownership. At present, most environmental protection legislation in Canada gives governments (through their environmental agencies) only a discretionary role *vis-à-vis* protection of the environment. That is, it *may* apply and enforce the legislation, but it *need not*. There are few obligations imposed on those who administer statutes.

However, the emerging public trust notion would impose duties to manage and use resources *in trust* for the public. It is already generally accepted that *governments* have public trust duties, in that land and resources owned by the government cannot be disposed of to private interests without taking into account the broad public interest. However, many argue that this notion should be applied to business as well, and to the land resources they own. While industries and developers would continue to be allowed the reasonable use of resources they own, their ownership and use would be qualified by their "public trustee" responsibilities.[2] Involved in this notion is in effect an evolution in our concept of ownership. The right to the private ownership and use of its land and resources by an industry would not be denied, but a new dimension would be added. That new dimension would be a responsibility to use it not only for private gain but also in the light of the common good. Consideration of the common good and the public heritage dimension of privately owned land and re-

sources would rule out, for example, disposal of one's industrial wastes in ways likely to create public harm or risk.

This general notion of a dimension of common ownership is not in reality entirely new to law. It is only being rediscovered in our times. It was already expressed in the Institutes of Justinian:

> By natural law the following things belong to all men, namely: air, running water, the sea, and for this reason the shores of the sea.[3]

The concept of public trust—of the environment as a public heritage—is one of the foundations of efforts on many fronts in recent years to establish environmental Bills of Rights....

They seek to shift at least some of the burden of proof from the plaintiff and Crown to the defendant and accused. Not only would a plaintiff, for example, not have to claim *personal* injury to have standing to bring an environmental action before a court, but if the activity complained of could be shown to endanger the environment, then the burden would shift to the alleged polluter to establish the safety of that activity.

From a "Homocentric" to an "Ecocentric" Ethic

A number of commentators have observed that the dominant environmental ethic both politically and intellectually until about the 1960s envisaged humans at the centre of the universe. Generally speaking that view made two assumptions as a result: that humans have dominion over all other forms of life and inanimate entities; and that we could and would make perpetually greater demands on the natural environment by way of production, consumption, and waste.[4] To a large extent, that "mankind at the centre" perspective characterized as well the arguments and positions of those pushing for a safer and cleaner environment. What counted as the measure of defensible environmental policies was the value of the environment to us—the need to protect it because it is indispensable to the satisfaction of human needs and desires. That view also fueled the environmental legislation in the United States and Canada. Harm to the environment was to be avoided and controlled, implicitly because we humans would otherwise be affected in some manner; continuing and expanding resource consumption and production would be constrained, our enjoyment of nature curtailed, and our health put at risk.

However, more recently environmentalists and others have underlined what they see as some serious limitations of that homocentric or "mankind at the centre" perspective, and many promoted instead an ecocentric or "environment at the centre" stance. They claim, for instance, that the older view was wrong to assume that we could have adequate environmental protection at no cost to our appetites, desires or life-styles—that we could continue and expand production, consumption and waste and at the same time have a safe and clean environment—that nature is infinitely resilient and flexible. They now argue that there are always costs, some payable now, some later, that some resources are not renewable, and that there are thresholds and limits to what can be used and destroyed in the environment and in each ecosystem. They maintain that there is a balance, harmony and interdependence in nature to be protected and respected for its own sake.

Some environmentalists also argue that, pushed to its logical conclusion, a policy of environmental protection based only on *human* goals and rights could progressively weaken claims for the protection of endangered aspects of the environment, the pollution or destruction of which would not constitute economic or aesthetic loss, or danger to human health. Some fear that as our capacity increases to supply by artificial means those human needs and desires now supplied by the natural environment, the checklist of those forms of life and inanimate entities in nature which we deem worthy of protecting would progressively shrink.

To some extent then, these and similar views constitute a shift away from a largely homocentric ethic, one which in effect seeks the protection of the environment *for its own sake*, quite apart from its relevance to humans. There are, of course, many important and laudable insights provided by proponents of this more recent stage of environmental concerns. At the very least, they further demonstrate that the environment itself in the view of many ought to be a legally protectable interest; but, as already suggested above, there remain some serious conceptual and practical obstacles to the provision of legal protection to the natural environment *for its own sake*, apart from considerations of human benefits, wishes, uses and health risks. It would amount to granting rights to nonhuman entities. From a practical standpoint, it is inconceivable that natural resources could ever be totally insulated from economic and political considerations. Nor is it evident that we cannot provide adequate protection for the natural environment itself by continuing to permit a homocentric ethic to underlie our environmental regulations and laws, but one which now gives more scope to the *quality* of human life, and to our responsibility of *stewardship* or trusteeship over the natural environment.

Conclusions

In view of the preceding analyses about fundamental values and interests, we are now able to make the first of our conclusions. At this point, this first set of conclusions will encompass only the matter of the particular environmental values and interests to which the *Criminal Code* could and should legitimately extend. The five options in this regard were described above....

1. The scope of a *Criminal Code* offence against the environment should not extend to protecting the natural environment for its own sake, apart from human values, rights and interests.

2. However, a fundamental value is seriously contravened by some instances of environmental pollution, one which can be characterized as the right to a safe environment, or the right to a reasonable level of environmental quality.

3. This value may not as yet be fully emerged or universally acknowledged, but its existence and shape are already largely discernible. In protecting it, the *Criminal Code* would be essentially reflecting public perceptions and expanding values traditionally underlined in the *Code*—the sanctity of life, the integrity of persons, and the centrality of human life and health. At the same time, the *Criminal Code* would be playing an educative and advocacy role by clearly articulating environmental concerns and dangers not always perceived as such, and by incorporating newer concerns such as quality of life and stewardship of the natural environment.

4. More specifically, the scope of a *Criminal Code* pollution offence should ex-

tend to prohibiting environmental pollution which seriously damages or endangers the *quality of the environment*, and thereby seriously harms or endangers *human life or health*.

5. The pollution activities prohibited by a *Code* offence should include not only those which are presently known to constitute immediate and certain health harms and risks, but also those *likely* to cause serious harm to human health in the foreseeable future.

6. The scope of a *Criminal Code* pollution offence should not normally extend to prohibiting pollution which deprives others of the *use and enjoyment* of a natural resource but causes no serious present or likely harm or risks to human health. Only by express exception should an interest other than life or health fall within the scope of such an offence. Such an exception would be, for example, when a form of pollution would deprive an entire community of its livelihood.

7. Environmental pollution which destroys or damages *private property* without, as a result, causing or risking serious harm to human life or health, should not fall within the scope of a *Code* offence against the environment, but should be the object of civil remedies or prosecuted as a crime against property.

Seriously Harmful or Endangering Conduct

...One explanation of the mechanics and implications of environmental damage and destruction is that provided by the ecosystem approach. That approach is not without its limitations when pushed to extremes, and it is not our intention to promote it or to justify legal prohibitions and reforms purely on the basis of one or another environmental school of thought. Nevertheless, some findings of ecologists are not disputed, and the general lines of the approach help to underline the potential seriousness of some environmental pollution.[5]

This relatively new approach is a synthesis of the insights and skills of a number of disciplines, especially biology, chemistry, geography and climatology. Whereas those and other fields study the threads of nature, the ecosystem approach studies its "whole cloth." Its proponents insist especially upon two points. They argue first of all that it is erroneous to speak of man *and* environment, or of man as *external* to the natural environment. Rather, humans are internal to, and partners with, the rest of nature. They argue, secondly, that serious harm done to one element in an ecosystem will invariably lead to the damage or even destruction of other elements in that and other ecosystems.

What ecologists mean by an "ecosystem" is any relatively homogeneous and delineated unit of nature in which nonliving substances and living organisms interact with an exchange of materials taking place between the nonliving and living parts. The term "ecosystem" is somewhat flexible and the boundaries between them somewhat arbitrary. Those boundaries are generally based upon what is most convenient for measuring the movement of energy and chemicals into and out of the system. Typical and important interrelated and overlapping ecosystems are: units of land along with the surrounding air and water, or lakes, or river basins, or forests, or climatic zones, or the earth itself or the biosphere (the outer sphere of the earth inhabited by living organisms and including lakes, oceans, soil and living organisms, in-

cluding man). Within each ecosystem there is, they maintain, a delicate balance and interdependence between all the elements. Systems can cope with and adapt to some interferences, but not others. The overall long-range effect of some intrusions is not yet known with certainty or in detail. Ecologists argue that ecosystems are now known to be subject to very definable and immutable processes, which impose corresponding ecological constraints. They stress two organizational rules, namely, the first two of the three laws of thermodynamics. The first rule (that of conservation of matter and energy) is that matter and energy cannot be destroyed, only *transformed*. The second (the law of entropy) is that all energy transformations are *degradations*, whereby energy is transformed from more organized to less organized forms. In simpler terms, they explain those rules by the following principles and examples.

The first is that *everything in the environment or individual ecosystems is related*. If one breaks a link in the food-chain, for example, or introduces a substance not biodegradable, there are consequences for the entire ecosystem. Examples of the serious and often irreversible harm are DDT and mercury. Since its massive use in the 1940s, the footsteps of DDT can be followed from wheat, to insects, to rodents, to larger animals and birds, and to man. In its wake it left whole species of animals more or less extinct or with serious reproductive problems. To illustrate the degree of interaction involved and the insignificance of time and distance, traces of DDT can now be found in the flesh of polar bears. The industrial discharge of *mercury* is another illustration. It has been followed from its discharge by pulp and paper industries into the air and water, to its transformation in the water into methyl-mercury by the water's micro-organisms, to its accumulation in the sediment of lakes or its absorption by the fish. Among its victims in the next stage, it is argued, have been the Indians of northern Ontario and Quebec, who eat the fish and are frequently inflicted with the horrors of what has come to be known as Minamata disease.

The second principle underlined by ecologists is that *unless neutralized, every contaminating substance remains harmful somewhere to something or someone* in the natural environment. Sooner or later we will pay, in some cases dearly, for discarding, for example, nonrecycled industrial toxins into rivers and dumps. Matter cannot be destroyed—only transformed. The atoms and molecules of matter are always preserved by ecosystems in some form. Moreover, if they are not or cannot be transformed, degraded, recycled or neutralized, it is an illusion to hope that that form will become a benign and harmless one.

Limitations of an Unqualified Ecosystem Approach

From the perspective of harm, however, there may be some difficulties and limitations of the ecosystem approach pushed to its extreme. It has been observed that some (by no means all) of its proponents are unjustifiably pessimistic and too rigorous. Some imply that each now stable and healthy ecosystem has inherent worth, and must be preserved exactly as it is, that any harm or modification to it would be immoral, and that all human impacts upon, or changes to, an aspect of the environment are necessarily unnatural. However, that view has at least three limitations.

(1) Viruses and Diseases: Good or Bad?

First of all, if every ecosystem, every species, is to be preserved and protected "as is" in its natural state, if human values, human judgement and human benefit are to be considered irrelevant, we would be forced to *tolerate many threats and diseases* generally perceived to be themselves harmful if not attacked and even wiped out if possible. An unqualified ecosystem approach pushed to its logical extreme might, for example, force a conclusion that the extinction of the smallpox virus was not a good thing, or that grasshoppers, mosquitoes, noxious weeds, various pests and disease organisms should not be combatted but protected, or that the building of human settlements was wrong because some ecosystems were necessarily harmed in the process. Few if any ecologists seem actually to intend these conclusions, but they do perhaps illustrate the sort of dilemmas implicit in attempts to determine and evaluate environmental harm, and the need to qualify the "deep ecology" stance in the light of some other considerations.

(2) The Adaptive Capacity of the Environment

A second limitation of an extreme and rigorous ecosystem approach used to measure environmental harm, is that ecosystems are not only in many respects vulnerable, but also *adaptive and evolutionary*. Up to a point and in some respects, ecosystems can respond to and accommodate change. Some man-made alterations of an element of the environment can, in particular cases, trigger adaptive responses. Ecosystems are not in all respects fixed; there is a degree of rhythm and fluctuation. It becomes important in this regard to weigh impacts of polluting contaminants and activities as to whether they are degradable and noncumulative (for example, mercury, lead, PCBs), reversible or irreversible, natural yet likely to cause damage to some environments in large concentrations (for example, sulphates, chlorides). There are undoubtedly good reasons for policy makers to give more attention to the "inherent worth" view of the natural environment, but this adaptive mechanism itself of ecosystems has an inherent worth and should be added to the calculations of harm. In some cases, the conclusion will be that a substance or activity goes well beyond the adaptive capacity of an ecosystem; in other cases it may not.

(3) Tolerating Pollution for Legitimate Social Purposes: Balancing the Human Health Standard.

There is yet a third and most important factor to be weighed in calculations of serious pollution harm, a factor more or less incompatible with an ecosystem approach which is strict and absolute. It is generally acknowledged in our political and economic system, and in our environmental policies and laws, that there are a number of legitimate social purposes which can justify, at least for a period of time, varying degrees of pollution, deterioration and risk—which permit downgrading the pollution harm and risk from serious and intolerable to less-than-serious and tolerable. It is not, of course, uncommon for the law to conclude that what would be reckless and unacceptable behaviour in some circumstances, can be justified if socially desirable for one reason or another. For example, a very risky medical operation can, in some circumstances, be acceptable and even desirable if it offers the only chance to save a life.

Primary among the goals and purposes implicitly or explicitly underlying environmental policies, regulations and statutes are economic ones. An environmental agency may judge, for example, that a particular existing industry should be allowed to exceed, at least for a specified time, the statutory emission standard for a particular contaminant, because there may be good reason to believe the expense of strict compliance will bankrupt the company and cause widespread unemployment. Similarly, it may be judged that the only way to secure the establishment of a new industry in an economically depressed area and to develop and market local resources is to permit it to do some widespread ecological damage, and/or, at least for a time, exceed by a considerable margin the statutory emission standards. It would, of course, be naive and unrealistic to assume that all such judgements are equally defensible, or that the economic viability and employment arguments of industry should be accepted uncritically by agencies. However, it would be equally naive and Utopian to expect that environmental decision-making can ever be completely insulated from economic and political considerations.

It should be noted that the mere emission of a particular contaminating substance beyond the standard established in the relevant statute or regulations need not in itself always imply serious (or even minor) environmental and health harm. In the first place, the standard itself may be open to legitimate debate as to its accuracy and appropriateness. In some cases the standard may, by some criteria, be too strict, or based upon uncertain evidence. On the other hand, it may be felt by some to be not strict enough. Secondly, it is at least the intention of regulation and standard makers to build into the emission standards a certain margin of safety.

The "social utility" and other factors just indicated demonstrate that judgements before or after the event about the types and degrees of pollution which will be characterized and treated as serious and intolerable, as opposed to minor and tolerable within regulated limits, are not and cannot be strictly and exclusively "scientific" in nature. Determinations of harm and degree of harm are to a large degree value-judgements, rather than scientific calculations. More precisely, such judgements are based upon criteria which themselves imply or import value-judgements. Therefore, these judgements about the acceptability of harm and risk should not be made only by the scientist as scientist.[6]

There is, then, a major distinction to be made between pollution offences and the "paradigm" (criminal) offences of homicide, assault and theft, as regards seriousness. The latter are *always* considered seriously harmful to individuals and fundamental societal values, and therefore criminal (if the *mens rea* conditions are met), no matter what the degree of injury or loss. However, especially given the "social utility" factor, it is possible at present for pollution which by some criteria is endangering to the environment (and human health) to be characterized in the final analysis as not serious and even tolerable. To characterize the harm and danger as not serious need not, of course, mean that the conduct should be subject to no legal prohibitions and sanctions, only that the conduct in question would not fall within the scope of the *Criminal Code*.

That balancing of the environmental risks involved in permitting harmful pollution, with (for example) the economic im-

plications of prohibiting it, is to at least some extent inescapable "before the event" in the formulation of environmental policies, standards and regulations. However, that same balancing is also legitimate "after the event," that is, in determining the seriousness of the alleged offence. At this stage, the social utility factor as a criterion of gravity can be one of the considerations in the choice among various compliance mechanisms authorized by the relevant statute, and in the decision about how rigorously to enforce the statute in this case, including whether or not to prosecute.

However, weighing the social utility of an alleged incidence of pollution to determine its seriousness is also inevitable if we go the further step being proposed in this Paper and characterize some of these activities as potentially *criminal in nature*. One of the criteria of pollution as a crime would be that it must be proved to be seriously harmful. That would be determined, at least in part, by whether conduct which is harmful or endangering by some scientific criteria, may in the final analysis be less than seriously harmful and endangering, or even justifiable and tolerable, in part because it promotes valid social goals. It has been suggested to us by one of those consulted that an alternate or more specific way of highlighting the social utility factor would be to make it a defence, or simply leave it to guide prosecutorial discretion. Both approaches appear to us essentially compatible with the analysis to this point. However, we feel that the jury may have a unique and important role to play in the balancing of harm and social utility.

In any event, the life and health of others cannot be traded off for other apparent benefits, whether economic or not. We do not permit such a trade-off for other criminal offences involving serious harms or dangers to human life and bodily integrity. That being so, we may formulate the following by way of a general criterion: (1) the more certain is the evidence or likelihood of present or future harm and danger to human life and health, and the more serious the nature of that harm and danger, the less legitimate and persuasive should be other socially useful goals as justifications for the pollution or for reducing its classification from serious to minor, and the more compelling would be arguments for the criminal nature of that activity; (2) the less likely are the serious present and future human health harms and dangers, and the more likely the interests affected are exclusively those of the use and enjoyment of the environment, the more relevant and legitimate is the weighing of other societal goals by way of mitigating its classification as potentially serious harm.

Notes

1   See generally on this approach, C.D. Stone, "Should Trees Have Standing?—Toward Legal Rights for Natural Objects" (1972), 45 *Southern California Law Review* 450; L.H. Tribe, "Ways Not to Think about Plastic Trees: New Foundations for Environmental Law" (1974), 83 *Yale Law Journal* 1315; D.P. Emond, "Co-operation in Nature: A New Foundation for Environmental Law" (1984) 22 *Osgoode Hall Law Journal* 323.

2   One of the strongest and earliest proponents of the relevance of this doctrine to environmental protection was Joseph Sax. See his *Defending the Environment: A Strategy for Citizen Action* (New York: Alfred A. Knopf, 1971). See also Constance D. Hunt, "The Public Trust Doctrine in Canada," in John Swaigen, ed., *Environmental Rights in Canada* (Toronto: Butterworths, 1981), pp. 151-94. A related approach encouraged by many argues for a new substantive right to environmental quality which could be enforced by government or any member of the public against business, or by any member of the public against the government. See John Swaigen and Richard

Woods, "A Substantive Right to Environmental Quality," in *Environmental Rights in Canada, supra*, pp. 195-241.

3   Institutes of Justinian, Book II, Title I, para. 1, in *The Civil Law*, a translation by S.P. Scott (Cincinatti: The Central Trust Company, 1932), vol. 2, p. 33.

4   See, for example, N. Morse and D.A. Chant, *An Environmental Ethic: Its Formulation and Implications* (Ottawa: Canadian Environmental Advisory Council, 1975); R. Cahn, *Footprints on the Planet: A Search for an Environmental Ethic* (New York: Universe Books, 1978).

5   For details on the meaning and significance of the ecosystems approach, see: E.P. Odum, *Fundamentals of Ecology*, 3rd ed. (London: Saunders, 1971); H.T. Odum, *Environment, Power and Society* (New York: Wiley, 1971); B. Commoner, *L'encerclement* (Paris: Le Seuil, 1972); P. Lebreton, *Les chemins de l'écologie* (Paris: Éditions Denoël, 1978); A. Schnaiberg, *The Environment* (Oxford: Oxford U. Press, 1980).

6   See T. Page, "A Framework for Unreasonable Risk in the Toxic Substances Control Act (TSCA)" in W. Nicholson, ed., *Management of Assessed Risk for Carcinogens* (1981), 363 *Annals of the New York Academy of Sciences*, New York.

Questions for Discussion

1   Should people who cause harm to the environment be made criminally liable for their actions? If so, should such liability ever extend to harms such as depriving people of the use and enjoyment of natural resources, or should it be limited to harm to life and health?

2   Does the claim that ecosystems have inherent value, independently of human beings, lead us to the conclusion that "the extinction of the smallpox virus was not a good thing, or that grasshoppers, mosquitoes, noxious weeds, various pests and disease organisms should not be combatted but protected"? How does the answer to this question affect our understanding of our relationship to the environment?

3   The Commission suggests that environmental agencies should sometimes judge that environmental considerations must lose out to economic ones. Under which circumstances, if any, would this be true?

Co-operation in Nature: A New Foundation for Environmental Law[1]

D. Paul Emond

The following selection contains an argument for a version of "deep ecology," according to which humans should view themselves as integral parts of the environment, who owe it respect and a sort of obligation. This "co-operative" approach is contrasted with the prevailing attitudes of domination and coercion. Emond argues that changes to the legal status of the environment may not be able to bring about the needed changes in attitude. An earlier part of this paper had acknowledged an intellectual debt to (yet some disagreement with) two groundbreaking articles, C. Stone's "Should Trees Have Standing?—Toward Legal Rights for Natural Objects" (1972), and L. Tribe's "Ways Not to Think About Plastic Trees: New Foundations for Environmental Law" (1974).

*   *   *

What is Wrong With Environmental Law?

What is wrong with environmental protection laws in Canada is what is wrong with *giving trees standing*: legal standing to go to court for the protection of natural objects offers few safeguards. It simply reaffirms the dominant-subservient relationship between people and trees. As for plastic trees, Fabricant offers a far more chilling prognosis than does Tribe, of where plastic trees will ultimately lead us:

[T]astes are bound to deteriorate further in the years ahead. For the values of future generations will be molded by the world into which they are born, and this could well be very different than ours because of the continued process of economic growth.... Our descendants will set environmental standards that we would view as intolerable....

If pollution is permitted to worsen over the centuries and eons, we can nevertheless suppose that life will adapt itself. "Living systems are systems that reproduce," yes; but as biologists define them, they are also systems "that mutate, and that reproduce their mutations." That is why living things "are endowed with a seemingly infinite capacity to adapt themselves to the exigencies of existence"—even in a *cesspool*.... But there is no certainty that human life will adapt and survive![2]

It may take centuries, even eons, for earth to become the cesspool that Fabricant fears, but that is no reason not to begin now the search for a better way, and to embody the first tentative steps of that search in our environmental protection laws. Such a process demands that we recognize the value of transcendence and immanence and try to reconcile the conflicting principles of each. More than that, it demands that we understand the reasons for environmental degradation, the misconceptions that underlie existing environmental protection laws, and the inherent value of laws based on the principle of co-operation rather than control and domination.

A. The Roots of the Pollution Problem

Pollution is a natural consequence of activity. As long as wastes generated by human activity are naturally assimilated or disposed of, there is no pollution problem. The problem arises because a growing population imposes demands on a planet with finite assimilative capacities. It may not be, as the Club of Rome study[3] predicted, a crisis, but pollution is nevertheless a serious concern that demands a more radical solution than some new "technological fix." The second cause, and I believe that it is related to the first, has to do with technology. Technology will solve and has solved many problems, especially those that arise from the pressures to generate more with less. Indeed, I have no doubt that its contribution to meeting present needs has, to date, far outweighed its costs. But the real impact of technology lurks ominously in the near future: mutation costs of insecticides on future generations; synergistic costs of combining two apparently harmless chemicals; and unforeseen second and third order effects of four wheel drive tractors, fertilizers and food additives.

A growing population, with growing demands to maximize individual wealth in a world with finite resources, will create environmental problems if left unchecked. Some mediating principle is needed to limit demand and ensure that "we do not despoil the environment that sustains us." The most persuasive analysis on environmental despoliation, at least as judged by its acceptance, has been written by the economist Hardin, in a provocative article entitled: *The Tragedy of the Commons.*[4] Hardin's ar-

ticle is important for two reasons: first, it gives credence to the assumption that pollution springs from people's unrestrained desire to improve their lot in society at the expense of others; secondly, it offers a "mediating principle" to control such destructive desires. Together, these two factors have strongly influenced environmental laws in Canada and the western world.

Hardin's important thesis is captured in the following quotations:

> The tragedy of the commons develops in this way. Picture a pasture open to all. It is to be expected that each herdsman will try to keep as many cattle as possible on the commons....
>
> As a rational being, each herdsman seeks to maximize his gain. Explicitly or implicitly, more or less consciously he asks, "What is the utility to me of adding one more animal to my herd?" This utility has one negative and one positive component.
> (1) The positive component is a function of the increment of one animal. Since the herdsman receives all the proceeds from the sale of the additional animal, the positive utility is nearly +P1.
> (2) The negative component is a function of the additional overgrazing created by adding one more animal. Since, however, the effects of overgrazing are shared by all herdsmen, the negative utility for any particular decision-making herdsman is only a fraction of -1.
> [T]he rational herdsman concludes that the only sensible course of action for him to pursue is to add another animal to his herd. And another; and another.... But this is the conclusion reached by each and every rational herdsman sharing a commons. Therein is the tragedy. Each man is locked into a system that compels him to increase his herd without limit—in a world that is limited....
>
> [N]atural selection favours the forces of psychological denial. The individual benefits as an individual from his ability to deny the

truth even though society as a whole, of which he is a part, suffers. Education can counteract the natural tendency to do the wrong thing, but the inexorable progression of generations requires that the basis for this knowledge be refreshed.[5]

Pollution is the tragedy of the commons in reverse, with the actors adding something to the commons (air, water, sound, view) rather than removing something from it. Again, Hardin describes the thought processes of the rational decision-maker in these circumstances:

The rational man finds that his share of the costs of the wastes that he discharges into the commons is less than the cost of purifying his wastes before releasing them. Since this is true for everyone, we are locked into a system of "fouling our own nest," so long as we behave only as rational, independent, free enterprisers.[6]

This theme has provoked a good deal of thinking and writing on pollution, all of which can be characterized as the search for "cost internalization." The questions have arisen in this way: how can the costs that polluters impose on the commons and all who use it (the victims) be shifted (internalized) to the polluter? Or, to ask the converse, how can the benefits of abatement be enjoyed by those who reduce pollution? Unless those who spend money on reducing pollution enjoy more of the benefits of less pollution, there will be little incentive to spend. This is the search for "benefit internalization." Both problems result from the common non-ownership features of our natural resources, and both evoke a search for ways of "privatizing the resource" so that use is monitored through price and costs and benefits are borne or enjoyed by those responsible.

Hardin's thesis, like most economic theory, purports to be steeped in *rational* human behaviour, with rationality determined objectively through empirical study of behaviour patterns, reinforced by everyday individual experience. How do people behave? What is our experience? According to Hardin, we are motivated by self-interest, irrespective of the consequences. Consequences are virtually irrelevant because adverse consequences are shared by all, while benefits are enjoyed by the individual actor. The desire for one to maximize self-interest exists even though the short-term gain that arises by putting another animal on the common may, ultimately, come at the expense of the long-term well being of all.

B. Pollution and Environmental Protection Laws

From this perception of the pollution problem it is clear that the appropriate "mediating principles" all lead to some form of control. Control of unrestrained self-interest and of competition among members of society will lead to the control of pollution. In a rather limited sense, the common law embraces just such a principle.

The concepts of property and private ownership, for example, limit access to the owner of the property or those who have the owner's permission. The nuisance doctrine *limits* use and exploitation to reasonable levels, with reasonableness determined by reference to the effect that the use may have on nearby occupants. The riparian rights doctrine *prohibits* water pollution to the detriment of downstream (or lake) riparian owners. Trespass *prohibits* direct and intentional interference by one with the use and enjoyment of the property of another. In each case the common law, if vig-

orously pursued and applied, limits or prohibits activities by some that are disadvantageous to others.

In such a world of competition and
struggle, co-operation among individuals
and communities is the exception rather
than the rule. Competition and struggle
dominate. The pursuit of individual self-interest is so strong that it is blind to the
long-term implications of such actions. In
other words, the war (competition) against
others is ultimately the war against self, and
thus the war of all against all. Such a
crassly Darwinian[7] view of the world, and
human participation in it, implies clearly
that the effectiveness of the common law is
weighed primarily in terms of its limiting
and prohibiting effects.

At the political level, legislatures have
been slow to subscribe to Hardin's call for
increased privatization of the environment.
One reason for this is that as the trustee of
the air, water and public lands, the government is the owner. It perceives no need to
secure protection through privatization.
More importantly, government owners have
quite different objectives from those that
are normally ascribed to the private sector.
In an effort to respond to growing public
demands, politically motivated owners will
facilitate access rather than restrict it, and
encourage rather than control use. The propensity to maximize present benefits in this
way is almost irresistible to a "four year"
politician. But, of course, increased access
and use only accentuate pollution and the
overuse of resources, thereby creating
countervailing pressures on government to
improve management and regulatory techniques. And, it does this with increasing
frequency. There are now a vast array of
licences, permits, orders, and approvals administered by ever-expanding departments
whose objectives are to "manage" private
exploitation of public resources by reconciling competing uses, and "optimize" and
"maximize" the utility of the environment
by subsidizing exploitation. Whatever the
goal, the effect is always the same: the environment is continually violated, while the
bureaucracy expands in size and scope, attempting to "manage" problems into solutions but failing miserably.

Like the common law, environmental
protection legislation is based on Hardin's
premise of insatiable self-interest and
human want. In response to political pressures, such wants are encouraged and accommodated (to the extent possible) by
government. Once the implications of accommodating unbridled "need" are widely
understood, countervailing pressures produce a plethora of pre- and post-controls on
virtually all human activity. This legislative
and bureaucratic schizophrenia explains
much of the dilemma facing the public
today.

Canadian environmental protection legislation also mirrors the common law in the
acceptance of two premises: 1) individual
users have the *right* to develop and exploit
the environment, that is, "to use it for their
own personal gain"; and 2) the propensity
to maximize individual wealth will, if left
unchecked, wreak havoc on the very resources needed to sustain such wealth maximization. Thus, environmental protection
legislation is both facilitative and restrictive. It encourages and facilitates exploitation, while at the same time it limits and
restricts the worst excesses of a pro-development policy. These two contradictory
principles underlie much environmental legislation in Canada today. A few examples
from the federal and provincial spheres will
suffice to illustrate the point.

The *Canada Water Act*[8] recognizes the increasing public demand for water resources and provides "means by which [such demand] may be met." The solution seems self-evident: "the conservation, *development* and *utilization* [of water resources] to ensure their *optimum wise use* for the *benefit of all Canadians*." Water pollution is primarily a threat to the "health, well-being and prosperity of the people of Canada" and secondarily to the "quality of the Canadian environment at large."[9] The *Arctic Waters Pollution Prevention Act*[10] is less blatant in its focus on development, but the pro-development bias exists. The preamble states that Canada has an *"obligation* to see that the natural resources of the Canadian Arctic are *developed* and *exploited*...in a manner that takes cognizance of Canada's responsibility for the welfare of Eskimo...and the preservation of the peculiar ecological balance."[11]

The ostensible purpose of both statutes is to balance development, utilization and exploitation for the benefit of Canadians against the quality of the environment and to preserve the ecological balance. The mechanism by which such objectives are achieved clearly betrays the extent to which development succeeds over preservation. *The Canada Water Act*, for example, through Comprehensive Water Resource Management Programs, follows a scheme of research, planning and project implementation to achieve an *"efficient* conservation, development and utilization of those waters" within the jurisdiction of the management program.[12] Water quality is to be secured through Water Quality Management Agencies, which have the power to prescribe appropriate water disposal practices and levy effluent discharge fees.[13] While both techniques may reduce water

pollution, they operate on the assumption that water pollution is best reduced by legalizing so-called "acceptable" levels of pollution. The *Arctic Waters Pollution Prevention Act* employs a similar licensing scheme. The deposit of waste in arctic waters is prohibited unless "authorized by regulations"[14] or "approved pursuant to Cabinet's power to set out, by order, the specifications for proposed work in the arctic."[15]

The federal statute long regarded as the most pro-environment, the *Fisheries Act*,[16] also "authorizes" pollution by specifying approved wastes and pollutants. Subsection 33(2), the pollution control provision, prohibits the deposit of "a deleterious substance of any type in water frequented by fish" *unless* the waste or pollutant is "authorized by regulations made by Cabinet under this or any other Act" (subsection 33(4)). The regulation-making power under subsection 33(13) is very broad, covering and potentially sanctioning almost every conceivable pollution situation.

Provincial legislation evidences the same clear intent of controlling pollution to facilitate development. British Columbia, for example, regulates potentially harmful development under the *Environment and Land Use Act*,[17] the *Environment Management Act*[18] and the *Waste Management Act*.[19] The whole thrust of its legislative approach is management to secure optimum use of the environment. A committee established under the *Environment and Land Use Act* has the duty:

(b) to ensure that all the aspects of preservation and maintenance of the natural environment are fully considered in the administration of land use, and minimize and prevent waste of these resources, and despoilation of the environment occasioned by that use.[20]

Under section 2 of the *Environment Management Act*, the duties, powers and functions of the minister extend to matters relating to the management, protection and enhancement of the environment, including:

(b) development of policies for the *management, protection* and *use* of the environment... [Emphasis added.]

(f) preparation and publication of environmental management plans...which may include...
   (i) flood control;
   (ii) drainage;
   (iii) soil conservation;
   (iv) water resource management.

The *Waste Management Act* is primarily a licensing mechanism whereby government managers are authorized to issue a permit to an applicant authorizing it to introduce waste into the environment or to store special waste subject to requirements for the protection of the environment if the manager considers it advisable.[21]

Nova Scotia offers a similar "pollution control by permit" approach to environmental protection. Although the pro-development bias noted in the British Columbia legislation is not present, the effect seems to be the same. The purpose of the *Environmental Protection Act* is "to provide for the preservation and protection of the environment."[22] Few jurisdictions offer such an unqualified and unequivocal statement that environmental protection is apparently the *only* purpose of the Act. But once such a laudable objective is reduced to pollution authorizing permits and licenses, the Act becomes pro-development. Like most other provincial jurisdictions Nova Scotia "controls" pollution through a sophisticated regime of permits and orders. Subsection 23(1) specifies that:

No person shall own, occupy, operate or be responsible for the operation of a plant, structure, facility, undertaking or thing that discharges, releases, deposits, drains, emits or threatens to allow the discharge...of waste into the environment or otherwise causes or tends to cause pollution unless he has obtained a permit from the Minister.

New facilities or alterations to existing facilities are regulated in a similar fashion under subsection 28(1). Polluters wishing to expedite the process or anxious to receive the immunity from prosecution that goes with an approved activity may propose a pollution "control program" under section 30. Like the permit, the control program is subject to ministerial approval. For those problems that cannot wait for regulation by permit, the Minister may act more expeditiously by way of an "order." The order (s.26(1)) may be used to, *inter alia*:

(a) cease contravention of the Act;

(b) limit or control the rate of addition, emission or discharge of the waste into the environment in accordance with the directions set out in the order;

(c) stop the addition, emission or discharge of the waste into the environment;
   ...

(f) install, replace or alter the equipment or thing designed to control or eliminate the addition, emission or discharge of the waste into the environment.

While this approach to environmental protection and pollution control offers the potential for comprehensive control of individual pollution problems, it is a level of control that is beyond the reach of the most ambitious department. For an agency with a limited and shrinking budget the degree of control achieved is minimal. Most departments issue permits primarily on the basis of what the *polluter* regards as feasible or realistic.[23] Some smaller polluters are vigorously pursued by government regulators, but activity at this low level merely serves to emphasize the inherent limitation of individual regulation of such a widespread problem.

Environmental protection legislation in Canada is misnamed: in the intent, protection is quite secondary. The desire to facilitate development by keeping environmental degradation within "tolerable" limits—usually expressed as "maximum permissible levels" of contaminants—is paramount. The legislation is utilitarian, not utopian. It lacks vision. Pollution is rationalized and, after the necessary permit is issued, legalized. Once a desired level of pollution has received the required statutory approval, the polluter is immune from quasi-criminal prosecution and effectively shielded from civil liability.[24] Everything turns on the licensing or approval process. And here, much of Tribe's criticism of existing laws is particular apt. The *best* environmental protection decision-making processes use the crude cost-benefit analysis of which Tribe is so contemptuous. More often, standards are set by regulators behind closed doors in close consultation with the "polluters," and without input from the public. In this way, industry concerns about competitive pricing, profitability and jobs soon squeeze environmental values out of the regulatory standards and guidelines, particularly if government regulators lack the resources to develop an independent view of the problem. The prospect of including "felt obligations" toward the environment is remote. Environmental laws offer little more than symbolic reassurance to an apprehensive public. They offer virtually nothing for the environment. They shift re-

sponsibility for pollution from the polluters to the regulators. Stone is ahead of his time. It is premature to talk about giving trees standing when our laws do not even give standing to many affected *people*!

Thus, under present legislation the *best* that can be hoped for is wise use of the environment by the public, and equally wise management of public use by the government. But wisdom is a scarce resource, particularly in a society motivated, as Hardin argues, by individual wealth maximization and regulated by large bureaucratic organizations with their own institutional priorities and preferences. Dedication to preserving the environment will only emerge from deeply committed people. Without commitment to environmental preservation the likely result is unrelenting pressure to exploit the environment and expand regulation and control by government under the guise of multiple and optimum use management. Nevertheless, much can be done within the existing legal framework to reduce our propensity to carelessly develop, exploit and utilize the environment. It is here that Stone and Tribe's theses offer refreshing new ideas.

The starting point for better legislation is the regulatory decision-making process. *All* who are affected must be heard from, not simply those whose property rights are jeopardized or those whose applications for the "necessary permit" are put into question. Public participation in the decision-making process must be more than symbolic. Decision-makers must not only *hear* the public, but also heed it. In other words, decision-makers must relinquish some of the powers which allow decisions as "they see fit." By fettering their discretion with clearly articulated decisional criteria, and making decisions that are responsive to the environmental issues and "felt obligations" of an increasingly apprehensive and troubled public, they go some distance to meet environmental concerns. Process, however, takes the analysis no further than to question the criteria that the decision-makers use. Again, Stone and Tribe have a good deal to contribute. Tribe's suggestion for improving cost-benefit analysis by strengthening and enhancing present analytic techniques is sensible. He calls for a re-examination of the processes by which all values are reduced to market values (prices), of the ways in which future fears are heavily discounted to present values, and of the propensity to ignore those adverse environmental effects that are widely diffused over space which affect no one in particular, but everyone in general. Stone takes Tribe's argument one step further into the realm of recognizing environmental rights. His focus is less on those concerns that find expression through the impact on environment users, and more on the effects of the environment as an environment. The process must not only factor in "felt obligations" that are not derived from use, but also adverse impacts on environments that are neither used nor enjoyed by anyone. Thus, a decision to permit the pollution of a river would have to take account of the impact on downstream riparian owners, fishermen and other communal and recreational users, but also the despoliation of the river and fish as living entities. Under Stone's scheme, not all rivers will be free of a pulp mill's effluent. But if the effluent will wreak "irreparable harm," or if the river is clear and pure and thus on the "endangered species" list, a decision to prohibit pollution is appropriate.

Finally, consideration must be given to what Tribe describes as the "means-ends fluidity problem": the ways in which effect is given to environmental goals will have enormous "feed back effects" on human goals. The present technique of legalizing pollution through licenses and permits to pollute rationalizes pollution. Once it is justified in this fashion, the rights are with the polluter, not the environment. The onus is on those who seek environmental protection to prove that a curtailment of such a right is necessary to protect environmental values. But, putting the onus of proof on those who seek protection, especially in an area in which strict proof must often await the findings of the epidemiologist, condemns the environment to perpetual domination by those who exploit it.

There are no legislative models in Canada that would take environmental protection to the lengths of Stone or Tribe's proposals. Two statutes from Ontario are, however, worth examining as acts that offer the first tentative steps toward such an approach. Neither can be described as "environmental protection" legislation. Rather they exhibit a resource development bias, but with a very strong respect for environmental values.

The *Niagara Escarpment Planning & Development Act*[25] was enacted to provide for the maintenance of the:

> Niagara Escarpment and land in its vicinity substantially as a continuous natural environment, and to ensure only such development occurs as is compatible with that natural environment. [Section 2]

This objective is to be achieved by a Commission through the development and implementation of a Niagara Escarpment Plan. Under section 8, the statutory objectives of the Plan are:

(a) to protect unique ecologic and historic sites;

(b) to maintain and enhance the quality of natural streams and water supplies;

(c) to provide adequate opportunities for outdoor recreation;

(d) to maintain and enhance the open landscape character of the Niagara Escarpment insofar as possible, by such means as compatible farming or forestry and by preserving the natural scenery;

(e) to ensure that all new development is compatible with the purpose of this Act.

The statute is area specific, but the concept has general application to resource-use environmental protection decision-making. The *Ontario Planning and Development Act*[26] offers a similar, more "balanced" approach to development, although there is less emphasis on environmental protection. Again, a plan is the key. Under the Act, a development plan is proposed, the definition of which includes:

[A] plan, policy and program...covering a development planning area designed to promote the optimum economic, social, environmental and physical condition of the area. [Subsection 1(a)]

and may contain:

(a) policies for the economic, social and physical development of the area covered by the plan in respect of,
(i) the general distribution and density of population,
(ii) the general location of industry and commerce, the identification of major land use areas and the provision of major parks and open space and the policies in regard to the requisition of lands,
(iii) the management of land and water resources,

(iv) the control of all forms of pollution of the natural environment

While neither statute has received much support from politicians, the approach to decision-making embodied in this type of legislation is commendable. The focus on planning ensures that decision-making is proactive rather than reactive; furthermore, the legislation mandates a full consideration of environmental values, both in terms of mitigating the adverse impact of development and maintaining and enhancing such values. The flaw in the legislation is what has debilitated all previous environmental legislation, that is, it assumes that society has the *right* to develop, exploit and control the environment, subject only to the *restrictions* and *regulations* that are imposed on the most unacceptable activity. There is acceptance of the premise that human self-interest is anti-environmental, thus demanding that all forms of activity be *controlled*. It perpetuates the myth of human domination over nature. The search is for a balance among competing self-interests, not a balance between people and their place in the environment.

Co-operation and Mutual Aid: A New Foundation for Environmental Protection

Like Stone, I begin with Charles Darwin.[27] Stone used Darwin to demonstrate that "the history of man's moral development has been a continual extension in the range of objects receiving his social instincts and sympathies,"[28] and from this he argued that the next logical extension of human sympathies was toward the animate and inanimate "objects" of the environment. The thesis is not as radical as it first appears.

For while affording such objects our "social instincts and sympathies" may seem laudable, it is, as I have argued, susceptible to argument in favour of continued domination of and control over such objects. Rather than begin with a position of *dominance* in which *rights are given* and *sympathies extended*, I prefer a starting point in which people are no more and no less than an integral part of the environment. Human relationships with the environment would then be based in a large part, on co-operation using principles of mutual aid. While this approach is not inconsistent with Darwin, it does require me to return to him and, with the assistance of the Russian writer Kropotkin, put Darwin's work in a different light.

At the risk of gross oversimplification, Darwin made two important contributions to the theory of evolution: struggle for existence and the idea of the natural selection, or as it is commonly referred to, survival of the fittest. Given such a theory, the environment was something within which struggle existed, and where survival was the ultimate goal. A preoccupation with these two themes will, if left unmoderated by Darwin's full work, clearly distort what he actually wrote. Natural selection is, as Darwin so well documented, a factor in evolution; indeed, survival of the fittest does describe the *successful* or *more advantageous* mutants. But, the reason for survival is unclear. It is not, as many have assumed, to dominate, control and master the environment, and those within it, but rather for the purpose of adapting the structure of each individual for the benefit of the whole community, if the community profits by the selected change.

Subsequent work on the theory of evolution has, of course, confirmed much of Darwin's work; but it has also offered a new perspective, a new emphasis. Petr Kropotkin's work *Mutual Aid: A Factor of Evolution*[29] offers an important focus and perspective on Darwin's work. First, Kropotkin emphasizes that the "theory of natural selection" is the most significant generalization of the nineteenth century. But while the struggle for life is an important factor in evolution, it does not deserve "commandment" standing. From Kropotkin's research into birds and the ways in which they assist one another, he concluded that the "sociability and social instinct in animals for the well being of species...was underrated."

Darwin recognized this fact, although many Darwinists, particularly social Darwinists, have chosen to ignore it. In the *Descent of Man*, Darwin describes how the struggle is replaced by co-operation, which in turn results in the development of intellectual and moral faculties which secure for species the best conditions of survival. Thus, the fittest are neither the physically strongest nor the most cunning, but "those who learn to combine so as mutually to support each other, strong and weak alike for the welfare of the community."[30] The inference is that co-operation, not competition and struggle, will generate communities that flourish and rear the greatest number of offspring. And this makes sense. Struggle and competition leave combatants impoverished in vigour and health, such that no progressive evolution of the species can be based on such a period of keen competition. Nor is competition and struggle necessarily the dominant feature of either underpopulated communities or those who enjoy an abundant lifestyle. In the first case, low population makes struggle unnecessary, in the second, the maintenance and preservation of the species is better secured through mutual aid and support. As Kropotkin wrote, "sociability is as much a law of nature as mutual struggle." And of these latter two, Kropotkin argued that mutual aid has the greater importance because:

> [I]t favours the development of such habits and characteristics as ensure the maintenance and further development of the species, together with the greatest amount of welfare and enjoyment of life for the individual, with the least waste of energy.[31]

Seen in this context, *struggle* is only one component in the evolution of the species, and while perhaps the most *important*, it is a baser, more primitive factor in evolution than co-operation.

What are the practical implications of redesigning our environmental protection laws around the twin principles of co-operation and mutual aid? While this is not the place to redraft the common law and statutes, a consideration of a new set of mediating principles may lead to important reforms in each area. First, I believe that the perception of the environmental crisis must change. In most circumstances little is served by labelling producers "polluters" and consumers "innocent victims." People are all polluters and all victims, connected by a web of activities and relationships. The problem truly is the war of all against all. Wars are not settled by more aggression and hostility. Settlement will only come through understanding and a commitment from everyone to solve the problem. Co-operation is better learned than imposed. With this view of "the problem," I believe that there is a larger role for public expenditures—both in terms of generating increased public awareness of the environment (responding to the preference shaping problems so well described in the excerpt from Fabricant, *supra*), and in terms of providing environmental protection *incentives* for existing and potential polluters. The coercive tactics presently employed lead inevitably to the polluter adopting strategies for the avoidance of laws, which ultimately create increased pressure for even stronger control and regulation. Incentives, on the other hand, will tend to produce compliance strategies. Compliance will, in my view, generate a growing sensitivity to environmental values, hopefully to the point where respect and obligation are fully internalized in both private and public decision-making.

Secondly, society's present preoccupation with development and exploitation must be re-examined. The efficiency logic of the cost-benefit analysis is important, but it is only one factor. There are others: responsibility, care and, as I have emphasized, co-operation. Mechanisms must be developed to ensure that the implications of human activity are learned, understood and respected. The legal implications of such a premise are an increased emphasis of fact finding, a reversal of the onus of proof, and an attempt to resolve development and conservation disputes in non-adversarial, non-hierarchical ways.

Fact finding provides the context within which environmental implications can be understood. In the face of uncertainty about adverse environmental impact, the *status quo* should prevail. While this may be regarded as an anti-development, anti-progress bias, it need not be so. Development or "transcendence," to use Tribe's word, is a necessary and integral part of life. But it must be *in context*. As an integral and interdependent part of our environment, development must *respect* "the land that sustains us." Domination, control, and the ethic of need and greed must give way to empathy, tolerance and the ethic of care and share. Taking the time to understand the impact of various decisions, to fully evaluate the human relationship to the environment will mean that some proposed projects will not proceed. There will be "costs" associated with such decisions. The benefits, however, are potentially enormous. By taking the time to watch, listen and understand, everyone can be "Pilgrims at Tinker Creek,"[32] connected to the land, rooted in a past, present and future. Humans can be both "grand manipulators and sacred observers."

Some progress has already been made to improve decision-making. Environmental assessment is beginning to demonstrate the value of planning, careful evaluation of potential adverse effects and subsequent monitoring of anticipated (and unanticipated) impacts.[33] But preoccupation with process condemns us to a principled way of deciding rather than principled decisions. Thus, proactive processes may generate little more than a plethora of consultants studies. Environmental management may simply be another label under which the environment is tamed to comply with preconceived notions of aesthetic values. And multiple use management offers a new banner to justify all forms of development, provided the project is properly engineered, the impact is "tolerable" and the environment is subsequently rehabilitated. Society needs a new set of substantive principles.

While I have already described the needed principles in terms of co-operation, respect and mutual aid, they can be reduced to specific legal concepts. Beginning first with the common law and private ownership, the verb "to own" must be transformed into its earlier meaning "to owe." Historically, "ownership" did not carry

with it the almost unrestricted right to exploit, but rather a series of obligations, some owed to the crown, some to the lord and some to the land itself. Put into a modern context, ownership must encompass responsibilities and obligations—not to maximize profit, but to occupy the land as a steward, respecting its integrity and preserving its value for both future generations and for its own worth. Furthermore, the oppressive logic of "reasonableness" that underlies both the nuisance and riparian rights doctrines must give way to the "unreasonableness" of environmental protection and preservation for its own sake. Reason and rationality will, if left unchecked, reduce the environment to a lowest common denominator of allegedly compatible uses. Not only are some uses unreasonable in any context, but *any* uses are unreasonable in some contexts. The law, with its pro-human bias, cannot recognize this fact. The reasonable use principle must, therefore, be replaced by one that recognizes that in some circumstances the best use is no use. How this can happen within the present legal framework is not obvious. Certainly reform will not come from within the legal system itself. Here again, there is an obvious role for publicly inspired and financed incentives to preserve and protect wetlands, rivers, forests and vistas. And as increased use shrinks these resources, the need for a mediating principle of preservation grows.

The first legislative steps toward co-operation in nature have already been taken. British Columbia recently passed ecological preserve legislation[34] where Crown land may be reserved for "ecological purposes" (section 2). The focus of the act is educational (subsection 2(a)) and preservationist (section 2). Ontario wilderness legislation[35] provides a similar focus on the need for a "single use" approach to some aspects of the environment. In conjunction with such enabling legislation, "single use" public authorities must be established for the express purpose of protecting the environment, not compromising it under the present multiple use approaches. Development oriented departments, and even those charged with environmental protection, offer, at best, a multiple use approach to conservation and protection. There is, in my opinion, a strong argument in favour of removing large tracts of public land from development pressures while building the "co-operation in nature" perspective into future activities.

At a more practical level, the present legislative approach of facilitating development to control it, of licensing pollution to legitimize it, must be stopped. This "assault" on domination, coercion and rationalization will not be easy. Respect and obligation are seen as vague, soft concepts while development is a firm concept embodied in progress and hard profits. Nevertheless, respect, obligation and co-operation promise to elevate both society and the environment simultaneously. As Tribe argued, "freedom can be realized only...[by] fidelity to organization." A new approach cannot be forced upon an unwilling or uncaring public. Environmental protection legislation must encourage and reward co-operation with a range of incentives that are not tied to use and exploitation.

These then are the beginnings of a new foundation for environmental protection laws. They owe much to the pioneering work of Stone and Tribe. But I have attempted to push my own analysis at least another step. Neither rights for natural objects nor a better process will necessarily produce the better world that society seeks. That world will only change when people cast off the yoke of competition and domination and embrace co-operation and mutual aid as the pre-eminent guiding principles.

Notes

1 I have titled the article, "Co-operation *in* Nature" rather than "Co-operation *with* Nature" to emphasize that people are an integral part of nature, rather than separate from it.

2 Fabricant, "Economic Growth and the Problem of Environmental Pollution," in Boulding, ed., *Economics of Pollution* (1971) 139 at 148-49.

3 Forrester and Meadow, *The Limits of Growth* (1971).

4 Hardin, *The Tragedy of the Commons* (1968), 162 Science 1243 at 1244-45.

5 *Ibid.*

6 *Ibid.*

7 And, I might add, distorted view of Darwin's thesis.

8 *Canada Water Act*, R.S.C. 1970, c. 5 (1st supp.). [Hereinafter referred to as *C.W.A.*]

9 *C.W.A.*, Preamble (emphasis added).

10 *Arctic Waters Pollution Prevention Act*, R.S.C. 1970, c. 2 (1st supp.). [Hereinafter referred to as *A.W.P.P.A.*]

11 *A.W.P.P.A.*, Preamble (emphasis added).

12 *C.W.A.*, s.4(e) (emphasis added).

13 *C.W.A.*, s.13.

14 *A.W.P.P.A.*, s.4.

15 *A.W.P.P.A.*, s.10.

16 *Fisheries Act,* R.S.C. 1970, c. 119 as amended (emphasis added).

17 *Environmental and Land Use Act*, R.S.B.C. 1979, c. 110. [Hereinafter referred to as *E.L.U.A.*]

18 *Environmental Management Act*, S.B.C. 1981, c. 14.

19 *Waste Management Act*, S.B.C. 1982, c. 41.

20 *E.L.U.A.*, s.3(b).

21 *E.L.U.A.*, s.9(1)-(2).

22 *Environmental Protection Act*, C.S.N.S. 1973, c. 6, s.3.

23 Castrilli and Lax, "Environmental Regulation-Making in Canada: Towards a More Open Pro-

cess," in Swaigen, ed., *Environmental Rights in Canada* (1972) 334 at 340ff.

24 Emond, "Defences and Remedies to Common-Law Causes of Actions in the Environmental Law Field," in Canadian Bar Association, *Environmental Law: Bringing and Defending Actions* (1984).

25 *Niagara Escarpment Planning and Development Act*, R.S.O. 1980, c. 316.

26 *Ontario Planning and Development Act*, R.S.O. 1980, c. 354.

27 Darwin, *supra* note 5.

28 Stone, *supra* note 2, at 450.

29 Kropotkin, *supra* note 6.

30 *Ibid.* at 2.

31 *Ibid.* at 6.

32 Aillard, *Pilgrims at Tinker Creek: A Mystical Excursion* (1974).

33 Emond, "Accountability and the Environmental Decision-Making Process: Some Suggestions for Reform," in Swaigen, ed., *supra* note 54, at 406.

34 *Ecological Reserve Act*, R.S.B.C. 1979, c. 101.

35 *Ontario Wilderness Areas Act*, R.S.O. 1980, c. 533.

Questions for Discussion

1 Is it possible for policies to be framed by human beings which do not pre-suppose some sort of dominance by humans over the environment?

2 How radically must people change their attitudes toward the environment? What role can government play in bringing about any needed changes?

Legal Rights for Nature: *The Wrong Answer to the Right(s) Question*

P.S. Elder

In the following article, Elder argues that there is no convincing reason to accept the view of the "deep ecologists" that there are subjects of moral value other than individual sentient creatures. Elder goes on to claim that the existing moral and legal systems are adequate for dealing with environmental problems.

*   *   *

Some years ago, Christopher Stone gave an affirmative answer to his own question, "Should Trees Have Standing?"[1] He was independently supported in this conclusion by Laurence Tribe.[2]

I reject Stone's claim that non-animal and perhaps non-living objects ought to have legal standing. The only stone which could be of moral concern and hence deserving of legal rights, is one like Christopher. This may tell today's "deep ecologist" that "anthropocentric" thinkers such as myself, are "shallow"; but epithets do not replace analysis.

In this essay, I will highlight the differences between "shallow" and "deep" ecology, and briefly criticize Stone's position. I will then claim that Stone and the deep ecologists, even if not philosophically confused, do not take us anywhere in solving environmental disputes, that conventional ethics and law do not already go.

Shallow and Deep Ecology

My disagreement with Stone reflects the current debate between the self-described deep ecologists and their shallow opponents.[3] Each term represents a constellation of views about how humans should relate to the natural order. Different camps coexist under each banner, but shallow ecologists tend to see moral value only in individual sentient creatures, if not solely in human beings. For this reason, they have been called "anthropocentric"[4] as opposed to the "ecocentric" views of deep ecologists. Different proponents in the latter group argue that not only sentient creatures, but all living things, all species, all ecosystems, possibly all things in the entire universe have inherent value and have moral significance independent of their use by human beings, or even of human existence. They decry the "species-ism" in the claim that human beings have unique moral importance. They also reject the "sentientism" which claims that some level of consciousness or capacity for experience is a prerequisiste for moral significance. Indeed, some ecologists have adopted a mystical, ineffable vision of the unity of all:

> [It] then follows...that the distinction between 'life' and 'lifeless' is a human construct. Every atom in this body existed before organic life emerged.... Remember your own childhood as minerals, as lava, as rocks?... We are the rocks dancing. Why do we look down on them with such a condescending air?[5]

Although I have neither the space nor the background to assess the many arguments for each species of shallow or deep ecology, I note that Stone is clearly deep and that I am shallow. Also, animal rights advocates like Tom Regan,[6] whose case rests on sentientism, are shallow ecologists.

Stone's Position

In his article, Stone is "quite seriously proposing that we give legal rights to forests, oceans, rivers and other so-called 'natural objects' in the environment—indeed to the natural environment as a whole."[7] He specifically limits himself to "non-animal but natural objects."[8] This extraordinary leap is based on the following implicit argument. Our environment is seriously degraded by human action which has been based upon a serious ethical mistake. We have failed to see that natural objects, both animate and inanimate, have moral worth in themselves. Our "anthropocentric" ethics value the natural world as a resource to be manipulated at will for human benefit, without regard for the rights of non-animate things. On such a view, even conservationists make anthropocentric utilitarian arguments. Creating rights for these things and allowing the appointment of guardians to invoke these rights will enable us to improve the environmental quality. Presumably for Stone, nothing short of this new "ethical" framework will enable us to do this.

In discussing the legal implications of his thesis, Stone describes what it means to be a holder of legal rights: first, no entity has a right "unless and until *some public authoritative body* is prepared to give *some amount of review* to actions that are colorably inconsistent with that 'right'"; secondly, "the thing can institute legal actions at his *behest*"; thirdly, "the court must take *injury to it* into account" and fourthly, "relief must run to the *benefit of it*."[9] Naturally, the inanimate object could institute proceedings only through its guardian.

Stone does admit that even if trees had rights, they could still be cut down on certain conditions. Indeed, the environment might have a different body of rights than humans.[10] He believes that an expansion of environmental impact assessment procedures would be a major step toward protecting rights of the environment.[11] Beyond procedural protection, however, Stone suggests that "some [relatively] absolute rights be defined for the environment by setting up a constitutional list of 'preferred objects.'"[12] Proposals threatening injury to them would "be reviewed with the highest level of scrutiny at all levels of government."[13] Also, Stone argues that plants can communicate their "needs,"[14] but does not explain how rocks can do so. He also believes that economic analysis can quantify loss either on a replacement cost basis or, in the case that is question-begging, on a normative basis of how much something should be valued. Payment into a trust fund for the environment would presumably follow development approval.[15]

Stone believes that this shift in conceptual framework would work into the language of judges and steer their thoughts in the right direction.[16] Perhaps, for example, the burden of proof would be interpreted "far more liberally from the point of view of the environment."[17] Stone even suggests that at the legislative level the natural environment should perhaps be given some sort of proportional representation.[18]

Criticism of Stone

Unfortunately, Stone never reveals why the natural environment has a moral claim. He argues that, since we have progressed morally by extending rights to blacks, women and children, and even to some animals that can suffer, we can (and should) progress further by giving plants and inanimate objects rights.[19] But this is obviously a non sequitur: people and plants are not in the same category, which would be necessary to justify such a conclusion. Even if the grass and plants "need" water, in the sense that they will die without it, why does it follow that we have a duty to water them? Do they have any moral importance?

Stone clearly believes they do, and that is the heart of the matter. But they lack any of the relevant characteristics which make persons of moral importance—awareness, self-consciousness, the ability to formulate goals, act to attain them and to appreciate their attainment. It is, therefore, a distortion of our concepts to claim that plants or non-living natural objects can "want" to survive or remain undisturbed. There is "nobody home" who would care, or who could suffer. And if they do not care, why should we? In short, to paraphrase Gertrude Stein, "When you get there, there's no *their* there."

Deep ecologists admit that trees and canyons lack the human characteristics which we all agree make people of moral importance. They deny, however, that these are the only criteria for an object to have value in and of itself. Yet, following Kant, does not the notion of value presuppose a rational conception of self as subject rather than object? This second order self-awareness or,

[R]eflective capacity of persons...makes them the *source of value*, the objects of moral concern. The reason that persons are the source of value is that the choice of an alternative must *matter* to the chooser; the choice must make the difference, it must be valued. The idea of a choice being valued is intelligible only if the choice is consistent with a concept of one's self.[20]

Stone uses another non sequitur when he argues that, since we can give rights to fictional entities such as corporations, and can create guardians for people who cannot speak for themselves, we can do so for the environment. Maybe we can; certainly these examples have met legal and individual needs in our complex society. The question, again, is why is it morally appropriate to do so? Stone is, remarkably, silent on the matter.

If it cannot matter to canyon or trees if they are irreparably damaged, how are their guardians to know what to argue on their behalf, other than by using their own values? Even if trees "want" less smog in the air, why would they want it? One answer might be to reduce biological strain and to allow the tree to grow bigger or produce more seeds. But equally, the tree could ask that other trees competing with it be cut down for the same reason. Down with survival of the fittest (and perhaps, implicitly, with wilderness)! Civilized trees, bears or deer might reasonably ask that they, like people, be protected from the dangers of the natural environment and be fed and watered by people through the long rigorous winter (or summer in arid regions). As Sagoff comments:

Are labour saving conveniences only good for people? Environmentalists always assume that the interests of those objects [rivers, mountains, lakes and other natural things] are *opposed to development*. How do they know this? Why wouldn't Mineral King want to host a ski resort, after doing nothing for a billion years? The seashore...indicates its willingness to entertain poor people...by becoming covered with great quantities of sand.[21]

At root, therefore, are the deep ecologists themselves not being "anthropocentric" in believing they know what is best for the natural environment? And, what if we disagree about what is best? In the case of an environment with rights, one can imagine government, industry and public interest groups litigating to see who will be named as guardian and thus give content to these "rights."

Suppose we agree with Stone that humans are indeed part of the biosphere and should not be seen as separate and apart. We could draw a radically different conclusion from his: people are a part of nature, and in manipulating the environment to their own ends have simply proven to be better suited for survival. Over the eons of natural processes, ninety-nine percent of species have already become extinct. Why may we now not cause other species to become extinct, by being the stronger competitor? The deep ecologists' answer, one assumes, is that we owe these species moral duties. Why? *Because we're different and the deep ecologists' case rests on this difference*. We are not simply "part of nature." We can understand morality. Indeed, it is the essence of being human which leads to respecting the rights of morally important beings.

Ordinary Ethics Gets Us There Too

The fundamental question is why moral obligations exist and toward whom. Stone is quite right to point out that we already accept obligations to other than fully aware human persons—to babies, idiots and to some extent human vegetables. Who then has rights?

This essay is meant only to show that Stone has not made his case; it is not intended to argue the case for ordinary morality. I would simply state my conclusion: first, that any self-conscious being who can have hopes and wishes about the future, weigh alternatives, freely choose among them and appreciate their attainment, is an object of moral concern. Second, a creature's capacity to feel pain (not merely show some physical reactions as plants and styrofoam cups do) clearly establishes its right not to have unnecessary suffering inflicted even if the creature is not in the first category. Third, there is no other category of morally relevant creatures or things. Thus, if whales, dolphins, apes or fruit flies can be shown to meet the first test, we cannot murder them for food or any other purpose nor can we enslave them. On the other hand, if they can feel pain, but cannot conceptualize (an impossibility to at least one serious thinker[22]) we can kill them for food and even experiment on them as long as they are not caused to suffer unduly.

These conclusions may not seem emotionally satisfying. Deep ecologists may even think such views can be held only by vandals or philistines. This is not so. They need not lead to pillage or to Coney Island. Many shallow ecologists, including myself, feel peace, delight and awe when in the wilderness. We respect life. We also feel great personal distress about the diminishing wilderness or impending extinction of beautiful animals or plants. But here are human reasons for us to let them or wilderness environments, survive—so that many people, shallow or deep, will not suffer anguish at their disappearance. Thus, rigorous environmental protection follows from shallow ecology as well as deep. Indeed, of

Arne Næss's seven characteristics of deep ecology, I can support at least five.[23]

Conventional Law Can Do It

Whether or not Stone's murky intuitive claims are philosophically sound, a great deal of philosophic and legal fuss can be avoided if our present, conventional legal notions can achieve the same result. Since all of law is a human construct, it follows that we can identify any matter of concern and legislate about it, if we want to. Whether or not non-humans have rights, only humans can be actors in the legal system and it must follow that only human concerns could ever be addressed by it. If society has the will to create rights for non-humans, we can *a fortiori* use sovereign legislating power to protect the environment by giving new rights to people.[24] A wide range of policy and legal techniques is available within existing legal and moral paradigms. For the moment, I will ignore the real problem, lack of political will; this exists whether or not a conceptual or merely technical shift is required.

Stone's main policy thrust seems to be an extension of environmental impact assessment and procedures to ensure a heavier weighting of environmental criteria.[25] Clearly, this can be done with our existing notions. Many suggestions have been made: legislate environmental criteria which must be considered by decision-makers and allow court challenges under broader rules of standing for failure to meet minimum standards of procedure or substance in decision-making;[26] guarantee the rights to public interest groups or concerned citizens to participate in open hearings with full information and financial aid to intervenors; extend environmental impact assessment to include the social and economic environments; and mandate a more searching inquiry of broad alternatives to the proposed project. For instance, decision-makers (and thus public hearing bodies) could be required to consider evidence that insulation and other energy conservation policies would be a cheaper "source" of new energy than developing tar sands or frontier hydrocarbons and, in addition, that conservation creates more employment.[27]

Further, the ambit of impact assessment could be extended to both private and public projects, and even to those which are individually insignificant if a predicted series of them would, in the aggregate, cause a significant impact. Programs or even legislative proposals would require assessment.[28] Funds for environmental mitigation or reclaimation could be established. Decision makers in all levels of government involved in this assessment could be required to use legislated criteria, which presumably Stone would favour. For example, projects having significant environmental impacts might be authorized only "if no feasible and prudent alternative exists" and "if all possible planning to minimize harm" has been done.[29]

It is widely agreed that our society has failed to protect its citizens adequately from harm caused by the production or use of many chemicals and from manufacturing processes. Technology assessment might prevent the production or use of new chemicals or processes until society is satisfied that no unreasonable long range human health problems or environmental damage will occur. Legislatively, a particular burden and standard of proof could be placed on the proponent of the technology; the weight of the burden could be statutorily defined. If scientific uncertainty and difficulty in the prediction of harm is inevitable,[30] development may have to be slowed down dramatically. Also, we must think more carefully about whether limited or pilot approvals should be considered.

In Canada, for instance, the law of standing has been a potential barrier in constitutional, public nuisance and administrative law disputes. Basically, the courts require that a person who sues must demonstrate a particular interest, usually property or person, which has been damaged or threatened, before the lawsuit can proceed. Although the rules, at least in constitutional cases, have been relaxed,[31] legislation can entirely abolish the standing problem if this is thought desirable. Also, lax pollution standards could become more restrictive. However, sophisticated judgement will be necessary to decide if the criminal law model is unsatisfactory.[32] Possibly effluent fees or regional pollution treatment authorities should be considered. Legislation such as *Michigan Environmental Protection Act*[33] can create a substantive right for any citizen to sue to prevent significant environmental harm and even to challenge the adequacy of agency standards. Numerous other techniques are available to the government to shape or even require or prevent behaviour: income tax deductions or credits; compulsory standards (zero pollutant discharge, if deemed feasible); subsidies; education, training and public information programs; pilot or demonstration programs; government procurement requirements; paid advertising; price setting; and constitutional amendments.

For example, the Charter of Rights and Freedoms could be amended to provide some form of a right to a healthy, safe environment. It should be remembered that, although this reform would protect only legal persons, preventing harmful pollutants protects many other species than our own.

No doubt other more imaginative legal innovations and prescriptions for radical social transformation can and should be developed. But enough has been said to suggest that the limiting factor in environmental protection is not the paucity of available legal techniques based on anthropocentric theories of rights. I cannot think of one environmental protection reform which is beyond present institutional or legal scope. Of course, this is not to imply that there exists the will to restore the environment to pristine condition or even that it is necessary to try to do so. But the debate on this is intelligible and capable of resolution within our traditional ethics. We do, however, need rigorous public debate about the failure in many spheres of policy to apply traditional moral principles of justice (rights) and consequentialist goals, such as maximized happiness or minimized suffering. Stone, Tribe and the deep ecologists are right when they criticize society for favouring values which in the long run are wrong, both from a prudential and a moral point of view. Polluters who fail to internalize their externalities are really solving their disposal or economic problems at the expense of others—the paradigm of ignoring other people's rights. And rights, properly understood, include more than protection of property and the physical person, although again taking these seriously would go far toward solving our problems. Persons have psychological needs, but ethical policy formulation can take these into account.

Environmental and social reform require decisions in the political process, and until the necessary shifts in public attitudes or values occur, the fundamental direction of our society will continue as it is. Participatory decision-making processes may allow us to argue the case for the conserver society, social control over production, zero discharge of highly toxic chemicals, and alternative energy. But, precisely because the legal techniques await policy decisions, it seems a waste of time for either Stone or myself to discuss in detail how legal techniques could help us clean up the environment, if there were the will. There is not. However, the collective lack of will need not render reformers impotent. Careful analysis and tireless political action are both badly needed. Ultimately, decision-makers, in appropriate circumstances, must be persuaded to favour environmental over other interests. Careful ethical analysis will be needed to show the thoughtful ones why they should. Once sound theory is in place, sophisticated political action will be needed to show the others why they had better follow such a lead.

But to return to Stone. He is also right to criticize the casual treatment of the world as a resource, a factory and a dump. It is, first of all, our home and as it is effectively a closed ecological system (save for energy from the sun), decision-makers owe us all a moral duty to respect our rights to "life, liberty and the security of the person."

Our present economic and political systems have failed us. Most people sense this, even if they cannot articulate it. It is now up to political, economic and environmental thinkers to show whether capitalism, socialism or a third, environmentally based political theory can provide guidance for the future. Personally, I doubt that a shared perception of environmental problems and of general prescriptions like decentralized, small-scale institutions, appropriate technology or the conserver society can unite people of the left, right and centre for very long. Ultimately, people will still have to choose who will own or control the means of production and how distribution will occur; "economistic"[34] analysis may not be sufficient, but it is necessary. This is why environmental political parties like the Green Party[35] may be doomed, even though they add other issues like feminism and nuclear disarmament to their program.

The Canadian mixed economy has tried brilliantly to fuse capitalism and socialism. Social welfare programs and Crown enterprises have been accepted by private capital as the price for the latter to remain fundamentally in control. We can opt for this mixed capitalist economy with social mobility for the most able, but in a future without continual growth, the present pattern of distribution will come under increased pressure. In light of these life and death decisions about toxic and carcinogenic pollutants, human starvation, oppression and the threat of nuclear holocaust, deep ecology's argument supporting rights for canyons, trees and mule deer is really a trivial pursuit. It is not the direction in which environmental political philosophy should go.

Postscript

In reading the editors' preface [to *Environmental Ethics: Volume II*], I am struck by the claim that my criticism of non-anthropocentrists is itself a non sequitur because they are "indulging...in theory construction." I think this suggestion is wrong.

First, I doubt that deep ecologists are constructing an entirely new theory such that criticism from within the traditional paradigm of ethics would be irrelevant or,

as the editors prefer, a non sequitur. If the deep ecologists' theory were unconnected with morality, it could never accommodate *any* let alone all of the present moral data. Indeed, "moral" would have no meaning like its present one. Nor coulod they claim, as they seem to do, that any one (morally) should support their theory.

To try to persuade people that deep ecology is a morally sureior theory is to admit its dependence on conventional ethical theory. It is also to demonstrate that the choice of theory rests on rational argument and that pointing contradictions and non sequiturs is legitimate. Unless deep ecology has also jettisoned logical rules like the principle of non-contradition (in which case the theory cannot even be expressed), rational dialogue entails justification. Justification of something morally just or right is "a matter of the mutual support of many considerations, of everything fitting together in one coherent view."[36]

As I argue here and in "Is Deep Ecology the Way?"[37] deep ecology fails this test.

Notes

1 *Southern California Law Review* 45 (1972): 450. Herinafter, "Standing."

2 Tribe, "Ways Not to Think About Plastic Trees: New Foundations for Environmental Law," *Yale Law Journal* 83 (1974): 1315.

3 Næss, "The Shallow and the Deep, Long-Range Ecology Movement. A Summary," *Inquiry* 16 (1973): 95.

4 "Anthropocentrism" is a somewhat misleading term. First, all environmental ethics are anthropocentric in that, as far as we know, they can only be prescribed and consciously followed by humans. Second, few people believe that only humans are the object of any moral concern whatever. Almost everybody accords some limited moral significance to those animals who we think are capable at least of having experience of pain and pleasure.

5 Seed, "Anthropocentrism?," in Sessions and Devall (eds.), *Ecophilosophy* 5 (1983): 11-12.

6 See Regan, *The Case for Animal Rights* (Berkely: The University of California Press, 1983).

7 "Standing," 456.

8 "Standing," 26n.

9 "Standing," 458 (emphasis in original).

10 "Standing," 458.

11 "Standing," 483-86.

12 "Standing," 486.

13 "Standing," 486.

14 "Standing," 471.

15 "Standing," 480.

16 "Standing," 488.

17 "Standing," 488

18 "Standing," 487.

19 "Standing," 450-57.

20 Thomas L. Harper and Stanley M. Stein, "Persons as the Source of Value: An Alternative Basis for Rational Planning," a paper presented to the Association of Collegiate Schools of Planning, San Francisco (October 1983): 3

21 Mark Sagoff, "On Preserving the Natural Environment," *Yale Law Journal* 84 (1974): 222 (words in brackets supplied).

22 Janet M. Keeping, *Pain*, unpublished Master's Thesis, Department of Philosophy, University of Calgary, 1977.

23 See note 3 above. I support the following five of Næss's seven normative principles of deep ecologists (all emphasis in the original):

1. "Rejection of the Man-in-environment image in favour of the *relational, total-field image.*" (p. 95.) Human[s] should not be seen as isolated from, but intrinsic to, the environment.

2. "*Principles of diversity and symbiosis.*" (p. 96.)

3. "Fight against *pollution and resource depletion.*" (p. 97.)

4. "*Complexity, not complication*" (p. 97), because of the existence of unifying principles which help us to explain ecosystems.

5. "*Local autonomy and decentralization.*" (p. 98.)

I disagree with:

1. "*Biosphere egalitarianism—in principle.*" (p. 95.) Næss believes that the equal right to live inheres in all living creatures not just humans subject to some rights of self-defence.

2. "*Anti-class posture*" (p. 96), but only if Næss means to imply that being anti-class involves a refusal to divide living creatures into those having, and those not having, moral significance.

24 The "supremacy of Parliament" may be subject to constitutionally protected rights, but if the constitution interferes with achieving social goals such as rigorous environmental protection, legal machinery exists which can amend the constitution.

25 "Standing," 482-85.

26 See P.S. Elder, "A Survey of Developments in American Environmental Law," in *Pollution Environmental Law Reference Material* (Toronto: Department of Continuing Education, Law Society of Upper Canada, 11 and 12 May, 1972): 149-50. Stone cites one of the same cases. *Scenic Hudson Preservation Conference v. Federal Power Commission*, 354 F. 2nd 608 (1965) (sub. nom., *Consolidated Edison Co. of New York Inc. v. Scenic Hudson Preservation Conference et al.*, cert. denied, 384 US 941, 86 S.Ct. 1462 (1966)) to show this is already happening. Curiously he takes developments in the law of standing as support for his position.

27 See P.S. Elder, *Heating Up Cold Lake—Public Participation and Esso Resources' Heavy Oil Project* (Faculty of Environmental Design, The University of Calgary, Occasional Paper Series, October 1981).

28 Section 102(c) of the *US National Environmental Policy Act* of 1969 requires environmental impact statement on "proposals for legislation and other major federal actions...."

29 This was the legislation binding on the US Secretary of Transportation in *Citizens to Preserve Overton Park Inc. v. Volpe*, 401 US 402, 91 S.Ct. 814 (1971). See Elder, "A Survey of Developments in American Environmental Law," 150.

30 See Thompson, "Water Law—The Limits of the Management Concept," in *Environmental Law in the 1980s: A New Beginning Proceedings* (Calgary: Canadian Institute of Resources Law, 1982), 45; and Howard R. Eddy, "Problems in Resolving Scientific Uncertainty Through Legal Process," *ibid.*, 131.

31 John Swaigen, "Environmental Law 1975-1980," *Ottawa Law Review* 12 (1980): 459. See this useful article for a discussion of various ideas referred to herein.

32 Thompson, "Water Law."

33 See Joseph L. Sax and Joseph F. Dimento, "Environmental Citizen Suits: Three Years' Experience Under the Michigan Environmental Protection Act," *Ecology Law Quarterly* 4 (1974): 1; John Swaigen and Richard E. Woods, "A Substantive Right to Environmental Quality," in Swaigen, (ed.), *Environmental Rights in Canada* (Toronto: Butterworths, Canadian Environmental Law Research Foundation, 1981), 195. This collection is fundamental to the area being discussed herein.

34 Murray Bookchin, *Toward an Ecological Society* (Montreal: Black Rose Books, 1980).

35 The Green Party is a well known political faction in Europe, especially in France and Germany. As well as being environmentalist, its members are deeply democratic (favouring concensus over majority rule) and tend to believe more in direct action than in Parliamentary representation. As well as environmentalism, they support feminism and nuclear disarmament.

   The existence of green parties (they are being organized in several provinces in Canada, including British Columbia, Alberta and Ontario) is a source of frustration to socialists who argue that they have the same program. However, "Greens" point out that many socialists support nuclear power, centralized planning and increase material production, all of which are anathema to many environmentalists.

36 John Rawls, *A Theory of Justice* (Cambridge: Harvard University Press, 1971), 23 and 579.

37 *Alternatives* 15 (April/May 1988): 70.

Questions for Discussion

1 Is Elder right to say that, in thinking they know what is in the interests of the environment, "deep ecologists" are being just as anthropocentric as "shallow ecologists"?

2 Is there more of a burden of proof on the "deep ecologists" to show that a whole new perspective is required, or on the "shallow ecologists" to show that the existing approach can handle environmental problems?

3 Elder claims that the existing legal system can provide adequate protection for the environment, but that what is required is a change in public attitudes. Can the law be used as a vehicle for changing attitudes, and if so, how?

Leaving Eden: To Protect and Manage the Earth

Summary: a new global economy

E.G. Nisbet

In the following selection, Nisbet argues that people should view their relationship to the environment as one of stewardship of our home. It is argued that existing practices must be reformed significantly, but that there is no reason why wealth cannot continue to increase if a clean source of energy can be found. Nisbet also notes some of the global aspects of environmental issues.

*   *   *

It is one of the greatest tragedies of today that man, having made himself autonomous, free of dependence on God as he thinks, has separated himself from Nature, and the more he knows, the greater the curse he can become to the Nature he was intended to

Ethical Issues

rule.... It is a Christian task...to treat whatever part of the world God may place us in as part of God's creation to which we owe a duty.

H.L. Ellison (1967), Comment on
Psalm 148

But who should begin? Who should break this vicious circle?...responsibility cannot be preached, only borne, and the only possible place to begin is with oneself.... Whether all is really lost or not depends entirely on whether or not I am lost.

Václav Havel, Letters to Olga, No.
142 (written from prison)

Is there no balm in Gilead?

Jeremiah 8:22

The word *economy* is derived from the Greek root *oikos*, meaning home. An economist is a person who is entrusted with the stewardship of the home. We now have a global economy, and we have become responsible for the stewardship of the planet. In a culture that can reach the limits of the solar system, there is no limit to growth in well-being except that imposed by stupidity, but despite our technical success we have not yet come to terms either with our power or with our responsibilities. The thesis of this book is simple: humanity now controls the Earth and has assumed the management of the planetary economy. Economics is no longer a matter of resources, exploitation, and production; global economics must now be based on the sound stewardship of our home. Only if we become guardians of the planet can the life of humanity improve.

The control of climate

For 4 billion years the Earth's surface environment has been self-managing. The natural controls on the environment have operated since the beginning of the geological record and have maintained the temperature so that the surface has neither frozen over nor boiled. As the solar input has grown and varied, the natural warming effect (the greenhouse effect) of the Earth's atmosphere has changed, so that the planet's surface temperature has stayed roughly constant. There have been warm periods and cold intervals, but the planet as a whole has never frozen, nor has it become so warm that life has died out.

Today, the human economy is of such scale that it has taken over the control of the globe, and humanity is beginning to determine the course of the global climate. Our influence is so profound that we are now powerful enough deliberately to change that climate. We are able, if we choose, easily to warm the planet, or, with somewhat more difficulty, to cool it. We can, if we wish, melt the polar ice; we can probably, if we like, create a semidesert in central North America; we may soon be able to impose rainfall on the Peruvian desert or drought in southern Africa. Climate, which is a long-term matter, is now technically under our control, although we cannot yet influence day-to-day weather on any significant scale.

In several ways human behavior now determines the climate. The products of our industrial activity are now important in terms of the total bulk of the atmosphere. Each year, we add trace gases to the atmosphere in such amounts that we have changed the composition of the air on a planetary scale. The addition is no longer simply local pollution; it constitutes an important part of the workings of the atmosphere, and we are rapidly losing track of what pristine nature was. Old air is a prized commodity, because we are now less and less able to characterize the natural environment. The atmosphere, from now on, will be what we make it to be.

The second major way in which humanity determines the planetary climate is in our control of the surface vegetation, the animal population, and the color of the Earth. Vegetation—everything from rainforest to plankton—is crucial to the global air-conditioning system. Plants help to cleanse, hydrate, and circulate the air. The processing system is enormously complex and subtle. The effect of vegetation on the water cycle and on the circulation of the air is poorly understood. Plants transpire water and in so doing they transfer energy into the air. The transfer of heat is so large that it is an important contribution to the energy driving the global air circulation. The northern forest and the tropical and subtropical dry forest are also important in helping to control the oxygen and carbon dioxide content of the air.

Clouds are immensely important in controlling the climate. Their impact on temperature is far more important than the direct effects of greenhouse gases or of vegetation. Small changes in greenhouse gases or in vegetation can change cloud distribution, and have extreme impact on the planetary climate. This is one of the nightmares of global change, that some small change in cloud patterns may induce a much larger catastrophe that transforms the world climate. Other nightmares include a runaway emission of methane from the Arctic hydrates, collapse of atmospheric hydroxyl concentration, a runaway increase

in pollutants, and the danger of change in sea circulation.

Humanity now controls around a third to a half of the primary biological production of the land. Large parts of all the continents except Antarctica are now our gardens in which we plant crops, cut forests, graze cattle, or burn grass. Aeschylus no longer speaks the truth: the air is heaven's protectorate no more. In taking over the direction of the continental surface, we have also become responsible for the atmosphere: the decision to remove forest in Borneo alters the weather in South Asia, the burning of the Amazon forest influences the jet stream over the United States. As yet, we do not understand the extent and significance of these effects, and we are so rapidly losing the natural world that it may be gone before we understand it. It is extremely important that *deforestation be stopped, and that agricultural practice, world-wide, be reformed so that good environmental management becomes a chief goal of human use of the land and seas.*

The response to challenge

A Luddite reaction to these problems would be to deny our duty of managing the planet, to smash our industries, and to return to a better, natural world. This would have the immediate consequence of consigning the poorer parts of the world to an existence without hope, in perpetual poverty, starvation, and disease, until enough people had died to restore the old pretechnological balance of nasty, brutish, and short lives. The "natural" Earth (if such a thing could be restored) would probably sustain less than a billion of the 5 billion people who now live. Fortunately for the poorer peoples of the Earth, this option is not possible since the most powerful nations are democracies, and the average electors will not decide to execute the poor. Nor will they cheerfully accept a government that orders them to go without fast foods, plastic packaging, cars, television, soft drinks, baseball caps, and the other marks of civilization. Any government which demands that these essentials be abandoned will be swiftly voted out of office. Persuasion, by subtle forces, is the only option. We cannot demolish our present industry *unless* we can replace it with a more attractive substitute.

The duty of economists as stewards of society is therefore to find alternatives to our present pattern of behavior in the richer and also in the poorer parts of the world, alternatives so attractive that they will actually be implemented. Any new global economic system must be capable of supplying energy to the richer nations and of providing food and some hope of an improvement in living standards to the poorer nations.

The generation of useful energy and the expending of it dominates the economic needs of the rich nations and is at the root of most atmospheric pollution. Given an adequate supply of energy, there is virtually no limit to the increase in wealth, if the energy is atmospherically clean and wealth is defined as the well-being of humanity in a stable biological environment. If energy is not clean, the increase in wealth is limited, and the environment is dangerously threatened. Some economists feel that the wealthy nations can simply carry on regardless, as we can always buy food even if rich farmers struggle and those of the poor nations fail. This is a valid, if amoral, point of view, but it ignores the strains on the social fabric of the rich nations that will come when they are faced with major internal agrarian changes; it also ignores the problem of innumerable starving migrants, legal and illegal, pounding on the gates closed at the borders.

Our energy at present is generated from coal, oil, natural gas, and hydroelectric and nuclear sources. Coal is unacceptable in atmospheric terms and must be abandoned. Oil and natural gas are slightly less noxious, but the carbon dioxide and methane they produce are unacceptable unless waste gas can be eliminated or reinjected into the ground. Hydroelectric power is attractive in moderation but it is not a very viable way of producing enough electricity to satisfy the planet. It is environmentally damaging and it is limited in its resources.

There are several sources of energy that do not alter the air. Solar energy is the most obvious possibility. At present it is very expensive and inefficient to produce, but it is likely that it will in future become much cheaper and more efficient. Much research is needed, urgently. Biomass burning is another form of solar power that, at first glance, is atmospherically neutral, as biologically fixed CO_2 is then burnt for energy. However, a very large area of land would be needed for biomass production if a significant part of humanity's energy came from this source. This land would have to be taken from agricultural land or from forest where it would otherwise support plants that would fix CO_2 on a rather longer term. The obvious short-term option, which is favored in this work, is nuclear energy. Nuclear power is the only major source of energy that is able to supply the planet for the next few decades without a massive reduction in the availability of electricity to the poorer nations. Over the longer term, solar energy will probably eventually be the chief support of the economy.

Finally, and most important, there is the option of energy conservation, which is laudable in the rich nations but anathema to poor countries that desperately need abundant electricity. In the short term, for the rich nations, conservation is the best and least expensive way of reducing emissions of greenhouse gases.

The generation of electrical power without the simultaneous generation of CO_2 or loss of CH_4 is not the whole answer to the problem of global change. Public transport is vitally important, especially when electrically powered. Cities ought to be reshaped so that individual transport is less needed. Endless suburbia and interminable rush hours are not necessary features of paradise. Neither is gasoline. We can use an alternative currency of energy, such as electricity or hydrogen produced from water by electricity.

A successful global economy of the period 2000-2050 may not be based on fossil fuels, as today. Instead it may be a nuclear-electric-hydrogen economy. In such an economy the electricity generated in nuclear power stations would be used to power industry and to produce hydrogen to power independent transport. Eventually, there would be a transition to solar power. In contrast, a global economy that continues to use fossil fuel is likely to be unsuccessful and will eventually fall to social unrest induced by climate change. Whatever the shape of the future, *it is important that the industrial economy should make no net emissions of CO_2, CH_4 or other pollutants* and that this state should be brought about soon.

The implementation of change

Can the global economy change? Do we possess the institutional structures to plan and implement change? The answer must be optimistic: the alternative is a new Dark Age. We now possess a rudimentary network of global economic management. We have a growing web of international meetings and organizations such as the G-7 group, the International Monetary Fund and World Bank, the General Agreement on Tariffs and Trade, the Organization for Economic Cooperation and Development, and so on. Competition between nations is moderated by a wide variety of formal and informal agreements to regulate world trade and currencies. It is through this web of international cooperation that a new global economy can be developed, in which formal treaties, such as the 1990 London agreement on atmospheric ozone, will be supplemented by bilateral and multilateral agreements on reducing greenhouse emissions, on using the debt of poor nations as an instrument for protecting tropical vegetation, and on research programs for understanding the biosphere. A new, environmentally sound global economy *can* be implemented, without great disruption, and without limiting the growth in wealth of the rich or poor nations. The alternative is global catastrophe.

At the source of the flood of disruption that is changing the Earth is the fountain of human births. The planetary ecosystem can only be sustained if the human population is stabilized. An ill-educated, poor, and fecund humanity can only destroy the fabric of nature. Poor people are not stupid people; they have many children for the good reason that it is advantageous to them. Children provide labor, economic benefit, and hope for a secure old age. Those nations that have halted the growth in their populations all have universal education, good health care, social security in old age, and women who are treated as the equals of men. *Population growth can be stopped, but only if there is a strong social will to remove the underlying causes of the growth.*

As a global society, humanity can choose a policy of little action now, followed by a massive forced change in our civilization in the early decades of the next century. Alternatively, we can change our economy in a series of relatively small shifts of behavior, beginning now, in the hope that over the next few decades we attain a balanced planet.

Our science may not be advanced enough to manage the Earth with success. For most of this century the earth sciences and biology have been reductionist. There have been triumphs—plate tectonics, DNA—but also there has been blindness. We study the geochemistry of ytterbium in great detail, but have no time to discover why the air is one-fifth oxygen. J.E. Love-lock, the most thoughtful planetographer of our age, has pointed this out: our scientific funding committees and our training drive us to minutiae, but not to knowledge. We do not yet understand the physiology of the Earth. Consequently, we cannot manage it. It is urgent that we study the biosphere, not just with computers but on the ground, in the air and from space.

But already we control our home; blind, humanity steers the globe. A crash may extinguish us. Without knowledge or vision to go on, we must stop and restore. If we learn to manage, we can drive the chariot of our civilization across the solar system. Should we not learn, what is left of the biosphere may simply excrete our remains from the wreckage of our planet.

Questions for Discussion

1   Is Nisbet correct that a return to a "natural" Earth would have too great a human cost to be desirable, even if it is possible?

2   Has the scientific community been too concerned with analyzing different parts of the natural world separately, rather than dealing with the planet as a whole?

The Politics of the Steady State

Charles Taylor

In this paper, Taylor claims that society must eventually reach limits beyond which it cannot pass: specifically, a population limit, a resource limit, and a pollution limit. These limits will impose the need for a "steady state," in which there is a stable population, a severe rationing of non-renewable resources, and a strict ban on at least some forms of pollution. Taylor argues that the transition to this unavoidable steady state will put severe strains on our society, and will force us to re-think our values, including our attitudes toward material goods.

*　　*　　*

In pondering the political possibilities and impossibilities of the steady state, we do not need to accept any of the predictions of disaster put forward recently concerning the future of mankind (although any one of these gloomy predictions may easily be close to the truth). We only have to accept the proposition that our present patterns of exponential growth in population and industrial development must somewhere hit against limits of three kinds:

a population limit beyond which the supply of basic necessities, especially food, cannot be assured for larger numbers;

a resource limit, where the supply of non-renewable resources is so reduced as first to make increasing consumption impossible and later to force us to do without altogether;

a pollution limit, whereby the ecologically harmful side effects of increased production become a danger to life.

There may also be other limits, such as a population-concentration limit, which may already have been reached in large conurbations today, well before the limit of food supply mentioned above. The close-packed concentration of tens of millions of human beings leads beyond a certain point to individual and social breakdown, expressed in 'anomic' violence, increasing mutual mistrust and hostility, more and more frenetic attempts to escape society by privatization, and perhaps other as yet unknown terrors.

But this latter limit is speculative, in the sense that there are indications but no solid evidence for it; and the exact shape of the three undeniable limits is very much a matter of dispute. For those who, like the authors of *The Limits to Growth*, are willing to put some kind of time span on our progress towards the limits there are always objectors who point to the possibilities of avoiding or pushing back the limits. For instance, if one of the big barriers we now threaten to run against is thermal pollution—that is, the addition to the earth's heat from the sun by internal sources of man-made heat through the burning of fossil fuels or the transforming of other kinds of energy (hydro-electric generation), thereby at some (unknown) point producing disastrous climatic changes—we can always hope that the switch to solar energy will allow us to meet all our growing energy needs from the sun's existing flows of heat.

The layman rapidly loses his way in these disputes and becomes incapable of arbitrating. And in this area we are all partly laymen, since the range of expertise and scientific knowledge required straddles so many fields that no one person can master them all. But however difficult it is to predict the detail, when we step back from these disputes we can surely see in general outline what the requirements must be for future human society. They spell the end of exponential quantitative growth.

For setting aside the cases where the ways around the limits proposed by the 'optimists' themselves have other unacceptable side-effects (e.g., energy through hydrogen fusion, which solves the problem of scarce resources but not at all those of thermal or other forms of pollution), the new ways can, no more than the old, open the way to unlimited exponential growth. For instance, the potential of solar and geothermal energy may be so large as to be, for our purposes, unlimited. But tapping these sources requires investment, and tapping them in ever-increasing amounts requires ever-larger investment and hence increasing use of other resources. Thus tapping solar heat for power purposes requires giving over some (at present quite large) parts of the earth's surface to reflectors, and this area obviously couldn't be increased beyond a certain point without hampering other essential uses or provoking harmful ecological effects.

The crude layman's intuition is that with so large and varied a number of limits awaiting us somewhere out there on our trajectory of exponential growth, our chances of missing *all* of them, by some dazzling manoeuvre worthy of a comic strip hero, are just about nil. It seems overwhelmingly likely that as we swerve our star-ship to avoid one we will charge into another. For the range of such limits is much wider and more multiform than the above neat three-fold classification suggests. There are many possible scenarios in which the world today may run into the hunger barrier, and there are a large number of essential resources which may run out. Above all, there is an indefinite number of lethal pollution effects or ecologically disastrous consequences of increased production. It is quite possible that the most lethal are as yet unknown to us. The scenario of a world rendered uninhabitable by human agency through a completely unforeseen chain of effects, dear to science fiction authors, is far from implausible. The wild optimists, the Buck Rogers of our growth

Odyssey, are dreaming of that sublime technological coup, the invention of the perfect gimmick, which infinitely increases potency without cost, satirized by Al Capp in the Valley of the Schmoon.

Sooner or later, we shall all have to live within economic systems which respect certain limits: 1) a stable population; 2) a severe rationing of non-renewable resources, the stock of which must ultimately sink to what can be recycled perpetually; 3) a ban on the increase of certain side-effects of production, such as the creation of heat or the emission of certain substances into soil, water, or atmosphere, so that any increase in production must be accompanied by more effective counter-action, such as the recycling of waste substances.

It might be thought that this reflection is too general. It applies to the world as a whole, but all this is going to hit the different countries and parts of the world at very different rates and times, and in very different ways. Population limit is a reality in Bangladesh but surely not in Canada, we might argue, with its immense spaces and sparse population. A similar point might be made about resource exhaustion, again considering our exceptional endowment. But quite apart from humanitarian considerations, this may be a very foolish line of thought. We are a relatively weak country, small in industrial and military might. The world may not let us go on enjoying our incredible advantage in natural endowment and go on living in the old pattern of unrestrained growth, while everyone else is forced into the new straitened mould. And besides this, a relatively generous endowment in space and resources doesn't free us from all of the multiform limits that we face. There are numerous pollution effects to which we are heir along with all other peoples (indeed, many pollution effects are more serious in the North, where lie large parts of our 'great open spaces'). Or again, we may not have reached the population limit in the sense that our food supply is inadequate; but if there is a population concentration limit, we may soon, in our large cities, be hitting the point at which the quality of social life rapidly deteriorates.

Hence we too will have one day to start thinking in terms of the steady state society, which we might define first as one which respects the three limits just mentioned. And for this we are grievously unprepared: respecting these limits means renouncing exponential quantitative growth.

Respecting the three limits doesn't mean that all growth is impossible. For there are qualitative changes which we understand as growth because we consider the end-result more valuable, even though they involve no greater use of material resources. Let us say that a firm improves the quality of the wallpaper it produces by improving its design, and this improvement consists entirely in a more aesthetically pleasing pattern, the actual use of materials being the same. This in some sense is growth in that people now have higher quality decoration in their houses. And it could even be measured as such in the gross national product (GNP), since we can imagine that the firm would charge more for this superior product.

Thus it is possible to increase the quantities of certain products by better design or by eliminating waste without needing increased resources as, for example, when a handy man builds a solar heater for his house out of waste products, or when we revert to an older design of clothes-peg which doesn't require the metal clasp.

These forms of growth, what we might call quality growth and greater economy,

remain possible even in the most stringently resource-pressed society. But what will be ruled out is long runs of continuing quantitative increases in production. Of course, not all resources will be limited: renewable ones and those of such great abundance that we need never worry will be there for the asking. But the expanding exploitation of these resources will require at some point either the increased use of non-renewable resources or will increase some pollution effect. To continue on the path of increased production will thus require greater efforts at counteraction, thus increasing costs. And since it is frequently the case (exemplified in *Limits to Growth*, p. 142, in the matter of reducing organic wastes from a beet sugar plant) that pollution control involves steeply mounting costs as it aims for more complete effectiveness, the increase in costs will be exponential.

The steady state society will thus allow for qualitative growth, for all growths in quantity due to new designs which are more economical in resource use, and for short runs of quantitative growth which make use of renewable or astronomically abundant resources (e.g., hydrogen) which can surge forward until they hit a limit in their use of non-renewable resources or in their pollution effects. But what would be impossible would be continuing exponential quantitative growth, where the production of one phase is the base from which the increased output of the next phase is generated by some continuing percentage of growth. And to rule this out is to rule out exponential growth altogether, since exponential qualitative growth is a meaningless category.

Of course, this notion of a steady state society is an idealization. It may be that we will never be all that strapped. Or—and this is, alas, more likely—it may be that we will be more catastrophically deprived, as we overshoot, run out of some essential resource, and have to cut back (a foretaste of which we came close to experiencing in the recent oil crisis). But to take the optimistic side, we will probably always have *some* non-renewable resources that we can still afford to be prodigal about; and there will always be *some* pollution effects which we can afford to be reckless about for a while. These will certainly lengthen our bursts of quantitative growth. But the steady state society must define the asymptote towards which we shall be inexorably forced to move.

We are lamentably unprepared for this steady state society. And this is because we are wedded to exponential growth. Exponential growth is measured, conceived, worried about, and celebrated in our societies by the figure for GNP. This is expected to grow each year by some hefty and sustained percentage. Much has been written of this almost ridiculous obsession with GNP, this idolatry of growth. But it is not just a weakness in the head of politicians, journalists, and academics (though all of these groups may be weak enough in the head); it is much more deeply rooted in our society, in its definitions of hope, the future, the good life—indeed in the very way in which we are integrated as a society.

Let us try to enumerate the ways in which exponential growth is essential to us. This is not an easy task, for some ways are hard to define, but the attempt I will make here will be enough to show how deep and wide it cuts.

1. Our society counts on continued growth to maintain full employment. This has been a feature of all 'capitalist' societies. Any serious drop in the rate of growth of GNP means stagnation, widespread un-employment, and distress, often very unfairly distributed with a much heavier incidence in the poor, under-developed regions.

2. Our society relies on growth to meet one of the most pressing demands made on it, that for a just and more equal distribution of benefits. Modern societies, having swept aside any of the previous ontological justifications for hierarchy or differential life predicaments, are faced with a continuing demand for the equalization of life chances. The surviving justifications for unequal distribution, based on merit, supposed contribution to society, or effort, are either becoming more transparently unacceptable (how can one estimate the value of *individual* effort, when the most productive enterprises of modern society are vast, interdependent, collective achievements?), or else fail to justify the existing degree and type of inequality (how can differences of merit justify hereditary structural disabilities, such as affect people in underprivileged regions and classes?).

Faced with the demand for greater equality, which our society in its own terms cannot gainsay, and therefore which is pressed more and more urgently and imperiously by those who feel themselves disadvantaged, our response has been to pin everything on growth. In a static economy, greater equality would mean redistribution, which would mean lowering the living standard of the better off to raise that of the poorer. But this is all the more unthinkable in our society in that the very definition of happiness and the good life in a technological civilization includes the progressive increase in prosperity over the life-cycle, and prosperity in turn is defined by the increased command over goods and services. To face our affluent classes with not only a standstill in income growth but an actual cut-back would be adding the unbelievable to the unacceptable. Static redistribution is hard to achieve, if not impossible, in any society; but in ours doubly so.

And so the only way that we can see to cope with the strains of inequality is to treat it with the spin-off effects of growth. The minimal or right-wing hope is that people on steadily rising incomes will not care too much that income disparities are remaining constant or even getting worse—in other words that others are getting richer. The maximal, or left-wing, hope is that a disproportionate share of growth can be steered to the less well-off so that income disparities can be reduced, but painlessly, since this time the rich are compensated (or anaesthetized) by rising incomes for the more rapid progress of the poor.

As a matter of fact, this latter hope has been cruelly disappointed both internationally and domestically in most industrialized countries. This seems to happen both because of the very mechanisms of exponential growth and because of the expectation of increased incomes mentioned above. An economy grows exponentially because the production of one year is the base for the increased production the following year by some non-secularly declining percentage of growth. But in real terms this means, of course, that most of the growth will happen where it has already happened. Thus world growth sees the industrialized nations pulling ahead of the underdeveloped ones by more and more frightening margins. And something similar tends to happen between regions in Canada, although it is to some extent offset by transfer payments, and government attempts at encouraging development.

At the same time, the affluent refuse to behave according to the left-wing scenario and not to mind or notice when a disproportionately high share of growth goes to the disadvantaged. The laws of exponential growth seem to hold in regard to expectations as well, and in our richer times we hear more gnashing of teeth about (non-corporate) welfare bums, more churlish resentment at any attempt at relative redistribution than in previous decades. The very ideology of growth, the very celebration of its benefits, seems to pre-empt its product through the rising demands of the powerful and affluent, so that mountains of munitions are piled up for a war on poverty which never begins.

But the failure of the egalitarian hope makes our reliance on growth all the more urgent and unavoidable. If greater equality evades us, then only rapid all-around growth can compensate the disadvantaged for their unjust plight (we hope). Affluent western economies may come to resemble rich men in the grip of a blackmailer; they will have to pay higher and higher sums to keep things quiet. And paying higher and higher sums means maintaining exponential growth.

3. This expectation of an endless increase in prosperity, which in the past has countered egalitarian hopes, can itself be seen as an independent form of addiction to exponential growth, since it would make the steady state very hard to bear for us even if we had no redistributional imperative. But it is hard to define this addiction and even harder to get to its roots. We can see it as defining the good life to include an ever-increasing command over goods and services, and an ever-increasing capacity to control nature for individual ends. This definition of the good life would, of course,

have seemed wicked if not incomprehensible to men of many previous epochs. But it seems to be very deeply rooted in our own. And as long as this is so, our adjustment to the steady state will be very difficult and painful.

What then are the roots of this addiction? In part, they lie in the sense, widespread in modern civilization, of what it is to be a human being: control over nature, the shaping of things to our freely chosen projects, with the attendant definition of autonomy as self-dependence, and the focus on the future, are of paramount importance. This, which has sometimes been referred to as 'the modern identity,' is very difficult to define exactly, especially in the narrow compass of this talk. But it should be listed as an independent mode of addiction to growth, because it operates in any modern technological society, even one where the increase in *individual* prosperity counted for nothing as in the ideal 'socialist' society (are there any such? perhaps China—for the present; certainly not the nations of the Soviet bloc). For these societies too would measure their success and their worth by production, by the steady increase of mastery over nature—in short by growth. A steady state society, on the other hand, requires that we accept, and hence come to value, a balance of some kind with our surroundings, one that will perhaps be constantly undergoing micro-reorderings from within as we strive for qualitative growth, but which will no longer offer the prospect of a linear increase in potency, let alone an exponential one.

The importance of this modern productive identity is also visible in our non-socialist societies in many other ways than just the expectation of rising prosperity. We too celebrate our collective triumphs over nature, such as the moon landing. We measure the health of our society by the rate of growth of GNP; we justify it as a producing society. And more important, this justifying image of ourselves as a vast interdependent enterprise of production is part of the essential rationale for social differentiation, one of the main underpinnings of social discipline, one of the things that holds our society together.

Indeed, we are very aware of this now, because this justifying image is weakening its hold on our minds, along with a weakening of the modern identity among a substantial part of the rising generation; partly as a result, we find that the disciplines and restraints on which we counted in the past are slipping. Contemporary industrial societies appear, more than in the immediately preceding decades, to be cockpits of struggle between groups seeking an acceptable level of income, privilege, or dignity, becoming more and more determined to achieve their objectives, and more indignant when they do not, and being less willing to compromise and restrain themselves in the name of supposed over-riding social goods.

But if the modern identity and its attendant sense of common social purpose is already slipping in this period of unprecedented growth, how will we accommodate to the steady state? It seems that we are committed to growth through the very underpinnings of our industrial society.

This brings us to our principal problem— the politics of the steady state. For the deeply disturbing prospect which arises from this list of our commitments to growth is that our present reasonably free, reasonably democratic, reasonably civilized polities might be casualties of the enforced shift to the steady state. If we can barely meet the demand for fairer shares through break-neck growth, how can we cope when growth is dramatically reduced and ceases to be exponential? Our society will fly apart.

Of course, 'fly apart' is a metaphor. Societies rarely fly apart. What happens when they cease to be able to hold together through a traditional set of institutions is that they mutate to another set in which force, violence, and coercion have a greater role. There is a coup, an army or police take-over; or great masses of citizens tacitly consent when a government destroys traditional liberties and takes dictatorial power.

The first *raison-d'être* for growth, that we count on it to maintain full employment, is not decisive. For the switch to a steady state would in fact call for a great effort, would force us to reintroduce labour-intensive technologies in some cases, and require a very important productive drive to retool us for the change; for instance, immense investment would be required in recycling technology and equipment, anti-pollution devices, and the like. The impact of scarcity, provided we are capable of any organized response at all, will require an immense redirection of our productive effort, comparable to wartime. Unless our economy collapses into chaos, and we allow progressive shortages just to disorganize production without any effort to reshape our economy, we should suffer no more than severe transitional unemployment (which may be bad enough, but not the same as another depression).

But the second and third rationales for growth addiction are of decisive importance. Our society, in which the good life is defined partly in terms of ever-increasing prosperity (that is, individual command over goods and services) and in which dif-

ferences of income, privilege, and life-chance become progressively less justifiable while they remain intractably undiminished, is already under severe strain. The strain is increased, as we saw, by the weakening of one of its most important justifying self-images, that of a society of interdependent producers. There seems to be an internal dynamic in this kind of society in which individuals and group feel justified in pressing increasing demands both in the name of equality and under their entitlement to ever-increasing prosperity. These demands are pressed more imperiously and often truculently, and less willingness to compromise or to heed appeals (spurious or genuine) in the name of the general welfare.

One of the more benign, or less malignant, manifestations of this growing free-for-all is the income scramble, which is part cause in almost all advanced industrial economies of the increasing rate of price inflation. But there are other, more terrifying forms. Members of some disadvantaged groups have resorted sporadically to terrorism. Admittedly, this happens where the issue is not just differences of income and privilege, but rather as part of a systematic denial of dignity and freedom to the group in question. But it would be wrong to see these two kinds of struggle, the utilitarian income scramble and the terroristic demand for rights, as necessarily two qualitatively different things, separated by water-tight compartments. Who has not heard these days the demand for higher incomes and more equality framed in the rhetoric of rights and liberation?

Still, it would take something to bring a society over the leap from the mere income scramble such as we see in contemporary Britain to the terrorist war of desperate minorities such as we see in Northern Ireland

(and now spilling over to Britain). But the kind of shock that might do it would be just such a forced, rapid transition to the steady state. In a society in which groups are intent on increasing their members' prosperity, and on at least maintaining their present rate of growth and sometimes increasing it, where this determination is fuelled by the widespread acceptance of the consumer-goods standard of happiness, what happens when growth must be slowed down? Income growth has to be halted, privileged groups become ever more determined to resist redistribution at all costs, disadvantaged groups become more desperate and combative, less willing to accept appeals to general social solidarity. At the same time everyone suffers the frustration of controls, for a society of increasingly scarce resources is one that requires rationing and restrictions. This cuts across one of the key features of individual prosperity as commonly understood, that in his increasing command over consumer goods the individual exercises increasing choice.

A crisis of this kind could possibly produce a mutation, a sudden rediscovery of social solidarity and common purpose, as did the evacuation from Dunkirk by Britain during the last war. I want to turn to explore what would be involved in this kind of transformation in a moment. But the frightening scenario I am considering here is that the society may face the crisis without any such regeneration. And here the prospect is of an increasing bitterness and desperation in the inter-group struggle, a greater and greater willingness to hold society to ransom by whatever means available, which may extend all the way to the means of violence. Terrorism only requires the action of small minorities; from the majority of a given group it only demands a certain

moral ambivalence, sufficient to avoid active collaboration with the forces of order, as in the situation existing in the Catholic ghettos of Ulster.

A society terrorized would 'fly apart.' Sooner or later, the majority of citizens, who only identify sporadically with the desperadoes, will be willing to abdicate whatever power they possess as an electorate and many of their traditional freedoms to a strong-arm government which will restore order. This change may not come in as spectacular, bloody, and revolting a way as the army coup in Chile (where society seems to have 'flown apart' for other reasons than those considered here); perhaps the Uruguayan case should be a more worrying precedent, where the power of democratic institutions can be slowly undermined with the tacit consent of a citizenry who have been through an extended experience of terrorism.

In this scenario either overt dictatorship or a society substantially more under authoritarian direction and control becomes the only 'solution,' the only way of imposing the necessary restrictions, the only way to impose *some* sharing of the social product which the groups cannot acquiesce to through free bargaining or accept out of social solidarity.

The question of the politics of the steady state can thus be more precisely put in this way: is there any way of avoiding this authoritarian scenario? Is there another way of meeting the transition to the steady state and the challenges of adjustment, by which we can preserve and perhaps even extend our liberties, our democratic institutions, and the level of civilized behaviour we have attained in our public life? Of course, a crucial part of what makes the difference, of what provokes, for instance, a Dunkirk spirit or its opposite, can never be adequately defined. But perhaps something can be said of the changes in institutions and publicly accepted goals which would be part of a more creative and civilized political response to the steady state.

The ensuing reflections are fragmentary and abstract but, fortunately, not entirely general. The focus of my questioning, sometimes unstated, sometimes stated, will be this country and its possibilities. The passages of general discussion of societies in the steady state are preparatory to putting a question about a particular society. If someone from another country were to engage in a general discussion about the steady state, he would probably focus on quite different things. There is no doubt an implied criticism here of my general considerations, but I don't know how to make them more genuinely universal without losing my bearings altogether.

Perhaps the place to start would be to ask how a steady state society can meet the demand for greater equality without lapsing into an authoritarian pattern. I think an essential condition of this would be the elaboration, partly by spontaneous convergence, partly by design, of a normal pattern of consumption which was accessible to the least affluent.

The major challenge to a steady state society comes as we saw from the fact that our present pattern of inequality is basically intolerable and is made provisionally tolerable only by rapid growth. But there are different patterns of inequality, and not all of them are equally intolerable or intolerable in the same way. There is, for instance, the inequality between the mass of the population on one hand and a handful of spectacularly privileged on the other. In certain circumstances this is felt by the majority to be absolutely unacceptable; for instance, where the minority enjoy their privileges by directly exploiting the masses, where they are landlords, say, and the majority are their rack-rented tenants; or where, even without exploitation, the life of the majority is felt as intolerable in itself, quite apart from any comparison; or where the privileged are exempt from certain necessary disciplines and sacrifices imposed on everyone else (e.g., they are evading taxation on a lavish scale like many American political leaders).

Outside these circumstances, however, this kind of inequality frequently does not evoke resentment or indignation. Multi-millionaires have generally not been resented in North American society, as the remains of a leisured aristocracy are generally not in Europe. No one is enraged when Howard Hughes rents himself a Central American republic, or Countess So-and-so marries into some dispossessed royal family. For this kind of behaviour has nothing to do with normal life. Not to be like that is not a deprivation for the great majority, even though many in fantasy may imagine themselves with the wealth and leverage of Howard Hughes.

Or again, there are societies with a deeply entrenched class division, where the classes have their different respective modes of life. This was the case in medieval and early modern Europe, as indeed it was in almost all large and complex societies until the last century or so. In this kind of society there are a number of different models of normal life, and although these differ in the wealth that men have at their disposal or in their ability to wield power or display themselves, these differences may not be resented by those less privileged because these capacities of wealth, power, and display are not part of *their* normal life.

What is intolerable about the inequality in a contemporary industrial society is that these societies have developed a single norm of acceptable life, but this norm is accessible only to about 60 to 75 per cent of the population. The non-affluent minority, a quarter to two-fifths of the population, are in a totally unacceptable position; they are unable to live by a standard which is defined universally as *the* normal standard of a decent life. And this standard becomes increasingly inescapable as modern societies dissolve and sweep away in their normal course of evolution all differentiated and heterogeneous sub-cultures; as mobility loosens the ties of regional and historic communities, as the pervasive single communications network penetrates deeper into everyone's life, as growth sweeps away older landmarks, and as the ideology of a producing society draws people away from their allegiance to the past and towards the future of increasing mastery over things.

This is not to say that another kind of diversity doesn't spring up, one of tastes, styles, avocations, even sexual mores, personal discipline. But this diversity is very fragile; people are not deeply anchored in their options of style or even sexual mores, as they were in regional and historical communities. And this diversity has an underlying common premise, that individuals *choose* among these different styles and mores, and they can choose because they have some minimum command as individuals over the shape of their lives, and they get this in our society by being consumers at or above a certain standard of living. Of course, there are objectors who want to reject this latter equation, who dream of and even may try to create a counter-society in which men can be individually free in a communitarian context in balance with nature. But this minority has been quite ineffective in actually creating an alternative (although its criticism has had a deep echo in the structure of our society and has contributed to its failure of nerve). And as has often been pointed out, this minority comes to a large degree from those who have already 'made it' on the consumer standard, and very frequently have a super-standard life to fall back on if things go wrong.

In our society the affluent three-fifths can hope to enjoy such things as a reasonably secure and non-demeaning job, decent housing, the full range of consumer durables, a holiday away from time to time (either travel or cottage), some chance for further education for their children. The rest face the grim prospect of missing out on these. And this is made absolutely intolerable by the fact that such possessions and possibilities are defined as the normal decent life. In part this is a function of the fact that the majority now enjoy them (even though it may be a bare majority). People with memories stretching back far enough have often remarked that even greater deprivation was in a way more bearable during the Depression because 'everyone' was then in the same boat. But it is also a creation of our modern society, with its inexorable action of sweeping away partial communities and imposing the single norm which suits the modern identity.

This pattern of inequality is intolerable in a way that the others—that of a deeply class-differentiated society, that of a small minority of spectacularly privileged—are not. This intolerable inequality is one of the major sources of strain, which we are easing temporarily through (at least the promise of) growth. But this pattern could not be sustained in a free society once it had reached the steady state.

A society forced to give up exponential growth, and which responded to this by freezing the existing pattern of distribution, or where necessary, rolling everyone back proportionately, would become a smouldering volcano. It would sooner or later have to abandon some of its free institutions and go over into an authoriatarian pattern, with a large, irresponsible apparatus for the maintenance of order. But at the same time a society which responded to the end of exponential growth by trying a radical levelling down would also provoke volcanic discontent. This solution, too, might only be possible under a dictatorship, and/or massive emigration of the better-off (as in the case of Cuba under Fidel).

When looked at in this way, the future of freedom looks gloomy indeed. And perhaps this is the most realistic perspective. But being a compulsive optimist, I would like to try to look at it another way. If we set aside for the moment the problem of the transition, where special factors may be in play, as I argue below, and focus on what new pattern of society could be potentially a free society, we can perhaps outline one which, however unlikely, is conceivable.

The kind of society which could be sustained under the stable state would be one in which the consumption standard defining a normal decent life would be available generally speaking, to the most disadvantaged. (I say 'generally speaking' for there will probably always be some special cases of disability or misfortune which the most dedicatedly egalitarian society will not be able to cope with.) I am assuming for the moment a single such standard, because it seems obvious that any attempt to recreate a class-differentiated society, besides being

undesirable, would be clearly impossible in a modern, technological, urbanized, communications-saturated civilization. Later on, however, we may lift this assumption to look at the possibility that a new *regional* differentiation may grow (or return), for this would obviously have special relevance for a country like ours.

This kind of standard for 'normal' life, in which there is no one left out below, as it were, exists of itself in some simple and relatively indigent societies. But clearly in our case it would have to be created. At present the normal standard is partly defined by a command over an ever-growing and ever-diversifying range of consumer goods and services, such that it is always economically unfeasible to provide it for everyone. If any range of goods is available for everyone then it cannot exhaust the standard; this is almost a corollary of the ideology of growth. What we would need in the steady state is a redefined, relatively static standard (one which grew only slowly and irregularly) which everyone could feasibly enjoy.

But how could such a thing be brought about? In terms of mechanism by a systematic policy of rationing and subsidies. What is necessary is some consensus about the commonly available standard, what goes to make it up: let us say, beyond a certain food budget, a certain quality of housing, some level of education, health care, availability of personal transport, possibility of travel, and so on. (Need I mention that this standard is utterly different from the minimum standards of welfare or other transfer payments of our present society, which are meant as survival minima and must be set well below the norm of decent living?)

The aim of public policy would be to ensure by a mixture of rationing and subsidy that the goods and services of this common standard are available at prices which everyone can meet (including, of course, zero price in the case of such services as education and health care). In some cases this could be done by allocating resources to producers (i.e., rationing at the producers' level) to ensure that the supply of certain goods is sufficient to keep its price down. In other cases it could be done by subsidy as well. And in some cases, where an essential resource was scarce, it might have to be rationed to the consumer, possibly at controlled prices.

The results of this (or at least the desired result) would be that the goods of the standard would be available to everyone's budget, but that the goods and services outside this range, being relatively starved of resources and unsubsidized, would be much more highly priced. Suppose that the standard includes some utility vehicle for personal transport (whether this is a car or some species of motor-bicycle will depend on how constrained we are for resources, relative pollution levels, and so on). Then some more luxurious vehicle would be spectacularly more expensive, and would in fact be purchased with their excess income by very few. This would not necessarily mean, of course, that there would be a minority of privileged with Cadillacs, expensive dwellings, holidays in Tahiti, and so on. This is a distinct possibility in almost any form of society. Luxuries may in fact be dispersed more widely, as some people find it possible to take a flyer on a Cadillac, others on an expensive house, others again on tours to Tahiti (which might even, in certain fortunate conditions, be part of the standard). What is essential to this pattern of distribution, however, is that the great majority be at or near the standard, so that,

if resources increase well beyond what is necessary to maintain it at present levels, the standard should be raised, rather than that the luxury sector be allowed to proliferate and so eventually create a new socially effective standard from which a substantial minority is left out below.

I can hear in advance the groans of my readers as they take in the import of these paragraphs. It looks as though in addition to the dangers of dictatorship I am holding out the prospect of a Byzantine society in which production and consumption are held in a static pattern by a myriad of controls, and in which the pattern of consumption is marked by the drab uniformity of the utility good. The economics of Byzantium combine with the taste of wartime Britain; we see the prospect of an endless diet of Brussels sprouts eaten under the watchful eye of the Eparch of Constantinople.

I can't say that I am unambiguously overjoyed at the prospect myself. But I have two contradictory things to say in partial mitigation: first, that things are going to be that bad anyway whatever we do; and second, that they don't need to be all that bad.

On the first point: we have to face the fact that when we hit the limits of scarce resources and unacceptable pollution levels, we shall *have* to start allocating resources and/or licences to produce. We saw this with the US oil crisis [in the mid-1970s]: gas was made more difficult to obtain for the private motorist in order to safeguard supplies for industry and heating. When we come to the limits of growth, this kind of allocation will become the rule rather than the exception. And in cases of great scarcity, we shall have to face consumer rationing as well.

This allocation by public policy will replace a more haphazard system in force today, loosely and misleadingly referred to as 'the market.' In fact, allocations are made today by business decisions, most often of large corporations who are operating within the limits of what they believe they can induce consumers to buy at generally managed prices. This doesn't mean, of course, that they operate in conditions of unlimited freedom; they have to contend on one side with scarcity and the claims of rivals to the same resources, on the other with the not always predictable boundary of consumer interests. But their freedom is that of self-designed growth through shaping demand within these boundaries.

It ought not to be thought a step backward if this system, whose global growth is haphazard, but whose partial consequences are determined by private and irresponsible concentrations of power, is replaced by public and responsible decision-making. And this is the more so if we reflect that the thrust of the present system is towards the entrenchment and extension of the consumer goods standard of happiness; for the condition of growth of corporations is the perpetual extension and diversification of consumer demand. These indeed are the major institutions which embody and sustain with all the power and influence at their command the religion of infinite productive growth, the conception of the good life as ever-increasing individual command over goods and services.

What is legitimately depressing about the prospect of the steady state society is not that the major allocations of resources between priorities will be conscious and public, but rather the perhaps terrible conditions of scarcity under which such choices will be made. It is this which will force us to forgo the endless proliferation of consumer goods. There will just not be enough resources. A freely proliferating consumer bonanza would be a privilege which only a few participated in, and which could in principle never 'trickle down' through the beneficent action of exponential growth. If anyone prefers a recreation of the society of Marie Antoinette to one in which priority is given to a universal standard, I regret I haven't the space here to argue the case in morals and political theory. I want just to make the point that such a society could only be held in that mould by force, and it would most likely end in the same way as its illustrious eighteenth-century-analogue.

But to come to the second point: things don't have to be that bad. A society with a universally available consumer standard can still be one in which there is lots of choice, good design, alternative designs, and alternative sources of design. With the standard 'package' people could obviously choose less consumer durables in order to have more interesting holidays. But beyond this, the goods of the standard, those which benefit from resource allocations or subsidies, don't have to be standardized. What has to be determined is the amount of resources used per unit. A 'utility' frigidaire, for instance, would be defined as one which did not exceed a certain budget of resources in its manufacture. Outside of that there need be no limit other than economic on the variety of designs or the number of firms public, co-operative, or private, doing the designing.

And beyond this we can hope that people might rediscover other ways of expressing and realizing variety and colour than those of the proliferating consumer society. Indeed, in view of the likely era of scarcity coming up we had better do so. But more of this below.

In short, my answer to those who find my scenario of a universal consumer standard gloomy is to point to the fact that the future will be gloomy willy-nilly, at least in the sense that our choices will be severely restricted. The growing consumer society will be an impossibility, except for a perhaps shrinking minority. The condition of a society which won't have to be held down by an irresponsible minority with a monopoly of force will be some such equalization as is adumbrated above. In a sense, the essential point I am putting forward is independent of the machinery of controls, allocations, and subsidies I referred to. It is that a society in which a substantial minority remains below the normal standard will be very unlikely to survive the steady state with its free institutions intact. A free society will have to have a universally available consumer standard, however this is realized. But I think it is clear that in the conditions of a technological society, it will have to be *realized*; it will not happen of itself. But once we accept this requirement of universality, we can see that with luck the prospect doesn't have to be all gloomy. Human happiness can survive the demise of the consumer society.

But we can't let optimism run away with us. A necessary condition of a steady state society with free institutions is probably some such universally available consumer standard. But this is far from being a sufficient condition. The dilemma we posed above remains intact. A universal standard society would represent a levelling down relative to our present society, and how can the affluent majority ever accept that? And if they can't, then how can this society be held together except by force? How does

it admit any more of free institutions than the society whose inequalities are frozen in a permanent mould?

In a way to speak of a redistribution by levelling down is to put the prospect in a misleading way. If anyone proposed such a thing today there would be armed insurrection by the affluent and powerful. But we are talking about a quite different predicament with two stages. There is the transition, when dire shortages begin to appear, and then there is the new mould of a more permanent steady state society.

The transition may be a period of crisis, in which a kind of Dunkirk spirit may prevail, as in wartime, when people are willing to take a drop in the standard of living and even level down 'for the duration.' Whether this will happen, or an unseemly and brutal scramble for the scarce resources, is hard to predict or to determine. It depends on a number of intangibles in a people's public life.

But whether there can be a steady state society which doesn't slip towards authoritarian control is a question which arises after the transition granted this is weathered with free institutions unimpaired. And what will be required will be a sort of mutation in society's generally accepted self-definitions, the general sense of the nature of the social bond and the kind of solidarity which binds people. This is always a very mixed and varied thing, very difficult to describe or articulate. In our society today it is a mixture of national and/or ethnic/linguistic common identities on the one hand, and some notion of society as an interdependent enterprise of production for the general benefit on the other.

What kind of definition would sustain an equal universal-standard society pressed by the limits of the steady state? It would have to be a society with a very strong sense of common purpose. For only societies which feel a powerful common purpose or a forceful sense of common identity accept willingly the discipline of equal shares. Many societies, including our own, have a notion of a level of indigence below which no one should be allowed to fall. But this is very much an unequal portion, conferred in virtue of obligations of charity or universal justice. The sense, however, that things must be shared more or less equally comes from the sense that people share a common lot or face a common task. This is why this spirit is often visible in wartime. For many centuries the models that writers had in mind when thinking of such societies were the Greek *poleis*, but in our day the state of Israel might be usefully thought of as an example. Here there is both the forceful identity and the urgent common task.

Perhaps the health, maybe the fate, of free institutions in the steady state of the future depends on whether our societies respond to the end of growth either as a challenging common task which binds them or as a disaster in which each must scramble for safety on his own. One writer (Heilbroner) uses the image of a sinking liner in which everything depends on whether the passengers co-operate and file down in order, or rush in panic for the lifeboats which thus sink and take everyone to their doom. But in a way this image is partially misleading. For it makes us focus on the short-term crisis, which will be rather like that on the sinking liner. What is more important is the long haul. And for this another, more long-term, more deeply rooted sense of common purpose will be necessary. Men will have to respond to the end of growth not just as a crisis which requires that we all pull together; rather they will

have to see in the new situation a new ideal form of life to be realized, and not just an occasion to show heroism in salvaging the old one. If we face the steady state as a set of challenging circumstances in which we are called on somehow to keep the flag aloft on endless production, we are probably lost. It is only if we come to see it as the occasion to realize a new kind of life in which the balance with nature is not a regrettable limit but an opportunity to express and realize new human possibilities that we shall be able to sustain the kind of public morale we will need to maintain the discipline of equality and hence free institutions.

In any case, a universal-standard society would have to be one with a strong sense of common purpose with the attendant sense of solidarity. Only in this context would the necessary degree of equality be seen as something acceptable. If we tried to make our present society more equal, there would be strong resistance from the affluent because they see such efforts as transfers in which they are forced to forgo income on behalf of essentially less productive people; and since they see the social bond largely as that of a co-operative enterprise of producers they don't see why they should support 'welfare bums.' But even in present society, affluent tax-payers don't have anything like so much resentment against what are perceived essentially as common enterprises. Even the much-maligned and cursed CBC is not resented in the same way as, say, laxer regulations on unemployment benefits.

But in another society with a stronger sense of common purpose, the allocations and subsidies which made the common standard universally available would be seen as common enterprises, essential to the goals of the society, rather than as transfers. Once they come to be seen in this latter light, the strains may become unbearable, as the resistance of the potentially affluent mounts. But seeing them this way is already to have lost some of the sense of common purpose; it is to see oneself as an individual bidding for scarce resources against rivals, rather than as the member of a common enterprise.

A universal-standard society would thus have to have this stronger purpose. And to this end, the advantage may lie with small societies or societies which can be meaningfully decentralized. For solidarity is difficult to maintain in very large societies, where relations are more and more mediated by bureaucratic structures and where masses of people feel an immense distance separating them from the decisions, achievements, and events which affect society as a whole.

And the advantage of smaller size is even more evident when we reflect on the conditions of maintaining free institutions. We saw that steady state societies will probably have to be much more planned and regulated than we are today. Their recurrent danger will be bureaucratic sclerosis, corruption, and exploitation by those in the know, accompanied by resignation, cynicism, and sporadic outbursts of violence on the part of the *administrés*. The only way to avoid this is to elaborate and keep alive mechanisms of consultation and popular decision in planning. How is the consensus on the universal consumer standard arrived at? How do we come to a common mind on this? Or is it the end just handed down from an administrative structure which we each feel too powerless or perhaps too confused and uncertain to fight?

Perhaps the drive towards Byzantinism will be unbeatable. But if it can be beaten, this will much more probably occur in small societies or societies which can be meaningfully decentralized—that is where the units of decentralization are not just arbitrarily carved out (as are most urban electoral constituencies or the boundaries of a development zone for example), but have a meaning in the common and differential sense of identity of those who live within them. The elaboration of a consensus, the discussion of alternatives, the referring back to citizens, are all potentially feasible in small units in a way that has no parallel in larger ones.

It is often said that we need to elaborate new techniques of consultation/decision, and that we need to apply our considerable communications technology, film, television, and so on, to this end. Some of the successes of social animation have shown the truth in this. But these are successes in small societies. In large societies this same communication technology can be as much a barrier as a link. When a mass of citizens feel an unbridgeable distance between them and the source and process of decision, television doesn't bridge the gap. Rather it becomes just another way of moulding the image of that process of decision as something essentially foreign and unknown directly to them.

Another condition of continued solidarity in a steady state society will probably be mobility, the ability to change profession during a lifetime or between generations. Turn-over of this kind is an important condition of a sense of equality, and this is essential to the sense of solidarity in societies which have evolved beyond class-differentiation.

Let us try to gather together the threads by returning to the central question, somewhat rephrased; as we enter the steady state society, is there any way of avoiding the strong trend towards an authoritarian and Byzantine society, towards the atrophy if not destruction of civil rights and the institutions of self-government, and the growth of an all-embracing irresponsible bureaucratic control of our lives?

I started to answer this question by asking how a steady state society could meet the demand for equality which seemed a condition of the continued unity without which self-governing institutions don't survive. The answer seemed to be a society with a universally available consumption standard. And a condition of this in turn would seem to be a society with a powerful sense of common purpose. In order to remain vitally self-governing in a steady state, a society will have to elaborate new ways of popular consultation and decision. And it should in addition be highly mobile. For all these reasons it had better be small or capable of meaningful decentralization.

But we could also run through our thumbnail portrait of the alternative society from this angle. Plainly, steady state societies will have to be planned and regulated as ours are not. There is not just the question of allocation of scarce resources discussed above; but the whole direction of technological development will have to be consciously guided towards a recycling technology, which will rely more heavily on abundant resources and forms of energy and production which respect certain pollution limits. A society like this can only avoid sclerosis and Byzantinism if it can compensate with a more vigorous participation by citizens in consultation and decisions. A society which is small and can

decentralize will have a great advantage in this.

But a society in this predicament can only combat Byzantinism by keeping open as well the opportunities for individual or small group initiative. And this, too, requires decentralization. It should be possible for people to elaborate new and original ways of living in balance with nature with a low use of energy and resources. The need for leeway to allow for different ways of realizing a steady state should eventually force us to reverse the trend towards the concentration of population in a few large urban centres. But the partial return to a larger number of smaller, more self-sufficient communities will probably be a technical imperative of the steady state in any case.

But what must go on binding society together, however decentralized into diverse communities, is the strong sense of being engaged in a common enterprise; for without this, diversification will soon mean striking inequality in access to essential common resources, and with this a free, self-governing society is in jeopardy.

It may indeed be very difficult to combine both decentralization and a strong sense of purpose, and this double requirement may push this sketch of an alternative future even farther towards the utopian fringe. But both these conditions seem essential to a free and participating society in the new predicament arising beyond the end of growth.

I'd now like to take up the question which has been the implicit focus of this discussion: what are our chances in this country of making the transition to a steady state without sliding into authoritarian or bureaucratic rule?

Well, we clearly have some advantages. First, we are a small society relatively speaking. But more important, since 22 millions is still a lot of people, we are a society which admits of meaningful decentralization. Indeed, this fact—that the constituent parts of Canada have a meaningful identity—has been our major political problem since the beginning and may indeed break the country up.

But it may turn out in the coming age to be a tremendous advantage. We only have to think of how difficult it will be in larger, more centralized nations to plan for the steady state without entrenching and extending a bureaucratic structure so distant and irresponsible that the vast majority will experience it only as an alien force. Decentralization in England, France, even the United States may be of no avail because the units will not have the identity which they need to function as units, where citizens sense enough of a common identity as members of that unit to want to participate in shaping its course.

But the division of Canada into provinces represents in most cases an important sociological reality. In some cases provinces, in others, groups of provinces, embody a distinct society, with a culture and history and in one case a language distinct from those dominant elsewhere. It is realistic to see these as units of autonomous planning—indeed, it would be very unrealistic to see our future any other way; Canada is an uncentralizable country. This is a fact that many reformers used to curse; they are now beginning to be grateful for it. For the chances of controlling a distant and irresponsible bureaucracy, although perhaps not great anywhere in the coming age, are infinitely greater in these smaller societies.

Planning in Canada for the steady state will obviously have to be greatly decentralized. For instance, the elaboration of the standard pattern of consumption could vary somewhat from region to region. Ultimately, it would be a healthy thing if our regions evolved away from the homogenization of their ways of life which has been steadily going ahead in past decades.

Decentralization we can have for the asking. But can we combine this with a common purpose? This has been our recurrent problem and it will return with a vengeance in the era of the steady state. And as ever one of the crucial determinants of the outcome will be the question of equality. For some of our most persistent and divisive inequalities have been interregional. A century of growth has not appreciably reduced them for reasons with which we are increasingly familiar and which were mentioned above. Left to itself exponential growth increases gaps, as we see on the international scene. The effect of interregional transfers by governments and migration in the last decades has probably been to offset this tendency so that the inequalities remain roughly the same. But here, as elsewhere, growth is now considered the palliative. Even if they cannot attain equality, poorer regions may feel an incentive to remain on board in order to participate in the growth of the larger Canadian economy. I believe that this incentive is the major counter-force to independence in Quebec; indeed, it may be the decisive factor preventing a majority of Québécois from opting out.

The coming era of scarcity will generate its own incentives for us to stick together: the need to pool resource endowments, the need to make a common front against an external world which will more and more press us to give up our resources quickly and cheaply. All this provides an important potential basis for co-operation and indeed makes it essential. But in politics the essential is not always the actual, and we will probably need to do much better in reducing inter-regional inequality if we are to generate the common purpose to realize this potential.

But the transitions to the steady state will give us an unprecedented chance to do better. Of itself, the new predicament may change the balance of economic importance of different occupations and hence regions. For instance, food production is almost certainly going to command a greater relative reward in the new dispensation.

But beyond this, the transition will involve a far-reaching transformation of our economy, as we have seen. We will have to shift our effort to quite different technologies, those of recycling, low resource use, and the offsetting of pollution effects. This by itself means the building up of whole new industries, a development of the same type as but on a larger scale than the growth of the computer and information-processing industry in the last decades. And in addition, the existing industries will have to transform their production pattern in important ways to meet the new requirements of resource utilization and pollution control. And all this will have to be done under public direction in a way that earlier transformations were not.

Will we be able to use this opportunity to disperse the new technologies and industries more evenly, so that all regions have some comparable part in their development? In a way, this is a much more hopeful prospect than that of dispersing an already developed industry by moving an extra branch plant out to a neglected area;

for this kind of development runs against an existing grain and is usually accomplished by lavish public bribes which turn out to be bad investments.

In the end the crucial question may be whether the will is there in the rich heartland of the country to back such a policy of dispersal. And whether this is so will depend on a number of things both intangible and unpredictable.

In a way this sums up our situation. We are in a rare, almost unique position to enter the new age beyond growth. We have not only the advantage of decentralization, but also the very substantial ones of great resource endowment, so that in many cases we can afford to ease ourselves into the new dispensation instead of being brutally hurled into it; of wide open spaces which make at least our pollution limits less immediately pressing than those of other countries, of great wealth per head in capital and technical know-how, so that we could ourselves design and effect many of the new industries and technologies which we require. We are in a relatively favoured international position.

Apart from the too great economic leverage which the United States has over us (admittedly not an inconsiderable factor) our principal obstacle to reacting in a timely and creative way to the coming crisis is an internal one. Canadians are still deeply wedded to the consumer society, and at the same time very uncertain of their own powers to pioneer a new economic mode of life. The consumer society itself is seen as largely an American creation from which we have benefitted by our integration into the American economy.

This integration tends to paralyse our will all the more in that it is piecemeal. Provincial governments agree to sell off various natural resources to multinational corporations, often on bad terms even for themselves, all too frequently on terms which further reduce our future freedom to respond intelligently as a society to the coming era of scarcity. When this mood is on them, provincial governments and electorates want to block any common initiatives towards a new conserving policy, and they do this in the name of development, through which they see their only conceivably economic salvation.

And this could be our fate. We could be incapable of creating a new structure to meet the new predicament, because we lack the will and above all the common will to do so. We could be hamstrung by what is potentially our greatest strength, our regional diversity. So that as pressures mount we could be thrown into a scramble for survival, in which some regions respond to the world's growing hunger for resources by selling them fast at astronomical prices, perhaps investing the proceeds in traditional technologies which won't be sustainable when the resources are gone (what good is a petrochemical plant if we burn all our oil for fuel?), while others cope with mounting scarcity by costly imports. The image of the sinking liner comes again irresistibly to mind.

Perhaps any sober prophet of the future would have to pick this gloomy prospect as the most likely one. But the compulsive optimist in me sees signs of another trend. There also are in Canada: a mounting concern about our economic integration into the United States; a very ill-defined but potentially powerful feeling about the land, particularly the North, and a sense that it is ecologically threatened; a growing resistance to resource management (or mismanagement) by the multinationals, and a sense

that it is not in our interest; a growing desire not to go the same way as the United States towards the ultimate of bigness and mobility, and the sacrifice of the past to the future. Some of these trends I may have imagined, and some I have exaggerated, but something like them is there.

The question is whether these diverse sentiments and aspirations—some of them hard-headed perceptions of interest, others which feed on our sense of identity and the way this is sustained by the past and what surrounds us (aspirations which can all too easily run into conflict)—can be brought together into a common objective, united in the project of an alternate society. This is by no means inevitable, but I do not believe it is impossible. But it will take a number of things, including two which are equally hard to produce to order; good luck and creative political leadership.

In the meantime, while the issue of the future society beyond growth still cannot be posed at the centre of our political life, we can nevertheless make partial gains. Any setback to the heedless and reckless development of our natural resources for export, any successful measure to safeguard the environment, any shift in our priorities towards the universal provision of a decent normal standard of life, puts us in a marginally better posture to face the coming transition. Perhaps the big difference, whether we respond creatively as a free society, will be determined by a number of small decisions, some of which we can make today.

Questions for Discussion

1   Is Taylor correct that a successful transition to a steady state would require a strong sense of community, which may not be prevalent in our current individualist society?

2   To what extent is our society's understanding of "the good life" tied to an assumption of continuous exponential growth? Does concern for the environment require us to change this understanding?

The Sinking Ark

N. Myers

Human beings have been responsible, directly or indirectly, for the extinction of many different species of plants and animals. In the following selection, Myers discusses the relationship between consumerism and such extinctions, and argues that environmental issues must be understood within a network of interdependent global problems. In particular, the relationship between the developed nations and the developing nations must be changed if we are to put an end to the extinction of species which is spiralling out of control.

*   *   *

Ask a man in the street what he thinks of the problems of disappearing species, and he may well reply that it would be a pity if the tiger or the blue whale disappeared. But he may add that it would be no big deal, not as compared with crises of energy, population, food and pollution—the "real problems." In other words, he cares about disappearing species, but he cares about many other things more: he simply does not see it as a critical issue. If the tiger were to go extinct tonight, the sun would still come up tomorrow morning.

In point of fact, by tomorrow morning we shall almost certainly have one less species on Planet Earth than we had this morning. It will not be a charismatic creature like the tiger. It could well be an obscure insect in the depths of some remote rainforest. It may even be a creature that nobody has ever heard of. A unique form of life will have been driven from the face of the earth for ever.

Equally likely is that by the end of the century we shall have lost 1 million species, possibly many more. Except for the barest handful, they will have been eliminated through the hand of man.

Extinction Rates

Animal forms that have been documented and recognized as under threat of extinction now amount to over 1000. These are creatures we hear much about—the tiger and the blue whale, the giant panda and the whooping crane, the orangutan and the cheetah. Yet even though 1000 is a shockingly large number, this is only a fractionally small part of the problem. Far more important are those many species that have not even been identified by science, let alone classified as threatened. Among the plant kingdom, these could number 25,000, while among animals, notably insects, the total could run to hundreds of thousands....

...By the time human communities establish ecologically sound life-styles, the fallout of species could total several million. This would amount to a biological débâcle greater than all mass extinctions of the geological past put together.

Loss to Society

We face, then, the imminent elimination of a good share of the planetary spectrum of species that have shared the common earth-home with man for millenia, but are now to be denied living space during a phase of a mere few decades. This extinction spasm would amount to an irreversible loss of unique resources. Earth is currently afflicted with other forms of environmental degradation, but, from the standpoint of permanent despoilation of the planet, no other form is anywhere so significant as the fallout of species. When water bodies are fouled and the atmosphere is treated as a garbage can, we can always clean up the pollution. Species extinction is final. Moreover, the impoverishment of life on earth falls not only on present society, but on all generations to come.

In scores of ways, the impoverishment affects everyday living right now. All around the world, people increasingly consume food, take medicines and employ industrial materials that owe their production to genetic resources and other startpoint materials of animals and plants. These pragmatic purposes served by species are numerous and growing. Given the needs of the future, species can be reckoned among society's most valuable raw materials. To consider the consequences of devastating a single biome, the tropical moist forests: elimination of these forests, with their exceptional concentration of species, would undermine the prospects for modernized agriculture, with repercussions for the capacity of the world to feed itself. It could set back the campaign against cancer by years. Perhaps worst of all, it would eliminate one of our best bets for resolving the energy crisis: as technology develops ways to utilize the vast amount of solar energy stored in tropical-forest plants each day, these forests could generate as much energy, in the form of methanol and other fuels, as almost half the world's energy consumption from all sources in 1970. Moreover, this energy source need never run dry like an oil well, since it can replenish itself in perpetuity.

Any reduction in the diversity of resources, including the earth's spectrum of species, narrows society's scope to respond to new problems and opportunities. To the extent that we cannot be certain what needs may arise in the future, it makes sense to keep our options open (provided that a strategy of that sort does not unduly conflict with other major purposes of society). This rationale for conservation applies to the planet's stock of species more than to virtually any other category of natural resources.

The situation has been well stated by Dr. Tom Lovejoy of the World Wildlife Fund:

> If we were preparing for a new Dark Age, and could take only a limited number of books into the monasteries for the duration, we might have to determine which single branch of knowledge would have the greatest survival value for us. The outstanding candidate would be biology, including its applied form such as medicine, agriculture, forestry and fisheries. Yet we are doing just the contrary, by busily throwing out the biology books before they have been written.

Many other biologists—switched-on scientists, not "case-hardened eco-nuts"—believe that man is permanently altering the course of evolution, and altering it for the worse. The result will be a grossly impoverished version of life's diversity on earth, from which the process of evolution will be unlikely to recover for many millions of years. And it is not going too far to say that, by eliminating an appreciable portion of earth's stock of species, humanity might be destroying life that just might save its own.

Species Conservation and Economic Advancement

There is another major dimension to the problem, the relationship between conservation of species and economic advancement for human communities.

As indicated, the prime threat to the species lies with loss of habitat. Loss of habitat occurs mainly through economic exploitation of natural environments. Natural environments are exploited mainly to satisfy consumer demand for numerous products. The upshot is that species are now rarely driven extinct through the activities of a few persons with direct and deliberate intent to kill wild creatures. They are eliminated through the activities of many millions of people, who are unaware of the "spill-over" consequences of their consumerist lifestyles.

This means that species depletion can occur through a diffuse and insidious process. An American is prohibited by law from shooting a snowy egret, but, by his consumerist lifestyle, he can stimulate others to drain a marsh (for croplands, highways, housing) and thereby eliminate the food supply for a whole colony of egrets. A

recent advertisement by a utility corporation in the United States asserted that "Something we do today will touch your life," implying that its activities were so far-reaching that, whether the citizen was aware or not, his daily routine would be somehow affected by the corporation's multifaceted enterprise. In similar fashion, something the citizen does each day is likely to bear on the survival prospects of species. He may have no wanton or destructive intent toward wildlife. On the contrary, he may send off a regular donation to a conservation organization. But what he contributes with his right hand he may take away with his half-dozen left hands. His desire to be a consumer as well as conservationist leads him into a Jekyll-and-Hyde role. Unwitting and unmalicious as this role might be, it becomes even more significant and pervasive every day.

Equally important, the impact of a consumerist lifestyle is not confined to the home country of the fat-cat citizen. Increasingly the consequences extend to lands around the back of the earth. Rich-world communities of the temperate zones, containing one-fifth of earth's population, account for four-fifths of raw materials traded through international markets. Many of these materials derive from the tropical zone, which harbors around three-quarters of all species on earth. The extraction of these materials causes disturbance of natural environments. Thus affluent sectors of the global village are responsible—unknowingly for sure, but effectively nonetheless—for disruption of myriad species' habitats in lands far distant from their own. The connoisseur who seeks out a specialty-import store in New York or Paris or Tokyo, with a view to purchasing some much-sought-after rosewood from Brazil, may be contributing to the destruction of the last forest habitat of an Amazon monkey. Few factors of the conservation scene are likely to grow so consequential in years ahead as this one of economic-ecologic linkages among the global community.

True, citizens of tropical developing countries play their part in disruption of natural environments. It is in these countries that most of the projected expansion of human numbers will take place, 85 percent of the extra 2 billion people that are likely to be added to the present world population of 4 billion by the end of the century. Of at least as much consequence as the outburst in human numbers is the outburst in human aspirations, supported by expanding technology. It is the combination of these two factors that will precipitate a transformation of most natural environments throughout the tropics. Equally to the point, impoverished citizens of developing nations tend to have more pressing concerns than conservation of species. All too often, it is as much as they can do to stay alive themselves, let alone to keep wild creatures in being.

Plainly, there is a lot of difference between the consumerdom of the world's poor majority and of the world's rich minority. For most citizens of developing countries, there is little doubt that more food available, through cultivation of virgin territories (including forests, grasslands, wetlands, etc.), would increase their levels of nutrition, just as more industrial products available would ease their struggle for existence in many ways. It is equally likely that the same cannot be said for citizens of the advanced world: additional food or material goods do not necessarily lead to any advance in their quality of life. The demand for products of every kind on the part of the

1 billion citizens of affluent nations—the most consummate consumers the world has ever known, many making Croesus and Louis XIV look like paupers by comparison—contributes a disproportionate share to the disruption of natural environments around the earth.

For example, the depletion of tropical moist forests stems in part from market demand on the part of affluent nations for hardwoods and other specialist timbers from Southeast Asia, Amazonia and West/Central Africa. In addition, the disruptive harvesting of tropical timber is often conducted by multinational corporations that supply the capital, technology and skills without which developing countries could not exploit their forest stocks at unsustainable rates. Such is the role of Georgia Pacific and Weyerhauser from the United States, Mitsubishi and Sumitomo from Japan and Bruyzneel and Borregaard fom Europe. Similarly, the forests of Central America are being felled to make way for artificial pasture-lands, in order to grow more beef. But the extra meat, instead of going into the stomachs of local citizens, makes its way to the United States, where it supplies the hamburger trade and other fast-food business. This foreign beef is cheaper than similar-grade beef from within the United States—and the American consumer, looking for a hamburger of best quality at cheapest price, is not aware of the spillover consequences of his actions. So whose hand is on the chainsaw?

A further source of destruction in tropical forests is the shifting cultivator. There are at least 140 million of these people, subsistence peasants who often have nowhere to sink a digging hoe except the virgin territories of primeval forests. Theirs is a form of agriculture that tends, by its very nature, to be inefficient: it is highly wasteful of forestlands.

It could be made intensive rather than extensive, and thus relieve the pressure on virgin forests, through the perquisites of modern agriculture, notably fertilizer to make a crop patch productive year after year. But since the OPEC price hike in 1973, the cost of petroleum-based fertilizer has been driven sky-high—and has been kept sky-high through inflated demand on the part of affluent nations (Americans and Europeans use as much fertilizer on their gardens, golf courses and cemeteries as is used by all the shifting cultivators of tropical forestlands). As long as the price of fertilizer remains beyond the reach of subsistence peasants, there is less prospect that they will change their agricultural practices. Part of the responsibility for this situation lies with the OPEC cartel, part with the excessively consumerist communities of the advanced world.

An Interdependent Global Community

Looked at this way, the problem of declining tropical forests can be seen to be intimately related to other major issues of an interdependent global community: food, population, energy, plus several other problems that confront society at large. It is difficult to make progress on all the others at the same time. This aspect of the plight of tropical forests—the inter-relatedness of problems—applies to the problem of disappearing species in general.

Similarly, the advanced-nation citizen can hardly support conservation of species while resisting better trade-and-aid relationships with developing nations. The decline of tropical forests could be slowed through a trade cartel of Tropical Timber Exporting Countries. If the countries in question could jack up the price of their hardwood exports, they could earn more foreign exchange from export of less timber. For importer countries of the developed world, the effect of this move would be a jump in the price of fine furniture, specialist panelling and other components of better housing. Would an affluent-world citizen respond with a cry of protest about inflation, or with a sigh of relief at improved prospects for tropical forests? For a Third-World citizen, it is difficult to see how a conservationist can be concerned with the International Union for Conservation of Nature and Natural Resources, without being equally concerned with the New International Economic Order.

A second example concerns paperpulp. There could soon be a shortage of paperpulp to match present shortages of fuel and food. The deficit could be made good through more intensive exploration of North American forests, or through more extensive exploitation of tropical forests—both of which alternatives might prompt outcries from environmental groups. A third alternative would be for developed-world citizens, who account for five-sixths of all paperpulp consumed world-wide, to make do with inadequate supplies, in which case the cost of newsprint would rise sharply. So perhaps a definition of a conservationist could be a person who applauds when he finds that his daily newspaper has once again gone up in price.

In accord with this view of the situation, this book emphasizes that problems of threatened species and disappearing forests can be realistically viewed only within a framework of relationships between the developed world and the developing world.

A prime conservation need everywhere, and especially in tropical regions, is for countries to set aside representative examples of their ecosystems in order to protect their stocks of species. In other words, to expand their present networks of parks, such as they are, by establishing systems of protected areas. However, many developing countries are in no position to designate large tracts of their territory as "off limits" to development. (Through their present efforts to safeguard the bulk of the earth's species, they in effect subsidize the rest of the global community.) If emergent regions of the tropics are to help protect the global heritage of species for the community at large, the community should see to it that their development prospects are not thereby penalized. In short, ways must be devised to make conservation programs economically acceptable and politically palatable for developing nations.

How Far Should We Go to Save Species?

Just as the whooping crane is not worth more than a mere fraction of the United States' GNP to save it, so the preservation of species in all parts of the planet, and especially in tropical regions, needs to be considered within a comprehensive context of human well-being. Anthropocentric as this approach may appear, it reflects the way the world works: few people would be willing to swap mankind, a single species, for fishkind with its thousands of species.

So the central issue is not "Let's save the species, come what may." Rather we should ask whose needs are served by conservation of species, and at what cost to whose opportunities for a better life in other ways. Instead of seeking to conserve species as an over-riding objective, we should do as much as we can within a framework of trying to enhance long-term human welfare in all manner of directions.

As we have seen, people already make "choices" concerning species. Regrettably they do not make deliberate choices after careful consideration of the alternatives. Rich and poor alike, they unconsciously contribute to the decline of the species, in dozens of ways each day. Not that they have malign intentions toward wild creatures. According to a 1976 Gallup Poll, most people would like to see more done to conserve wildlife and threatened species— 87 percent in the United States, 89 percent in Western Europe, 85 percent in Japan, 75 percent in Africa, and 94 percent in Latin America (though only 46 percent in crowded India). Subsistence communities of the developing world have limited scope to change the choice they implicitly make through their ways of making a living. Rich-world people, by contrast, have more room to maneuver, and could switch to a stronger expression of their commitment in favor of species. Meantime, through their commitment to extreme consumerism, they in effect express the view that they can do without the orangutan and the cheetah and many other species—and their descendants, for all ages to come, can likewise do without them. In theory, they would like the orangutan and the cheetah to survive in the wild, but in practice they like many other things more. However unwittingly, that is the way they are making their choice right now.

Fortunately, affluent-world citizens will have plenty of scope to make a fresh choice. They may find it turns out to be no easy choice. If they truly wish to allow living space for millions of species that existed on the planet before man got on his hind legs, they will find that entails not only a soft-hearted feeling in support of wildlife, but a hard-nosed commitment to attempt new lifestyles. While they shed a tear over the demise of tropical moist forests with their array of species, they might go easy on the Kleenex....

How Species Arrive and Disappear

The evolutionary process that throws off new species, speciation, has been under way virtually since life first appeared. As a species encounters fresh environments, brought about by factors such as climatic change, it adapts, and so alters in different ways in different parts of its range. Eventually a new form becomes differentiated enough to rank as a new species. The parent form, if unable to fit in with changed circumstances, disappears, while the genetic material persists, diversified and enriched.

By contrast, some species are not so capable at the process of adaptation and differentiation. This applies especially to those that have become so specialized in their lifestyles that they cannot cope with transformed environments. They fade away, and their distinctive genetic material is lost forever.

Since life began about 3.5 billion years ago, vast amounts of unique genetic formulations have been eliminated. The total number of species that is believed to have existed is put at somewhere between 100 and 250 million,[1] which means that the present stock of species, estimated at 5-10 million, represents between 2 and 10 percent of all species that have ever lived on earth. It also means that extinction is not

only a biological reality, but it is a frequent phenomenon under natural circumstances. Moreover, whereas the process of speciation is limited by the rate of genetic divergence, and so generally throws up a new species only over periods of thousands or millions of years, the process of extinction is not limited by any such constraint, and can occur, through man's agency, within just a year or two, even less.

How many species have existed at each stage of evolutionary history is only roughly known. The fossil record is so limited that it is a pitiful reflection of past life. But it now appears likely that, after a gas cloud solidified into the present planet approximately 6 billion years ago, earth remained lifeless for another 2.5 billion years. When life eventually appeared, it left virtually no trace of its existence for a long time, except for micro-fossils of early algae such as have been found in Swaziland. Not until about 1500 million years ago did nuclear-celled organisms appear, and not until about 700 million years ago, following an outburst of evolutionary activity during the Cambrian period, did most modern phyla become recognizable. This array of species diversified only gradually, or even remained pretty constant, for the best part of 400 million years, until it crashed spectacularly with the extinction of many marine organisms towards the end of the Permian period. Thereafter the abundance and variety of species steadily increased, until a further mass extinction during the late Cretaceous period, 70 million years ago, put an end to around one-quarter of all families, including the dinosaurs and their kin. Since that time the trend has been generally towards ever-greater diversity of species. In short, the evolutionary record does not show a steady upward climb in earth's total of species, rather a series of step-wise increases. The current stock of species is reckoned to be 10 or even 20 times larger than the stock of species inhabiting the Paleozoic seas before the Permian crash.[2]

During the past few million years, however, extinction rates seem to have speeded up. At the time of the late Pliocene, some 5 million years ago, there may have been one-third more bird species than today.[3] During the early Pleistocene, around 3 million years ago, a bird species probably had an average life expectancy of 1.5 million years. This span progressively contracted until, by the end of the Pleistocene, it could have amounted to only 40,000 years.[4] Equally likely is that the pace of speciation has probably speeded up, and full speciation among certain classes of birds could now be far more rapid than the quarter of a million years once believed necessary. Indeed, it conceivably takes place in as little as 15,000 or even 10,000 years.

The house sparrow, introduced into North America in the 1850s, has thrown off a number of clear subspecies during the course of only 110-130 generations.[5] In certain circumstances, for instance when new variations are radiating from an unspecified ancestor, a new plant species can evolve, it is estimated, in only 50-100 generations.[6] (Experiments with fruit flies, under special laboratory conditions that serve to "force the pace," show that speciation can occur in less than a dozen generations.) Among mammals, with generally slower breeding rates than birds, the average life expectancy for a species could now be, under natural circumstances, around half a million years.

Man's Impact on Extinction Rates

More recently, extinction has stemmed increasingly from the hand of man. For much of his last 50,000 years as a hunter-gatherer, primitive man, perhaps in conjunction with climatic upheavals, proved himself capable of eliminating species through over-hunting and through habitat modification by means of fire.[7] In the main, the process was relatively rare and gradual. By around the year A.D. 1600, however, man became able, through advancing technology, to disrupt extensive environments ever more rapidly, and to employ modern weapons to over-hunt animals to extinction in just a few years. It is from this recent watershed stage that man's impact can no longer be considered on a par with "natural processes" that lead to extinction. Of course, this is not to say that natural extinction is not still taking place. The Labrador duck appears to have disappeared through no discernible fault of man, while the white-nosed saki of Brazil has been losing more of its range to other Amazon monkeys than to man.

To reduce the history of species on earth to manageable proportions, suppose the whole existence of the planet is compressed into a single year. Conditions suitable for life do not develop for certain until May, and plants and animals do not become abundant (mostly in the seas) until the end of October. In mid-December, dinosaurs and other reptiles dominate the scene. Mammals, with hairy covering and suckling their young, appear in large numbers only a little before Christmas. On New Year's Eve, at about five minutes to midnight, man emerges. Of these few moments of man's existence, recorded history represents about the time the clock takes to strike twelve. The period since A.D. 1600, when man-induced extinctions have rapidly increased, amounts to 3 seconds, and the quarter-century just begun, when the fallout of species looks likely to be far greater than all mass extinctions of the past put together, takes one-eighth of a second—a twinkling of an eye in evolutionary times.

It is sometimes suggested that, as some sort of compensation for the outburst of extinctions now under way, two evolutionary processes may gather pace, one a natural process and the other contrived by man. The argument in support of the first process is that as species disappear, niches, or "ecological living space," will open up for newly emerging species to occupy. In fact so many vacant niches could appear that they might well stimulate a spurt of speciation. Sound as this argument is in principle, it is a non-starter in practice. The present process of extinction, vastly speeded up, will not lead to anything near a similarly speeded up process of speciation. As natural environments become degraded under man's influence, there will be few areas with enough ecological diversity to encourage many new species to emerge. Furthermore, as natural environments become homogenized, there will be little geographical isolation of populations, and hence little reproductive isolation of genetic reservoirs, to enable speciation to continue as it would under less disturbed conditions.

The second argument deals with man-contrived speciation. Opportunities are now emerging to synthesize genes in the laboratory by combining segments of the master molecule of life, DNA, from different species. This opens the way to creation of forms of life distinct from any that now exist. Regrettably this argument too is not valid. Producing a new species will be costly in the extreme, far more so than con-serving the gene pool of virtually any species in its natural habitats. Moreover, a synthetic species may not be adapted to conditions outside the laboratory, in which case it may either quickly be eliminated or may encounter no natural controls to restrict its increase.

Meantime, man's activities, especially his mis-use and over-use of natural environments, continue to drive species extinct at an increasing rate. From A.D. 1600 to 1900, man was certainly accounting for one species every 4 years. From the year 1900 onwards, the rate increased to an average of around one per year. These figures refer, however, almost entirely to mammals and birds; and they are limited to species which man knows have existed and which man knows have disappeared. When we consider the other 99 percent of earth's stock of species, the picture appears far different from a "mere" one species per year.

...[I]t is likely that during the last quarter of this century we shall witness an extinction spasm accounting for 1 million species. The total fallout could turn out to be lower; it could also, and more probably, turn out to be higher. Taking 1 million as a "reasonable working figure," this means an average of over 100 extinctions per day. The rate of fallout will increase as habitat disruption grows worse, i.e. toward the end of the period. Already, however, the process is well underway. In the region where rainforest destruction is most advanced, Southeast Asia, we can expect a wave of extinctions by the mid-1980s. Thus it is not unrealistic—in fact, probably optimistic—to say that we are losing one species per day right now. Within another decade, we could be losing one every hour.

Notes

1 Brodkorb, B.P., 1971, Origin and evolution of birds, *Avian Biology* 1:19-55.

2 Gould, S.J., 1975, Diversity through time, *Natural History* 84 (8):24-32: Stebbins, G.L., 1971, *Processes of Organic Evolution*, Prentice-Hall, Englewood Cliffs, New Jersey.

3 Fisher, J. and Peterson, R.J., 1964, *The World of Birds*, Macdonald Publishers, London.

4 Moreau, R.E., 1966, *The Bird Faunas of Africa and Its Islands*, Academic Press, New York.

5 Johnstone, R.F. and Selander, R.K., 1971, Evolution in the house sparrow, *Evolution* 25:1-28.

6 Huxley, A., 1974, *Plant and Planet*, Allen Lane Publisher, London.

7 Martin, P.S. and Wright, H.E. (editors), 1967, *Pleistocene Extinctions: The Search for a Cause*, Yale University Press, New Haven, Connecticut.

Questions for Discussion

1 Why should we be concerned with the loss of species, as opposed to limiting our concern to individual sentient beings? Is this a *moral* concern, or is it of some other type (e.g. aesthetic)? Does it matter that extinction is, to some extent, a "natural" phenomenon?

2 Myers claims that the possible uses of genetic materials for medicines, food, and industrial purposes make them among our most valuable resources. How should we balance such potential benefits against more certain immediate benefits of land-use, etc?

3 How much limitation on consumerism should be imposed in the name of environmental concern? If some such change is desirable, how should it be brought about?

Future Generations: The Non-Identity Problem

D. Parfit

One of the major arguments put forward for preserving the environment now is that we should be concerned for future generations. In the following selection, Parfit points out that the decisions we make today will affect not only the quality of life of people in the future, but also who those people will be. He considers the possibility that no future person will be harmed by our actions, since those particular people would not even have existed if not for our actions. This puzzling observation makes it harder to specify what is wrong in exploiting the environment for present-day well-being at the expense of the future.

*   *   *

How Lowering the Quality of Life Might Be Worse for No One

Suppose that we are choosing between two social or economic policies. And suppose that, on one of the two policies, the standard of living would be slightly higher over the next century. This effect implies another. It is not true that, whichever policy we choose, the same particular people will exist in the further future. Given the effects of two such policies on the details of our lives, it would increasingly over time be true that, on the different policies, people married different people. And, even in the same marriages, the children would increasingly over time be conceived at different times. As I have argued, children conceived more than a month earlier or later would in fact be different children. Since the choice between our two policies would affect the timing of later conceptions, some of the people who are later born would owe their existence to our choice of one of the two policies. If we had chosen the other policy, these particular people would never have existed. And the proportion of those later born who owe their existence to our choice would, like ripples in a pool, steadily grow. We can plausibly assume that, after three centuries, there would be no one living in our community who would have been born whichever policy we chose. (It may help to think about this question: how many of us could truly claim, 'Even if railways and motor cars had never been invented, I would still have been born'?)

How does this produce a problem? Consider

Depletion. As a community, we must choose whether to deplete or conserve certain kinds of resources. If we choose Depletion, the quality of life over the next three centuries would be slightly higher than it would have been if we had chosen Conservation. But it would later, for many centuries, be much lower than it would have been if we had chosen Conservation. This would be because, at the start of this period, people would have to find alternatives for the resources that we had depleted. It is worth distinguishing two versions of this case. The effects of the different policies would be as shown below.

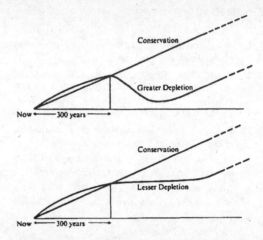

We could never know, in such detail, that these would be the effects of two policies. But this is no objection to this case. Similar effects would sometimes be predictable. Nor does it matter that this imagined case is artificially simple. The case raises the questions which arise in actual cases.

Suppose that we choose Depletion, and that this has either of the two effects shown in my diagram. Is our choice worse for anyone?

Because we chose Depletion, millions of people have, for several centuries, a much lower quality of life. This quality of life is much lower, not than it is now, but than it would have been if we had chosen Conservation. These people's lives are worth living; and, if we had chosen Conservation, these particular people would never have existed. Suppose that we do not believe that causing to exist can benefit. We should ask, 'If particular people live lives that are worth living, is this worse for these people than if they had never existed?' Our answer must be No. Suppose next that we believe that causing to exist can benefit. Since these future people's lives will be worth living, and they would never have existed if we had chosen Conservation, our choice of Depletion is not only not worse for these people: it *benefits* them.

On both answers, our choice will not be worse for these future people. Moreover, when we understand the case, we know that this is true. We know that, even if it greatly lowers the quality of life for several centuries, our choice will not be worse for anyone who ever lives.

Does this make a moral difference? There are three views. It might make all the difference, or some difference, or no difference. There might be no objection to our choice, or some objection, or the objection may be just as strong.

Some believe that *what is bad must be bad for someone*. On this view, there is no objection to our choice. Since it will be bad for no one, our choice cannot have a bad effect. The great lowering of the quality of life provides no moral reason not to choose Depletion.

Certain writers accept this conclusion.[1] But it is very implausible. Before we consider cases of this kind, we may accept the view that what is bad must be bad for someone. But the case of Depletion shows, I believe, that we must reject this view. The great lowering of the quality of life must provide *some* moral reason not to choose Depletion. This is believed by most of those who consider cases of this kind.

If this is what we believe, we should ask two questions:

(1) What is the moral reason not to choose Depletion?

(2) Does it make a moral difference that this lowering of the quality of life will be worse for no one? Would this effect be *worse*, having greater moral weight, it it *was* worse for particular people?

Our need to answer (1), and other similar questions, I call the Non-Identity Problem. This problem arises because the identities of people in the further future can be very easily affected. Some people believe that this problem is a mere quibble. This reaction is unjustified. The problem arises because of superficial facts about our reproductive system. But, though it arises in a superficial way, it is a real problem. When we are choosing between two social and economic policies, of the kind that I described, it is *not true* that, in the further future, the same people will exist whatever we choose. It is therefore *not true* that a choice like Depletion will be against the interests of future people. We cannot dismiss this problem with the pretence that this *is* true....

Causing Predictable Catastrophes in the Further Future

...Consider

The Risky Policy. As a community, we must choose between two energy policies. Both would be completely safe for at least three centuries, but one would have certain risks in the further future. This policy involves the burial of nuclear waste in areas where, in the next few centuries, there is no risk of an earthquake. But since this waste will remain radioactive for thousands of years, there will be risks in the distant future. If we choose this Risky Policy, the standard of living would be somewhat higher over the next century. We do choose this policy. As a result, there is a catastrophe many centuries later. Because of geological changes to the Earth's surface, an earthquake releases radiation, which kills thousands of people. Though they are killed by this catastrophe, these people will have had lives that are worth living. We can assume that this radiation affects only people who are not yet conceived, and that its effect is to give these people an incurable disease that will kill them at about the age of 40. This disease will have no effects before it kills.

Our choice between these two policies will affect the details of the lives that are later lived. In the way explained above, our choice will therefore affect no one who will later live. After many centuries there would be no one living in our community who, whichever policy we chose, would have been born. Because we chose the Risky Policy, thousands of people are later killed. But if we had never chosen the alternative Safe Policy, these particular people would never have existed. Different people would have existed in their place. Is our choice of the Risky Policy worse for anyone?

We should ask, 'If people live lives that are worth living, even though they are killed by some catastrophe, is this worse for these people than if they had never existed?' Our answer must be No. Though it causes a predictable catastrophe, our choice of the Risky Policy will be worse for no one.

Some may claim that our choice of Depletion does not have a bad effect. This cannot be claimed about our choice of the Risky Policy. Since this choice causes a catastrophe, it clearly has a bad effect. But our choice will not be bad for, or worse for, any of the people who later live. This case forces us to reject the view that a choice cannot have a bad effect if this choice will be bad for no one.

In this case, the Non-Identity Problem may seem easier to solve. Though our choice is not worse for the people struck by the catastrophe, it might be claimed that we harm these people. And the appeal to people's rights may here succeed.

We can deserve to be blamed for harming others, even when this is not worse for them. Suppose that I drive carelessly, and in the resulting crash cause you to lose a leg. One year later, war breaks out. If you had not lost this leg, you would have been conscripted, and killed. My careless driving therefore saves your life. But I am still morally to blame.

This case reminds us that, in assigning blame, we must consider not actual but predictable effects. I knew that my careless driving might harm others, but I could not know that it would in fact save your life. This distinction might apply to our choice of the Risky Policy. Suppose we know that, if we choose this policy, this may in the distant future cause many accidental deaths. But we have overlooked the Non-Identity Problem. We mistakenly believe that, whichever policy we choose, the very same people will later live. We therefore believe that our choice of the Risky Policy may be very greatly against the interests of some future people. If we believe this, our choice can be criticized. We can deserve blame for doing what we *believe* may be greatly against the interests of other people. This criticism stands even if our belief is false—just as I am as much to blame even if my careless driving will in fact save your life.

Suppose that we cannot find Theory X [*Ed. Note:* Parfit uses "Theory X" to refer to the theory about future people which we ought to accept, whatever that may turn out to be.], or that X seems less plausible than the objection to doing what may be greatly against the interests of other people. It may then be better if we conceal the Non-Identity Problem from those who will decide whether we increase our use of nuclear energy. It may be better if these people believe falsely that such a policy may, by causing a catastrophe, be greatly against the interests of some of those who will live in the distant future. If these people have this false belief, they may be more likely to reach the right conclusions.

We have lost this false belief. We realize that, if we choose the Risky Policy, our choice will *not* be worse for those people whom the catastrophe later kills. Note that this is not a lucky guess. It is not like predicting that, if I cause you to lose a leg, this will later save you from death in the trenches. We know that, if we choose the Risky Policy, this may in the distant future cause many people to be killed. But we also know that, if we had chosen the Safe Policy, the people who are killed would never have been born. Since these people's lives will be worth living, we *know* that our choice will not be worse for them.

If we know this, we cannot be compared to a careless driver. What is the objection to our choice? Can it be wrong to harm others, when we know that our act will not be worse for people harmed? This might be wrong if we could have asked these people for their consent, but have failed to do so. By failing to ask these people for their consent, we infringe their autonomy. But this cannot be the objection to our choice of the Risky Policy. Since we could not possibly communicate with the people living many centuries from now, we cannot ask for their consent.

When we cannot ask for someone's consent, we should ask instead whether this person would later regret what we are doing. Would the people who are later killed regret our choice of the Risky Policy? Let us suppose that these people know all of the facts. From an early age they know that, because of the release of radiation, they have an incurable disease that

will kill them at about the age of 40. They also know that, if we had chosen the Safe Policy, they would never have been born. These people would regret the fact that they will die young. But, since their lives are worth living, they would not regret the fact that they were ever born. They would therefore not regret our choice of the Risky Policy.

Can it be wrong to harm others, when we know *both* that if the people harmed knew about our act, they would not regret this act, *and* that our act will not be worse for these people than anything else that we could have done? How might we know that, though we are harming someone, our act will not be worse for this person? There are at least two kinds of case:

(1) Though we are harming someone, we may also know that we are giving to this person some fully compensating benefit. We could not know this unless the benefit would clearly outweigh the harm. But, if this is so, what we are doing will be better for this person. In this kind of case, if we are also not infringing this person's autonomy, there is no objection to our act. There is no objection to our harming someone when we know both that this person will have no regrets, and that our act will be clearly better for this person. In English Law, surgery was once regarded as justifiable grievous bodily harm. As I argued [elsewhere], we should revise the ordinary use of the word 'harm.' If what we are doing will not be worse for some other person, or will even be better for this person, we are not, in a morally relevant sense, harming this person.

If we assume that causing to exist can benefit, our choice of the Risky Policy is, in its effects on those killed, like the case of the surgeon. Though our choice causes these people to be killed, since it also causes them to exist with a life worth living, it gives them a benefit that outweighs this harm. The objection to our choice cannot be that it harms these people.

We may instead assume that causing to exist cannot benefit. On this assumption, our choice of the Risky Policy does not give to the people whom it kills some fully compensating benefit. Our choice is not *better* for these people. It is merely *not worse* for them.

(2) There is another kind of case in which we can know that, though we are harming someone on the ordinary use of 'harm,' this will not be worse for this person. These are the cases that involve overdetermination. In these cases we know that, if we do not harm someone, this person will be harmed at least as much in some other way. Suppose that someone is trapped in a wreck and about to be burnt to death. This person asks us to shoot him, so that he does not die painfully. If we kill this person we are not, in a morally relevant sense, harming him.

Such a case cannot show that there is no objection to our choice of the Risky Policy, since it is not relevantly similar. If the catastrophe did not occur, the people killed would have lived for many more years. There is a quite different reason why our choice of the Risky Policy is not worse for these people.

Could there be a case in which we kill some existing person, knowing what we know when we choose the Risky Policy? We must know (*a*) that this person will learn but not regret the fact that we have done something that will cause him to be killed. And we must know (*b*) that, though this person would otherwise have lived a normal life for many more years, causing

him to be killed will be neither better nor worse for him. ((*b*) is what we know about the effects of our choice of the Risky Policy, if we assume that, in doing what is a necessary part of the cause of the existence of the people killed by the catastrophe, we cannot be benefiting these people.)

Suppose that we kill some existing person, who would otherwise have lived a normal life for many more years. In such a case, we could not *know* that (*b*) is true. Even if living for these many years would be neither better nor worse for this person, this could never be predicted. There cannot be a case where we kill some existing person, knowing what we know when we choose the Risky Policy. A case that is relevantly similar must involve causing someone to be killed who, if we had acted otherwise, would never have existed.

Compare these two cases:

Jane's Choice. Jane has a congenital disease, that will kill her painlessly at about the age of 40. This disease has no effects before it kills. Jane knows that, if she has a child, it will have this same disease. Suppose that she can also assume the following. Like herself, her child would have a life that is worth living. There are no children who need to be but have not been adopted. Given the size of the world's population when this case occurs (perhaps in some future century), if Jane has a child, this will not be worse for other people. And, if she does not have this child, she will be unable to raise a child. She cannot persuade someone else to have an extra child, whom she would raise. (These assumptions give us the relevant question.) Knowing these facts, Jane chooses to have a child.

Ruth's Choice. Ruth's situation is just like Jane's, with one exception. Her congenital disease, unlike Jane's, kills only males. If Ruth pays for the new technique of in vitro fertilization, she would be certain to have a daughter whom this disease would not kill. She decides to save this expense, and takes a risk. Unluckily, she has a son, whose inherited disease will kill him at about the age of 40.

Is there a moral objection to Jane's choice? Given the assumptions in the case, this objection would have to appeal to the effect on Jane's child. Her choice will not be worse for this child. Is there an objection to her choice that appeals to this child's rights? Suppose we believe that each person has a right to live a full life. Jane knows that, if she has a child, his right to a full life could not possibly be fulfilled. This may imply that Jane does not violate this right. But the objection could be restated. It could be said, 'It is wrong to cause someone to exist with a right that cannot be fulfilled. This is why Jane acts wrongly.'

Is this a good objection? If I was Jane's child, I would regret the fact that I shall die young. But, since my life is worth living, I would not regret that my mother caused me to exist. And I would deny that her act was wrong because of what it did to me. If I was told that it *was* wrong, because it caused me to exist with a right that cannot be fulfilled, I would *waive* this right.

If Jane's child waives this right, this undermines this objection to her choice. But, though *I* would waive this right, I cannot be certain that, in all such cases, this is what such a child would do. If Jane's child does not waive his right, the appeal to this right may perhaps provide some objection to her choice.

Turn now to Ruth's choice. There is clearly a greater objection to *this* choice. This is because Ruth has a different alternative. If Jane does not have a child, she will not be able to raise a child; and one fewer life will be lived. Ruth's alternative is to pay for the technique that will give her a different child whom her disease will not kill. She chooses to save this expense, knowing that the chance is one in two that her child will be killed by this disease.

Even if there is an objection to Jane's choice, there is a greater objection to Ruth's choice. This objection cannot appeal only to the effects of Ruth's actual child, since these are just like the effects of Jane's choice on Jane's child. The objection to Ruth's choice must appeal in part to the possible effect on a different child who, by paying for the new technique, she could have had. The appeal to this effect is not an appeal to anyone's rights.

Return now to our choice of the Risky Policy. If we choose this policy, this may cause people to exist who will be killed in a catastrophe. We know that our choice would not be worse for these people. But, if there is force in the objection to Jane's choice, this objection would apply to our choice. By choosing the Risky Policy, we may cause people to exist whose right to a full life cannot be fulfilled.

The appeal to these people's rights may provide some objection to our choice. But it cannot provide the whole objection. Our choice is, in one respect, unlike Jane's. Her alternative was to have no child. Our alternative is like Ruth's. If we had chosen the Safe Policy, we would have had different descendants, none of whom would have been killed by released radiation.

The objection to Ruth's choice cannot appeal only to her child's right to a full life. The same is therefore true of the objection to our choice of the Risky Policy. This objection must in part appeal to the effects on the possible people who, if we had chosen differently, would have lived. As before, the appeal to rights cannot wholly solve the

Non-Identity Problem. We must also appeal to a claim like Q, which compares two different sets of possible lives. [*Ed. Note:* Q, or the "Same Number Quality Claim," states that "If in either of the two outcomes the same number of people would ever live, it would be bad if those who live are worse off, or have a lower quality of life, than those who would have lived." Parfit believes that some such principle, widened to include the fact that we can influence the *number* of people who ever live, must be accepted. Nevertheless, he believes there are some serious difficulties with any such principle, which appeals to the well-being of possible people.]

It may be objected: 'When Ruth conceives her child, it inherits the disease that will deny it a full life. Because this child's disease is inherited in this way, it cannot be claimed that Ruth's choice kills her child. If we choose the Risky Policy, the causal connections are less close. Because the connections are less close, our choice kills the people who later die from the effects of released radiation. That we kill these people is the full objection to our choice.'

This objection I find dubious. Why is there a greater objection to our choice because the causal connections are less close? The objection may be correct in what it claims about our ordinary use of 'kill.' But, as I argued [elsewhere], this use is morally irrelevant. Since that argument may not convince, I add

The Risky Cure for Infertility. Ann cannot have a child unless she takes a certain treatment. If she takes this treatment, she will have a son, who will be healthy. But there is a risk of one in two that this treatment will give Ann a rare disease. This disease has the following features. It remains dormant for twenty years, is undetectable, kills men but does not harm women, and is in-

fectious. The following is therefore true. If Ann takes this treatment and has a healthy son, there is a chance of one in two that in twenty years she will infect her son with a disease that will kill him twenty years later, or when he is about forty. Ann chooses to take this treatment, and she does later infect her son with this fatal disease.

On the objection stated above, there is a strong objection to Ann's choice, which does not apply to Ruth's choice. Because the causal connections are less close, Ann's choice kills her son. And she knew that the chance was one in two that her choice would have this effect. Ruth knows that there is the same chance that her child will die at about the age of 40. But, because the causal connections are so close, her choice does not kill her son. According to this objection, this difference has great moral relevance.

This is not plausible. Ruth and Ann both know that, if they act in a certain way, there is a chance of one in two that they will have sons who will be killed by a disease at about the age of forty. The causal story is different. But this does not make Ann's choice morally worse. I believe that this example shows that we should reject this last objection.

The objector might say: 'I deny that, by choosing to take the Risky Cure, Ann kills her son.' But, if the objector denies this, he cannot claim that, by choosing the Risky Policy, we kill some people in the distant future. The causal connections take the same form. Each choice produces a side-effect which later kills people who owe their existence to this choice.

If this objection fails, as I believe, my earlier claim is justified. It is morally significant that, if we choose the Risky Policy, our choice is like Ruth's rather than Jane's.

It is morally significant that, if we had chosen otherwise, different people would have lived who would not have been killed. Since this is so, the objection to our choice cannot appeal only to the rights of those who actually later live. It must also appeal to a claim like Q, which compares different sets of possible lives. As I claimed earlier, the appeal to rights cannot wholly solve the Non-Identity Problem.

Conclusions

I shall now summarize what I have claimed. It is in fact true of everyone that, if he had not been conceived within a month of the time when he was conceived, he would never have existed. Because this is true, we can easily affect the identities of future people, or *who* the people are who will later live. If a choice between two actual social policies will affect the standard of living or the quality of life for about a century, it will affect the details of all the lives that are later lived in our community. As a result, some of those who later live will owe their existence to our choice of one of these two policies. After three centuries, this will be true of everyone in our community.

This fact produces a problem. One of these two policies may, in the further future, cause a great lowering of the quality of life. This would be the effect of the policy I call Depletion. This effect is bad, and provides a moral reason not to choose Depletion. But, because of the fact just mentioned, our choice of Depletion will be worse for no one. Some people believe that a choice cannot have bad effects if this choice will be worse for no one. The Case of Depletion shows that we must reject this view. And this is shown more forcefully by the Case of the Risky Policy. One effect of choosing this policy is a catastrophe that kills thousands of people. This effect is clearly bad, even though our choice will be worse for no one.

Notes

1 See T. Schwartz, 'Obligations to Posterity,' in Sikora and Barry.

Questions for Discussion

1 Does the fact that the policy of Depletion and the Risky Policy will not be bad for anyone mean that it is morally acceptable to adopt such policies? Why or why not?

PART 5

cultural, linguistic, and aboriginal rights

It is still fairly common to refer to the relationships between Canada as a whole and the various cultures to which individual Canadians belong in terms of the image of the "Canadian Mosaic." This is contrasted with the image of a "melting pot" in which people merge their identities to become all one new culture. In the "mosaic" model, each group maintains its own identity while at the same time it joins with other groups. The result is "multiculturalism"—a plurality of cultures (or sub-cultures) within the whole.

This may sound like a very appealing ideal, but it is not without problems. For one thing, there may be cases in which conflict arises because different cultural groups want or need things which are not compatible. It is difficult to provide a systematic, non-discriminatory method for adjudicating such issues.

Another problem is that cultures may need positive steps on the part of government in order to preserve their integrity, or sometimes to continue to survive at all. Even with the goal of a multicultural mosaic, there may well be a dominant culture which tends to submerge others. To what extent is society at large obliged to provide assistance for particular cultures? Is this simply a matter for market forces, in which it is left up to individual members of the culture in question to decide whether to take the steps necessary to preserve it, or to assimilate into the "dominant culture"? Or should the government provide, for example, financial support for cultural institutions? And should the government make allowances in its own dictates for cultural difference, such as allowing Sikhs to wear turbans when doing so deviates from the standard RCMP uniform?

It might make a difference, in answering these questions, which cultural group's fate is at stake. One might think that, from a legal point of view, there is no distinction between people on the basis of culture in Canada today, but that is not entirely accurate. For example, the Separate School Board system across the country ensures the continuation of Catholic and (in Québec) Protestant education, but does not necessarily make similar provisions for other faiths. Furthermore, there are enshrined protections for some linguistic groups and not others. Part of the legacy of the Trudeau government of the late 1960s and 1970s is official bilingualism, according to which individuals are to be guaranteed access to services (at least from the government) in either French or English anywhere in the country. Similarly, various government sources of money are available for both official languages in places where they constitute a minority language.

Why are these groups protected rather than others? Is it simply a matter of numbers? Would that mean, for example, that in parts of the country where languages other than the two "official" languages (say, Ukrainian or Chinese) are very common, the government should make sure it accommodates these groups? Is it rather a matter of history—the idea that Canada was "founded" by these groups, which therefore have a special entitlement to protection? In that case, one might well ask what the status should be of various First Nations languages, such as Ojibway and Cree.

These issues have been prominent in Canadian political life for a long time, and at times seem to threaten to tear the country apart. Moreover, they are not unique to Canada—there are many countries in the world which have struggled to find the right balance between cultural diversity and national homogeneity. Sometimes—as in Yugoslavia and Ireland—these struggles have taken the form of bloody warfare, and even attempts to draw boundaries and establish separate nations have often proven messy and complicated.

This chapter will explore some aspects of this issue, concentrating on the Canadian experience. In this country, the most obvious cultural distinction historically has been that between the French and the English. Even within that distinction, there has been the issue of who should be allowed to speak for the French—the combination of Francophone Canadians, including those living in predominantly English-speaking parts of the country, or the province of Québec, in which French is the majority language. The French-English distinction is not the only one within this country, however, and others have been getting more attention in recent years. Issues about turban-wearing RCMP officers or reparations for rights violations of Japanese Canadians during the war also have received considerable attention.

Another complex and important set of issues has to do with the cultural integrity of the various groups of aboriginal peoples in Canada. Historically, these groups stand in a very different relation to the dominant culture than do any of the cultures which have immigrated to this land. Indeed, part of the complexity of the issues connected with aboriginal rights today has to do with questions of what happens when different cultures, complete with different understandings of things such as the relationship between people and the land they live on, come into contact with each other. Is the dominant culture entitled to impose its understandings and its interpretations of laws and principles on the other culture?

Aboriginal people have also always been treated differently by Canadian law. Treaties (where they exist) were often interpreted to suit the purposes of the government and non-aboriginal settlers and developers rather than the aboriginal peoples, or were blatantly violated. Also, the government has taken direct control of many aspects of the lives of aboriginal people through the Indian Act. Many would argue that these facts have contributed greatly to the social problems facing aboriginal people today. What steps, if any, is the government obliged to take to reverse the effects of these policies? To what extent should members of a present generation feel obliged to compensate for past injustices? Are aboriginal groups entitled to "self-determination" (or "self-government"), and if so, what does that mean within a broader Canadian context?

These are some of the most important issues connected with the relationships between individuals, the cultures they belong to, and society as a whole. Some of these issues pose serious questions for political theory in general. Can a society such as Canada's, with its traditional emphasis on tolerance and the value of individual choice, find an appropriate place for the value of cultural membership and one's identification as a member of a group? Is there room for the existence of officially recognized "distinct societies" within one nation? Can justice be satisfied purely in terms of individual rights, or should society take notice of such things as "collective rights"? Can protection of cultural groups be consistent with the ideal of a "colour-blind" constitution which advocates equality for all? To what extent can cultural groups violate equality rights in order to preserve their identity (for example, by drawing distinctions between women and men within the cultural group)? Is the very concept of an individual right the product of a specific culture, which should not be applied wholesale to other cultures?

All of these questions are touched upon in the readings which follow.

Indian Nations: Determination or Termination

Union of British Columbia Indian Chiefs position paper statement

---

Leaders of Canadian aboriginal peoples have often made formal statements which help clarify their beliefs, both political and spiritual. The following is one such statement.

*   *   *

Indian Nations in Canada were never conquered. European traders, and in later years, settlers, were made to feel welcome in a land and environment which was alien to them. Throughout years of European settlement and expansion Indian Nations sought a mutual accommodation, one that would permit a bountiful land to be shared to the benefit of all.

Indian rights to land, resources, culture, language, a livelihood and self government

are not something conferred by treaties or offered to Indians as concessions by a beneficent government. These are the rights which Indian Nations enjoy from time immemorial. THESE RIGHTS ARE PREEXISTING AND INVIOLABLE. A CANADIAN CONSTITUTION CAN ACCOMMODATE INDIAN RIGHTS— IT CANNOT DIMINISH, ALTER OR ELIMINATE THEM.

Indian Nations understand the constitution to be a pact among founding peoples, among which we include ourselves. We understand our special constitutional relationship with the Federal Government to be in the nature of a partnership with the federative system, which was intended to permit us to survive and prosper as Indian Nations, while contributing to Canada's total development.

Sons of the Pilgrims Anniversary

John Quincy Adams

John Quincy Adams, who would later become president of the United States, made the following remarks in 1802. In them, he states a fairly common view of the time about the legitimacy of appropriation of land which was seen as being used inefficiently by its aboriginal inhabitants.

*   *   *

There are moralists who have questioned the right of Europeans to intrude upon the possessions of the aborigines in any case and under any limitations whatsoever. But have they maturely considered the whole subject? The Indian right of possession itself stands, with regard to the greatest part of the country, upon a questionable foundation. Their cultivated fields, their constructed habitations, a space of ample sufficiency for their subsistence, and whatever they had annexed to themselves by personal labor, was undoubtedly by the laws of nature theirs. But what is the right of a huntsman to the forest of a thousand miles over which he has accidentally ranged in quest of prey? Shall the liberal bounties of Providence to the race of men be monopolized by one of ten thousand for whom they were created? Shall the exuberant bosom of the common mother, amply adequate to the nourishment of millions, be claimed exclusively by a few hundred of her offspring? Shall the lordly savage not only disdain the virtues and enjoyments of civilization himself, but shall he control the civilization of a world? Shall he forbid the wilderness to blossom like the rose? Shall he forbid the oaks of the forest to fall before the ax of industry and rise again transformed into the habitations of ease and elegance? Shall he doom an immense region of the globe to perpetual desolation, and to hear the howlings of the tiger and the wolf silence forever the voice of human gladness? Shall the fields and the valleys which a beneficent God has framed to teem with the life of innumerable multitudes be [con]demned to everlasting barreness? Shall the mighty rivers poured out by the hands of nature as channels of communication between numerous nations, roll their waters in sullen silence and eternal solitude to the deep? Have hundreds of commodious harbors, a thousand leagues of coast, and a boundless ocean been spread in the front of this land, and shall every purpose of utility to which they could apply be prohibited by the tenant of the woods? No, generous philanthropists! Heaven has not been thus inconsistent in the works of its hands. Heaven has not thus placed at irreconcilable strife its moral laws with its physical creation.

Questions for Discussion

1 Can people who do not use land efficiently lose their claim to it? If so, are they entitled to compensation? How is "efficiency" to be defined?

Justice in our Time

Pierre E. Trudeau

In June of 1969, the Canadian government issued a "Statement of the Government of Canada on Indian Policy," (commonly known as the "White Paper") in which it proposed to repeal all laws suggesting differential treatment of aboriginal peoples, and phase out the Department of Indian Affairs. This statement marked an important turning point in the history of aboriginal peoples in this country. In a famous speech a little over a month after the statement's release, Prime Minister Trudeau tried to explain the government's position.

*   *   *

Remarks on Aboriginal and Treaty Rights.

Excerpts from a Speech Given August 8th, 1969, Vancouver, British Columbia

I think Canadians are not too proud about their past in the way in which they treated the Indian population of Canada and I don't think we have very great cause to be proud.

We have set the Indians apart as a race. We've set them apart in our laws. We've set them apart in the ways the governments will deal with them. They're not citizens of the province as the rest of us are. They are wards of the federal government. They get their services from the federal government rather than from the provincial or municipal governments. They have been set apart in law. They have been set apart in the relations with government and they've been set apart socially too.

So this year we came up with a proposal. It's a policy paper on the Indian problem. It proposes a set of solutions. It doesn't impose them on anybody. It proposes them—not only to the Indians but to all Canadians—not only to their federal representatives but to the provincial representatives too and it says we're at the crossroads. We can go on treating the Indians as having a special status. We can go on adding bricks of discrimination around the ghetto in which they live and at the same time perhaps helping them preserve certain cultural traits and certain ancestral rights. Or we can say you're at a crossroads—the time is now to decide whether the Indians will be a race apart in Canada or whether it will be Canadians of full status. And this is a difficult choice. It must be a very agonizing choice to the Indian peoples themselves because, on the one hand, they realize that if they come into the society as total citizens they will be equal under the law but they risk losing certain of their traditions, certain aspects of a culture and perhaps even certain of their basic rights and this is a very difficult choice for them to make and I don't think we want to try and force the pace on them any more than we can force it on the rest of Canadians but here again is a choice which is in our minds whether Canadians as a whole want to continue treating the Indian population as something outside, a group of Canadians with which we have treaties, a group of Canadians who have as the Indians, many of them claim, aboriginal rights or whether we will say well forget the past and begin today and this is a tremendously difficult choice because, if—well one of the things the Indian bands often refer to are their aboriginal rights and in our policy, the way we propose it, we say we won't recognize aboriginal rights. We will recognize treaty rights. We will recognize forms of contract which have been made with the Indian people by the Crown and we will try to bring justice in that area and this will mean that perhaps the treaties shouldn't go on forever. It's inconceivable, I think, that in a given society one section of the society have a treaty with the other section of the society. We must be all equal under the laws and we must not sign treaties amongst ourselves and many of these treaties, indeed, would have less and less significance in the future anyhow but things that in the past were covered by treaties like things like so much twine or so much gun powder

and which haven't been paid this must be paid. But I don't think that we should encourage the Indians to feel that their treaties should last forever within Canada so that they be able to receive their twine or their gun powder. They should become Canadians as all other Canadians and if they are prosperous and wealthy they will be treated like the prosperous and wealthy and they will be paying taxes for the other Canadians who are not so prosperous and not so wealthy whether they be Indians or English Canadians or French or Maritimers and this is the only basis on which I see our society can develop as equals. But aboriginal rights, this really means saying, "We were here before you. You came and you took the land from us and perhaps you cheated us by giving us some worthless things in return for vast expanses of land and we want to re-open this question. We want you to preserve our aboriginal rights and to restore them to us." And our answer—it may not be the right one and may not be one which is accepted but it will be up to all of you people to make your minds up and to choose for or against it and to discuss with the Indians—our answer is "no."

If we think of restoring aboriginal rights to the Indians well what about the French who were defeated at the Plains of Abraham? Shouldn't we restore rights to them? And what about though the Acadians who were deported—shouldn't we compensate for this? And what about the other Canadians, the immigrants? What about the Japanese Canadians who were so badly treated at the end or during the last war? What can we do to redeem the past? I can only say as President Kennedy said when he was asked about what he would do to compensate for the injustices that the Negroes had received in American society. We will be just in our time. This is all we can do. We must be just today.

Questions for Discussion

1 Is Trudeau right to suggest that it is impossible to make up for past injustices, and that we must simply start now and be "just in our time"?

2 Are there any relevant differences between the government's relationship to aboriginal peoples, and to other minorities in Canada?

Indian Women and the Law in Canada: Citizens Minus

Kathleen Jamieson

The government's position in the White Paper met with an unforeseen amount of opposition, especially from aboriginal leaders, in light of which the White Paper was eventually withdrawn. In the first of the two following excerpts, Kathleen Jamieson describes this reaction. In the other excerpt, she outlines the political climate surrounding the legal case of Jeannette Lavell a couple of years later. The Indian Act had specified that Indian women who married non-Indians lost their status as Indians, whereas men who married non-Indians bestowed their Indian status on their spouses. Lavell protested this apparent violation of her equality rights, and the resulting Supreme Court case is a classic example of conflict of legal principles, with significant political overtones.

*　　　*　　　*

The Minister of Indian Affairs, Jean Chrétien, in what came to be called the "White Paper," proposed a new deal for Indians. This policy paper deplored the disadvantaged position of Indians and suggested to remedy this a total revision of the Indian Act and the gradual phasing out of the Department of Indian Affairs over five years; the paper also proposed that there should be increased provincial involvement (which had been suggested in the Hawthorne-Tremblay Report) in the Administration of Indian Affairs. It is significant, if not ominous, in the light of subsequent provincial government reaction to the issue of Indian women's rights, that this paper begins: "To be an Indian is to be a man with a man's needs and abilities."[1]

Some eighteen meetings on changes to the Act had been held with Indians prior to this proposal. When the Indians were presented with the "White Paper" on June 25, 1969, however, there was an immediate and outright rejection of its content. In the first reaction of June 26th, ten Indian Chiefs from across Canada issued a statement declaring that though they did not question the Minister's "good will" they could only "view this as a policy designed to divest us of our aboriginal, residual and statutory rights. If we accept this policy and in the process lose our rights and our lands, we become willing partners in cultural genocide."[2]

"It is apparent to us," they said, "that while there was a show of consultation, neither the Minister nor his Department really heard and understood the Indian people."[3]

At this time two factors strengthened the Indians' position. First, Indians' aspirations to special rights based on aboriginal rights had been given a strong impetus by the imminent settlement of the Alaska native land claims by the US government. Secondly, the formation of the National Indian Brotherhood with a membership limited to status Indians in 1968 also seemed to make for a more united Indian political front than had hitherto been possible. It was ironical, though perhaps inevitable, that successful political cohesion depended on Indian Act categories.

The "White Paper," however, had provided real cause for alarm in that it did indeed seem to attempt to play down treaty rights and deny aboriginal land rights: "These aboriginal claims to land are so general and undefined that it is not realistic to think of them as specific claims capable of remedy except through a policy and program that will end injustice to Indians as members of the Canadian community."[4]

Prime Minister Trudeau fanned the flames by stating two months later in a speech in Vancouver: "But aboriginal rights, this really means saying, 'We were here before you!'...Our answer...is 'no.'" He then defended the "White Paper" as an attempt to rescue Indians from "the ghetto in which they live."[5] "Canadians," he said, "were not proud of their treatment of Indi-

ans in the past and had no reason to be so," but he promised "We will be just in our time. This is all we can do. We must be just today."[6]

But to the Indians this was not justice and this government was not really saying anything new. The "Just Society" and the policy of "integration" which Prime Minister Trudeau and his government were now espousing were only another formulation of assimilation, which had always been the stated intention of every Canadian government. The difference was that Indians were now determined that they would no longer be dictated to by anyone....

The [Lavell] case, which became a political vehicle for both the government and the Indians, came before the Supreme Court of Canada in 1973, when Jeannette Lavell contested her loss of Indian Status under the section 12(1)(b) of the Indian Act. The basis of the case...was that the discriminatory provisions of this section of the Indian Act were contrary to the Canadian Bill of Rights.

The government had just published a "White Paper" proposing that the Indian Act should be phased out.[7] But a strong Indian political front was emerging, apparently determined to wring from the government redress for past injustices. Insistence on the retention of the Indian Act was regarded as a crucial part of this strategy by the Indian leaders. As Harold Cardinal put it, "We do not want the Indian Act retained because it is a good piece of legislation, it isn't. It is discriminatory from start to finish. But it is a lever in our hands and an embarrassment to the government, as it should be.... We would rather continue to live in bondage under the *Indian Act* than surrender our sacred rights."[8] The Indian Act was thus transformed from the legal instrument of oppression which it had been since its inception into a repository of sacred rights for Indians. The opposition of Indian leaders to the claim of Lavell became a matter of policy to be pursued at all cost by government and Indians together because it endangered the Indian Act.

Jeannette Lavell lost her case, but the consequences were far-reaching. The issue of Indian women's status under section 12(1)(b) acquired, for many people, the dimensions of a moral dilemma—the rights of all Indians against the rights of a minority of Indians, i.e. Indian women. The case created a united Indian front on the "untouchable" nature of the Indian Act. And finally, the federal government's eagerness to support the major Indian political associations (most of which seem to have almost exclusively male executives and memberships) against Lavell established a basis for continued government-Indian interaction, which had been in deadlock since the conflict over the government "White Paper" of 1969. The rapport generated during the Lavell case was, after a short period of gestation, to give birth in 1975 to a joint NIB-Cabinet consultative committee to revise the Indian Act.

The government gave an undertaking to the NIB that no part of the Indian Act would be changed until revision of the whole Act is complete, after full process of consultation. The result of this gentleman's agreement has been that until very recently, a powerful blanket of silence was imposed on discussion of the status of Indian women and the topic began to assume an extra dimension. It became taboo and unwise in certain circles even to mention the subject. Despite the fact that the Indian Act continues to discriminate against them on the basis of race, sex and marital status, and is

contrary to the most fundamental principles of human rights, Indian women who have dared to speak out against it have been seen by many as somehow threatening the "human rights" of Indians as a whole.

The fact that Indian women in Canada who have lost their status are expected to accept this oppression compounds and perpetuates the injustice and has clear parallels in other societies where discriminatory practices and legislation permit the victimization of one group by another....

A curious twist to the issue has now developed. Despite the fact that Section 12(1)(b) is part of an Indian Act which was developed by previous federal governments without consultation with the Indian peoples, and despite the fact that this kind of discrimination against Indian women was never part of Indian cultural tradition, as later chapters of this study will show, the government is now placing the onus for the continuing existence of this discrimination squarely on the shoulders of the Indians and their representatives, the NIB.

Thus we find in a nationally-read newspaper the recent headline: "Indians' leaders warned to halt discrimination against women." The article then begins, "Justice Minister Ronald Basford has warned Indian leaders that Parliament is not going to tolerate 'for too long' the discrimination against women contained in the Indian Act."[9]

The Honourable Marc Lalonde, the Minister responsible for the Status of Women, in February 1978, informed a meeting of women delegates from across Canada that the issue of discrimination against Indian women is complicated and that "Discrimination against women is a scandal but imposing the cultural standards of white society on native society would be another scandal."[10]

This "two scandals" argument is another version of the "moral dilemma," but this time discrimination against women is argued as being Indian custom and for the government to impose other values prohibiting discrimination would be scandalous.

Of the many and varied arguments that have been used to justify the continued existence of this legislation, this product of the 1970s is the most insidious.

Notes

1 Government of Canada, *Statement of the Government of Canada on Indian Policy, 1969* (Ottawa, 1969), p. 3

2 National Indian Brotherhood, *Statement on the Proposed New "Indian Policy,"* press release, July [sic] 26, 1969.

3 Ibid., p. 5

4 Government of Canada, op. cit., p. 11

5 Cumming, Peter A. and Mickenberg, Neil H., *Native Rights in Canada* 2nd edition (Toronto: Indian-Eskimo Association of Canada in association with General Pulishing Co., 1972), p. 263

6 Ibid.

7 Chrétien, Hon. Jean, *Indian Policy, Statement of the Government of Canada* (Ottawa, 1969). Afterwards called the "White Paper."

8 Cardinal, Harold, *The Unjust Society* (Edmonton: M.G. Hurtig, 1961), p. 140.

9 *The Globe and Mail*, May 26, 1977.

10 *The Globe and Mail*, February 17, 1978.

Questions for Discussion

1 Should cultural groups within Canada have the power to enforce measures which seem to conflict with equality rights, in the interests of cultural integrity?

Group Rights Versus Individual Rights in the Charter

The Special Cases of Natives and the Québecois

F.L. Morton

In the following article, Morton describes some of the tensions between principles included in the Canadian Constitution. In particular, he discusses the possible conflicts between protections of specific groups and individual rights, discussing a number of landmark Canadian legal cases in the process.

*   *   *

Introduction

With the adoption of the Charter of Rights in 1982, the political issues raised by government policies toward minorities in Canada became inextricably linked with the constitutional issues raised by the equality rights provisions of section 15. What were once essentially policy issues to be resolved through the political accommodation of the parliamentary process have taken on a new constitutional dimension and are now subject to judicial resolution. The mandates of section 15 reinforce but also complicate Canadian public policies toward minority groups. This paper identifies and analyzes the political and legal problems raised by section 15 for government policy toward two specific minority groups—natives and the Québecois.

Historically, Canadian public policies toward minorities can be roughly placed into three distinct categories: non-discrimination, special treatment based on a group's unique legal status, and group self-government. The notion of minority group rights as the right against discrimination is the oldest and most fundamental, and is shared by all other liberal democracies. Despite the rubric of "group right," its focus is essentially individualistic. It attempts to assure that individuals are not arbitrarily discriminated against by the government because of their membership in a racial, ethnic, or religious minority group. This policy has always been an integral part of the "rule of law" in Canada's unwritten constitution. (Dawson 1969:77,78) It was given explicit statutory force in the 1960 Bill of Rights, and has been made part of Canada's written constitution by the "equality before the law" clause of section 15.

A new and much broader scope was added to the meaning of non-discrimination and legal equality by section 15. Additional language was used to extend its original meaning of non-discrimination in the "application and administration of the law" to a substantive meaning of non-discriminatory laws. The additional rights to equality "under the law" and "equal protection of the law" were added to proscribe the use of certain designated minority group charac-

teristics as legislative classifications, or at least to place a heavy burden of proof on the government to justify the use of such classifications before the courts. The additional equality right to the "equal benefit of the law" was intended to prohibit laws or policies that have a discriminatory or unequal impact upon minority groups. (Hogg 1982:51)

The notion of minority group rights as a group's possession of a special legal status is also well-entrenched in Canadian law and politics. Unlike the non-discrimination right, which essentially is the claim of an individual to be treated the *same* as everyone else *regardless* of minority group membership, special legal status amounts to the claim of an individual to be treated *differently* than everyone else *because* of minority group membership. The British North America Act proclaimed special denominational rights with respect to religious education (s. 93) and language rights (s. 130). These were reaffirmed and, in the case of language rights, extended by sections 16-23 and section 29, respectively, of the Charter. Section 91(24) of the B.N.A. Act clearly authorized Parliament to create a special legal status for Indians and the governance of affairs on Indian reserves, which Parliament has done in the form of the Indian Act. Section 25 of the Charter reaffirms the validity of a special legal status for Indians, and, together with section 35, goes on to recognize and protect "existing aboriginal and treaty rights." A novel form of special legal status—known as "affirmative action"—is given constitutional legitimacy by the second part of section 15. Section 15(2) authorizes the government to designate certain groups as "disadvantaged," and to enact laws, programs, and activities designed to better the condition of such groups. Its recognized purpose is to create a category of exceptions to the non-discrimination principle of section 15(1).

The third and final notion of minority group rights is the right of a group to be self-governing. While not explicitly recognized in the B.N.A. Act, the form of federalism was clearly adopted to accommodate regional demands for a degree of self-government. In the case of Quebec, the concept of provincial rights has always had added significance because of the ethnic, linguistic, and religious homogeneity of that province's Francophone majority. With varying degrees of intensity, Quebec governments have always maintained that the protection of Quebec's provincial rights is equivalent to the protection of the French minority's rights within Canada. (See section 4, below.) Native groups have long claimed a similar right to self-government, and now argue that this right is recognized in the declaration of "aboriginal rights" in sections 25 and 35 of the Charter. (See section 3, below.)

There are strong tensions and sometimes outright conflicts between these three different kinds of minority group policies. To grant special education status to Catholics and Protestants is to deny "equal" treatment to other religious groups. Does a law that treats individuals differently because of their race or sex constitute an undesirable form of invidious discrimination or a desirable form of special treatment justified by special needs? Does the right to group self-government allow groups to enact discriminatory policies within their jurisdiction?

In the past, in the absence of a constitutionally entrenched equality rights clause, responsibility for reconciling these competing demands and values rested with the federal and provincial legislatures. A government was able to pursue a pragmatic mixture of these different kinds of policies. It need not have worried about such tensions and conflicts, other than the political unpopularity that they might incur. The Charter changes this. Under section 15, a minority group member, representing either himself or his group, may challenge a government policy, or absence of policy, as violating one of the various equality rights mandated by section 15. In deciding these cases, judges will be forced to choose between the competing notions of minority rights. After April 17, 1985, the date that section 15 takes effect, all government policies respecting minority groups will potentially be subject to judicial review and possible reversal by the courts.

The equality rights section of the Charter raises a number of personal problems for government policies toward minorities. This paper addresses only one: the tension between group rights and individual rights as it affects public policy toward natives and French Canadians in Quebec. Both of these groups share the conception of *their* group rights as a form of the right to self-government and self-determination. Unlike a group such as women, whose putative goal is economic and social assimilation into the Canadian mainstream, Natives and French Canadians (or at least their leaders) define their goals as avoiding such assimilation and maintaining their group identity through the process of self-government. In both instances this leads to conflicts with the competing conception of non-discrimination as the basic principle of group equality.

Through an analysis of these two groups, this paper argues that the courts have been given a nearly impossible task in reconciling the group rights and individual rights requirements of Canada's amended constitution. Legally, it is suggested that the courts will be unable to devise a "principled" approach to interpreting the section 15 equality rights clause of the Charter. Judges will be forced to make so many exceptions to the non-discrimination principle of the section 15 equality clause that the exceptions will destroy the rule. Without the support of principle, judicial interpretation will degenerate into an *ad hoc* style of judicial decision making, a practice likely to erode the courts' authority. Politically, it is suggested that the Charter places the courts in an equally difficult position, by creating inevitable conflicts between group rights and individual rights, in which competing parties are not willing to accept an adverse decision.

Native Rights: Self-Government and Cultural Autonomy Versus Individual Freedom

The social situations in *Brown v. Board of Education* and the instant cases are, of course, very different, but the basic philosophic concept is the same. The Canadian Bill of Rights is not fulfilled if it merely equates Indians with Indians in terms of equality before the law, but can have validity and meaning only when...it is seen to repudiate discrimination in every law of Canada by reasons of race, national origin, colour, religion or sex...[1]

These were the words of Justice Emmett Hall in the 1969 *Drybones* case, a case which voided a conviction under section 94(b) of the Indian Act as a violation of the 1960 Bill of Rights guarantee to "equality before the law." They were broad indeed, and, together with the opinions of five other judges, they were hailed as ush-

ering in a "brave new world" of Canadian jurisprudence. Parliamentary supremacy was to be replaced, or at least modified, by the new primacy of the 1960 Bill of Rights, interpreted and enforced by a vigilant Supreme Court. Discrimination in government policy on any of the prohibited grounds could now be successfully attacked through the courts.

These hopes and expectations were shortlived. They were dashed by a series of subsequent Supreme Court decisions that revived and reinstated Dicey's interpretation of "equality before the law" as a procedural not a substantive requirement—as equality in the application and administration of laws, not equal laws. In a 1975 case that effectively completed the destruction of the *Drybones* legacy, Justice Beetz attempted to explain the source of the Court's difficulties with the equality clause:

> The principle of equality before the law is generally hostile to the very nature of status and it is no easy task to reconcile the two in Canada when the one is enshrined in a quasi-constitutional statute and the other forms part of the fundamental law of the land. This the courts have attempted to do in *Drybones* and *Lavell*.[2]

The experience under the 1960 Bill of Rights demonstrated a basic incompatibility between the tradition of "group rights" in Canadian political experience and an American-style equality clause. The tradition of group rights entails the use of status classifications, while a non-Diceyean equality principle prohibits such classifications. The unhappy experience of the Bill of Rights notwithstanding, the framers of the new Charter of Rights and Freedoms have now compressed these two contrary principles into Canada's written constitution.

No area of law caused more problems for judicial interpretation of the 1960 Bill of Rights than the Indian Act. Three of the five major equality decisions of the Supreme Court dealt with provisions or effects of the Indian Act: *Drybones, Lavell* and *Canard*.[3] The Court's inability to reconcile the special status conferred through the Indian Act and authorized by the B.N.A. Act with a substantive defintion of "equality before law" effectively undermined the potential for any American-style, *Brown v. Board* equality jurisprudence under the 1960 Bill of Rights. Unwilling to adopt a definition of "equality before the law" that would deny the validity of the Indian Act, the Court quickly abandoned the broad, substantive notion of "equality before the law" articulated in *Drybones*, and returned to the procedural definition of Dicey.

The drafters of the equality clause of the Charter went to great lengths to avoid a repeat of this experience. In addition to the traditional right to "equality before the law," section 15 goes on to proclaim rights to equality "under the law...equal protection (of the law) and equal benefit of the law." This "new improved," four-tier equality clause was designed to make it clear to even the most traditional of judges that the Charter requires much more than the Bill of Rights precedents provide. It is intended, in short, to resurrect Justice Hall's brave new vision articulated in *Drybones*: "to repudiate discrimination in every law of Canada by reason of race, national origin, colour, religion or sex."

Since the Indian Act is clearly a law that discriminates "by reason of race," does this mean that it is now (or will be in 1985, when section 15 takes effect) unconstitutional? The answer, one hopes, is certainly not. There are insuperable legal and political obstacles to such an interpretation. Legally, the use of Indian status is certainly authorized by the terms of section 91(24) of the B.N.A. Act, "to make laws for...Indians, and Lands reserved for Indians." In addition, sections 25 and 35 of the Constitution Act, 1981, proclaim the continued validity of any and all aboriginal and treaty rights of native peoples. This constitutional sanction for the continued use of race as a legislative classification, combined with the "reasonable limitations" clause of section 1 of the Charter, would seem to provide more than enough legal support for the continued validity of the Indian Act.

The political obstacle is even more obvious. Neither the federal government, nor native groups themselves, would allow the Indian Act to be unilaterally cast out by a group of judges claiming to enforce the equality provisions of the Charter of Rights. While neither party may be content with the status quo under the Indian Act, each has a vested interest in participating directly in any process that changes the status quo.

Does the Charter thus solve the problem that so perplexed the judges under the Bill of Rights? Is Justice Beetz's lament in *Canard* no longer applicable? Civil libertarian enthusiasts certainly think so. For the reasons reviewed above, the Indian Act can be treated as *sui generis*, "a special and limited exception" to the non-discrimination command of section 15. This answer can be provisionally accepted, but it raises in turn a second question. How many exceptions can a constitutional principle have before it ceases to be a principle? Constitutional principles, after all, are supposed to lay down the basic ground rules for the conduct of government. At what point do the exceptions swallow the rule? We will return to this problem at the end of the paper.

The guarantees of existing aboriginal and treaty rights in sections 25 and 35 of the Constitution Act, 1982, may resolve the problem of reconciling the Indian Act with the non-discrimination principle of section 15. But they raise even more serious problems. Just what these "aboriginal rights" mean in practice is notoriously ambiguous. At a minimum they include only the existing rights and privileges bestowed by positive law and treaties. At a maximum, many native leaders claim that "aboriginal rights" include the right to complete self-government and political autonomy, on large tracts of land presently under the control of non-Indians, and all this on the basis of natural or "higher" law. (Flanagan 1984; and Sanders 1983:225)

The native claims to self-government and political autonomy pose critical problems for the application of the Charter of Rights, and especially the equality clause, to the "internal" policy affairs of Indian bands. This "right to self-government" essentially means the right of native groups to conduct all the internal affairs of the band free from "outside" interference, including judicial interference. This is a problem, because inevitably some of these internal practices and policies will conflict with the provisions of the Charter.

The fundamental freedoms (s. 1) and equality sections of the Charter are designed for a "liberal" society, a society that accepts the "natural equality" of all members, and a corresponding right to participate equally in the process of government. A liberal society relegates religion to a secondary or "private" matter, and prohibits any direct government support of religion or punishment of "nonbelievers." It places a premium on the rights of the individual and not the group. Individual liberty, including the use of private property, cannot be restricted legitimately, unless it can be shown that they directly harm some other individual. Suffice it to say that most of these concepts are absent from, if not in direct conflict with, the traditions and values of native societies. These non-European, and thus non-liberal, traditions and values would inevitably, and in some cases purposely, be included in the internal policies of self-governing Indian bands. Indeed, a central purpose of the native claim to self-government, free from "outside" interference, is precisely to protect and to promote aspects of traditional native culture that are perceived to be threatened by the norms and practices of Canadian society.

The conflict between native rights as the right to greater self-government and the Charter is not merely hypothetical. The *Lavell* and *Bedard* cases, and the ensuing controversy, are a good example of this problem. Lavell and Bedard were both Indian women who married non-Indians and, pursuant to s. 12(1)(b) of the Indian Act, lost their Indian status. There is no similar loss of status for Indian men who marry non-Indians. Lavell and Bedard argued that s. 12(1)(b) discriminated against them on the basis of sex, and thus violated the "equality before the law" provision of the 1960 Bill of Rights. The Supreme Court rejected this argument by interpreting the Bill of Rights as requiring only equality in "the application and administration of the law." Since Lavell and Bedard were treated the same as all other Indian women, there was no proscribed inequality of treatment.

Referred to as the "*Plessy v. Ferguson* of Canadian civil liberties," this case has become something of a "cause célèbre" amongst civil libertarians and feminist groups. The *Lavell* decision marked the beginning of the end of the broad, non-discrimination principle announced in *Drybones*, and is, along with the *Bliss* case, the direct cause of the four-tier wording of the "new improved" equality clause in section 15 of the Charter. Feminists and civil libertarians were determined to guarantee that when the next *Lavell* and *Bliss* cases arrived at the Supreme Court, they would be decided very differently.

That day may not be far off. In the 10 years since the *Lavell* decision, there has been no legislative resolution of the controversy. Despite many promises (and eventually threats) by the federal government to amend the Indian Act, s. 12(1)(b) remains intact. The reason is intense opposition by native leaders to any changes to s. 12(1)(b) without accompanying financial assistance and additional land to accommodate the potential influx of an estimated 15,000 Indian women and 57,000 Indian children. While the federal government has indicated a willingness to pick up the financial costs associated with such a policy change—costs estimated at $35 million for the first year and amounting to $312.1 million by year 40 of the program—provincial governments have been unwilling to cede disputed land claims that make up the second half of the package.[4] Without both, Indian leaders refuse to cut a deal. The result has been an absolute stalemate, as witnessed by the failure of the second Constitutional Conference on Aboriginal Rights in March, 1984.

While native leaders have tirelessly denounced both the federal and provincial governments for creating and prolonging this admittedly discriminatory practice, they have been equally adamant about not allowing the issue to be resolved by the courts.

Eleven of the twelve Indian associations that intervened in the original *Lavell* case supported the legal validity of s. 12(1)(b). Native leaders have repeatedly rejected the idea that it is simply an issue of "individual rights." (Cardinal, 1977: 109-112). George Manuel, president of the National Indian Brotherhood, pointedly identified the native's fear of any judicial involvement in this issue: "...we cannot accept a position where the only safeguards we have can be struck down by a court that has no authority to put something better in its place." (Manuel and Posluns 1974:241) In the wake of the bitterly unsuccessful March, 1984 Constitutional Conference, the Assembly of First Nations ran half-page advertisements in major Canadian newspapers declaring:

> Although the problem has been described as discrimination against women, sexual equality is not the issue.... The proposed change to eliminate discrimination would create more serious problems than it solves, as it only addresses one of the many and varied problems confronting First Nations. This is a complex matter involving real issues such as the rights of individual First Nations to determine their own citizenship, the preservation of their cultural identities and the right to exercise self-government.[5]

While the same advertisement went on to claim that, "We have always believed in and practiced sexual equality," and blame the federal government for creating the problem, the fact remains that Indian leaders prefer the status quo to any court-ordered solution. Unilateral control of band membership is an essential element of the collective right to self-government embraced by the native conception of "aboriginal rights." While they may be willing to bargain with the federal government for changes in band membership in exchange for financial and land claims compensation, they are vehemently opposed to any unilateral "judicial law reform" under section 15 of the Charter.

As a result, s. 12(1)(b) is a Charter case just waiting to happen, and there is no doubt that it will. There are disenfranchised Indian women such as Mary Two-Axe Early, formerly from the Mohawk Caughnawaga reserve, who have actively campaigned for abolition of s. 12(1)(b), with or without the consent of native leaders. According to Two-Axe, native leaders have too many other priorities. "They are worried about land claims. How many years will it take them to worry about us?"[6] Feminist groups strongly support this position, and are willing and able to organize and pay for the required lawsuits.

How, it must be asked, are Canadian judges supposed to decide this case? Legally, both sides can point to explicit Charter language supporting their case: Indian leaders to the guarantee of "aboriginal rights" in sections 25 and 35; disenfranchised Indian women and feminist groups to the non-discrimination principle in section 15. Politically, neither side is willing to accept an adverse decision. A decision either way will be bitterly condemned by the losing side, and possibly not complied with by native leaders.

Group Rights as Provincial Rights: The Case of the Québécois

The concept of group rights is hardly new in Canadian law and politics. It can be traced back to the terms under which Canada's two founding nations, the English and the French, agreed to union, or rather, confederation. The British North America Act provided three different constitutional protections for collective or minority rights. The section 93 denominational school provisions were intended to protect the Protestant minority in Quebec and the Catholic minority in the other provinces. Similarly, section 133 provided protection for the English-speaking minority within Quebec and the French-speaking minority within Canada in the conduct of the affairs of the new national government. Finally, and perhaps most importantly, section 92 as a whole, and especially subsection 13, provided for the protection of the French minority in Canada as a whole, by providing a significant degree of political autonomy for Quebec, the home of over 85 percent of all French-speaking Canadians.

The political history of Canada since 1867 might well be summarized as the struggle between which of these two ways of protecting and expressing the "French fact" in Canada should prevail. From Laurier's refusal to intervene in the Manitoba school crisis in the 1890s to Trudeau's confrontation with Levesque in the 1980 Quebec Referendum, the alternatives of an essentially provincial presence versus a national presence have competed with one another for dominance, especially among French Canadian leaders.

The Charter of Rights now overlays a constitutional principle of non-discrimination on this 100-year tradition of collective rights for French and English, Catholic and Protestant minorities. It thus raises in a new form the dilemma complained of by Justice Beetz in *Canard*: how to reconcile the constitutional prohibition of legal status—assigning different rights to individuals based upon their ethnic background or religious affiliation—with other clauses of the constitution that explicitly provide for such treatment.

In the context of this well-established tradition of collective or group rights, the Charter raises two very distinct kinds of problems. The first is the more obvious but less serious problem of how to deal with the claims of ethnic or religious groups that do not, or choose not to, fit into either the English Protestant or French Catholic legal categories. If Catholics have a right to direct their property taxes to Catholic schools, should not Jews or Fundamentalist Christians enjoy "equal right"? When an ethnic group comes to dominate a certain neighbourhood or community, should they not have an "equal right" to educate their children in their mother tongue? These claims are certainly given added plausibility by section 27 of the Charter, which declares that the Charter "shall be interpreted in a manner consistent with the preservation and enhancement of the multicultural heritage of Canadians."

Under the traditional Diceyean interpretation of "equality before the law," these claims could be dispensed with easily. But as we have already seen, the "new improved" equality clause of the Charter is purposely stacked with language to discourage a merely procedural interpretation. Individuals are guaranteed the additional rights of "equal protection and equal benefit of the law." And there is little question that a provincial education act that allocates property taxes to the Catholic schools but no other denomination hardly provides the "equal benefit of the law." Once again, Canadian judges are confronted with a dilemma.

There are basically three possible solutions to this problem. The first would be to abolish, by judicial fiat, any and all preferential treatment of linguistic or religious minorities. This would be the most consistent and thus the most "judicial" application of the non-discrimination principle of section 15, and is essentially the constitutional practice in the United States.[7] Of course, this approach is neither legally nor politically feasible in present-day Canada. Legally, section 93 of the B.N.A. Act is still the law of the land. Moreover, it is reinforced by section 29 of the Charter, which affirms all traditional "rights or privileges guaranteed by or under the Constitution of Canada in respect of denominational, separate or dissentient schools." The political furor created by such a decision need not be elaborated.

A second option would be for the courts to embark on a broad course of judicial policy making, ordering provinces and school districts to accommodate the demands of linguistic and religious minorities on an "equal" footing with English Protestant and French Catholic minorities. While this may well be unavoidable in cases raising section 23 claims to English or French language educational facilities, the judges would be well advised to steer clear of setting innovative education policies for other minorities under section 15 of the Charter. While principle would again be served by this approach, it raises a host of practical difficulties. In addition to the obvious problem of judicial control of the public purse, the American school desegregation experience strongly suggests that when judges take over the administration of school systems, neither the judges nor the schools prosper. (Glazer 1974) Finally, given the proven cautiousness of the Canadian judiciary in civil liberties cases, it is highly improbable that this approach would be adopted in the forseeable future.

The third option, and the one most likely to be adopted, is simply to maintain the status quo. This is not only the path of least resistance politically, but it can be defended on the basis of tradition, combined with the "reasonable limits" clause of section 1.[8] This course of action does not preclude a province or a school board from voluntarily expanding its school policies to accommodate other ethnic or religious minorities in Canadian society. It simply states that there are no "rights" in these matters, but only questions of policy, properly determined by local political accommodation.

The drawback to this approach is that it is yet another exception to the non-discrimination principle of section 15. In effect, this approach says to other ethnic or religious minorities, "Sorry, you came too late. Only French and English, Catholics and Protestants, enjoy any special educational rights in this country." While this solution is defensible on policy grounds and a prudent course of action for the judges, it further erodes the claim that section 15 establishes a *judicially enforceable* non-discrimination policy. How many exceptions can a principle have before it ceases to be a principle?

The second problem is the accurate perception of the Charter as a direct challenge to the claim of Quebec to be the true or best representative of French interests in Canadian politics and society. This is a more serious problem than the first, because it drags the courts into an area where the political battle lines are old and well established, and places the courts squarely on the side of the federal government. Once again the Charter places the courts, especially the Supreme Court, in an exceedingly difficult position. The Charter explicitly authorizes the courts to enforce the enumerated rights against any offending provincial legislation. Yet any attempts to do so against Quebec legislation will be widely regarded within the province as further attacks on and erosion of the collective rights of French Canadians. The perception of the Supreme Court as impartial and politically neutral will be damaged, and thus its authority within Quebec further diminished.

Quebec's misgivings about the Charter have been eloquently summarized by Gordon Robertson:

> As far as the point about collective rights is concerned, it seems to me that it would be a mistake to assess the protection of collective rights only in terms of clauses like section 92(13) or section 93 or section 133 of the BNA Act, that formally and directly protect specific rights. The powers of the government of Quebec are seen in Quebec as being in themselves important protections of the collective rights of the French-speaking people of the province. Those people in Quebec constitute eighty-five percent of the French-speaking people of Canada. Their continuity as a vibrant, healthy, French-speaking society is seen as a *sine qua non* for the survival of French-speaking communities in the rest of Canada. In short, the rights and powers of the government of Quebec become a very important instrument of protection for the entire French-speaking minority in Canada. (McKercher 1983:149)

The Charter, he concludes, actually "diminishes the powers of the Assemblée Nationale de Québec."

This is essentially the view of [then] Premier Levesque and his Parti Québecois, who have treated the Charter with open contempt. Because they did not consent to the constitutional amendments of which the Charter was one part, they regard the entire Constitution Act, 1982, as itself "unconstitutional" and illegitimate. Their contempt for the Charter was manifested in Bill 62, enacted in June, 1982, immediately after the Charter took effect. Taking advantage of the section 33 legislative override clause in an unanticipated and extreme form, Bill 62 purports to exempt retroactively and in a blanket-fashion all existing Quebec statutes from sections 2 and 7 to 15 of the Charter.[9]

This view of the meaning and desirability of collective rights as provincial rights in Canadian politics is certainly not unanimous. As M. James Penton has effectively argued, "from an historical standpoint collective rights have often become collective wrongs for those groups not in the mainstream of Canadian politics." (McKercher 1983:174) Penton documents this claim through such examples as Quebec's persecution of the Jehovah's Witnesses during the forties; the prairie province's mistreatment of Catholics and Francophones and, more recently, discriminatory legislation directed at Hutterites, Mennonites, and Doukhobors; and anti-Chinese legislation at various times in British Columbia. From Penton's perspective, there is an irreconcilable tension between individual rights and group rights, and he is generally critical of the Charter's various concessions to the latter, especially the section 33 legislative override. On balance, however, he sees the various protections of individual rights as "a major buttress in defense of civil liberties in Canada," and hails the Charter's "enactment and entrenchment as a positive step in the history of our nation." (McKercher 1983:183)

The judges are left with the task of trying to reconcile these two very different views on the relative meaning and desirability of collective rights and individual rights in the Canadian polity. This will be no easy task, for underlying these opposing judgements are two very different understandings of the very meaning and purpose of politics. Penton's views, which are basically those of all civil libertarians, are based on a very individualistic view of society and a radical narrowing of the purpose of government. Individual liberty is the primary political fact, and government's main purpose is to protect its exercise from infringement by other individuals or the government itself. There are no collective or group rights, other than the collective right of the entire society to be governed by their consent, because there are no collective goods, other than the sum of all disparate individual goods. Each individual defines for himself the meaning of "the good life," or happiness. What in pre-liberal thought was called the "health of the soul" is banished from the public agenda and made a purely private affair. The function of the state is reduced to providing security—collective security from hostile foreign nations, and domestic security for the "life, liberty, and property" of each individual citizen.

Such is the political theory implicit in those sections of the Charter championed by its civil libertarian supporters, and it is a very liberal, and a very American, view of political life. Needless to say, it does not fit comfortably with the Canadian political experience. As Hartz, Horowitz, Grant and others have all said in different ways, Canada has retained a sense of collective good, a "tory touch," a sense that the political whole is more than the sum of its parts. This is especially true of Quebec nationalism, and a central purpose of the federal form of government has been to give scope and life to the different regions' sense of collective identity and purpose.

It is in the context of this dimension of Canadian political experience that the protests of the Quebec nationalists find their source and moral force. For them, group rights do not mean the right of an individual not to be discriminated against because of his race or religion. Rather, in the words of André Tremblay,

> To my mind, collective rights mean justice for minorities who want to survive, who want to develop. I am not against the protection of individual rights, but Quebec's legitimate demands for collective rights have yet to be met.... What worries me is that this constitution is the product of confrontation and means few collective rights, less justice for minorities, and more bitterness for Quebec. (McKercher, 1983:142)

Tremblay's remarks make arguably clear that the Quebec nationalist understanding of the purpose of politics is not limited to a narrow Lockean liberalism of the protection of individual liberty. It includes facilitating the "survival" and "development" of a collective way of life, a shared language and a shared culture. This "politics of culture" is a modern version of the old "regime politics" rejected and eventually overthrown by modern political liberalism. And as the founders of modern liberalism well understood, when a government undertakes actively to promote through law and public policies a distinctive "way of life," it inevitably impinges on the sense of equal treatment and equal participation of those minorities who are not part of the community and who do not share in their sense of collective good. The "politics of culture" presupposes a homogeneous community, while the Charter is designed to protect the equal treatment of individuals in a heterogeneous society.[10]

Predictably, the conflict between the political liberalism of the Charter and the "regime politics" of the Levesque nationalists has already come to a head in a Charter of Rights case. The Quebec Association of Protestant School Boards has challenged the constitutional validity of the French language education sections of Bill 101, the centrepiece of the Levesque government's language and culture program.[11] Since the section 23 education language rights provisions are not subject to any provincial override, the Levesque government has been forced to fight this issue in the courts. It lost at trial and again on appeal in the Quebec courts, and the case is now pending decision by the Supreme Court of Canada.

Unlike other institutions of government decision making, the Supreme Court must provide an answer to this dispute. It cannot call for a Royal Commission to study the matter, or call a first ministers conference to negotiate a compromise settlement. It must make a ruling and make it now. Since the language of relevant Charter sections is relatively clear on this issue, the Court will almost certainly rule against the challenged education provisions of Bill 101, and thus the heart of the Parti Québécois agenda.

While the Supreme Court's decision is quite predictable in this case, the response of the Quebec government is not. Will Levesque comply with such a decision? Andre Tremblay has pointedly stated the Parti Québecois perspective: "The question is, to what extent is the minority bound to respect a decision which will remove its collective rights?" (McKercher 1983:142) If compliance is not forthcoming, would the federal government "force" compliance? More interesting still, could the federal government force Quebec to obey?[12]

It is these latter questions—and their disturbing implications—that point to the risks involved in "constitutionalizing," or, what is the same thing, "judicializing" issues of fundamental political disagreement. Do collective rights mean "justice for minorities who want to survive, who want to develop"? Or are collective rights a code word for discrimination against minorities? If Canadian society cannot answer this question, it is very doubtful that the Supreme Court can.

American experience sheds some light on the problems involved in "constitutionalizing" issues of fundamental political disagreement. In the 1857 *Dred Scott* case, the American Supreme Court tried to resolve once and for all the slavery issue that had divided the new American nation since its founding. The result was the formation of the Republican Party, a wholly regional party, the election of a Republican—that is, a regional—president three years later, and the beginning of a civil war. Almost one hundred years later, in the *Brown v. Board of Education* case, the American Supreme Court once again attempted to impose a solution to the legacy of slavery—the legal system of racial desegregation in the South. Despite strong "states' rights" protests, this Supreme Court decision was obeyed, but only after President Eisenhower called in the National Guard to force the integration of Central High School in Little Rock, Arkansas. If Quebec refuses to comply with the Supreme Court's decision in the Bill 101 case, would Canadians support a similar form of federal enforcement?

The point is not that the US Court's decision in *Brown v. Board* was a mistake. Obviously it was a most necessary decision. Try to imagine contemporary American society without it. The point is that the decision had a high cost—the destruction of the remaining constitutional supports of states' rights and federalism. "States' rights" was the constitutional vehicle for segregation, and it had to be destroyed if "equal protection of the laws" was to be enforced. Americans (the majority of whom lived outside the South) were willing to pay this price. Would a majority of Canadians be willing to pay a similar price to enforce bilingual education in Quebec?

A still more relevant political precedent can be drawn from Canadian political history. Historian Kenneth McNaught, in describing Sir Wilfrid Laurier's decision not to use the federal government's power to legislate a settlement to the Manitoba School Crisis in the 1890s, writes:

Knowing that the principal shoal to avoid was a permanent division on racial lines, he saw also that "rights" depended more upon mutual accommodation than upon law. (McNaught, 1960:187)

Historically, the federal structure of Canada's political system has served arguably well to facilitate such political accommodations. Unfortunately, judicial interpretation of "entrenched rights" is a uniquely ill-suited process for this purpose.

Conclusion

The courts have been given a near impossible task in reconciling the group rights and individual rights provisions of the Charter. The language of section 15, combined with the other guarantees of group rights, new and old, simply point in different directions. There is no single "principle of equality" that the judges can appeal to as a ground for their decisions. Recommendations for tests of "judicial balancing of competing values" just obfuscate this prob-

lem, and come from civil liberties enthusiasts whose "result oriented" jurisprudence
permits them to ignore this problem.

The logical problems of interpreting
section 15 are further compounded by political problems. If the judges simply ignore
the four-tier wording of the equality clause
and persist in a Diceyean interpretation of
equality as equality in the application and
administration of the law (which at least has
the merit of permitting on principle "affirmative action" policies), they will be exco-
riated by civil libertarian groups, feminists,
academic legal commentators, and the
press. If, on the other hand, the courts
strike out with "bold" and "creative" substantive interpretations of the equality guarantees, sweeping aside "archaic" and
"overbroad" legislative classifications, they
will shortly butt up against the cold reality
of the section 33 legislative override power.
Provincial political leaders are not likely to
be reluctant to use their section 33 override
powers to disobey "legally" court decisions
that are generally perceived as contrary to
common sense, sound policy, or both.

The courts are thus in a very difficult
situation. No matter what they do with section 15, they will be roundly condemned by
one faction or another. This unenviable predicament provokes the obvious question of
why—or how—did this ever happen in the
first place? The answer seems to be in the
political wheeling and dealing by the Trudeau government during the constitution-
making process of 1980 to 1982. Their
protestations of innocence notwithstanding,
the federal negotiators not only traded "fish
for rights," but they also traded "rights"
for timely political support against the
"Gang of Eight." The original wording of
section 15 and some of the legal rights sections were significantly broadened in the direction advocated by feminist and civil liberties groups. In the end, the Charter had
something for everyone—a politician's
dream come true, but a judicial nightmare.

Before contemptuously dismissing Trudeau for creating such a legal and political
morass, it must be asked whether there
might not be some method in his madness.
For whatever his vices might be, nobody
has ever accused the Prime Minister of
being stupid. Upon closer analysis, there
are really two different categories of
"group rights" in the Charter: the section
15 equality rights and the sections 16-23
minority language and education rights.
The principal difference is that the former
are all subject to the section 33 legislative
override, while the latter are not. This rein-
forces the view that Trudeau's "concessions" to feminists and other civil
libertarian groups on the wording of section
15 and certain of the legal rights sections
were tactical maneuvers designed to gain
wider political support for the overall constitutional package. It also suggests that
perhaps from Trudeau's perspective, they
were not very significant concessions.

From this perspective, the fundamental
or preferred freedoms of the Charter are
not the universal rights and freedoms associated with the practice of liberal democracy everywhere, but rather those rights
and freedoms that are unique to Canadian
experience. Rather than "cluttering up" the
Charter as some commentators have critically remarked, these uniquely Canadian elements may be its heart and soul. Nor,
perhaps, is it coincidence that they correspond closely to, and indeed promote,
Trudeau's vision of a more unified Canada
based on a national policy of bilingualism.

Notes

1 *The Queen v. Drybones* S.C.R. 282 (1970).

2 *Attorney-General of Canada v. Canard*, 52 D.I.R. (3d) 548 (1975).

3 The other two cases are *Regina v. Burnshine*, 44 D.L.R. (3d) 584 (1974), and *Bliss v. Attorney-General of Canada* 92 D.L.R. (3d) 417 (1979).

4 These figures are from Minister for Indian Affairs, John Munro's "secret report" of September, 1983, "Amendments to Remove the Discriminatory Sections of the Indian Act." The unwillingness of provincial leaders to cede disputed land claims was predicted in this report, and demonstrated at the Constitutional Conference of March, 1984. See *Calgary Herald*, March 10, 1984, "Ministers' Meet Collapses."

5 See *Calgary Herald*, April, 1984.

6 *Calgary Herald*, March 10, 1984.

7 This is certainly true as far as religious sects are concerned. Historically it has been true of race as well, until the beginning of "affirmative action" policies in the late sixties. Much of the opposition to "affirmative action" comes from old-style American liberals (now known as "neo-conservatives") who see it as a dangerous deviation from the "colour-blind" constitutional policy announced in *Brown v. Board of Education* in 1954.

8 The section 23 educational language rights are quite explicit, and cannot be avoided by the courts.

9 It was originally speculated that Bill 62 was itself unconstitutional, but it recently withstood a legal challenge. See *Re: Alliance des Professeurs de Montréal et al. v. A.-G. Québec,* Superior Court of Québec, unreported.

10 For an insightful elaboration of the "non-liberal" character of the Parti Québecois' culture policies, see Rainer Knopff's two articles: "Language and Culture in the Canadian Debate: The Battle of the White Papers," *Canadian Review of Studies in Nationalism* (Spring, 1979): 66-82; and "Liberal Democracy and the Challenge of Nationalism in Canadian Politics," *Canadian Review of Studies in Nationalism* (Spring, 1982): 23-42.

11 *Québec Association of Protestant School Boards et al. v. A.-G. Québec* 140 D.L.R. (3d) (1982), 23-42.

12 These questions are all raised but of course not answered in the "roundtable" section of McKercher, (1983): 139-150.

References

Cardinal, Harold. *The Rebirth of Canada's Indians.* Edmonton: Hurtig Publishers, 1977.

Dawson, R. MacGregor. *The Government of Canada.* Revised by Norman Ward, 4th edition. Toronto: University of Toronto Press, 1963.

Flanagan, Thomas. "What are Aboriginal Rights, and Do They Exist?" Paper presented at the Western Canadian Legal History Conference, University of Calgary. April 25-27, 1984.

Glazer, Nathan. *Affirmative Discrimination.* New York: Basic Books, 1974.

Hogg, Peter. *Canada Act 1982 Annotated.* Toronto: Carswell, 1982.

Manuel, George and Michael Posluns. *The Fourth World — An Indian Reality.* Toronto: Collier-Macmillan Canada, 1974.

McKercher, William R., ed. *The US Bill of Rights and the Canadian Charter of Rights and Freedoms.* Toronto: Ontario Economic Council, 1983.

McNaught, Kenneth. *The Pelican History of Canada.* London: Penguin Books, 1960.

Sanders, Douglas. "Prior Claims: An Aboriginal People in the Constitution of Canada." In Stanley M. Beck and Ivan Bernier, *Canada and the New Constitution: The Unfinished Agenda.* Vol. 1. Montreal: The Institute for Research on Public Policy, 1983.

Questions for Discussion

1 Is it possible to reconcile "equality" with protection of specific groups within Canada?

2 Is it better for conflicts about group and individual rights to be resolved in parliament, or in the courts?

Liberalism in Culturally Plural Societies

Will Kymlicka

The following is excerpted from a book in which Will Kymlicka tries to find the appropriate value of community within a liberal framework.

*　　*　　*

So far...I have not made any explicit distinction between two different kinds, or different aspects, of community. On the one hand, there is the political community, within which individuals exercise the rights and responsibilities entailed by the framework of liberal justice. People who reside within the same political community are fellow citizens. On the other hand, there is the cultural community, within which individuals form and revise their aims and ambitions. People within the same cultural community share a culture, a language and history which defines their cultural membership.

Now clearly these two may simply be aspects of the same community: those people who have the same citizenship may also have the same cultural membership. A political community may be coextensive with one cultural community, as is envisaged in the 'nation-state,' and this seems to be the situation implicitly assumed in most contemporary political theory. But the two forms of community may not coincide: the political community may contain two or more groups of people who have different cultures, speaking different languages, developing different cultural traditions. This is the situation in multinational, or cultur-

ally plural, states, and these form the vast majority of the world's states (Connor, 1972 pp. 319-21, van den Berghe, 1981 p. 62).

How should liberals respond to a situation of cultural plurality? Clearly the answer depends on the role cultural membership plays in liberal theory. But this is not a simple matter, and immediately raises a number of questions. What does it mean for people to 'belong' to a cultural community—to what extent are individuals' interests tied to, or their very sense of identity dependent on, a particular culture? And what follows from the fact that people belong to different cultures—do people have a legitimate interest in ensuring the continuation of their own culture, even if other cultures are available in the political community? If they do have such an interest, is it an interest which needs to be given independent recognition in a theory of justice?

These are all questions which arise most pressingly in a culturally plural state, but they go to the heart of the liberal conception of the relationship between self and community. And they give rise to an important political issue: the rights of minority cultures. In [what follows] I use the question of minority rights, and in particular the rights of the aboriginal population in Canada and the United States, as a focal point for exploring these questions about the role of cultural membership in liberal theory.

Aboriginal rights are a part of political life in North America, and perhaps they are the most familiar example of minority rights to the Anglo-American world. Yet they are very much at odds with some of our common self-perceptions. While the United States is often viewed as a 'melting-pot,' without permanently distinct minority cultures, this is clearly not true of the aboriginal population. There is a system of reservations for the American Indian population, within which the members of particular Indian communities have been able (to a greater or lesser degree) to protect their culture. But their ability to do so has rested on having, as a community, unusual rights and powers. The reservations form special political jurisdictions over which Indian communities have certain guaranteed powers, and within which non-Indian Americans have restricted mobility, property, and voting rights.

This scheme for the protection of a minority culture is often treated as an exception, an issue which arises prior to, or outside the bounds of, liberal theory. But it is far from unique in contemporary liberal democracies. It is similar to legislation which establishes special political and social rights for aboriginal peoples in Canada, New Zealand, and Australia as well. And these are similar to many of the special measures of political and cultural autonomy for minorities in the multicultural countries of Western Europe, such as Belgium and Switzerland. And if we look beyond Western liberal democracies to many African, or

Eastern-bloc, countries, the story is very similar. On all continents, in countries of all ideological stripes, we find cultural minorities that have a distinct legal and political status. In these countries, individuals are incorporated into the state, not 'universally' (i.e. so that each individual citizen stands in the same direct relationship to the state), but 'consociationally' (i.e. through membership in one or other of the cultural communities). Under consociational modes of incorporation, the nature of people's rights, and the opportunities for exercising them, tend to vary with the particular cultural community into which they are incorporated. And the justification for these measures focuses on their role in allowing minority cultures to develop their distinct cultural life, an ability insufficiently protected by 'universal' modes of incorporation.

How should liberals respond to these kinds of measures for minority cultures? They may seem, at first glance, to be inconsistent with liberal theories of justice, and that indeed is the common presumption. But, if so, that is a serious matter, for these measures have been important to the political legitimacy, and very stability, of many multicultural countries. Wars have been fought in order to gain or protect these measures. Removing them would have a profound effect on the political culture of these countries, and on the lives of the members of the minority cultures.

It's surprising, then, that liberal theorists haven't explicitly defended, or even discussed, this implication of their theories....

Why is it commonly supposed that liberals must oppose special status for minority cultures? Liberal opposition is often explained in terms of an alleged conflict between individual and collective rights. This is exhibited in recent debates concerning the constitutional definition of the special status of the aboriginal peoples of Canada (i.e. Indian, Inuit, and Métis). This special status was recognized, but left undefined, in Section 35 of the 1982 Constitution Act. Greater specification of this status was to be reached through a series of annual constitutional conferences between government and aboriginal leaders. There was a general consensus that aboriginal peoples should be self-governing, in contrast to the paternalistic legislation under which reservation life had been regulated in detail for decades. But aboriginal leaders said that the principle of aboriginal self-government must include the recognition of certain collective rights, rights which need to be weighed alongside and balanced against more traditional individual rights. For example, self-government would include the ability of aboriginal communities to restrict the mobility, property, and voting rights of non-aboriginal people. Many government officials, on the other hand, demanded that aboriginal self-government operate in a way that leaves intact the structure of individual rights guaranteed elsewhere in the constitution. So the initial agreement soon gave way to disagreement over the relationship between individual and collective rights. (These differences have, so far, proven too great to overcome, and the constitutional rights of aboriginal peoples in Canada remain undefined.)

The accepted wisdom is that liberals must oppose any proposals for self-government which would limit individual rights in the name of collective rights. I think that is a mistake, one that has caused serious harm to the aboriginal population of North America, and to the members of minority cultures in other liberal democracies. This chapter will explore some of the reasons why liberals have opposed collective rights for minority cultures[1]....

What explains the common liberal opposition to such minority rights? It's not difficult to see why liberals have opposed them. Liberalism, as I've presented it, is characterized both by a certain kind of *individualism*—that is, individuals are viewed as the ultimate units of moral worth, as having moral standing as ends in themselves, as 'self-originating sources of valid claims' (Rawls 1980 p. 543); and by a certain kind of *egalitarianism*—that is, every individual has an equal moral status, and hence is to be treated as an equal by the government, with equal concern and respect (Dworkin 1983 p. 24; Rawls 1971 p. 511). Since individuals have ultimate moral status, and since each individual is to be respected as an equal by the government, liberals have demanded that each individual have equal rights and entitlements. Liberals have disagreed amongst themselves as to what these rights should be, because they have different views about what it is to treat people with equal concern and respect. But most would accept that these rights should include rights to mobility, to personal property, and to political participation in one's community. The new Canadian Charter of Rights and Freedoms embodies these liberal principles, guaranteeing such rights to every citizen, regardless of race or sex, ethnicity or language, etc. (Asch, pp. 86-7; Schwartz ch. 1).

There seems to be no room within the moral ontology of liberalism for the idea of collective rights. The community, unlike the individual, is not a 'self-originating source of valid claims.' Once individuals have been treated as equals, with the respect and concern owed them as moral beings, there is no further obligation to treat the communities to which they belong as equals. The community has no moral existence or claims of its own. It is not that community is unimportant to the liberal, but simply that it is important for what it contributes to the lives of individuals, and so cannot ultimately conflict with the claims of individuals. Individual and collective rights cannot compete for the same moral space, in liberal theory, since the value of the collective derives from its contribution to the value of individual lives.

The constitutional embodiment of these liberal principles, in Canada and elsewhere, has played an important role in many of liberalism's greatest achievements in fighting against unjust legislation. For example, in the *Brown v. Board of Education* case, ([1954] 347 US 483), the Fourteenth Amendment of the American Constitution, guaranteeing equal protection of the law to all its citizens, was used to strike down legislation that segregated blacks in the American South. The 'separate but equal' doctrine which had governed racial segregation in the United States for sixty years denied blacks the equal protection of the law. That case dealt solely with segregated school facilities, but it was a major impetus behind the removal of other segregationist legislation in the 1950s, the passage of the Civil Rights and Voting Rights Acts in the 1960s, and the development of mandatory busing, 'head start,' and affirmative action programs in the 1970s; which in turn were the catalyst for similar programs to benefit other groups—Hispanics, women, the handicapped, etc. Indeed, "its educative and moral impact in areas other than public education and, in fact, its whole thrust toward equality and opportunity for all men has

been of immeasurable importance" (Kaplan p. 228). The 'thrust' of this movement was sufficiently powerful to shape non-discrimination and equal protection legislation in countries around the world, and it provided the model for various international covenants on human rights (especially the Convention on the Elimination of All Forms of Racial Discrimination, adopted by the UN General Assembly in 1965). It also underlies the prominent philosophical accounts of liberal equality.

The history of these developments is one of the high points of Western liberalism in the twentieth century, for there is a powerful ideal of equality at work here in the political morality of the community—the idea that every citizen has a right to full and equal participation in the political, economic, and cultural life of the country, without regard to race, sex, religion, physical handicap—without regard to any of the classifications which have traditionally kept people separate and behind.

The logical conclusion of these liberal principles seems to be a 'colour-blind' constitution—the removal of all legislation differentiating people in terms of race or ethnicity (except for temporary measures, like affirmative action, which are believed necessary to reach a colour-blind society). Liberal equality requires the 'universal' mode of incorporating citizens into the state. And this indeed has often been the conclusion drawn by courts in Canada and the United States.

This movement exercised an enormous influence on Canadian Indian policy as well (Berger 1984 p. 94). The desirability of a colour-blind constitution was the explicit motivation behind the 1969 proposals for reforming the Indian Act in Canada. In 1968 Pierre Trudeau was elected Prime

Minister of Canada on a platform of social justice that was clearly influenced by the American political movements. Canada didn't have a policy of segregating blacks, but it did have something which looked very similar. As in the United States, the native Indian population was predominantly living on segregated reserves, and was subject to a complex array of legislation which treated Indians and non-Indians differentially. While every Indian had the right to live on the land of her band, there were restrictions on her ability to use the land, or dispose of her estate as she saw fit, and there was a total prohibition on any alienation of the land. The reservation system also placed restrictions on the mobility, residence, and voting rights of non-Indians in the Indian territory; and in the case of voting rights, the restriction remained even when the non-Indian married into the Indian community. There were, in other words, two kinds of Canadian citizenship, Indian and non-Indian, with different rights and duties, differential access to public services, and different opportunities for participating in the various institutions of Canadian government.

Dismantling this system was one of the top priorities of Trudeau's 'Just Society' policy, and early in 1969 the government released a White Paper on Indian Policy which recommended an end to the special constitutional status of Indians (DIAND 1969). The government proposed that the reservation system, which had protected Indian communities from assimilation, be dismantled. Indians would not, of course, be compelled to disperse and assimilate. They would be free to choose to associate with one another, and co-ordinate the way they used their resources in the market, so as to preserve their way of life. Freedom of association is one of the individual rights to be universally guaranteed in a colour-blind constitution. But they would receive no legal or constitutional help in their efforts. Legislation discriminating against non-Indians in terms of property-rights, mobility rights, or political rights would not be allowed.

From its very conception to the choice of language in the final draft, the policy reflected the powerful influence of the ideal of racial equality which was developing in the United States and the United Nations. Paraphrasing UN human rights instruments, the authors said that the policy rested "upon the fundamental right of Indian people to full and equal participation in the cultural, social, economic and political life in Canada," and this required that the legislative and constitutional bases of discrimination be removed (DIAND 1969 pp. 201-2). Echoing the *Brown* decision, the policy proposed that Indians no longer receive separate services from separate agencies, because "separate but equal services do not provide truly equal treatment" (DIAND 1969 p. 204). Echoing Justice Harlan's famous dictum that the American Constitution should be colour-blind, the Canadian proposal said that "The ultimate aim of removing the specific references to Indians from the constitution may take some time, but it is a goal to be kept constantly in view" (DIAND 1969 p. 202). Perhaps it was the weight of all this normative authority that gave the authors such a sense of righteousness. It is, they said, 'self-evident' that the constitution should be colour-blind, an "undeniable part of equality" that Indians should have equal access to common services; "There can be no argument.... It is right" (DIAND 1969 pp. 202-3).

It is worth emphasizing that the issue was not about temporary measures to help Indians overcome their disadvantaged position in the broader society. While not all liberals are prepared to allow even temporary measures which differentiate on the basis of race or ethnicity, the government proposal followed the more common view that measures such as affirmative action are acceptable. But they are acceptable precisely because they are viewed as appropriate or necessary means to the pursuit of the ideal of a colour-blind constitution. Affirmative action of this sort appeals to the values embodied in that ideal, not to competing values. The issue posed by the special status of Canada's Indians, therefore, was not that of affirmative action, but "whether the granting of permanent political rights to a special class of citizens (rather than special rights on a temporary basis) is possible within an ideology that maintains the principle of equality of consideration" (Asch p. 76). And for the liberal architects of the 1969 proposal, the answer was that liberal equality was incompatible with the permanent assigning of collective rights to a minority culture.

The proposal was immediately applauded by the media, even by opposition parties, as a triumph for liberal justice. Indians, on the other hand, were furious, and after six months of bitter and occasionally violent Indian protest, the policy was withdrawn. In the words of one commentator, the policy was a response "to white liberal demands from the public, not to Indian demands" (Weaver 1981 p. 196). But liberals have only reluctantly retreated from that policy, despite the almost unanimous opposition it received from the Indians themselves. Liberals fear that any deviation from the strict principle of equal individual rights would be the first step down the road to apartheid, to a system where some individuals are viewed as first-class citizens and others only second-class, in virtue of their race or ethnic affiliation. These fears are strengthened when liberals see white South African leaders invoke minority rights in defence of their system of apartheid, and compare their system of tribal homelands to our system of Indian reservations and homelands (*International Herald* p. 2; *Toronto Star* p. B3). If we allow Indians to discriminate against non-Indians in the name of their collective rights, how can we criticize white South Africans for discriminating against blacks in the name of their collective rights?...

The crucial difference between blacks and the aboriginal peoples of North America is, of course, that the latter value their separation from the mainstream life and culture of North America. Separation is not always perceived as a 'badge of inferiority.' Indeed, it is sometimes forgotten that the American Supreme Court recognized this in the *Brown* desegregation case. The Court did not reject the 'separate but equal' doctrine on any universal grounds. The Court ruled that, in the particular circumstances of contemporary American white-black relations, segregation was perceived as a 'badge of inferiority.' The lower motivation of black children in their segregated schools was a crucial factor in their decision. But in Canada, segregation has always been viewed as a defence of a highly valued cultural heritage. It is forced *integration* that is perceived as a badge of inferiority by Indians, damaging their motivation. While there are no special problems about motivation on segregated reserve schools, the drop-out rate for Indians in integrated high schools was over 90 per cent, and in most areas was 100 per cent for post-secondary education (Cardinal 1977 p. 194; Gross p. 238).

Michael Gross distinguishes the case of blacks and Indians this way:

> Where blacks have been forcibly *excluded* (segregated) from white society by law, Indians—aboriginal peoples with their own cultures, languages, religions and territories—have been forcibly *included* (integrated) into that society by law. That is what the [Senate Subcommittee on Indian Education] meant by coercive assimilation—the practice of compelling, through submersion, an ethnic, cultural, and linguistic minority to shed its uniqueness and mingle with the rest of society. (Gross p. 244)

Gross argues that the "integration of Indian children in white-dominated schools had the same negative educational and emotional effects which segregation was held to have on blacks in *Brown*" (Gross p. 245). Therefore, the 'underlying principle' which struck down legislated segregation of blacks (i.e. that racial classifications harmful to a racial minority are unconstitutional) would also strike down legislated integration of Indians (Gross p. 248).[2] Assimilation for the Indians, like segregation for the blacks, is a badge of inferiority which, in the words of the Senate Subcommittee, fails "to recognize the importance and validity of the Indian community" and which results in a "dismal record" of "negative self-image [and] low achievement" as the "classroom and the school [become] a kind of battleground where the Indian child attempts to protect his integrity and identity as an individual by defeating the purposes of the school" (Gross p. 242). Similar situations arise when Indians have to assimilate later in life, e.g. at work.

But to say that segregation is preferred by the Indians is not to say it is, or even could be, the natural result of the interplay of preferences in the market. On the contrary, the viability of Indian communities depends on coercively restricting the mobility, residence, and political rights of both Indians and non-Indians. It is this which raises the need for the minority rights that are decried by many liberals, rights that go beyond non-discrimination and affirmative action.

These special needs are met, in Canada, by two different forms of aboriginal community arrangements (Asch, ch. 7). In the reservations of southern Canada, where the population is high and land scarce, the stability of Indian communities is made possible by denying non-Indians the right to purchase or reside on Indian lands (unless given special permission). In the north, however, they are creating political arrangements for the Indian and Inuit population which would have none of these restrictions. Under these arrangements, non-aboriginal people will be free to take jobs, buy land, and reside as long as they want; the inhospitability of the environment ensures that aboriginal people are not likely to be outnumbered by non-aboriginal permanent residents. However, northern Canada is rich in resources, and development projects will often bring in huge influxes of temporary resident workers. While very few, if any, of these workers are likely to remain in the north for more than seven years, so that the aboriginal people will continue to constitute the majority of permanent residents, at any one time non-aboriginal people may well form the majority. If non-aboriginal transient workers were allowed to vote, they would probably decide to use public money to provide amenities for themselves—movie theatres, dish antennas for television reception, even a Las Vegas-styled resort. Since many aboriginal people in the north are dependent on short-term work projects due to the seasonal nature of most economic activity in the area, such a policy could force them to move into localities dominated by whites, and to work and live in another culture, in a different language. Transient residents might also use their voting power to demand that public services and education be provided in their own language, at the expense of the provision of services and education in aboriginal languages.[3]

To guard against this, aboriginal leaders have proposed a three-to-ten-year residency requirement before one becomes eligible to vote for, or hold, public office, and a guaranteed 30 per cent aboriginal representation in the regional government, with veto power over legislation affecting crucial aboriginal interests. If this scheme proved unable to protect aboriginal communities, they would have the power to impose even greater restrictions, most likely on immigration, and thereby move closer to the southern model, which avoids the necessity of restricting voting rights by simply denying non-aboriginal people a chance to gain residence. In other words, there is a continuum of possibilities, involving greater or lesser guarantees of power for aboriginal people, and greater or lesser restrictions on the mobility and political rights of non-aboriginal people (see Bartlett, and Lyon pp. 48-65, for some of the variants). Aboriginal groups have demanded the restrictions they believe to be necessary to protect their communities.

Historically, the evidence is that when the land on which aboriginal communities are based became desirable for white settle-ment and development, the only thing which prevented the undesired disintegration of the community was legally entrenched non-alienability of land. Indeed the most common way of breaking open stubbornly held Indian land for white settlement was to force the Indians to take individual title to alienable land, making the pressure on some individuals to sell almost unbearable, partly because Indians were financially deprived (and hence in need of money to meet the basic needs of the family), and also because they were culturally ill-equipped to understand the consequences of having (or selling) title to land (Sanders 1983a pp. 4-12; Kronowitz et al. pp. 530-1; MacMeekin p. 1239). Such measures to endow individual title are usually justified as giving Indians greater choice. The White Paper, for example, proclaimed that "full and true equality calls for Indian control and ownership of reserve land...[this] carries with it the free choice of use, retention, or of disposition" (DIAND 1969 p. 209). The Minister responsible for the policy said he was only trying to give Indians the same freedom to manage their own affairs as other Canadians (Bowles et al. p. 215). But Indians have as much free choice over the use of their land as the average renter has over her public-housing apartment. Indeed rather more, since the Indian bands are like cooperatively-managed apartment buildings. Moreover, unlike renters, Indians get a per capita share of the band's funds if they choose to leave the reservation. The reservation system can thus combine considerable freedom of individual choice over the use of one's resources with protection of the community from the disintegrating effects of the collective action problem that would result were the costs of maintaining the community borne individually. Whatever the motivation for the endowing of individual title, the effect has been to sacrifice the Indian community in order to protect the mobility rights of individual non-Indians.

But the reservation system causes a problem in the case of mixed marriages. Every member of an Indian band has the right to reside on the band reserve—not the right to buy land on the reserve, since that land can't be bought or sold, but the right to be allocated a plot of land to live on. If the band population grew at a natural rate from purely intra-band marriages, there wouldn't be a problem. But when there are a substantial number of marriages to people from outside the band, if the majority of such mixed couples prefer to live on the reserve (as they do), then there will soon be a problem of overcrowding. Unless there is the possibility of expanding the land-base, some mechanism is needed to control the membership.

In the United States, they use a blood criterion. Only those with a certain proportion of Indian blood can be full members of the band, so non-Indian spouses never acquire membership, nor do the children if they have less than the required proportion. Non-members never acquire the right to participate in band government, and should the Indian spouse die, they have no right to residence and so can be evicted; while non-member children must leave the reserve at the age of eighteen. In Canada, the obvious drawbacks of the blood criterion are replaced by a kinship system; everyone in a nuclear family has the same status. If one person in the family has membership, they all do, and so all have full non-contingent rights of residence and participation in band government. Clearly, however, not every mixed family can have membership—that

would create over-population. If some non-Indians gain membership for themselves and their children by marrying an Indian, there must also be some Indians who give up membership for themselves and their children by marrying a non-Indian. In Canada, until recently it has been Indian women who lose status upon entering into a mixed marriage.

There is an obvious trade-off here—sexual equality for family integrity. There are other models for regulating membership (Sanders 1972 pp. 83-7; Manyfingers) some of which are more equitable. But all options have this in common; if the land-base is fixed and over-population threatens, some Indians will not legally be able to marry a non-Indian and have him or her move in and become a full and equal member of the community. Again, there is a continuum of possibilities involved: some proposals allow non-Indian spouses to vote but not to hold office, others allow non-member spouses and children to remain after the death of the Indian spouse but not to vote, etc. (DIAND, 1982). In all cases there are restrictions on the marriage and voting rights of both Indians and non-Indians: these are viewed as the concomitants of the reservation system needed to protect Indian cultural communities.

There are also controversial measures concerning language rights. The Charter of Rights and Freedoms guarantees to all Canadian citizens the right to a public education in either of the two official languages (English or French), and to deal with all levels of government in either of these languages, where numbers permit. Aboriginal leaders have sought exemption from this. Allowing new residents in the community to receive education and public services in English would weaken the long-term viability of the community. Not only will new residents not have to fully integrate into the minority culture, the establishment of an anglophone infrastructure will attract new anglophone arrivals who may have no interest in even partial integration into the aboriginal community. This is a concern for French-Canadians in Quebec, who want to limit access to English-language schools for people moving into the province. On the other hand, parents will demand their right to a publicly funded education in English so that their children will not be at a disadvantage if they choose to enter the historically dominant and privileged social, political, and economic life in English Canada.

This is just a partial survey of some of the aspects of the aboriginal rights question in Canada. The arrangements are not uniform across the country, and they are all in a state of flux as a result of the unfinished constitutional negotiations. But we can at least get a sense of the basic issues raised for a liberal theory of justice. The common element in all these measures is that some of the recognized rights and liberties of liberal citizenship are limited, and unequally distributed, in order to preserve a minority culture. And we could tell similar stories about the goals and effects of minority rights schemes in other countries, notwithstanding their many variations.

As we've seen, many liberals treat these measures as obviously unjust, and as simple disguises for the perpetuation of ethnic or racial inequality. But once we recognize the differences between these measures and the segregation of blacks, judgements of fairness become more complex, and our intuitions concerning individual and collective measures may be divided.

What underlies this conflict of intuitions? At first glance, someone might suppose that the conflict is between 'respect for the individual' and 'respect for the group.' On this view, to endorse minority rights at the expense of individual rights would be to value the group over the individual. But there is another, and I believe more accurate, view of our intuitions. On this view, both sides of the dilemma concern respect for the individual. The problem is that there are two kinds of respect for individuals at stake here, both of which have intuitive force.

If we respect Indians as Indians, that is to say, as members of a distinct cultural community, then we must recognize the importance to them of their cultural heritage, and we must recognize the legitimacy of claims made by them for the protection of that culture. These claims deserve attention, even if they conflict with some of the requirements of the Charter of Rights. It may not seem right, for example, that aboriginal homelands in the north must be scrapped just because they require a few migrant workers to be temporarily disenfranchised at the local level. It doesn't seem fair for the Indian and Inuit population to be deprived of their cultural community just because a few whites wish to exercise their mobility rights fully throughout the country. If aboriginal peoples can preserve their cultural life by extending residency requirements for non-aboriginal people, or restricting the alienability of the land-base, doesn't that seem a fair and reasonable request? To give every Canadian equal citizenship rights without regard to race or ethnicity, given the vulnerability of aboriginal communities to the decisions of the non-aboriginal majority, does not seem to treat Indians and Inuit with equal respect. For it ignores a potentially devastating problem faced by aboriginal people, but not by English-Canadians—the loss of cultural membership. To insist that this problem be recognized and fairly dealt with hardly sounds like an insistence on racial or ethnic privilege.

Yet if we respect people as Canadians, that is to say as citizens of the common political community, then we must recognize the importance of being able to claim the rights of equal citizenship. Limitations on, and unequal distribution of, individual rights clearly impose burdens. One can readily understand the feeling of discrimination that occurs when an Indian woman is told she can't get a publicly funded education in English for her child (or when a white man is told that he can't vote in the community he resides in or contributes to).

There is, I think, a genuine conflict of institutions here, and it is a conflict between two different considerations involved in showing respect for persons. People are owed respect as citizens and as members of cultural communities. In many situations, the two are perfectly compatible, and in fact may coincide. But in culturally plural societies, differential citizenship rights may be needed to protect a cultural community from unwanted disintegration. If so, then the demands of citizenship and cultural membership pull in different directions. Both matter, and neither seems reducible to the other. (Indeed, when Charles Taylor wanted to illustrate the ultimate plurality of moral value, he chose precisely this conflict between equality for Indians *qua* members of a cultural community and equality for Indians *qua* citizens of the political community: C. Taylor 1988 p. 25.)

The special status of aboriginal people can be viewed as an acceptable, if imperfect, resolution of this conflict. Such conflicts are, in fact, endemic to the day-to-day politics of culturally plural societies,

and various schemes of minority rights can be understood and evaluated in this light.

Liberalism, as commonly interpreted, doesn't recognize the legitimacy of one half of this dilemma. It gives no independent weight to our cultural membership, and hence demands equal rights of citizenship, regardless of the consequences for the existence of minority cultures. As Taylor has said: "The modern notion of equality will suffer no differences in the field of opportunity which individuals have before them. Before they choose, individuals must be interchangeable; or alternatively put, any differences must be chosen" (C. Taylor 1979 p. 132). This conception of equality gives no recognition to individuals' cultural membership, and if it operates in a culturally plural country, then it tends to produce a single culture for the whole of the political community, and the undesired assimilation of distinct minority cultural communities. The continued existence of such communities may require restrictions on choice and differentials in opportunity. If liberal equality requires equal citizenship rights, and equal access to a common 'field of opportunity,' then some minority cultures are endangered. And this, I believe, does not respond to our intuitions about the importance of our cultural membership.

If we are troubled by this failure of liberal theories to do justice to our institutions about the importance of cultural membership, two responses are possible. One response is to say that liberals have misinterpreted the role that cultural membership can or must play in their own theory. On this view, the correct interpretation of liberalism does not require universal incorporation or a colour-blind constitution, and liberals should accept the possible legitimacy of minority rights. The other response is to accept that liberalism accords no role to cultural membership, and precludes minority rights, but then say that liberalism is incomplete, or perhaps entirely inapplicable to the case of minority rights at stake. On this view, we should seek some other moral theory or set of values which will recognize the importance of cultural membership and the legitimacy of minority rights.

Supporters of aboriginal self-government in Canada have tended to adopt this second approach, defending aboriginal rights *against* liberalism. Liberalism is said to be incomplete or inapplicable for a number of reasons: some claim that the aboriginal population has special rights because their ancestors were here first (Cardinal 1969; Dene Nation; Robinson and Quinney); others claim that Indians and Inuit are properly viewed as 'peoples' under international law, and so have the right of self-determination (Sanders 1983*a* pp. 21-5; Robinson and Quinney pp. 141-2; L.C. Green p. 346); some claim that aboriginal peoples have a different value system, emphasizing the community rather than the individual, and hence group rights rather than individual rights (Ponting and Gibbins 1986 p. 216; Little Bear, Boldt, and Long p. xvi; Svensson pp. 451-2); yet others suggest that aboriginal communities *themselves* have certain rights, because groups as well as individuals have legitimate moral claims (Boldt and Long 1985 pp. 343-5). These are all common ways of defending aboriginal rights against liberalism, by locating our intuitions in favour of them in some non-liberal theory of rights or values.[4]

However, I think that the first response—the attempt to reconcile minority rights and liberal equality—is worth consid-

ering, whether one's first commitment is to liberalism, or to minority rights....

The current liberal hostility to minority rights is, I [shall] argue, misguided. However, it is not the result of any simple or obvious mistake, and identifying the problem requires looking deep into the liberal view of the self and community. And even if we recognize the problem, there is no simple or obvious way to correct it within a liberal theory of justice. The issue for liberal theory is not as simple as Trudeau once suggested, in response to a question about his reasons for advancing and then withdrawing the 1969 proposal:

> We had perhaps the prejudices of small 'l' liberals and white men at that who thought that equality meant the same law for everybody, and that's why as a result of this we said 'well let's abolish the Indian Act and make Indians citizens of Canada like everyone else. And let's let Indians dispose of their lands just like every other Canadian. And let's make sure that Indians can get their rights, education, health and so on, from the governments like every other Canadian.' But we learned in the process we were a bit too abstract, we were not perhaps pragmatic enough or understanding enough. (Quoted in Weaver 1981 p. 185.)

I shall argue that the problem isn't just one of pragmatism or prejudice. The idea of collective rights for minority cultures doesn't just conflict with the pre-reflective habits or prejudices of liberals. It seems in direct conflict with some of the most fundamental liberal principles, even in their most theoretically sophisticated formulations. And so the search for a liberal defence of minority rights will take us back into the heart of liberal theory....

Notes

1   One terminological point concerning the specific example of minority rights or special status that I am using: the issue of minority rights is raised in many countries by the presence of aboriginal peoples who have been conquered, colonized, or simply overrun by settlers from other countries and continents. The rights of Canada's aboriginal peoples are, therefore, representative of a major class of minority rights questions. However, the term 'aboriginal rights' is sometimes used in a more restricted sense, to refer solely to those rights which flow from original occupancy of the land. Hence some writers distinguish between the 'aboriginal rights' of aboriginal peoples (e.g. land claims) and their 'national rights,' 'minority rights,' or 'human rights' (e.g. to cultural freedom, self-determination, language rights, etc.)— e.g. Barsh and Henderson 1982 p. 76. But this restricted usage is uncommon, and I shall be using 'aboriginal rights' to refer to the rights of aboriginal peoples, not simply to those rights which aboriginal people have because they are the original occupants of the land.

One of the most important aspects of minority rights claims concerns the ability of minority cultures to restrict the mobility or voting rights of non-members. In the context of Canada's aboriginal people, this is invariably phrased as a matter of whether aboriginal communities can restrict the rights of 'whites.' The historical basis for this usage is obvious, and it has become an unquestioned part of the political vocabulary of the debate over aboriginal rights. But it is important to note that 'whites' is not being used as a racial term—many people who are racially white have become members of aboriginal communities (by marriage or adoption), and Canadians who are not members of aboriginal communities have diverse racial ancestry (including aboriginal ancestry). The terms 'aboriginal' and 'white' refer to cultural membership, not race. 'White' has simply become a general label for those Canadians who are not members of aboriginal communities. Hence many of the aboriginal people who demand restrictions on the mobility of 'whites' have some white ancestry, and many of the people whose mobility is being restricted have some aboriginal (or black, or Asian, etc.) ancestry.

2   Similarly, the principles underlying the Supreme Court decisions which struck down legislation redrawing political boundaries so as to *exclude* blacks from political subdivisions (e.g. *Gomillion*

v. Lightfoot [1960] 364 US 339) would seem to argue against legislation to *include* Indians in political subdivisions which are unrepresentative and therefore harmful to their interests (Gross p. 250).

3   This is precisely what happened to the Métis in Manitoba, and to the Hispanic population in the American Southwest, during the second half of the nineteenth century. These groups formed a majority in their respective regions, and had rights to public services and education in their own languages. But once their regions became incorporated into the larger Canadian and American federations, these groups became outnumbered by anglophone settlers, who quickly proceeded to take away those rights (see J. Weinstein pp. 46-7 on the Métis; Glazer 1975 p. 25 and 1983 p. 277 on the Spanish-speaking population of the Southwest). Aboriginal self-government proposals have been designed with these dangers and historical precedents in mind. (J. Weinstein p. 47; Purich p. 229).

4   I shall discuss the weakness of the last two arguments (about the different value systems of aboriginal peoples, and the moral standing of communities) [elsewhere]. I am unsure what to say about the first two, partly because they in fact have many variants, some of which contradict others. But I should say something about them, since they are important not only in Canada, but in the emerging international norms concerning aboriginal rights.

The fact of original occupancy is invoked to defend at least two different aboriginal claims. The first is 'aboriginal title' (i.e. ownership or usufructuary rights over land and natural resources), the second is sovereignty. I'll discuss sovereignty together with the self-determination argument, since they raise similar questions of international law.

The 'aboriginal title' claim, by itself, does not justify permanent special political status, unless it is further claimed that "the ownership of the land is the fundamental concept on which other rights, including the right to self-government, are based" (Sanders, 1983*b* pp. 328-9). This is in fact the argument amongst some aboriginal groups whose land-base is secure and legally recognized. However, the emphasis on aboriginal title raises a number of questions. Firstly, it is far from clear why it matters who first acquired a piece of land, unless one is inclined to a Nozick-like theory of justice (Lyons; McDonald 1976). Aboriginal communities were, of course, unjustly deprived of much of their land when whites settled, and those injustices have lingering effects which warrant some form of compensation. But that is not yet a reason why the ultimate goal shouldn't be some form of equality of resources for all the citizens of the country, rather than any permanent special status. Secondly, if self-government is supposed to flow from aboriginal title, then there may not be any grounds to demand that the federal government fund aboriginal self-government (Lyon pp. 13-14). Finally, it won't justify either land or self-government for some aboriginal groups, who for various (and often historically arbitrary) reasons lack recognizable title (Robinson and Quinney pp. 51, 86; Opekokew).

The sovereignty claim says that because aboriginal nations were here first, and have not officially relinquished their sovereignty, therefore, as a matter of international law, domestic Canadian law does not apply to aboriginal communities. Any relationship between the federal government and the aboriginal communities must be concluded by what are essentially state-to-state treaties. On the self-determination view, aboriginal peoples are entitled to the same right to self-determination that previously colonized peoples claim under Article 1 of the International Covenant on Civil and Political Rights. The two views often go hand in hand (e.g. Robinson and Quinney), but they are distinct, since aboriginal communities could have sovereignty even if they are not 'peoples' under international law, or they could be 'peoples' even if they do not have sovereignty under international law.

However, neither claim has heretofore been explicitly recognized in international law. Aboriginal rights have instead been viewed as coming under Article 27 of the Covenant, dealing with minority rights (see e.g. United Nations 1983 pp. 94-104), which is roughly how I have been treating them. Most aboriginal leaders have been concerned to change that pattern (see e.g. Sanders 1983b pp. 21-5; Barsh 1983 pp. 91-5, 1986 pp. 376-7; Kronowitz et al. pp. 598-600; L.C. Green p. 346; Robinson and Quinney pp. 141-2), although some people have thought Article 27 sufficient (e.g. Svensson p. 438). Aboriginal advocates rightly point out that international rulings have been quite arbitrary in limiting the recognition of sovereignty or peoplehood to overseas colonies (the 'Blue Water Thesis'), while denying it to internal groups who share many of the same historical and social features (e.g. Barsh 1983 pp. 84-91).

But since advocates of self-determination and sovereignty views are not in fact seeking a sovereign state, it is not immediately clear what rests on the distinction between Article 1 and Article 27 rights. Article 27 has occasionally been interpreted as merely requiring non-discrimination against minorities. But the recent Capotorti report on the international protection of minority rights decisively rejects that view, and insists that special measures for minority cultures are required for 'factual equality,' and that such measures are as important as non-discrimination in 'defending fundamental human rights' (Capotorti pp. 40-1, 98-9). If the goal is not a sovereign state, then Article 27 may be as good as Article 1 in arguing for the right of minority cultures to freely develop and express their own culture. As Wirsing notes, recent changes in the interpretation of Article 27 go 'some distance towards closing the gap' between the expectations of minority cultures and the concessions of the international community (Wirsing 1980 p. 228). And while elimination of the 'Blue Water Thesis' in regard to the definition of 'peoples' would eliminate some arbitrariness, it would also essentially eliminate the category of 'minorities' (most groups which have sought special measures under Article 27 would constitute peoples, not minorities, according to the definitions offered by some aboriginal groups—e.g. the Mikmaq proposal quoted in Barsh 1983 p. 94.)

One worry aboriginals have about Article 27, even on an expansive reading, concerns not the content of the rights it may accord to minorities, but the question of who *delegates* the rights. They are aware of the vulnerability created by the American system of aboriginal rights, in which self-government "is a gift, not a right...a question of policy and politics" (Kronowitz et al. pp. 533, 535; cf. Barsh 1983 p. 103). Some aboriginal leaders believe that claims to sovereignty are needed to avoid this vulnerability (see e.g. Robinson and Quinney p. 123). But others say that such claims heighten misunderstanding and prevent the negotiation of adequate guarantees. "The maximum height on the government side is generated by the word 'sovereignty'; and on the aboriginal side, by the word 'delegated.' Somewhere between the two lies an area of potential agreement" (M. Dunn p. 37).

Since Article 1 has not been applied to the aboriginal peoples of North America, and since Article 27 may still be too weak, some aboriginal groups have been pressing for the recognition of a specifically aboriginal category between those of 'peoples' and 'minorities,' in which self-determination is neither sovereign nor delegated (see Moore pp. 27-8; Kronowitz *et al.* pp. 612-20; Barsh 1986 pp. 376-8; Sanders 1983*b* pp. 28-9). The question of whether self-government is delegated or not is clearly important, but it is somewhat distinct from the questions I am addressing. If aboriginal rights to self-determination are not delegated, or indeed if aboriginal communities retain their legal sovereignty, then aboriginals should be able to reject the substantive provisions of a Canadian government proposal for self-government, should they view them as unjust. My question is the prior one of evaluating the justice of the provisions. And it may be that the same substantive provisions would be just whether aboriginal groups are viewed as peoples, or as minorities, or as their own third category. The different categories would affect not only the justice of their claims, but their domestic and international ability to negotiate for those just claims.

Even if aboriginal peoples have substantive claims which cannot be derived from Article 27, in virtue of aboriginal title or legal sovereignty, it is still important for liberals to determine what is owed minorities under that article. Even if aboriginal peoples have special rights beyond those owed them as a minority culture, liberals should ask what they (or other minorities) are owed just in virtue of plural cultural membership. In any event, it is doubtful whether all North American aboriginal groups could qualify as sovereign or self-determining peoples under international law. So a liberal defence of minority rights, if one can be found, would be a helpful argument for many aboriginal groups, and may be the only argument available for some of the groups.

References

Asch, M. (1984). *Home and Native Land: Aboriginal Rights and the Canadian Constitution*. Toronto: Methuen.

Barsh, R. (1983). 'Indigenous North America and Contemporary International Law.' *Oregon Law Review*. Vol. 62.

————. (1986). 'Indigenous Peoples: An Emerging Object of International Law.' *American Journal of International Law*. Vol 80.

Barsh, R., and Henderson, J.Y. (1982). 'Aboriginal Rights, Treaty Rights, and Human Rights: Indian Tribes and Constitutional Renewal.' *Journal of Canadian Studies*. Vol 17.

Bartlett, R. (1986). *Subjugation, Self-Management and Self-Government of Aboriginal Lands and Resources in Canada*. Kingston, Ont.: Institute of Intergovernmental Relations.

Berger, T. (1984). 'Towards the Regime of Tolerance.' In *Political Thought in Canada: Contemporary Perspectives*. Ed. S. Brooks. Toronto: Irwin Publishing.

Boldt, M., and Long, J.A. (1985). 'Tribal Philosophies and the Canadian Charter of Rights and Freedoms.' In *The Quest for Justice: Aboriginal People and Aboriginal Rights*. Eds. Boldt, M., and Long, J.A. Toronto: University of Toronto Press.

Bowles, R., Hanley, J., Hodgins, B., and Rawlyk, G. (1972). *The Indian: Assimilation, Integration or Separation?* Scarborough, Ont.: Prentice-Hall.

Capotorti, F. (1979). *Study on the Rights of Persons Belonging to Ethnic, Religious and Linguistic Minorities*. UN Doc. E/CN 4/Sub. 2/384 Rev. 1.

Cardinal, H. (1969). *The Unjust Society*. Edmonton: Hurtig Publishers.

————. (1977). *The Rebirth of Canada's Indians*. Edmonton: Hurtig Publishers.

Connor, W. (1972). 'Nation-Building or Nation-Destroying?' *World Politics*, Vol. 24.

Dene Nation (1977). 'A Proposal to the Government and People of Canada.' In *Dene Nation: The Colony Within*. Ed. M. Watkins. Toronto: University of Toronto Press.

DIAND (Department of Indian Affairs and Northern Development). (1969). 'A Statement of the Government of Canada on Indian Policy.' In Bowles *et al.* (1972).

————. (1982). 'The Elimination of Sex Discrimination from the Indian Act.' R32-59/1982. Ottawa.

Dunn, M. (1986). *Access to Survival: A Perspective on Aboriginal Self-Government for the Constituency of the Native Council of Canada*. Kingston, Ont.: Institute of Intergovernmental Relations.

Dworkin, R. (1983). 'In Defense of Equality.' *Social Philosophy and Policy*, Vol. 1.

Glazer, N. (1975). *Affirmative Discrimination: Ethnic Inequality and Public Policy*. New York: Basic Books.

————. (1983). *Ethnic Dilemmas: 1964–1982*. Cambridge, Mass.: Harvard University Press.

Green, L.C. (1983). 'Aboriginal Peoples, International Law and the Canadian Charter of Rights and Freedoms.' *Canadian Bar Review*, Vol. 61.

Gross, M. (1973). 'Indian Control for Quality Indian Education.' *North Dakota Law Review*, Vol. 49.

International Herald Tribune (1985). 'Botha Rejects Plea From Within Party to End Home School Segregation.' 3 Oct.

Kaplan, J. (1964). 'Comment on "The Decade of School Desegregation".' *Columbia Law Review*, Vol. 64.

Kronowitz, R., Lichtman, J., McSloy, S., and Olsen, M. (1987). 'Toward Consent and Cooperation: Reconsidering the Political Status of Indian Nations.' *Harvard Civil Rights–Civil Liberties Review*, Vol. 22.

Little Bear, L., Boldt, M., and Long, J. (1984). *Pathways to Self-Determination: Canadian Indians and the Canadian State*. Toronto: University of Toronto Press.

Lyon, N. (1984). *Aboriginal Self-Government: Rights of Citizenship and Access to Government Services*. Kingston, Ont.: Institute of Intergovernmental Relations.

Lyons, D. (1981). 'The New Indian Claims and Original Rights to Land.' In *Reading Nozick: Essays on* Anarchy, State and Utopia. Ed. J. Paul. Totowa, NJ.: Rowman and Littlefield.

McDonald, M. (1976). 'Aboriginal Rights.' In *Contemporary Issues in Political Philosophy*. Eds. W. Shea and J. King-Farlow. New York: Science History Publications.

MacMeekin, D. (1969). 'Red, White and *Gray*: Equal Protection and the American Indian.' *Stanford Law Review*, Vol. 21.

Manyfingers, M. (1986). 'Determination of Indian Band Membership: An Examination of Political Will.' *Canadian Journal of Native Studies*, Vol. 6.

Moore, K. (1984). *The Will to Survive: Native People and the Constitution*. Val d'Or, Que.: Hyperborea Publishings.

Opekokew, D. (1987). *The Political and Legal Inequalities Among Aboriginal Peoples in Canada*. Kingston, Ont.: Institute of Intergovernmental Affairs.

Ponting, J., and Gibbins, R. (1986). 'An Assessment of the Probable Impact of Aboriginal Self-Government in Canada.' In *The Politics of Gender, Ethnicity, and Language in Canada*. Eds.

A. Cairns and C. Williams. Toronto: University of Toronto Press.

Rawls, J. (1971). *A Theory of Justice*. London: Oxford University Press.

————. (1980). 'Kantian Constructivism in Moral Theory.' *Journal of Philosophy*. Vol. 77.

Robinson, E., and Quinney, H. (1985). *The Infested Blanket: Canada's Constitution—Genocide of Indian Nations*. Winnipeg: Queenston House.

Sanders, D. (1972). 'The Bill of Rights and Indian Status.' *University of British Columbia Law Review*. Vol. 7.

————. (1983*a*). 'The Re-Emergence of Indigenous Questions in International Law.' *Canadian Human Rights Yearbook 1983*. Toronto: Carswell.

————. (1983*b*). 'The Rights of the Aboriginal Peoples of Canada.' *Canadian Bar Review*. Vol. 61.

Schwartz, B. (1986). *First Principles, Second Thoughts: Aboriginal Peoples, Constitutional Reform and Canadian Statecraft*. Montreal: The Institute for Research on Public Policy.

Svensson, F. (1979). 'Liberal Democracy and Group Rights: The Legacy of Individualism and Its Impact on American Indian Tribes.' *Political Studies*. Vol. 27.

Taylor, C. (1979). *Hegel and Modern Society*. Cambridge: Cambridge University Press.

————. (1988). *Justice After Virtue*. Legal Theory Workshop Series, Faculty of Law, University of Toronto. WS 1987-88 no. 3.

Toronto Star (1986). 'Botha's Warning.' 28 Sept.

United Nations Human Rights Committee. (1983). *Considerations of Reports Submitted by States Parties under Article 40 of the Covenant: Canada*. CCPR/C/1/Add. 62.

van de Berghe, P. (1981). *The Ethnic Phenomenon*. New York: Elsevier.

Weaver, S. (1981). *Making Canadian Indian Policy*. Toronto: University of Toronto Press.

Weinstein, J. (1986). *Aboriginal Self-Determination off a Land Base*. Kingston, Ont.: Institute of Intergovernmental Relations.

Wirsig, R. (1980). 'Cultural Minorities: Is the World Ready to Protect Them?' *Canadian Review of Studies in Nationalism*. Vol 7.

Questions for Discussion

1 Should "liberals" oppose any proposals which would limit individual rights in the name of collective rights?

2 Is "community" valuable only for what it contributes to the lives of individuals?

Aboriginal Peoples and the Canadian Charter

Mary Ellen Turpel

The following is excerpted from an article in which Turpel raises doubts about the applicability of a legal system based on a particular culture (European) to other cultures, in particular those of aboriginal peoples.

*   *   *

The Rights Paradigm

The whole fabric of rights discourse constitutes the more subtle level at which the undifferentiated legal framework displays its cultural imagery. The struggle over the division of social, political, and economic power in Canadian society has been formulated by the Charter as a set of rights claims or as a dispute over rights in order to give it constitutional currency. Even multiculturalism operates as an interpretive rider on rights analysis in the Charter. Sections 25 and 27 of the Charter, the interpretation provisions on aboriginal and treaty rights and multiculturalism, are said to take account of cultural differences in constitutional human rights conflicts.[1] It is significant to note that these are provisions within a rights-focused framework of legal analysis. Consequently, any consideration of cultural differences suggested by sections 25 and 27 will be formulated within the predetermined mode of reasoning, central to Anglo-European legal discourse, of rights claims or claims against the state. These provisions do attempt to address differences or "otherness," from within the dominant or prevalent method of resolving legal conflicts. It is noteworthy, however, that they are construed as exceptional or special provisions within the rights-based dominant style of analysis. Hence, we are in the realm of the special, exceptional, or "other" in section 25, and arguably in section 27, rather than in the realm of the fundamentally different, incongruous, or incommensurable. Arguments for multiculturalism are particularly offensive because they presume differences to be "minority" matters that are manageable, interpretively, from within the majority-conceived scheme of the Charter. This is an aberration to aboriginal people because it does not recognize the fundamental challenge presented by cultural difference to the rights approach to social conflicts.[2]

Because the rights regime is dominant, sanctioned and elevated as the supreme law, it must filter all conflicts through its categories and conceptual apparatus. The rights regime dominates the culturally different interpretive communities by using its own conceptual framework to apply the provisions of the Charter to "others" even though these provisions may be interpreted in a "special" way. It decides for those it doesn't understand, using a framework that undermines their objectives. It performs a levitation trick by transforming differences into rights within the supreme law of Canada.

To what extent can a rights paradigm of analysis be viable universally? Is it shared by culturally different peoples? I suggest that the "rights" analysis and imagery is a projection of an exclusionary cultural or political self-image. In situating this assertion in the context of aboriginal peoples, I am faced with the fact that rights discourse has been widely appropriated by aboriginal peoples in struggles against the effects of colonialism, and that we have been encouraged to do so. Here it is important to distinguish arguments that are made for aboriginal peoples by legal scholars who do not share a common ancestry or culture with those for whom they write, from the much smaller body of literature by aboriginal persons.[3] This distinction is critical because just as cultural difference is acknowledged, aboriginal peoples are faced with a response, at least from the legal community that is ostensibly "supportive," that unwittingly perpetuates their domination through a false reconciliation of differences. For example, in the introduction to a pair of recent articles by W. Pentney, one finds a general disclaimer to the effect that his work on the Charter was written from the perspective of a supporter and that it is entirely conceivable that many aboriginal peoples would not share/understand his perspective.[4] However, in the text, this modesty seems to be effaced by the legal analysis advanced. He constructs an argument that by-passes cultural differences and advances a thesis that assumes that if only better legal tests were developed to balance collective and individual rights, and more care were taken to define aboriginal rights, the problems with the culturally hegemonic self-image of the Charter could be conceivably resolved.[5] The task is frequently formulated as one of better thinking, more rigorous analysis, and consciousness-building in order to decide how to "apply" the constitution to aboriginal peoples. This style, even, as here, in its best-intentioned form, has provoked frustration and criticism from aboriginal writers, many of whom would suggest that the legal arguments simply mask social and political conflicts between aboriginal peoples and the Canadian state, concealing the painful experiences of aboriginal peoples under bureaucratic rule. An expression of the sense of domination felt by aboriginal people when someone from "outside" the cultural framework sets out to solve and reconcile conflicts is expressed in an article by Patricia Monture.[6] She writes:

Following this tradition of oral history and storytelling, I want to share one of my experiences with you. Like most other academics, I spent at least a little bit of my time going to conferences, listening to other people, and learning and sharing what we are thinking. This is a story about a conference I attended, a legal conference, that I want to tell you. It is also a story about anger. My anger is not unique to this conference;

it is paralleled at many other conferences I have been to and the classes I have been to, most other days in my life, so it is an important story.... [She relates her reaction to a discussion of a racial incident].... *This is my life*. I do not have any control over the pain and brutality of living the life of a dispossessed person. I cannot control when that pain is going to enter my life. I had gone away for this conference quite settled with having to deal with racism, pure and simple. But, I was not ready to have my pain appropriated. I am pretty possessive about my pain. It is my pain. I worked hard for it. Some days it is all I have. Some days it is the only thing I can feel. Do not try to take that away from me too. That was what was happening to me in that discussion. My pain was being taken away from me and put on the table and poked and prodded with these sticks, these hypotheticals. "Let's see what happened next." I felt very much under a microscope, even if it was not my own personal experience that was being examined.[7]

Monture's description of pain at having racism discussed dispassionately, or as a technical or unconflicted analysis is interesting because it points to the inability of legal categories and descriptions to account for the lived experiences of aboriginal peoples in Canada. Moreover, it suggests the possibility that assistance aimed at human rights progress may actually be part of the oppression aboriginal peoples experience.[8]

It is interesting to me that, in other disciplines, apart from law, cultural differences have been approached in a way that is contrary to current legal analyses. They have not been "interpreted" as gaps in one's knowledge of a discipline or discourse, waiting to be filled with conceptual bridges and extensions, but rather as irreconcilable or irreducible elements of human relations. Barbara Johnson, for example, in a recent work on literary theory, observes

the following of her experience of difference:

If I perceive my ignorance as a gap in knowledge instead of an imperative that changes the very nature of what I think I know, then I do not truly experience my ignorance. The surprise of otherness is that moment when a new form of ignorance is suddenly activated as an imperative.[9]

The perception of cultural difference as an imperative that may loosen or shift the paradigm of knowledge, rather than a cognitive gap to be filled, is one that has not yet been taken seriously in legal analysis or interpretation vis-à-vis the cultural differences of aboriginal peoples. What would the implications of a Johnson-type sensibility be for the legal discourse? I contend that it would problematize the conceptual basis of the rights paradigm in Canadian legal analysis because concepts, such as the rule of law, human rights, and judicial impartiality, would be seen more as culturally-specific beliefs rather than universally applicable concepts. As Raymond Williams suggests of this shift for political theory and literature:

When the most basic concepts—the concepts, as it is said, from which we begin—are suddenly seen to be not concepts but problems, not analytic problems either but historical movements that are still unresolved, there is no sense listening to their sonorous summons or their resounding clashes. We have only, if we can, to recover the substance from which their forms were cas[t].[10]

Williams captures, in my view, the effect of the imperative of cultural difference. When we think of cultural differences between aboriginal peoples and the Canadian state and its legal system, we must think of these as problems of conceptual reference for which there is no common grounding or authoritative foothold. Necessarily, we can't "decide" the substance of cultural differences from a position of a particular institutional and conceptual cultural framework; each culture is capable of sensitivity to the basic condition of difference, and should develop cross-cultural relations accordingly. To what extent is the rights paradigm of constitutional analysis a conceptual framework for the toleration of, or sensitivity toward, cultural difference? To answer this question at least two lines of inquiry need to be pursued: what is the conceptual-historical basis of the rights paradigm, and how do aboriginal peoples use rights terminology?

The human rights paradigm in Canadian constitutional discourse is clearly a product of the political theories of natural rights developed in Europe during the seventeenth century. Despite recurring references to a collectivist orientation of society, most often cited in attempts to differentiate Canada from the United States, individualism arguably derived from Locke and Hobbes underpins the Charter.[11] While I do not want to suggest that an exploration of the origins of the paradigm is dispositive in any way, it does seem significant that the rights conception developed in Europe, and especially for Canadian constitutional purposes, in England in the later seventeenth century. Moreover, the conceptual basis of rights analysis in notions of property and exclusive ownership are critical factors in the tension between rights discourse and cultural difference.

Thomas Hobbes and John Locke developed theories of "natural rights" based on the argument that one key purpose for entering civil society was the protection of private property. Locke suggested that every *man* (and emphasis should be on *man* because Locke should be infamous for his theory that society was naturally patriarchal) possesses a right of property ownership. This right, he reasoned, flowed logically from the fact that human beings are God's property. He argued that people enter into "civil society" for the central, and negatively conceived, purpose of protecting their interest or claim to private property against random attack from other persons.

The idea of the absolute right to property, as an exclusive zone of ownership, capable of being transmitted through the family (through males according to the doctrine of "primogenitor"), is arguably the cornerstone of the idea of rights in Anglo-American law. Rights are seen as a special zone of exclusion where the individual is protected against harm from others. Obviously, this is a highly individualistic and negative concept of social life based on the fear of attack on one's "private" sphere. It provides something of a basis, however, for all ideas about rights—the idea that there is a zone of absolute individual rights where the individual can do what she chooses. As Roberto Unger has suggested:

> The right is a loaded gun that the rightholder may shoot at will in his corner of town.... The property right was the very model of right generally. The consolidated property right had to be a zone of absolute discretion. In this zone, the rightholder could avoid any tangle to claims to mutual responsibility. It was natural that this conception of right should be extended to all rights.[12]

The imagery of the property-based right to exclude surfaces rather revealingly in Charter rights jurisprudence. With property rights metaphors at hand, the Supreme Court of Canada in the recent *Morgentaler*

Ethical Issues

case on the Criminal Code provisions on abortion, suggested that

> [t]he Charter is predicated on a particular conception of the place of the individual in society. An individual is not a totally independent entity disconnected from the society in which he or she lives. Neither, however, is the individual a mere cog in an impersonal machine in which his or her values, goals, and aspirations are subordinated to those of the collectivity. The individual is a bit of both. The Charter reflects this reality by leaving a wide range of activities and decisions open to legitimate government control while at the same time placing limits on the proper scope of that control. Thus, the rights guaranteed in the Charter erect around each individual, metaphorically speaking, an invisible fence over which the state will not be allowed to trespass.... The role of the courts is to map out, piece by piece, the parameters of the fence.[13]

The metaphors of the fence, mapping, and trespassings are so property-specific and exclusionary in character that they can only be construed as symptoms of acute Locke-jaw.

Notions of protection from social/legal intrusion, a classical concept of liberty, seem to have a common conceptual origin in or nexus with property rights. The idea that rights are necessary to protect one's "rightful" corner of town, to restrain the ill-intentioned from depriving someone of their corner, is also an important justificatory argument for rights claims in contemporary legal and political theory. The extension of this notion of a natural right to property to other forms of social relations (and conceptions of the private) arguably precedes the rights paradigm formalized in the Charter. It emphasizes a liberal conception of social life where the maximization of wealth and happiness through self-inter-

est is the guiding creed. Ironically, liberal notions of property and self-interest regulate the general character of Canadian political discourse. They are likewise evident in legal texts and in their interpretation where debates over individualism and collectivism find expression.[14]

There is no policy that is purely individualistic or purely collectivist. A binary coupling of these characteristics implies a kind of dialectical hierarchy. I would suggest that the individual description is integrally privileged in the rights paradigm and that collectivist considerations are merely supplementary. However, I would take issue with some scholars on their projection of "society" as an either-or, and caution against an attempt to typify, for example, an aboriginal society in such a fashion.[15]

The Canadian human rights system, and in particular the Charter, having been distanced in time from what I would construe as the conceptual basis of rights theories—that is, the natural right to individual ownership of property—seems a little less hostile to and perhaps even supportive of cultural difference, especially since so much is said of aboriginal matters in the context of interpretations of provisions of the Charter. Some scholars argue extensively that the Charter has recognized certain collective rights, such as aboriginal rights and language rights, and that this has taken legal conceptions of rights in Canada far beyond the "individualistic" basis of rights that find their origin in property notions.

There are two aspects of the collective rights stream of legal scholarship on the Charter that I would call into question in the context of cultural difference. The first is the tendency to conceptualize collective rights, and arguments for collectivist considerations, as "oughts": perhaps persuasive, but at this point only apologies for suggested directions. Scholars in this camp serve as wishful legislative "spin doctors." The second is the extent to which these arguments are responsive to cultural differences vis-à-vis aboriginal peoples when made on their behalf, presuming that aboriginal peoples can unproblematically engage in the abstract, adversarial legal process for the "granting" of such rights. In other words, the problem, identified earlier, is that of using an(other) language and conceptual apparatus (the Canadian legal system) to further an understanding of a different system of belief.

On the first issue, I would suggest that if current political and economic arrangements are any indication, the scope for respect of cultural differences is more theoretical than actual in the case of aboriginal peoples.[16] The main difference which is tolerated, albeit with considerable strain, in Canadian federalism is the French linguistic/cultural difference inside of Quebec and, to a lesser extent, outside of that province. Indeed, the tale of two founding nations present at Confederation, accepted uncritically in Canadian legal discourse, while often trotted out in support of "collective rights"-style arguments, is a position particularly disrespectful of the cultural and political differences of aboriginal peoples.[17] For the most part, Canada is defined politically as two primary and distinct cultures and languages that form the centrepiece of nationhood, with multiple decorator cultures as embellishing addenda. This is not to belittle the differences that have been nominally formalized in legislation, but to question why cultural difference means different compared with either or both of the two privileged solitudes.[18]

One can understand why aboriginal peoples reacted so strongly to the distinct society clause, section 2(1)(b), of the 1987 constitutional (Meech Lake) accord.[19] As the Assembly of First Nations suggested in their reaction to the clause:

It perpetuates the idea of a duality in Canada and strengthens the myth that the French and English peoples are the foundation of Canada. It neglects the original inhabitants and distorts history. It is as if the peoples of the first nations never existed. It suggests that historically and presently as well the French peoples in Quebec form the *only* distinct society in Canada. The amendment fails to give explicit constitutional recognition to the existence of first nations as distinct societies that also form a fundamental characteristic of Canada.... We were told for five years that governments are reluctant to entrench undefined self-government of aboriginal peoples in the constitution. Yet, here is an equally vague idea of a "distinct society" unanimously agreed to and allowed to be left to the courts for interpretation.[20]

Apart from the apparent subterfuge of the Meech Lake Accord, the collective rights position is put forth with built-in restrictions in legal scholarship. For example, Joseph Magnet, in an article on collective rights, suggests that

[t]he spirit of Canada's constitution is rooted in the principle of bi-nationality. Canada's federal system proceeds directly from the requirements of a bi-national state.[21]

Perhaps the tolerance of a collective difference within Confederation is the result of the scope of that difference. Could it be that differences will be tolerated, respected, and even formally enshrined provided they are differences arising from a common (European) ancestry?

Some arguments for collective rights view them as logical extensions of real—

that is, individual rights. In this line of reasoning, individual rights serve as the conceptual source of collective rights. Hence, by common sense, constitutional provisions that protect individual rights will protect collectivities. Even those of such persuasion would not seriously suggest that the Charter is strictly (textually) an individualist document.[22] But the extent to which one can argue that there is any framework, conceptual and institutional, within which to seek recognition of such diverse collective-based interests is, in my view, very limited at present. Furthermore, the extent to which it would be desirable to do so, especially for aboriginal peoples, is questionable given the issue raised earlier of the ability of the rights paradigm to deal with cultural differences. As Canada pins multiculturalism on its chest, the dominant European culture continues presumptively to set the terms of tolerance for collective differences.

Notes

1 These sections provide:

Section 25: The guarantees in this Charter of certain rights and freedoms shall not be construed so as to abrogate or derogate from any aboriginal, treaty or other rights or freedoms that pertain to the aboriginal peoples of Canada including (1) any right of freedoms that have been recognized by the Royal Proclamation of October 7, 1763, and (b) any rights or freedoms that now exist by way of land claims agreements or may be so acquired.

Section 27: This Charter shall be interpreted in a manner consistent with the preservation and enhancement of the multicultural heritage of Canadians.

Also, section 35, in Part II of the Constitution Act, 1982, provides:

(1) The existing aboriginal and treaty rights of the aboriginal peoples of Canada are herby recognized and affirmed.

(2) In this Act, aboriginal peoples of Canada includes the Indian, Inuit and Métis peoples of Canada.

(3) For greater certainty, in subsection (1) "treaty rights" includes rights that now exist by way of land claims agreements or may be so acquired.

(4) Notwithstanding any other provision of this Act, the aboriginal and treaty rights referred to in subsection (1) are guaranteed equally to male and female persons.

2 As D. Sanders, "Article 27 and Aboriginal Peoples of Canada," (in *Multiculturalism and the Charter: A Legal Perspective*. Toronto: Carswell, 1987.) suggests (p. 156),

Frequently Indian leaders have rejected the terms "ethnic" or "cultural minority" as inadequate to describe the special situation of indigenous peoples. They assert a uniqueness which they feel is denied by terms that equate them to Irish Catholics or Chinese. The rejection of such categories was rather sharply put by Brooklyn Rivera, the Miskito Indian leader from Nicaragua, when he said "Ethnic groups run restaurants; we are nations of people."

3 Examples in the former category are numerous and part of a growth industry. See, as a sampling, Cumming, "Rights of Indigenous Peoples: A Comparative Analysis" (1974), 68 *ASIL Proc.* 265; B. Morse, *Aboriginal Self-Government in Australia and Canada* (Kingston: Institute of Intergovernmental Relations, 1984); Sanders, "Aboriginal Peoples and the Constitution" (1981), 19 *Alberta L.R.* 410; Slattery, "The Constitutional Guarantee of Aboriginal and Treaty Rights" (1983), 8 *Queens L.J.* 232; and Wildsmith, "Pre-Confederation Treaties," in Morse, ed., *Aboriginal Peoples and the Law* (Ottawa: Carleton University Press, 1985), 122. Scholarship in the aboriginal community includes, as a sampling, B. Richardson, ed. *Drumbeat: Anger and Renewal in Indian Country* (Summerhill Press, 1989); G. Manuel and M. Posluns, *The Fourth World: An Indian Reality* (Don Mills: Collier-Macmillan, 1974); V. Deloria, Jr. and C. Lytle, *The Nations Within: The Past and Future of American Indian Sovereignty* (New York: Pantheon Books, 1984); Henderson, "Unravelling the Riddle of Aboriginal Title" (1977), 5 *Am. Indian L. Rev.* 75; Chartier, "Aboriginal Rights and Land Issues: The Métis Perspective," in Boldt and Long, eds., *The Quest for Justice: Aboriginal Peoples and Aboriginal Rights* (Toronto: University of Toronto Press, 1985), 54; Monture, see infra note [6]; and Gunn-

Allen, *The Sacred Hoop* (Boston: Beacon Press, 1986).

4   William Pentney, "The Rights of the Aboriginal Peoples of Canada in the Constitution Act, 1982: Part I—The Interpretive Prism of Section 25" (1988), 22 *U.B.C.L.Rev.* 21, and "Part II Section 35: The Substantive Guarantee" (1988) 22 *U.B.C.L.Rev.* 207.

5   Pentney, ibid., in Part II, at 278, concludes by suggesting that:

> The key challenge that remains is to translate the theoretical generalities presented here into arguments in concrete cases, for it is only by this process that sections 25 and 35 of the Constitution Act, 1982 can serve to enhance the rights of the aboriginal peoples of Canada.

And in Part I, at 59, he concludes that:

> The illustrations...should operate in a Charter case. It is an interpretive prism, and the refraction which it provides will protect the rights and freedoms of the aboriginal peoples of Canada.

6   Patricia Monture, "Ka-Nin-Geh-Heh-Gah-E-Sa-Nonh-Yah-Gah" (1986), 2 *C.J.W.L.* 159.

7   Ibid., at 160 and 163-64.

8   For an explanation of this idea in another cultural context, see A.D. Freeman, "Legitimizing Racial Discrimination Through Anti-discrimination Law: A Critical Review of Supreme Court Doctrine" (1978), 62 *Minn.L.Rev.* 1049. Freeman's dialogue (at 1049-50, footnotes omitted) in his analysis attempts to capture he ironical effect of anti-discrimination law:

> THE LAW: "Black American rejoice! Racial Discrimination has now become illegal."
> BLACK AMERICANS: "Great, we who have no jobs want them. We who have lousy jobs want better ones. We whose kids go to black schools want to choose integrated schools if we think that would be better for our kids, or want enough money to make our own schools work. We want political power roughly proportionate to our population. And many of us want houses in the suburbs."
> THE LAW: "You can't have any of those things. You can't assert your claim against society in general, but only against a named discriminator, and you've got to show that you are an individual victim of that discrimination and that you were intentionally discriminated against. And be sure to demonstrate how that discrimination has caused your problem, for any remedy must be coextensive with the violation. Be careful your claim does not impinge on some other cherished American value, like local autonomy of the suburbs, or previously distributed vested rights, or selection on the basis of merit. Most important, do not demand any remedy involving racial balance or proportionality; to recognize such claims would be racist."

9   Barbara Johnson, *A World of Difference.*

10   Raymond Williams, *Marxism and Literature,* (Oxford: Oxford University Press, 1981), at 213.

11   Whose two most important works, respectively are: John Locke, *Two Treatises of Civil Government* (1690) and Thomas Hobbes, *Leviathan* (1651)

12   Roberto Unger, *The Critical Legal Studies Movement* (Cambridge: Harvard University Press, 1986), at 36 and 38.

13   Madame Justice Wilson writing in *Morgentaler, Smoling & Scott v. The Queen & Attorney General of Canada,* [1988] 1 S.C.R. 30, at 164; (1988) 82 N.R. 1, at 116; and (1988) 44 D.L.R. (4th) 385, at 485.

14   I do not want to get embroiled in the individualist versus collectivist description of Canadian society. See for example Patrick Monahan, *Politics and the Constitution: The Charter, Federalism and the Supreme Court of Canada* (Toronto: Carswell, 1987).

15   Ibid. Although Monahan does not explicitly do so, his employment of the metaphor of society, which implies a kind of totality of Canada, would seem to overlook cultural differences and their relation to the binary of individual versus collective.

16   Here I would note that the scholarly legal arguments suggesting Canada is a society respectful of difference, and indeed built on it, are largely reflective of a body of historical work along the same theme. It is interesting to me that this body of literature tends to focus on French-English differences ("two solitudes") as the primary cultural difference in Canada, generally effacing the arguably more radical (non-European) difference between either of those cultures and the First Nations. See, for example, A.R.M. Lower, "Two Ways of Life: The Primary Antithesis of Canadian History," in R. Cook, C. Brown and C. Berger, eds., *Contemporary Approaches to Canadian History* (Toronto: University of Toronto Press, 1987), at 1.

17 See Manuel and Posluns, *The Fourth World*, supra note [3], who ask:

> Why should there be a different kind of equality for us Indian people than for the other groups of Canadians who share both a common history and a common territory in the way a province occupies a single territory? Yet I can only imagine that our relationship with this land and with one another is far deeper and more complex than the relationship between the people of any province and their institutions, or one another. Nor can the Indian peoples be brushed off with the multi-cultural broom to join the diverse ethnic groups that compose the Third Element of Canada, that is, those who are neither French nor English.

18 I am reminded of the bitter closing remarks of Métis leader Jim Sinclair at the final failed sessions of First Ministers' constitutional discussions on Aboriginal Rights in March 1986 when he prophesied that the Prime Minister and Premiers who had rejected aboriginal peoples would soon "take care of their own" and bring Quebec explicitly into constitutional agreement. Of course, within a year, that same congenial confederation family left Meech Lake with an accord recognizing Quebec as a distinct society in Canada.

19 This section of the Accord provides that the Constitution of Canada shall be interpreted in a manner consistent with "the recognition that Quebec constitutes within Canada a distinct society."

20 Assembly of First Nations, position paper on the Meech Lake Accord, 1987 (unpublished).

21 Joseph Magnet, "Collective Rights, Cultural Autonomy and the Canadian State" (1986), 32 *McGill L.J.* 170, at 172.

22 The individualist-collectivist debate in many ways betrays the descriptive poverty of so much constitutional scholarship. Two absolutist, parable-like claims are cast as either/or. Evidently, scholars feel quite strongly that one or the other should prevail. However, I would question the validity of this restricting choice and its cultural relativity. See Monahan, supra note [14], at 95, and Schwartz, *First Principles, Second Thoughts: Aboriginal Peoples, Constitutional Reform and Canadian Statecraft* (Montreal: Institute for Research on Public Policy, 1986), at 366.

Questions for Discussion

1 Is Turpel correct that human rights are not universal, but rather products of a particular culture which cannot properly be imposed on other cultures?

Twenty Years of Disappointed Hopes

Georges Erasmus

Georges Erasmus, writing as National Chief of the Assembly of First Nations, wrote the following as part of a book describing direct actions taken by Canadian aboriginal peoples in defense of what they believed they were entitled to.

*   *   *

As people of the First Nations of Canada we have a vision of the sort of country we want to live in and to build in collaboration with other Canadians. It is certainly not the sort of country we have now, one in which our people have been relegated to the lowest rung on the ladder of Canadian society; suffer the worst conditions of life, the lowest incomes, the poorest education and health; and can envision only the most depressing of futures for our children.

We do believe, however, that our situation can be turned around. We believe not only that we can rescue ourselves from these depressing conditions, but that, in the process, we can contribute enormously to the health, effectiveness, and decency of Canada, benefiting every person who lives in this country.

To do so we have to go back to the agreement made in the Two-Row Wampum Treaty signed between First Nations and the newly arrived Europeans in 1664.

All across North America today First Nations share a common perception of what was then agreed: we would allow Europeans to stay among us and use a certain amount of our land, while in our own lands we would continue to exercise our own laws and maintain our own institutions and systems of government.

We all believe that that vision is still very possible today, that as First Nations we should have our own governments with jurisdiction over our own lands and people.

We should decide about and benefit from the type of development we want in our own territories, not have such development forced on us to serve outside interests.

We should have tribal courts run by our own people. We should administer our own child-care and social services. We should take control over our own education, as we have already begun to do.

In this visionary Canada we would be free to express in our actions our tremendous concern for the environment, to undertake our traditional role as protectors of Mother Earth. Once our jurisdiction was recognized we would clear up pollution and prevent further degradation in our own territories, and we would establish sustainable economies that would consider the long-term future of our children and grandchildren.

In this Canada our treaties would be recognized as the sacred documents they are supposed to be and would be properly implemented in accordance with the full spirit and intention of the original terms and conditions. In effect, then, we would be participants in a bilateral arrangement with the federal government. Provinces would no longer have authority over us in our own lands, and whenever federal-provincial agreements were negotiated, we would be included, accorded a role similar to that of the provinces today.

We realize that what we are asking for requires new perceptions among Canadians of the characteristics of our country. But we believe that the changes we propose can be easily accommodated in the Canadian confederation as it exists now. Within that structure of different orders of government and distinct founding peoples, we would be regarded as a third participant, a separate founding nation, exercising control over its own territories.

Under such a system, we would not, of course, make laws for other territories, any more than, say, Quebec makes laws for Alberta. But our relationship with the federal government would be different. The honour of the Crown was pledged to preserve the best interests of the aborigines, and in 1867 a section was included in the British North America Act intended to enable the federal government to act as a buffer between the First Nations and the provinces, which were emerging as the new power-brokers.

In our vision of a better Canada, the federal government would continue to act as trustee, safeguarding the spirit and intent of the treaties and of past undertakings. Our problem has been that the federal government has largely abrogated that role. Yet, the continuing validity of that original Royal Proclamation has recently been reaffirmed in the justice system, and the proclamation itself included in the new Canadian constitution....

We are keenly aware that the system we propose is not without the potential for problems; however, we believe that our interests and those of the people we live among are similar. We know that, in the modern world, no man, no race, no group or nation, is an island. Our vision of a better Canada rests on a foundation of co-operation among peoples.

Most of our people live in the Canadian hinterland, part of the country that has long been held hostage by the metropolitan centres. We know that non-Indians in the hinterland—whether special-interest groups, school districts, hospital boards, or municipal councils—need more resources, just as we do. And we understand that when we manage to win recognition of our right to self-government, with jurisdiction over non-Indian residents within the boundaries of our areas, it will be our mandate to ensure the equitable distribution of all benefits and responsibilities. One group of our people has vivid experience of this.

A year or two ago the Gitanmax, Kispiox, Kitwanga, and Moricetown bands of the Gitksan Wet'suwet'en Nation in British Columbia, 8,000 in number, passed a set of by-laws that gave them a great deal of power over the fishery in their reserves. As these by-laws were not disallowed by the federal government, they became, in fact, the law. The 25,000 non-native population of the area, especially those downstream, perceived that they were affected by our by-laws. An alliance was formed between the provincial government and local sport and commercial fishermen (with heavy lobbying in their favour from the Department of Fisheries and Oceans) that sought and won a court injunction, placing the by-laws in abeyance. So the victory of our people in winning more power over activities within our own lands was short-lived, temporarily nullified by actions of the surrounding majority.

Yet, these possible future difficulties are not insurmountable, merely obstacles to be overcome.

Enough of Outside Control and Manipulation

One thing we do know for sure is that control and manipulation from outside our communities have been the rule for many decades, and such a system of governance has certainly not worked; in fact, it has created an intolerable level of social and economic disorder among us. What we want is self-reliance, self-control, internal growth. We want to start a process of healing. We want to contribute to North American society, through better education, higher rates of employment and literacy, less dependence on welfare, and finally through a determined attack on the youth suicides, family abuse, alcoholism, and social dissolution that blight so many of our communities today.

We believe that to confront all these problems is not only in our interest, but in the interests of all Canadians. In fact, demographics indicate that as the national birthrate in Canada falls, and ours remains high, we are destined to become an ever-larger percentage of the Canadian workforce, estimated in at least one province to reach 40 per cent within a decade or so. This fact alone is one good reason why it is necessary to improve the educational levels of our people, and why there was such an immediate and strong reaction from young aboriginal people early in 1989 when the full impact of the funding cuts for our post-secondary education became fully understood throughout the country.

We cannot believe that our vision of a Canada in which we play a special and constructive role is so far removed from the wishes of ordinary Canadians as to be unattainable. Yet, in our struggle to achieve this goal, we have, in recent years, met with nothing but set-backs. It would not be an exaggeration to say that governments have exhibited a certain paranoia in response to our proposals. This paranoia seems to stem partly from economics: governments are afraid of what our proposals might cost. However, the hidden costs of ignoring them—welfare payments, health charges, unemployment insurance, not to mention the fact that so many of our people are unable to contribute as they should to the economy and cultures of Canada—are already immense.

Even more threatening to governments than the perceived monetary costs of our proposals is what they see as a loss of power. That is where a sort of paranoia is evident: governments cannot contemplate anything that might lead to a reduction in their powers, even when the application of that power over First Nations communities across the country has appalling results....

The evidence shows that since the rise of the modern Indian political movement, governments have consistently underrated the seriousness of the claims for land, resources, and self-government that could be mounted by the people of First Nations in all parts of Canada. So little attention was paid to these claims in the first half of this century that a cabinet document of the late 1960s suggested the Canadian government could settle all aboriginal land claims in the country for $11 million. A more recent estimate has put the figure at $4.8 billion. Though there is far more involved than money, the difference between the two figures is a measure of the unreality of the traditional response of Canadian society to aboriginal claims. And it is, perhaps, an explanation of the panic that seems to seize contemporary Canadian politicians in face of our demand for just treatment.

The fact is that, for generations, Canadian governments have treated us as a disappearing race, and have administered us accordingly. "I want to get rid of the Indian problem," Deputy Superintendent of Indian Affairs Duncan Campbell Scott told the House of Commons in the early 1920s. "Our object is to continue until there is not a single Indian in Canada that has not been absorbed into the body politic, and there is no Indian question, and no Indian department." Nothing could have been clearer than that.

"Before a quarter of a century is gone, perhaps, the savages will be no more than a memory!" wrote a Quebec civil servant in 1897. "Is it wise to sacrifice, for needs that are more fictional than real of this race that is leaving, the interests of the majority of the state?" His argument was repeated, virtually verbatim, by a judgement of the Quebec Court of Appeal in 1974 in the case brought by the James Bay Cree against the Quebec government's hydro-electric project.

We native people have been subject to such reasoning throughout our history. Yet, we have not disappeared; we have survived, as we have done since long before the appearance of Europeans, against no matter what odds. Unfortunately, to the present day, governments have been unconscionably slow in coming to terms with the fact that we will always be here, and that our claims for justice, land, resources, and control over our own affairs will never go away and must be fairly and honourably dealt with....

Comprehensive Claims: Discriminatory, Dilatory, and Unjust

The Royal Proclamation of 1763 stated clearly that the Crown should be the only body to deal with First Nations' land, and this had to be done before such land could be used by others. In many parts of the country this issue was never dealt with: in violation of the proclamation, in large parts of the Maritimes, all of Quebec and British Columbia, and many other parts of Canada as well, land was occupied by settlers without any prior negotiation with the First Nations who had always occupied it.

In theory, the comprehensive claims policy promised a solution to this problem; in practice, the way the policy has been administered has been not only unjust, but discriminatory towards and burdensome for our people.

Only three comprehensive claims were negotiated in the first ten years of the policy: the James Bay Agreement (1975) and the Northeastern Quebec Agreement (1978), both negotiated somewhat independently of the claims process, and that of the

Inuvialuit of the Mackenzie River delta (1984).

Six other claims (the maximum that the government will negotiate at any one time) remain unresolved at time of writing, and it may be noted that none of them has been on the table for less than ten years. Another nineteen claims have been accepted for negotiation, eight are under review, and another twenty are expected to be submitted. So, with fifty-three claims either submitted or awaiting access to the process, at the present rate it will take 160 years to resolve these problems.

A fundamental problem is that First Nations and the federal government have approached negotiations with different viewpoints and objectives. The government, in its search for finality in all agreements, has viewed the process as one in which an aboriginal group fully cedes, surrenders, and extinguishes all of its rights flowing from its aboriginal title and ownership of the land, in return for which the government returns to aboriginal people some small portion of rights within the land-claims agreement.

As First Nations, however, we believe that our aboriginal title includes ownership and jurisdiction over all lands and resources within our traditional areas. For us, claims resolution is a process of determining what land, resources, and jurisdiction will be shared with the governments of Canada. For us, the process is not one of negotiating extinguishment of our aboriginal rights, but of arriving at an equitable agreement on sharing.

Our people find it fundamentally unjust that we should be required as a condition of entering negotiations to surrender the very rights on which our entire case is based. Such is required of no other group in Canadian society. A second stumbling-block has been the refusal of government to deal, as part of the claims process, with the governing powers that First Nations will have over their lands when the negotiations are completed.

Not Only Land, but Jurisdiction over It

Land, and jurisdiction over land, go hand in hand. We have been pressing for fair land settlement to provide the basis for an economically viable life for our people, but we have also insisted on our right to aboriginal self-government over that land. By this we mean our right to exercise jurisdiction over our traditional lands, resources, and people. We must share in the benefits that come from the resources of the land, and we must make decisions in the best interests of our people, the land, and its resources. Government has accepted such jurisdiction as a goal, but has given it a much more restricted interpretation than we know is necessary.

We have also found it inequitable, to say the least, that, in the claims process, the federal government has taken it upon itself to act as judge, jury, advocate, prosecutor, and defendant—a totally unprecedented move, as far as I know, in Canadian negotiation....

[T]he federal government has blocked progress at the negotiating table, and in a bullying and defiant way has challenged First Nations to go to court if we do not like what we are offered, even though they know that aboriginal people do not have the resources to fight long legal battles. The Gitksan Wet'suwet'en court case illustrates the difficulties of this route. Two other examples are pertinent: after the Teme-Au-gama Anishnabai managed, in 1973, to impose a land caution over 110 townships in Northern Ontario, asserting aboriginal ownership, the Ontario government changed the legislation to preclude other First Nations from using the same tactic. Ten years later, when the Lubicon went to court to try for the same thing, the Alberta government retroactively changed the legislation to ensure that the band's action would fail. (These same tactics have been used by the South African apartheid government to deny the rights of Africans.)

Similarly, in 1985, the Supreme Court of Canada confirmed the right of Mi'kmaq Indians to hunt under a treaty of 1752, which the court declared to be in effect. Yet, in 1988, in defiance of that ruling, provincial game officers arrested and charged thirteen Mi'kmaq who were hunting outside the provincial hunting season, and have vowed to continue to prosecute Mi'kmaq citizens who exercise their rights.

In our view the Mi'kmaq case should have provided an opportunity for the federal government to begin bilateral negotiations with our people to redefine the terms of many of the old treaties. Instead, the government has chosen to ignore it. Even more absurdly, the minister has acted as if the treaty was with J.M. Simon (the Mi'kmaq who won the case) and not with all Mi'kmaqs. According to this reasoning, every Mi'kmaq would have to go to court to prove that he is descended from those who signed the 1752 treaty. This is the attitude of a federal government that is supposed to be there to protect the rights of aboriginal people.

These are only a few of the anomalies that have made the claims process unworkable.

The Conservative Government Reneges on Its Promises

We conducted intense lobbying on these issues during the 1984 election and after it; at first, we had some hope that the new Mulroney government would honestly try to improve matters, and meet us half-way. Their first minister of Indian Affairs, David Crombie, had a task force make a thorough study of the comprehensive land claims policy. The recommendations of this task force, released in March 1986, met a number of our objections to the present process, and was broadly acceptable to us and to other Canadians who keep close watch over these matters. It suggested, for example, that aboriginal rights should be recognized and affirmed as a matter of principle in every agreement, and the policy of extinguishing aboriginal rights in agreements should be abandoned.

The task force said the government's aim to reach "finality" in each agreement (which, incidentally, is shared by First Nations, who do not want to have to go back to square-one every time they need to affirm their rights) should be met by "balancing the need for certainty in the orderly development of land and resources with the need for flexibility in the evolving relationship between aboriginal groups and governments in Canada." Such "balancing" could be done, the task force suggested, by having agreements reviewed on a periodic basis to determine whether they continue to meet the objectives of the parties.

Finally, since land and jurisdiction are so intimately connected, the task force agreed with us that First Nations' self-government should be negotiated as part of the claims process: such practice would be consistent with the constitutional recognition

and affirmation of aboriginal rights and with the government's commitment to self-government.

Our hope that these recommendations would improve matters was dashed with the precipitate removal of Mr. Crombie from the Indian Affairs portfolio. Within months the new minister, Bill McKnight, had issued a revised comprehensive-claims policy, which virtually ignored the task force recommendations and was even more reactionary than what we had before. At the Assembly of First Nations, we described it at the time as yet another government invitation to aboriginal people to commit suicide.

The new policy further restricts the claims process by requiring the active participation of the provinces south of the sixtieth parallel. This is part of an obvious effort to expand the bilateral federal-aboriginal relationship confirmed in 1763 into a tripartite federal-provincial-aboriginal relationship. The policy is seen by First Nations as an effort to set up a good guy—bad guy scenario, where the provinces play the bad guy (as at First Ministers' meetings), with the federal government as the good guy encouraging First Nations to take what they can get because of the regressive provincial stand. It is also in direct conflict with the letter and intent of the Proclamation, which explicitly acknowledged that the interests of the colonies (now provinces) were diametrically opposed to those of First Nations.

Also, the new federal policy imposes a "municipal model" of self-government powers for First Nations that encroach on federal or provincial powers, even though it is clear that our communities need many of the powers exercised by these two levels of government if we are to function effectively and succeed in the immense task of revivifying the life of our people.

Furthermore, throughout the new policy document, First Nations are characterized, not as "Nations or Tribes," as recognized by the Royal Proclamation, but as just another interest group in Canadian society, whose interests are recognized, but whose rights are not protected....

The Constitutional Process: A Dead-End

Native people in Canada will not soon forget the contempt with which we were treated in the long negotiations leading up to the patriation of the Canadian constitution in 1982; or the equally contemptuous treatment we have received since negotiations to define our rights broke down in 1987.

We watched with mixed feelings as the national debate on the constitution proceeded in the first years of this decade. On the one hand, we were very much aware that any constitutional change might adversely affect the treaties that our forebears had signed with Great Britain before Canadian confederation; on the other hand, we were hoping that the inclusion of aboriginal and treaty rights in the constitution would, for the first time, signal our place in confederation....

Our People Treated As an After-Thought

Our high hopes...for a just and honourable resolution of our problems have been sorely betrayed in the seven years since the Constitution Act was passed recognizing and affirming our aboriginal rights.

Indeed, even before the act was passed, we had a striking demonstration of how expendable we apparently are in the eyes of the nation's provincial premiers.

First, we were included in the proposed deal but then, when Trudeau finally did get nine of the premiers on board (without Quebec), the proposed constitution that they would agree to no longer included aboriginal rights. We had been dropped as if we were no more than an after-thought.

When this happened we renewed our lobbying—in fact, what we had done previously was nothing compared with the work we now did. We formed coalitions across the country such as we had never known before, and organized tremendous effort to put pressure on the premiers and prime minister. Eventually they agreed to put the clause recognizing and affirming aboriginal rights back into the charter, but with the word "existing" added—"the existing aboriginal and treaty rights of the aboriginal peoples of Canada are hereby recognized and affirmed"—in an obvious effort to limit the meaning of the clause. Included also was an amendment that was intended to shut us up—that the details and definition of our rights would be resolved through a conference.

Now began a phase, lasting about five years, in which we did seem to be included in the constitution. The conference we held with the First Ministers, in March 1983, was an occasion of immense symbolic significance for our people. Almost 450 years after the arrival of the first Europeans, we at last had the opportunity to discuss our future face to face with them, nation to nation. For the last 150 years we had seen our cultures and languages suppressed and our economy undermined. We had been impoverished while the newcomers became enriched. Through all this time, though absent from the country's political agenda, we had never ceased to believe in, and stubbornly to affirm, our ancient rights.

So, our people turned up for this meeting in Ottawa with a proper sense of its solemnity and significance. Our leaders were in full regalia; we opened each day with public prayers arising from traditional ceremonies; we handed the traditional pipe of peace around the table. We believed we were gathered to do something that First Nations have always done—to discuss great issues with the objective of arriving at a consensus satisfactory to both sides.

It was clear from the first that the European side did not share our leaders' attitudes. But, in that first meeting, we did manage to get agreement on a constitutional amendment requiring a five-year negotiating process in which three further meetings would be held between First Nations and First Ministers. The agenda proposed for these meetings included four items: equality rights; aboriginal title and aboriginal rights; treaties and treaty land and resources; and aboriginal or self-government.

But, by the time the last of these three meetings was held, in March 1987—they began under the Liberals and ended under the Conservatives, who were firmly pledged to resolve outstanding issues—we had not succeeded in dealing with any of the agenda items.

What happened in that last meeting was shocking to all native people in Canada. When negotiations arrived at a stalemate, Prime Minister Mulroney, who, along with most of the premiers, insisted that self-government could not be enshrined in the constitution until it was clear what self-government meant, had a number of choices. He could have extended the pro-

cess without amendment of the constitution by announcing a continuing series of meetings, as an act of political will; or, he could have adjourned the meeting for a couple of years, to grapple with the problem of Quebec's position in relation to the constitution, and then come back to us.

But what he chose to do instead was to come back into the conference in the middle of the day, throw up his hands, and announce there was nothing further he could do. He told the country it was all over, even before our allotted time for the conference had run out.

Within less than a month he played a totally different role when he gathered the same First Ministers at Meech Lake to consider the place of Quebec. He said he was locking the door, they'd work all night long, if necessary; they weren't getting out of the lodge, would have to stay two or three days, until they agreed to resolve the question of Quebec.

First Nations' leaders were astounded to see that, at Meech Lake, Mulroney and the same premiers signed a vague and imprecise accord, the details of which were to be worked out by 1990. [*Ed. Note:* They did not succeed in working this out, and the Meech Lake accord fell through, partly as a result of the delaying tactics of Elijah Harper, an aboriginal MPP in Manitoba.] There are obviously two standards that the prime minister and premiers follow: one for themselves, and another for aboriginal peoples.

It seems to us in retrospect that the Meech Lake accord was already in the works when they decided to give up so easily on defining our rights: they didn't want any agreement among the nine premiers that might conceivably prejudice their coming agreement with Quebec.

Since then, all we have been able to get out of the federal government is a promise that, if and when the day comes that there are enough provincial governments in favour of amendments covering aboriginal rights, then the process will be renewed. But that process, with its countless meetings with officials and ministers from all across the country, could not produce consensus.

So, what we have run into is a complete dead-end: in our view the prime minister has adopted a hypocritical approach. He takes the view that, for aboriginal people, constitutional amendments will somehow come out of the air. We will all, simultaneously across the country, at some magical future time, arrive at a meeting of minds without putting any work into it. But, at the same time, he has no similar illusions on any other subject. The Meech Lake accord constitutionally entrenches two First Ministers' meetings every year on other subjects.

A Racist Double-Standard

So, we believe—heavy-heartedly, I may say—that his position is extremely racist, and reveals a double-standard....

I have to say that when we realized the immense concessions the prime minister made to the provinces in the Meech Lake accord, and compared them with his refusal even to consider such concessions towards aboriginal people, the level of frustration among our people rose considerably. Quebec could be recognized as a distinct society, but not, apparently, the First Nations, who were here long before any Quebeckers or any other European set foot on the continent. We, too, have our own languages, our own cultures, our own ways of life.

How, one might ask, could we be more distinct than we are? The whole process was not only a negation of our high hopes when we entered negotiations, but a caricature of our traditional methods for resolving conflict and reaching consensus....

An Effort to Educate the Public

Our people have tried in every case to explain the facts clearly to non-native people and to persuade them that the positions we have taken are in the long-term best interests of the whole community. For example, Chief Gary Potts, of the Teme-Augama Anishnabai who live in the Temagami area of Ontario, has repeatedly brought it to public attention that, at the present rate of cutting, there are only five years' worth of logging left in the forests his people are trying to defend, even if the government should permit the companies access to them. The native purpose is not to shut down the economy of the area, as their opponents claim. Rather, the long-term public interest lies in saving the remaining trees and collaborating on a forestry regime that is sustainable over the long term. These educational efforts have had a great deal of success: every environmental group in Ontario is opposing the extension of logging roads into this last remaining stand of timber. Yet, the Ontario government continues to bow down before the four hundred jobs that are at stake. If they would take a longer view they would realize it would be far cheaper to compensate the loggers for the few years of work they have left, and get on with re-creating the economy of the area on a more viable basis.

Similarly with road blockades undertaken in various parts of the country. The Haida who blocked the way to forests that were about to be clear-cut on the Queen Charlotte Islands attracted nation-wide support, not only on human-rights grounds, but because they were also battling for a more sustainable approach to the economy of their lands. The Lubicon of northern Alberta attracted support not only throughout Canada, but all over the Western world. In their effort to boycott the Olympic art show, "The Spirit Sings," they conducted an educational campaign that affected the outlook of hundreds of museum curators, anthropologists, and archaeologists, not to mention members of the public.

In Barriere Lake, Quebec, the Algonquins, one summer day in 1988, slowed traffic near their reserve and held what they called an "information toll": in six hours they obtained 1,400 signatures from passing motorists who supported the Algonquin aim to replace the present destructive forest- and water-exploitation of their lands with a more sustainable economy that will benefit all sectors of society into the far-distant future. In each case our people have tried to organize well for non-violent, effective action, and at the same time to educate the public about what they are doing and why.

We have pointed out to representatives of the Canadian government that, if they are really serious about protecting the Canadian environment, and want to do something to stop future destruction of the ecological balance, the best way to do it would be to recognize as quickly as possible the legitimate claims to aboriginal title that First Nations are making across the country. Given control of our own territories, we would immediately instil project-by-project decision-making, and there is no way in the world that our people would be making the kinds of decisions that are now destroying wildlife habitat, decimating for-

ests and off-shore resources, and degrading soil, air, and water. We have proven that this is so by the programs that we are trying to have accepted in many parts of the country. In almost every case these ideas have been rejected by governments, almost without serious consideration. Given a choice between dealing with aboriginal ideas of conservation and sustainability, and the exploitive ideas of huge corporations, the government never shows any hesitation in choosing the latter.

In the face of all these discouragements, in a speech in 1988 I warned about the dangers that lie ahead if our people are to be continually frustrated in their efforts to resolve their problems. If a serious attempt is not soon made to resolve a wide range of problems such as those outlined in these pages; if educational, housing, and economic difficulties in so many of our communities are not overcome, we can certainly expect a more aggressive response, especially from younger people. They will begin to take a critical attitude to leaders such as me who have been trying for years to resolve our problems through negotiation, but have been getting nowhere.

Our populations are increasing rapidly. As well, some 100,000 to 150,000 people who had lost their Indian status through the policy of "enfranchisement" have been reinstated and are now able to return to their reserves.

I warned in my speech that Canadians could not expect our people to remain peaceful for ever. In reaction, some said I was encouraging violence, though that was the farthest thing from my mind. I was trying to get the Canadian public and governments to become aware that conditions among aboriginal people, already by far the most disadvantaged group in Canada, are not improving, and that this situation is leading to frustration. Many people, however, have said I was correct, and they have restated my warning from one end of the country to the other; still others have said that I understated the case, and that we may have already run out of time....

Education

We urge that a major study on native education, which the Assembly of First Nations has recently completed, should be fully implemented by the federal government. A first step would be immediate recognition that First Nations have jurisdiction over their own education, and that it is not a provincial responsibility.

We believe that education should be recognized as a treaty right, and that the funding needed to develop a native-education system at least equal to that of Canadians should be made available. To do that, of course, would require special funding to enable our people to catch up to the general standards of Canadians in a number of areas (including such things as the literacy rate and the ratio of graduate students and practising professionals to the general population), with special provision for development and protection of First Nations languages and cultures.

To this end we also urge creation of an aboriginal languages institute, with an endowment of $100 million, to fund community-controlled and -initiated language programs. The model for such a government-sponsored program exists in the Maori Language Nests developed in Aoteoroa (New Zealand), where the object is to bring Maori children to proficiency in their own language before they enter school.

Justice

The recommendations made by the Native Law section of the Canadian Bar Association for major changes to make the Canadian justice system much more sensitive to aboriginal needs should be implemented, but, more than that, a separate native justice system should be recognized and created right across the country, as part of First Nations' self-government. Already some First Nations, such as Saddle Lake in Alberta, and Akwesasne in Ontario and Quebec, have begun to move in that direction, having established their own tribal courts and their own legal code. These tribal courts differ from the Canadian justice system in that they mediate and conciliate between parties, rather than forcing confrontation between adversaries.

Self-Government

[T]he central need if we are to reverse the trend that maintains so many of our communities in poverty and alienation, is the attainment of our right to govern ourselves.

There has to be a very genuine shift in the attitude of Canadians on this question. In our view, the provincial and federal governments should recognize and support the concept that aboriginal people will govern themselves, and do everything in their power to move in that direction. This is not impossible, as I pointed out earlier: it is already the common practice of the US government, and there is no reason it could not become so in Canada.

This would mean, specifically, that federal/provincial programs would accept aboriginal governments as similar in status to the provinces, so that, in future, federal funding of programs for native people would no longer go through the provinces, but would go directly from the federal government to the First Nations themselves.

To this end there would be bilateral First Nations/federal arrangements in a whole range of services—child care, family services, education, environment, and many others for which the federal government now doles out money to the provinces, who then pass it on to First Nations communities, after taking a healthy slice of it for administration. Such a changed system would be a saving to the country, and would ensure that more money goes to where it is intended, and most needed.

Conclusions

This may appear to be a formidable list of changes, both in attitude and policies, that we are demanding of Canadians. We are, however, becoming a little tired of hearing the repeated expressions of shame and dismay over the "national tragedy" of Canada's treatment of its native people. It is time to move to action.

We do not believe any thoughtful Canadian can be happy with the present situa-

tion. Change is needed, and it is needed quickly. We cannot afford to lose another generation of our children to alienation, low self-esteem, glue-sniffing, alcohol, suicide, and the many other horrors that afflict so many of our communities.

We wish to fulfil that vision of a better Canada with which this book opens. We realize that all people, within and without Canada, are bound together in a complex, rapidly changing world. We think our traditions and the cultures we have inherited have much to say that is of value as we all try to deal with the forces of change.

We know from bitter experience that others do not know what is best for us. We are engaged in a fight we will never give up, a fight to implement the policies we know will help us lift ourselves above our present problems. We hope for and welcome the support of other people in Canada in that struggle.

Question for Discussion

1 What should the Canadian government's policy be concerning aboriginal self-determination?

PART 6

free speech, censorship, and pornography

It has become a commonplace of what might be called "modern liberal democracies" that freedom of expression is an important right of each individual. This right has not always been officially recognized in the history of these nations, and there is a long history of debate over it. Indeed, in many parts of the world today this right is not recognized, although it is enshrined in the rights documents of most international organizations including the United Nations. It is sometimes thought that nations can be divided into those which are politically advanced enough to recognize this right, and those which are not. However, all societies place *some* restrictions on the content and form of what people may say, and the circumstances in which they are allowed to say it, so the situation is not quite as straightforward as it might seem.

In Canada, legal limitations on speech include: government guidelines on broadcasting and advertising; laws against libel, slander, and perjury; a law against distribution of hate propaganda; restrictions concerning the publication of official secrets, especially in time of war or other such emergency; and the prohibition of speech acts such as the famous example of yelling "Fire!" in a crowded theatre.

There may appear to be overwhelming justifications for at least some of these restrictions on speech. Other values, such as national security, need to be protected in society, and it is quite possible that some of these may appear to be of more pressing importance than individual speech. From a philosophical perspective, however, interesting questions arise about what these values might be which can conflict with the right to free speech. Asking these questions also requires one to ask *why* free speech is considered valuable in the first place—what value is *that* right supposed to protect? And once one has admitted that the right is not absolute, it then becomes an interesting question where the limits are. Not surprisingly, there are some cases in which it is not clear which side of the principle a given form of expression lies on, and people disagree about whether certain sorts of acts constitute protected speech acts or not.

Any restriction on freedom of expression, especially in a written or visual form, may be considered censorship. Such restriction need not take the form of an outright prohibition of the work, although some people would want to reserve use of the word for this case. Other actions which might be considered censorship include making it more difficult for people to gain access to certain materials (by such measures as restrictions on manner and places of sale, or heavy taxation), or allowing only some individuals to have access to certain materials (such as those over a certain age). A fairly recent proposal in the United States (the so-called "Minneapolis Ordinance") suggested the alternative of allowing people who believe they have been harmed by pornography to sue the producers and/or distributors of those materials for damages. All of these provisions can be more or less restrictive, and these gradations of degree can have a significant impact on the accessibility of the materials concerned. It is worth bearing in mind that even in this sense censorship is not a clear-cut issue.

The main debates about censorship, however, revolve around certain sorts of expression, and the question of whether they should be considered protected speech. One prominent area of this dispute has to do with the notion of "hate literature" or "hate propaganda." The Canadian Criminal Code contains provisions (Sections 318 and 319) against advocating genocide and against public incitement of hatred against any identifiable group. What reasons can be given for prohibiting people from stating their beliefs publicly in these areas? Are these reasons strong enough to justify the very intrusive measures of the criminal law? Should we be willing to trust the machinery of the law to administer this law wisely, or is there too much danger that the rights of some individuals will be violated? Perhaps most importantly, what sorts of statements would violate the provision? How "public" does an incitement need to be, and what is to count as an "identifiable group"? These are some of the questions at stake here, and they tend to involve a balance between the right to free expression and perhaps the right to privacy as well, on the one hand, and various social goods such as public order, and perhaps rights of unspecifiable members of various potential target groups, on the other.

Another prominent area of dispute concerning free expression has to do with the notion of obscenity and the maintenance of public moral standards. Many people have argued that any society must protect its moral standards in order to survive. Similarly, it might be argued that a society has an obligation to do all it can to help its members flourish as human beings, and this may include watching out for their moral interests (in a sort of gentle paternalism). If these beliefs are correct, they may provide a justification for limitations on the freedom of expression when such expressions may tend to compromise the moral standards of the society. On the other hand, one might believe that society as a whole benefits when people are allowed to challenge its existing beliefs. Also, there is the question of whether we want to trust the machinery of the law to decide which particular expressions are permissible.

This issue of the protection of public morals leads naturally to a discussion of pornography. This is perhaps the most hotly debated subject within the issue of freedom of expression. Yet there is little agreement about what pornography *is*, or even whether it is best understood as a form of expression at all.

Is producing pornography an instance of free speech? In the classic cases, free speech has been understood as an attempt to put forward an unpopular political view or challenge to prevailing beliefs. It seems clear that producers of pornography are usually driven by a desire to provide entertainment, and/or to make a profit, more than by any political motives, although there are inevitably cases where the distinction is not clear. Does it matter for the purposes of free speech what the intention of the speaker is? And who gets to decide what the "real" intention is? If intention is important, then it may well be that at least some pornography does not amount to protected speech, and the "censorship" debate may be short-circuited.

It is worth noting some of the difficulties in even finding a definition of the term "pornography." The word itself comes from ancient Greek and means, literally speaking and writing about the lives of prostitutes (and, by extension, their patrons). Its modern meaning has clearly changed somewhat, but there is disagreement about its proper usage. At some times "pornography" has been taken to refer to sexually explicit depictions which are still within prevailing social standards, as contrasted with "obscenity." Recently, however, it has been more common (especially in the light of feminist criticism) to use "pornography" to refer to unacceptable forms of sexual depiction, as opposed to "erotica" which may be equally explicit but not be considered offensive. There is still considerable disagreement, however, about what is "offensive."

Some people view any very explicit sexual materials as unacceptable, while others believe there must be further elements present. Examples of such other elements might include: the conjunction of violence with sex, the presence of the *intent* to arouse, the presence of something which tells lies about human sexuality, or the inclusion of elements which seem to recommend degrading or abusive behaviour. Some people might wonder whether these elements are necessary features of pornography, or just indicators that pornography may be present. Indeed, some would deny that materials need to be sexually explicit in order to be "pornographic"—for example, the use of women's bodies to sell commercial products might be viewed as pornographic even if the depiction is not overtly sexual. It is also possible to ask for clarification of some of the crucial terms, such as defining what constitutes a "lie" about human sexuality, or what sorts of behaviour are degrading. One interesting question one might ask is: Can a person be degraded (and thereby harmed) even if that person does not perceive the activity to be degrading? This question introduces the notion of "false consciousness." This notion also leads to other questions about when a person can be understood to have consented to his or her participation in the production of pornography. Does it matter how many other meaningful options were available? Does it matter if the person "consenting" is a child? Is there a reliable way to ensure that the producers use models, etc. *only* for things to which they have consented?

Clearly, finding a definition of pornography is itself a difficult problem. It is worth noting, in reading various authors' views about pornography, that they may have different definitions of the term in mind.

Often discussions of pornography have focused not on whether it is bad in itself, but rather on whether large-scale availability of pornography will have bad consequences. As suggested above, some people worry that the presence of pornography tends to undermine the general moral fabric of a society, including (for example, in contemporary Canada) providing a challenge to the traditional vision of the nuclear family.

Some people who *want* to challenge traditional values nevertheless worry about the consequences of pornography. For example, there is the concern that consumption of pornography tends to encourage men (or at least some men) to commit sexual assault. Alternatively, it has been suggested that pornography might provide an alternative sort of sexual release for would-be rapists, and thereby actually reduce the incidence of sexual assault. There has been quite a bit of interesting research aimed at trying to determine whether pornography does tend to have these effects, and the resulting evidence is unclear. People on each side of the issue can cite studies which seem to provide some support for their views. But it is also not clear how much of the issue hinges on such research.

It might be argued that, even if only one man were led to commit rape as a result of consuming pornography, that would be enough reason to justify censorship. This sort of assertion raises complex questions about how to balance foreseen risks to some individuals with expected benefits to large numbers of others. In the case at hand, it might be argued that the severe harm of being sexually assaulted could not be outweighed by *any* number of people who benefit from the "entertainment" value of pornography. It should be noted, however, that people *might* be inspired to commit violent crimes by a wide variety of stimuli (many of which would not be seen as stimulating in this way by most members of society), and it could be asked whether it is possible or desirable to try to control every possible such source.

Many people would argue that, even if pornography does not directly induce men to sexual assault, it does help foster attitudes toward sexuality, and toward women in general, which society would be better off without. Indeed it is generally assumed that what people see or read has an effect on how they think and act. That is why some people recommend reading great literature and why many parents try to monitor the television their children watch. It might seem surprising if pornography did not have some effect on the thoughts and actions of those who consume it. It is very difficult to tell how significant such an effect might be, however, and in particular whether the effect is significant enough (and undesirable enough) to warrant bringing in the coercive force of the criminal law. Trying to censor materials for such reasons might also lead to limitations on romance novels, violent films, advertisements, and many other facets of popular culture. One might believe that such limitations would be a good idea, but it is not a decision to be taken lightly.

On Liberty

John Stuart Mill

John Stuart Mill was one of the best known British philosophers of the nineteenth Century. The argument in his book On Liberty *has been one of the most influential in shaping the political climate of societies such as modern Canada. The following excerpts are from chapters two and three of that book, in which he offers a classic defense of freedom of expression.*

*   *   *

Of Thought and Discussion

...If all mankind minus one were of one opinion, and only one person were of the contrary opinion, mankind would be no more justified in silencing that one person than he, if he had the power, would be justified in silencing mankind. Were an opinion a personal possession of no value except to the owner, if to be obstructed in the enjoyment of it were simply a private injury, it would make some difference whether the injury was inflicted only on a few persons or on many. But the peculiar evil of silencing the expression of an opinion is that it is robbing the human race, posterity as well as the existing generation—those who dissent from the opinion, still more than those who hold it. If the opinion is right, they are deprived of the opportunity of exchanging error for truth; if wrong, they lose, what is almost as great a benefit, the clearer perception and livelier impression of truth produced by its collision with error.

It is necessary to consider separately these two hypotheses, each of which has a distinct branch of the argument corresponding to it. We can never be sure that the opinion we are endeavoring to stifle is a false opinion; and if we were sure, stifling it would be an evil still.

First, the opinion which it is attempted to suppress by authority may possibly be true. Those who desire to suppress it, of course, deny its truth; but they are not infallible. They have no authority to decide the question for all mankind and exclude every other person from the means of judging. To refuse a hearing to an opinion because they are sure that it is false is to assume that *their* certainty is the same thing as *absolute* certainty. All silencing of discussion is an assumption of infallibility. Its condemnation may be allowed to rest on this common argument, not the worse for being common....

The objection likely to be made to this argument would probably take some such form as the following. There is no greater assumption of infallibility in forbidding the propagation of error than in any other thing which is done by public authority on its own judgement and responsibility. Judgement is given to men that they may use it. Because it may be used erroneously, are men to be told that they ought not to use it at all? To prohibit what they think pernicious is not claiming exemption from error, but fulfilling the duty incumbent on them, although fallible, of acting on their conscientious conviction. If we were never to act on our opinions, because those opinions may be wrong, we should leave all our interests uncared for, and all our duties unperformed. An objection which applies to all conduct can be no valid objection to any conduct in particular. It is the duty of governments, and of individuals, to form the truest opinions they can; to form them carefully, and never impose them upon others unless they are quite sure of being right. But when they are sure (such reasoners may say), it is not conscientiousness but cowardice to shrink from acting on their opinions and allow doctrines which they honestly think dangerous to the welfare of mankind, either in this life or in another, to be scattered abroad without restraint, because other people, in less enlightened times, have persecuted opinions now believed to be true. Let us take care, it may be said, not to make the same mistake; but governments and nations have made mistakes in other things which are not denied to be fit subjects for the exercise of authority: they have laid on bad taxes, made unjust wars. Ought we therefore to lay on no taxes and, under whatever provocation, make no wars? Men and governments must act to the best of their ability. There is no such thing as absolute certainty, but there is assurance sufficient for the purposes of human life. We may, and must, assume our opinion to be true for the guidance of our own conduct; and it is assuming no more when we forbid bad men to pervert society by the propagation of opinions which we regard as false and pernicious.

I answer, that it is assuming very much more. There is the greatest difference between presuming an opinion to be true because, with every opportunity for contesting it, it has not been refuted, and assuming its truth for the purpose of not permitting its refutation. Complete liberty of contradicting and disproving our opinion is the very condition which justifies us in assuming its truth for purposes of action; and on no other terms can a being with human faculties have any rational assurance of being right....

In the present age, which has been described as "destitute of faith, but terrified at skepticism"[1]—in which people feel sure, not so much that their opinions are true as that they should not know what to do without them—the claims of an opinion to be protected from public attack are rested not so much on its truth as on its importance to society. There are, it is alleged, certain beliefs so useful, not to say indispensable, to well-being that it is as much the duty of the governments to uphold those beliefs as to protect any other of the interests of society. In a case of such necessity, and so directly in the line of their duty, something less than infallibility may, it is maintained, warrant, and even bind, governments to act on their own opinion confirmed by the general opinion of mankind. It is also often argued, and still oftener thought, that none but bad men would desire to weaken these salutary beliefs; and there can be nothing wrong, it is thought, in restraining bad men and prohibiting what only such men would wish to practice. This mode of thinking makes the justification of restraints on discussion not a question of the truth of doctrines but of their usefulness, and flatters itself by that means to escape the responsibility of claiming to be an infallible judge of opinions. But those who thus satisfy themselves do not perceive that the assumption of infallibility is merely shifted from one point to another. The usefulness of an opinion is itself matter of opinion—as disputable, as open to discussion, and requiring discussion as much as the opinion itself. There is the same need of an infallible judge of opinions to decide an opinion to be noxious as to decide it to be false, unless the opinion condemned has full opportunity of defending itself. And it will not do to say that the heretic may be allowed to maintain the utility or harmlessness of his opinion, though forbidden to maintain its truth. The truth of an opinion is part of its utility. If we would know whether or not it is desirable that a proposition should be believed, is it possible to exclude the consideration of whether or not it is true? In the opinion, not of bad men, but of the best men, no belief which is contrary to truth can be really useful; and can you prevent such men from urging that plea when they are charged with culpability for denying some doctrine which they are told is useful, but which they believe to be false? Those who are on the side of received opinions never fail to take all possible advantage of this plea; you do not find *them* handling the question of utility as if it could be completely abstracted from that of truth; on the contrary, it is, above all, because their doctrine is "the truth" that the knowledge or the belief of it is held to be so indispensable. There can be no fair discussion of the question of usefulness when an argument so vital may be employed on one side, but not on the other. And in point of fact, when law or public feeling do not permit the truth of an opinion to be disputed, they are just as little tolerant of a denial of its usefulness. The utmost they allow is an extenuation of its absolute necessity, or of the positive guilt of rejecting it....

[I]t is not the minds of heretics that are deteriorated most by the ban placed on all inquiry which does not end in the orthodox conclusions. The greatest harm done is to those who are not heretics, and whose whole mental development is cramped and their reason cowed by the fear of heresy. Who can compute what the world loses in the multitude of promising intellects combined with timid characters, who dare not follow out any bold, vigorous, independent train of thought, lest it should land them in something which would admit of being considered irreligious or immoral? Among them we may occasionally see some man of deep conscientiousness and subtle and refined understanding, who spends a life in sophisticating with an intellect which he cannot silence, and exhausts the resources of ingenuity in attempting to reconcile the promptings of his conscience and reason with orthodoxy, which yet he does not, perhaps, to the end succeed in doing. No one can be a great thinker who does not recognize that as a thinker it is his first duty to follow his intellect to whatever conclusions it may lead. Truth gains more even by the errors of one who, with due study and preparation, thinks for himself than by the true opinions of those who only hold them because they do not suffer themselves to think. Not that it is solely, or chiefly, to form great thinkers that freedom of thinking is required. On the contrary, it is as much and even more indispensable to enable average human beings to attain the mental stature which they are capable of. There have been, and may again be, great individual thinkers in a general atmosphere of mental slavery. But there never has been, nor ever will be, in that atmosphere an intellectually active people. When any people has made a temporary approach to such a character, it has been because the dread of heterodox speculation was for a time suspended. Where there is a tacit convention that principles are not to be disputed, where the discussion of the greatest questions which can occupy humanity is considered to be closed, we cannot hope to find that generally high scale of mental activity which has made some periods of history so remarkable. Never when controversy avoided the subjects which are large and important enough to kindle enthusiasm was the mind of a people stirred up from its foundations, and the impulse given which raised even persons of the most ordinary intellect to something of the dignity of thinking beings....

Let us now pass to the second division of the argument, and dismissing the supposition that any of the received opinions may be false, let us assume them to be true and examine into the worth of the manner in which they are likely to be held when their truth is not freely and openly canvassed. However unwillingly a person who has a strong opinion may admit the possibility that his opinion may be false, he ought to be moved by the consideration that, however true it may be, if it is not fully, frequently, and fearlessly discussed, it will be held as a dead dogma, not a living truth.

There is a class of persons (happily not quite so numerous as formerly) who think it enough if a person assents undoubtingly to what they think true, though he has no knowledge whatever of the grounds of the opinion and could not make a tenable defense of it against the most superficial objections. Such persons, if they can once get their creed taught from authority, naturally think that no good, and some harm, comes of its being allowed to be questioned. Where their influence prevails, they make it nearly impossible for the received opinion to be rejected wisely and considerately,

though it may still be rejected harshly and ignorantly; for to shut out discussion entirely is seldom possible, and when it once gets in, beliefs not grounded on conviction are apt to give way before the slightest semblance of an argument. Waiving, however, this possibility—assuming that the true opinion abides in the mind, but abides as a prejudice, a belief independent of, and proof against, argument—this is not the way in which truth ought to be held by a rational being. This is not knowing the truth. Truth, thus held, is but one superstition the more, accidentally clinging to the words which enunciate a truth....

If, however, the mischievous operation of the absence of free discussion, when the received opinions are true, were confined to leaving men ignorant of the grounds of those opinions, it might be thought that this, if an intellectual, is no moral evil and does not affect the worth of the opinions, regarded in their influence on the character. The fact, however, is that not only the grounds of the opinion are forgotten in the absence of discussion, but too often the meaning of the opinion itself. The words which convey it cease to suggest ideas, or suggest only a small portion of those they were originally employed to communicate. Instead of a vivid conception and a living belief, there remain only a few phrases retained by rote; or, if any part, the shell and husk only of the meaning is retained, the finer essence being lost. The great chapter in human history which this fact occupies and fills cannot be too earnestly studied and meditated on....

It still remains to speak of one of the principal causes which make diversity of opinion advantageous, and will continue to do so until mankind shall have entered a stage of intellectual advancement which at present seems at an incalculable distance. We have hitherto considered only two possibilities: that the received opinion may be false, and some other opinion, consequently, true; or that, the received opinion being true, a conflict with the opposite error is essential to a clear apprehension and deep feeling of its truth. But there is a commoner case than either of these: when the conflicting doctrines, instead of being one true and the other false, share the truth between them, and the noncomforming opinion is needed to supply the remainder of the truth of which the received doctrine embodies only a part. Popular opinions, on subjects not palpable to sense, are often true, but seldom or never the whole truth. They are a part of the truth, sometimes a greater, sometimes a smaller part, but exaggerated, distorted, and disjoined from the truths by which they ought to be accompanied and limited. Heretical opinions, on the other hand, are generally some of these suppressed and neglected truths, bursting the bonds which kept them down, and either seeking reconciliation with the truth contained in the common opinion, or fronting it as enemies, and setting themselves up, with similar exclusiveness, as the whole truth. The latter case is hitherto the most frequent, as, in the human mind, one-sidedness has always been the rule, and many-sidedness the exception. Hence, even in revolutions of opinion, one part of the truth usually sets while another rises. Even progress, which ought to superadd, for the most part only substitutes one partial and incomplete truth for another; improvement consisting chiefly in this, that the new fragment of truth is more wanted, more adapted to the needs of the time than that which it displaces. Such being the partial character of prevailing opinions, even when resting on a true foundation, every opinion which embodies somewhat of the portion of truth which the common opinion omits ought to be considered precious, with whatever amount of error and confusion that truth may be blended. No sober judge of human affairs will feel bound to be indignant because those who force on our notice truths which we should otherwise have overlooked, overlook some of those which we see. Rather, he will think that so long as popular truth is one-sided, it is more desirable than otherwise that unpopular truth should have one-sided assertors, too, such being usually the most energetic and the most likely to compel reluctant attention to the fragment of wisdom which they proclaim as if it were the whole....

I do not pretend that the most unlimited use of the freedom of enunciating all possible opinions would put an end to the evils of religious or philosophical sectarianism. Every truth which men of narrow capacity are in earnest about is sure to be asserted, inculcated, and in many ways even acted on, as if no other truth existed in the world, or at all events none that could limit or qualify the first. I acknowledge that the tendency of all opinions to become sectarian is not cured by the freest discussion, but is often heightened and exacerbated thereby; the truth which ought to have been, but was not, seen, being rejected all the more violently because proclaimed by persons regarded as opponents. But it is not on the impassioned partisan, it is on the calmer and more disinterested bystander, that this collision of opinions works its salutary effect. Not the violent conflict between parts of the truth, but the quiet suppression of half of it, is the formidable evil; there is always hope when people are forced to listen to both sides; it is when they attend only to one that errors harden into prejudices, and truth itself ceases to have the effect of truth by being exaggerated into falsehood. And since there are few mental attributes more rare than that judicial faculty that can sit in intelligent judgement between two sides of a question, of which only one is represented by an advocate before it, truth has no chance but in proportion as every side of it, every opinion which embodies any fraction of the truth, not only finds advocates, but is so advocated as to be listened to.

We have now recognized the necessity to the mental well-being of mankind (on which all their other well-being depends) of freedom of opinion, and freedom of the expression of opinion, on four distinct grounds, which we will now briefly recapitulate:

First, if any opinion is compelled to silence, that opinion may, for aught we can certainly know, be true. To deny this is to assume our own infallibility.

Secondly, though the silenced opinion may be an error, it may, and very commonly does, contain a portion of truth; and since the general or prevailing opinion on any subject is rarely or never the whole truth, it is only by the collision of adverse opinions that the remainder of the truth has any chance of being supplied.

Thirdly, even if the received opinion be not only true, but the whole truth; unless it is suffered to be, and actually is, vigorously and earnestly contested, it will, by most of those who receive it, be held in the manner of a prejudice, with little comprehension or feeling of its rational grounds. And not only this, but, fourthly, the meaning of the doctrine itself will be in danger of being lost or enfeebled, and deprived of its vital effect on the character and conduct: the dogma

becoming a mere formal profession, inefficacious for good, but cumbering the ground and preventing the growth of any real and heartfelt conviction from reason or personal experience....

Of Individuality, as One of the Elements of Well-Being

Such being the reasons which make it imperative that human beings should be free to form opinions and to express their opinions without reserve; and such the baneful consequences to the intellectual, and through that to the moral nature of man, unless this liberty is either conceded or asserted in spite of prohibition; let us next examine whether the same reasons do not require that men should be free to act upon their opinions—to carry these out in their lives without hindrance, either physical or moral, from their fellow men, so long as it is at their own risk and peril. This last proviso is of course indispensable. No one pretends that actions should be as free as opinions. On the contrary, even opinions lose their immunity when the circumstances in which they are expressed are such as to constitute their expression a positive instigation to some mischievous act. An opinion that corn dealers are starvers of the poor, or that private property is robbery, ought to be unmolested when simply circulated through the press, but may justly incur punishment when delivered orally to an excited mob assembled before the house of a corn dealer, or when handed out among the same mob in the form of a placard. Acts, of whatever kind, which without justifiable cause do harm to others may be, and in the more important cases absolutely require to be, controlled by the unfavorable sentiments, and, when needful, by the active interference of mankind. The liberty of the individual must be thus far limited; he must not make himself a nuisance to other people. But if he refrains from molesting others in what concerns them, and merely acts according to his own inclination and judgement in things which concern himself, the same reasons which show that opinion should be free prove also that he should be allowed, without molestation, to carry his opinions into practice at his own cost....

Notes

1 The quotation is from Thomas Carlyle, "Memoirs of the Life of Scott," reprinted in his *Critical and Miscellaneous Essays*, 7 vols.; London, 1869, vol. VI, p. 46.

Questions for Discussion

1 Mill's main argument is that allowing free speech will have the best consequences for society as a whole. Is this always necessarily the case?

2 It has been suggested that Mill's defense of free speech seems to assume that society is a sort of "debating society," in which people are rational and jointly pursue truth. To what extent should his endorsement of free speech be revised if in fact many people in society are given to persuasion by emotional arguments rather than rational ones?

3 Mill would allow some restriction on free speech, as in his example of the crowd outside the corn dealer's house. What principle is at work justifying this restriction? Are there other "exceptions" to Mill's basic argument?

Hate Propaganda

Law Reform Commission of Canada

In the following piece, the Canadian Law Reform Commission considers whether the existing legislation against distribution of hate propaganda should be changed. It examines the justification of the law, and several possible complications and ambiguities. It also considers whether the law against hate propaganda should cover pornography, and concludes that it should not.

*   *   *

[C]rimes of hate propaganda need special justification. Prohibiting the promotion of hatred conflicts with freedom of expression,[1] perhaps the most fundamental value in our society. As Thomas Berger has stated: "Freedom of speech is in a sense man's calling, the necessary condition of all other freedoms."[2]

However, even freedom of expression is not absolute. For example, our criminal law has justifiably recognized that it is a crime to counsel another to commit a crime, to commit perjury, to commit contempt of court, and to defraud by deceit. As Oliver Wendell Holmes remarked: "The most stringent protection of free speech would not protect a man in falsely shouting fire in a theatre, and causing a panic."[3]

On the other hand, our criminal law has refused to prohibit expressions which, although hurtful, are not seriously harmful. For example, not every vulgar abuse or insult is a crime. Instead, crimes which do catch insults are restrictively defined as to place or person—such as causing a disturbance in or near a public place, or the type of contempt of court known as scandalizing the court. There is just one exception to this—our present crime of defamatory libel which covers insult to any person. But the original rationale for this crime was the belief that libels would likely cause a breach of the peace. This rationale is now archaic, and for this among other reasons, we have recommended abolition of this crime.

In effect, the general principle underlying crimes which limit freedom of expression seems to be that words should be prohibited only when they cause or threaten to cause serious harm, such as personal injury (for example, incitement to murder), damage to an important institution (for example, perjury or contempt of court, which damages the criminal justice system), and property loss (for example, fraud).

Do our crimes of hate propaganda fall within this general principle? There are three kinds of crimes to examine here: (1) crimes dealing with genocide; (2) crimes dealing with promoting hatred; and (3) the crime of publishing false news....

Crimes of Promoting Hatred

Unlike advocating genocide and publishing false news, crimes of promoting hatred pose major problems. The crimes of promoting hatred referred to here are those two offences created in the present section 281.2 of the *Code*: (1) inciting hatred against any identifiable group where such incitement is likely to lead to a breach of the peace; and (2) the wilful promotion of hatred against any identifiable group.

These crimes of promoting hatred raise four major issues: (1) Do such expressions of hatred cause a substantial enough harm to warrant repression by the criminal law? (2) Assuming the need to create these offences, should they extend to individuals as well as groups? (3) Which groups should these crimes protect? (4) What restrictions should be placed on these crimes?

The Harm Involved

Because the harm involved relates to hatred, it is necessary to understand what hatred means. There is no *Code* definition of "hatred." But this is not a defect in this legislation. The ordinary meaning of the word will suffice. Hatred is not mere passive dislike. *The Shorter Oxford Dictionary* defines hatred to include "active dislike, detestation; enmity, ill will, malevolence." *Le petit Robert* defines "la haine" as "sentiment violent qui pousse à vouloir du mal à [quelqu'un] et à se réjour du mal qui lui arrive." In effect, hatred is enmity.

Promoting enmity is clearly dysfunctional to society. It stirs up hatred among social groups. It can even lay the foundation for physical attacks upon persons or property. Preventing such harm justifies the use of the criminal law.

Individuals or Groups?

Clearly, promoting hatred about an individual can cause serious harm. For example, he or she could be the victim of character assassination. Arguably, a consistent approach in dealing with the promotion of hatred requires that protection should extend to individuals as well as groups. Indeed, some have argued that an expansion of some kind is needed to catch those who deliberately avoid coming within the hate propaganda crimes by directing their hostility against something less than entire groups.[4]

Forceful as this argument is, we do not accept it, for three reasons. First, less social damage is caused when the attack is made upon a specific individual rather than a group. Second, a person would not be able to escape liability when the attack, ostensibly against a subgroup, is in fact an attack against the group itself.[5] Third, unlike an attack upon a group, a hateful attack upon an individual's reputation gives rise to an adequate civil remedy: a defamation suit. Given these factors, it is consistent with the fundamental principle of using the criminal law with restraint to continue to restrict these crimes to protect only identifiable groups.

Which Groups?

In a principled *Code*, one would expect that the groups chosen for protection would be selected on the basis of principle, rather than on an *ad hoc* basis.

Clearly, one would not want to protect all identifiable groups for two reasons. First, it would create a vague offence. Potentially, the number of groups within any society is infinite. Any "identifiable group" would include not just socially important groups (for example, religious groups), but also socially unimportant groups (for example, all fans of "Star Trek"). Second, such an expansion would infringe unjustifiably upon freedom of expression. Making a crime that could conceivably catch challenging and hostile views made against political or economic groups intrudes into the heated discussions on matters of public in-

terest so vital to the health of any democratic society.

Accordingly, these crimes should protect only those socially important groups which are an integral part of the Canadian social fabric and which are most capable of being harmed by hatred directed against them.

Which groups are these? Certain groups have been harmed by hate propaganda in the past—for example, ethnic, religious, or racial groups. Others might be harmed in the future—for example, the mentally handicapped, or the elderly.

Unfortunately, while the principle seems obvious, it will not do to create an open-ended definition of "identifiable group" in line with this principle; for then the crime becomes too vague. As a result, we are forced to rely upon an *ad hoc* list of groups which fall within this principle.

The question then is, Which list? The present one, or another? An excellent way to select criteria for protecting groups from hatred is to choose criteria which are clearly prohibited grounds of discrimination under Canadian law. While such criteria can be found in various human rights codes,[6] the strongest statement of protection from discrimination is found in subsection 15(1) of the Charter. Although open-ended, this guarantees equality rights to individuals characterized by the specifically enumerated criteria of "colour, race, ethnic origin, religion, national origin, sex, age, or mental or physical disability." If the Charter protects against individual discrimination on the basis of these specific criteria, it is entirely reasonable that groups characterized by the same criteria be protected by the criminal law when they are subjected to vicious expressions of hatred.

Of the new criteria for identifying groups proposed here, the most notable is probably that of "sex." No doubt, judges will encounter two major arguments in this regard; first, that the expanded crime will now catch pornography; and second, that it will now catch hatred directed against homosexuals and lesbians.

While not binding on judges, our view is that our proposal to protect sexual groups should have two qualifications. First, the recommended inclusion of sexual groups is not proposed to combat the evil inherent in pornography. For several reasons, we believe that the evil of pornography is best dealt with by way of clearly defined pornography offences, not by way of crimes of hate propaganda.[7] Instead, only the most vicious kinds of woman hating and, incidentally, man hating—that is, those done intentionally—will be caught.

Second, groups identifiable on the basis of "sexual orientation" are not intended to be included within the "sex" category. But should such groups be protected? Admittedly, "sexual orientation" is not specifically set out within subsection 15(1) of the Charter. However, the open-ended provisions of subsection 15(1) arguably do protect against discrimination on the basis of "sexual orientation." Indeed, the recent Report of the Parliamentary Committee on Equality Rights supports this view.[8] But more important, in recent history, homosexuals have been subjected to hateful attacks which led to their physical harm. After all, homosexuals were also victims of the genocidal policies of the Nazis.[9] Nonetheless, we would welcome further public feedback before making a specific recommendation on this issue.

What Restrictions?

...The crucial issue involving *mens rea* is whether the crime should retain the word "wilfully" or an equivalent phrase which makes the crime effectively one of specific intent, or whether "wilfully" should be dropped altogether to create a crime of recklessness. The preferred view of many persons, as reflected in *Equality Now* and the Fraser Committee report, is that the "wilfully" requirement must be dropped.

With respect, we do not share this view. The principle of restraint requires lawmakers to concern themselves not just with whom they want to catch, but also with whom they do not want to catch. For example, removing an intent or purpose requirement could well result in successful prosecutions of cases similar to *Buzzanga*, where members of a minority group publish hate propaganda against their own group in order to create controversy or to agitate for reform. This crime should not be used to prosecute such individuals.

In effect, this crime should be used only to catch the most extreme cases of fomenting hatred, when the accused is motivated by enmity. Accordingly, we recommend that this crime should continue to be one of intent or purpose. This is best achieved by removing the "wilfully" requirement and substituting in its place an "intentionally" or "purposely" requirement. This change in wording would not result in any change to the *mens rea* requirement for this crime as set out in *Buzzanga and Durocher*,[10] but it would avoid the problems inherent in the word "wilfully," which has been defined inconsistently in criminal law.[11]

Should there be a defence of truth for the crime? As the law now stands, there is. Some consultants argued that truth should not be a defence because it does not out-weigh the harm caused.

This raises an important policy issue: When should the criminal law punish a person for publishing the truth? One can concede that there are occasions when the criminal law should do so. For example, our revised crime of intentionally fomenting hatred in a public place has no defence of truth, nor any other defences. But the reason for denying defences there is that an immediate threat to public peace exists—the likelihood of harm to a person or damage to property.

By contrast, the crime of intentionally fomenting hatred does not require the existence of an immediate threat to the public peace. Thus, it is broader in scope. Here, the criminal law must respect truth as a fundamental value. Otherwise, we put at risk not just hatemongers but also legitimate scholars who, for a variety of motives, inject themselves into areas of controversy by publishing factually accurate material critical of socially important groups within our society.

What about the remaining defences?[12] Are they needed? Undoubtedly, many persons believe that the present range of defences is too broad, that it prevents the crime from being effective. For example, two of the remaining defences—those of an opinion on a religious subject and of a purpose to remove feelings of hatred—require that the accused act in "good faith." Some argue that all that "good faith" means is that the accused honestly believe what he or she says, thus permitting the sincere fanatic to raise a successful defence.

Nonetheless, our view is that the defences, rather than operating to acquit the accused when he or she wilfully promotes hatred, appear more to be examples of not wilfully promoting hatred.[13] If a person wilfully or intentionally foments hatred, it seems that the person acts in bad faith, not good faith. By analogy, for the defence of qualified privilege in defamation law, a person does not act in good faith even when he or she honestly believes the defamation, if the dominant motive is to give vent to personal spite, ill will, or some other improper purpose.[14] Indeed, cases such as *Keegstra* and *Buzzanga* suggest that where a person has in fact wilfully promoted hatred, judges and juries are reluctant to find that the defences apply to acquit the accused.[15]

Are these defences needed, however, as long as this crime remains one of intent or purpose? There is an important psychological advantage in retaining these defences because they reflect how highly our society values freedom of expression. After all, these remaining defences existed beforehand elsewhere in the *Code* as defences to other crimes which limit freedom of expression—namely, blasphemous libel, defamatory libel, and sedition.[16] They were created as defences here out of caution to ensure that statements of fact or opinion expressly permitted in other contexts would not be caught by this crime, and to ensure that minority groups would not be prosecuted under a crime designed to protect them. Therefore, they should be retained.

Should the crime of fomenting hatred (and, incidentally, the offence of advocating genocide) continue to require the consent of the Attorney General as a pre-condition to prosecution?

Because it is unclear exactly what does foment hatred, without safeguards there could be unwarranted prosecutions. For example, a complaint was made in Alberta in 1984 that the movie, "Red Dawn," about a fictional Communist invasion of the United

States, promoted hatred against Russians and Cubans.[17] In 1975, some young people were arrested by Toronto police for distributing leaflets saying "Yankee go home."[18]

In general, safeguards are provided, initially by the requirement that an information be laid before a justice of the peace, later by the power of the Crown to stay a prosecution. But is freedom of expression so fundamental to our society that it is justifiable to take special care to ensure that the power to prosecute crimes which limit freedom of expression will not be abused?

On the one hand, requiring the consent of the Attorney General prior to a prosecution is an effective safeguard to prevent at the outset the cost and burden of a criminal trial, especially in an area of political sensitivity. On the other hand, this requirement of consent can prevent those who are victims of hate propaganda from launching a prosecution. For example, Ernst Zundel was prosecuted under section 177 because the Ontario Attorney General refused to give his consent to prosecute him for wilful promotion of hatred.[19]

Whether there should be the requirement of the consent of the Attorney General for certain crimes is one of the issues being studied in a forthcoming Working Paper on the Powers of the Attorney General. For this reason, we defer making any recommendations on this issue as it relates to crimes of hate propaganda until that study is completed.

Conclusion

There is no easy solution to the problem of spreading hatred. Even among civil libertarians who believe strongly in protecting freedom of speech, opinion is divided as to whether these crimes are necessary.

These proposals may not meet with overwhelming approval from the public. On the one hand, visible minorities may regard with dismay the decision to retain, for the revised offence of fomenting hatred, the *mens rea* requirement of intent or purpose and all the existing defences. On the other hand, civil libertarians may be disappointed that we did not advocate abolition of the offence of wilfully promoting hatred, and indeed may shudder at the proposal to expand the definition of "identifiable group" to protect those groups enumerated specifically in subsection 15(1) of the Charter. Both sides may argue that the Commission has failed to act boldly and imaginatively on an important social issue.

Nonetheless, the proposals made here are entirely consistent with our view that, while the criminal law should uphold fundamental values, it should nonetheless be applied with restraint.

Admittedly, the very existence of these crimes of fomenting hatred is open to two fundamental objections. First, they encroach upon freedom of expression in an unjustifiable manner. In other words, restricting freedom of expression for some restricts freedom of expression for all. Second, they may not do what they are expected to do. After all, the Weimar Republic had crimes of hate propaganda; yet Hitler still came to power.

The crimes proposed in this Paper, however, infringe upon freedom of expression in a justifiable manner by ensuring that only the most serious kinds of hatred are caught by the criminal law. Moreover, these crimes will do what they are expected to do, in two ways: first, by underlining the fundamental values of equality and dignity; second, by deterring others from engaging in such activity.

Admittedly, too, the restricted definition of these crimes is open to the fundamental objection that they do not propose adequate legal controls on the propagation of hatred.

The issue here, however, is to what extent the *criminal law* must be used to combat fomenting hatred against identifiable groups. Given its coercive and brutal nature, criminal law must be used with restraint. It should be used as the last resort, not the first. Of course, our society can use other means to deal with the spreading of hatred. The work of human rights commissions is all-important in helping to eliminate attitudes which support discrimination. Perhaps a more effective way to deal with fomenting hatred would be to ensure that these commissions play a stronger role in combating such attitudes. But the role of the criminal law must be limited to preventing the most harmful hatreds being aimed at clearly socially important groups. Otherwise, in the name of fighting hatred, our society runs the risk of creating unjustifiable repression.

Pornography and Hate Propaganda

Many feminists assert that pornography promotes hatred against women. As Susan Brownmiller states, "[p]ornography is the undiluted essence of anti-female propaganda."[20] Indeed, some point out the similarities between pornography directed against women, and hate propaganda directed against Jews and Blacks.[21]

The Fraser Committee accepted this argument. So, in addition to a highly detailed three-tier system of criminal controls on pornography, it proposed the use of the hate propaganda section 281.2 of the *Code* to help deal with the evil inherent in pornography. As the Committee stated:

If one accepts the argument that pornography is an expression of misogyny, then use of the hate propaganda section of the *Code* in this connection is particularly attractive. If the evil seen in pornography is the communication of an untrue message which expresses or propagates hatred against women, it seems logical that this *Code* provision, and not one dealing with sexual morality, should be aimed against it.[22]

In examining the harm caused by pornography, the Fraser Committee emphasized the harm it causes to the constitutionally entrenched value of equality. But, to remain consistent with this argument, it recommended that the offence be expanded to include all those groups specifically enumerated in section 15 of the Charter.[23]

However, the Committee recognized that for this section to be effective in combatting the evil of pornography, other changes had to be made. First, the "wilfully" requirement had to be removed. As the Committee stated:

In the area of pornography, a wilfulness requirement would place an almost impossible burden on the prosecutor. The effect of material may be to engender hatred of women, but persons may all too readily establish that this was not done "wilfully." The motive behind the publication may be described as sexual entertainment, or even profit; even an unattractive motive, other than hatred, would serve to defeat a prosecution where specific intent was required.[24]

Second, the requirement of the Attorney General's consent to a prosecution had to be removed.[25] Third, the offence should be redefined to include any visible representation.[26]

Nonetheless, the proposed reform of the hate propaganda crimes outlined in this Paper would not be effective in dealing with the harm caused by pornography, because an "intentionally" or "purposely" requirement for the revised offence of fomenting hatred is required. This would effectively prevent prosecutions under section 281.2 for pornography, except, perhaps, in the most extreme circumstances.

The debate over using crimes of hate propaganda to deal with pornography highlights certain problems.

The first problem concerns the assumption that pornography promotes hatred against women just as, say, a white racist promotes hatred against Blacks. Some object to this evaluation. For example, Ryan states:

> [T]he whole subject of pornography is intimately and inextricably related to the biological sexual urges of the human animal.... Hate is sometimes present as a motive, but the motivation is complex and is at least partly based on the sexual urge.... It [pornography] should not be broken up and in part confused with racial and religious hatred, which spring from other roots.[27]

The second problem is that expanding the hate propaganda crimes to catch pornography by adding the category of "sex" to the definition of "identifiable group" also catches non-pornographic statements of misogyny. But what other statements are misogynistic? An arguably extreme position is that taken by Andrea Dworkin:

> Antifeminism is always an expression of hating women: it is way past time to say so, to make the equation, to insist on its truth.... It is right to see woman hating, sex hatred, passionate contempt in every effort to subvert or stop an improvement in the status of women on any front, whether radical or reform.... This is true when the antifeminism is expressed in opposition to the Equal Rights Amendment or to the right to abortion on demand or to procedures against sexual harassment or to shelters for battered

women or to reforms in rape laws. This is true whether the opposition is from the Heritage Foundation, the Moral Majority, the Eagle Forum, the American Civil Liberties Union, the Communist Party, the Democrats, or the Republicans.[28]

The third problem is that an offence which is expanded to catch reckless promotions of hatred against a sexual group catches not just woman hating, but also man hating. There is a danger that the offence could be used to prosecute radical feminists for promoting hatred against men. For example, Varda Burstyn points out that:

> [I]n December, 1984, Joe Borowski, a former Manitoba cabinet minister and well-funded anti-abortion crusader, announced his intention to seek charges against *Herizons*, a Winnipeg-based feminist magazine, for a cartoon showing a construction site exploding, supposedly as a result of women's revenge against the workers. He has stated that this cartoon represents 'violence against men.'[29]

The fourth problem is, assuming that specific offences against pornography are to be created in our new Code, will ensuring that crimes of hate propaganda also catch pornography be a substantially useful addition to the law? Admittedly, the Fraser Committee believed that its proposed revision of subsection 281.2(2) would complement its three-tiered scheme to deal with pornography.[30] But it is also clear that for the crime of promoting hatred to be effective in combatting pornography, it would have to catch much the same conduct as the specific crimes of pornography. Two issues arise. First, if there are specific crimes of pornography, then is there really a need to catch the conduct elsewhere? Second, while it may not complement specific crimes of pornography to some extent, could not the crime of promoting hatred be used to undercut the safeguards provided by the more specific offences of pornography? What if a private prosecutor is determined to prosecute, and realizes that the crime of promoting hatred fails to provide the same defences as the pornography offences?

In effect, the principle of restraint in the application of the criminal law compels this Commission to deal with pornography, not under hate propaganda offences, but rather only under specific offences of pornography.[31] Such an approach enables the criminal law to define with better precision the kind of pornography it wishes to catch. It also prevents a possible misuse of the criminal law by preventing prosecutions which could have a chilling effect upon freedom of expression.

Notes

1   Recently, some have argued that expressing hatred against an identifiable group is not part and parcel of the "freedom of expression" guarantee of paragraph 2(*b*) of the Charter. Nowhere is this more clearly stated at present in Canadian law than by Quigley J. in *R. v. Keegstra, supra*, note 37, p. 268. He initially concludes:

'[F]reedom of expression' as used in s. 2(*b*) of the Charter does not mean an absolute freedom permitting an unabridged right of speech or expression. In particular, I hold that s. 281.2(2) of the *Criminal Code* does not infringe upon the freedom of expression granted by s. 2(*b*) of the Charter.

If promoting hatred against an unidentifiable group is not part of "freedom of expression" from the outset, the effect is that it is unnecessary to determine whether crimes of hate propaganda are a demonstrably justifiable reasonable limit upon freedom of expression by resort to section 1 of the Charter.

With all due respect, we disagree with this approach. Freedom of expression is not defined restrictively by paragraph 2(*b*) of the Charter. Therefore, any kind of expression should fall within its ambit. This includes expressions made in public or in private, expressions of reason, expressions of passion—love as well as hate—expressions which help, and expressions which harm. To argue that some expressions are not part of the "freedom of expression" guarantee of paragraph 2(*b*) of the Charter could result in a patchwork of different degrees of protection for different kinds of speech, devoid of consistency and principle. How are courts to distinguish between expressions which do not initially fall within the "freedom of expression" guarantee, and those which do, but can be curtailed by resort to the reasonable limitation clause of section 1 of the Charter? Could not one avoid trying to meet the criteria imposed by the section 1 limitation clause by holding that the expression is not protected by paragraph 2(*b*)?

Finally, this approach is unnecessary. While it is used by the United States Supreme Court (for example, for hate propaganda in the now arguably outdated case of *Beauharnais v. Illinois, supra*, note 92, there is a necessary reason for doing so: there is no limitation clause in its Bill of Rights. But section 1 of the Charter permits demonstrably justifiable reasonable limits upon any Charter freedom or right, including freedom of expression. Therefore, there is no need to resort to the argument that "freedom of expression" means only those which are constitutionally protected.

2   T. Berger, *Fragile Freedoms* (Toronto: Clarke, Irwin, 1981), p. 134.

3   *Schenck v. United States,* 249 US 47 (1919), p. 52.

4   See, for example, the statement by The Honourable Roy McMurtry, Attorney General for Ontario to the Parliamentary Special Committee on Participation of Visible Minorities in Canadian Society, October 20, 1983. He argues, at page 11, that comments directed solely to a certain segment of the racial or religious group would not be caught even though the effect would tend to produce hatred against the entire group, for example, the word "zionist." This argument is referred to in *Equality Now, supra*, note 67, at page 71.

5   *Equality Now, supra*, note 67, p. 71, states:

The Committee does not believe that the Criminal Code has to be amended to deal with this problem. This type of material is subject to criminal sanction because it defiles an identifiable group in a general sense and not because it attacks all members of an identifiable group. Even if such hate propaganda purports to caricature only a part of a racial group, it should still be subject to prosecution under the present provisions of the Criminal Code in appropriate circumstances.

6   A list of Canadian human rights legislation is provided in Schedule A to this Paper.

7   These reasons are outlined in Schedule B to this Paper.

8   Report of the Parliamentary Committee on Equality Rights, *Equality Rights for All* (Ottawa: Supply and Services, 1985), p. 29. Some legal commentators have also reached the same conclusion. See, for example, J.E. Jefferson, "Gay Rights and the Charter" (1985), 43:1 *U.T. Faculty L.R.* 70; and N. Duplé, "Homosexualité et droits à l'égalité dans les Chartres canadienne et québécoise" (1984), 25 *C. de D.* 801.

9   For a harrowing account of the persecution of the homosexuals of Western Europe under the Nazis, see F. Rector, *The Nazi Extermination of Homosexuals* (New York: Stein and Day, 1981). Homosexuals were required to wear triangular pink cloth patches in the concentration camps for identification, and were treated savagely. Rector estimates that at least 500,000 gays died in the Holocaust (p. 116). Yet, he points out that this genocide of homosexuals "still lies buried as a virtual historical secret" (p. 111).

10 In *Buzzanga and Durocher, supra,* note 33, the Ontario Court of Appeal defined "wilfully" in the context of promoting hatred to mean (a) having the conscious purpose to promote hatred or (b) foreseeing that the promotion of hatred was certain or morally certain the result. This definition corresponds with the definition of intent/purpose for crimes requiring intent/purpose in this Commission's upcoming tentative draft Code.

11 See J. Fortin and L. Viau, *supra* , note 35, pp. 140-2.

12 Aside from truth, the three remaining defences in subsection 281.2(3) of the *Criminal Code* are:

(*b*) if, in good faith, he expressed or attempted to establish by argument an opinion on a religious subject;

(*c*) if the statements were relevant to any subjects of public interest, the discussion of which was for the public benefit, and if on reasonable grounds he believed them to be true; or

(*d*) if, in good faith, he intended to point out, for the purpose of removal, matters producing or tending to produce feelings of hatred towards an identifiable group in Canada.

13 See Cohen's analysis of these defences in *supra,* note 4, pp. 775-7.

14 For an excellent analysis of this issue in defamation law, see *Horrocks v. Lowe,* [1975] A.C. 135 (H.L.).

15 For example in *Buzzanga and Durocher, supra,* note 33, Martin J.A. stated at page 389, "The exemption contained in s. 281.2(3)(*d*) is, in my view, provided out of abundant caution, and where a person has 'wilfully' promoted hatred, the cases in which the exemption may successfully be invoked must be comparatively rare."

Also, in the *Keegstra* case, Keegstra was convicted of wilfully promoting hatred notwithstanding the existence of these defences: see Mertl and Ward, *supra,* note 36.

16 See *Criminal Code,* ss. 260(3), 273, 61(*d*).

17 See the editorial, "Red Yawn," *Edmonton Journal,* Thursday, September 13, 1984, p. A6.

18 See Mertl and Ward, *supra,* note 36, p. 38.

19 See Ryan, *supra* , note 46, p. 339.

20 S. Brownmiller, *Against Our Will* (New York: Bantam Books, 1976), p. 443. See also: A. Dworkin, *Pornography: Men Possessing Women* (New York: Putnam, 1981); and L. Lederer, ed. *Take Back the Night: Women on Pornography* (New York: Morrow, 1980).

21 See, for example, S. Griffin, *Pornography and Silence* (New York: Harper Colophon Books, 1981), pp. 156-99.

22 Fraser Committee, *supra,* note 56, Vol. 1, p. 319.

23 *Ibid.,* pp. 320-2.

24 *Ibid.,* p. 323.

25 *Ibid.,* p. 322.

26 *Ibid.,* pp. 323-4.

27 Ryan, *supra,* note 46, pp. 349-50. For additional criticism of this general view of pornography as promoting hatred, see also B. Faust, *Women, Sex, & Pornography* (London: Melbourne House, 1980), and L. Duggan, N. Hunter and C. Vance, "False Promises: Feminist Antipornography Legislation in the US" in V. Burstyn, ed., *Women against Censorship* (Vancouver: Douglas & McIntyre, 1985), p. 130.

28 A. Dworkin, *Right-Wing Women* (New York: Wideview/Perigee, 1983), pp. 196-7.

29 Burstyn, *supra,* note 146, p. 159. For a newspaper report of this incident, see the *Winnipeg Free Press,* Tuesday, December 4, 1984, p. 3.

30 Fraser Committee, *supra,* note 56, p. 324.

31 Janet Erasmus, in *Pornography: Obscenity Re-examined* (October 1985), an unpublished Background Paper on pornography prepared for the Law Reform Commission of Canada, also recommends against using the hate propaganda crime of promoting hatred for pornography prosecutions.

Questions for Discussion

1 The law states that the promotion of hatred against a recognizable group is criminal only if the content of the expression is not truthful, and the accused "wilfully" promotes the hatred. Are these requirements too restrictive?

2 Are the Commission's reasons for saying pornography should not fall under hate propaganda legislation convincing?

R. v. Keegstra

Supreme Court of Canada Chief Justice Dickson

One of the first serious tests of the hate propaganda legislation in court was in the case of R. v. Keegstra, which went to the Supreme Court of Canada. Chief Justice Dickson here discusses whether section 319 of the Criminal Code, which forbids hate propaganda, is justifiable in light of its apparent conflict with the right to freedom of expression (section 2(b)).

*   *   *

[T]he presence of hate propaganda in Canada is sufficiently substantial to warrant concern. Disquiet caused by the existence of such material is not simply the product of its effectiveness, however, but stems from the very real harm which it causes. Essentially, there are two sorts of injury caused by hate propaganda. First, there is the harm done to members of the target group. It is indisputable that the emotional damage caused by words may be of grave psychological and social consequence. In the context of sexual harassment, for example, this Court has found that words can in themselves constitute harassment.... In a similar manner, words and writings that wilfully promote hatred can constitute a serious attack on persons belonging to a racial or religious group....

A second harmful effect of hate propaganda which is of pressing and substantial concern is its influence upon society at large.... It is...not inconceivable that the active dissemination of hate propaganda can attract individuals to its cause, and in the process create serious discord between various cultural groups in society. Moreover, the alteration of views held by the recipients of hate propaganda may occur subtly, and is not always attendant upon conscious acceptance of the communicated ideas. Even if the message of hate propaganda is outwardly rejected, there is evidence that its premise of racial or religious inferiority may persist in a recipient's mind as an idea that holds some truth, an incipient effect not to be entirely discounted....

In my opinion, it would be impossible to deny that Parliament's objective in enacting s. 319(2) is of the utmost importance. Parliament has recognized the substantial harm that can flow from hate propaganda, and in trying to prevent the pain suffered by target group members and to reduce racial, ethnic and religious tension in Canada has decided to suppress the wilful promotion of hatred against identifiable groups....

At the core of freedom of expression lies the need to ensure that truth and the common good are attained, whether in scientific and artistic endeavors or in the process of determining the best course to take in our political affairs. Since truth and the ideal form of political and social organization can rarely, if at all, be identified with absolute certainty, it is difficult to prohibit expression without impeding the free exchange of potentially valuable information. Nevertheless, the argument from truth does not provide convincing support for the protection of hate propaganda. Taken to its extreme, this argument would require us to permit the communication of all expression, it being impossible to know with absolute certainty which factual statements are true, or which ideas obtain the greatest good. The problem with this extreme position, however, is that the greater the degree of certainty that a statement is erroneous or mendacious, the less its value in the quest for truth. Indeed, expression can be used to the detriment of our search for truth; the state should not be the sole arbiter of truth, but neither should we overplay the view that rationality will overcome all falsehoods in the unregulated marketplace of ideas. There is very little chance that statements intended to promote hatred against an identifiable group are true, or that their vision of society will lead to a better world. To portray such statements as crucial to truth and the betterment of the political and social milieu is therefore misguided.

Another component central to the rationale underlying s. 2(b) concerns the vital role of free expression as a means of ensuring individuals the ability to gain self-fulfillment by developing and articulating thoughts and ideas as they see fit. It is true that s. 319(2) inhibits this process among those individuals whose expression it limits, and hence arguably works against freedom of expression values. On the other hand, such self-autonomy stems in part from one's ability to articulate and nurture an identity derived from membership in a cultural or religious group. The message put forth by individuals who fall within the ambit of s. 319(2) represents a most extreme opposition to the idea that members of identifiable groups should enjoy this aspect of the s. 2(b) benefit. The extent to which the unhindered promotion of this message furthers free expression values must therefore be tempered insofar as it advocates with inordinate vitriol an intolerance and prejudice which views as execrable the process of individual self-development and human flourishing among all members of society.

Moving on to a third strain of thought said to justify the protection of free expression, one's attention is brought specially to the political realm. The connection between freedom of expression and the political process is perhaps the linchpin of the s. 2(b) guarantee, and the nature of this connection is largely derived from the Canadian commitment to democracy. Freedom of expression is a crucial aspect of the democratic commitment, not merely because it permits the best policies to be chosen from among a wide array of proffered options, but additionally because it helps to ensure that participation in the political process is open to all persons. Such open participation must involve to a substantial degree the notion that all persons are equally deserving of respect and dignity. The state therefore cannot act to hinder or condemn a political view without to some extent harming the openness of Canadian democracy and its associated tenet of equality for all.

The suppression of hate propaganda undeniably muzzles the participation of a few individuals in the democratic process, and hence detracts somewhat from free expression values, but the degree of this limitation is not substantial. I am aware that the use of strong language in political and social debate—indeed, perhaps even language intended to promote hatred—is an unavoidable part of the democratic process. Moreover, I recognize that hate propaganda is expression of a type which would generally be categorized as "political," thus putatively placing it at the heart of the principle extolling freedom of expression as vital to the democratic process. Nonetheless, expression can work to undermine our commitment to democracy where employed to propagate ideas anathemic to democratic values. Hate propaganda works in just such a way, arguing as it does for a society in which the democratic process is subverted and individuals are denied respect and dignity simply because of racial or religious characteristics. This brand of expressive activity is thus wholly inimical to the democratic aspirations of the free expression guarantee.

Indeed, one may quite plausibly contend that it is through rejecting hate propaganda that the state can best encourage the protection of values central to freedom of expression, while simultaneously demonstrating

dislike for the vision forwarded by hate-mongers. In this regard, the reaction to various types of expression by a democratic government may be perceived as meaningful expression on behalf of the vast majority of citizens. I do not wish to be construed as saying that an infringement of s. 2(b) can be justified under s. 1 merely because it is the product of a democratic process; the Charter will not permit even the democratically elected legislature to restrict the rights and freedoms crucial to a free and democratic society. What I do wish to emphasize, however, is that one must be careful not to accept blindly that the suppression of expression must always and unremittingly detract from values central to freedom of expression....

I am very reluctant to attach anything but the highest importance to expression relevant to political matters. But given the unparalleled vigour with which hate propaganda repudiates and undermines democratic values, and in particular its condemnation of the view that all citizens need be treated with equal respect and dignity so as to make participation in the political process meaningful, I am unable to see the protection of such expression as integral to the democratic ideal so central to the s. 2(b) rationale. Together with my comments as to the tenuous link between communications covered by s. 319(2) and other values at the core of the free expression guarantee, this conclusion leads me to disagree with the opinion of McLachlin J. [in dissent] that the expression at stake in this appeal mandates the most solicitous degree of constitutional protection. In my view, hate propaganda should not be accorded the greatest of weight in the s. 1 analysis.

As a caveat, it must be emphasized that the protection of extreme statements, even where they attack those principles underlying the freedom of expression, is not completely divorced from the aims of s. 2(*b*) of the Charter. As noted already, suppressing the expression covered by s. 319(2) does to some extent weaken these principles. It can also be argued that it is partly through a clash with extreme and erroneous views that truth and the democratic vision remain vigorous and alive.... In this regard, judicial pronouncements strongly advocating the importance of free expression values might be seen as helping to expose prejudiced statements as valueless even while striking down legislative restrictions that proscribe such expression. Additionally, condoning a democracy's collective decision to protect itself from certain types of expression may lead to a slippery slope on which encroachments on expression central to s. 2(*b*) values are permitted. To guard against such a result, the protection of communications virulently unsupportive of free expression values may be necessary in order to ensure that expression more compatible with these values is never unjustifiably limited.

None of these arguments is devoid of merit, and each must be taken into account in determining whether an infringement of s. 2(*b*) can be justified under s. 1. It need not be, however, that they apply equally or with the greatest of strength in every instance. As I have said already, I am of the opinion that hate propaganda contributes little to the aspirations of Canadians or Canada in either the quest for truth, the promotion of individual self-development or the protection and fostering of a vibrant democracy where the participation of all individuals is accepted and encouraged. While I cannot conclude that hate propaganda deserves only marginal protection

under the s. 1 analysis, I can take cognizance of the fact that limitations upon hate propaganda are directed at a special category of expression which strays some distance from the spirit of s. 2(*b*), and hence conclude that "restrictions on expression of this kind might be easier to justify than other infringements of s. 2(*b*).."...

Having made some preliminary comments as to the nature of the expression at stake in this appeal, it is now possible to ask whether s. 319(2) is an acceptably proportional response to Parliament's valid objective. As stated above [this part of the case is set out in Part I], the proportionality aspect of the *Oakes* test requires the Court to decide whether the impugned state action: i) is rationally connected to the objective; ii) minimally impairs the Charter right or freedom at issue; and iii) does not produce effects of such severity so as to make the impairment unjustifiable....

Section 319(2) makes the wilful promotion of hatred against identifiable groups an indictable offence, indicating Parliament's serious concern about the effects of such activity. Those who would uphold the provision argue that the criminal prohibition of hate propaganda obviously bears a rational connection to the legitimate Parliamentary objective of protecting target group members and fostering harmonious social relations in a community dedicated to equality and multiculturalism. I agree, for in my opinion it would be difficult to deny that the suppression of hate propaganda reduces the harm such expression does to individuals who belong to identifiable groups and to relations between various cultural and religious groups in Canadian society.

Doubts have been raised, however, as to whether the actual effect of s. 319(2) is to undermine any rational connection be-

tween it and Parliament's objective....
[T]here are three primary ways in which
the effect of the impugned legislation might
be seen as an irrational means of carrying
out the Parliamentary purpose. First, it is
argued that the provision may actually promote the cause of hate-mongers by earning
them extensive media attention. In this
vein, it is also suggested that persons accused of intentionally promoting hatred
often see themselves as martyrs, and may
actually generate sympathy from the community in the role of underdogs engaged in
battle against the immense powers of the
state. Second, the public may view the suppression of expression by the government
with suspicion, making it possible that such
expression—even if it is hate propaganda—
is perceived as containing an element of
truth. Finally, it is often noted...that Germany in the 1920s and 1930s possessed and
used hate propaganda laws similar to those
existing in Canada, and yet these laws did
nothing to stop the triumph of a racist philosophy under the Nazis.

If s. 319(2) can be said to have no impact in the quest to achieve Parliament's admirable objectives, or in fact works in
opposition to these objectives, then I agree
that the provision could be described as
"arbitrary, unfair or based on irrational
considerations,."... In my view, however,
the position that there is no strong and evident connection between the criminalization
of hate propaganda and its suppression is
unconvincing....

It is undeniable that media attention has
been extensive on those occasions when s.
319(2) has been used. Yet from my perspective, s. 319(2) serves to illustrate to the
public the severe reprobation with which
society holds messages of hate directed towards racial and religious groups. The ex-

istence of a particular criminal law, and the
process of holding a trial when that law is
used, is thus itself a form of expression,
and the message sent out is that hate propaganda is harmful to target group members
and threatening to a harmonious society....

In this context, it can also be said that
government suppression of hate propaganda
will not make the expression attractive and
hence increase acceptance of its contents.
Similarly, it is very doubtful that Canadians
will have sympathy for either propagators
of hatred or their ideas. Governmental disapproval of hate propaganda does not invariably result in dignifying the suppressed
ideology. Pornography is not dignified by
its suppression, nor are defamatory statements against individuals seen as meritori-
ous because the common law lends its
support to their prohibition....

As for the use of hate propaganda laws
in pre-World War Two Germany, I am
skeptical as to the relevance of the observation that legislation similar to s. 319(2)
proved ineffective in curbing the racism of
the Nazis. No one is contending that hate
propaganda laws can in themselves prevent
the tragedy of a Holocaust.... Rather, hate
propaganda laws are one part of a free and
democratic society's bid to prevent the
spread of racism, and their rational connection to this objective must be seen in such a
context....

...[I]n light of the great importance of
Parliament's objective and the discounted
value of the expression at issue I find that
the terms of s. 319(2) create a narrowly
confined offence which suffers from neither
overbreadth or vagueness. This interpretation stems largely from my view that the
provision possesses a stringent *mens rea* requirement, necessitating either an intent to
promote hatred or knowledge of the sub-

stantial certainty of such, and is also strongly supported by the conclusion that the meaning of the word "hatred" is restricted to the most severe and deeply-felt form of opprobrium. Additionally, however, the conclusion that s. 319(2) represents a minimal impairment of the freedom of expression gains credence through the exclusion of private conversation from its scope, the need for the promotion of hatred to focus upon an identifiable group and the presence of the s. 319(3) defences. [These are: (a) truth; (b) good faith opinion on a religious matter; (c) public interest; (d) good faith attempt to point out, so as to remove, matters producing feelings of hatred toward an identifiable group.] As for the argument that other modes of combatting hate propaganda eclipse the need for a criminal provision, it is eminently reasonable to utilize more than one type of legislative tool in working to prevent the spread of racist expression and its resultant harm....

The third branch of the proportionality test entails a weighing of the importance of the state objective against the effect of limits imposed upon a Charter right or guarantee. Even if the purpose of the limiting measure is substantial and the first two components of the proportionality test are satisfied, the deleterious effects of a limit may be too great to permit the infringement of the right or guarantee in issue.

I have examined closely the significance of the freedom of expression values threatened by s. 319(2) and the importance of the objective which lies behind the criminal prohibition. It will by now be quite clear that I do not view the infringement of s. 2(b) by s. 319(2) as a restriction of the most serious kind. The expressive activity at which this provision aims is of a special category, a category only tenuously connected with the values underlying the guarantee of freedom of speech. Moreover, the narrowly drawn terms of s. 319(2) and its defences prevent the prohibition of expression lying outside of this narrow category. Consequently, the suppression of hate propaganda affected by s. 319(2) represents an impairment of the individual's freedom of expression which is not of a most serious nature.

It is also apposite to stress yet again the enormous importance of the objective fueling s. 319(2), an objective of such magnitude as to support even the severe response of criminal prohibition. Few concerns can be as central to the concept of a free and democratic society as the dissipation of racism, and the especially strong value which Canadian society attaches to this goal must never be forgotten in assessing the effects of an impugned legislative measure. When the purpose of s. 319(2) is thus recognized, I have little trouble in finding that its effects, involving as they do the restriction of expression largely removed from the heart of free expression values, are not of such a deleterious nature as to outweigh any advantage gleaned from the limitation of s. 2(b).

Questions for Discussion

1 Is the potential harm of hate propaganda great enough to override the right to free expression?

Whose Body? Whose Self?   *Beyond Pornography*

Myrna Kostash

In this article, Kostash maintains that pornography should not be considered simply a matter of expression, on a par with the expression of political dissidence. She argues that women are right to fear pornography, and that, although there are reasons to be concerned about any form of censorship, pornography should be added to the list of cases in which the freedom of expression is not absolute.

*   *   *

Annals of the Boys' Club. When Larry Flynt, publisher of *Hustler* magazine, was convicted a few years ago of obscenity charges in the United States, several luminaries of the arts world, including novelist Gore Vidal and filmmaker Woody Allen, came to his defence. They called him an "American dissident," a designation which made their association of his tribulation with that of Soviet dissidents, Andrei Sakharov and Alexander Solzhenitsyn, irresistible. "Look," they were saying, liberal banners unfurled, "the authoritarian Soviet state represses free thought, the puritanical American state represses sexual expression." The implication was clear: those who would defend the fastnesses of the human imagination must take a stand here, at the line where the bureaucratic thought-police decree their interests (in this case, sexual discipline) have been trespassed.

It shall be left up to the reader to judge the appropriateness of the comparison between the situation of Soviet intellectuals and an American skin-magazine publisher, but this much can be said: the possibility that a pornographer is a *victim* of society is the fruit of a mid-Sixties mentality. Which is to say of a pre-feminist mentality. For it is thanks to the feminist movement of the last decade that we are now in a position to understand that obscenity and pornography, far from being a release from the sexual repression that bedevils our culture, do in fact trade in the same coin: contempt for women and traffic in our sexuality.

Larry Flynt is no dissident. He is a pimp.

*   *   *

Unfortunately, this perception alone resolves nothing. For women, the current debate about what does and does not represent sexual and intellectual freedom spins around a truly anguishing dilemma. On the one hand, the historical challenge (up to and including the sexual liberation skirmishes of the Sixties) to age-old taboos that govern sexual behaviour have been moments in women's ongoing struggle with the patriarchy—its family, its marketplace, its state. One has only to think of the exuberance with which the women's movement smashed the conspiratorial silence that had muffled the issues of female masturbation, female orgasm and lesbianism to understand how campaigns for the right to sexual self-expression have served us well.

When we have repudiated notions of "virginity" and "chastity," have denounced the sexual double standard ("Higamous, hogamous, women are monogamous; hogamous, higamous, men are polygamous"), have exposed the fallacies of "biological destiny," have censured the publicization of female masochism, we have in effect joined the struggle for the right to determine the nature and practice of our own sexuality.

In so doing, we have stood up in the same forum with those who, for instance, defended the publication of *Lady Chatterly's Lover* or *Body Politic*, or the distribution of *Pretty Baby*, or liberal amendments to the Criminal Code. This, then, is the anguish and the confusion: now *Hustler* and worse, have entered the forum, on the grounds that pornography too smashes taboos and constraints. Do we feminists contradict ourselves when we say we hate and fear it?

The dilemma is deepened by the compelling arguments of civil libertarians that the "freedom to read," and indeed the "freedom of the imagination," are in the public interest, even when these freedoms are employed to produce or consume pornography. This is all the more cogent when the freedom to read comes under attack, as in the case of Ontario school boards' banning of Margaret Laurence's *The Diviners* from school bookshelves; and the freedom to publish, as in parliamentary denunciations of the Canada Council's funding of publishers of "pornographic" poetry, "offensive to anyone with even a shred of decency," an idiotic allusion to Talonbooks and the work of poet bill bissett.[1] And when a small-town Ontario newspaper complains that such writers' "offerings are nothing more than a succession of gutter language, usually not even in sentence structure,"[2] we see how perilously close the attack on the allegedly pornographic comes to an attack on the artistic avant-garde as a whole.

Well, we say, *we* know what we mean by "pornography" and it isn't bill bissett; fair enough, but we are not in control of the public definition. *They* are, the MPs, the police, the judges—and feminists, as well as civil libertarians, have every right to fear that *their* definition casts a wide net indeed: shall we see public burnings of *Our Bodies, Our Selves*?

No, say the civil libertarians, not if we insist that the freedom to read and to publish is absolute and indivisible. Feminists cannot have it both ways—the restrictions on the distribution of "snuff" films, for instance, but the lifting of restrictions on, say, the Official Secrets Act.

On the other hand, of course, are the demands of the women's liberation movement. Reproductive freedoms: access to safe abortion and birth control and the right to give birth without trauma and insult. Freedom from rape and sexual abuse. Lesbian rights. Day care. Maternity rights, and so on. All those instances of the decolonization of our bodies.

How can we take these up and *not* hate and fear pornography?

Pornography: "the representation of sexual images, often including ridicule and violence, which degrades human beings for the purpose of entertaining or selling products."[3] The definition must be attempted, just as the definition of other modes of oppression and exploitation—racism, sexism, imperialism—have been risked and from that have entered our political lexicon. Else we risk wallowing in the subjectivities of perception, ambivalence and other temptations of liberalism ("Obscenity is in the eye of the beholder"), as though pornography does not take place out there in society, in social transactions between men and women. Pornography: from the Greek "to write about prostitution." At its root, then, the mercantile notion of the (usually) female body as a commodity. The territory of a commercial transaction. Pornography: a graphic metaphor for sex as the power that one (male) person wields over the destiny of another and the hostility that such an imbalance of power provokes.

What are its elements? Sadomasochism: the woman's body is subjected to various bondages, abuses, humiliations, from which she is often seen to extract her own pleasure. Misogyny: contempt for the female and her chastizement. Fascism: the male "lover" is frequently costumed as a militaristic superman, triumphing over the female subhuman, particularly where she is non-Aryan. Phallocentrism: the pornographic scenario is organized, overwhelmingly, around the penis and its ejaculation. Voyeurism: the deployment of the woman's body so as to excite the viewer.

What is its message? That sexual violence is pleasurable to men and that women desire or at least expect this violence. That women are "bad," their femaleness ridiculous, even foul, their submission appropriate. That male sexual (and political) satisfaction requires the diminution of female energy.

The images. The female torso disappears into a meat grinder. The woman, bound and gagged, splayed across the bed. The concubine, trussed up like a chicken, and raped. The girl-child, receiving foamy "come" on her eyelids and cheeks.

Enough.

Now begins the hard part. Must not our definition—images of ridicule and violence—also include the ostensibly artistic, the "art" photography of a Les Krims (a breast, cut off, is stuck to a table and dribbles blood) or the "arresting" acrylics of a James Spenser (a woman in black lace panties, her languid nudity an advertisement for her availability and for the flesh's uselessness, her body long since deprived of animation)? Must not our definition—for the purpose of entertainment or selling products—include almost the whole of popular culture and mass advertising in which the fragments of the female body are made to represent the desirability of a given product for consumption or for sale? Must not our definition—that which degrades the human being—now also include all those representations of coercion in which one person loses power to another's (aggressive) will, images which are pervasive in a male supremacist culture, which is to say are present in the merely sexist and in the pleasurably erotic?[4]

The definition, it turns out—but has anybody another that is more useful?—includes just about the whole of the iconography of everyday heterosexual life. The question becomes: what is *not* pornographic?

The answer to that lies in the realms of the utopian, or at best in the purely intimate or in the pockets of feminist subculture. For the non-pornographic, or the erotic, is about our, women's, vision of the sexually *possible*. In the best of possible worlds how would we represent sex? (What would art look like? Publicity? Movies?) With tenderness, affection, respect, with humour, playfulness. We would take delight in the sensuous detail, we would caress, we would be open psychically to the "lunar," to that part of our nervous system which is intuitional, which apprehends patterns, which is artistic. The "erotica" which corresponds to this ideal would represent freely chosen sexual behaviour in which the partners would serve each other's (and Eros's!) pleasure equally and in which the "I love you" is made flesh. How does it go? "With this body I thee honour...."

Feminist descriptions of the non-pornographic are necessarily as vague, evasive, dreamy as this for we have only recently allowed ourselves the luxury of contemplating sexual happiness, as opposed to the sexual terror of our environment. It is not easily done. Everywhere we turn we see our need for "romance" distorted as the ostensibly "erotic," which is in fact a thinly-veiled invitation to further violence. I'm thinking of the movies in which "provocative" women are murdered; blue jeans ads in which young girls are offered up to adult men; fashion layouts in which the limbs of the models are bruised in the jaws of snarling dogs. This is the so-called "pretty porn," the means by which the pornographic fantasy, heretofore closeted in hard-core literature and imagery, acquires access to the broad public. "Pretty porn" softens us up, as it were; it creates a tolerance for the explicitly sadistic and, like a callous, dulls our nerve endings so that we are no longer repelled. The image has become normal. Full frontal female nudity—this used to be considered porn—is now a standard of the Hollywood film and *Playboy*; the horse we flogged in the early Seventies now seems positively pastoral compared to the stuff in cellophane wrappers. For women, such de-sensitization is grotesque: we have somehow to make our way through the city *as though* pornography had nothing to do with us. For to acknowledge that it does is to let in the nightmare: "to be unknown, and hated," as Susan Griffin writes.[5]

But let it in we must, for to know the nature of the beast is the end of illusion and the beginnings of politics. Consider: *Hustler* magazine has seven million readers a month; six of ten bestselling monthlies are "men's entertainment" magazines; there are 260 different periodicals available in the United States devoted to child porn; pornography, in short, is a $4 billion industry.[6] Is this a problem for women? It is true that, even in Canada, rape is increasingly accompanied by sexual sadism and mutilation. Now where do rapists get their ideas? While current research on the relationship between pornography and aggression is far from conclusive, one way or the other, we do know that more than 50 studies involving 10,000 children have demonstrated over the years a consistent relationship between the amount of television violence consumed by the child and her/his level of aggression.[7] We have it from Drs. Neil Malamuth and James Check at the University of Manitoba that, when "effects of pornographic violence were assessed in responses to a lengthy questionnaire the findings indicated that heightened aggressiveness persists for at least a week."[8]

Of course, as it has been said, women do not need "proof" of laboratory research to know that the pervasiveness of the pornographic image is a threat to our well-being. In the image is an education: by it, men and women alike are instructed in the power men have over women, a power which extends along the whole desperate continuum of male privilege, from conjugal rights to pimping, from sexual harassment to rape-murder. By it women themselves are blamed for what has happened to them:

we are venal, we are stupid, we are uppity, we deserve what we get.

The *political* content of these representations of sexuality—that male authority is normal and can only be challenged at enormous risk—is obscured by the fact that, in our culture, relations of dominance and submission between men and women are seen as *sexy*. Power is an eroticized event, masked as titillation. Which is to say it is experienced as something intimate, domestic, personal. We literally don't see it. Two men are grappling on the floor, fingers at the throat, teeth biting into flesh: they are fighting. A man and a woman are grappling on the floor, teeth bared and her clothing ripped: they are making love.

*   *   *

Having come this far in our disillusionment, our work is cut out for us. Some feminist groups, organized explicitly to challenge the *consensus* that the pervasiveness of porn represents, have taken the beast by the horns. In San Francisco, Women Against Violence in Pornography and the Media (WAVPM) have picketed shops selling *Hustler*, have conducted tours for women through the Tenderloin, the porn district (no more averting our eyes from the scenarios of our humiliation), have put together a consciousness-raising slideshow and guided women through the "speaking bitterness" sessions which follow. In Toronto, Women Against Violence Against Women (WAVAW) demonstrated at Metro and City executive committee meetings to demand that the film *Snuff*[9] be banned. Twenty men and women invaded the cinema, smashed the projector and staged a sit-in until five of their number were arrested. And all over North America similar groups have demonstrated to "take back the night" from the merchants of sexual ghoulishness, repeatedly making the connection between porn and all other violence done women—rape, battery, forced sterilization, back-alley abortions—that cements the foundations of our social structures.

Such campaigns immediately raise the hackles of those to whom the issue of pornography is one not of sexual politics (who has the power to do what to whom) but of society's right to uncensored opinion. Briefly, they argue that "the realm of the imagination should not be subject to government control"[10] and that one must always be careful to draw the line between "personal" rights (we do have the right to freedom from physical attack, say) and "intellectual" rights (we all have the right to say aloud what we think without fear of reprisal). Even those who are as nauseated as any WAVAW member by pornography point out that men do not rape just because they see pictures, for the pictures are simply "metaphors" for what is already taking place in society. Besides, as long as women have little political power *qua* women, the demand for censorship of pornographic materials reproduces our powerlessness: somebody else, not us, will be the censors. In any event, as Alberta's attorney general put it to the Alberta Status of Women, "...it is impossible to pass a law or laws governing every imaginable human activity. Laws unfortunately do not prevent all undesirable activity, but merely make them illegal."

In reply, feminists have argued that the claim that pornography exists solely in the realms of the imagination or of self-expression is specious: it is an extensively public phenomenon, an *event* in the social situation of the sexes. Certainly the Nazis understood this when, having occupied

Poland, they flooded the bookstalls with porn to demoralize the population. And certain disenchanted Scandinavians understand it when, for all the availability of "liberating" porn, they still refer to themselves as "sexual invalids" and admit that from 1960 to 1978 rape was up 60 percent.[11]

Feminists have further argued that the right to "free speech" in practice extends only to those who have the money to buy it: the publishers, the producers, the politicians, the consumers. Those without money, women's groups for instance, must resort to other practices—leafleting, picketing, rallying, marching—which are, of course, denounced by liberals as "interferences" in the freedom of speech. Feminists ask: *whose* freedom?

All kinds of limitations already exist on "freedom of speech": laws relating to libel, slander, perjury, copyright, advertising, incitement. We accept them; *we* acknowledge that this freedom is not absolute. Therefore, the "right" to produce and consume pornography must be curtailed if our *women's* right to freedom from slander and injury is to be respected.[12]

In any event, it comes down to this: the woman's liberation movement, like all collectivist appeals to social transformation, is impatient with the claims of civil libertarians. It seeks not mere individual rights but social justice.

Justice must be seen to be done. It is within the *realpolitik* of the streetwise women's movement that each woman activist make her own decision about what she is prepared to do to smash the gloomy tyranny of porn. Already the agenda is drawn up. Consumer campaigns, public education, vigilante squads, agit-prop (protests that provoke public debate). Feminist-informed research (to establish once and for all the

connection between pornography and behaviour). Agitation for changes in the law relating to obscenity, as in "a law based on new standards which would entrench the physical and sexual autonomy of women and children within the law"[13] (although it is debatable how that which is not true in society—the sexual autonomy of women and children—can be guaranteed by law).

Feminists must also refine their arguments with their critics. There remains the longstanding liberal defence of pornography as an "isolated act," harmlessly "indulged in" by individuals free to choose their own "lifestyle." Feminists say: we want to live in an order where what we do and think has consequences. Leftists, ostensibly pro-feminist, have defended pornography on the various grounds that it is a "revolutionary aesthetic" (in which case it is the social protest of an idiot), that it is the "erotica" of the working class (in fact, pornography is a capitalist success story and is consumed overwhelmingly by middle-class men), that *Penthouse*, say, is anti-establishment (in fact, the fantasies purveyed by skin magazines *replicate* the deadening relations of the family place, the workplace, the marketplace). Rightists, lining up to burn skin magazines and smash rock records, are, however, on a moral crusade against sexual explicitness and are no friends of women. Against the feminist demand for women's right to sexual self-determination, the Right poses the stability of the patriarchal family, the iniquity of homosexuality and the sanctity of the chaste. We have been through that scenario before.

Through such refinements, women in the anti-porn movement may even come to a vision of what is possible beyond pornography. Pornography celebrates the atomization and irresponsibility of the person in the pretence that what one does as a sexual being has nothing to do with anything else, neither with the sexual partner nor with society. Beyond this morbidity, the gentle, laughing, administering embrace of sensual camaraderie presents itself: the longed-for alternative to the social tyrannies of passivity and mechanization. Beyond pornography lies the *polis*, the political space of the aggrieved in which we may finally overwhelm those forces that would circumscribe our vigour and our compassion.

*   *   *

At the University of California in Berkeley I am sitting in a journalism class. The instructor, writer Valerie Miner, has invited a representative from WAVPM to present the "consciousness-raising" slide-show on pornography. We watch it in disbelieving silence. Then the class is split up—the male students are invited to discuss the presentation in a separate room.

The women talk. So *that's* pornography. I've never really looked. Do men *really* want it? You know, it isn't just weirdos buying this stuff, it's our brothers and boyfriends (six, ten, fifteen million a month!), they're harbouring these fantasies, it's like a, well, barrier between us, isn't it? Do we have to accept it? How do we teach our men that this stuff hurts us without alienating them? Wait a minute, there's a "porn" for women too: all those romances of the super-feminine heroine overpowered by the dark, passionate lover. Remember *Wuthering Heights*? (Giggles)

I am thinking; my God, women have to be *taught* to like and live with men; our first, instinctual feeling toward them is fear.

Fear. The discussion takes an interesting turn. Away from the pornographic images we have just seen to anecdotes about fear. One story after another. Of being followed. Of obscene phone calls. Of being afraid to live alone, to go out at night, to answer the doorbell. "Women are such scairdy cats," the women say, "why are we so dumb, so afraid all the time?" And then more stories.

Fear. Suddenly all the intellectual and political anguish provoked by the threat of pornography has dissolved into one simple perception. Pornography is about women being afraid. While there is pornography, we are not safe. It is not a question of learning to "live with it": we are dying with it.

Notes

1   Quoted in *ACP Notebook*, No. 13 (July 1978), p. 2.

2   *Ibid.*, p. 8.

3   Valerie Miner, "Fantasies and Nightmares: The Red-Blooded Mass Media," unpublished paper, p. 3.

4   I am aware that almost all discussion of the issue of pornography concerns itself only with the photographic image, as though we accept the written word and the painting as "self-expression" but the unmediated image—the ultra-realistic depiction of gross materiality, not form—as dangerous and offensive. The photograph seems to reproduce reality and erases the distinction between fantasy and what is actually possible. Since this is true of any photograph, the next question is: is *any* photographic representation of women in a male supremacist culture *ipso facto* sexist and exploitative? Two British writers pursue this. "Pornography is a site for the struggle over the representations of women.... Is it more acceptable to view the image of a woman at work than a nude playmate? Why?" (Mary Bos and Jill Pack, "Porn, Law and Politics," *Camerawork* No. 18). Perhaps because work, for all its exploitation of the worker's labour power, does not *as an image* deny the dignity of the worker. The image of the female, however, has carried the burden of mean-

ing of everything from original sin to commodity fetishism. The image of the female connotes venality.

5 Susan Griffin, *Rape: The Power of Consciousness* (New York: Harper and Row, 1979), p. 51.

6 The figures are American. No Canadian ones are available.

7 Miner, op. cit., p. 11.

8 *New York Times*, September 30, 1980.

9 The film purports to show the actual mutilation and death of an actress.

10 The Writers' Union of Canada, "Obscenity Brief" (in respect to Bill C-51), January 1970.

11 Cited in "Fallout from the Sexual Revolution," *Maclean's*, 1981.

12 It is worth noting, however, that in the eleven years since the enactment of the Hate Propaganda Act (governing the "irrational and malicious abuse of certain identifiable minority groups" or an attack on such groups in "abusive, insulting, scurrilous and false terms") there have been only two charges laid under it. The first was against people distributing "Yankee Go Home" leaflets at a Shriners' Parade in Toronto. The second was against two men distributing anti-French Canadian handbills. In the latter case an appeal resulted in an acquittal. Cited in "Group Defamation in Canada," Jeanne Hutson, *Carleton Journalism Review*, Winter 1980.

13 Debra Lewis, *Kinesis*, April-May, 1979.

Questions for Discussion

1 Is there any way to distinguish between the "expression" of political dissidents, or of artists, on the one hand, and the "expression" of producers of pornography, on the other?

2 Is Kostash right that the message of pornography is that femaleness is ridiculous or bad, and that women desire or expect sexual violence?

3 Is Kostash right that pornography is a matter of sexual politics and power relationships in society, and not simply "fantasies" or "entertainment" lying solely in the realm of imagination?

Pornography: The Other Side

Ferrel Christensen

Ferrel Christensen is one of the leaders of Educators and Counsellors Against Censorship. In these selections from his Pornography: The Other Side, *he criticizes some of the arguments which have been raised against pornography.*

*　　*　　*

In the continuing clamor over pornography, the claims most often heard are these: (1) it is evil so it should be banned, and (2) it is evil but censorship is a greater evil. The other side—that pornography is not in itself morally bad—is rarely defended. The purpose of this essay is to present some of the evidence for that other side. In fact, it will be argued that the current anti-pornography campaign is in many ways itself morally evil. This will be a startling claim to many, but that is largely because they have been given so little opportunity to see the whole picture. Actually, pornography itself is not the fundamental issue; opposition to it is only a symptom of more general beliefs about sex that are tragically mistaken. Though such a complex subject cannot be completely circumscribed in one short essay, most of the essentials of the debate are treated here.

Standard Moral Objections: Debasement and Exploitation

In the next few sections we will look briefly at some of the reasons commonly given in making the claim that pornography is *intrinsically* evil; i.e., that it is bad in itself, independently of any good or ill it might later lead to. The question of whether it causes harmful attitudes or behavior in those who use it will be delayed until the second half of this essay. Let us begin by making the following observation: that where beliefs are produced by nonrational influences, such as wishful thinking or indoctrination, the mind typically attempts to create a rational basis for them, after the fact. As an example, certain human cultures have a tradition of disfiguring the teeth (blackening them, filing them down, even knocking them out); and when people of one such group were asked why that should be a desirable thing to do, they replied that having natural-looking teeth would make them "like *animals*." A large arsenal of such rationalizations has been employed in the attempt to justify this society's traditional attitudes about sexuality, including pornography. In general, now, one thing that exposes an argument as a mere rationalization is the fact that it is so clearly fallacious, once it is actually examined. Often, for instance, those who employ it wouldn't think of making the same claim in relevantly similar situations. (Animals eat food and care for their young; does that mean humans should not? The capacity to

destroy all life is uniquely human—does that mean it would be a good thing to do?) In other cases, the reasoning is seen to require a distortion of the facts in order to be convincing. Indeed, some such claims are virtually empty of factual content: they are mere shibboleths, which one has learned to say on cue but which describe nothing in reality. This is exactly the situation, we shall see, in regard to the standard moral objections against pornography. They all reveal an any-stick-will-do abandonment of critical judgement.

To begin with a variation on the "animal" *motif*, a common charge against pornography is that it is "dehumanizing." On the contrary, nothing is any more human than sexual fantasies and feelings, along with their representation and vicarious enjoyment in various media of expression. If anyone is trying to dehumanize us in this regard, it is those who would denigrate our sexuality and its celebration: they are denying a significant part of our humanity. As was hinted above, this sort of argument is evidently based on the assumption that anything uniquely or specially human is good, or that whatever is typical of animals is inferior. And once again, it is absurd. Alas, selfishness, arrogance and hatred are as human as generosity and compassion. It may be that we have a greater capacity than other animals for emotions such as the latter, but the same is true of the former. Those who employ the argument know little about human *or* animal nature. They typically assume that things like love, sex with love, monogamy or long-term bonding are peculiarly human, but they are wrong on every count.

The reasoning is often based on an erroneous view that animals and humans are utterly different in their natures: moved by blind instinct vs. emotion and intelligence. In truth, all the dissimilarities are differences in degree, not in kind—mostly degree of intelligence. Even conscience (guilt, etc.) is found in some other animals, as any dog-owner should know. But even if some traits are uniquely human, that does not mean they are good; they must be evaluated on their own merits. A second belief sometimes underlying this assumption is a misunderstanding of evolution: the idea that it is a benevolent force whose goal is to produce ever more noble creatures. But this is contrary to all of our scientific understanding. For example, once more, romantic love is not an emotion that nature values for its own sake; its ultimate "purpose" is the same as that of lust, to help propagate the species or the genes. None of this implies that there *are* no noble feelings, of course. What does constitute genuine goodness and moral rightness has already been briefly mentioned here, and will continue to be discussed.

Another standard accusation is that the persons involved in sexually explicit portrayals are thereby treated "like objects." Now, it isn't at all clear what this is supposed to mean. Or even whether it means anything at all, once again. It has come to be repeated so ritualistically, without explanation, that it appears to have no more descriptive content than "son of a bitch": it expresses the speaker's anger or contempt but nothing more. After all, "sex object" sounds like a contradiction in terms: objects don't have sexuality, but people do. Of course, to charge angrily that pornography treats people as sexual *beings* would have no negative impact, so that isn't said. Notice in this connection how seductively easy name-calling is. Anything can be made to sound awful by an appropriate choice of ep-

ithets. For example, one might charge that in a love relationship, or a movie about one, human beings are treated as "emotionally security blankets." Or it might be said that to expect sexual exclusivity from a mate is to treat him or her like private property, i.e., like an object one possesses. Such claims would be no more mindless than this familiar rhetoric.

Nevertheless, let us examine various things that might be meant by the objectification charge, to see if any of them are at all cogent. Sometimes what is intended is fetched pretty far. For example, there is the claim that since pornographic photos or movies are themselves objects, those who are portrayed in them are *ipso facto* treated or regarded as objects by the viewer. It doesn't seem to occur to those who talk this way that the same charge would apply equally well to pictures, movies and books of any *other* kind, including love stories. With similar foolishness, it might be alleged that a little girl's doll treats people as passive objects to be used and manipulated.

At other times, what the objection alludes to is the fact that those depicted in sexual materials are not personally known to the reader or viewer, or that the sex portrayed is itself between strangers. (Sex with a stranger is an extremely common fantasy of both men and women, and whirlwind romance with a stranger is *the* major love-story theme.) Here the claim is that sex, even fantasy sex, with someone one doesn't already know intimately is "impersonal" or "depersonalized," hence treats the other as an object rather than a person. That non-sequitur evidently rests on an equivocation between the words "person" and "personal": the latter refers either to what is unique or to what is not publicly shared about an individual, the former to the general fact of personhood. In this confused thinking, then, if one is not treated as a uniquely special person one is not treated as a person at all. The absurdity of the argument is also evident from the fact that it would render objectionable most *non*-sexual interactions with other people, along with (again) all other media presentations. Consider how bizarre it would be, for instance, to say that giving compassionate help to someone is depersonalized, treats that person as an object, if she or he is a stranger. If pornography *or* "casual" sex is to be condemned, it will have to be on more rational grounds than these.

At least part of the motive for all the talk about objects, clearly, is the fact that the human body is involved; it is (among other things) a physical object. And the portrayal of the body, hinting at or engaged in the physical activity of sex, is a central characteristic of pornography, while the arousal or satisfaction of desires toward the body is its *raison d'être*. Hence it seems pretty obvious that our long standing tradition of devaluing the physical body, and physical sex in particular, underlies this charge. But it is a serious and destructive error. Having a body is just as much a part of being a person as is having intelligence or emotions. Attraction to the former no more treats someone as a non-person than does attraction to one of the latter. Some of those who use the "object" rhetoric sound as if they have been alienated from their own bodies, from an essential part of their being.

Once again, most of that tradition about the body is dead and buried in the 1980s, with its emphasis on beauty and bodily health; only the suspicions about sex linger on. The result is an inconsistency of attitude that is revealed by the claim before us. For pictures of clothed people are no less pictures of bodies—the clothes themselves are mere inanimate objects. And video movies of, say, exercise classes (a bunch of "anonymous panting playthings"?) are just as much a focus on the physical body and its activities as is one involving sexual activity. But charges of treating people as objects are never raised against them. To realize how contradictory common thinking is on this matter, one has only to consider the general importance of close physical contact in human life: deprecatory remarks about the body are never made when the subject is the value of just being held. In a similar vein, a lover of things like painting and ballet would never grant that their purely physical nature makes them an unfitting source of emotional gratification.

As for the gratification itself—the pleasure or satisfaction derived from various sources like these—standard beliefs on this topic reveal parallel confusions. For instance, the traditional claim that sexual feelings are "merely physical" while others are "spiritual" is another serious error. One has only to reflect carefully on some of these other emotions to realize that they are also physical sensations; they are merely felt in a different part of the body, notably the face and chest. And as has already been hinted, *all* of our feelings are mediated by chemicals in the brain. Love and lust belong equally to the body and the soul. Along with the sharp dichotomy between humans and animals, the picture of a noble soul trying to control a rebellious body is obsolete, if not morally obstructive.

Sometimes the claim of objectification takes forms that are particularly fatuous. It is said, for example, that pornography reduces its subjects to a "collection of body parts."[1] Go look through any of a great number of *non*erotic magazines, and you will find ads and articles featuring pictures of hair, ears, feet, hands, etc. all by themselves. (They may be selling anklets or fungicide, or discussing the cause of lower back pain.) But they are never condemned for reducing people to their organs. The real reason for attacking the showing of sex organs, once again, is that they alone among body parts are considered shameful. Moreover, it is certainly not the case that displaying them all by themselves is the point of pornography. Most males and a small minority of females are biologically primed to focus especially on them, but only as part of the wider bodily *gestalt*. (The face is another body part, it should be noticed, and special attraction to it is universal.) In fact, it is the traditional aversion to nudity that comes closest to fitting the derogatory description under discussion. By decreeing that only certain parts may be shown or appreciated, it divides them off from the rest; it prevents us from enjoying our whole selves. In any case, the biologically healthy attraction to certain areas of the body is no more degrading to a person than interest in his or her personality, intelligence or moral character—no one would charge that a special interest in one of the latter carves a person up into pieces.

This leads us to another way of interpreting the "object" charge, one that clearly is intended by some who make it. It isn't the fact that pornography displays bodies and bodily activities, but that they are *all* it presents, that is supposed to "objectify" those involved. It treats people as if they were "*nothing but* sexual objects," the claim is often worded. Similar charges abound. Pornography presents a "one-dimensional view of life," it is said; it "re-

duces its subjects to their bodies and their physical appetites, rather than treating them as whole human beings," or "carries the tacit message that sex is all they're good for." Now it is quite true that most pornography has a very limited scope; it contains little else besides sex. (To some, in fact, that is a defining characteristic of it.) This is due in part to the fact that overt sexuality has traditionally been excluded from socially respectable portrayals of human experience; it has been driven out into a realm by itself. But it does not follow from its limited content that pornography treats its subjects as if they were nothing but sexual entities.

The absurdity of this new charge, together with its rationalizing nature, is once again revealed by the fact that no similar claim is made in analogous cases. All of our media presentations, to a greater or lesser degree, are specialized in their content. From sporting events to symphonies, they portray a "one-dimensional view of life" indeed—and many people spend an awful lot of their time enjoying such things. But is there anything wrong with that? Among the periodicals you will find magazines specializing in sports, food, romance, entertainment, hobbies, fashion, etc. Shall we say that such publications don't portray people as whole human beings? Do fashion magazines, for example, turn their models into human mannequins, just a bunch of clothing racks? (To mimic some of the purpler prose we hear denouncing pornography.) For that matter, do traditional movies and novels, which scrupulously avoid frank eroticism, deny our completeness by ignoring *that* important aspect of us? Human wholeness in no way precludes focusing on one aspect of ourselves at a time. And if there is some *special* reason why sex should only be portrayed in combination with other things, this argument again fails to give it. Fallacious arguments about personhood aside, these parallel cases also reveal that many who complain pornography portrays nothing but sex would find its explicitness offensive regardless of the rest of the content; for some this objection is only a pretext.

Underlying this charge against pornography, very often, is the wider claim that sexual desire toward another person, or even mutually between persons, is "objectifying" unless certain other sorts of feeling are present as well. But its status as a rationalization is also clear. We never hear the converse claim, that (say) desiring another's companionship but not his or her sexuality treats that individual as less than a whole person—even though the interest is no less partial. More generally, the fact that certain aspects of an individual should be of special or sole interest to someone does not imply that that person has no other human worth. Shall we say that students treat a professor as a mere intellect-object, because their only reason for coming to her or him is to learn about (say) history or logic? Does their limited interest mean they think that's all he or she is good for? Only ideologically induced blindness leads people to say such things in a sexual context.

It is instructive to consider one specific example of the "whole person" charge. (From Beatrice Faust's book *Women, Sex and Pornography*. Overall, Ms. Faust's treatment of the subject is unusually level-headed and well informed.) Contrasting the similar scenes of men watching a stripper and young women getting excited over a rock music star, the writer says, "Men react impersonally to the stripper's body and sexual aura; girls react to the pop star

as a person, not as a sexy body." Aside from its standard confusion of being personal with being a person, even the distinction this statement makes regarding the former is spurious. Male celebrities standardly report that before they achieved that status they got no special attention from women—yet they haven't changed *as persons*. Nor is there anything particularly personal about the star's highly contrived aura or stage persona; the girls are excited by the artificial image and high status of an individual they've never even met. In fact, one's body is clearly more unique and intrinsic to one's self than status or fame; it is *more* personal. But the important point here is that there is nothing disrespectful about the reaction to the star *or* to the stripper. Neither in any intelligent sense treats him or her as other than a complete human being.

There is one more thing that could be meant, and manifestly often is meant, by the charge that pornography treats people as objects. It is that those who enjoy such presentations do not care about the welfare of the subjects portrayed, about their needs or feelings as human beings. There is only one thing to be said in response to this charge: it is a vicious libel. Sexual desire, including its expressions involving pornography, represents a need, not an attitude. And there is nothing intrinsically uncaring about a need—though of course, any need can be accompanied by callous attitudes or pursued in a callous way. On the part of some, the error here would seem to lie in confusing romantic love with human love: they think that feeling sexual desire without the former sort of emotional involvement just *is* being cold and uncaring. Now, human love is the essence of morality, whereas romantic attachment is only one need or desire among many. For a person who feels the latter yearning, it is important that it be met, but it is no more inherently noble than any other interpersonal need. The truth in this matter, in fact, is just the reverse of what has been charged. It is those who despise the sexual and emotional makeup of others—their greater need for sex, or greater emotional independence, or both—who reveal a lack of caring and human concern.

Closely similar to the accusation of callousness is another that often accompanies it. Explicitly sexual presentations, it is said, "exploit" their subjects; the latter are simply "used" for the gratification of one's own selfish desires. Once again, the underlying attitudes here transcend the specific issue of pornography. Of all the things that people desire for themselves, and all the ways in which they wish to satisfy needs or get pleasure from others, it is uniquely the sexual ones that are regarded in this culture as inherently selfish. This has become such a kneejerk response, in fact, that people don't stop to ask whether the charge is really appropriate in a given case. So let us remind ourselves of the meaning of the word: to exploit a person is to get something from him or her in a way that is hurtful or unfair. Whatever else may be good or bad about the situation, if it is consensual and equally beneficial, it is not exploitive. To illustrate this inconsistency of attitudes toward different sources of pleasure, consider something one observes not infrequently: a woman's eyes lighting up at the sight of a cute baby in a magazine or on TV. "Oh, what a darling little thing!" she may say, focusing intently. She is getting pleasure for herself from the visual experience, and perhaps fantasizing getting pleasure from a real child. Is this being exploitive? Does it

mean she regards babies as mere objects for her gratification? Of course not. Indeed, her desires include *sharing* pleasure with the infant of her fantasy.

Yet it is no different from this, for normal persons, in the sexual enjoyment of others—whether in fantasy or in real life. Sexual desire is fundamentally a desire for mutual pleasure. Nothing is any more gratifying, or more sexually exciting, than to have one's erotic interest returned. Hence it is hardly surprising that the commonest theme of male-oriented erotic movies is that of women who are uninhibited in seeking sex. She wants him the same way he wants her! Its appeal rests precisely on the fact that it makes the need and pleasure equal and mutual. To be sure, attempts to satisfy sexual needs can and often do employ exploitive means. (Though this seems to be less common in sex-positive cultures, where satisfying such needs is much less difficult. To a degree, at least, the attitude that sex is exploitive is self-fulfilling.) People with unmet needs will often settle for less than the mutual ideal. But this is true of all other strong desires as well, including romantic love—as is made plain by the scheming manipulations so often engaged in by jealous or insecure spouses and lovers. In fact, it is germane to point out here that false moral charges are themselves used in the selfish manipulation of other persons. If some can convince others that the latter's desires are ignoble, they can more easily get what they want instead. This motive seems to underlie a lot of negative attitudes involving sexuality; the reader should keep it in mind as we continue.

Sometimes sexually frank performances and materials are called exploitive on the grounds that, even if all those directly involved enjoy their experience, it still offends the deep feelings of others to know they exist. "Sex is sacred and personal," it is said; "its privacy should not be violated." These third-party arguments are often tinged with hypocrisy. It is the censors who want to invade the personal lives of others, to tell them what they may participate in making or what they may use even in private. More to the point, once again, it is hard to see why we shouldn't apply the same reasoning to many other things. Does a television show like *The Waltons* exploit families or family living? Does it invade family privacy? (What could be more sacred or personal than that?) Such comparisons make it clear that sex and nudity are covered up because they are considered shameful, not because they are seen as sacred. Feelings of shame are the reason sex is regarded as private and personal, not the other way around. And those conditioned feelings have no more ultimate claim on our moral values than any other taboos we have inherited. Even with these emotions as they now are, however, the argument is fallacious. Both drama and psychology texts lay bare the most personal of human affairs; but so far from being evil, that can be highly rewarding. What is apt to be bad, by contrast, is invading the privacy of individuals in real life, in contrast to staged portrayals. Consider the television cameras staring brazenly at a grief-stricken couple as they watch their daughter die in the explosion of the Challenger: *that* is obscene.

The notion of exploitation also appears in a different sort of claim, one involving the commercial aspect of most pornography. The idea that making money by portraying sex is illegitimate has become so common that the term "sexploitation" is recognized by everyone. We hear nothing about commercial exploitation of the family, however, even though programs like *The Cosby Show* presumably make a lot of money for their sponsors. "Porn makes profit from women's bodies!" shouts one slogan. And the construction industry makes money from the bodies of men— what does *that* tell us? Actors and models of every other type perform their services for pay, and make money for their employers, to almost no one's dismay. No reason why sex should be so different in this regard is ever given. In a similar vein, the buying of sexual materials is often equated with the buying of sex itself. Yet we never hear it said that spending money to read or watch love stories makes a "commodity" of love. Sex is also said to be besmirched when erotic portrayals appear in magazines that are full of advertising for consumer goods—ignoring the fact that magazines on any other subject are also loaded with such ads. The attempt to sell things by associating them directly with sex, love, friendship, or anything else people find desirable is standard in advertising these days. That is arguably objectionable, but is not immediately relevant to our topic.

In addition to claims that it is immoral, pornography is frequently accused of being inherently bad in other ways. Explicit sex is "ugly," it is said, or "not really erotic." Beyond the failure to realize how fully mere conditioning is responsible for their aesthetic reactions, what these speakers reveal is their ego-centredness. "My tastes, the tastes of my group, are true and beautiful; what turns me on is genuinely erotic. But as for you...."[2] On the other hand, much of the explicitly erotic literature and movies traditionally produced would seem inferior to the tastes of nearly everyone: they are very cheaply made. But clearly, this is an artifact of the low level of social acceptability of really explicit pornography. If it were even as "respectable" as media violence has always been (consider the high levels of both artistic excellence and brutality in, say, *Hill Street Blues*), much more of it would be produced by those who make quality films and magazines—as is indeed already the case for mildly and implicitly sexual productions.

In a similar vein, many detractors of pornography decry the sad tawdriness of the peep-show parlors. In this they are partly right, though perhaps not in the way they think. There you will often find men who are painfully shy or sexually inhibited, men whom women regard as unattractive or as losers, military men cut off from other sources of female companionship, men who are physically or psychologically impaired, old and middle-aged men whose biological cravings defy social dogma by yearning for young women, young men whose female acquaintances don't want sex, and so on. What they all have in common is a powerful need and an inability, temporary or long-term, to get "the real thing." So they accept a poor substitute, a commercial fantasy. (And it's said that *they* are exploiters, of the women who make money from their plight!) Sad and tawdry indeed. But what is amazing is not the pornography-foes' indifference to that suffering: "Let them eat cake" is often the attitude of those not in need toward those who are. Nor is it their failure to grant that a poor substitute is better than nothing at all. It is the tacit or explicit message that somehow pornography is the cause of the sad situation. Like many another social epiphenomenon, it gets the blame for problems whose real source lies in nature or in the structure of society.

The supply of arguments for the intrinsic badness of sexual explicitness goes on and on, but the foregoing are common and representative. And they are all worthless. The fact is that all the standard "moral" arguments against pornography and sex for its own sake are logical fallacies of one kind or another. That such patent rationalizations have been convincing to so many is a testament to the power of socialization, once again. It is very, very difficult even to recognize the real sources of, much less to consciously overcome, the beliefs one has been indoctrinated with and the feelings one has been conditioned to have; they seem so natural, so obviously right. But the price humanity has always had to pay for such blindness is a terrible one. Summoning the will to be honest in this regard is not only the moral thing but the only intelligent thing to do, for the sake of the welfare of all—as we shall continue to see.

Degrading Content

Another special issue which is often aired regarding sexual portrayals is that of degradation. Or at least that of women: just as there is a tradition of special concern over violence against them, there is a wider view that affronts to the dignity of women are more reprehensible than those affecting men. Now, the primary topic discussed in this essay so far has been whether or not sexual openness or explicitness is degrading in itself; that general question needs no further treatment. But it is often charged that much pornography is genuinely debasing, over and above its sexual frankness. In fact, many anti-pornography groups claim that they are not opposed to portrayals of nudity or sexual behavior as such; it is merely the degrading ones that they abhor—though they insist that the latter are very common. For example, the conservative Commission on Pornography appointed by US Attorney-General Edwin Meese declared in its *Final Report* that non-violent but degrading material "constitutes somewhere between the predominant and the overwhelming portion of what is currently standard fare heterosexual pornography."[3] That charge, involving as it does specific types of sexual depiction, does require further analysis.

Actually, this new claim is very often highly misleading, if not deliberately deceitful. "We're only opposed to *degrading* sex" certainly sounds reasonable, and is manifestly designed to reassure the public that its makers aren't just motivated by traditional prudishness. When we read the fine print, however, it frequently turns out that most of what they include under this rubric *is* objected to for its sexual content; scenes that are at all explicit (e.g. with genital close-ups) rather than soft-focus or merely suggestive, or that don't contain sufficient aesthetic content or affectionateness, or whose sole purpose is to display nudity (pin-ups), etc. Some of these people are simply not being honest about their views. Others' attitudes do differ from traditional ones, but only in degree, only in the amount of explicitness or disinhibition or unredeemed sex they find tolerable.

There is one charge in this category that is worthy of special mention. It derives from the fact, discussed earlier, that the women of pornography typically display strong sexual desire or responsiveness; they show high levels of excitement and enthusiasm, engaging in sex readily and enjoying a variety of sexual acts or partners or both. The accusation is made, not only that this misrepresents women in general, but that it is degrading to them to be portrayed in

such a manner. Often those who make the charge engage in hyperbole or distortion, saying pornography views women as "dirty whores," or at least as "nymphomaniacs" who are "hysterical" over sex. And once again, some even insist the debasement is deliberate, motivated by a desire to degrade all women. It has already been pointed out here that sexual fantasies don't make a statement of fact about any real women, much less about all. But what if they did? Are such depictions really degrading to anyone?

What is most astonishing about these accusations, in this day and age, is their totally unselfconscious endorsement of a double standard of sexual behavior. The men of pornography are equally randy and uninhibited—a fact that the accusers occasionally admit, as an afterthought. But it is only complained that women are shown as "sexually undiscriminating" and "hypersexual." And only women are said to be degraded by being so portrayed. It is even alleged that such depictions will lead to a loss of respect for women (but not men) in general, hence to sexist discrimination and mistreatment of numerous kinds. This is absurd; such treatment certainly might be caused by the double standard these people embrace, but it can hardly be blamed on portrayals that treat men and women alike. The main point here, however, is this: it is not at all genuinely degrading, to a man *or* to a woman, to be or to be seen as highly sexual. A strong love of sex is no more evil than a strong love of sports, or of music. To have erotic desires that are lower than average may (or may not) be unfortunate, but no one considers it morally evil; an unusually high enthusiasm for sex should be regarded no differently. Only those who find such enthusiasm bad would object to anyone's being "stereotyped" as having it; otherwise it would be no worse than being represented as honest, or as liking lasagna....

Many charges of degradation in pornography are straightforward extensions of the traditional attitude that sex itself is degrading. But there are claims, involving certain special types of portrayal, that the debasement is independent of the sexual content. The Meese Commission listed three general kinds of depiction that they felt encompass the "degrading" category: portraying persons as "existing solely for the sexual satisfaction of others," or as being "in decidedly subordinate roles," or engaging "in sexual practices which would to most people be considered humiliating."[4] As described, such scenes might indeed be objectionable; it will be of value for us to consider these cases one at a time.

That first phrase, unfortunately, is more rhetorical than descriptive; it isn't at all clear what it comes to, and no examples were given. But charges of this type are often levelled against pornography, including ordinary pin-ups. And they are generally absurd. Though posing for a photograph of any kind typically involves making oneself as appealing as possible, only in the case of pictures of nude females is this considered a sign of existing merely to satisfy others. Another standard complaint is about portrayals of fellatio. These people are usually stone silent about those of cunnilingus, even though they are also a staple of hard-core sex films: that shows a man giving pleasure to a woman. But neither act is at all totally one-sided, since, once again, such a large factor in sexual excitement is the excitement of the other person.

In other contexts, what is seemingly meant by rhetoric like this is the flip side of that "nymphomaniac" charge. This time, on the grounds that no woman would engage so readily in sex, or in so much sex or in certain types of sex, for her own enjoyment, it is concluded that she is doing it only to satisfy men. That is to say, many insist on re-interpreting scenes of highly sexed women as cases of the women merely accommodating the men. They are reading traditional stereotypes of females as passive, compliant and non-sexual into scenes where they are obviously anything but; the "nymphomaniac" charges are exaggerated but at least more honest. Quite naturally, now, men fantasize about women who enjoy sharing things they themselves would like. But equally, women's romantic fantasies typically have men engaging in and enjoying things that the women want. So the main problem here is this: in some people's eyes, a fantasy doesn't count as portraying equality between the sexes unless it involves men's desires becoming like women's, rather than the other way around. But there is nothing genuinely wrong with either. For all that, even the fact that male tastes are typically celebrated in pornography is hardly inevitable. The laws of the marketplace decree that a larger female interest in sexual portrayals would change their content—a process that has already begun in the case of video movies.

This is not to deny that a one-sided selfishness is ever found in pornography—or in real sex. There certainly are men and women whose pleasure in receiving things from the opposite gender (security, affection, *or* sex) is not contingent upon the latter's pleasure. But only a small proportion of pornography genuinely reflects these attitudes. This is so in spite of the fact that the making of such materials, unlike that portraying women's fantasies, has been left largely in the hands of people whose social sensitivities are not very keen. But even if certain depictions do contain a one-sided concern for male pleasure, it is a gross exaggeration to describe them in terms like "existing only to serve men," or even to consider them degrading rather than merely selfish and inconsiderate. And they can hardly compare to the message of this society's chivalric sexism, that women's needs and wishes are more noble than those of men. Indeed, it is precisely the failure of pornography to accede to this social attitude that so distresses traditionalists and some feminists.

Actually, the charge under discussion here is only one manifestation of a wider distortion in the views of sexist feminists. They claim that women in this society are constantly serving men, whereas men never do anything to help or please women. This is a complex topic, but there is far less truth to that claim than is commonly supposed. Indeed, their perception of such things often contains a further double standard. If men are shown being solicitous to women—e.g., opening doors for them—the "message" is that women are helpless children; if they are shown doing things for men, it is that women exist only to serve. In summary, this first category of "degrading" pornography is almost wholly the product of the sorts of paranoia and excuse-fishing that we have encountered before. We will have to look elsewhere for examples of genuine debasement.

* * *

Let us turn to the second alleged type of degrading portrayal, in which someone is shown in a definitely subordinate role. Ob-jections to this kind of thing arise from concern over traditional male dominance and female passivity. This is a problem that must not be taken lightly; eliminating the power imbalance between the sexes is central to the cause of equality for women. Unfortunately, some have become hypersensitive to the issue, reading such imbalances into innocent situations. And they have done this with a vengeance in the case of pornography. For example, it is often claimed that emotional passivity, not just the physical stillness required in posing for a camera, is reflected in ordinary pin-ups. And a reclining nude is said to be doubly passive and helpless—never mind that the only comfortable way to have sex is lying down, to them the posture represents submission, not sex. (On the question of whether the "missionary position" subordinates women, of course, the extremist feminists and the traditionalists part company.) This mindset also leads to some revealing doublethink. For instance, if a male is shown having consensual sex with more than one female, they're automatically his "harem"; if it is a woman with two or more men, it's a "gang rape."

One of the more incredible charges of this type is that sexual portrayals of interracial couples are racist, no matter how equally they are actually depicted. (This is also ironic, since in earlier years a common objection to men's magazines was that they were racist for only showing white women.) The rationale here is that the social power imbalance between the different races means that any such depiction inherently involves dominance. If that conclusion followed, it would bode even worse for a *real* sexual relationship between members of different races, including marriage. What makes this claim especially disturbing is the fact that abhorrence of interracial sex is such an integral part of real racism. "Would you want your sister to marry one?" used to be the presumed clincher in defenses of segregation. And under Hollywood's old Hays Code, not only sex but any depiction of interracial couples was strictly prohibited. If racial dominance is really endorsed, in pornography or anywhere else, that certainly is bad. But the idea that depicting interracial sexuality is inherently evil is itself tinged with racism.

False charges aside, it certainly is true that some pornography depicts men who are dominant and women who are passive, to one degree or another. In this, however, it is merely reflecting the reality in this culture: from dating to kissing and embracing to sex itself, males are still forced by female passivity to take the more active role. (Notice then how this particular objection clashes with an earlier one: it comes dangerously close to complaining that pornography is *too* true to life!) Moreover, sexual depictions of this type are only doing what others often do, from adventure stories to romance novels. To single out sexual portrayals for special blame for something that is so universal reveals that the real objections lie elsewhere. (The footnote on p. 330 of the Commission's *Final Report* suggests that they were desperate to find power imbalances. The alleged pornographic theme, "He is ready to take. She is ready to be taken," describes equally well the large majority of love scenes in romantic novels and movies.) In fact, however, pornography on the whole treats women and men more alike and more equal than the entertainment media in general do. So far from being passive, once again, most of the women portrayed in it are sexually assertive.

This was borne out by the study of hard-core videotapes made in Vancouver. It found that in only fourteen percent of the sexual scenes was the activity less than completely mutual; in these, the team of male and female coders felt that at least one of the participants was playing "a more dominant or directive role," "a more assertive role in directing the course of the interaction." In nearly half of these cases the woman was more dominant than the man—which sounds more egalitarian than mainstream movies. Notice also that this description doesn't sound particularly serious; extreme subordination was evidently quite uncommon. That being so, it isn't clear that even this much dominance is very objectionable. Many independent women report that they sometimes like to be dominated in the bedroom—"but not anywhere else!" Evidently, they do not see this as having consequences for their non-sexual lives. If they are right, a mild power imbalance in depictions of sexual activity is not a threat to women's equality. Notice also that this attitude appears to be part of a more general one: women often speak of the emotional value of being held by a man, but not of *doing* the holding. It is not clear that there is anything bad about this, however. Only those who feel threatened by all gender differences will automatically reject it.

What about that small minority of cases of extreme dominance in sexual portrayals, then? They fall into several categories, which will need to be considered separately.... First of all, there is the standard macho novel. Liberally sprinkled with scenes of rape and men pushing women around, they certainly are objectionable for their portrayal of women, *and* men. Most of these would not rightly be classed as pornography, since sex is not their central focus. As for those that would, the point here is that they are only the erotic segment of a larger category of fantasies, those expressing the power-desires of lower class males. Denied access to the money and status of the entrenched social structure, these men compensate with a tough-guy self image. So the characters in these stories ride roughshod over other males as well; general dominance is the theme, not just the subjection of women. To pretend, as many do, that this mistreatment of women is a natural outgrowth of the portrayal of sex is a serious distortion of the facts. Its cause and cure lie elsewhere.

Another variety of genuine subjugation involves a special paraphilia. What is known as "dominance and submission" is practiced by a tiny sexual subculture. (*The Story of O* provides a well-known illustration. This and another paraphilic specialization, "bondage and discipline," are often both classed as subcategories of sadomasochism.) The causes of such desires are obscure. The Freudian hypothesis that they trace back to the love-and-helplessness relationship of a child to its parents is plausible, but hard evidence is not easy to get. What does seem clear is that they are not in general produced by a wider desire to subjugate women, as some have charged. Indeed, the majority of the males in this category desire the submissive role. (They want a "dominatrix.") This is reportedly reflected in the sexual materials published for these people: in a survey of such magazines, one researcher found submissive males in roughly thirty percent more of the cases.[5] The extremist claim that "porn is about power, not about sex" is absurd, once again; but it is even false in regard to paraphilic dominance and submission. For

the individuals who have these feelings, power or its lack is what *causes* sexual arousal. The former is only a means to the latter—just the reverse of this charge.

But isn't that sort of activity, or its portrayal, evil nonetheless? To answer, we must realize again that paraphilic behavior like this is nearly always just play-acting; it is practiced by mutual consent and for mutual enjoyment. Moreover, its practitioners' non-sexual lives tend to be quite normal. Disturbing to others though they naturally are, these desires are not in general a reflection of forces or feelings that are a threat, to women or anyone else. And they certainly are not common. One study of "adult" book shops in New York City found that about seventeen percent of their magazine covers depicted bondage or domination, but this figure is misleadingly high. First, materials that cater to more unusual sexual tastes are concentrated in these stores; the big-selling sex magazines are sold in more socially acceptable outlets. Second, this particular survey counted titles, rather than separate issues or the number of copies of the latter; but publications portraying more deviant activities tend to be produced only once (in spite of the "Vol. 1, No. 1" they may carry).[6] Unlike the last one, this variety of depicted dominance should be of little concern to the women's movement.

The oppression of women by men down through history is a fact to be deplored. But feminists too frequently ignore the power that women exercise over men. Humans are highly social beings, whose behavior is more often influenced by the opinions of others than by superior physical strength. And in the matter of controlling others through approval and disapproval, women exercise very great power. This influence is especially great in the formative years of early childhood, since the bulk of socialization at that age is done by women: mothers, day-care workers, school teachers, etc. More directly, women have traditionally controlled men by getting other men to do it for them, from gallant knights vying for their favors to modern politicians vying for their votes. In fact, an often-effective way of exercising power over others is precisely by exaggerating one's lack of power, by playing victim. Social reality is much more complex than feminist theories generally allow.

The power of women is nowhere more in evidence than in regard to love and sex: the fact that this culture's moral standards match the needs of its females better than those of its males has been mentioned here repeatedly. In the last century, the women's "purity crusade" created laws against pornography, prostitution and male homosexual acts, also birth control and abortion. Without a single vote, the women involved were able to shame male legislators into doing what the crusaders perceived as being in women's best interests.[7] It is certainly true that the extreme double standard maintained previous to that time by the males in power was oppressive to women; but the comstockery that replaced it was oppressive to everyone. In a more direct way, men's greater need for sex puts control into the hands of women. "All that power," marvels Ms. Friday in describing the control this gives adolescent females over their male peers. Some women are oblivious to this situation, while others exploit it—just as some males exploit females' greater need for love.

The manner in which these facts are reflected in sexual fantasies is extremely important to our discussion. For once more,

their purpose is often to make the world seem better than it is in real life. Hence it is not surprising that some male fantasies would "turn the tables" in this relationship. Those occasional scenes in which a woman is so strongly aroused that she begs for sex make a transparently clear statement of male powerlessness in this regard. Similarly, pornographic portrayals in which men dominate women—*and* those that are the other way around—appear to represent attempts by males to cope with the feelings of helplessness and frustration. Such things must be understood for what they really are, not simplemindedly denounced as yet another manifestation of patriarchy.

Notes

1   For those who have seen it, the one thing in all the world that is best described by this familiar rhetoric is artist Judy Chicago's tableful of plastic vaginas, *The Dinner Party*. But male sexual desire isn't involved, so it is politically acceptable to many if not all feminist foes of pornography. Had it appeared in *Hustler* instead of in feminist circles, it would no doubt be standardly cited by them as a paradigm of the male objectification of women. Traditionalists, of course, are scandalized by it.

2   To satisfy the reader's curiosity, the explicit scenes of hard-core pornography do not appeal to me; I find them very unaesthetic. (I also detest the taste of baked squash and fresh onions.) But I have decent, caring friends who get great pleasure from them, including some who use them to augment loving marital relationships.

3   From pp. 334-5 in the *Final Report* of the Attorney General's Commission on Pornography (hereafter, *AGCP*).

4   P. 331. The religiously conservative Meese Commission was of course silent about the subordination of women many insist is endorsed by the Bible.

5   From Alan Soble's *Pornography: Marxism, Feminism and the Future of Sexuality*, p. 19.

6   The survey was by Dietz and Evans, in the *American Journal of Psychiatry*, 139:11. (Having been co-authored by one of the commissioners, this ar-

ticle may also throw more light on the question of which acts they considered non-dominating but still degrading; see the chart on p. 1494.) The information that such magazines are not produced once is from Robin Badgley *et al.*, *Sexual Offences Against Children*.

7 For example, see Sheila Rothman's book *Woman's Proper Place*.

Questions for Discussion

1 Much of Christensen's argument takes the form of a comparison of pornography with other aspects of popular culture, suggesting pornography is no more offensive. Christensen uses this to claim pornography is acceptable. Could one use the same point to establish that much of popular culture should be changed?

2 One of Christensen's points is that those who attack pornography have been influenced by an unreasonable traditional view that a woman's nudity is more degrading than a man's nudity, or that the same actions or attitudes can be shameful in a woman but not in a man. Is he right? Does it matter to his argument whether most consumers of the pornography see it in those terms?

Pornography is a Civil Rights Issue

Andrea Dworkin

Andrea Dworkin is one of the best known feminist supporters of legal measures against pornography. She and Catharine MacKinnon were the framers of the "Minneapolis Ordinance." This ordinance was designed to make trafficking in pornography a violation of civil rights (for which a victim might sue) rather than an obscenity offense. She was called as a witness before the United States Attorney General's Commission on Pornography to present her views. The following is taken from her testimony before that commission.

*   *   *

MS DWORKIN: Thank you very much. My name is Andrea Dworkin. I am a citizen of the United States, and in this country where I live, every year millions and millions of pictures are being made of women with our legs spread. We are called beaver, we are called pussy, our genitals are tied up, they are pasted, makeup is put on them to make them pop out of a page at a male viewer. Millions and millions of pictures are made of us in postures of submission and sexual access so that our vaginas are exposed for penetration, our anuses are exposed for penetration, our throats are used as if they are genitals for penetration. In this country where I live as a citizen real rapes are on film and are being sold in the marketplace. And the major motif of pornography as a form of entertainment is that women are raped and violated and humiliated until we discover that we like it and at that point we ask for more.

In this country where I live as a citizen, women are penetrated by animals and objects for public entertainment, women are urinated on and defecated on, women and girls are used interchangeably so that grown women are made up to look like five- or six-year-old children surrounded by toys, presented in mainstream pornographic publications for anal penetration. There are magazines in which adult women are presented with their pubic areas shaved so that they resemble children.

In this country where I live, there is a trafficking in pornography that exploits mentally and physically disabled women, women who are maimed; there is amputee pornography, a trade in women who have been maimed in that way, as if that is a sexual fetish for men. In this country where I live, there is a trade in racism as a form of sexual pleasure, so that the plantation is presented as a form of sexual gratification for the black woman slave who asks please to be abused, please to be raped, please to be hurt. Black skin is presented as if it is a female genital, and all the violence and the abuse and the humiliation that is in general directed against female genitals is directed against the black skin of women in pornography.

Asian women in the country where I live are tied from trees and hung from ceilings and hung from doorways as a form of public entertainment. There is a concentration camp pornography in this country where I live, where the concentration camp and the atrocities that occurred there are presented as existing for the sexual pleasure of the victim, of the woman, who orgasms to the real abuses that occurred, not very long ago in history.

In the country where I live as a citizen, there is pornography of the humiliation of women where every single way of humiliating a human being is taken to be a form of sexual pleasure for the viewer and for the victim; where women are covered with filth, including feces, including mud, including paint, including blood, including semen; where women are tortured for the sexual pleasure of those who watch and do the torture, where women are murdered for the sexual pleasure of murdering women, and this material exists because it is fun, because it is entertainment, because it is a form of pleasure, and there are those who say it is a form of freedom.

Certainly it is freedom for those who do it. Certainly it is freedom for those who use it as entertainment, but we are also asked to believe that it is freedom for those to whom it is done.

Then this entertainment is taken, and it is used on other women, women who aren't in the pornography, to force those women into prostitution, to make them imitate the acts in the pornography. The women in the pornography, sixty-five to seventy percent of them we believe are victims of incest or child sexual abuse. They are poor women; they are not women who have opportunities in this society. They are frequently runaways who are picked up by pimps and exploited. They are frequently raped, the rapes are filmed, they are kept in prostitution by blackmail. The pornography is used on prostitutes by johns who expect them to replicate the sexual acts in the pornography, no matter how damaging it is.

Pornography is used in rape—to plan it, to execute it, to choreograph it, to engender the excitement to commit the act. Pornography is used in gang rape against women. We see an increase since the release of *Deep Throat* in throat rape—where women show up in emergency rooms because men believe they can penetrate, deep-thrust, to the bottom of a woman's throat. We see increasing use of all elements of pornography in battery, which is the most commonly committed violent crime in this country, including the rape of women by animals, including maiming, including heavy bondage, including outright torture.

We have seen in the last eight years an increase in the use of cameras in rapes. And those rapes are filmed and then they are put on the marketplace and they are protected speech—they are real rapes.

We see a use of pornography in the harassment of women on jobs, especially in nontraditional jobs, in the harassment of women in education, to create terror and compliance in the home, which as you know is the most dangerous place for women in this society, where more violence is committed against women than anywhere else. We see pornography used to create harassment of women and children in neighborhoods that are saturated with pornography, where people come from other parts of the city and then prey on the populations of people who live in those neighborhoods, and that increases physical attack and verbal assault.

We see pornography having introduced a profit motive into rape. We see that filmed rapes are protected speech. We see the centrality of pornography in serial murders. There *are* snuff films. We see boys imitating pornography. We see the average age of rapists going down. We are beginning to see gang rapes in elementary schools committed by elementary school age boys imitating pornography.

We see sexual assault after death where frequently the pornography is the motive for the murder because the man believes that he will get a particular kind of sexual pleasure having sex with a woman after she is dead.

We see a major trade in women, we see the torture of women as a form of entertainment, and we see women also suffering the injury of objectification—that is to say we are dehumanized. We are treated as if we are subhuman, and that is a precondition for violence against us.

I live in a country where if you film any act of humiliation or torture, and the victim is a woman, the film is both entertainment and it is protected speech. Now that tells me something about what it means to be a woman citizen in this country, and the meaning of being second class.

When your rape is entertainment, your worthlessness is absolute. You have reached the nadir of social worthlessness. The civil impact of pornography on women is staggering. It keeps us socially silent, it keeps us socially compliant, it keeps us afraid in neighborhoods; and it creates a vast hopelessness for women, a vast despair. One lives inside a nightmare of sexual abuse that is both actual and potential, and you have the great joy of knowing that your nightmare is someone else's freedom and someone else's fun.

Now, a great deal has happened in this country to legitimize pornography in the last ten to fifteen years. There are people who are responsible for the fact that pornography is now a legitimate form of public entertainment.

Number one, the lobby of lawyers who work for the pornographers; the fact that the pornographers pay lawyers big bucks to fight for them, not just in the courts, but in public, in the public dialogue; the fact that lawyers interpret constitutional principles in light of the profit interest of the pornographers.

Number two, the collusion of the American Civil Liberties Union with the pornographers, which includes taking money from them. It includes using buildings that pornographers own and not paying rent, it includes using pornography in benefits to raise money. It includes not only defending them in court but also doing publicity for them, including organizing events for them, as the Hugh Hefner First Amendment Awards is organized by ACLU people for *Playboy*. It includes publishing in their magazines. It includes deriving great pride and economic benefit from working privately for the pornographers, while publicly pretending to be a disinterested advocate of civil liberties and free speech.

I want you to contrast the behavior of the ACLU in relation to the pornographers with their activities in relation to the Klan and the Nazis. The ACLU pretends to understand that they are all equally pernicious. But do ACLU people publish in the Klan newsletter? No. Do they go to Nazi social events? No. Do they go to cocktail parties at Nazi headquarters? No, they don't, at least not yet.

Finally, they have colluded in this sense, that they have convinced many of us that the standard for speech is what I would call a repulsion standard. That is to say we find the most repulsive person in the society and we defend him. I say we find the most powerless people in this society, and we defend *them*. That's the way we increase rights of speech in this society.

A third group that colludes to legitimize pornography are publishers and the so-called legitimate media. They pretend to believe that under this system of law there is a First Amendment that is indivisible and absolute, which it has never been.

As you know, the First Amendment protects speech that has already been expressed from state interference. That means it protects those who own media. There is no affirmative responsibility to open communications to those who are powerless in the society at large.

As a result, the owners of media, the newspapers, the TV networks, are comfortable with having women's bodies defined as the speech of pimps, because they are protecting their rights to profit as owners, and they think that that is what the First Amendment is for.

I am ashamed to say that people in my profession, writers, have also colluded with the pornographers. We provide their so-called socially redeeming value, and they wrap the tortured bodies of women in the work that we do.

Fourth, politicians have colluded with the pornographers in municipalities all over this country. They do it in these ways:

Zoning laws do not keep pornography out of cities. They are an official legal permission to traffic in pornography. And as a result politicians are able to denounce pornography moralistically while protecting it through zoning laws.

Zoning laws impose pornography on poor neighborhoods, on working-class neighborhoods, on neighborhoods where people of color live, and all of those people have to deal with the increase in crime, the terrible harassment, the degradation of the quality of life in their neighborhoods, and the politicians get to protect the property values of the rich. There is an equal protection issue here: why the state makes some people pay so other people can profit.

But that issue has never been raised. We have never been able to sue a city under the equal protection theory, because lawyers are on the other side. Lawyers belong primarily to pornographers, and the people who live in these neighborhoods that are saturated with pornography are powerless people. They don't even have power in their own municipalities.

In addition, what pornographers do in municipalities is that they buy land that is targeted for development by cities. They hold that land hostage. They develop political power through negotiating around that land. They make huge profits, and they get influence in local city governments.

Five, not finally but next to the last, a great colluder with the pornographers was the last presidential Commission on Obscenity and Pornography. They were very effective in legitimizing pornography in this country. They appeared to be looking for a proverbial ax murderer who would watch pornography and within twenty-four or forty-eight hours go out and kill someone in a horrible and clear way. The country is saturated with pornography, and saturated with violence against women, and saturated with the interfacing of the two. And the Commission didn't find it.

None of the scientific research that they relied on to come to their conclusions is worth anything today. It's all invalid. I ask you to take seriously the fact that society does not exist in a laboratory, that we are talking about real things that happen to real people, and that's what we are asking you to take some responsibility for.

Finally, the ultimate colluders in the legitimizing of pornography, of course, are the consumers. In 1979 we had a $4-billion-a-year industry in this country. By 1985 it was an $8-billion-a-year industry. Those consumers include men in all walks of life: lawyers, politicians, writers, professors, owners of media, police, doctors, maybe even commissioners on presidential commissions. No one really knows, do they?

And no matter where we look, we can't find the consumers. But what we learn is the meaning of first-class citizenship, and the meaning of first-class citizenship is that you can use your authority as men and as professionals to protect pornography both by developing arguments to protect it and by using real social and economic power to protect it.

And as a result of all this, the harm to women remains invisible; even though we have the bodies, the harm to women remains invisible. Underlying the invisibility of this harm is an assumption that what is done to women is natural, that even if a woman is forced to do something, somehow it falls within the sphere of her natural responsibilities as a woman. When the same things are done to boys, those things are perceived as an outrage. They are called unnatural.

But if you force a woman to do something that she was born to do, then the violence to her is not perceived as a real violation of her.

In addition, the harm to women of pornography is invisible because most sexual abuse still occurs in private, even though we have this photographic documentation of it, called the pornography industry.

Women are extremely isolated, women don't have credibility, women are not believed by people who make social policy.

In addition, the harm of pornography remains invisible because women have been historically excluded from the protections of the Constitution; and as a result, the violations of our human rights, when they don't occur the same way violations to men occur, have not been recognized or taken seriously, and we do not have remedies for them under law.

In addition, pornography is invisible in its harm to women because women are poorer than men and many of the women exploited in pornography are very poor, many of them illiterate, and also because there is a great deal of female compliance with brutality, and the compliance is based on fear, it's based on powerlessness and it is based on a reaction to the very real violence of the pornographers.

Finally, the harm is invisible because of the smile, because women are made to smile, women aren't just made to do the sex acts. We are made to smile while we do them.

So you will find in pornography women penetrating themselves with swords or daggers, and you will see the smile. You will see things that cannot be done to a human being and that are done to men only in political circumstances of torture, and you will see a woman forced to smile.

And this smile will be believed, and the injury done to her as a human being, to her body and to her heart and to her soul, will not be believed.

Now, we have been told that we have an argument here about speech, not about women being hurt. And yet the emblem of that argument is a woman bound and gagged and we are supposed to believe that that is speech. Who is that speech for? We have women being tortured and we are told that that is somebody's speech? Whose speech is it? It's the speech of the pimp, it is not the speech of a woman. The only words we hear in pornography from women are that women want to be hurt, ask to be hurt, like to be raped, get sexual pleasure from sexual violence; and even when a woman is covered in filth, we are supposed to believe that her speech is that she likes it and she wants more of it.

The reality for women in this society is that pornography creates silence for women. The pornographers silence women. Our bodies are their language. Their speech is made out of our exploitation, our subservience, our injury and our pain, and they can't say anything without hurting us, and when you protect them, you protect only their right to exploit and hurt us.

Pornography is a civil rights issue for women because pornography sexualizes inequality, because it turns women into subhuman creatures.

Pornography is a civil rights issue for women because it is the systematic exploitation of a group of people because of a condition of birth. Pornography creates bigotry and hostility and aggression towards all women, targets all women, without exception.

Pornography is the suppression of us through sexual exploitation and abuse, so that we have no real means to achieve civil equality; and the issue here is simple, it is not complex. People are being hurt, and you can help them or you can help those who are hurting them. We need civil rights legislation, legislation that recognizes pornography as a violation of the civil rights of women.

We need it because civil rights legislation recognizes the fact that the harm here is to human beings. We need that recognition. We need civil rights legislation because it puts the power to act in the hands of the people who have been forced into pornographized powerlessness, and that's a special kind of powerlessness, that's a powerlessness that is supposed to be a form of sexual pleasure.

We need civil rights legislation because only those to whom it has happened know what has happened. They are the people who are the experts. They have the knowledge. They know what has happened, how it's happened; only they can really articulate, from beginning to end, the reality of pornography as a human rights injury. We need civil rights legislation because it gives us something back after what the pornographers have taken from us.

The motivation to fight back keeps people alive. People need it for their dignity, for their ability to continue to exist as citizens in a country that needs their creativity and needs their presence and needs the existence that has been taken from them by the pornographers. We need civil rights legislation because, as social policy, it says to a population of people that they have human worth, they have human worth, that this society recognizes that they have human worth.

We need it because it's the only legislative remedy thus far that is drawn narrowly enough to confront the human rights issues for people who are are being exploited and discriminated against, without becoming an instrument of police power to suppress real expression.

We need the civil rights legislation because the process of civil discovery is a very important one, and it will give us a great deal of information for potential criminal prosecutions, against organized crime, against pornographers, and I ask you to look at the example of the Southern Poverty Law Center and their Klanwatch Project, which has used civil suits to get criminal indictments against the Klan.

Finally, we need civil rights legislation because the only really dirty word in this society is the word "women," and a civil rights approach says that this society repudiates the brutalization of women.

We are against obscenity laws. We don't want them. I want you to understand why, whether you end up agreeing or not.

Number one, the pornographers use obscenity laws as part of their formula for making pornography. All they need to do is provide some literary, artistic, political or scientific value and they can hang women from the rafters. As long as they manage to meet that formula, it doesn't matter what they do to women.

And in the old days, when obscenity laws were still being enforced, in many places—for instance the most sadomasochistic pornography—the genitals were always covered because if the genitals were always covered, that wouldn't kick off a police prosecution.

Number two, the use of the prurient interest standard—however that standard is construed in this new era, when the Supreme Court has taken two synonyms, "lasciviousness" and "lust," and said that they mean different things, which is mind-boggling in and of itself. Whatever prurient interest is construed to mean, the reaction of jurors to material—whether they are supposed to be aroused or whether they are not allowed to be aroused, whatever the instructions of the court—has nothing to do with the objective reality of what is happening to women in pornography.

The third reason that obscenity law cannot work for us is: what do community standards mean in a society when violence against women is pandemic, when according to the FBI a woman is battered every eighteen seconds and it's the most commonly committed violent crime in the country? What would community standards have meant in the segregated South? What would community standards have meant as we approached the atrocity of Nazi Germany?

What are community standards in a society where women are persecuted for being women and pornography is a form of political persecution?

Obscenity laws are also woman-hating in their construction. Their basic presumption is that it's women's bodies that are dirty. The standards of obscenity law don't acknowledge the reality of the technology. They were drawn up in a society where obscenity was construed to be essentially writing and drawing; and now what we have is mass production in a way that real people are being hurt, and the consumption of real people by a real technology, and obscenity laws are not adequate to that reality.

Finally, obscenity laws, at the discretion of police and prosecutors, will keep obscenity out of the public view, but it remains available to men in private. It remains available to individual men, it remains available to all-male groups; and whenever it is used, it still creates bigotry, hostility and aggression towards all women. It's still used in sexual abuse as part of sexual abuse. It's still made through coercion, through blackmail and through exploitation.

I am going to ask you to do several things. The first thing I am going to ask you to do is listen to women who want to talk to you about what has happened to them. Please listen to them. They know, they know how this works. You are asking people to speculate; they know, it has happened to them....

Questions for Discussion

1   Dworkin suggests that it is impossible to separate pornography from a whole pattern of power imbalances and violence against women in our society. Is she right?
2   Should legislation concerning pornography be framed in terms of violation of civil rights, rather than obscenity?

Feminism, Moralism, and Pornography

Ellen Willis

Willis writes from a feminist perspective, but is very suspicious of any attempts to censor pornography. She warns against a tendency to repeat elements of the traditional views of the proper role of women in the current feminist campaign against pornography. She also raises some questions about how those who are opposing pornography try to define what they are opposed to.

*   *   *

For women, life is an ongoing good cop—bad cop routine. The good cops are marriage, motherhood, and that courtly old gentleman, chivalry. Just cooperate, they say (crossing their fingers), and we'll go easy on you. You'll never have to earn a living or open a door. We'll even get you some romantic love. But you'd better not get stubborn, or you'll have to deal with our friend rape, and he's a real terror; we just can't control him.

Pornography often functions as a bad cop. If rape warns that without the protection of one man we are fair game for all, the hard-core pornographic image suggests that the alternative to being a wife is being a whore. As women become more "criminal," the cops call for nastier reinforcements; the proliferation of lurid, violent porn (symbolic rape) is a form of backlash. But one can be a solid citizen and still be shocked (naively or hypocritically) by police brutality. However widely condoned, rape is illegal. However loudly people proclaim that pornography is as wholesome as granola, the essence of its appeal is that emotionally it remains taboo. It is from their very contempt for the rules that bad cops derive their power to terrorize (and the covert approbation of solid citizens who would love to break the rules themselves). The line between a bad cop and outlaw is tenuous. Both rape and pornography reflect a male outlaw mentality that rejects the conventions of romance and insists, bluntly, that women are cunts. The crucial difference between the conservative's moral indignation at rape, or at *Hustler*, and the feminist's political outrage is the latter's understanding that the problem is not bad cops or outlaws but cops and the law.

Unfortunately, the current women's campaign against pornography seems determined to blur this difference. Feminist criticism of sexist and misogynist pornography is nothing new; porn is an obvious target insofar as it contributes to larger patterns of oppression—the reduction of the female body to a commodity (the paradigm being prostitution), the sexual intimidation that makes women regard the public streets as

enemy territory (the paradigm being rape), sexist images, and propaganda in general. But what is happening now is different. By playing games with the English language, anti-porn activists are managing to rationalize as feminism a single-issue movement divorced from any larger political context and rooted in conservative moral assumptions that are all the more dangerous for being unacknowledged.

When I first heard there was a group called Women Against Pornography, I twitched. Could I define myself as Against Pornography? Not really. In itself, pornography—which, my dictionary and I agree, means any image or description intended or used to arouse sexual desire—does not strike me as the proper object of a political crusade. As the most cursory observation suggests, there are many varieties of porn, some pernicious, some more or less benign. About the only generalization one can make is that pornography is the return of the repressed, of feelings and fantasies driven underground by a culture that atomizes sexuality, defining love as a noble affair of the heart and mind, lust as a base animal urge centered in unmentionable organs. Prurience—the state of mind I associate with pornography—implies a sense of sex as forbidden, secretive pleasure, isolated from any emotional or social context. I imagine that in utopia, porn would wither away along with the state, heroin, and Coca-Cola. At present, however, the sexual impulses that pornography appeals to are part of virtually everyone's psychology. For obvious political and cultural reasons nearly all porn is sexist in that it is the product of a male imagination and aimed at a male market; women are less likely to be consciously interested in pornography, or to indulge that interest, or to find porn that turns them on. But anyone who thinks women are simply indifferent to pornography has never watched a bunch of adolescent girls pass around a trashy novel. Over the years I've enjoyed various pieces of pornography—some of them of the sleazy Forty-second Street paperback sort—and so have most women I know. Fantasy, after all, is more flexible than reality, and women have learned, as a matter of survivial, to be adept at shaping male fantasies to their own purposes. If feminists define pornography, per se, as the enemy, the result will be to make a lot of women ashamed of their sexual feelings and afraid to be honest about them. And the last thing women need is more sexual shame, guilt, and hypocrisy—this time served up as feminism.

So why ignore qualitative distinctions and in effect condemn all pornography as equally bad? WAP organizers answer—or finesse—this question by redefining pornography. They maintain that pornography is not really about sex but about violence against women. Or, in a more colorful formulation, "Pornography is the theory, rape is the practice." Part of the argument is that pornography causes violence; much is made of the fact that Charles Manson and David Berkowitz had porn collections. This is the sort of inverted logic that presumes marijuana to be dangerous because most heroin addicts started with it. It is men's hostility toward women—combined with their power to express that hostility and for the most part get away with it—that causes sexual violence. Pornography that gives sadistic fantasies concrete shape—and, in today's atmosphere, social legitimacy—may well encourage suggestible men to act them out. But if *Hustler* were to vanish from the shelves tomorrow, I doubt that rape or wife-beating statistics would decline.

Even more problematic is the idea that pornography depicts violence rather than sex. Since porn is by definition overtly sexual, while most of it is not overtly violent, this equation requires some fancy explaining. The conference WAP held in September was in part devoted to this task. Robin Morgan and Gloria Steinem addressed it by attempting to distinguish pornography from erotica. According to this argument, erotica (whose etymological root is "eros," or sexual love) expresses an integrated sexuality based on mutual affection and desire between equals; pornography (which comes from another Greek root—"porne," meaning prostitute) reflects a dehumanized sexuality based on male domination and exploitation of women. The distinction sounds promising, but it doesn't hold up. The accepted meaning of erotica is literature or pictures with sexual themes; it may or may not serve the essentially utilitarian function of pornography. Because it is less specific, less suggestive of actual sexual activity, "erotica" is regularly used as a euphemism for "classy porn." Pornography expressed in literary language or expensive photography and consumed by the upper middle class is "erotica"; the cheap stuff, which can't pretend to any purpose but getting people off, is smut. The erotica-versus-porn approach evades the (embarrassing?) question of how porn is *used*. It endorses the portrayal of sex as we might like it to be and condemns the portrayal of sex as it too often is, whether in action or only in fantasy. But if pornography is to arouse, it must appeal to the feelings we have, not those that by some utopian standard we ought to have. Sex in this culture has been so deeply politicized that it is impossible to make clear-cut distinctions between "authentic" sexual impulses and those conditioned by patriarchy. Between, say, *Ulysses* at one end and *Snuff* at the other, erotica/pornography conveys all sorts of mixed messages that elicit complicated and private responses. In practice, attempts to sort out good erotica from bad porn inevitably come down to "What turns me on is erotic; what turns you on is pornographic."

It would be clearer and more logical simply to acknowledge that some sexual images are offensive and some are not. But logic and clarity are irrelevant—or rather, inimical—to the underlying aim of the anti-porners, which is to vent the emotions traditionally associated with the word "pornography." As I've suggested, there is a social and psychic link between pornography and rape. In terms of patriarchal morality both are expressions of male lust, which is presumed to be innately vicious, and offenses to the putative sexual innocence of "good" women. But feminists supposedly begin with different assumptions—that men's confusion of sexual desire with predatory aggression reflects a sexist system, not male biology; that there are no good (chaste) or bad (lustful) women, just women who are, like men, sexual beings. From this standpoint, to lump pornography with rape is dangerously simplistic. Rape is a violent physical assault. Pornography can be a psychic assault, both in its content and in its public intrusions on our attention, but for women as for men it can also be a source of erotic pleasure. A woman who is raped is a victim; a woman who enjoys pornography (even if that means enjoying a rape fantasy) is in a sense a rebel, insisting on an aspect of her sexuality that has been defined as a male preserve. Insofar as pornography glorifies male supremacy and

sexual alienation, it is deeply reactionary. But in rejecting sexual repression and hypocrisy—which have inflicted even more damage on women than on men—it expresses a radical impulse.

That this impulse still needs defending, even among feminists, is evident from the sexual attitudes that have surfaced in the anti-porn movement. In the movement's rhetoric pornography is a code word for vicious male lust. To the objection that some women get off on porn, the standard reply is that this only shows how thoroughly women have been brainwashed by male values—though a WAP leaflet goes so far as to suggest that women who claim to like pornography are lying to avoid male opprobrium. (Note the good-girl-versus-bad-girl theme, reappearing as healthy-versus-sick, or honest-versus-devious; for "brainwashed" read "seduced.") And the view of sex that most often emerges from talk about "erotica" is as sentimental and euphemistic as the word itself: lovemaking should be beautiful, romantic, soft, nice, and devoid of messiness, vulgarity, impulses to power, or indeed aggression of any sort. Above all, the emphasis should be on *relationships*, not (yuck) *organs*. This goody-goody concept of eroticism is not feminist but feminine. It is precisely sex as an aggressive, unladylike activity, an expression of violent and unpretty emotion, an exercise of erotic power, and a specifically genital experience that has been taboo for women. Nor are we supposed to admit that we, too, have sadistic impulses, that our sexual fantasies may reflect forbidden urges to turn the tables and get revenge on men. (When a woman is aroused by a rape fantasy, is she perhaps identifying with the rapist as well as the victim?)

At the WAP conference lesbian separat-
ists argued that pornography reflects patriarchal sexual relations; patriarchal sexual
relations are based on male power backed
by force; ergo, pornography is violent.
This dubious syllogism, which could as easily be applied to romantic novels, reduces
the whole issue to hopeless mush. If all
manifestations of patriarchal sexuality are
violent, then opposition to violence cannot
explain why pornography (rather than romantic novels) should be singled out as a
target. Besides, such reductionism allows
women no basis for distinguishing between
consensual heterosexuality and rape. But
this is precisely its point; as a number of
women at the conference put it, "In a patriarchy, all sex with men is pornographic."
Of course, to attack pornography, and at
the same time equate it with heterosexual
sex, is implicitly to condemn not only
women who like pornography, but women
who sleep with men. This is familiar
ground. The argument that straight women
collaborate with the enemy has often been,
among other things, a relatively polite way
of saying that they consort with the beast.
At the conference I couldn't help feeling
that proponents of the separatist line were
talking like the modern equivalents of
women who, in an era when straightforward prudery was socially acceptable,
joined convents to escape men's rude sexual demands. It seemed to me that their re-
vulsion against heterosexuality was serving
as the thinnest of covers for disgust with
sex itself. In any case, sanitized feminine
sexuality, whether straight or gay, is as
limited as the predatory masculine kind and
as central to women's oppression; a major
function of misogynist pornography is to
scare us into embracing it. As a further incentive, the good cops stand ready to assure

us that we are indeed morally superior to
men, that in our sweetness and nonviolence
(read passivity and powerlessness) is our
strength.

Women are understandably tempted to
believe this comforting myth. Self-righ-
teousness has always been a feminine
weapon, a permissible way to make men
feel bad. Ironically, it is socially acceptable
for women to display fierce aggression in
their crusades against male vice, which
serve as an outlet for female anger without
threatening male power. The temperance
movement, which made alcohol the symbol
of male violence, did not improve the position of women; substituting porn for demon
rum won't work either. One reason it won't
is that it bolsters the good girl—bad girl
split. Overtly or by implication it isolates
women who like porn or "pornographic"
sex or who work in the sex industry. WAP
has refused to take a position on prostitution, yet its activities—particularly its support for cleaning up Times Square—will
affect prostitutes' lives. Prostitution raises
its own set of complicated questions. But it
is clearly not in women's interest to pit
"good" feminists against "bad" whores (or
topless dancers, or models for skin magazines).

So far, the issue that has dominated
public debate on the anti-porn campaign is
its potential threat to free speech. Here too
the movement's arguments have been full
of contradictions. Susan Brownmiller and
other WAP organizers claim not to advocate
censorship and dismiss the civil liberties
issue as a red herring dragged in by men
who don't want to face the fact that pornography oppresses women. Yet at the same
time, WAP endorses the Supreme Court's
contention that obscenity is not protected
speech, a doctrine I—and most civil liber-

tarians—regard as a clear infringement of First Amendment rights. Brownmiller insists that the First Amendment was designed to protect political dissent, not expressions of woman-hating violence. But to make such a distinction is to defeat the amendment's purpose, since it implicitly cedes to the government the right to define "political." (Has there ever been a government willing to admit that its opponents are anything more than anti-social troublemakers?) Anyway, it makes no sense to oppose pornography on the grounds that it's sexist propaganda, then turn around and argue that it's not political. Nor will libertarians be reassured by WAP's statement that "We want to change the definition of obscenity so that it focuses on violence, not sex." Whatever their focus, obscenity laws deny the right of free expression to those who transgress official standards of propriety— and personally, I don't find WAP's standards significantly less oppressive than Warren Burger's. Not that it matters, since WAP's fantasies about influencing the definition of obscenity are appallingly naive. The basic purpose of obscenity laws is and always has been to reinforce cultural taboos on sexuality and suppress feminism, homosexuality, and other forms of sexual dissidence. No pornographer has ever been punished for being a woman-hater, but not too long ago information about female sexuality, contraception, and abortion was assumed to be obscene. In a male supremacist society the only obscenity law that will not be used against women is no law at all.

As an alternative to an outright ban on pornography, Brownmiller and others have advocated restricting its display. There is a plausible case to be made for the idea that anti-woman images displayed so prominently that they are impossible to avoid are coercive, a form of active harassment that oversteps the bounds of free speech. But aside from the evasion involved in simply equating pornography with misogyny or sexual sadism, there are no legal or logical grounds for treating sexist material any differently from (for example) racist or anti-Semitic propaganda; an equitable law would have to prohibit any kind of public defamation. And the very thought of such a sweeping law has to make anyone with an imagination nervous. Could Catholics claim they were being harassed by nasty depictions of the pope? Could Russian refugees argue that the display of Communist literature was a form of psychological torture? Would pro-abortion material be taken off the shelves on the grounds that it defamed the unborn? I'd rather not find out.

At the moment the First Amendment issue remains hypothetical; the movement has concentrated on raising the issue of pornography through demonstrations and other public actions. This is certainly a legitimate strategy. Still, I find myself more and more disturbed by the tenor of antipornography actions and the sort of consciousness they promote; increasingly their focus has shifted from rational feminist criticism of specific targets to generalized, demagogic moral outrage. Picketing an anti-woman movie, defacing an exploitative billboard, or boycotting a record company to protest its misogynist album covers conveys one kind of message, mass marches Against Pornography quite another. Similarly, there is a difference between telling the neighborhood news dealer why it pisses us off to have *Penthouse* shoved in our faces and choosing as a prime target every right-thinking politician's symbol of big-city sin, Times Square.

In contrast to the abortion rights movement, which is struggling against a tidal wave of energy from the other direction, the anti-porn campaign is respectable. It gets approving press and cooperation from the New York City government, which has its own stake (promoting tourism, making the Clinton area safe for gentrification) in cleaning up Times Square. It has begun to attract women whose perspective on other matters is in no way feminist ("I'm anti-abortion," a participant in WAP's march on Times Square told a reporter, "but this is something I can get into"). Despite the insistence of WAP organizers that they support sexual freedom, their line appeals to the anti-sexual emotions that feed the backlash. Whether they know it or not, they are doing the good cops' dirty work.

Question for Discussion

1   Is Willis right to suggest that feminists should view the distinction between "erotica" and "pornography" as being dangerously close to the traditional dichotomy of "good girls" and "bad girls"?

PART 7

employment equity

The subject of this chapter has been described by several different names, such as "employment equity," "affirmative action," "differential hiring," "preferential treatment," or "reverse discrimination." Sometimes the name one picks is affected by one's attitude toward the practice—a person who is against it might call it "reverse discrimination," hoping that the negative connotations of the word "discrimination" will carry over, whereas a person who is in favour might choose "affirmative action" with the idea that the positive connotations of "affirmative" will influence the reader. Often the practice gets different names in different places, and so people simply pick up whatever is current in their area. It is also possible that people use different labels to cover slightly different meanings—since this concept is the subject of philosophical debate, there is (as always) some scope for disagreement about exactly what sort of practices the name is meant to describe. It is not usually necessary to differentiate between the different terms, and we can usually agree with the statement in the Royal Commission Report that "Ultimately, it matters little whether in Canada we call this process employment equity or affirmative action, so long as we understand that what we mean by both terms are employment practices designed to eliminate discriminatory barriers and to provide in a meaningful way equitable opportunities in employment." (Judge R. Abella, *Equality in Employment, A Royal Commission Report*, 1984, Government of Canada.)

The fundamental idea of employment equity is that some steps be taken to provide advantages for members of traditionally disadvantaged groups to enhance their ability to participate fully in the social and economic life of the community. Discussion has tended to focus on opportunity to gain employment directly, but others issues such as access to education are also relevant.

Formulating the notion of employment equity immediately draws attention to some of the problems philosophers might want to consider in connection with it. For example, what is the definition of a "traditionally disadvantaged group"? Existing legislation has targeted four main groups: women, Native people, disabled persons, and visible minorities. However, these groups (at least the latter three) often have fuzzy boundaries, and some definition is needed of who does and who does not fit within them. Furthermore, one might ask whether there are sufficient reasons for singling out these groups as entitled to special benefits, when many other groups (e.g. Jews, Irish Catholics, etc.) have also been traditionally disadvantaged. Finally, there is a very important question which must be asked about why individuals might be thought to qualify for compensatory advantages simply in virtue of being members of groups which have been disadvantaged. If a group has been discriminated against, does it follow that every member of that group has been discriminated against? Should individuals have to demonstrate that they personally have been discriminated against? Will employment equity programs reach those who have suffered most from discrimination?

This formulation of the concept raises questions about defining the steps which might be taken to improve the lot of the disadvantaged. One aspect of this, of course, will involve determining what sorts of steps are likely to improve the situation. If discrimination (whether systematic or particular) could be eliminated simply by having someone get up and say "I don't think we should discriminate any more," it is doubtful that anyone would object. The real-life situation is obviously much more complex than this, and the proposed "remedies" often both require much more drastic measures, and prove to be difficult to assess in terms of effectiveness. The philosophical perspective may be useful in establishing what the test of success should be—should the goal be proportional representation immediately? A long-term shift in that direction? How does this compare with a meritocracy in which the most qualified people always get the job? (Asking this question does not imply that the existing state of affairs is such a meritocracy.) Do beneficiaries of employment equity programs suffer loss of self-esteem, and if so how important is such loss for assessing the programs?

Certainly one of the important questions in considering employment equity is "does it work?" Once goals have been established (such as improving the equality of a society), it is important to consider what means are most likely to help achieve the goal. However, these questions are largely empirical, and are not the primary interest of the question from the philosophical perspective. Philosophers are much more likely to be interested in figuring out whether it is morally acceptable to pursue the means called for. Suppose everyone agreed that it would be desirable if there were more equality (or a different type of equality) in society, and that means X, Y, and Z would be likely to bring about this goal. It would not follow immediately that X, Y and Z ought to be pursued. For example, someone might point out that pursuing policy X would violate his or her rights, or someone might claim that policy Y would bring about so much unhappiness as to outweigh the gain in equality. Much of the philosophical debate has centred around questions like this: what (if any) are the limits society faces in pursuing the goal of employment equity?

This subject also raises questions about what one thinks the role of government should be. Is government merely a neutral observer, mediating conflicts of interests between individuals? Does government have a positive duty to try to do what is best for its citizens? If government is to try to do what is in the best interests of the people, is this to be done by giving them what they want now, or by trying to judge what is in the people's long term interests, even if they do not see things the same way? Or perhaps government should strive to improve the moral quality of its citizens. How one views the role of government will affect what one's view will be of questions such as how far the government can intervene in order to bring about a desired state of affairs.

Finally, the issue of employment equity raises questions about what it is for a person to "deserve" a particular benefit of harm. What sort of "qualifications" are relevant in deciding who should get a given job? Do people have a right to be evaluated on one basis rather than another? What are the relative values of different properties such as talent, effort, the ability to be a role model, or previous accomplishment? In short, what criteria should be used in determining who will get a particular job, place in school, promotion, and so on? All these questions focus the philosopher's consideration of this moral issue.

Outline of the Employment Equity Act

Government of Canada

In 1986, the Government of Canada passed an Employment Equity bill, designed to help remedy inequalities in employment in Canada. The following is from a government paper published when the law was proposed, outlining the purpose and specifications of the act.

* * *

Purpose of the Act

The proposed Employment Equity Act is set in the context of growing government awareness of the need to affirm the rights of individuals, along with the recognition that certain groups within Canadian society do not share equally in the economic and social benefits gained from employment.

The purpose of this piece of legislation is to achieve equality in employment in recognition of the fact of the employment disadvantage suffered by some groups.

For the purposes of implementing Employment Equity, certain individuals or groups who are at an employment disadvantage are designated to benefit from Employment Equity. Programs to benefit those groups are permitted under section 15 of the Canadian Human Rights Act and under Section 15, subsection 2, of the Canadian Charter of Rights and Freedoms.

The designated groups are women, aboriginal peoples, persons with disabilities and persons who are, because of their race or colour, in a visible minority in Canada.

Employment Equity is a new term to express the result to be achieved—equality in employment—as well as the means to obtain it. Employment Equity is related to both equal opportunity programs and affirmative action.

Over the recent past, equal opportunity and affirmative action programs have been established voluntarily in different levels of government and private business in Canada.

Equal opportunity encourages employers to eliminate barriers affecting certain groups and thereby provide equal access to employment, training and promotion. Affirmative action provides a rational analytic process for employers to examine their human resources and employment systems, enabling decisions for remedying problems of target group under-representation where necessary.

Employment Equity is a results-oriented program which seeks evidence that employment situations for the designated groups are improving, indicated by their greater numerical representation in the workforce, improvement in their employment status, occupations, and salary levels in jobs for which they are available and qualified.

Employer's Duty

The Act provides a section to require employers to implement Employment Equity, and to describe the major elements of an Employment Equity program. General concepts are included as necessary components.

1. Identifying and eliminating any employment practice which has the effect of excluding members of designated groups.

Examples of such employment practices are:

- height or weight requirements;
- inflated educational requirements;
- training women for their current position while training men for promotion;

- lack of developmental or bridging positions out of clerical or other dead-end occupations;
- lack of accommodation for disabled employees; and
- reliance on formal as opposed to practical training experience.

2. Implementing new policies and practices with the objective of positively encouraging or facilitating the participation of the excluded groups.

Examples of such positive practices are:

- establishing experience equivalence and recruiting on that basis rather than according to formal education requirements;
- using target group associations or newspapers for selective recruitment of designated group members;
- creation of bridging positions to move employees from dead-end occupations into other categories;
- design of specific training, utilizing methods appropriate for designated group members, on-the-job training or special accommodation for disability, to enable movement of designated group members;
- provision of cooperative car pools or transportation;
- provision for job assignment programs to prepare a group of promotable employees;
- provision of, or assistance for, child care arrangements.

3. Making appropriate accommodation for members of designated groups to enable their entry into areas from which they had previously been excluded.

4. Setting up a program to ensure that the composition of the employer's person-

nel reflects the composition of the relevant pool of available workers, that is, the work-force.

Appropriate representation of designated group members is measured for: the geographic location of each employer; each occupational category; each of the designated groups; the recruitment area that is appropriate for each occupational group; and the appropriate group from which promotions are made. The appropriate degree of representation of target group members in an employer's organization is the degree of representation that reflects the demographic composition of the relevant recruitment (and promotion) population. The reference point in the population is those who are in the work force or would be if they were not excluded by employment barriers, those qualified for the work, those eligible (by reason of the necessary permit, license, union membership, etc.), and those within a reasonable recruitment or promotion area.

Employment Equity and Economic Growth

Background Paper

Government of Canada

The government also provided a background paper to discuss the extent of inequality in Canada, and the ways in which employment equity legislation might be expected to improve the situation. What follows is the government's account of the barriers facing each of the designated groups as of the time of proposing the employment equity legislation.

*　　　*　　　*

Despite a decade of voluntary affirmative action programs and equal opportunity laws, there has been little progress in the overall economic advancement of women in the labour force. Nevertheless, the trend is such that women's participation in the labour force is growing apace. In 1974, the participation rate of women between the ages of 25 and 54 years was 48 percent, and by 1984, that had jumped to 66.7 percent.

Women do not receive a fair return for their economic contributions. In 1984, women working full-time earned only 64 cents for every dollar earned by men. Women's occupational options are so narrow that fully three-quarters of employed women work in only five of the twenty-two major occupational groups. Most of these jobs are not only low-paying, but also dead-end, offering limited scope for advancement. In addition, structural changes due to microelectronics, automation and other technological developments threaten many of those jobs held by women. Women in 1984 accounted for 71 percent of all part-time workers, but part-time work provides fewer job benefits, security or promotional opportunities than full-time work. Historically, women's unemployment rate has always been higher than that of men.

The constraints to attaining full parity in the labour market include: a wage system which devalues jobs performed by women in the paid labour force; economically limiting job segregation and occupational concentration; lack of training opportunities and upward mobility....

Discriminatory barriers in employment compound the disadvantages to which disabled persons are subject. In addition to reduced opportunities for training, education and employment, disabled persons face a range of obstacles to the realization of their potential as productive workers.

Foremost is the attitude of many nondisabled persons: there is widespread misunderstanding and under-rating of the abilities of disabled persons.

There are other barriers. Inflated job standards often have a screening out effect. Only a careful examination of the content of a job can determine whether standards that eliminate the entry of disabled persons are truly essential to performance on the job. An advanced computer professional, for example, who, because of cerebral palsy, cannot fit the disc into the machine, should not be excluded from a job in which using the keyboard is obviously more important than inserting the disc. Thus, the job can be adjusted to provide assistance in fitting the disc—while retaining the skills of a competent worker.

Some barriers have to do with access to buildings or to work areas within buildings. People confined to wheelchairs are simply unable to get to certain places unless provision is made to accommodate them. Other barriers have to do with hours of work and methods of work. Since people with some

disabilities may not be able to do an eight-hour shift, it might be necessary to adjust the hours so that such persons, otherwise qualified, can work and contribute. Again, a whole range of technical aids permit people with vision or hearing problems, or other disabilities, to perform tasks which some employers might assume were impossible....

Native people face attitudinal and cultural barriers to their equitable participation in the economy. Racial intolerance and misunderstanding, unnecessary educational requirements for jobs and training and elaborate screening systems, tend to eliminate Native applicants. Native people generally have less formal education than non-Natives and less experience in highly skilled jobs in the labour market.

Native communities should stand to benefit from employment opportunities created by mining, exploration and other resource development activities in Northern communities. Experience, however, has not been conducive to sustaining hope for economic benefits. Faced with needing skilled workers unavailable in the neighbouring Native communities, employers frequently recruit non-Natives in the south.

The low Native labour force participation rates, high unemployment, low income and education levels are the results of numerous complex factors in operation for many years. The inequity faced by Native people in the labour market has severe social and economic effects, not only on Natives themselves, but on the Canadian economy as well. Without active measures to achieve equity in employment for Native people, the situation will not improve....

Research attests to the existence both of prejudicial attitudes to non-whites and systemic discrimination based on racial factors. A study released in January 1985 indicates that white job applicants receive three job offers for every one made to blacks. An adverse impact is apparent even when non-whites are highly trained and are in high-demand occupations. A June 1983 study of whites, blacks and Asian holders of master's degrees in business administration demonstrated that although the blacks and Asians sent more job applications and went to more interviews, they received fewer job offers than white applicants. The same study noted a 26 percent difference in income between white business professionals and similarly experienced visible minority counterparts.

There are a number of employment barriers that apply not exclusively to visible minorities but which, when combined with racial prejudice, exacerbate the difficulties. Thus, language, dress, religion, foreign credentials, cultural differences, and the requirement of "Canadian experience" can serve to sharpen the disadvantages experienced by visible minorities.

Employment problems vary also in accordance with the national origin of some visible minority groups. Recent immigrants from non-English or non-French speaking countries must first surmount a language barrier. Such immigrants are more concerned initially with services or programs to facilitate their entry into the job market than they are with racial prejudice.

Questions for Discussion

1   Is it legitimate to use statistics to establish unjust treatment of designated groups within society?

2   To what extent should measures to improve employment equity be optional for employers, as opposed to required?

3   The government suggests that employment equity would both do a better job of respecting people's rights, and improve the productive efficiency of the Canadian work-force. Are both of these elements necessary in order to justify a policy of employment equity?

Black Americans' Views of Racial Inequality

The Dream Deferred

Lee Sigelman and Susan Welch

There is considerable disagreement about the meaning of "employment equity" or "affirmative action," and often people's attitudes toward it seem to change depending on how it is defined. The following selection explores some of the aspects of this difference. It is based on comparative studies of blacks and whites in the United States. Of course, those findings may not carry over directly into Canada, but it is useful to see some of the ways in which different attitudes break down.

*   *   *

Jobs, education and affirmative action

Prior to the passage of the Civil Rights Act, job discrimination was the type of discrimination blacks resented most. In 1963, more blacks (30 percent) listed employment discrimination as affecting them than mentioned any other form of discrimination, with educational discrimination (11 percent) placing a distant second. Well over half believed their pay was lower than a white doing the same work would receive (Brink and Harris, 1964: 194). In another 1963 survey, 58 percent of blacks cited equal job opportunity as the highest priority for immediate government action; voting rights and school desegregation finished far behind, at 13 percent each, while only three percent mentioned integration of public accommodations (Schwartz, 1967). And in yet another 1963 survey, blacks rated the right to hold the same jobs as whites highest among "rights wanted by almost all Negroes" (Schwartz, 1967).

The Civil Rights Act outlawed discrimination in employment, but a quarter of a century after the passage of that landmark legislation blacks continue to lag in occupational status and pay. Although many potential solutions to this problem have been proposed, there still is no consensus about how to overcome job-related discrimination. There is, among both blacks and whites, a consensus that "Negroes should have as good a chance as white people to get any kind of job"; indeed, by the early 1970s agreement with this question had become so nearly unanimous that pollsters simply stopped asking it. Although this question now seems quite innocuous, as late as 1964 most whites actually disagreed with it, explicitly rejecting the principle of equal employment opportunity (Schuman et al., 1985: 74-5). Today the issue is not whether blacks deserve an equal chance, but how equal job opportunities are to be won.

On the question of means—of specific programs for integrating the workplace—consensus splinters. Indeed, affirmative action, a general label for a variety of procedures intended to open up job opportunities to minorities, women, and the physically handicapped, ranks alongside busing and abortions as one of the most heated public policy issues of our times. Many affirmative action procedures, such as the requirements that job vacancies be openly listed and that criteria for employment be related to the job skills needed, are not especially controversial, although numerous controversies have arisen about their application in particular circumstances. Other aspects of affirmative action have sparked great controversy. The use of numerical hiring goals has led to charges that "quota systems" are being established, and the implementation of hiring plans has fueled apprehension about "reverse discrimination" against white males.

Are blacks highly supportive of affirmative action? At least one scholar (Jacobson, 1983) has concluded that they are, but we recommend proceeding with great caution when analyzing public opinion on a topic as multi-faceted as affirmative action. It is a truism that "what the public thinks" about a particular issue depends on how the issue is framed, and that truism has never been more apt than in the case of affirmative action, where so much depends on the specific aspect of the policy respondents are asked to consider and the precise phrasing of the question. Depending on the question asked and on the specific language used, one could truthfully say that as many as 96 percent of all blacks and 76 percent of all whites are in favor of affirmative action. But equally correctly one could say that as few as 23 percent of all blacks and 9 percent of all whites support affirmative action. These dramatic differences stem from the great diversity of questions asked in opinion surveys, diversity that makes trend analyses of support for affirmative action nearly impossible.

Even within a single survey, opinions vary greatly depending on question wording. In the 1984 NBES, for example, 57 percent of a sample of 1,150 blacks agreed and 38 percent disagreed that "Minorities should be given special consideration when decisions are made about hiring applicants for jobs." Three questions later, 72 percent agreed that "Job applicants should be judged solely on the basis of test scores and other individual qualities." Admittedly, the phrase "and other individual qualities" is ambiguous, but it does seem clear that blacks, like whites, believe in merit as the major criterion in hiring while also wanting to make opportunities more available to minorities.

In Table 1, we catalogue responses to an array of survey questions concerning affirmative action that have been asked since the late 1970s. Wide variability is evident in these responses, but some patterns are evident amid that variability. First, the aspects of affirmative action that blacks see as most desirable also win the greatest approval among whites, and the aspects blacks like least are rejected most often by whites. Although the black-white differential in agreement with these items ranges from 5 to 40 percentage points, blacks and whites rank these options in much the same order; in fact, across the thirteen items the correlation between the percentage of

blacks agreeing and the percentage of whites agreeing is almost perfect.

In general, blacks appraise affirmative action most positively when responding to questions that either specifically mention that no quotas are involved or are worded in a vague, nonthreatening manner (e.g., the items about giving minorities and women a "chance" and allowing them to "get ahead," neither of which alludes to quotas or preferential treatment). Most blacks also look favorably upon training programs. Responding to questions like these, upwards of 75 percent of blacks say they support affirmative action. Responding to the same questions, whites are also highly supportive; on each of the first six questions more than 60 percent of white respondents express support for affirmative action.

On the other hand, affirmative action finds few supporters, black or white, when the idea of giving minorities special treatment to make up for past discrimination is directly contrasted with hiring solely on the basis of merit (see also Bolce and Gray, 1979; Lipset and Schneider, 1978; Sackett, 1980). Presented with such a choice, only about one black in four supports special treatment, and not even one white in ten does so.

Thus, most blacks agree with most whites on eight of the thirteen items in Table 1—the first six and the last two. On all eight of these questions, blacks are more supportive of affirmative action than whites are, but there is no fundamental disagreement between blacks and whites about what is most acceptable and what least so.

On the seventh item in Table 1, which concerns the idea that employers should reserve positions for hiring qualified blacks, three blacks in four and a bare majority of

---

Table 1. Support for affirmative action in employment, blacks and whites, 1977-1988 (in %)

	Blacks	Whites
Affirmative action programs that help blacks get ahead should be supported (1980-G)	96	76
Agree that after years of discrimination only fair to set up special programs to ensure that women and minorities and given every chance to have equal opportunities in employment and education (1978-H)	91	71
Favor affirmative action programs in employment for blacks, provided there are no rigid quotas		
(1978-H)	89	67
(1988-H)	78	73
Approve of requiring large companies to set up special training programs for members of minority groups (1977-NYT)	88	63
Favor affirmative action programs in employment for blacks, provided there are no rigid quotas (1988-H)	78	73
As long as no quotas, makes sense to give special training and advice to women and minorities so they can perform better on the job (1978-H)	77	70
Employers should set aside places to hire qualified blacks and other minorities (1980-G)	73	51
Approve of requiring businesses to hire a certain number of minority workers (1977-NYT)	64	35
Approve of requiring some corporations to practice affirmative action, sometimes requiring special preference to minorities or women when hiring (1978-C)	58	35[a]
Approve Supreme Court decision allowing employer to set up special training and promotion program for minorities and women (1978-H)	56	36
Support Court ruling allowing employers to favor women and minorities in hiring over better qualified men and whites (1987-G)	56	25
Support giving blacks preference in getting jobs over equally qualified whites because of past discrimination against blacks (1984-GJ)	49	9
To make up for past discrimination, women and minorities should be given preferential treatment in getting jobs and places in college as opposed to mainly considering ability as determined by test scores (1985J, 1984G)	23	10[a]

Notes: The correlation between the percentage of blacks supporting a given policy and the corresponding percentage of whites is .92.

a   The survey is of the entire public, not just whites. *Sources*: H = Louis Harris and Associates, G = Gallup Poll, NYT = *New York Times*, C = Cambridge Survey Research, summarized by Lipset and Schneider (1978), J = Lawrence Johnson and Associates and Metro Research Services, summarized by Lichter (1985), GJ = Gallup Joint Center Poll.

whites agree. This contrasts with the response pattern on the next item, where most blacks support but most whites oppose requiring businesses to hire a certain number of minority workers. The disparity in responses evoked by the seventh and eighth items may seem odd, given the overlapping content of the two items, but the seventh question merely suggests that employers "should" set aside places for minorities, while the eighth inquires about "requiring" businesses to do so. Moreover, the seventh question also refers to hiring "qualified" blacks, but the eighth makes no mention of qualifications. Together, these wording differences seem sizable enough to account for the observed disparity in responses.

There is substantial black-white disagreement on three other items. The differential is greatest (40 percentage points) on a 1984 item asking whether because of past discrimination, blacks should be given job preference over "equally qualified whites"—an idea endorsed by about half of black respondents but only one white in ten. There is also racial discord on a question concerning a Supreme Court decision allowing employers to set up special training and promotion programs for minorities and women. Ordinarily, we suppose that most people would assent to this sort of "soft" scenario "allowing" employers to set up training and promotion programs. However, not only is the wording of the question quite lengthy and complex,[1] but the question points out that critics of the Court ruling alleged that whites and males were victims of reverse discrimination and that seniority rights would be violated. These cues seem to have triggered negative responses among whites.

A third item over which there is great disagreement between blacks and whites concerns a 1987 Supreme Court ruling that it is permissible for an employer to hire a woman instead of a man who scored slightly higher on a screening test. Unfortunately for the sake of gauging support for the Court's decision, the Gallup Poll oversimplified the issue by asking whether employers should be able to favor women and minorities in hiring over "better qualified" men and whites. Unless a screening test were extraordinarily reliable, a difference of only a few points would presumably say virtually nothing about the relative qualifications of the two job applicants. Nonetheless, even though it does not fairly represent the substance of the Court's holding, this item taps into respondents' reactions to preferential treatment, and we learn from it that many Americans find the idea of bypassing a "better qualified" applicant repugnant; just over half of blacks and only a quarter of whites are willing to say that the "better qualified" applicant should not get the job.[2]

The general patterns we have observed in blacks' attitudes toward affirmative action in employment are echoed in their attitudes toward affirmative action in education, shown in Table 2. On three of these six items, blacks are strongly supportive of affirmative action, while on the other three most blacks oppose affirmative action practices. Again, the specific wording of the items greatly influences support. Blacks overwhelmingly favor affirmative action when no quotas are involved (the first item), when black applicants are qualified and no mention is made of qualified whites being turned away (the second item), and when only vague reference is made to "special consideration to the best minority students" (the third item). Most blacks reject affirmative action when it is specifically

---

Table 2. Support for affirmative action in education, blacks and whites, 1976-1980 (in %)

	Blacks	Whites
Favor affirmative action in higher education for blacks, provided there are no rigid quotas (1978-H)	91	68
Colleges and universities should set aside a certain number of positions to admit qualified blacks and other minorities (1980-KS)	84	60
Approve of a college giving special consideration to best minority applicants to help more get admitted (1977-CBS/NYT)	64	35
Approve of a school reserving a certain number of places for qualified minority applicants even if some qualified white applicants wouldn't be admitted (1977-CBS/NYT)	46	32
Choose black applicant for last opening to law school in a case where a white student has better college record but both black and white meet qualifications (1976-H)	42	14
Approve of medical school lowering its standards to enroll black medical student who may not have the right qualifications but shows real promise (1976-H)	37	10

Sources: H = Louis Harris and Associates, KS = Kluegel and Smith, CBS/NYT = CBS News/*New York Times*.

---

noted that qualified whites would be turned away (the fourth and fifth items) and when it is assumed that the black applicant is unqualified (the sixth item). Even under the latter conditions, however, a sizable minority of blacks still supports affirmative action.

Again, whites are less supportive of these affirmative action practices, though most do support affirmative action as described in the first and second questions. Only about one white in three endorses giving "special consideration to the best minority applicants" or reserving places for qualified minorities when some qualified whites must be turned away. Even fewer whites favor the affirmative action procedures pinpointed in the last two items: choosing a black over a better qualified white and lowering standards for unqualified blacks. On these items, as on the earlier questions on affirmative action in the workplace, blacks are 20 to 30 percent more supportive of affirmative action than are whites.

Explaining attitudes on affirmative action

The key to understanding public opinion on affirmative action has been said to lie in the distinction between compensatory action and preferential treatment (Lipset and Schneider, 1980). Thus understood, compensatory action involves "measures to help disadvantaged groups catch up to the standards of competition set by the larger society," while preferential treatment involves "suspending those standards and admitting or hiring members of disadvantaged groups who do not meet the same standards as white males" (41). Relatively few whites, Lipset and Schneider argue, object to compensatory action, but most renounce policies involving preferential treatment. In other words, most whites are said to be willing "to provide minorities with a starting point on the inside lane" but still believe that "ultimately the race must go to the swift" (Sackett, 1980: 22).

We doubt that the distinction between compensatory action and preferential treatment holds the key to understanding attitudes toward affirmative action, especially since compensatory action is a form of preferential treatment and preferential treatment is a type of compensatory action. The picture that emerges from our data is much more complex than Lipset and Schneider's distinction. The main elements in this picture are as follows.

First, both whites and blacks support programs designed to allow minorities to "get ahead," to deliver training, to provide equal opportunities, and to extend affirmative action as long as no quotas are involved. Second, blacks but not whites favor general "affirmative action" strategies even when quotas are not explicitly disavowed. Third, blacks tend to be divided and whites to be negative about affirmative action policies that pass over equally or more qualified whites. Finally, most members of both races oppose preferential hiring when such preferences run afoul of the principle of merit.

More generally, supporters of affirmative action consider it necessary in order to make up for past racism and to ensure that blacks have a fair chance at jobs and higher educational opportunities. Opponents argue that because affirmative action inappropriately focuses on group characteristics rather than individual qualifications, it may lead to people being admitted to college or being hired even though they are less qualified than others who are passed over. These rationales for supporting or opposing affirmative action are reflected in Table 3, which summarizes what blacks and whites think would happen in the absence of affirmative action.

Three blacks in four say that affirmative action is needed to ensure that blacks get a "fair shake" and, more concretely, to forestall a dropoff in black access to jobs and education. Only one black in five sees affirmative action as inevitably leading to reverse discrimination against white males.

Only 42 percent of blacks consider preferential treatment—the aspect of affirmative action whites find most objectionable—fair. The enthusiasm blacks display for affirmative action, then, is clearly not premised on endorsement of preferential treatment. This enthusiasm, in fact, can be said to hold in spite of blacks' qualms about the principle of preferential treatment. Obviously, for most blacks affirmative action is not a synonym for preferential treatment.

In stark contrast to most blacks, most whites do not agree that without affirmative action blacks would be denied a "fair shake" or that blacks' opportunities for schooling and jobs would be adversely affected. This view is, of course, quite consistent with the widespread perception among whites, that racial discrimination is not really much of a problem in this country. Beyond this, many whites consider affirmative action undesirable as well as unnecessary: 40 percent of whites believe that it leads to reverse discrimination, twice as high as the black proportion, and most

Table 3. Perceptions of the consequences of affirmative action, blacks and whites, 1978 and 1980 (in %)

	Blacks	Whites
Without affirmative action blacks would not get a fair shake		
Agree	74	26
Without quotas there will be a slowing of hiring of blacks		
Agree	75	45
Unsure	11	13
Without affirmative action, women and minorities will fail to get their fair share of jobs and education		
Agree	73	42
Unsure	16	19
Affirmative action is bound to lead to reverse discrimination against white men		
Agree	20	40
Unsure	20	15
Preferential treatment (setting aside places to hire qualified blacks) is fair		
Agree	42	35

Notes and Sources: Question wordings and sources (in order): "Unless quotas are used, blacks and other minorities just won't get a fair shake." (Harris, 1978). "In business and education, without set quotas there will be a slowing down in the hiring of blacks and other minorities" (Harris, 1978). "If there are no affirmative action programs helping women and minorities in employment and education, then these groups will continue to fail to get their share of jobs and higher education, thereby continuing past discrimination in the future" (Harris, 1978). "Once affirmative action programs for women and minorities are started, the result is bound to be reverse discrimination against white men" (Harris, 1978). "Do you personally feel that such preferential treatment [for blacks] is/would be fair, unfair" (Kluegel and Smith, 1980).

whites, like most blacks, do not believe that preferential treatment is fair.

On the other hand, when we add to the whites who support affirmative action on the first three items in Table 3 the fairly substantial number who are uncertain, we see that most whites at least are open to the possibility that progress toward racial equality would be slower in the absence of affirmative action.

These data suggest that in addition to assessing the effects of affirmative action differently, many blacks and whites actually define affirmative action differently. Most blacks concede that preferential treatment is unfair, but still support the other components of affirmative action. Most whites also consider preferential treatment unfair, but whites are more likely than blacks to regard preferential treatment as a central component of affirmative action. Large minorities of whites support affirmative action only when they are assured that no quota system or preferential treatment is involved.

Many whites simply do not see any need for affirmative action since they do not perceive that much racial discrimination exists. This denial, compounded by the tendency to view themselves as potential victims of "reverse discrimination," goes far toward explaining why so many whites bitterly oppose affirmative action. On the other hand, blacks, most of whom have personally experienced discrimination, are more likely to consider affirmative action a necessary tool for black advancement.

Notes

1 The stem of this question actually contains 101 words, upholding the tradition that survey questions about the Supreme Court's affirmative action decisions are generally complex. Harris polls in particular tend to ask long, complicated questions describing a case and laying out the issues. Providing background information may seem useful, since most people know little or nothing about a given Supreme Court decision. However, long, complicated questions tend to confuse respondents (See Converse and Presser, 1986: 11-13, 24-5).

Another extremely complicated Harris item on affirmative action related to the Court's 1978 *Bakke* decision (Louis Harris and Associates, 1978). The 171-word stem of this item informed respondents that the Court had held against quotas and in favor of special consideration for members of disadvantaged races: "Recently, the U.S. Supreme Court handed down a decision in the Bakke case. A white man, Alan Bakke, claimed that he was refused admission to a University of California medical school because the school automatically set aside 16 out of 100 places in the freshman class for non-whites, even if on their tests the non-whites scored below whites who applied. The Supreme Court decided that Bakke had been the victim of reverse discrimination and should be admitted to the medical school. The Court also decided that such rigid quotas as setting aside 16 out of 100 places for non-whites are not proper or legal. At the same time, the Court made clear that students from less advantaged races may be given special considerations on racial grounds. In effect, then, the Supreme Court decided that strict quotas are out, and affirmative action could be used to make up for past discrimination against racial minorities. All in all, do you personally favor or oppose the U.S. Supreme Court decision in the Bakke case?"

Seventy-seven percent of the white respondents and 29 percent of the black respondents said they favored the decision, with 23 percent of the blacks and 11 percent of the whites indicating uncertainty. Unfortunately, it is not apparent which aspect of the Bakke decision, as summarized in the Harris question, would have struck a particular respondent as more salient—the Court's rejection of strict quotas or its general endorsement of affirmative action. In light of the other evidence we have analyzed on whites' attitudes toward affirmative action, it seems likely that whites were indicating support for the overturning of quotas. However, black support for quotas has never been strong, so it is difficult to know the basis of the overwhelmingly negative black reaction to the question.

2 In the facts of the specific case, it appeared that the white woman candidate had a lower test score than the leading white male candidate only because of a more subjective oral interview conducted by a panel of men who had never hired a woman for a professional position. We doubt that this can be translated into a more general rule about hiring the "less qualified" under other circumstances.

Questions for Discussion

1 What is the relationship between a) programs which aim at allowing members of traditionally disadvantaged groups to "get ahead," b) quotas for employment or education, and c) the principle of merit?

Justified Inequality?

An Exchange on Preferential Treatment

Robert L. Simon and Sara Ann Ketchum: Exchange from *Analysis*

In the following exchange, Simon and Ketchum debate the applicability of facts about groups to decisions about individuals who are members of those groups.

*   *   *

Statistical Justifications of Discrimination

Robert L. Simon

A. 80% of the candidates who score poorly on Test *T* will fail to graduate from the university due to academic deficiencies. Therefore, the university is justified in refusing to admit *any* candidate who scores poorly on *T*.

B. 80% of women lack the physical strength to perform job *J*. Therefore, employers are justified in refusing to consider *any* women as candidates for *J*.

C. 80% of the members of group *G* are victims of past injustice. Therefore, compensatory programs are justified in providing benefits to *all* members of *G*.

Sara Ann Ketchum and Christine Pierce recently criticized arguments of kind *B* (*Analysis* 36, no. 2, 91-5). They allow that "statistical differences between the sexes would indicate that justice does not require equal distribution of women and men...within given job categories." But they deny that "all women may justifiably be discriminated against in hiring if sufficiently fewer women than men are qualified" (92,93). On the other hand, James Nickel has defended arguments of kind *C* (*Analysis* 34, no. 5, 154-60). Nickel argues

that while preferential discrimination in favor of black persons as a group may not be justifiable by ideal principles of compensatory justice, it can be justified by administrative or pragmatic factors. Where there is a high correlation between being a victim of social injustice, there is a pragmatic justification for compensating all members of the group in question. It would just be too costly and difficult to evaluate cases on an individual basis. Nickel concedes that the pragmatic approach "may result in a certain degree of unfairness" but maintains that "it does not help to decrease administrative costs so that more resources can be directed to those in need" (James Nickel, "Classification by Race in Compensatory Programs," *Ethics* 84, no. 2 [1974], 148; see also his "Preferential Policies in Hiring and Admissions," *Columbia Law Review* 75, p. 534).

Can one justifiably reject arguments such as *B*, which use statistical generalizations to justify discrimination *against* a particular group, yet accept arguments such as *C*, which use similar generalizations to justify discrimination *in favor* of a particular group? I will argue that to the extent that one agrees with Ketchum and Pierce in rejecting the use of statistical generalizations to justify discrimination against persons of a particular sex or race, one is committed to rejection of Nickel's pragmatic defense of preferential discrimination as well. Either there is no difference between the two or, if there are differences, they are not such as to justify any difference in evaluation of the arguments.

Consider an at least relatively benign use of statistical generalizations, such as that found in *A*. Surely, the university's policy is an acceptable one, at least if either it is impossible to tell whether any given candidate of the kind in question will wind up in the 80% who fail or the 20% who succeed, or if it is excessively costly to make such fine distinctions, and no other relevant information about the candidates is easily obtainable.

If such pragmatic considerations are sufficient to justify the use of statistical generalizations as a basis for discrimination in all contexts then *B* and *C* would be as acceptable as *A*. Discrimination for and against particular groups would be justifiable on cost accounting grounds alone. But then, the price of accepting Nickel's argument for preferential discrimination, given the appropriate empirical claims about efficiency, is that we are committed to accepting arguments of kind *B*, given similar empirical claims about efficiency. But if, as is surely the case, arguments from efficiency do not justify discrimination against women or blacks, then arguments from efficiency for preferential discrimination in favor of women and blacks are unacceptable as well (at least where such preferential treatment in favor of group members requires a denial of positions to non-members).

One might reply, however, that there is an important difference between *A* and *C*, on the one hand, and *B* on the other. For it can be argued that discrimination directed against persons of a particular race or sex as such is inherently invidious and degrading and so cannot be justified by arguments that may be acceptable in more innocuous contexts. Although Nickel's pragmatic approach would disfavor some white persons, its *intent* is not to discriminate against whites as such but rather is to extend certain benefits to the unjustly victimized. Similarly, the intent of the university in *A* is not to practice systematic and pervasive discrimination against previously low achievers who could nevertheless do university level work. Rather, it is to serve more efficiently the university's high priority educational goals.

This reply will not do, however, for *B* would remain objectionable even if the intent of employers is not to discriminate against women as such but only to maximize profits. To distinguish in the way suggested between *A* and *C*, on the one hand, and *B* on the other, is to countenance discrimination against a particular race or sex whenever the purpose of such discrimination is in itself benign, e.g. to maximize profits.

Nickel himself argues that correlations appealed to by racists (and presumably by sexists as well) are spurious (*Analysis* 34, no. 5, 156ff.) However, Ketchum and Pierce acknowledge that there may in fact be some statistical differences between the sexes in areas relevant to job qualifications. And some tests used to select among job applicants have had an adversely disproportionate effect on blacks.[1] So the issue of whether statistical generalizations justify discrimination against individuals remains even when false and invidious generalizations cited by racists are left out of the picture.

Perhaps, however, the difference between *B* and *C* lies not in the *intent* to discriminate but in actual discriminatory effect. That is, given past invidious discrimination against a group, even benignly motivated discrimination now practiced against that group is likely to stigmatize members of the affected group and, at the very least, continue to perpetuate that group's unfairly imposed subordinate position. Thus, discrimination against blacks is so objectionable precisely because it contributes to or at least perpetuates the effect of past discrimination in creating an especially disadvantaged caste. Discrimination against whites has no such effect, for whites do not constitute an especially disadvantaged caste, nor is preferential discrimination likely to reduce them to such a state.

While such an argument might be quite strong in a world of sharp and clear caste distinctions, contemporary western society is not such a world. For what the argument implies is "that the white majority is monolithic and so politically powerful as not to require the...safeguards afforded minority racial groups. But the white majority is pluralistic, containing within itself a multitude of religious and ethnic minorities—Catholics, Jews, Italians, Irish, Poles, and many others who are vulnerable to prejudice and who to this day suffer from the effects of past discrimination."[2] Discrimination against individual members of such groups may perpetuate the psychological, social and economic effects of past discrimination. And while these effects may be more serious on the average for blacks, it is just the propriety of jumping from premises about the average to conclusions about individuals that is at issue.

Finally, it may be suggested that the difference between *B* and *C* lies in the difference in cost of obtaining the data that would make reliance on statistical generalizations unnecessary. Thus, it is relatively easy to test individuals for strength but relatively difficult to find out just what degree of injustice a particular individual may have suffered. Thus, *B* is unacceptable precisely because it is so easy to avoid appeals to statistical generalizations in the context at hand. On the other hand, *C* at least has a plausible claim to acceptability just because of the difficulty of getting the relevant information about individual cases.

While there may well be this difference between *B* and *C*, it is not a significant difference. Thus, we would find arguments of kind *B* objectionable even it was quite difficult to verify claims about the strength of particular individuals. This can be brought out by comparing *B* and *A*. Surely, the savings in cost would have to be far higher to warrant appeal to statistical generalizations to justify discrimination against women or blacks than to justify the use of standardized tests in university admissions.

This can be brought out more clearly if we consider an alternative to the use of Test *T* in the admissions process. Suppose that the university finds that the presence in an applicant's background of (i) a family which has been mired in poverty for generations, (ii) a father who lacks a university education and (iii) a family history of diabetes is an excellent predictor of academic failure. Suppose further that it actually is less costly to verify the presence of these factors in particular cases than to administer *T*. But even given the above suppositions, we surely would think it *unfair* if the university promulgated a rule to the effect that candidates who satisfied (i), (ii) and (iii) would be eliminated from consideration *without even being given the chance to take the test.* On the contrary, each individual at least has a claim to be considered on his or her individual abilities and talents. Even if (i), (ii), and (iii) turn out to be better predictors than *T*, *T* is morally relevant to the making of academic decisions in a way that they are not. It is the refusal to allow certain students even to try for admission, when based on ascriptive grounds, that is unjust or unfair. Thus, it is not simply the *cost* of obtaining information that is at stake. The *kind* of information obtained and employed is morally relevant as well. (Similarly, even if it could be shown that certain genetic irregularities were excellent indicators of criminal tendencies in individuals, detention of individuals with such genetic irregularities prior to the commission of any crime would be unfair. This is particularly true if the purpose of such prior detention was simply to cut the costs of police work involved in finding a fleeing criminal.)

Likewise, since *B* and *C* replace consideration of morally relevant data with identification of ascriptive characteristics, they are similar in a morally significant way. Each involves a significant degree of unfairness to individuals. Now, it may be that in some contexts avoidance of excessive costs should take precedence over avoidance of unfairness. But if that is so, avoidance of the same amount of cost will count as much in favor of discrimination against blacks and women as in favor of discrimination benefiting blacks and women.

Accordingly, even if *B* and *C* are different in the way suggested, it is far from clear that this difference is sufficient to demonstrate the moral acceptability of *C* and the moral unacceptability of *B*. The gains in efficiency involved may not be sufficient to compensate for the unfairness to individuals. And, at the very least, the price of opting for efficiency with respect to *C* is that of acknowledging that similar gains in efficiency would warrant discrimination against the very groups compensatory policies are designed to benefit. Given the nature of the price, we should be especially wary of accepting the claims of efficiency at the price of fairness.

Isn't there a difference, however, between sacrificing justice to efficiency *in order to right a wrong* and making a similar sacrifice for efficiency's sake alone? And isn't *that* the difference between *B* and *C*? That is, Nickel's argument may be interpreted as having moral as well as pragmatic force. The point of using Nickel's approach, on this interpretation, is to minimize injustice by providing compensation to a high proportion of those who are entitled to it at costs which impose a less severe burden on the rest of the community than would implementation of ideal principles of compensatory justice.

However, this kind of response begs one of the crucial issues at stake. For surely one of the major points at issue in the debate over preferential discrimination is whether such treatment creates new injustice by substituting group considerations for evaluation of individual cases. Indeed if, as I have suggested, the substitution of ascriptive criteria for consideration of individual cases does involve a significant degree of unfairness to individuals, then it will not be easy to show that the pragmatic approach minimizes injustice. Nickel is not entitled simply to *assume* that any injustice involved is outweighed *on the scales of justice* by the compensatory benefits provided. That the pragmatic approach cuts costs of administration is indeed initially plausible. That it minimizes injustice as well is far more controversial and thus requires significant additional support.

The price, then, of shifting from a strategy of increasing efficiency to one of minimizing injustice is that of decreased initial credibility and consequent assumption of a far heavier burden of proof.

Perhaps that burden can be met. Or perhaps alternate justifications of preferential treatment for groups are acceptable. It seems to me that those are the issues on which debate should focus. Appeal to statistical generalizations will not help us here. If such appeals are understood as appeals to efficiency, they are vulnerable to the sorts of objections raised earlier. If they are understood as appeals to justice, they simply raise at a new level the very questions about fairness to individuals that the appeal to the administrative approach was designed to help us avoid.

Logically, then, one cannot have it both ways. If purely pragmatic appeal to statistical generalizations can justify preferential discrimination in favor of women and black persons, then, given corresponding gains in efficiency, it can justify discrimination against those groups as well. In each kind of case, fairness to individuals requires consideration of relevant factors, but in each kind of case the appeal is to ascriptive classifications instead. But the price of appealing pragmatically to ascriptive considerations in one kind of case is that of logical commitment to similar appeals in similar contexts in the other kind of case. Even given significant gains in predictive power and efficiency, this sort of commitment is one of which we ought to be exceedingly wary. The moral status of discrimination remains the same, even though its victims and beneficiaries may change.

I am grateful to the National Endowment for the Humanities and the Center for Advanced Study in the Behavioral Sciences for their support of my work. I am also indebted to Brian Barry, Elizabeth Ring and the Editor [of *Analysis*] for helpful comments on an earlier draft.

Notes

1 Whether such tests are constitutional if there is no intent on the part of those giving it to discriminate is an issue that has been considered by the United States Supreme Court. In *Washington v. Davis*, the Court held that it was not sufficient to show simply that more black than white applicants had failed a qualifying examination for police recruits; in addition, the Court required that the plaintiffs demonstrate a racially discriminatory purpose.

2 This passage, quoted from Professor Lavinsky's contribution to the "DeFunis Symposium," *Columbia Law Review* (1975), 520, 527, was quoted favorably by the Supreme Court of California in *Allan Bakke v. the Regents of the State of California* in which it overthrew the University of California at Davis's program of preferential admission to medical school for black applicants.

Evidence, Statistics and Rights: A Reply to Simon

Sara Ann Ketchum

In a recent paper in *Analysis*, Christine Pierce and I argued that being a member of a group, a high percentage of which are unqualified, is not in itself a disqualification for a job.[1] For example, individual women whose physical strength is not known should not be disqualified from job J on the grounds that, for example, 80 percent of women lack the strength to perform job J. In response to our paper, Robert Simon[2] has charged that this claim is in conflict with an argument for compensatory programs such as the one offered by James Nickel.[3] Nickel argues that compensation is due to victims of past discrimination in the form of programs of special benefits. Although such programs are justified on the basis of injuries suffered, the administrative basis for the distribution of benefits will most likely be a characteristic such as race rather than proof of suffering (155). White males will suffer injustice, according to Simon, "where such preferential treatment in favor of group members requires a denial of positions to non-members" (38).

I

I will agree with Simon that the argument which Nickel presents for compensatory programs would not be a particularly good argument for preferential hiring. However, the major weakness of Nickel's argument is also a weakness of Simon's analysis. That is, they both assume that the connection between being black in a white-supremacist society and having suffered injustice is properly represented by the notion of statistical correlation, that the alternatives are requiring proof of suffering or distributing on the basis of a characteristic which is merely statistically correlated with being a victim of injustice. Thus, as Simon presents Nickel's argument, the relevant characteristic of the group to be compensated is that, for example, 80 percent of its members have suffered injustice.

A comparison of two examples would show that the statistical correlation between group membership and injustice does not represent the connection assumed by defenders of compensatory programs. Imagine the following two societies:

A. In society *A* there is an established pattern of white supremacy such that blacks are treated unjustly because they are black. That is, the fact that an individual is black is a reason, either covert or overt, for treating him or her unjustly. By some peculiar acci-

dental circumstance, or by some weakness or failure of the system of white supremacy, 20 percent of the blacks in this society have never suffered an injustice—they are immune not only to racism, but also to any other system of injustice prevalent in the society.

B. In society *B*, being black is never a social reason for being unjustly treated. There is no history or present practice of racism, black slavery, etc. However, there are practices of discrimination against three groups, and only three groups—for example, people over 65, members of a particular religious group, say, Baptists, and people who come from a particular region. Because of accidental demographic patterns, 80 percent of blacks belong to one or the other of these groups and suffer the injustices levelled against these groups. But, within these groups, blacks and whites are treated exactly the same—that is a 70-year-old black would be treated the same as a 70-year-old white and a 30-year-old black would be treated exactly the same as a 30-year-old white, etc.

The argument Simon portrays would entail that we have just as much reason for assigning benefits on the basis of race in society *B* as in society *A*. And, although Nickel makes it clear that he intends to be dealing only with *A*, his analysis does not adequately capture the difference. But the defense of compensatory programs always takes place within a historical context, and Nickel is simply assuming that context. It would be more appropriate to assume that the characteristic which should be connected to the injustice and, hence, relevant to the distribution of compensatory benefits would be something like the following (I will call it *C*, for short):

C: Being an *X* in a *Y*-supremacist society, where the superiority of *Y*'s is defined in terms of the inferiority of *X*'s.

The Y-supremacy might include, but not be exhaustively described by: discrimination in favor of Y's against X's in hiring, access to education and other goods; a systematic ideology of the inferiority of X's and the superiority of Y's; a systematic concentration of political and economic power in the hands of Y's and exclusion of X's from such power, etc.

The connection between characteristic C and the property of having suffered injustice is not a merely empirical correlation. There is a logical or conceptual connection which cannot be captured by any statistical statement. The empirical question is whether or not a given society is Y-supremacist and the degree and pervasiveness of the Y-supremacy. Statistics are relevant as evidence that a specific society is Y-supremacist, but they are not sufficient. The claim that a society is Y-supremacist implies that there are practices, institutions and habits of action and thought which are (i) about the relative social position appropriate to X's and Y's or about the relative capacities of X's and Y's, and (ii) productive of unjust equalities between X's and Y's.

Thus, I would agree with Simon that, in cases where there is a mere statistical correlation between being X and having suffered injustice it would probably not be appropriate to distribute compensatory benefits on the basis of being X. I disagree, however, with Simon's assumption that this is an appropriate description of either present-day American racism or present-day American sexism. Thus, I would not agree that the failure of this argument would constitute a point against the practice of distributing compensatory benefits on the grounds of being a black in a white-supremacist society such as our own. In such a program, one would not be distributing benefits on

the basis of race or sex *per se* (for example, a black from a black African country might not be due any compensation for racism) but on the basis of one's past and present social status.

II

Simon seems to assume without argument that the white males who would get jobs if there were no policy of preferential treatment have a right to those jobs, and that those jobs would be, so to speak, "stolen" from them by the blacks and women who are hired on such a policy. The first thing to point out is that a policy which is preferential in intent may not be preferential in effect. Employers who are, as one should expect them to be, influenced in their thinking by the society in which they were raised and live might hire qualified blacks only if they thought they were giving preference to blacks, by the same mechanism which leads them to think of themselves as turning down unqualified blacks when they refuse to hire qualified blacks.

The problems that remain even if we assume that the policy is one that has a preferential effect and not just a preferential intent, are perhaps more serious. Let us suppose, for a particular job which requires advanced education, that under a system of blind review or an impartial merit system the proportion of white males to blacks and women hired would be roughly equivalent to their distribution in the candidate pool (that is, people with the appropriate degrees). Say the proportion is 2 percent black and 15 percent female. Suppose further that a policy of preferential hiring would increase those percentages to 5 percent and 20 percent, respectively. Thus, approximately 13 percent of white males who would have gotten jobs on the policy of blind hiring would not get jobs with preferential hiring. However, even with preferential hiring of this degree the proportion of white males in the profession will be several times their proportion in the population—that is, white males, who are a minority of the population, will hold a large majority of the professional positions. If we are not to assume that there are vast differences in innate abilities between blacks and whites and between men and women, then it seems reasonable to believe that the disproportionate number of white males in the applicant pool is a result of discrimination and of white male supremacy. That is, most of the difference between the percentage of white males with the appropriate training and the percentage of white males in the population is a result of past discrimination in their favor and of social and political advantages created by racism and sexism. Since, even with preferential hiring, the proportion of white males hired is considerably larger than the proportion of white males in the population, it is reasonable to assume that even such a policy of preference will grant many white males jobs they would not have received if the system had been non-discriminatory from the beginning.

Let us consider a job candidate, Mr. White, who: (i) will get job X, or some better job Y, if the discrimination in favor of white males continues; (ii) would have gotten job X if a policy of blind review or an unbiased application of the merit principle were used in the hiring practice and were based on present qualifications the possession of which is, in part, related to past discriminatory policies; and (iii) would not have been in the applicant pool at all (that is, would not have received the necessary training) if there had been no discrimination

in favor of white males in the process through which he has obtained his education. Thus, he would not have received job X, if there had been no discrimination in his favor.

Simon assumes that Mr. White has a *right* to job X (or that an injustice would be done in denying him job X), although not to job Y. His assumption implies that, although Mr. White does not have a right to have discrimination in his favor continued, he does have a right to the perquisites of whatever position he has already gained from past discrimination in his favor.

Much is often made of the fact that Mr. White is not morally responsible for the injustices from which he is benefiting. But, surely, this is not sufficient to show that he has a right to benefit from these injustices. His lack of responsibility for such injustices is only relevant to the question of whether or not he should be punished for them or be required to make reparation for them. If Mr. White is prevented from benefiting from past injustices by others in his favor, it is inappropriate to claim that this constitutes his being punished or asked to make reparation. If this analysis is right, then, the suffering that Simon claims the young white males to be paying for the sins of their elders turns out to be the suffering of those who would not be able to benefit as much from past injustices as they had hoped or expected. This may be genuine and even innocent suffering, but it is not the suffering of the victim of present injustice.

Moreover, if the hiring goals are not compensatory—that is, if the goal is to hire roughly the same percentage of blacks who are in the qualified applicant pool—Mr. White's position is even shakier. In that case, the white males who do not get jobs under the system of goals will be even more likely to include those who not only would not have had the training had there never been discrimination, but would also not have gotten the job in question, if, given the present distribution of qualifications, racism were to disappear suddenly and miraculously from the hiring practice. Mr. White is then in a position of having to show that the probability and moral seriousness of his not being hired for extraneous reasons is greater than the probability and moral seriousness of some black's not being hired because of racism if the goals were not present. If we assume that there is a greater probability that white males will be unjustly treated under nonpreferential goals than that members of groups discriminated against will be unjustly treated if we allow past practices to continue, we are presupposing that members of groups discriminated against in the applicant pool are generally less qualified than white males. Unless we assume that employers will not be able to find well qualified blacks or women in proportion to their percentage in the applicant pool, nonpreferential goals should not give us any a priori reason for suspecting unfairness to white males.

Perhaps even more important is the fact that Simon's discussion does not even touch on the major use of statistics in affirmative action law as it applies to hiring—that is, the use of statistical comparisons between the qualified applicant pool and hiring decisions as evidence of discrimination.[4] He never explains what system he is comparing preferential hiring to (although his remarks suggest that the alternative he has in mind is a perfect meritocracy run by unbiased ideal observers). Thus, he never confronts the problem of practical means of reducing discrimination. Nor does he offer any argument for the claim that the use of either

preferential or nonpreferential goals will produce, for whites, more injustice than any alternative system of preventing racial discrimination would produce or allow for blacks. (He at least suggests that whatever alternative he has in mind would not involve the use of statistical goals even as evidence.)

Thus, although there may be rights which would be violated if a policy of preferential hiring were to be adopted, Simon is obscuring the issue by assuming a priori that the white males who would not get jobs under such a program would, in virtue of that fact, be unjustly treated. Of course there is the more radical criticism that the likely outcome of such programs would be to increase the discrimination against those groups discriminated against which are not included in the compensatory program (for example, white male second-generation immigrants). But this is not an objection to the principle of distributing compensatory benefits on the basis of being a member of a group which has been discriminated against. It is rather a cautionary note about the practical application of such a principle. As such, it would not be appropriate to the conclusion Simon draws from his arguments.

An earlier version of this paper was presented at Hamilton College.

Notes

1   "Implicit Racism," *Analysis* 36, no. 2 (1976), 92, 93.

2   "Statistical Justifications of Discrimination," *Analysis* 38, no. 1 (1978), 37-42.

3   "Should Reparations Be to Individuals or to Groups?" *Analysis* 34, no. 5 (1974), 154-60.

4   See Gertrude Ezorsky, "Hiring Women Faculty," *Philosophy & Public Affairs* 7, no. 1 (Fall, 1977), 82-91.

Rights, Groups and Discrimination: A Reply to Ketchum

Robert L. Simon

In a recent paper ("Statistical Justifications of Discrimination," *Analysis* 38, no. 1 [January 1978], 37-42) I claimed that arguments like *A* below

> A. 80% of the members of group *X* were victims of past discrimination. Therefore, for purposes of administrative convenience, all members of *X* should be regarded as eligible for compensatory benefits.

are logically parallel to arguments like *B*:

> B. 80% of women are physically incapable of performing task *T*. Therefore, for purposes of administrative convenience, no women ought to be considered as candidates for *T*.

I concluded that since *B* is unacceptable, and since *A* is logically parallel to *B*, *A* is unacceptable as well. Accordingly, the so-called administrative defense of preferential treatment, which presupposes the acceptability of arguments like *A*, fails (see James Nickel, "Should Reparations Be to Individuals or Groups?" *Analysis* 34, no. 5 [April 1974], 154-60.)

In reply, Sara Ann Ketchum claims that I am committed to a faulty analysis of race and sex discrimination and that I "seem to assume without argument that the white males who would get jobs if there were no policy of preferential treatment have a right to those jobs and that those jobs would be so to speak 'stolen' from them...on such a policy" ("Evidence, Statistics and Rights: A Reply to Simon," *Analysis* 39, no. 3 [June 1979], 150). Since I neither presented an analysis of race or sex discrimination nor advanced a view as to the rights of the most qualified job applicant, I fail to discern why Ketchum attributes these views to me or thinks they are relevant to my original argument.[1] However, as Ketchum's rejoinder does raise substantial questions about the issue I did address, the acceptability of inferences from premises about groups to conclusions about treatment of individuals, I believe her arguments are worth pursuing further.

Ketchum relies on such an inference at a particularly key point. For she argues that since white males as a group have acquired advantages from unjust discrimination against women and minorities, preferential treatment of particular women and minorities over particular white males is justified. "The suffering that Simon claims the young white males to be paying for the sins of their elders turns out to be the suffering of those who would not be able to benefit as much from past injustices as they had hoped or expected."[2]

At least two questions need to be raised about this argument. First, is it true that *all* white males have secured *net* advantages from unjust discrimination against women and minorities? Second, if such a claim is true, does it follow that preferential treatment of women and minorities is justified as a means of nullifying the unfairly gained advantages of white males?

Surely, there are strong grounds for doubting the claim that all white males have secured net advantages from sex and race discrimination. For one thing, such systematic and pervasive forms of injustice may have contributed to a social climate in which other forms of injustice, some of which have victimized white males, have flourished. Consider, for example, the alleged connection between racial discrimination and economic exploitation of whites in the pre-Civil-War South. Moreover, as Alan Goldman has pointed out, discrimination entails inefficiency (the best candidates are not hired or admitted) and such inefficiency may have harmed some white males more than discrimination against others helped them (Goldman, *Justice and Reverse Discrimination*, 108-9). Still other white males may have to overcome insidious forms of discrimination themselves and may have claims to redress of their own. Indeed, some affluent white females may have benefited more from systems of injustice and exploitation than have some white males.

Accordingly the claim that all white males have secured net advantages from past discrimination (or that they have in all cases secured more of an advantage than any woman) is open to serious objection. Thus unless Ketchum means to advance arguments like *A* and *B*, and argue from statistical correlation, her argument appears to rest on a doubtful premise. Even if *most* white males have (however inadvertently) secured net advantages from past discrimination against women and minorities, it does not follow that *every* white male may legitimately be disadvantaged by policies of preferential treatment. For the white male disadvantaged by such a policy may not be among the subclass of white males who have profited from the victimization of others.

Suppose, however, that in fact *all* white males have secured net advantages from past unjust discrimination. It hardly *follows* that the kinds of preferential treatment by race and sex now at issue in hiring or graduate school admission are justified. For one thing, such practices impose the costs of redress arbitrarily. If all white males are liable, it is hardly fair that a small proportion

pay the entire cost of restitution while the overwhelming majority give up nothing. More important, even if all white males have benefited, they have not all benefited *equally*. Yet, preferential treatment imposes costs according to one's relative lack of qualifications in the market, not degree of benefit received.[3] Indeed, those adversely affected are those with relatively weak records, precisely those who would tend to have benefited least from past injustice or have been victims of it themselves.[4]

What this suggests is that generalizations about groups do not easily lend themselves to direct support of conclusions about the just treatment of individuals. If we are to treat similar cases similarly, we must be sensitive to the differences as well as the resemblances between group members. At the very least, at this point in the debate over preferential treatment much more argument than Ketchum provides is needed if her position is to avoid the kinds of objections sketched above.

At this point, however, it may be objected that I have unjustifiably assumed an individualist framework of discussion. For isn't it Ketchum's point that discrimination of a systematic and pervasive kind affects individuals in virtue of their *group* membership? If so, the very point of so called "reverse discrimination" is not to deal out fair redress on an individual basis but to restore to victimized groups the social and economic position they would have held in the absence of systematic injustice.

If this is Ketchum's point, it seems to me to parallel Paul Taylor's recent defense of group compensation ("Reverse Discrimination and Compensatory Justice," *Analysis* 33, no. 6 [June, 1973], 177-82). I will not add to the criticisms of that view that have been advanced elsewhere except to suggest that even if our goal is compensation of groups we must still be as fair as possible to individuals in the process. Thus, Taylor's original proposal calls for *society* to compensate victimized groups. I have argued above, however, that the kinds of preferential treatment currently at issue imposes costs arbitrarily on *individuals*. Accordingly, an appeal to group considerations along lines advanced by Taylor will not support Ketchum's position. It is unfair that arbitrarily selected individuals pay the entire cost of promoting equality of groups.

I have suggested, then, that excluding particular white males from consideration for various benefits simply because white males as a group have benefited from past injustice raises serious issues about stereotyping and insensitivity to individual circumstances. Appeal to statistical correlations will not help us avoid these issues for the reasons given earlier in my paper. Accordingly I conclude that, for all Ketchum has said, present recommendations for preferential treatment by race or sex raise many of the same questions of injustice that properly apply to the invidious discrimination practiced for so long against women and minorities.

Notes

1   In fact, I find Ketchum's own analysis of systematic and pervasive discrimination quite attractive. And while I do think the most qualified applicant has a *prima facie* right to the job, I do not see that my original argument relies on such a claim. More important, I believe such a right can be overridden for a variety of reasons, including compensatory ones. Finally, in no sense do I believe beneficiaries of preferential treatment have stolen, or "stolen," jobs from the most qualified applicants. For useful discussion of the rights of the most qualified job applicant, see Chapter 2 of Alan H. Goldman's *Justice and Reverse Discrimination* (Princeton, 1979).

2   Surely the most Ketchum is entitled to claim is that white males expect and hope to profit from a system that in fact operates unjustly. She is not entitled to claim, at least not without providing some supporting evidence, what her language suggests: namely, the entirely different claim that white males intend and hope to profit from what they perceive as injustice.

3   I have made a similar point about the beneficiaries of preferential treatment in my "Preferential Hiring: A Reply to Judith Jarvis Thomson," *Philosophy & Public Affairs* 3, no. 3 (1974), 315. This point also counts against the acceptability of Ketchum's inference from the claim that every member of certain victimized groups has been injured by systematic discrimination to the acceptability of a system of preferential treatment which awards benefits according to qualifications, not degree of injury suffered.

4   Goldman makes a similar point about the beneficiaries of preferential treatment, in his *Justice and Reverse Discrimination*, 90-1.

Questions for Discussion

1   Are there any significant differences between the three cases Simon describes (A, B, and C)?

2   Is it legitimate to claim that the existence of disproportionately many white males in the employment pool establishes that those white males have benefited from systematic discrimination?

3   Simon claims that preferential treatment in hiring will harm the wrong people in society (those who have benefited least from past discrimination). Is he right, and if so, how significant is this as an objection to preferential treatment?

Have We a Right to Non-Discrimination?

Jan Narveson

In this selection, Jan Narveson argues against legally enforced employment equity programs, on the grounds that employers are not under an obligation to hire anyone at all, and therefore cannot be under an obligation to hire one person rather than another.

*   *   *

Prefatory

Discrimination stands very high on the list of what is currently accounted injustice. Indeed, the pages of North American journals, at least, tend to be filled with articles addressing the issue of whether *reverse* discrimination is justified or not; but that discrimination itself is unjust is scarcely ever questioned. The point of the present essay is to question it anyway. I largely share the tendency to regard much of what is currently regarded as discriminatory as a bad thing, something to condemn and certainly to avoid. I am much less certain, though, that it is in addition something to prohibit by the machinery of the law. At a minimum—and this is the motivation for the essay—I am puzzled. So the reader may construe the following investigation as an invitation to come forth with a clear account of the matter, at any rate, for I am quite sure that none has as yet been given. And that seems to me to be a very bad thing. When we prohibit the activities of voluntary and rational human beings, we ought, one would think, to have a clear and compelling reason for it. The current tendency seems to be to assume that the

wrongness of discrimination is self-evident. That attitude, I am sure we'll agree, will not do.

Initial Definitions

Discrimination requires three persons at a minimum: (1) the Discriminator, (2) the Discriminatee, the person discriminated against, and (3) the parties who have been favored in comparison with the discriminatees; perhaps we can call this class the Beneficiaries. Further, there has to be some characteristic possessed by the second class of persons on account of which they are treated less well than the third: being black, or a woman, or a foreigner, or non-Christian for instance. This property we might call the Discriminandum. Finally, note the expression 'discriminated *against*.' It is essential to the idea of discrimination, I take it, that the discriminatee is treated badly, adversely, or at any rate less well than the Beneficiaries.

All these are necessary conditions. I believe we have a sufficient condition if we add that to discriminate against someone is to treat that person in the undesirable way in question *because* the person has the property in question. But we should perhaps make room for a notion, presumably lower on the scale of moral culpability, of inadvertent discrimination. Here, the persons badly treated are not intentionally singled out for their possession of the Discriminandum in question; but it turns out that the class distinguished by possession of it is, nevertheless, coming out on the short end of the stick just as if they were intentionally thus singled out.

As with so many of the expressions we employ in day-to-day moral activity, it would be possible to expend time and energy deliberating about whether the word 'discriminate' is *logically* condemnatory or not. I don't think this time would be well spent. Smith may be complimented for being a discriminating judge of wine, or of music; Jones may be condemned for his discriminatory practices in business. I believe we can readily enough identify a sense of 'discrimination' which is logically neutral on the moral issue, and indeed, the proposed definition assembled above really is so. Confining ourselves to the more dominant intentional sense of the term, let us begin as follows:

D_1: A discriminates against B in relation to C by doing x = (def.) There is a property, K, such that B has K, C does not have K, and A treats B worse than C by doing x, and does so *because* B is a K.

That A treats B worse than C is not, itself, a morally significant fact—a point I shall expand on below. And—as I shall also be at pains to point out—there are obvious cases of treatment fitting the above which no one would take to be unjust. There are two suggestions to consider for expanding the above in such a way as to bring it more nearly into line with that use of the term in which the current controversies are

couched. Each deserves some further treatment of its own. Meanwhile, the partial definition given so far may serve as the basis for raising the important questions. What we want to know is: what values of K and x are such that to do x to a K *rather* than a non-K and *because* the person in question is a K, rather than a non-K make the doing of x unjust?

Incidentally, I will tend to favor the term 'unjust' for these purposes because my main interest is in the moral status which would ground restrictive *legislation*. Whether some lesser charge than injustice might be brought against one who discriminates is not a matter I shall be much concerned to explore.

Non-Basic Discrimination

One way in which D_1 can be expanded would be by restricting the value of our act-variable, x, in such a way as to guarantee that discrimination is unjust. There are two ways to do this (at least). One would go like this:

D_2: A discriminates against B in relation to C by doing x = (def). B is a K, C a non-K, and because B is a K, A does x to B *and x is unjust.*

This makes discrimination unjust by definition, but also trivializes the matter. What we want to know is whether there are acts x, such that x is unjust because x is discriminatory. We do not wish to know whether there are acts, x, such that x is unjust because x is unjust.

A more interesting way might go like this:

D_3: A discriminates against B in relation to C by doing x = (def). A does x to B and not to C because B is a K and C isn't a K, and x consists in harming B, e.g. by killing, torturing, maiming, depriving of rightful property, etc.

I leave an 'etc.' in this definition because my intention is to incorporate into the definition of discrimination a restriction on x to acts which are generally recognized to be morally wrong (and, indeed, are morally wrong, in my view). But I don't wish to incorporate a use of the term 'unjust' in the definition. The idea is to identify discrimination with the doing of evil acts, even though the evilness of those acts is not logically part of the description of those acts. (I have failed even so, in view of the reference to "depriving of rightful property"; finding a non-tendentious description of violations of property rights is not easy, and I request that this failing be overlooked for present purposes.)

D_3 makes discrimination wrong, all right, and it is not trivial either. But it has a different and crucial defect. For the restriction on the range of acts to be considered discriminatory according to it is now such that discriminatory acts are wrong, all right, but not *because* they are discriminatory. For they would be wrong even if they *weren't* discriminatory. We may call such acts acts of "non-basic" discrimination. Now, there are plenty of examples of non-basic discrimination, and indeed, I think that most examples of discrimination which one might be inclined to go to as paradigm cases of it would be non-basic discriminations. Think of black people being lynched, or Jews sent to the gas chambers at Auschwitz, for instance. It is quite true that the reason why these people were thus treated is that they were black or Jews, and quite true that they were discriminatory. But surely what makes it wrong to lynch an innocent person is not that that's no way to

treat a *black* person, but rather that it's no way to treat *any* innocent person.

A good deal of the progress which, I think we'd all agree, has been made in the treatment of other races in North America (at least) in the last few decades has taken the form of getting people to appreciate that the basic principles of morality are colorblind. We think there are basic human rights, held by everybody of whatever race, color, etc., and we are at the point where even sheriffs in small towns in Alabama could probably be got to subscribe to that thesis, at least in point of lip service and maybe to some degree in action as well. All this is very real progress, and insofar as the hubbub about discrimination is about this sort of thing, the hubbub is justified. The trouble is, it seems clear that what I have called non-basic discrimination is not the sort of thing which we need [in order] to show that discrimination as such is wrong—that there is anything that is wrong just *because* it is discriminatory. 'Discrimination,' given our new definition, D_3, has yet to signify a basic wrong, something which we have a right that others not do something to us which we wouldn't have had anyway.

There is, no doubt, an interesting question on the matter of whether non-basic acts of discrimination are *worse* because they are discriminatory. It has been suggested to me[1], for instance, that if the Nazis had gassed people at random, or by lot, rather than picking on the Jews in particular, then that would strike us as being hideous and awful, but not *unjust*, or at least not *as* unjust as what actually happened. It is unclear to me whether this is so or not. Perhaps one reason why one might think so is that we tend to connect injustice with *unfairness*, and it may be agreed that it is unfair to gas people for being Jews, leaving non-Jews intact. And that defect could be rectified by establishing a lottery. But on the other hand, a just community will surely be just as concerned to prevent random gassing of innocent people as it will to prevent selective gassing of them, will it not?

Suppose that instead of gassing you because you are a Jew, I gas you because I dislike your taste in ties. Is this in the same boat, or not? Or suppose I gas you because I have embezzled your money and don't want you to tell the authorities I have done so. Gassing people at random is in one sense more terrible than any of these, in the same way that terrorism in general is terrible: it might befall anyone at any time. But all of these things are terrible, and I doubt that there's any point in trying to say in the abstract which is worst. In general, I suspect that the reason we are so impressed with the case of the Jews is twofold. First, antisemitism is popular, for some reason, whereas anti-tiewearing (to the point of gassing) is virtually unheard of, and random gassing is exceedingly rare, though random violence is not. And second, antisemitism is *divisive*. It sets people against each other. Policies of antisemitism will tend to produce in many people the attitude that there is actually something wrong with being Jewish, that Jewishness is a property which literally deserves extermination, or whatever. There is therefore a public interest reason for worrying about antisemitism that isn't there in regard to the other two practises.

Moral Irrelevance

The most popular candidate for a principle of non-discrimination, no doubt, would be one which makes use of the notion of "moral irrelevance." On this view, discrimination would be defined in some such way as the following:

D₄: A discriminates against B in relation to C by doing x = (def). A does x to B and not to C because B is a K and C is not, and K-ness is *morally irrelevant* to treating people in way x.

What is meant by 'moral irrelevance' here? I suppose that a property of a person is morally relevant to a manner of treatment if it is the case that by virtue of having that property, one is morally entitled to a certain sort of treatment. And indeed, we do frame some exceedingly high-level, abstract-sounding moral principles in some such manner as that. To use the words of Sidgwick, for instance: "If a kind of conduct is right...for me...is not right...for someone else, it must be on the ground of some difference between the two cases, other than the fact that I and he are different persons."[2] This suitably self-evident-seeming idea readily lends itself to evolution into a principle about the treatment of others: if I am to treat B differently from C, then there has to be some difference, other than the fact that B is B and C is C, which justifies this difference of treatment.

Principles as abstract as this have some well-known demerits. Those, for instance, who practice racial discrimination are certainly not treating B differently from C just because C is a different person from B. They are treating B differently from C because (for instance) B is black and C isn't. Obviously a thicker theory about which properties are relevant to which sorts of treatment is required. But I think the plot can be thickened before we get into detail on that matter. We need at a minimum to distinguish two different levels of moral relevance. (1) A property might be morally relevant in the sense that we are morally *required* to treat people who have it differently from people who don't. Or (2) a property might be morally relevant only in the sense that it is morally *permissible* to treat people who have it differently from people who don't. And we may agree straight off that there must be morally relevant properties grounding any differences of treatment in the *second* sense. For after all, if it is not morally permissible to treat B differently from C, then no doubt it is wrong to treat them differently; and if we confine ourselves to the sorts of wrongness which ground restrictive laws, unjust-making wrongnesses, then it is obvious that moral relevance in sense (2) is a necessary condition for treating people justly. But it is also trivial to say that, after all. What, however, about sense (1)?

It does, I must say, seem perfectly obvious that in order to justify difference of treatment of two persons, B and C, there does *not* need to be a *morally* relevant difference between them in sense (1). I do not mean merely that we might find different ways of treating B and C which treat them equally well, so that neither has any complaint coming on the score of having been less well treated. I mean, more interestingly, that we may very well treat one person less well than another without a hint of injustice, and without appealing to any differences between them which are morally relevant in the stronger sense. Moreover, I think we can find examples of this type which are also frankly discriminatory in the sense not only of D_4, but also relative to current thinking, in that they discriminate along the very lines which figure in many of our laws as well as private judgements.

Such, for instance, seems to me to be the case with marrying and offering to marry. It seems to me that there are virtually no morally relevant characteristics in this whole area. Suppose I decide to marry Jane on the ground that she has lovely blue eyes, while Nell has to make do with plain ol' brown ones. Well, where is the duty to marry blue-eyeds rather than brown-eyeds? Obviously nowhere: so do I perform an injustice to Nell in so behaving? I think not. Nor is the situation any different if we think of the standard Discriminanda currently in the public eye. If I marry Amanda because she is black, I do not behave unjustly to Sue who is white; or if I marry Cathy because she is of the same religious persuasion as I—or because she is of a different persuasion, for that matter—I do not *thereby* wrong the unfortunate (or fortunate?) candidates who are thus rejected.

Similarly with friendship. If I like A because he is intelligent and charming, while refraining from befriending B because he is uninteresting, I do not thereby wrong B, despite the total lack of any moral duty to befriend all and sundry, or to befriend the intelligent, or the charming. In short, I think it clear that the general claim that we can justify treating one person less well than another only by invoking "morally relevant" characteristics in the interesting sense distinguished above simply will not wash.

It is manifestly clear that we can act well or badly, and in particular, intelligently or unintelligently, in these contexts. You may certainly criticize my taste if I marry someone because of the color of her eyes, or her skin, or even her choice of religion, perhaps. These decisions may be personally justified or not. But morally? It would take a special background to bring morality into it. Perhaps you have been dating Jane all this time, leading her to expect that you like people such as her, indeed leading her to expect a proposal from you; and instead, you may turn around and propose to some total stranger. You may owe her an explanation. Or perhaps you promised your dear ol' Mum that you'd marry a fellow Seventh Day Adventist, and now you've gone and proposed to a Buddhist, yet. There's no end of what might bring moral considerations into these matters. But my point is that so far as it goes, morality has no bearing on it: marry whom you like, and Justice will not blink an eye, though Prudence might turn around and quietly vomit.

Is There Basic Discrimination?

Further reflection on the foregoing discussion of moral relevance raises the interesting question whether there really is any such thing as what I have implicitly identified as Basic discrimination. Non-basic discrimination, we recall, is where there is something wrong with what you are doing to B *anyway*; the fact that you do it to him because he is the possessor of some property (not common to all moral persons) which does not qualify him for that treatment is not needed in order to condemn the action in question. Basic discrimination, then, would be where your act of treating B worse than C is wrong, not because it is to do something to B which you have no right to do anyway, but because it unjustly discriminates between B and C. What we would need here, evidently, is a principle calling upon us to do certain things to certain people if we also do them to certain others, but where there is in itself nothing wrong with doing it to anyone.

Yet there seems something odd about this. Here is something I can do to some-one, something which there is no inherent moral objection to doing. Call this act x. Often x will be some negative action, a *non*action such as not offering the person in question a job. There is also, we are assuming, *no* moral duty to do not-x, to refrain from x, to *anyone*. How, then, can it suddenly be unjust if I choose to do x to B, and not-x to C? Doing it, to anyone, is not wrong; nor is doing it, to anyone, a moral duty, required. Nobody has the right that I do it to him or refrain from doing it to him. How can it be that it is, under the circumstances, wrong to do it to B rather than C?

The most interesting current context, I take it, is employment. We have in general no obligation to hire anybody for anything; nor have we in general any obligation to refrain from hiring anybody for anything. Yet it is widely supposed that if A hires C rather than B because C is, say, a male, or white, despite B's equal competence, then A has done B an injustice, and the law may properly descend upon A and make him toe the line of equality. Why? So interesting are these contexts that I propose to discuss them on their own for a few pages.

Public/Private

To begin with, we had better immediately take account of a distinction plainly relevant in this connection, namely the distinction between hiring in the public sector and private hiring. I mean this to be a conceptual distinction. Some might argue that the public sector is a fraud, or at any rate that there ought to be no such thing: you name it and "the public" has no right doing it. Others might say the same thing about the private sector. I do not intend either to affirm or deny either view here. I only wish to point out that if we acknowledge a public sector, it is easy enough to see why discrimination there would be something to make a fuss about.

The reason is simple enough. Suppose there are services which any member of the public has a right to, *vis-à-vis* the public generally. He has that right, then, *qua* member of the public. Moreover, those offering it to him are also acting as agents of the public. Now, the public consists of *everybody*. If, then, there is some service to which one is entitled *qua* member of the public, clearly it will be wrong for any agent of the public to give it to C but withhold it from B, so long as both are members of the relevant public. If there is a limited resource which the public is to expend—medical services, say—it is held that this is a public matter, so that all and only the medically needy have a claim on it, and demand exceeds supply, then it is also plausible to hold that the resources ought to be proportioned equally to the need, or perhaps that we ought to maximize the public health, but in any case not on a basis which favors some irrelevantly distinguished group in society. In fact, the criteria of relevance will be quite clear: if there is some need N to which some service S of the public is to cater, then factors other than N are irrelevant when it comes to administering S.

Prima facie, we also have a case for insisting that the agents administering S hire only on the basis of competence. If the idea is to maximize the satisfaction of N, then if applicant B promises to promote that goal better than C at the same cost, then the public would seem to have a right that B be hired rather than C. (The situation gets messy when we ask whether the public has the right that its servants reflect, say, the racial composition of the public they are to serve, particularly when perhaps the typical applicants from one readily-distinguished group are less competent than those of some other, since now there will be a clash between considerations of efficiency, which the public has a right to, and the interest in an equal share of the action, which it may also have a right to. But we will not press these issues further here.)

What is important about the invocation of the public here is that it gives us a basis for nondiscrimination which again does not clearly show discrimination to be a *basic* injustice. For it seems, again, that if B can successfully claim to have been discriminated against in the public sector, there is also a claim on B's part to that which he was denied by virtue of the discriminatory act in question. It is not the case that there is no obligation to provide the service for which hiring is being done. On the contrary, the thesis is that the public has the duty to provide the service, and is also entitled to it, on a basis that is equal as between persons of one color and another, one sex and another, etc.

But this is not true of the private sector in general. In that sector, the assumption is that those who hire do so in pursuit of private gain, or perhaps some other sort of private satisfaction. There is no obligation to set up any business whatever, no obligation to offer any particular service, or any service at all. That somebody didn't get hired by you, a private employer, is *prima facie* not something he can complain about, since you have no obligation to hire anybody at all—neither that person nor any other. More interestingly, it is by no means clear that he can complain even if he was of superior competence as compared with his competitors. Since you have no obligation to hire at all, it is hard to see why you should have an obligation to hire the most competent. What if you don't care about competence? Perhaps you'd rather that your employees were attractive, or devout Catholics, or tee-totalers, or males. So what? Again, it seems to me: if there is no right to a job at all, how can there be a right that people like you be hired rather than people like anybody else, if anyone is hired at all?

Again, there are certainly considerations of prudence; and it is possible that some will see considerations of morality entering here too. Let us see, beginning in particular with prudence. We turn, briefly, to the question of the economics of discrimination. Too briefly, no doubt, but the matter can afford some instruction anyway.

Dollars and Discrimination

Let us first consider the matter on what are usually thought of as classical assumptions, *viz.*, that everyone in the market is an economically rational agent interested in maximizing his dollar returns. (This assumption, as will be noted below, is unclear even if true; but one thing at a time. One good reason for starting with this assumption is that some people seem to think that discrimination is actually *caused* by the motive of gain.) Such agents will buy at the lowest price available for a given level of quality in the product, and will sell whatever they have to sell, e.g. their labour power, at the highest available price. If A wants an x and B, a black person, offers it to him at a lower price than C, who is white, then A will buy from the black person. (It should be noted that although, as I say, I will be questioning the above assumptions in some respects, there is plenty of empirical evidence that consumers, whether of labour or other things, will in-

deed buy from people they ostensibly despise if the price is right.)

Consider, then, the case of the Little Goliath Motor Company, a firm which makes no bones about its basic purpose: profit. And consider any position in this firm, call it P, forwarding some function, F, within this noble enterprise. The primary purpose of making money will determine both which subordinate functions will be values of F and, together with an understanding of how F fits in with the rest of the operation, the criteria of better and worse performance at P. The more efficiently per unit of pay F is fulfilled, the lower will be the firm's cost per unit, or the higher the quality, or some mix of the two; in either case it will do better on the market, being able to sell cheaper or higher quality goods than the competition, if the latter don't do as well on these scores. Applicants for P, therefore, will rationally be judged by those criteria.

Enter another classical assumption, *viz.*, that such factors as race and sex make no difference to efficiency on the part of employees. (Again, it is an assumption which is often certainly false to fact, but, again, one thing at a time.) On this assumption, the people down at Little Goliath will not do well to have any interest in the race or sex of their applicants. For, imagine what happens if they do. They begin, let us suppose, prefering whites or males. Preferring them means that they will hire them instead of females or blacks (or whatever). Now this presumably means that it will hire a less efficient white male at the same wage as it could get a more efficient black or female for the job at hand; which is equivalent, economically speaking, to paying more for an equally efficient one. On classical assumptions, what happens next?

Well, the more persistently enterprising Universal Motor Co. up the road will begin to hire females and blacks, doing equally good work, for lower wages; it is in a position to do this, since the Goliath people insist on turning away perfectly good females with an interest in taking the best-paying job they can get. If this keeps up, and if, as our assumptions dictate, motor car purchasers are interested in quality for price rather than the color or sex of those who put the product together, then we shall expect the Universal people to do well, and the Goliath people to do badly.

Perhaps a case at a classier level will be still more perspicuous. Most firms, we are told, much prefer males to females for executive positions; and we are told that this is in fact sheer prejudice, females being equally capable. Under the circumstances, we should expect cagey firms to be soon staffed, in their higher reaches, with high-powered women at half the pay which their competitors have to offer their all-male staffs. If all firms were rational and our assumption about the relative abilities of the sexes correct, we should eventually see executives of both sexes at the same salaries more or less everywhere.

The moral is generalizable: if the criterion of discrimination in hiring is that criteria other than those relevant to job-performance are used for the sorting of candidates, then in free-market conditions, with economically rational consumers, the non-discriminating firm will be better. Discrimination does not pay.

Might things go severely otherwise? Might the assumptions be badly wrong? The situation is unclear. We can certainly imagine cases in which consumers are not out to maximize their returns. If consumers insist on buying grapes picked by unionized labour, we are into another ball game: not that storeowners really *mind* having customers who prefer paying more to paying less for the same goods, but it is all slightly puzzling. Likewise, it is possible that people would want to know whether the soap they buy was wrapped by lily-white rather than ebony hands. Possible, though unlikely. More likely, of course, is discrimination in service industries where the customer comes into direct contact with the supplier. People might like black waiters and butlers better than white ones, or pretty stewardesses better than plain though efficient ones, or whatever. In all such cases, economics will not erode discrimination. It will instead lead to the members of favoured classes being better off than members of unfavoured ones; and whether, for instance, wages in given industries will tend to equalize in a longish run is imponderable. But it should certainly be noted that there is no clear tendency toward reinforcing preexisting patterns of social discrimination, as anyone who has recently attempted to procure the services of Leontyne Price or Oscar Peterson will be acutely aware.

It is also essential to point out that the most scandalous cases in the past have been anything but cases of free market operation. Black slavery in the American South was *not* a free market institution. Neither is the situation in South Africa, where wage differentials between black and white workers are reinforced not only by law, but by unions.

I should like to explore this aspect of the matter much further, but space does not permit. Instead, I wish to turn to another crucial matter, closely related to that just discussed and, I think, offering perhaps the most puzzling challenge of all to those who think that there is a clear and straightforward underlying principle behind current attitudes about discrimination.

The Purposes of Firms

Competence is assessed by the criteria relevant to performance of the function which the position in question is to serve. Which functions are to be served, depends in turn on the ultimate purpose of the firm in which the position is situated. Some firms are out to make money; but not all. Let us address ourselves to a couple of relevant cases. One of my favorites, for starters, is a small nonprofit organization known as the Equadorian Friendship Society. The E.F.S. has as its purpose the forwarding of friendship among Equadorians, and this purpose is not notably served by hiring, say, Bolivian janitors and secretaries, or even French chefs. We may well imagine that the management down at the E.F.S. will substantially prefer less competent Equadorians to more competent Bolivians when screening applications for those and other positions, right up to Vice President depending, no doubt, on the condition of its finances. But who is to say that the firm is acting irrationally in such practices? After all, it might be argued, given the purpose of this particular firm, that it is *not* efficient, looked at from the higher point of view, to hire Bolivian secretaries, however efficient they may be *qua* secretary. Under the circumstances, the hiring of Bolivians, however competent, is less than utterly Friendly.

Another of my favorites among these specialized nonprofit establishments is the Black Muslim Church of America, which may be presumed to look considerably askance at applicants of the Occidental persuasion for positions in their clergy, however eloquent and dedicated. The point, again, may be made that given the purposes of the firm, what would otherwise be discriminatory is legitimate, indeed efficient and thus mandatory. Thus it may be argued that these firms do not really violate the canon of hiring only on the basis of relevant competence: competence, as I say, is dictated by the purposes of the organization.

At this point, two questions loom before us. Both should tax us mightily, I think. The first point may be furthered by bringing up another example dear to my heart: the Irish-Canadian Distilleries Corporation. This amiable organization lets it be known to all and sundry that although it is happy to turn an honest dollar, it also has a pronounced interest in maximizing the percentage of persons of Irish descent amongst its employees, even if this should cut into profits a bit. For its purpose is not simply to make money—this, they imply, is a motive reserved for the low of mind, such as the denizens of the Highlands. It is, rather, to be a sort of marginally profitable Irish-Canadian Friendly Society, a high purpose for which, indeed, its commercial product is peculiarly suitable. Its otherwise inefficient hiring practices, when viewed from this higher perspective, turn out to be perfectly efficient after all, and therefore, on the standard view which seems to prevail about what is "morally relevant," quite free of any taint of discrimination.

The second question follows naturally enough, *viz.*: what's so great about efficiency, anyway? Why not accuse those firms which hire exclusively on the basis of competence of discriminating unjustly against the incompetent? Why should competence be thought a "morally relevant characteristic"? It is not, incidentally, thought to be so when it comes to such elementary matters as the right to vote, or indeed, to stand for Parliament. From the point of view of the employer, of course, competence is highly desirable. So indeed is it from the point of view of the consumer. But why should only that point of view count? Aren't we supposed to be adumbrating an impartial standard of justice?

Advertising of Positions

One possible account of the injustice thought to be inherent in discriminatory hiring, and to some extent applicable in other contexts as well, is that those who are excluded for apparently irrelevant reasons have been dealt badly with because their expectations, engendered by the advertisement for the position or such other description of the opportunity regarding which the discrimination has taken place, have been disappointed. An applicant may well say, "Look, I've come all this way, taken all this time and trouble to get this job interview, and now you tell me that no X-ians will be considered. Why didn't you say so in the first place?"

Complaints of this kind, where applicable, may certainly be well-taken, and sometimes could be a basis for a claim of compensation. But so far as the general issue of a basic right to nondiscrimination is concerned, it is surely too weak to do the job many people feel there is to be done. For one thing, it would be hard to specify the number of factors on the basis of which a candidate might be rejected in any satisfactorily general way. After all, if there is just one job and many candidates, several are going to be disappointed, however excellent the reasons for their rejection. And

more generally, it is surely not true that the case against discrimination, in the minds of the many who think it a major context for social concern, would always be settled just by wording advertisements appropriately. The claim is that it's wrong to impose the condition that No Irish Need Apply, however well advertised that condition may be. We shall have to look elsewhere to find any deep principles against discrimination. (Nor should it be assumed *a priori* that we will succeed.)

Current Practice

It is perhaps not entirely out of order to ask whether our current practices in this area make all that much sense, taken in large. For one thing, it does seem as though discrimination is in fact quite all right when practiced by the allegedly downtrodden against the allegedly mighty majority (though the term 'majority' has come to have a somewhat non-literal usage, in view of the fact that, e.g., white Anglo-Saxon males must by now make up rather a small percentage of the Canadian or American populace, and women an outright majority). And do we not tolerate, indeed expect and encourage, discrimination as between members of our own family and others when it comes to the distribution of various economic and social benefits, including jobs, education beyond what is provided by the public, and so forth?

Another area in a more public quarter has to do with the matter of nationalism. At one time, discrimination on grounds of nationality was one of the standard bad examples, along with discrimination on grounds of sex, race and religion. But recently, one hears less about nationality, perhaps for the reason that every government so flagrantly violates any principle along this line. Not only public employers, but also employers in the private sector, are routinely required to discriminate very strongly against citizens of other countries (in Canada, this is true even of immigrants, whom employers are often required to rank second to citizens for employment). Goods made by foreign firms are, of course, routinely discriminated against by means of tariffs and other restrictions. Even the freedom to marry foreigners has been abridged by some nations, and immigration restrictions having this effect are not uncommon.

I have already mentioned churches in connection with employment. But the existence of organizations with special purposes seems quite generally to raise a question about the intent of nondiscrimination principles, for do not organizations routinely distinguish between members and non-members, persons who share their goals and persons who do not? And why on earth shouldn't they—indeed, how could they not do so? But that is just the point. A clear principle distinguishing between all these myriad cases of intentionally prejudicial bestowing of important benefits and the ones popularly frowned upon as discriminatory is what we need and, it seems to me, do not have.

A Note on Utilitarianism

Those who have felt that nondiscrimination is a basic right have often, I think, supposed that it is a right which exceeds the reach of utilitarianism. Partly for this reason, it is of some interest to observe that, while it is, if the foregoing arguments are as strong as I am so far persuaded they are, extremely difficult to find a plausible deep principle going beneath the level of utilitarian considerations, it is not difficult to give a pretty plausible account of our practices and currently professed principles in utilitarian terms. For one thing, the distinction between private and public in the hiring arena, which figures strongly in the foregoing, does not have all that much status for the utilitarian. From his point of view, one might say *all* activities are "public" in the sense that the public has a legitimate interest in how they are carried on. If there is to be a private sector at all, from that point of view, it is because the public interest is served better by making some things private. That the wealth of a society is promoted by private enterprise, if true, is certainly important and creates a presumption in favor of private enterprise; but then, in cases where it is not so promoted, the utilitarian has no scruples about putting it back in the hands of the public. And if some other important public interest besides wealth comes into the picture, then the utilitarian will simply consider whether this other interest is sufficient to outweigh the lost prosperity resulting from catering to it, if indeed that is what would happen.

What other utilities might be at stake? Prominent among them, surely, are two, or perhaps two sides of a single one. First, there is the sheer fact that those discriminated against *feel* badly done by. If the public is upset by a certain practice—or indeed, if a smallish minority is upset by it, given that it is upset enough—then that creates at least some presumption in favor of altering the practice. And secondly, it is fair to argue that discriminatory practices, particularly in areas of such substantial concern to people as hiring, are socially divisive, as was noted in [the section on Non-Basic Discrimination]. If sizable groups of people are clamoring for advancement, while others characteristically are preferred in those respects, even at some cost in efficiency, then the tendency will be for bad feeling to exist between the groups in question, and we may expect trouble. The fact that we can't identify, in principle and in general, any characteristics and range of practices such that the doing of those things to people with those characteristics and the nondoing of them to people without them is fundamentally wrong doesn't matter all that much; if we can deal with the situation pretty effectively with rather vague and unsatisfactorily messy principles, that is better than ignoring the problem.

It is to be expected, if utilitarianism is our guide, that there will be no stable list of Discriminanda such that nondiscrimination principles would always be stated in terms of them, nor any particular social context, such as hiring, where the wrongness of discrimination is permanently to be abhorred. It will depend on social conditions. Fifty years from now, perhaps some quite new contexts, new Discriminanda, will be where the focus of concern falls. And if we are interested in capturing current "intuitions" and predicting the way things will go, this aspect of utilitarianism seems likely to stand us in pretty good stead.

But there are more shortcomings. Naturally, the basic status of utilitarianism itself is one of them. Nor is it evident that the whole job to be done is to account for current practices; and if currently held beliefs are what are to be accounted for, then there is the widespread feeling that the right to nondiscrimination does not wait upon social interest for its confirmation to consider: is that part of what is to be accounted for, or isn't it? More importantly, however, is that it seems to me questionable what the real outcome of utilitarianism is on such issues.

To see this, we need to distinguish between two views about the operation of utilitarianism, or perhaps about its application. We might call these the "crude" versus the "sophisticated" form. The crude variety, which I have tacitly appealed to above, has it that we weigh any old interest, however derived. If interests in strawberry jam count, and interests in Mahler symphonies, so do interests in wife-beating, in keeping up with the Joneses, and in one's neighbors all being attired in identical seersucker suits. The sophisticated type, however, does not easily allow such interests to count, or discounts them as compared with others. If interests in others' having such-and-such interests count, and if interests in others having such-and-such relations to oneself count equally, that seems to make way for the kind of objections to utilitarianism trotted out in the standard textbooks and Introductions to Philosophy. And the difficulty is that it seems that the kind of interests catered to in nondiscrimination principles are of that kind. In order to get very much weight behind the thesis that social utility will be further enhanced by A's electing to have B work for him rather than C, despite the fact that he'd rather have C, we have to attach a good deal of weight to the intensity of B's feelings of indignation at not being equally considered by A, and more weight to the fuss which will be caused by the objections of B's cohorts, etc. If, on the other hand, we simply attend to what appears to be the fact, that whichever A hires, A will be doing that person a favor, but if he hires the one he likes he will in addition create more utility for himself, then it is unclear that we should allow the further fact that B doesn't like the situation to count.

It is characteristic of utilitarianism that once one sees there are competing sources of utility to take into account, and these are not easily estimated, the argument could be taken either way. And often, the very utility being counted is due to the pre-existing moral beliefs of the persons involved. If B had the attitude that A has a perfect right to hire whomever he pleases, there wouldn't *be* the various political utilities to which the argument of crude utilitarianism appeals. And this means that utilitarianism may not be of much use in this matter after all.

And a Note on Contractarianism

Another of the most important theoretical bases for social philosophy to have been taken seriously in recent times, as well as times past, is the suggestion that the principles of justice are the principles for the structuring of society which would be accepted by rational individuals on a long-term basis, or perhaps an impartial one. Indeed, I would be inclined to argue this way myself. But some who have been of this persuasion have evidently supposed that principles of nondiscrimination are among those which would most fundamentally be opted for in this way; and unfortunately, I fail to see that this is obvious.

Presumably a main source of this view that nondiscrimination would have such a status is the fact, which is not in dispute here, that the fundamental principles chosen would be, so to speak, color-blind (and sex-blind, etc.). Unfortunately, as has been in effect argued above, this is very far from supporting the very strong principles which are here being questioned. For it is one thing to say that the fundamental principles of morality will not favour any groups as compared with any other (except, of course, that it will disfavour those who don't comply with them), and quite another

to say that those principles will require individuals not to favour other individuals on the basis of sex, color, race, religion, taste in wines, or whatever, when it comes to doing things for them. When we are contracting for general rights, after all, we are contracting to give up certain liberties. The strategy of contractualism is to pick out those liberties which we are better off giving up, and thus to argue that the rational person will be prepared to do so, in exchange for certain benefits which cannot be had without giving up those liberties. In the case of the liberty to kill, or in general to inflict harms on people, it is plausible to argue that the advantage of being free from such depredations at the hands of others will outweigh, in any even modestly longish run, the disadvantage of giving up the liberty to commit them oneself. But it is a different story when what is at issue is how one is to dispose of one's various positive assets, one's capacity to benefit others. Here it is *not* plausible to argue that every rational person *must* find it to his or her advantage to forego the liberty to decide who will be the beneficiary of such activities, in return for the benefit of being assured of having an equal chance, along with others who differ in various respects, of winding up as the beneficiary of some other people's similar activities.

It has been the habit of Rawls and of theorists persuaded by his general views to speak rather vaguely about opportunities for realizing the benefits which one's 'society' has to offer. The trouble with this, as Nozick was at pains to argue, is that it seems to assume that society is a kind of organized club with certain rather specific purposes which all members in good standing must be interested in promoting, and having a variety of assets at its disposal for the promotion of these purposes. But since this is fairly obviously not so, and fairly obviously therefore not something which we can simply assume, it is clear that one would have to argue for the claim that everyone *ought* to look at it that way. And I don't see how such an argument is to go through in general. But 'in general' is what we are talking about here. It is not to the point to observe that many people would see advantage in so viewing the matter, for manifestly some would not, and given that that is so, there is surely no prospect of a general agreement, reaching to all rational persons, on the point.

Even if we suppose that some progress along that line is possible, there is a further problem about the relevance of our results to the present issue. Suppose, for instance, that we can make some kind of case for, say, an assured minimal income for all—already an extremely implausible assumption. But still, although that would, by the reasoning of [the section "Public/Private"], provide the basis for nondiscrimination in the administration of the program for securing that minimum to all, it does not seem possible that it would provide a basis for nondiscrimination as between candidates for very high-paying positions, or even most positions. Presumably the minimum must be set somewhere below the average income from employment, and then we have the question of why everyone's entitlement to this minimum should carry with it an entitlement to nondiscrimination at any of the levels above it.

Most contractualist arguments about social minima *et al* in any case run up against another problem. If people were so interested in security, including the particular kinds of security which nondiscrimination laws provide, why wouldn't they buy into insurance which provided that kind of security? Or form clubs whose members would agree to boycott those who practiced the types of discrimination they wished to avoid? Why, in short, are the kinds of benefits which nondiscrimination presumably provides of a type which justifies coercive methods for seeing to it that *all* persons avoid practicing the types of discrimination in question—not only those who do see it as a benefit, but also those who see it as just the reverse? Given contractarian premises, one would have thought that if one has one's choice between enabling some good to be brought about by voluntary efforts among those who want it and a system of imposing it by force, if need be, on all alike, the former would be preferable. When we disagree, the rational thing for us both to do is agree to disagree—*not* agree that something called 'society' will declare one of us out of bounds and impose the other's view on him willy-nilly.

A Note on Logic

The principal argument in the foregoing effort to establish that the foundations of our attitudes toward discrimination are insecure and obscure has been of the following general form: We do not (it is admitted) have any obligation to do anything of the kind in question—appointing to a position, say— to anybody at all; so why do we have an obligation not to do it to one person rather than another? If I don't owe *anybody* a certain benefit, X, how is it that I can owe it to everyone that if I do give it to some person other than he, it will not be because he has certain properties but rather because he has certain others? If I owe it to no one at all, then why can't I give it to whomever

I please, since the option is to give it to nobody whatever?

The question arises how we are to formulate the principle thus implicitly appealed to. Very generally, no doubt, the idea is that found in Hobbes, to the effect that "Obligation and Liberty...in one and the same matter are inconsistent." However, there is the question of specifying the 'matter' in question. Perhaps it is the case that even though I have no obligation to do x to A or to B, I have an obligation to do it to A in preference to B if at all, because in doing x to B I would not simply be doing x, but also something else, y, which is forbidden. The trouble is, though, that in the foregoing I have argued that the cases in which there clearly is this other description of my act, this other fact about it, in virtue of which it is obligatory on me not to do it, we have what I called "non-basic" discrimination, and this, I observed, doesn't seem to be sufficient to account for standard attitudes and practices on this subject. Were it the case that, in declining to give the job to A, one also hit him over the head or heaped insults upon him, that would be wrong; but that is not the behavior at issue. It is felt that it is wrong to decline to give it to A at all, if A is in fact "better qualified" than B and one simply prefers to have B for extraneous reasons such as that one simply likes B, or people like B in certain respects, better than A or people like A in certain respects.

A slightly formalized representation of the principle behind the argument would go, perhaps, something like this:

(1) A's preferring B to C in context H consists in A's doing x to B rather than to C, if at all.

(2) A's being obliged to prefer B to C in context H = A's being obliged to do x to B rather than C, if at all.

(3) A's not being obliged to do x at all = A's not being obliged to do x to any person whatever, for any reason, i.e., there is no class of persons such that A is obliged to do x to any member of that class.

(4) Context H involves some purpose, P, such that pursuit of P would give a reason to prefer B to C.

(5) But A has no obligation to pursue P *at all*. (If P were obligatory, then A would have some obligation to do x to someone, if available. But by hypothesis, A has no such obligation.)

(6) Therefore (by 5), A has no obligation to prefer anyone to anyone with respect to x; and hence not to prefer B to C.

If this is right, then it also appears that there is no such thing as obligatory *basic* nondiscrimination. If we were obliged to prefer one person to another *vis-à-vis* doing of some act x, that would imply that we had some obligation to do x, or pursue some purpose such that x promoted it, though other acts y could be done instead, or in general to perform kinds of acts of which x was an example.

Do we think this to be so? I am hard put to decide, but let us consider a few examples. Many of us would accept a general obligation to treat our children equally, for instance: if we have some limited resource—money, for instance—which we can devote to promoting their welfare, we feel some obligation to divide that resource equally, or in such a way as to promote their respective welfares equally. True: but it is also true that we have an obligation to promote their welfare *at all*. How much is, of course, not entirely easy to say, but suppose that we say we are to promote each child's welfare maximally within some limit. If we have this for *each* of them, and the resources are only sufficient for some level short of what we would ideally like, then it is readily concluded that we should split the resource more or less equally, or aim at equal welfares. But if we had no such obligation at all, it is hard to see how any of them could reasonably complain if he or she were always passed over in favor of others.

In general, it seems to me that the claim to *equal treatment* rests on an assumption that there are equal *claims to that kind of treatment*; and hence, that there *are* claims to that kind of treatment. The right to *equal opportunity*, in particular, rests on an assumed *right to opportunity*. In the absence of the latter, it is hard to see how we can make much sense of the former.

A Note on Prejudice

One final matter should be mentioned. Very often, certainly, treatment of different large groups that is markedly unequal in the various respects we have in mind when we talk of 'discrimination' is based on beliefs about the relative merits of those different groups. When those beliefs are without foundation, we bring in the notion of 'prejudice,' of judging people's merits before we actually know the relevant facts—if any. The subject of prejudice invites special comment; and doubtless some, though I think not all, of the prevailing beliefs about discrimination are accounted for on the basis of their relation to it. The following observations seem especially pertinent here.

(1) We must bear in mind that not all discrimination will be due to prejudice. Perhaps Brown doesn't believe that all X-ians are shiftless, immoral, or whatever; he may simply not much care for X-ians, or he may care for members of his own race (etc.) more. There is a difference between an attitude based on an unreasoned or baseless belief, on the one hand, and on no belief at all, on the other.

(2) When the attitudes in question are based on beliefs, those beliefs are, of course, capable of being rationally appraised. Now sometimes—we ought to recognize—they might be based on pretty decent evidence. It may not be obvious that the different races, sexes, etc., do have the same degree of allegedly relevant properties. Possibly it is a matter on which reasonable people may differ. Where this is so, it is at least clear that one cannot convict, say, an employer who turns out to employ a quite different percentage of X-ians from that which X-ians bear to the whole population, of discrimination straight off. Perhaps the X-ians *are* a lot better, or a lot worse, at that sort of job than the average other person. (Obviously there might still be discrimination, for perhaps the employer follows a policy of not even considering X-ians, when in fact a modest percentage of them are better at the job thatn a lot of X-ians. This raises further questions, prominent among them being how much trouble an employer could reasonably be required to go to to test persons directly rather than going by obvious qualities, such as sex, which are quite well correlated with them.) At any rate, the point is that we cannot assume *a priori* that various abilities and whatnot are distributed in a population independently of the popular discriminanda; it simply isn't an *a priori* matter.

(3) Even where it is quite clear that prejudice is at work, there are two questions to raise about it. In the first place, there is the question whether it is right to

persecute people for their beliefs. We do not do so, or at least we profess to believe that we have no right to do so, in the case of religious beliefs, even though those beliefs are always, strictly speaking, baseless, and even though they often lead to very substantial kinds of discriminatory treatment. In the second place, and more important at least in practice, there is the fact that once the foundations, or lack of them, of a belief are out in the open where critics can assail them, it is not easy to maintain that belief with a perfectly straight face for very long. Why should we assume so readily that the proper way to deal with actions based on beliefs we think are baseless, illogical, or confused is by making laws against those actions? We can hardly think that generally appropriate. Do we not, after all, have a pretty well-grounded suspicion that most people's practical beliefs are baseless, illogical, and/or confused? (Including, it will doubtless turn out, most of our own?) And are we not agreed that one does not properly outlaw the entertaining of that belief: that in fact the proper way to deal with it is to *refute* it, much to the psychic stress of the person who holds it?

At the risk of being embarrassingly obvious, I would just note that if we were to take seriously the suggestion that it is unjust to hold baseless beliefs, then any principle of freedom of religion would evidently have to go by the boards. Most religions, after all, are almost self-consciously mysterious, and do not even pretend to offer sound reasons, persuasive to any rational being, for holding their main tenets. For all that, these beliefs are obviously dangerous. It takes little investigation of history to see that any number of wars, including perhaps most of the messier ones, have been fought partly or wholly on religious grounds. If the sort

of prejudices often leading to discrimination are a public menace, surely religion is even more so. Yet which tenets of liberalism have pride of place over religious freedom?

It may be urged that there is a difference between allowing someone to hold a belief and allowing him to act on it. Anyone seriously urging a strong principle of freedom of thought or of speech needs to make such a distinction, since otherwise he will find himself in the embarrassing position of having to allow any degree of iniquity whenever the agent in question does it on conscientious grounds. In those cases, of course, we need to establish the iniquitousness of the acts in question on independent grounds; and by and large, my argument in this paper has been that it is unclear that we have such grounds. Meanwhile, it in any case remains that employers frequently cannot be said to have clearly unreasonable grounds for their discriminatory beliefs; and when this is so, it is difficult to see how we could proceed against them on the ground that their beliefs were, as we in our wisdom have decreed, false. And on the other hand, we do allow people to act on their religious beliefs, within broad limits, and those beliefs don't have nearly so much to be said for them as some of the beliefs on which prejudices are based.

There is one particular kind of prejudice-supporting belief of which we may, I would agree, make a special case. This is the kind which consists in holding that certain groups of people are, without further explanation, "morally inferior." A belief so expressed might, of course, be an empirically based one, to the effect that the incidence of certain standardly recognized types of immoral behavior is greater in that group than in others—which in any case, of course, would not justify across-the-board discrimination against members of that group. But the case I have in mind does not involve an explicable belief of that kind. It consists instead of simply holding that the group in question is not morally deserving of normally good treatment or of ordinary rights. Such a belief, we may certainly agree, is not only unintelligible but also immoral. It is unintelligible because it requires that there be a special, empirically undetectable property or set of properties that render their possessors eligible for inclusion in the moral community, and it is in principle erroneous to suppose that there is any such feature or features. And it is immoral because it would make it impossible for an accused person to defend himself against the "charge" of "inferiority" of that kind, even though its purpose is to justify the kind of treatment that is only properly administered to persons guilty of genuinely immoral behavior. But as with the kind of beliefs discussed previously, it must again be pointed out that persons engaging in that kind of treatment of others without a supportable charge of that kind are themselves guilty of violating the rights of others. What is wrong with the behavior in question is not that that is its motive, and it is unclear that the motive in question *adds* to the iniquity of the behavior. But certainly the spreading of such "beliefs," since it *can* only be used to promote evil behavior, may be condemned strongly enough.

Summary

The thesis of this essay is that the case for regarding discrimination, properly so called, as an injustice has not been clearly supported in western thought, despite its enormous impact on western practice. "Discrimination properly so called" marks

an essential distinction here, for much discriminatory behavior, termed 'non-basic' in the foregoing, is undoubtedly wrong but not wrong by virtue of being discriminatory: killing or injuring people who are innocent of any morally sustainable crime is wrong, whatever the motive. But that leaves a great deal that *is* "properly so called," where the discrimination consists only in treating some people less well than others, and doing so for a reason that is not morally relevant, in the strong sense of that term in which a morally relevant distinction morally requires a corresponding distinction in treatment. Not giving one person rather than another a job in a company of which you are the owner, and where your reason for preferring the other has nothing to do with competence at that job, is an example. What is anomalous about classifying such behavior as unjust, I have argued, is that there seems to be no *duty* to give anyone the job, in general; how, then, can it be unjust not to give it to one person rather than another? That is the central puzzle, and it seems to me to remain unanswered.

Cases can be made for the wrongness of what is ordinarily called discrimination on indirect grounds having to do with social harmony and the like. But such cases, unlike what can be said in the case of non-basic discrimination, run up against a serious barrier, *viz.*, the principle of liberty. To require persons to perform all sorts of actions despite the fact that the actions they might instead prefer are not literally harmful to anyone is surely to violate their liberty. It has been assumed throughout that that is a serious point against any requirement or prohibition, and perhaps some would be inclined to deny that it is. Arguing against those people would get us into another essay, and thus I let the case rest at this point.

Notes

1   In private conversation with G.A. Cohen.
2   Henry Sidgwick, *The Methods of Ethics*, 7th ed. (Indianapolis/Cambridge: Hackett, 1981), p. 379.

Questions for Discussion

1   Narveson claims that it would be wrong to discriminate in the public sector, but not necessarily in the private sector. Does this distinction hold up?

2   Does Narveson's argument suggest that, if there is no obligation to do something, then a person who is nevertheless going to do that thing cannot be obliged to do it one way rather than another? Is this a reasonable claim?

Taking Rights Seriously   *Reverse Discrimination*

Ronald Dworkin

In the following selection, Dworkin tries to sort out an apparent contradiction which has emerged in modern "liberalism" between claims that it is wrong to distinguish between people on the basis of skin colour, gender, etc., and that governments must take steps to promote certain identifiable groups so as to remedy inequalities. He does this by means of a comparison of two American legal cases involving availability of university spaces (Sweatt and DeFunis). Dworkin argues that liberals can consistently oppose racial discrimination against traditionally disadvantaged groups, and support differential treatment.

*   *   *

1.

In 1945 a black man named Sweatt applied to the University of Texas Law School, but was refused admission because state law provided that only whites could attend. The Supreme Court declared that this law violated Sweatt's rights under the Fourteenth Amendment to the United States Constitution, which provides that no state shall deny any man the equal protection of its laws.[1] In 1971 a Jew named DeFunis applied to the University of Washington Law School; he was rejected although his test scores and college grades were such that he would

have been admitted if he had been a black or a Filipino or a Chicano or an American Indian. DeFunis asked the Supreme Court to declare that the Washington practice, which required less exacting standards of minority groups, violated his rights under the Fourteenth Amendment.[2]

The Washington Law School's admissions procedures were complex. Applications were divided into two groups. The majority—those not from the designated minority groups—were first screened so as to eliminate all applicants whose predicted average, which is a function of college grades and aptitude test scores, fell below a certain level. Majority applicants who survived this initial cut were then placed in categories that received progressively more careful consideration. Minority-group applications, on the other hand, were not screened; each received the most careful consideration by a special committee consisting of a black professor of law and a white professor who had taught in programs to aid black law students. Most of the minority applicants who were accepted in the year in which DeFunis was rejected had predicted averages below the cutoff level, and the law school conceded that any minority applicant with his average would certainly have been accepted.

The *DeFunis* case split those political action groups that have traditionally supported liberal causes. The B'nai Brith Anti-Defamation League and the AFL-CIO, for example, filed briefs as *amici curiae* in support of DeFunis' claim, while the American Hebrew Women's Council, the UAW, and the UMWA filed briefs against it.

These splits among old allies demonstrate both the practical and the philosophical importance of the case. In the past liberals held, within one set of attitudes, three propositions: that racial classification is an evil in itself; that every person has a right to an educational opportunity commensurate with his abilities; and that affirmative state action is proper to remedy the serious inequalities of American society. In the last decade, however, the opinion has grown that these three liberal propositions are in fact not compatible, because the most effective programs of state action are those that give a competitive advantage to minority racial groups.

That opinion has, of course, been challenged. Some educators argue that benign quotas are ineffective, even self-defeating,

because preferential treatment will reinforce the sense of inferiority that many blacks already have. Others make a more general objection. They argue that any racial discrimination, even for the purpose of benefiting minorities, will in fact harm those minorities, because prejudice is fostered whenever racial distinctions are tolerated for any purpose whatever. But these are complex and controversial empirical judgements, and it is far too early, as wise critics concede, to decide whether preferential treatment does more harm or good. Nor is it the business of judges, particularly in constitutional cases, to overthrow decisions of other officials because the judges disagree about the efficiency of social policies. This empirical criticism is therefore reinforced by the argument that even if reverse discrimination does benefit minorities and does reduce prejudice in the long run, it is nevertheless wrong because distinctions of race are inherently unjust. They are unjust because they violate the rights of individual members of groups not so favored, who may thereby lose a place as DeFunis did.

DeFunis presented this moral argument, in the form of a constitutional claim, to the courts. The Supreme Court did not, in the end, decide whether the argument was good or bad. DeFunis had been admitted to the law school after one lower court had decided in his favor, and the law school said that he would be allowed to graduate however the case was finally decided. The Court therefore held that the case was moot and dismissed the appeal on that ground. But Mr. Justice Douglas disagreed with this neutral disposition of the case; he wrote a dissenting opinion in which he argued that the Court should have upheld DeFunis's claim on the merits. Many universities and colleges have taken Justice Douglas's opinion as handwriting on the wall, and have changed their practices in anticipation of a later Court decision in which his opinion prevails. In fact, his opinion pointed out that law schools might achieve much the same result by a more sophisticated policy than Washington used. A school might stipulate, for example, that applicants from all races and groups would be considered together, but that the aptitude tests of certain minority applicants would be graded differently, or given less weight in overall predicted average, because experience had shown that standard examinations were for different reasons a poorer test of the actual ability of these applicants. But if this technique is used deliberately to achieve the same result, it is devious, and it remains to ask why the candid program used by the University of Washington was either unjust or unconstitutional.

2.

DeFunis plainly has no constitutional right that the state provide him a legal education of a certain quality. His rights would not be violated if his state did not have a law school at all, or if it had a law school with so few places that he could not win one on intellectual merit. Nor does to [sic] have a right to insist that intelligence be the exclusive test of admission. Law schools do rely heavily on intellectual tests for admission. That seems proper, however, not because applicants have a right to be judged in that way, but because it is reasonable to think that the community as a whole is better off if its lawyers are intelligent. That is, intellectual standards are justified, not because they reward the clever, but because they seem to serve a useful social policy.

Law schools sometimes serve that policy better, moreover, by supplementing intelligence tests with other sorts of standards: they sometimes prefer industrious applicants, for example, to those who are brighter but lazier. They also serve special policies for which intelligence is not relevant. The Washington Law School, for example, gave special preference not only to the minority applicants but also to veterans who had been at the school before entering the military, and neither DeFunis nor any of the briefs submitted in his behalf complained of that preference.

DeFunis does not have an absolute right to a law school place, nor does he have a right that only intelligence be used as a standard for admission. He says he nevertheless has a right that race *not* be used as a standard, no matter how well a racial classification might work to promote the general welfare or to reduce social and economic inequality. He does not claim, however, that he has this right as a distinct and independent political right that is specifically protected by the Constitution, as is his right to freedom of speech and religion. The Constitution does not condemn racial classification directly, as it does condemn censorship or the establishment of a state religion. DeFunis claims that his right that race not be used as a criterion of admission follows from the more abstract right of equality that is protected by the Fourteenth Amendment, which provides that no state shall deny to any person the equal protection of the law.

But the legal arguments made on both sides show that neither the text of the Constitution nor the prior decisions of the Supreme Court decisively settle the question whether, as a matter of law, the Equal Protection Clause makes all racial classifications unconstitutional. The Clause makes the concept of equality a test of legislation, but it does not stipulate any particular conception of that concept.[3] Those who wrote the Clause intended to attack certain consequences of slavery and racial prejudice, but it is unlikely that they intended to outlaw all racial classifications, or that they expected such a prohibition to be the result of what they wrote. They outlawed whatever policies would violate equality, but left it to others to decide, from time to time, what that means. There cannot be a good legal argument in favor of DeFunis, therefore, unless there is a good moral argument that all racial classifications, even those that make society as a whole more equal, are inherently offensive to an individual's right to equal protection for himself.

There is nothing paradoxical, of course, in the idea that an individual's right to equal protection may sometimes conflict with an otherwise desirable social policy, including the policy of making the community more equal overall. Suppose a law school were to charge a few middle-class students, selected by lot, double tuition in order to increase the scholarship fund for poor students. It would be serving a desirable policy—equality of opportunity—by means that violated the right of the students selected by lot to be treated equally with other students who could also afford the increased fees. It is, in fact, part of the importance of DeFunis's case that it forces us to acknowledge the distinction between equality as a policy and equality as a right, a distinction that political theory has virtually ignored. He argues that the Washington Law School violated his individual right to equality for the sake of a policy of greater equality overall, in the same way that double tuition for arbitrarily chosen

students would violate their rights for the same purpose.

We must therefore concentrate our attention on that claim. We must try to define the central concept on which it turns, which is the concept of an individual right to equality made a constitutional right by the Equal Protection Clause. What rights to equality do citizens have as individuals which might defeat programs aimed at important economic and social policies, including the social policy of improving equality overall?

There are two different sorts of rights they may be said to have. The first is the right to *equal treatment*, which is the right to an equal distribution of some opportunity or resource or burden. Every citizen, for example, has a right to an equal vote in a democracy; that is the nerve of the Supreme Court's decision that one person must have one vote even if a different and more complex arrangement would secure the collective welfare. The second is the right to *treatment as an equal*, which is the right, not to receive the same distribution of some burden or benefit, but to be treated with the same respect and concern as anyone else. If I have two children, and one is dying from a disease that is making the other uncomfortable, I do not show equal concern if I flip a coin to decide which should have the remaining dose of a drug. This example shows that the right to treatment as an equal is fundamental, and the right to equal treatment, derivative. In some circumstances the right to treatment as an equal will entail a right to equal treatment, but not, by any means, in all circumstances.

DeFunis does not have a right to equal treatment in the assignment of law school places; he does not have a right to a place just because others are given places. Individuals may have a right to equal treatment in elementary education, because someone who is denied elementary education is unlikely to lead a useful life. But legal education is not so vital that everyone has an equal right to it.

DeFunis does have the second sort of right—a right to treatment as an equal in the decision as to which admissions standards should be used. That is, he has a right that his interests be treated as fully and sympathetically as the interests of any others when the law school decides whether to count race as a pertinent criterion for admission. But we must be careful not to overstate what that means.

Suppose an applicant complains that his right to be treated as an equal is violated by tests that place the less intelligent candidates at a disadvantage against the more intelligent. A law school might properly reply in the following way. Any standard will place certain candidates at a disadvantage as against others, but an admission policy may nevertheless be justified if it seems reasonable to expect that the overall gain to the community exceeds the overall loss, and if no other policy that does not provide a comparable disadvantage would produce even roughly the same gain. An individual's right to be treated as an equal means that his potential loss must be treated as a matter of concern, but that loss may nevertheless be outweighed by the gain to the community as a whole. If it is, then the less intelligent applicant cannot claim that he is cheated of his right to be treated as an equal just because he suffers a disadvantage others do not.

Washington may make the same reply to DeFunis. Any admissions policy must put some applicants at a disadvantage, and

a policy of preference for minority applicants can reasonably be supposed to benefit the community as a whole, even when the loss to candidates such as DeFunis is taken into account. If there are more black lawyers, they will help to provide better legal services to the black community, and so reduce social tensions. It might well improve the quality of legal education for all students, moreover, to have a greater number of blacks as classroom discussants of social problems. Further, if blacks are seen as successful law students, then other blacks who do meet the usual intellectual standards might be encouraged to apply, and that, in turn, would raise the intellectual quality of the bar. In any case, preferential admissions of blacks should decrease the difference in wealth and power that now exists between different racial groups, and so make the community more equal overall. It is, as I said, controversial whether a preferential admissions program will in fact promote these various policies, but it cannot be said to be implausible that it will. The disadvantage to applicants such as DeFunis is, on that hypothesis, a cost that must be paid for a greater gain; it is in that way like the disadvantage to less intelligent students that is the cost of ordinary admissions policies.[4]

We now see the difference between DeFunis's case and the case we imagined, in which a law school charged students selected at random higher fees. The special disadvantage to these students was not necessary to achieve the gain in scholarship funds, because the same gain would have been achieved by a more equal distribution of the cost amongst all the students who could afford it. That is not true of DeFunis. He did suffer from the Washington policy more than those majority applicants who were accepted. But that discrimination was not arbitrary; it was a consequence of the meritocratic standards he approves. DeFunis's argument therefore fails. The Equal Protection Clause gives constitutional standing to the right to be treated as an equal, but he cannot find, in that right, any support for his claim that the clause makes all racial classifications illegal.

3.

If we dismiss DeFunis's claim in this straightforward way, however, we are left with this puzzle. How can so many able lawyers, who supported his claim both in morality and law, have made that mistake? These lawyers all agree that intelligence is a proper criterion for admission to law schools. They do not suppose that anyone's constitutional right to be treated as an equal is compromised by that criterion. Why do they deny that race, in the circumstances of this decade, may also be a proper criterion?

They fear, perhaps, that racial criteria will be misused; that such criteria will serve as an excuse for prejudice against the minorities that are not favored, such as Jews. But that cannot explain their opposition. Any criteria may be misused, and in any case they think that racial criteria are wrong in principle and not simply open to abuse.

Why? The answer lies in their belief that, in theory as well as in practice, *DeFunis* and *Sweatt* must stand or fall together. They believe that it is illogical for liberals to condemn Texas for raising a color barrier against Sweatt, and then applaud Washington for raising a color barrier against DeFunis. The difference between these two cases, they suppose,

must be only the subjective preference of liberals for certain minorities now in fashion. If there is something wrong with racial classifications, then it must be something that is wrong with racial classifications as such, not just classifications that work against those groups currently in favor. That is the inarticulate premise behind the slogan, relied on by defendants of DeFunis, that the Constitution is color blind. That slogan means, of course, just the opposite of what it says: it means that the Constitution is so sensitive to color that it makes any institutional racial classification invalid as a matter of law.

It is of the greatest importance, therefore, to test the assumption that Sweatt and DeFunis must stand or fall together. If that assumption is sound, then the straightforward argument against DeFunis must be fallacious after all, for no argument could convince us that segregation of the sort practiced against Sweatt is justifiable or constitutional.[5] Superficially, moreover, the arguments against DeFunis do indeed seem available against Sweatt, because we can construct an argument that Texas might have used to show that segregation benefits the collective welfare, so that the special disadvantage to blacks is a cost that must be paid to achieve an overall gain.

Suppose the Texas admissions committee, though composed of men and women who themselves held no prejudices, decided that the Texas economy demanded more white lawyers than they could educate, but could find no use for black lawyers at all. That might have been, after all, a realistic assessment of the commercial market for lawyers in Texas just after World War II. Corporate law firms needed lawyers to serve booming business but could not afford to hire black lawyers, however skillful, because the firms' practices would be destroyed if they did. It was no doubt true that the black community in Texas had great need of skillful lawyers, and would have preferred to use black lawyers if these were available. But the committee might well have thought that the commercial needs of the state as a whole outweighed that special need.

Or suppose the committee judged, no doubt accurately, that alumni gifts to the law school would fall off drastically if it admitted a black student. The committee might deplore that fact, but nevertheless believe that the consequent collective damage would be greater than the damage to black candidates excluded by the racial restriction.

It may be said that these hypothetical arguments are disingenuous, because any policy of excluding blacks would in fact be supported by a prejudice against blacks as such, and arguments of the sort just described would be rationalization only. But if these arguments are, in fact, sound, then they might be accepted by men who do not have the prejudices the objection assumes. It therefore does not follow from the fact that the admissions officers were prejudiced, if they were, that they would have rejected these arguments if they had not been.

In any case, arguments such as those I describe were in fact used by officials who might have been free from prejudice against those they excluded. Many decades ago, as the late Professor Bickel reminds us in his brief for B'nai Brith, President Lowell of Harvard University argued in favor of a quota limiting the number of Jews who might be accepted by his university. He said that if Jews were accepted in numbers larger than their proportion of the popula-

tion, as they certainly would have been if intelligence were the only test, then Harvard would no longer be able to provide to the world men of the qualities and temperament it aimed to produce, men, that is, who were more well-rounded and less exclusively intellectual than Jews tended to be, and who, therefore, were better and more likely leaders of other men, both in and out of government. It was no doubt true, when Lowell spoke, that Jews were less likely to occupy important places in government or at the heads of large public companies. If Harvard wished to serve the general welfare by improving the intellectual qualities of the nation's leaders, it was rational not to allow its classes to be filled up with Jews. The men who reached that conclusion might well prefer the company of Jews to that of the Wasps who were more likely to become senators. Lowell suggested he did, though perhaps the responsibilities of his office prevented him from frequently indulging his preference.

It might now be said, however, that discrimination against blacks, even when it does serve some plausible policy, is nevertheless unjustified because it is invidious and insulting. The briefs opposing DeFunis make just that argument to distinguish his claim from Sweatt's. Because blacks were the victims of slavery and legal segregation, they say, any discrimination that excludes blacks will be taken as insulting by them, whatever arguments of general welfare might be made in its support. But it is not true, as a general matter, that any social policy is unjust if those whom it puts at a disadvantage feel insulted. Admission to law school by intelligence is not unjust because those who are less intelligent feel insulted by their exclusion. Everything depends upon whether the feeling of insult is produced by some more objective feature that would disqualify the policy even if the insult were not felt. If segregation does improve the general welfare, even when the disadvantage to blacks is fully taken into account, and if no other reason can be found why segregation is nevertheless unjustified, then the insult blacks feel, while understandable, must be based on misperception.

It would be wrong, in any case, to assume that men in the position of DeFunis will not take *their* exclusion to be insulting. They are very likely to think of themselves, not as members of some other minority, such as Jews or Poles or Italians, whom comfortable and successful liberals are willing to sacrifice in order to delay more violent social change. If we wish to distinguish *DeFunis* from *Sweatt* on some argument that uses the concept of an insult, we must show that the treatment of the one, but not the other, is in fact unjust.

4.

So these familar arguments that might distinguish the two cases are unconvincing. That seems to confirm the view that Sweatt and DeFunis must be treated alike, and therefore that racial classification must be outlawed altogether. But fortunately a more successful ground of distinction can be found to support our initial sense that the cases are in fact very different. This distinction does not rely, as these unconvincing arguments do, on features peculiar to race or segregation, or even on features peculiar to issues of educational opportunity. It relies instead on further analysis of the idea, which was central to my argument against DeFunis, that in certain circumstances a policy which puts many individuals at a disadvantage is nevertheless justified because it makes the community as a whole better off.

Any institution which uses that idea to justify a discriminatory policy faces a series of theoretical and practical difficulties. There are, in the first place, two distinct senses in which a community may be said to be better off as a whole, in spite of the fact that certain of its members are worse off, and any justification must specify which sense is meant. It may be better off in a *utilitarian* sense, that is, because the average or collective level of welfare in the community is improved even though the welfare of some individuals falls. Or it may be better off in an *ideal* sense, that is, because it is more just, or in some other way closer to an ideal society, whether or not average welfare is improved. The University of Washington might use either utilitarian or ideal arguments to justify its racial classification. It might argue, for example, that increasing the number of black lawyers reduces racial tensions, which improves the welfare of almost everyone in the community. That is a utilitarian argument. Or it might argue that, whatever effect minority preference will have on average welfare, it will make the community more equal and therefore more just. That is an ideal, not a utilitarian, argument.

The University of Texas, on the other hand, cannot make an ideal argument for segregation. It cannot claim that segregation makes the community more just whether it improves the average welfare or not. The arguments it makes to defend segregation must therefore all be utilitarian arguments. The arguments I invented, like the argument that white lawyers could do more than black lawyers to improve commercial efficiency in Texas, are utilitarian, since commercial efficiency makes the community better off only if it improves average welfare.

Utilitarian arguments encounter a special difficulty that ideal arguments do not. What is meant by average or collective welfare? How can the welfare of an individual be measured, even in principle, and how can gains in the welfare of different individuals be added and then compared with losses, so as to justify the claim that gains outweigh losses overall? The utilitarian argument that segregation improves average welfare presupposes that such calculations can be made. But how?

Jeremy Bentham, who believed that only utilitarian arguments could justify political decisions, gave the following answer. He said that the effect of a policy on an individual's welfare could be determined by discovering the amount of pleasure or pain the policy brought him, and that effect of the policy on the collective welfare could be calculated by adding together all the pleasure and subtracting all of the pain it brought to everyone. But, as Bentham's critics insisted, it is doubtful whether there exists a simple psychological state of pleasure common to all those who benefit from a policy or of pain common to all those who lose by it; in any case it would be impossible to identify, measure, and add the different pleasures and pains felt by vast numbers of people.

Philosophers and economists who find utilitarian arguments attractive, but who reject Bentham's psychological utilitarianism, propose a different concept of an individual and overall welfare. They suppose that whenever an institution or an official must decide upon a policy, the members of the community will each prefer the consequences of one decision to the consequences of others. DeFunis, for example, prefers the consequences of the standard admissions policy to the policy of minority preference Washington used, while the blacks in some urban ghetto might each prefer the consequences of the latter policy to the former. If it can be discovered what each individual prefers, and how intensely, then it might be shown that a particular policy would satisfy on balance more preferences, taking into account their intensity, than alternative policies. On this concept of welfare, a policy makes the community better off in a utilitarian sense if it satisfies the collection of preferences better than alternative policies would, even though it dissatisfies the preferences of some.[6]

Of course, a law school does not have available any means of making accurate judgements about the preferences of all those whom its admissions policies will affect. It may nevertheless make judgements which, though speculative, cannot be dismissed as implausible. It is, for example, plausible to think that in post-War Texas, the preferences of the people were overall in favor of the consequences of segregation in law schools, even if the intensity of the competing preference for integration, and not simply the number of those holding that preference, is taken into account. The officials of the Texas law school might have relied upon voting behavior, newspaper editorials, and simply their own sense of their community in reaching that decision. Though they might have been wrong, we cannot now say, even with the benefit of hindsight, that they were.

So even if Bentham's psychological utilitarianism is rejected, law schools may appeal to preference utilitarianism to provide at least a rough and speculative justification for admissions policies that put some classes of applicants at a disadvantage. But once it is made clear that these utilitarian arguments are based on judgements about the actual preferences of members of the community, a fresh and much more serious difficulty emerges.

The utilitarian argument, that a policy is justified if it satisfies more preferences overall, seems at first sight to be an egalitarian argument. It seems to observe strict impartiality. If the community has only enough medicine to treat some of those who are sick, the argument seems to recommend that those who are sickest be treated first. If the community can afford a swimming pool or a new theater, but not both, and more people want the pool, then it recommends that the community build the pool, unless those who want the theater can show that their preferences are so much more intense that they have more weight in spite of the numbers. One sick man is not to be preferred to another because he is worthier of official concern; the tastes of the theater audience are not to be preferred because they are more admirable. In Bentham's phrase, each man is to count as one and no man is to count as more than one.

These simple examples suggest that the utilitarian argument not only respects, but embodies, the right of each citizen to be treated as the equal of any other. The chance that each individual's preferences have to succeed in the competition for social policy, will depend upon how important his preference is to him, and how many others share it, compared to the intensity and number of competing preferences. His chance will not be affected by the esteem or contempt of either officials or fellow citizens, and he will therefore not be subservient or beholden to them.

But if we examine the range of preferences that individuals in fact have, we shall see that the apparent egalitarian character of a utilitarian argument is often deceptive. Preference utilitarianism asks officials to attempt to satisfy people's preferences so far as this is possible. But the preferences of an individual for the consequences of a particular policy may be seen to reflect, on further analysis, either a *personal* preference for his own enjoyment of some goods or opportunities, or an *external* preference for the assignment of goods and opportunities to others, or both. A white law school candidate might have a personal preference for the consequences of segregation, for example, because the policy improves his own chances of success, or an external preference for those consequences because he has contempt for blacks and disapproves social situations in which the races mix.

The distinction between personal and external preferences is of great importance for this reason. If a utilitarian argument counts external preferences along with personal preferences, then the egalitarian character of that argument is corrupted, because the chance that anyone's preferences have to succeed will then depend, not only on the demands that the personal preferences of others make on scarce resources, but on the respect or affection they have for him or for his way of life. If external preferences tip the balance, then the fact that a policy makes the community better off in a utilitarian sense would *not* provide a justification compatible with the right of those it disadvantages to be treated as equals.

This corruption of utilitarianism is plain when some people have external preferences because they hold political theories that are themselves contrary to utilitarianism. Suppose many citizens, who are not themselves sick, are racists in political theory, and therefore prefer that scarce medicine be given to a white man who needs it rather than a black man who needs it more. If utilitarianism counts these political preferences at face value, then it will be, from the standpoint of personal preferences, self-defeating, because the distribution of medicine will then not be, from that standpoint, utilitarian at all. In any case, self-defeating or not, the distribution will not be egalitarian in the sense defined. Blacks will suffer, to a degree that depends upon the strength of the racist preference, from the fact that others think them less worthy of respect and concern.

There is a similar corruption when the external preferences that are counted are altruistic or moralistic. Suppose many citizens, who themselves do not swim, prefer the pool to the theater because they approve of sports and admire athletes, or because they think that the theater is immoral and ought to be repressed. If the altruistic preferences are counted, so as to reinforce the personal preferences of swimmers, the result will be a form of double counting: each swimmer will have the benefit not only of his own preference, but also of the preference of someone else who takes pleasure in his success. If the moralistic preferences are counted, the effect will be the same: actors and audiences will suffer because their preferences are held in lower respect by citizens whose personal preferences are not themselves engaged.

In these examples, external preferences are independent of personal preferences. But of course political, altruistic, and moralistic preferences are often not independent, but grafted on to the personal preferences they reinforce. If I am white and sick, I may also hold a racist political theory. If I want a swimming pool for my own enjoyment I may also be altruistic in favor of my fellow athlete, or I may also think that the theater is immoral. The consequences of counting these external preferences will be as grave for equality as if they were independent of personal preference, because those against whom the external preferences run might be unable or unwilling to develop reciprocal external preferences that would right the balance.

External preferences therefore present a great difficulty for utilitarianism. That theory owes much of its popularity to the assumption that it embodies the right of citizens to be treated as equals. But if external preferences are counted in overall preferences, then this assumption is jeopardized. That is, in itself, an important and neglected point in political theory; it bears, for example, on the liberal thesis, first made prominent by Mill, that the government has no right to enforce popular morality by law. It is often said that this liberal thesis is inconsistent with utilitarianism, because if the preferences of the majority that homosexuality should be repressed, for example, are sufficiently strong, utilitarianism must give way to their wishes. But the preference against homosexuality is an external preference, and the present argument provides a general reason why utilitarians should not count external preferences of any form. If utilitarianism is suitably reconstituted so as to count only personal preferences, then the liberal thesis is a consequence, not an enemy, of that theory.

It is not always possible, however, to reconstitute a utilitarian argument so as to count only personal preferences. Sometimes personal and external preferences are so inextricably tied together, and so mutually dependent, that no practical test for measuring preferences will be able to discriminate the personal and external elements in any individual's overall preference. That is especially true when preferences are affected by prejudice. Consider, for example, the associational preference of a white law student for white classmates. This may be said to be a personal preference for an association with one kind of colleague rather than another. But it is a personal preference that is parasitic upon external preferences: except in very rare cases a white student prefers the company of other whites because he has racist, social, and political convictions, or because he has contempt for blacks as a group. If these associational preferences are counted in a utilitarian argument used to justify segregation, then the egalitarian character of the argument is destroyed just as if the underlying external preferences were counted directly. Blacks would be denied their right to be treated as equals because the chance that their preferences would prevail in the design of admissions policy would be crippled by the low esteem in which others hold them. In any community in which prejudice against a particular minority is strong, then the personal preferences upon which a utilitarian argument must fix will be saturated with that prejudice; it follows that in such a community no utilitarian argument purporting to justify a disadvantage to that minority can be fair.[7]

This final difficulty is therefore fatal to Texas' utilitarian arguments in favor of segregation. The preferences that might support any such argument are either distinctly external, like the preferences of the community at large for racial separation, or are inextricably combined with and dependent upon external preferences, like the associa-

tional preferences of white students for white classmates and white lawyers for white colleagues. These external preferences are so widespread that they must corrupt any such argument. Texas' claim, that segregation makes the community better off in a utilitarian sense, is therefore incompatible with Sweatt's right to treatment as an equal guaranteed by the Equal Protection Clause.

It does not matter, to this conclusion, whether external preferences figure in the justification of a fundamental policy or in the justification of derivative policies designed to advance a more fundamental policy. Suppose Texas justifies segregation by pointing to the apparently neutral economic policy of increasing community wealth, which satisfies the personal preferences of everyone for better homes, food, and recreation. If the argument that segregation will improve community wealth depends upon the fact of external preferences; if the argument notices, for example, that because of prejudice industry will run more efficiently if factories are segregated; then the argument has the consequence that the black man's personal preferences are defeated by what others think of him. Utilitarian arguments that justify a disadvantage to members of a race against whom prejudice runs will always be unfair arguments, unless it can be shown that the same disadvantage would have been justified in the absence of the prejudice. If the prejudice is widespread and pervasive, as in fact it is in the case of blacks, that can never be shown. The preferences on which any economic argument justifying segregation must be based will be so intertwined with prejudice that they cannot be disentangled to the degree necessary to make any such contrary-to-fact hypothesis plausible.

We now have an explanation that shows why any form of segregation that disadvantages blacks is, in the United States, an automatic insult to them, and why such segregation offends their right to be treated as equals. The argument confirms our sense that utilitarian arguments purporting to justify segregation are not simply wrong in detail but misplaced in principle. This objection to utilitarian arguments is not, however, limited to race or even prejudice. There are other cases in which counting external preferences would offend the rights of citizens to be treated as equals and it is worth briefly noticing these, if only to protect the argument against the charge that it is construed ad hoc for the racial case. I might have a moralistic preference against professional women, or an altruistic preference for virtuous men. It would be unfair for any law school to count preferences like these in deciding whom to admit to law schools; unfair because these preferences, like racial prejudices, make the success of the personal preferences of the applicant depend on the esteem and approval, rather than on the competing personal preferences, of others.

The same objection does not hold, however, against a utilitarian argument used to justify admission based on intelligence. That policy need not rely, directly or indirectly, on any community sense that intelligent lawyers are intrinsically more worthy of respect. It relies instead upon the law school's own judgement, right or wrong, that intelligent lawyers are more effective in satisfying personal preferences of others, such as the preference for wealth or winning law suits. It is true that law firms and clients prefer the services of intelligent lawyers; that fact might make us suspicious of any utilitarian argument that is said not to depend upon that preference, just as we are suspicious of any argument justifying segregation that is said not to depend on prejudice. But the widespread preference for intelligent lawyers is, by and large, not parasitic on external preferences: law firms and clients prefer intelligent lawyers because they also hold the opinion that such lawyers will be more effective in serving their personal preferences. Instrumental preferences, of that character, do not themselves figure in utilitarian arguments, though a law school may accept, on its own responsibility, the instrumental hypothesis upon which such preferences depend.[8]

5.

We therefore have the distinctions in hand necessary to distinguish *De Funis* from *Sweatt*. The arguments for an admissions program that discriminates against blacks are all utilitarian arguments, and they are all utilitarian arguments that rely upon external preferences in such a way as to offend the constitutional right of blacks to be treated as equals. The arguments for an admissions program that discriminates in favor of blacks are both utilitarian and ideal. Some of the utilitarian arguments do rely, at least indirectly, on external preferences, such as the preference of certain blacks for lawyers of their own race; but the utilitarian arguments that do not rely on such preferences are strong and may be sufficient. The ideal arguments do not rely upon preferences at all, but on the independent argument that a more equal society is a better society even if its citizens prefer inequality. That argument does not deny anyone's right to be treated as an equal himself.

We are therefore left, in *DeFunis*, with the simple and straightforward argument with which we began. Racial criteria are not necessarily the right standards for deciding which applicants should be accepted by law schools. But neither are intellectual criteria, nor indeed, any other set of criteria. The fairness—and constitutionality—of any admissions program must be tested in the same way. It is justified if it serves a proper policy that respects the rights of all members of the community to be treated as equals, but not otherwise. The criteria used by schools that refused to consider blacks failed that test, but the criteria used by the Washington University Law School do not.

We are all rightly suspicious of racial classifications. They have been used to deny, rather than to respect, the right of equality, and we are all conscious of the consequent injustice. But if we misunderstand the nature of that injustice because we do not make the simple distinctions that are necessary to understand it, then we are in danger of more injustice still. It may be that preferential admissions programs will not, in fact, make a more equal society, because they may not have the effects their advocates believe they will. That strategic question should be at the center of debate about these programs. But we must not corrupt the debate by supposing that these programs are unfair even if they do work. We must take care not to use the Equal Protection Clause to cheat ourselves of equality.

Notes

1 *Sweatt v. Painter*, 339 U.S. 629, 70 S. Ct. 848.
2 *DeFunis v. Odegaard*, 94 S. Ct. 1704 (1974).
3 See Chapter 5 (of *Taking Rights Seriously*)
4 I shall argue later in this Chapter that there are circumstances in which a policy violates someone's right to be treated as an equal in spite

of the fact that the social gains from that policy may be said to outweigh the losses. These circumstances arise when the gains that outweigh the losses include the satisfaction of prejudices and other sorts of preferences that it is improper for officials or institutions to take into account at all. But the hypothetical social gains described in this paragraph do not include gains of that character. Of course, if DeFunis had some other right, beyond the right to be treated as an equal, which the Washington policy violated, then the fact that the policy might achieve an overall social gain would not justify the violation (See Chapter 6 of *Taking Rights Seriously*). If the Washington admissions procedure included a religious test that violated his right to religious freedom, for example, it would offer no excuse that using such a test might make the community more cohesive. But DeFunis does not rely on any distinct right beyond his right to equality protected by the Equal Protection Clause.

5 In the actual *Sweatt* decision, the Supreme Court applied the old rule which held that segregation was constitutionally permitted if facilities were provided for blacks that were 'separate but equal.' Texas had provided a separate law school for blacks, but the Court held that that school was by no means the equal of the white school. *Sweatt* was decided before the famous *Brown* case in which the Court finally rejected the 'separate but equal' rule, and there is no doubt that an all-white law school would be unconstitutional today, even if an all-black law school were provided that was, in a material sense, the equal of that provided for whites.

6 Many economists and philosophers challenge the intelligibility of preference utilitarianism as well as psychological utilitarianism. They argue that there is no way, even in principle, to calculate and compare the intensity of individual preferences. Since I wish to establish a different failing in certain utilitarian arguments, I assume, for purposes of this essay, that at least rough and speculative calculations about overall community preferences can be made.

7 The argument of this paragraph is powerful, but it is not, in itself, sufficient to disqualify all utilitarian arguments that produce substantial disadvantages to minorities who suffer from prejudice. Suppose the government decides, on a utilitarian argument, to allow unemployment to increase because the loss to those who lose their jobs is outweighed by the gain to those who would otherwise suffer from inflation. The burden of this policy

will fall disproportionately on blacks, who will be fired first because prejudice runs against them. But though prejudice in this way affects the consequences of the policy of unemployment, it does not figure, even indirectly, in the utilitarian argument that supports that policy. (It figures, if at all, as a utilitarian argument against it.) We cannot say, therefore, that the special damage blacks suffer from a high unemployment policy is unjust for the reasons described in this essay. It may well be unjust for other reasons; if John Rawls is right, for example, it is unjust because the policy improves the condition of the majority at the expense of those already worse off.

8   No doubt the preference that some men and women have for intellectual companions is parasitic on external preferences; they value these companions not as a means to anything else, but because they think that intelligent people are better, and more worthy of honor, than others. If

such preferences were sufficiently strong and pervasive we might reach the same conclusion here that we reached about segregation: that no utilitarian argument purporting to justify discrimination against less intelligent men and women could be trusted to be fair. But there is no reason to assume that the United States is that intellectualistic; certainly no reason to think that it is intellectualistic to the degree that it is racist.

Questions for Discussion

1   Is Dworkin right to suggest that a person's skin colour, etc., could be seen as one of the desired qualifications for a position just as easily as a person's intelligence or industriousness?

2   Does Dworkin give a coherent account of what is required in order to be "treated as an equal"?

acknowledgements

1 distribution of scarce resources

World Health Organization, definition of "health" Reprinted with permission.

R. Munson, "Selection Committee for Dialysis" in R. Munson (ed.) *Intervention and Reflection: Basic Issues in Medical Ethics*, 3rd Edition (Belmont, CA: Wadsworth, 1988) pp. 477-481. Reprinted with permission.

M. Lockwood, "Quality of Life and Resource Allocation," in J.M. Bell & S. Mendus (eds.) *Philosophy and Medical Welfare* (Cambridge, UK: Cambridge University Press, 1988) pp. 33-55. Reprinted with permission.

R. Nozick, *Anarchy, State and Utopia* [selection from chapter 7, section 1] Reprinted with permission.

T. Govier, "The Right to Eat and the Duty to Work," first printed in *Philosophy of the Social Sciences*, Vol. 5 (1975) pp. 125-143; as reprinted (with some deletions) in J.E. White (ed.), *Contemporary Moral Problems*, 3rd Edition (St. Paul, MN: West Publishing Co., 1991) pp. 197-207. Reprinted with permission.

G. Hardin, "Living on a Lifeboat," copyright 1974 American Institute of Biological Sciences [reprinted in many collections, including J.E. White (ed.), *Contemporary Moral Problems*, 3rd Edition, pp. 185-197]. Reprinted with permission.

P. Singer, "Rich and Poor," in Singer, *Practical Ethics* (Cambridge: Cambridge University Press, 1979), pp. 158-181. Reprinted with permission.

2 the beginning and end of life

Old Canadian Abortion Law

Part of the Morgentaler decision overturning that law, as printed in J.E. Bickenbach (ed.) *Canadian Cases in the Philosophy of Law* (Peterborough, Ont.: Broadview Press, 1991). Reprinted with permission.

Proposed 1990 Abortion Law

A.A. McLellan, "Abortion Injunction Vacated: Daigle v. Tremblay," in *Constitutional Forum*, Vol. 1 No. 2, Winter 1990, pp. 9-11. Reprinted with permission.

C. Overall, "Abortion," Ch. 4 of her *Ethics and Human Reproduction: A Feminist Analysis* (London: Allen & Unwin, 1987), pp. 68-87. © Christine Overal, 1987 Reprinted with permission.

B.M. Dickens, "Comparative Judicial Embryology: Judges' Approaches to Unborn Human

Life," in *Canadian Journal of Family Law*, Vol. 9, No. 1, Fall 1990, pp. 180-192. Reprinted with permission.

A.L. Caplan, "The Ethics of In Vitro Fertilization" [in R.T. Hull (ed.) *Ethical Issues in the New Reproductive Technologies* (Belmont, CA: Wadsworth, 1990), pp. 96-109]; originally in *Primary Care*, Vol. 13, No. 2, pp. 241-253, reprinted with the permission of W.B. Saunders Co. and the author.

President's Commission for the Study of Ethical Problems in Medicine and Biomedical and Behavioral Research, "Why 'Update' Death?" from their *Defining Death: Medical, Legal and Ethical Issues in the Determination of Death* (Washington, DC: U.S. Government Printing Office, 1981) [as printed in T.L. Beauchamp & L. Walters (eds.), *Contemporary Issues in Bioethics*, 3rd ed. (Belmont, CA: Wadsworth, 1989) pp. 150-153. Reprinted with permission.

J. Gay-Williams, "The Wrongfulness of Euthanasia," in R. Munson (ed.), *Intervention and Reflection: Basic Issues in Medical Ethics*, 3rd Edition (Belmont, CA: Wadsworth, 1988) pp. 168-171. Reprinted with permission.

R. Brandt, "A Moral Principle About Killing," in M. Kohl (ed.), *Beneficent Euthanasia* (Buffalo, NY: Prometheus Books, 1975) pp. 106-114. Reprinted with permission.

J. Lavery, "When Merely Staying Alive is Morally Intolerable," *Globe and Mail* editorial, Tuesday January 7, 1992. Reprinted with permission.

3 the moral status of non-human animals

Canadian law against cruelty to animals.

J. Feinberg, "The Rights of Animals and Unborn Generations," in his *Rights, Justice, and the Bounds of Liberty: Essays in Social Philosophy* (Princeton, NJ: Princeton University Press, 1980), pp. 159-184; first published in W.T. Blackstone (ed.) *Philosophy and Environmental Crisis* (Athens, GA: University of Georgia Press, 1974), pp. 43-68. Reprinted with permission.

R.G. Frey, "Rights, Interests, Desires and Beliefs," first published in *American Philosophical Quarterly*, Vol. 16 No. 3, July 1979, pp. 233-239; reprinted in D. VanDeVeer & C. Pierce (eds.) *People, Penguins, and Plastic Trees: Basic Issues in Environmental Ethics* (Belmont, CA: Wadsworth, 1986) pp. 40-46. Reprinted with permission.

P. Singer, "Animal Liberation," originally in *New York Review of Books*, April 1973, pp. 17-21 as a review of S. Godlovith, R. Godlovith, and J. Jarris (eds.) *Animals, Men and Morals* [reprinted many places including D. VanDeVeer & C. Pierce (eds.) *People, Penguins, and Plastic Trees: Basic Issues in Environmental Ethics*, pp. 24-32]. Reprinted with permission.

R. Crisp, "Utilitarianism and Vegetarianism," in *The International Journal of Applied Technology*, Vol. 4, No. 1, Spring 1988, pp. 41-49. Reprinted with permission.

J. Barber, "Trapped," in *Domino* (Globe and Mail Magazine), Sept. 1990 pp. 81-83, 98, 100, and 102. Reprinted with permission.

4 resources and the environment

Law Reform Commission Working Paper on Environmental Crime.

D.P. Emond, "Co-operation in Nature: A New Foundation for Environmental Law," in *Osgoode Hall Law Journal*, Vol. 22, No. 2, pp. 323-348. Reprinted with permission.

P.S. Elder, "Legal Rights for Nature: The Wrong Answer to the Right(s) Question," in R. Bradley and S. Duguid (eds.), *Environmental Ethics: Volume II* (Burnaby, BC: Institute for the Humanities, Simon Fraser University, 1989), pp. 107-119 [previous version in *Osgoode Hall Law Journal*, Vol. 22, No. 2, pp. 285-295.] Reprinted with permission.

E.G. Nisbet, selection from *Leaving Eden: To Protect and Manage the Earth* (Cambridge: Cambridge University Press, 1991), pp. 294-299. Reprinted with permission.

C. Taylor, "The Politics of the Steady State," in A. Rotstein (ed.), *Beyond Industrial Growth* (Toronto: University of Toronto Press, 1976). Reprinted with permission.

N. Myers, selection from *The Sinking Ark* (Oxford: Pergamin Press, 1980), pp. 3-13, 27-31. Reprinted with permission.

D. Parfit, "Future Generations: The Non-Identity Problem," from Parfit, *Reasons and Persons* (Oxford: Clarendon Press, 1984), pp. 361-363, 371-378. Reprinted with permission.

Liberalism, Community, and Culture (Oxford: Clarendon Press, 1989), pp. 135-161. Reprinted with permission.

M.E. Turpel, a few pages from "Aboriginal Peoples and the Canadian Charter: Interpretive Monopolies, Cultural Differences," printed in R.F. Devlin (ed.) *Constitutional Interpretation*, pp. 126-131 (article is on pp. 123-156). Reprinted with permission.

G. Erasmus, "Twenty Years of Disappointed Hopes," selected portions of the introduction and conclusion from B. Richardson (ed.), *Drumbeat: Anger and Renewal in Indian Country* (Toronto: Summerhill Press Ltd., Assembly of First Nations, 1989). Reprinted with permission.

5 cultural, linguistic, and aboriginal rights

Union of B.C. Indian Chiefs position paper statement, Oct. 1980, *Indian Nations: Determination or Termination*. Reprinted with permission.

J.Q. Adams, "Sons of the Pilgrims Anniversary," Dec. 22, 1802.

P.E. Trudeau, "Justice in our Time" speech, printed in P.A. Cumming & N.H. Mickenberg (eds.) *Native Rights in Canada*, 2nd edition (Toronto: Indian-Eskimo Association of Canada, in assoc. with General Publishing Co. Ltd., 1972) pp. 331-332. Reprinted with permission.

K. Jamieson, *Indian Women and the Law in Canada: Citizens Minus* (Ottawa: Minister of Supply and Services, 1978), pp. 77-78 and pp. 2-4. Reprinted with permission.

F.L. Morton, "Group Rights Versus Individual Rights in the Charter: The Special Cases of Natives and Quebecois," in N. Nevitte & A. Kornberg (eds.) *Minorities and the Canadian State* (Oakville, ON: Mosaic Press, 1985). Reprinted with permission.

W. Kymlicka, "Liberalism and Culturally Plural Societies," (somewhat edited) Ch. 7 of his

6 liberalism, censorship, and pornography

J.S. Mill, selected passages from *On Liberty*, ed. E. Rapaport (Hackett, 1978).

Law Reform Commission, Working Paper 50, *Hate Propaganda*, 1986.

Excerpts from R. v. Keegstra, as printed in Bickenbach (ed.) *Canadian Cases in the Philosophy of Law* (Peterborough, Ont.: Broadview Press, 1991).

M. Kostash, "Whose Body? Whose Self? Beyond Pornography," in M. Fitzgerald, C. Guberman, and L. Wolfe (eds.), *Still Ain't Satisfied!: Canadian Feminism Today* (Toronto: The Women's Press, 1982), pp. 43-54. Reprinted with permission.

F.M. Christensen, selected passages from *Pornography: The Other Side* (Westport, Conn.: Praeger Publishers, 1990). Reprinted with permission.

A. Dworkin, "Pornography is a Civil Rights Issue," from *Letters From A War Zone, Writings 1976-1987* (New York: E.P. Dutton, a division of Penguin, 1989) pp. 276-307. Reprinted with permission.

E. Willis, "Feminism, Moralism, and Pornography" [in A. Snitow, C. Stansell, & S. Thompson (eds.), *Powers of Desire: The Politics of Sexuality* (New York: New Feminist Library, Monthly Review Press, 1983), pp. 460-467]; originally in the *Village Voice*, Oct. and Nov. 1979 [copyright Ellen Willis]. A later version of this article will appear in *Beginning to See the Light: Sex, Hope and Rock and Roll* by Ellen Willis, to be published by Wesleyan University Press/University Press of New England. Reprinted with permission of the author.

7 employment equity

Canadian Government, "Outline of the Employment Equity Act."

Canadian Government, background paper, "Employment Equity and Employment Growth."

Sigelman & Welch, selection from *Black Americans' Views on Racial Inequality* (Cambridge: Cambridge University Press, 1991). Reprinted with permission.

R.L. Simon, "Statistical Justifications of Discrimination," in *Analysis*, Vol. 38 No. 1, January 1978. Reprinted with permission.

S.A. Ketchum, "Evidence, Statistics, and Rights: A Reply to Simon," in *Analysis*, Vol. 39 No. 3, June 1979. Reprinted with permission.

R.L. Simon, "Rights, Groups, and Discrimination: A Reply to Ketchum," in *Analysis*, Vol. 40 No. 2, March 1980. Reprinted with permission.

J. Narveson, "Have We a Right to Non-Discrimination?" in D. Poff & W. Waluchow (eds.) *Business Ethics in Canada*, 2nd edition (Scarborough, ON: Prentice-Hall Canada, 1987), pp. 279-294. Reprinted with permission.

R. Dworkin, "Reverse Discrimination," from his *Taking Rights Seriously* (London, UK: Gerald Duckworth & Co., 1977). Reprinted with permission.